THE FINEST B

WRITTEN AB

JOHN TOLAND HAS GIVEN

THE DEMON A HUMAN FACE . . .

"He managed to talk to many Germans who would not normally have granted an interview to an American . . . as a result, Toland has shed much fresh light on the strange, part captivating, part repellent personality of Hitler, by going to the people who knew him from his childhood onward."

The New York Times Book Review

"A SIGNIFICANT CONTRIBUTION TO THE HISTORY OF OUR TIME . . ."

The National Observer

"THE BEST PICTURE YET OF HITLER AS A PERSON AND POLITICIAN . . . impressive narrative power . . . it has added in good measure to our knowledge of history's most demonic and enigmatic figures."

Houston Chronicle

Also by John Toland
Published by Ballantine Books:

BUT NOT IN SHAME

ADOLF HITLER

HITLER: THE PICTORIAL DOCUMENTARY OF HIS LIFE

NO MAN'S LAND

John Toland

BALLANTINE BOOKS • NEW YORK

 Published in the United States by Ballantine Books, a division of Random House, Inc., New York, and simultaneously in Canada by Random House of Canada Limited, Toronto.

Library of Congress Catalog Card Number: 74-25126

ISBN 0-345-31784-X

Grateful acknowledgment is made for permission to quote portions from the following:

The Young Hitler I Knew by August Kubizek. Copyright © 1954 by Paul Popper and Company. Reprinted by permission of the publisher, Houghton Mifflin Company, Boston.

Hitler's Secret Conversations, 1941–1944, edited by H. R. Trevor-Roper, translated by Norman Cameron and R. H. Stevens. Copyright © 1953 by Farrar, Straus and Young, Inc. Reprinted with the permission of Farrar, Straus & Giroux, Inc., and of George Weidenfeld & Nicolson Ltd., London.

The Testament of Adolf Hitler: The Hitler-Bormann Documents, February–April 1945, edited by François Genoud and translated by R. H. Stevens. Copyright © 1959, Libraire Arthème Fayard; English edition published by Cassell & Co., Ltd. Reprinted by permission of A. D. Peters & Co., Ltd.

Hitler's Interpreter by Paul Schmidt. Copyright © 1951 by Opera Mundi, Inc. Reprinted by permission of Opera Mundi, Inc.

Douze ans auprès d'Hitler: Confidences d'une secrétaire particulière d'Hitler, recorded by Albert Zoller. Copyright © 1949 by Éditions René Julliard. Reprinted by permission of Éditions René Julliard.

Manufactured in the United States of America

First Ballantine Books Edition: November 1984

Contents

LIST OF MAPS

Foreword

Adolf Hitler was probably the greatest mover and shaker of the twentieth century. Certainly no other human disrupted so many lives in our times or stirred so much hatred. He also inspired widespread adoration and was the hope and ideal of millions. The passage of more than forty-four years since his end has done little to alter the perspective of either enemies or true believers. Today we see the other leaders of his era—Roosevelt, Churchill, Mussolini, Stalin—in a different, more objective light but the image of Hitler has remained essentially the same. To the few who remained his faithful followers he is a hero, a fallen Messiah; to the rest he is still a madman, a political and military bungler, an evil murderer beyond redemption whose successes were reached by criminal means.

As one of those whose life was altered by Hitler, I have done my utmost to subdue my own feelings and to write of him as if he had lived a hundred years ago. I interviewed as many as possible of those who knew Hitler intimately—both worshipers and deriders. Many agreed to talk freely and at length about the unhappy past. Gone was the reluctance of past years to discuss the Führer and his actions for fear their views might be distorted. I conducted more than two hundred and fifty interviews with his adjutants (Puttkamer, Below, Engel, Günsche, Wünsche and Schulze); his secretaries (Traudl Junge and Gerda Christian); his chauffeur (Kempka); his pilot (Baur); his doctors (Giesing and Hasselbach); his favorite warriors (Skorzeny and Rudel); his favorite architects (Speer and Giesler); his first foreign press secretary (Hanfstaengl); his military leaders (Manstein, Milch, Dönitz, Manteuffel and Warlimont); the women he most admired (Leni Riefenstahl, Frau Professor Troost and Helene Hanfstaengl). All but a dozen of these interviews were recorded on tapes which presently are stored in the Library of Congress for safekeeping. All those interviewed whose accounts are included in the book read the passages about themselves and not only made corrections but often added illuminating comments.

Significant new documents, reports and studies have also been utilized to help unravel the mystery of Hitler: the dossiers of the U.S. Army Counter-Intelligence Command, including one agent's interview with Hitler's sister Paula; unpublished documents in the U.S. National Archives such as a secret psychiatric report on Hitler in 1918; the unpublished documents from the British Government Archives; the recently discovered Göring-Negrelli correspondence of 1924–25 which sheds new light on Nazi-Fascist relations; the secret speeches of Himmler; and unpublished diaries, notes and memoirs including the revealing recollections of Traudl Junge, Hitler's youngest secretary.

My book has no thesis, and any conclusions to be found in it were reached only during the writing, perhaps the most meaningful being that Hitler was far more complex and contradictory than I had imagined. "The greatest saints," observed one of Graham Greene's characters, "have been men with more than a normal capacity for evil, and the most vicious men have sometimes narrowly evaded sanctity." Deprived of heaven, Adolf Hitler chose hell—if, indeed, he knew the difference between the two. To the end, obsessed by his dream of cleansing Europe of Jews, he remained a Knight of the Hakenkreuz, a warped archangel, a hybrid of Prometheus and Lucifer.

Victory in the West

GERMANY BETWEEN WARS
NORTH SEA
GREAT BRITAIN
London
Southampton
Dover
ENGLISH CHANNEL
HOLLAND
Amsterdam
Rotterdam
Antwerp
Ypres
Werwick
Fromelles
Lille
Brussels
BELGIUM
Arras
Cambrai
SOMME R.
Le Havre
Compiègne
OISE R.
AISNE R.
Paris
Rheims
Versailles
MARNE R.
SEINE R.
Verdun
LUXEMBOURG
Montoire
FRANCE
SAÔNE R.
Bremen
Hanover
Essen
RUHR
Düsseldorf
GER
Cologne
RHINE R.
Coblenz
Frankfurt am Main
RHINELAND
MAIN R.
Saarbrücken
SAAR
Heidelberg
Stuttgart
ALSACE-LORRAINE
Strasbourg
SWITZERLAND
Lausanne
Geneva
Vichy
Lyon
RHÔNE R.
Milan
Turin
ITALY
Genoa
Marseille
Toulon
MEDITERRANEAN SEA
N
0 Miles 100
palacios

Copenhagen
SWEDEN
DENMARK
BALTIC SEA
Memel
LITHUANIA
FREE CITY OF DANZIG
Königsberg
EAST PRUSSIA
Lübeck
POLISH CORRIDOR
Pasewalk
ODER R.
VISTULA R.
Berlin
Frankfurt an der Oder
Poznan
Warsaw
Brest-Litovsk
Beelitz
N Y
ELBE R.
POLAND
Leipzig
Weimar
Dresden
Breslau
UPPER SILESIA
ODER R.
SUDETEN
Eger
Cracow
Prague
Pilsen
Nuremberg
Brno
CZECHOSLOVAKIA
DANUBE R.
Spital
Urfahr
Braunau
Munich
Leonding
Linz
Vienna
Bratislava
Lambach
Tegernsee
Salzburg
Berchtesgaden
Budapest
Innsbruck
AUSTRIA
BRENNER PASS
HUNGARY
Trieste
Zagreb
Venice
Fiume
DANUBE R.
Belgrade
YUGOSLAVIA
ADRIATIC SEA
Sarajevo

GREAT BRITAIN
London
Dover
Amsterdam
HOLLAND
Brussels
BELGIUM
Cologne
GER
LUXEMBOURG
ATLANTIC OCEAN
NORMANDY
Paris
OCCUPIED FRANCE
Montoire
Munich
BRENNER PASS
SWITZERLAND
Ascona
Vichy
Geneva
L. COMO
L. MAGGIORE
VICHY FRANCE
Milan
Biarritz
Hendaye
Marseille
Florence
Toulon
St. Tropez
PORTUGAL
Lisbon
Madrid
SPAIN
CORSICA
Rome
Anzio
SARDINIA
Gibraltar
Ceuta
SP. MOROCCO
PANTELLERIA
Bône
Bizerte
Algiers
Rabat
Port Lyautey
Oran
Bougie
Medjez el Bab
Tunis
Casablanca
Tebessa
Kasserine
MOROCCO
ALGERIA
Gabès
Mareth
TUNISIA
Tripoli
N
0
Miles
300

Berlin
Warsaw
U. S. S. R.
OCCUPIED POLAND
NY
Kiev
Prague
SLOVAKIA
Vienna
Bratislava
Budapest
HUNGARY
Odessa
ROMANIA
Sevastopol
Yalta
Trieste
Bucharest
BLACK SEA
Belgrade
YUGOSLAVIA
ADRIATIC SEA
BULGARIA
Sofia
Istanbul
Foggia
Tirana
Naples
Taranto
ALBANIA
Ankara
Salerno
GREECE
TURKEY
Messina
Athens
Gela
Syracuse
SICILY
MALTA
CYPRUS
CRETE
MEDITERRANEAN SEA
Derna
El Gazala
Tobruk
Matruh
Alexandria
Benghazi
Salum
El Alamein
Cairo
SUEZ CANAL
El Agheila
EGYPT
LIBYA

THE RUSSIAN FRONT
Line of Nov. 15, 1941
Deepest German Penetration
0 Miles 200
N
WHITE SEA
FALKENHORST
FROM NORWAY
FINLAND
MANNERHEIM
L. ONEGA
FINNISH
L. LADOGA
Helsinki
BALTIC SEA
GULF OF FINLAND
Volkhov
Tallinn
Leningrad
Tikhvin
ESTONIA
Novgorod
RUSSIAN COUNTEROFFENSIVE WINTER 1942
Pskov
Riga
LATVIA
KUECHLER
Kalinin
Yaroslavl
VOLGA R.
Gorki
LITHUANIA
LEEB
Velikiye Luki
Dvinsk
Moscow
Kaunas
Vyazma
U. S. S. R.
Tula
Smolensk
Kaluga
BOCK
Minsk
KLUGE
Bryansk
Penza
Orel
Brest-Litovsk
Pinsk
Mogilev
POLAND
RUNDSTEDT
Saratov
Kursk
Voronezh
Gomel
BATTLE OF STALINGRAD, NOV. '42 - JAN. '43
DON R.
Belgorod
Kiev
Lvov
Kharkov
WEICHS
Werwolf
Vinnitsa
DNIEPER R.
Stalingrad
VOLGA R.
Lugansk
Dnepropetrovsk
ROMANIAN
DON R.
Krivoy Rog
Nikolaevsk
Rostov
Odessa
SEA OF AZOV
LIST
ROMANIA
Krasnodar
Stavropol
Bucharest
Constanza
Sevastopol
Novorossisk
BULGARIA
Grozny
BLACK SEA
Palacios

PART 1

I, VISIONARY

Chapter One

DEEP ARE THE ROOTS

1889 – 1907

1

Hitler rarely talked about his family but to a few confidants he did confess an inability to get along with his father, a dictatorial man. While he revered his mother, a quiet, soft soul, it soon became evident that the former would be the dominating force in his life. Both parents came from the Waldviertel, a rural area of Austria, northwest of Vienna, not far from the present Czechoslovakian border and, according to one member of the family, there was Moravian blood in the line. Hitler was an unusual name for an Austrian and quite possibly it was derived from the Czech names "Hidlar" or "Hidlarček."

Hitler's father was born on June 7, 1837, in the village of Strones. His mother was a forty-two-year-old unmarried woman, Maria Anna Schicklgruber. Strones was too small to be a parish and so the baby was registered in Döllersheim as Aloys Schicklgruber, "Illegitimate." The space for the father's name was blank, generating a mystery that remains unsolved: he probably was a man from the neighborhood. There is the slight possibility that Hitler's grandfather was a wealthy Jew named Frankenberger or Frankenreither; that Maria Anna had been a domestic in this Jewish household at Graz and the young son had got her pregnant.

When Alois (as his name would be spelled henceforth) was

almost five, Johann Georg Hiedler, an itinerant millworker from nearby Spital, married Maria. But her little son continued to have a blighted family life; she died five years later and the stepfather apparently resumed his drifting. Alois consequently was brought up by Hiedler's brother Johann Nepomuk at house number 36 in Spital. This farmhouse and the one next door would play an important role in the life of young Adolf Hitler, for here, in this isolated village, he spent half a dozen pleasant summer holidays.

The situation in Spital became intolerable for Alois and at thirteen he "laced his tiny knapsack and ran away from his home." This is the touching, if accurate, scene later painted by his son Adolf in *Mein Kampf*. "A desperate decision to take to the road with only three gulden for travel money, and plunge into the unknown." He worked his way to the mecca of venturesome youth, Vienna, where he became apprenticed to a shoemaker, but five years later, after learning this trade, he decided to become "something better" so enlisted in the frontier guards. This made him a civil servant, a step above the priesthood. He studied diligently, passed a special examination, and by the time he was twenty-four was promoted to a supervisory rank, an exceptional honor for a boy from the Waldviertel. Promotions came regularly to the ambitious Alois and in 1875 he was made a full inspector of customs at Braunau on the Inn River, just across from Germany.

No one was prouder of Alois' success than the man who had brought him up, Johann Nepomuk Hiedler. No Hiedler had ever risen so high. There was no son to carry on the name of Hiedler and on a late spring day in 1876 Johann decided to do something about it. On June 6 his son-in-law and two other relatives made the short trip to the town of Weitra where they falsely testified before the local notary that "Hiedler's brother"—they spelled his name "Hitler"—"had several times stated in their presence and before his death [in 1857] as his last and unchangeable will" that he had fathered an illegitimate son, Alois, and wanted him made his legitimate son and heir.

Perhaps the change of name from Hiedler to Hitler was carelessness, but more likely it was a cunning peasant trick to becloud the issue. The next day Johann Nepomuk Hiedler traveled with his three relatives to Döllersheim where the original birth record of Alois was registered. After examining the document signed by the three witnesses, the elderly parish priest affirmed from the parish marriage book that a man named

Georg Hiedler had indeed married a girl named Schicklgruber in 1842. And so he agreed to alter the birth register. But he must have been reluctant or leery. Although he changed the "illegitimate" to "legitimate" and crossed out "Schicklgruber" in the space for the child's name, he failed to write in another name. In the last space, in extremely cramped writing, he penned: "It is confirmed by the undersigned that Georg Hitler whose name is here entered as Father, being well known to the undersigned, did accept paternity of the child Aloys, according to the statement of the child's mother, and did desire his name to be entered in the register of baptisms of this parish." He himself signed the names of the three witnesses and each, in turn, made his mark, a cross.

The amendments on the register were neither dated nor signed. The parish priest had reason to be devious. Not only had he written in the father's name as "Hitler," instead of the "Hiedler" appearing in the marriage book, but he must have known the entire procedure was illegal on two counts: a deceased man could not be recognized as a father except by legal proceedings; moreover, the mother had to corroborate the facts.

To the girls of Spital, Alois must have cut a dashing figure in his uniform, close-clipped military haircut, bushy eyebrows, sweeping *Kaiserbart* (handlebar) mustache, and two fiercely jutting tufts of hair on either side of a clean-shaven chin. He too had an eye for the girls. Like his legal father, he had already sired an illegitimate daughter. Nor had marriage to the daughter of an inspector in the imperial tobacco monopoly been much of a restraint to amorous adventures. After all, she was sickly and fourteen years his senior.

One of the most attractive Spital girls was Johann Nepomuk Hiedler's granddaughter, Klara Pölzl, a sweet-faced, quiet sixteen-year-old. She was slim, almost as tall as stocky Alois, with abundant dark brown hair and even features. Whether it was love at first sight or simply a desire to provide his ailing wife with a willing housemaid, he managed to persuade the family to let Klara follow him to Braunau. She was installed with the Hitlers in an inn where Alois was already carrying on an affair with a kitchen maid, Franziska (Fanni to the customers) Matzelsberger.

This situation was too much for Frau Hitler. She left Alois and was granted a legal separation. Now it was Fanni's turn to enter the Hitler ménage and she established herself more as common-law wife than mistress. She was only too aware of how tempting a pretty maid could be to the susceptible Alois and one of her first acts was to get rid of Klara. Two years later, in 1882, Fanni gave birth to a boy, like his father, illegitimate.

The following year Hitler's estranged wife died of consumption and he married Fanni. The ceremony was timely. Within two months a second child, Angela, was born. At last Alois had a legitimate child, even if conceived illegitimately. He also accepted legal responsibility for the boy, who became Alois Hitler, Jr. Fanni, restored to respectability, was no happier since Alois, Sr., once more showed signs of wandering affections. Like her predecessor, she contracted a serious lung ailment and was forced to leave Braunau for the country air of a nearby village. Since this left Alois alone on the top floor of the Pommer Inn with two infants, it was only logical for him to seek help from his attractive niece. Once more the compliant Klara was installed in the Pommer Inn and this time she became housemaid, nursemaid and mistress. Adolf Hitler's mother-to-be was such a goodhearted girl she also did her best to help restore Fanni to health, visiting her frequently. Curiously, Fanni welcomed the ministrations of her rival.

In the summer of 1884 the wretched life of Fanni ended. Predictably, the next lady in waiting in the Hitler household was already pregnant. Alois wanted to marry Klara; she could care for his two children and he was genuinely fond of her. But the Church forbade their marriage since, by the fake legitimization, his own father and Klara's grandfather were brothers. Alois appealed to the local priests for a special dispensation from Rome. It was granted within the month, undoubtedly because of Klara's pregnancy. And at the first possible moment, on the morning of January 7, 1885, Alois and his niece were married.

Remarkably, the untidy private life of Alois had never interfered with his professional duties. He continued to be an efficient and honest public servant, esteemed by colleagues and superiors alike. He held himself in the same high esteem although his local reputation was not good; extramarital affairs in such a small town inevitably became common gossip. Among the ugly rumors was one that he had bought a coffin for his first wife while she was still alive.

Klara flourished in her new role as *Hausfrau*. She was a model housekeeper and completely devoted to Alois, Jr., and Angela, treating them as if they were her own. Four months after the ceremony she gave birth to a son, and within two years to a girl and another boy. The youngest died within a few days of birth and shortly afterward both of the older children contracted diphtheria and succumbed. The tragedy was hard for Klara to bear.

The death of three children apparently affected her regular rate of pregnancy and it was not until April 20, 1889, that the fourth child was born. He was one quarter Hitler, one quarter Schicklgruber, one quarter Pölzl, and one quarter uncertain. In the baptismal registry he was entered as "Adolfus Hitler." Later Klara claimed that Adolf was a sickly baby and that she always lived in fear of also losing him, but their housemaid remembered Adolf as a "very healthy, lively child who developed very well."

In either case, Frau Hitler lavished love and attention on her boy and, as a result, probably spoiled him. Life went on placidly at the Pommer Inn. The father spent more time with his cronies and his hobby, beekeeping, than he did at home, but he apparently had ceased his sexual wanderings—or at least was becoming more discreet.

When Adolf was three years and four months old his father was promoted and the family moved to Passau, a good-sized city down the Inn on the German side of the river, where the customs inspection office was located. Living in a German city and playing with German children made a lasting mark on the youngster. The distinctive lower Bavarian dialect, for instance, would remain his mother tongue. It reminded him, he recalled, "of the days of my childhood."

Frau Hitler had not become pregnant again and it has been suggested that in overcompensating the "sickly" child she was still nursing him. It was not until Adolf was almost five that the next child, Edmund, was born. At last Adolf was freed from his mother's constant surveillance, and almost complete freedom came shortly after when his father was reassigned to Linz. The family, apparently because of the newborn baby, stayed in Passau and the five-year-old Adolf now could play endlessly with the German children or wander at will for hours, his own master.

For a year he reveled in this carefree life. Then in the spring of 1895 the family was reunited in Hafeld, a small farm community some thirty miles southwest of Linz. They lived in a farmhouse situated on nine acres of gently rolling fields. The property established the Hitlers near the top of local society.

A month later the six-year-old Adolf was further separated from his possessive mother by entrance into a small *Volksschule* (primary school) several miles away at Fischlam. The regimentation of education was reinforced within a few weeks by rigorous supervision at the hands of his father, who had just retired, after forty years of service, to a life of modest comfort as a minor country gentleman.

It was a pretty house on a slight rise, almost completely hidden by an orchard of fruit and walnut trees and flanked by a brook, artificially straight, churning with clean water. Despite the new restrictions, Adolf must have led a happy life in such pleasant surroundings, for there was no lack of neighboring children for companionship.

It took Adolf and his half sister Angela more than an hour to walk to school, a rigorous trip for a small boy. The building, "shabby and primitive," was separated into two classrooms, one for the boys and one for the girls. The Hitler children made a good impression on the master, who remembered Adolf as "mentally very much alert, obedient, but lively." Moreover both children "kept the contents of their school bags in exemplary order."

"It was at this time that the first ideals took shape in my breast," Hitler wrote in *Mein Kampf*, an account with the usual exaggeration of an autobiography. "All my playing about in the open, the long walk to school, and particularly my association with extremely 'husky' boys, which sometimes caused my mother bitter anguish, made me the very opposite of a stay-at-home." Even at this age he could express himself vocally and before long he became "a little ringleader."

In the months to come his position at home became increasingly difficult. Retirement was proving to be a drudgery for Alois since he had no talent for farming. To add to the aggravation, another child, Paula, was born in the late fall of 1896. With five children, including a crying infant, in the cramped quarters, Alois probably drank more heavily than usual and certainly became quarrelsome and irritable.

As for young Alois, life at Hafeld had become unbearable. He felt not only mistreated by his father but neglected by his stepmother and out of this deprivation came a deep resentment of his half brother Adolf. "He was imperious and quick to anger from childhood onward and would not listen to anyone," he told an interviewer in 1948, still resentful after fifty-two years. "My stepmother always took his part. He would get the craziest notions and getaway with it. If he didn't have his way he got very angry. . . . He had no friends, took to no one and could be very heartless. He could fly into a rage over any triviality."

Feeling abused and rejected, Alois, Jr., followed in the footsteps of Alois, Sr., and ran away from home at the age of fourteen, never to return in his father's lifetime. His vengeful elder retaliated by reducing the boy's inheritance to the legal minimum. A few months later the disgruntled country gentleman sold the burdensome farm for the more enjoyable town life of Lambach half a dozen miles away. For six months the family lived on the third floor of the Gasthof Leingartner just opposite the imposing Benedictine monastery. Freed from farm chores, Adolf's existence also became more palatable and he did well at the modern school. His marks were excellent and in the last quarter of the school year 1897–98 he had twelve 1's, the highest grade. He also had a good natural singing voice and on certain afternoons attended the choir school at the monastery, under the tutelage of Padre Bernhard Gröner. On the way he had to pass by a stone arch in which was carved the monastery's coat of arms—its most prominent feature a swastika.

At this time he became "intoxicated" with that "solemn splendor of brilliant church festivals." The abbot became his idol and he hoped to join the Church himself, one aspiration that curiously met his anti-clerical father's approval. Adolf later told Frau Helene Hanfstaengl that "as a small boy it was his most ardent wish to become a priest. He often borrowed the large kitchen apron of the maid, draped it about his shoulders in vestment fashion, climbed on a kitchen chair and delivered long and fervent sermons." His devout mother would certainly have welcomed such a career, but Adolf's interest in things priestly ended as quickly as it began. Before long he was caught smoking.

Lambach proved to be as dull as the farm to the restless Alois and in 1899 he bought a snug house across from the cemetery wall in Leonding, a village on the outskirts of Linz. The house was no larger than usual but the location was far more to Alois' taste. Leonding had 3000 inhabitants and took on an air of civilization from its proximity to Linz with the latter's theaters, opera house and imposing government buildings. The local companionship was more congenial.

With Alois, Jr., gone from home, it was Adolf who bore

the brunt of the father's discipline. It was he, recalled Paula Hitler, "who challenged my father to extreme harshness and who got his sound thrashing every day. He was a scrubby little rogue, and all attempts of his father to thrash him for his rudeness and to cause him to love the profession of an official of the state were in vain. How often on the other hand did my mother caress him and try to obtain with her kindness, where the father could not succeed with harshness!"

In a show of rebellion Adolf decided to run away from home. Somehow Alois learned of these plans and locked the boy upstairs. During the night Adolf tried to squeeze through the barred window. He couldn't quite make it, so took off his clothes. As he was wriggling his way to freedom, he heard his father's footsteps on the stairs and hastily withdrew, draping his nakedness with a tablecloth. This time Alois did not punish with a whipping. Instead he burst into laughter and shouted to Klara to come up and look at the "toga boy." The ridicule hurt Adolf more than any switch and it took him, he confided to Frau Hanfstaengl, "a long time to get over the episode."

Years later he told one of his secretaries that he had read in an adventure novel that it was a proof of courage to show no pain. "I then resolved never again to cry when my father whipped me. A few days later I had the opportunity of putting my will to the test. My mother, frightened, took refuge in front of the door. As for me, I counted silently the blows of the stick which lashed my rear end." From that day on, so Hitler claimed, his father never touched him again.

Even at the age of eleven there was something in the thin-faced youngster's look that set him apart from his fellows. In the class picture that year of the Leonding Volksschule he sits in the center of the top row, several inches taller than his comrades, chin up, arms crossed. With his glint of rebellion, his cocky assuredness, he is patently the top boy. He was breezing through school with little effort and had already discovered another talent. He could draw. A picture of Wallenstein dated March 26 of that year, 1900, indicates a budding talent as an artist. In the classroom he would spend some of his study time surreptitiously sketching. A boy named Weinberger once watched in wonder as Hitler recreated from memory the castle of Schaumberg.

At recess and after school he remained the leader. He had already resided in more places than most of his comrades would visit in their lives and they saw him as a man of the world. In play he was inspired by the adventure stories he was devouring by James Fenimore Cooper and his German imitator, Karl May. The latter had never been to America, but his tales of noble Indians and hardy cowboys were accepted as gospel by generations of German and Austrian boys.

It was about this time that he found more significant stimulation in two illustrated magazines devoted to the Franco-Prussian War of 1870. He pored over the words and pictures. "It was not long before the great historic struggle had become my greatest inner experience," he claimed in *Mein Kampf*, which occasionally twisted the truth for political purposes. "From then on I became more and more enthusiastic about everything that was in any way connected with war or, for that matter, with soldiering."

The Boer War, which broke out that same year, also inspired him with Germanic patriotism as well as providing play material. For hours he led his Boers into "hot battle" against those unfortunate ones who had to portray the English. Often he would become so involved that he kept his father waiting an hour or so for the tobacco he was supposed to pick up at the store. The result, recalled Weinberger, was a "hot" reception at home. These adventurous days perhaps helped shape the course of Hitler's career. "Woods and meadows," he once wrote, "were the battlefields on which the 'conflicts' which exist everywhere in life were decided."

That year six-year-old Edmund died of measles. Four deaths were almost too much for Klara to bear, and—with Alois, Jr., gone—there was only one son to carry on the family name. Coming as Adolf was completing his last year at the Volksschule, this latest domestic tragedy heightened the conflict between father and son. Alois wanted the boy to follow his example and tried to inspire him with stories from his own life as a civil servant. His son yearned to be an artist but for the time kept this revolutionary plan to himself and without argument accepted his father's plan for the next step in his education. He was eligible to enroll either in a *Gymnasium*, which placed emphasis on classical education and prepared a student for university, or in a *Realschule*, which was more technical and scientific. The practical Alois decided on the latter and Adolf acquiesced since such a school also had a course in drawing.

From the beginning Adolf did poorly. No longer the leader, the brightest, the most talented, he was overwhelmed by his surroundings. The other students tended to look down on boys from a country suburb; and the personal interest and attention he had received from teachers in the smaller schools were not to be found in such a large institution. In that year's class picture he again was perched on the top row but gone was the cocky Adolf; in his place sat a lost, forlorn youngster.

Retreating into his shell, he showed increasing lack of interest in schoolwork. "I thought that once my father saw how little progress I was making at the Realschule, he would let me devote myself to my dream, whether he liked it or not." This explanation in *Mein Kampf* could be either an excuse or a reason for his failure to be promoted because of deficiencies in mathematics and natural history. His detractors claim his failure was due to inherent laziness but it was just as likely a form of revenge against his father, some emotional problem, or simply unwillingness to tackle uncongenial subjects.

The next year, however, Adolf changed tactics and showed a marked improvement in the classroom. Older than his mates, he once more became the leader. "We all liked him, at desk and at play," said Josef Keplinger. "He had 'guts.' He wasn't a hothead but really more amenable than a good many. He exhibited two extremes of character which are not often seen in unison, he was a *quiet* fanatic."

For some reason Adolf took his Germanism far more seriously than the others, perhaps as a rebellion against his father, who was a stout advocate of the Habsburg regime. Once Keplinger accompanied him part of the way home, up the steep Kapuzinerstrasse. At the top of the hill Hitler stopped before a small chapel. "You are not a *Germane* [old German]," he bluntly told Keplinger. "You have dark hair and dark eyes." His own eyes, he noted proudly, were blue and his hair (at that time, according to Keplinger) was light brown. He was already entranced with the heroic figures of German mythology and at the age of twelve attended his first Wagnerian opera, *Lohengrin*, at the Linz Opera House. He was "captivated at once" as much by the Germanic feelings it aroused in him as by the music.

On January 3, 1903, Alois left home for his morning visit to the Gasthaus Stiefler. No sooner had he seated himself at the table for regular patrons than he remarked that he wasn't feeling very well. Moments later he died—of pleural hemorrhage. He was buried two days later in the church cemetery in sight of the Hitler house. On the gravestone was attached an oblong picture of the former customs official, eyes fixed determinedly ahead. "The sharp word that fell occasionally from his lips could not belie the warm heart that beat beneath the rough exterior," read the commendatory obituary notice in the Linz *Tagespost*. "At all times an energetic champion of law and order and universally well informed, he was able to pronounce authoritatively on any matter that came to his notice."

2

Contrary to popular belief, Alois did not bequeath his family a life of penury. At the time of his death he was receiving a pension of 2420 kronen, a sum considerably more substantial than that received, for example, by the principal of a Volksschule. The widow was granted half of this amount as well as a lump sum equivalent to a quarter of one year's pension. In addition, each child would receive 240 kronen annually "until its 24th birthday or until it becomes self-supporting, whichever shall be the earlier."

The remarkable change in the little house was the absence of tension. Gone was the authoritarian shadow cast by Alois. Adolf, almost fourteen, was the man of the family. Klara attempted to carry out the wishes of her husband concerning the boy, but her only weapon was entreaty. Needless to say, this was no deterrent to Adolf's dream; whenever anyone asked what he was going to be, the answer was invariably, "A great artist."

Even the gentle influence of his mother was diminished at the beginning of the spring term when Adolf was permitted to room in Linz so that he wouldn't have to endure the long daily trip to school. He was installed in the home of an elderly lady, Frau Sekira, with five other schoolboys. Here he became known for his reserve, always using the formal *Sie*, not only with the landlady but with his peers. While this change of locale did little to improve his low standing in school, it did give him more time for drawing and reading.

The desultory school year ended with a failure in mathematics and Frau Hitler was informed that her son would again have to repeat a year unless he passed a special examination in the fall. This cast only momentary gloom on the household, for that summer they were all invited to Spital for a vacation. With two large, old-fashioned trunks filled with clothes and dishes, the Hitlers set off by train for the country. They were met in Weitra by Klara's brother-in-law, Anton Schmidt, who drove them to the tiny settlement of Spital in his oxcart. It was a pleasant summer. Klara found companionship and sympathy in her family, and Adolf, who contrived to avoid work in the fields, would occasionally play with the Schmidt children. Often he spent his time reading and drawing. These pursuits already had marked him as a peculiar youngster; he preferred living in his own dream world. When it rained Adolf was forced to stay in the children's room. "On such occasions," recalled Maria Schmidt, "he often paced up and down or drew or painted and was very angry if he was interrupted. He pushed me out of the room and if I cried outside, he tried to get his mother to give me some tea or something else. We often teased Adolf Hitler and threw something against the window when he was inside, whereupon he quickly jumped out and chased us."

Adolf had succeeded in passing his make-up exam and was now involved in the demanding work of the Third Form. His most difficult subject was French, which he would condemn years later as a "complete waste of time." Professor Hümer, the French teacher, had mixed feelings about young Adolf. "He had definite talent, though in a narrow field," he recalled. "But he lacked self-discipline, being notoriously cantankerous, wilful, arrogant and irascible. He had obvious difficulty in fitting in at school. Moreover, he was lazy; otherwise, with his gifts, he would have done much better. In freehand sketching his style was fluent and he did well in scientific subjects. But his enthusiasm for hard work evaporated all too quickly." Dr. Hümer had more than a passing interest in Adolf since he also taught him German and was the class adviser. "He reacted with ill-concealed hostility to advice or reproof; at the same time, he demanded of his fellow-pupils their unqualified subservience, fancying himself in the role of leader, at the same time indulging in many a less innocuous prank of a kind not uncommon amongst immature youths."

The history professor—Leopold Pötsch—did manage to make an impression on the secretive youngster. Adolf was fascinated by his lectures on the ancient Teutons, which were illustrated by colored slides. "Even today," Hitler wrote in *Mein Kampf*, "I think back with gentle emotion on this gray-haired man, who by the fire of his narratives, sometimes made us forget the present; who, as if by enchantment, carried us into past times and, out of the millennial veils of mist, molded dry historical memories into living reality. On such occasions we sat there, often aflame with enthusiasm, and sometimes even moved to tears."

That year Adolf failed in French. In the autumn his make-up exam was given a passing mark but only on condition that he not return to the Linz school for the Final Form. The nearest Realschule was some twenty-five miles away in Steyr. Once again Adolf would be forced to live away from home. Frau Hitler and the fifteen-year-old journeyed to Steyr where she found a little room for him at the home of the Cichini family. From the beginning Adolf was unhappy. He detested the new town and the view from his room was sinister. "I often used to practice shooting rats from the window." Adolf spent more time shooting rats, reading and drawing than on schoolwork. As a result his grades for the first semester suffered. While he received an "excellent" in gymnastics and "good" in freehand drawing, he was only "adequate" in two favorite subjects, history and geography, and failed mathematics and German. He would go to ridiculous lengths to avoid schoolwork. Upon arriving in class one morning with a huge scarf tied around his neck, he pretended to have lost his voice and got himself sent home.

Despite all this, his marks gradually improved and he was informed he could graduate if he returned in the fall for a special examination. Adolf brought this relatively good news to his mother on a sultry day in July 1905. She had sold the farm at Leonding, scene of so much turmoil and unhappiness, and now lived in a rented flat in a dour stone-faced building at Humboldtstrasse 31 in the middle of Linz. The year away from his mother's protective care had brought a marked change in Adolf's appearance. He was no longer a boy but a youth with unruly hair, the rudiments of a mustache and the dreamy expression of a romantic young bohemian. One of his classmates in Steyr, named Sturmberger, caught all of this in a pen-and-ink drawing that could have been entitled "Portrait of the Artist as a Young Man."

He was greeted as a hero by the adoring Klara, and mother and son resumed their warm relationship. Shortly they left with Paula for another summer in Spital. Here the youth was stricken by a lung infection (the family had a history of respiratory diseases). This illness brought mother and son even closer together and the summer, despite its problems, must have been a pleasant change for both of them after Adolf's exile in Steyr.

By the time the Hitlers left the country, the youth was well enough to return to Steyr for his make-up examination on September 16. He passed; and that night he and several comrades celebrated with a secret wine party, which left him dead drunk. "I've completely forgotten what happened during the night." He only remembered being wakened at dawn on the highway by a milkwoman. Never again would he suffer such humiliation. It was the first and last time he got drunk.

Despite the certificate, Hitler could not face his *Abitur*, the final examination for a diploma; in fact, the mere thought of additional schooling at an *Oberrealschule* or technical institute was repugnant. Using his lung condition as an excuse—"suddenly an illness came to my help"—he persuaded Klara to let him discontinue his studies.

With no father and no school to deter him, the sixteen-year-old was free to drift, his own master, a despiser of authority. It was an escapist existence. Adolf read voraciously, filled sketchbooks with drawings, went to museums, the opera and the waxworks. No longer did he seek out companionship; no longer was he the leader of childhood games. He wandered the streets of Linz, solitary but not lonesome—his mind churning with dreams of the future. The company of others became tedious. Late in the fall of 1905 he finally met someone he could tolerate. August Kubizek, son of an upholsterer, also had a dream: he would be a world-famous musician. Already he could play the violin, viola, trumpet and trombone and was studying musical theory at Professor Dessauer's School of Music. One evening the two young men met at the opera. Kubizek noted that Hitler was reserved, meticulously dressed. "He was a remarkably pale, skinny youth, about my own age, who was following the performance with glistening eyes." Kubizek himself had a sensitive look and with his high forehead, curly hair and dreamy eyes seemed destined for an artist's life.

Together Adolf and Gustl (Hitler refused to call his new friend "August") began attending almost every opera performance. Other nights they would stroll along the Landstrasse, Adolf twirling his ever present black ivory-handled cane. Once Kubizek got up the nerve to ask his uncommunicative companion if he worked. "Of course not," was the gruff reply; a "bread-and-butter job" was not for him.

Since Hitler did not like talking about himself, their conversation centered on music and art in general. One day, however, Adolf abruptly drew out a black notebook to read a poem he had just written; a little later he showed his new friend several drawings and designs, then confessed he was going to be an artist. Determination at such an age impressed Kubizek ("I was thrilled by the grandeur which I saw here"), and from that moment his admiration for Hitler approached hero-worship. Although his recollections, consequently, are often exaggerated and sometimes even fictionalized, no comrade knew the young Hitler so intimately.

While the two had much in common, they were of conflicting temperaments. Kubizek considered himself "adaptable and therefore always willing to yield," while Hitler was "exceedingly violent and high-strung." These differences only solidified the friendship. Kubizek, a patient listener, relished his own passive role, "for it made me realize how much my friend needed me." Hitler warmed to such a sympathetic audience and would often make speeches "accompanied by vivid gestures, for my benefit alone." These orations, usually delivered when they were walking through the fields or on some deserted woodland path, reminded Kubizek of an erupting volcano. It was like a scene on the stage. "I could only stand gaping and passive, forgetting to applaud." It took some time before Kubizek realized his friend was not acting but was "in dead earnest." He also discovered that all Hitler could stand was approval and Kubizek, enthralled more by Adolf's oratory than by what he said, readily gave it.

In the spring of 1906 one of Adolf's dreams was realized; his mother allowed him to visit Vienna, the mecca of art, music and architecture. For a month he roamed the romantic old city (he probably stayed with his godparents, Johann and Johanna Prinz) totally enthralled. He kept Gustl posted. "Tomorrow I go to the opera to see *Tristan*, the day after to *Flying Dutchman*, etc.," he wrote on a three-sectioned postcard on May 7. "Even though I find everything very fine, I am longing for Linz again. To the Stadttheater today." A second postcard, sent the same day, pictured the Royal Opera House. Adolf found the interior uninspiring. "Only when the mighty waves of sound roll through space and the whistling of the wind yields to the frightful rushing billows of sound does one feel nobility and forget the gold and velvet with which the interior is overloaded." These lines were typical of the budding artist—atrocious grammar mixed with poetic imagery, grandiose but sensitive sentiments.

Adolf returned to Linz more dedicated than ever to a life of art and architecture. He insisted that Gustl share this dream, finally persuading him to go into partnership on a ten-kronen state lottery ticket. Hitler talked endlessly of how their winnings should be spent. They would rent the entire second floor of a large house across the Danube and work in the two rooms farthest apart so that Gustl's music should not be a distraction. Adolf himself would furnish every room, create the murals and design the furniture. Their apartment, he daydreamed, would become the headquarters for a circle of dilettantes. "There we would make music, study, read—above all, learn; the field of German art was so wide, said my friend, that there could be no end to the study of it." There was a final delightful and revealing provision: "A lady of exquisite culture would preside over the household as 'chatelaine,' but this educated lady would have to be sedate in temperament and years in order that no expectations or intentions should be aroused of a kind unwelcome to us." This fantasy, like most, was dissolved by reality: their ticket did not win.

After another uneventful summer vacation in Spital, highlighted by his present of a magic lantern to the Schmidt children, Adolf resumed his existence as budding artist and dreamer. In early October he began taking piano lessons from Gustl's teacher. Paula recalled her brother "sitting for hours at the beautiful Heitzmann grand piano my mother had given him." No expense was too great for such a son. It was about this time that Hitler revealed himself to Kubizek in a startling new role. It occurred on the evening they first saw Wagner's *Rienzi*. The story of the hero's rise and fall as tribune of Rome had a curious effect on Adolf. Ordinarily he began criticizing the performers or musicians once the final curtain dropped. This night he not only said nothing but rebuked Kubizek to silence with "a strange, almost hostile glance." Hitler strode into the street, silent, paler than usual, the collar of his black overcoat turned up against the November chill. Looking "almost sinister," he led his puzzled companion to the top of a steep hill. Suddenly he grasped Kubizek's hands tightly. Eyes "feverish with excitement," he began speaking in a hoarse, raucous voice. It seemed to Kubizek as if another being had taken over his friend—"it was a state of complete ecstasy and rapture, in which he transferred the character of Rienzi, without even mentioning him as a model or example, with visionary power to the plane of his own ambitions." Till now Kubizek had been convinced that his friend's true goal was to be an artist or perhaps an architect. This Adolf was a complete stranger, ranting as if possessed of "a special mission which one day would be entrusted to him"—a call from the people to lead them to freedom. This scene may have been one of Kubizek's fictions, but it surely reflected the state of mind of his romantic friend.

The vision on the hill was followed by a moody period in which he felt as rejected and injured as a Dostoevski hero. He could have stepped out of the pages of *The Adolescent*. The piano lessons stopped within four months. Kubizek felt it was because "those dull, monotonous finger exercises did not suit Adolf at all," but it was more likely occasioned by the ill-health of Klara Hitler. On January 14, 1907, two weeks before Adolf's last piano lesson, his mother called on Dr. Edward Bloch, a Jewish physician known locally as the "poor people's doctor." In a quiet, hushed voice she complained of a pain in her chest; it kept her awake night after night. An examination indicated that Frau Hitler had "an extensive tumor of the breast." Dr. Bloch did not tell the patient she had cancer but the following day he summoned Adolf and Paula. Their mother was "a gravely ill woman," and the only hope, and that but a slight one, was surgery. Bloch was touched by Adolf's reaction. "His long, sallow face was contorted. Tears flowed from his eyes. Did his mother, he asked, have no chance? Only then did I recognize the magnitude of the attachment that existed between mother and son."

The family decided to risk an operation and Klara Hitler entered the hospital of the Sisters of Mercy in Linz on January 17. The next day Dr. Karl Urban removed one of her breasts. By this time Aunt Johanna—a hunchback, irascible but always on hand—had arrived from Spital to keep house for the children. For nineteen days Klara recuperated in a third-class ward at three kronen a day; she could have afforded more comfortable quarters but, typically, economized on herself. The three flights to the apartment on the Humboldtstrasse were too difficult for Klara to climb and late that spring the family moved across the Danube to the suburb of Urfahr into three rooms on the second floor of an attractive stone building at Blütengasse 9. It was a quiet, pleasant neighborhood, a short ride on the streetcar across the long bridge to Adolf's favorite haunts.

The youth had a new preoccupation. He fell in love. Until then his relationship with girls had been trifling. During one vacation in Spital, for example, there had been a brief encounter in a barn with a girl who was milking a cow, but when she showed a willingness to go further, Adolf had rushed off, knocking over a large pot of fresh milk. While strolling the Landstrasse with Kubizek, they had approached a "distinguished looking girl, tall and slim," with thick fair hair swept into a bun, a young Valkyrie. Adolf excitedly gripped his companion's arm. "You must know," he said resolutely, "I'm in love with her." Her name was Stephanie Jansten; and she too lived in Urfahr. He composed numerous love poems to her, including one entitled *Hymn to the Beloved*, and read them all to his faithful Gustl. Adolf confessed he had never spoken to her but that eventually "everything would be clear without as much as a word being exchanged."

When Stephanie continued to ignore Hitler's presence he imagined she was angry with him (she was about to become engaged to a lieutenant, and it would come as a complete surprise to learn years later that Hitler had been her devoted admirer). Despondent, he swore he could bear it no longer. "I will make an end of it!" He decided to jump off the bridge into the Danube. But Stephanie would have to go with him in a suicide pact. He devised a plan complete in every detail, with appropriate dialogue for everyone, including Kubizek, who must witness the tragic event.

It was a convenient love affair for a susceptible youth of imagination. Success would have led to marriage and the end of an artistic career; failure only contributed to another pleasurably painful fantasy. More important matters soon put Stephanie in the background. Adolf's creative drive had made a turn from art to architecture. He was still an indefatigable water colorist, but these paintings, while pleasantly executed with a degree of talent, could not satisfy the ideas and emotions seething inside him. "Adolf never took painting seriously," said Kubizek; "it remained rather a hobby outside his more serious aspirations." His architectural designs, on the other hand, gave expression to an irresistible urge to create as well as a sense of order that was almost obsessive. He was driven to alter the shape of Linz. He would stand in front of the new cathedral, praising some features, criticizing others. He redesigned structure after structure in a passion for improvement. "He gave his whole self to his imaginary building and was completely carried away by it." As he ranged the streets with his one-man captive audience, Hitler pointed out features that must be changed, then explained in detail what had to be done. The town hall was uninspiring and he envisioned in its place a stately modern structure. He would also completely remodel the ugly castle, restoring it to its original grandeur. The new museum did please him and he returned time and again to admire its marble frieze, which depicted historical scenes. But even this had to be changed; he would double the length to make it the longest frieze in Europe.

His life had become one of isolation. Hitler slept late and stayed in the house most of the day reading, painting and designing. The downstairs neighbor, the wife of the postmaster, would see him leave the house after 6 P.M. and, on his return from his adventures with Kubizek, hear him pace around the living room until early morning. One day her husband suggested Adolf enter the postal service but he replied that he was going to be a great artist someday. "When it was pointed out that he lacked the necessary means and connections for this, he replied briefly: 'Makart and Rubens worked themselves up from poor circumstances.'"

Adolf was restless; and Linz had no more to offer him. He yearned for the world outside, specifically Vienna. He tried to convince his mother that he should be allowed to enter the Academy of Fine Arts. Klara was pressed from the other side by arguments from her son-in-law and Josef Mayrhofer, the children's guardian. Both insisted that it was time the boy selected a respectable profession. Mayrhofer even found a baker who was willing to take Adolf as an apprentice.

But Klara could not resist her son's passionate pleas and that summer he was allowed to withdraw his patrimony, some seven hundred kronen, from the Mortgage Bank of Upper Austria. This was enough for a year in Vienna, including tuition at the academy. Adolf's victory was marred by a deterioration in his mother's health and he probably left home with emotions of guilt, regret and exultation. But examinations for the Academy of Fine Arts were held only in early October and if he didn't go to Vienna now his career would have to be postponed another year.

Adolf took his exam at the academy with confidence. The verdict was shocking: "Test drawing unsatisfactory." When the stunned young man asked for an explanation the rector assured him that his drawings "showed my unfitness for painting, and that my ability obviously lay in the field of architecture."

It took the downcast Hitler a few days to realize what Kubizek had already guessed—his painting was only a hobby and his true destiny was as an architect. The road ahead seemed insurmountable; entrance in the Academy's School of Architecture depended on a diploma from the building school and to enter this institution he needed a diploma from Realschule. Determined to succeed, yet depressed by the difficulties, he spent the next weeks aimlessly, reading for hours in his little room, attending the opera and wandering the streets to admire the buildings.

In Urfahr, Klara Hitler was dying. The postmaster's wife wrote Hitler and he rushed back. On October 22 he again consulted Dr. Bloch, who revealed that drastic treatment was necessary to save the patient's life. Klara, it seemed, had been operated on too late and "there were already metastases in the pleura." The treatment, continued Dr. Bloch, was not only dangerous—large doses of iodoform on the open wound—but extremely expensive. Money was no object to Adolf and he agreed to remunerate Dr. Bloch for the iodoform in advance, while promising to pay for the treatment itself later.

Kubizek was startled when Adolf unexpectedly turned up at his home, deathly pale, eyes dull. After explaining what had brought him from Vienna, Hitler burst into a diatribe against doctors. How could they say his mother could not be cured? They simply were incapable of curing her. He was staying home, he said, to help take care of his mother since his half sister, Angela, was expecting a second child. Kubizek was surprised that his friend didn't even ask about Stephanie, nor did Adolf mention her for some time, "so deeply engrossed" was he with his mother.

By November 6 she was receiving an almost daily dosage of iodoform. It was an agonizing procedure. Gauze was saturated with iodoform (which had a nauseating, clinging, "hospital" odor) and then folded around the open wound. Not only did the iodoform burn its way into the tissues but once it entered the system the patient could not swallow. Klara's throat burned and yet she could not quench this burning thirst since all liquids tasted like poison.

Hitler devoted himself to his mother, sharing the household duties with the postmaster's wife, Paula and Aunt Johanna. Klara had been installed in the kitchen since it alone was heated all day. The cupboard had been removed and replaced by a couch. Adolf slept here so he could be in constant attendance. During the day he was part-time cook and Frau Hitler confided to Kubizek with pride that her appetite had never been better. At these words her usually pale cheeks colored. "The pleasure of having her son back and his devotion to her had transfigured the serious, worn face."

In the cold, damp days that followed, Kubizek could not believe the change in Hitler. "Not a cross word, not an impatient remark, no violent insistence on having his own way." Adolf "lived only for his mother" and even took over as man of the house. He would scold Paula for doing poorly at school and one day made her swear solemnly to their mother that she would henceforth be a diligent pupil. Kubizek was deeply impressed by this uncharacteristic behavior. "Perhaps Adolf wanted to show his mother by this little scene that he had meanwhile realized his own faults."

Each waking hour was filled with pain for Klara. "She bore her burden well," recalled Dr. Bloch, "unflinchingly and uncomplaining. But it seemed to torture her son. An anguished grimace would come over him when he saw pain contract her face." On the evening of December 20 Kubizek found Frau Hitler, mouth drawn and eyes sunken, sitting up in bed, supported by Adolf to ease the pain. Hitler motioned his friend to leave. As he started out, Klara whispered, "Gustl." Usually she addressed him as Herr Kubizek. "Go on being a good friend to my son when I'm no longer here. He has no one else."

By midnight it was apparent that the end was near but the family decided not to disturb Dr. Bloch. Klara was beyond his help. In the dark early morning hours of December 21—in the glow of a lighted Christmas tree, according to Hitler—she died quietly. After daylight, Angela asked Dr. Bloch to come to the Blütengasse and sign the death certificate. He found Adolf, face wan, at his mother's side. On a sketchbook was a drawing of Klara, a last memory. Dr. Bloch tried to ease Hitler's grief by saying that in this case "death had been a savior." But Adolf could not be comforted. "In all my career," recalled Dr. Bloch, who had witnessed many deathbed scenes, "I never saw anyone so prostrate with grief as Adolf Hitler."

Chapter Two

"THE SCHOOL OF MY LIFE"

DECEMBER 1907–MAY 1913

1

The morning of December 23, 1907, was damp and foggy. Klara was carried out of Blütengasse 9 in a "hard polished wooden coffin with metal corners" and the hearse headed down the slushy street to a church. After a short service the little funeral cortege—hearse and two carriages—proceeded slowly across the Danube and over the hill to Leonding. She was buried, as she wished, beside her husband, with her own name inscribed on his marker. The family, all in black, stood silently in the misty graveyard, within sight of the snug little house they had once occupied. Adolf in a long black overcoat held a black top hat. He seemed even paler than usual to Gustl, his face "stern and composed."

Christmas Eve was lugubrious for the Hitlers. The family made a formal visit to Dr. Bloch to settle the medical bill. The total was 359 kronen, of which 59 kronen had already been paid on account. It was a considerable sum, representing more than ten per cent of Klara's estate, but it was extremely reasonable since it included seventy-seven home and office visits and forty-seven treatments, most of them with iodoform. The balance was paid with profuse thanks. The sisters talked while Adolf, wearing black suit and loosely knotted tie, stared at the floor, a shock of hair tumbling over his forehead. Finally he grasped the doctor's hand and looked directly at him. "I shall be grateful to you forever," he said and bowed. "I wonder if today he recalls this scene," wrote Dr. Bloch thirty-three years later in *Collier's*. "I am quite sure that he does, for in a sparing sense Adolf Hitler had kept his promise. Favors were granted to me which I feel were accorded to no other Jew in all Germany or Austria."

In February, Adolf returned to Vienna. Five days later Gustl followed him. Hitler was delighted to meet his friend at the station. He kissed him on the cheek. He took one handle of the heavy bag, Kubizek the other, and they emerged into the turmoil of the city. It was already dark but electric arc lights made the station plaza "as bright as day."

They passed through the wide entrance of Stumpergasse 29, an imposing structure, crossed a small courtyard to its humbler annex and struggled up dark stairs to a room on the second floor. Sketches were scattered everywhere. Adolf spread a newspaper over the table and brought out his own sparse food supply—milk, sausage and bread. Kubizek shoved these aside and, like a magician, produced from his canvas bag roast pork, freshly baked buns, cheese, jam and a bottle of coffee. "Yes," Hitler is supposed to have exclaimed, "that's what it is to have a mother!"

Since the room was too small for two *and* a piano, the persuasive Adolf convinced the owner to give up her own large room and move into his. The young men agreed to pay twenty kronen a month, double the original rent. The grand piano took up more space than imagined and, since pacing was a requirement for Adolf, the furniture had to be rearranged to give him a promenade three strides in length.

Within two days Gustl had registered at the Academy of Music and passed the entrance examination. "I had no idea I had such a clever friend," was Hitler's curt comment. Nor was he interested in hearing about Kubizek's progress in the weeks to follow. He made a scene when Gustl was visited by a fellow student, a pretty young girl, and after she left, delivered a tirade, as he paced back and forth, "about the senselessness of women studying." Kubizek had "the impression that Adolf had become unbalanced. He would fly into a temper at the slightest thing." Nothing Gustl did seemed to suit Adolf, "and he made our life together very hard to bear. . . . He was at odds with the world. Wherever he looked he saw injustice, hate and enmity."

The underlying reason was Hitler's own rejection and this

came into the open when he suddenly burst into a bitter denunciation of the Academy of Fine Arts. "... a lot of old-fashioned fossilized civil servants, bureaucrats, devoid of understanding, stupid lumps of officials. The whole Academy ought to be blown up!" His face was livid; his eyes ("There was something sinister about them") glittered with hatred. Then he finally revealed that he had been thrown out, turned down. "What now?" asked the concerned Kubizek. Hitler sat down at the table and began to read a book. "Never mind," was the calm reply.

About a week after Hitler left Linz, his guardian Herr Mayrhofer was informed by the Pensions Office that the two orphans, Paula and Adolf Hitler, would each be granted three hundred kronen a year until they reached the age of twenty-four. Mayrhofer was authorized to divide the entire six hundred kronen a year as he saw fit and he decided to give each orphan twenty-five kronen a month.

This regular sum, equivalent to some six current American dollars, undoubtedly gave renewed hope to Hitler but, assuming that he still had most of the six hundred and fifty kronen from his patrimony, life would still have been spartan. His roommate later insisted that Hitler often went hungry. "For days on end he could live on milk and bread and butter only." Kubizek never knew how much money Adolf had and assumed he was secretly ashamed of how little it was. "Occasionally, anger got the better of him and he would shout in fury, 'Isn't this a dog's life.'"

The money Hitler saved on food and other economies—he "pressed" his trousers, for example, under the mattress—enabled him to go to the Burgtheater or the Opera several times a week. Nor would Hitler sit in the gallery with girls—"all they were after was flirting." He made Kubizek stand with him in the promenade, where women were not admitted, at the considerable cost of two kronen a ticket. They never saw the end of the longer operas, since they had to leave at 9:45 P.M. in time to get home before the entrance to Stumpergasse 29 was closed. Otherwise they would have to tip the concierge. Back in their own room Hitler would force Kubizek to play on the piano what they had missed.

Hitler never tired of hearing Wagner. Even when Gustl wanted to see a first-class production of Verdi at the Royal Opera, Adolf insisted on dragging his friend to the People's Opera for a second-rate Wagner production. The music would transport him and was "that escape into a mystical world which he needed in order to endure the tensions of his turbulent nature." Together they saw Adolf's favorite opera, *Lohengrin*, ten times. *Die Meistersinger* similarly entranced Hitler.

The two young men also spent many evenings at concerts for which Kubizek, as a student at the Academy, got free tickets. Gustl was surprised when Adolf began "developing a taste for symphonic music" and a particular fondness for the Romanticists—Weber, Schubert, Mendelssohn and Schumann. Other favorites included Bruckner, Beethoven and Grieg, whose Piano Concerto in A Minor never failed to move him.

Lack of money did not dim the luster of their Vienna. It was the golden era for opera and music. Vienna was the capital of an empire in its final years of flowering, a polyglot center with no common tongue and a population gathered from the four corners of Austria-Hungary. It was a brilliant, cosmopolitan city where joy of life ran hand in hand with a sense of impending doom. This seat of the Habsburg dynasty was German in tradition, yet unique among metropolises. It was a capital not only of banking and finance but also of fashion and culture. Unlike Germany, it was a melting pot of incongruous peoples. "Swamped for long centuries by the Slavs, the Magyars, and the Italians," commented one contemporary reporter, "this town, they say, has no longer a drop of German blood." There was a Bohemian theater, an Italian opera, singers from France and clubs for the Polish; and in some cafés there would be Czech, Slav, Polish and Hungarian newspapers but not one in German. You might be "a German of pure breed, but your wife will be a Galician or a Pole, your cook a Bohemian, your nursemaid as Istriote or a Dalmatian, your valet a Serb, your coachman a Slav, your barber a Magyar, and your tutor a Frenchman. . . . No, Vienna is not a German town."

Hitler and Kubizek would leave their room on the Stumpergasse, often with empty stomachs, pass through dingy middle-class streets to the center of the city with its "splendid mansions of the nobility with garishly attired servants in front and the sumptuous hotels." Adolf became increasingly rebellious, railing endlessly at the social injustice of all that unearned wealth. What bothered him more than hunger was the filth of the bug-infested room on the Stumpergasse. Hitler, Kubizek recalled, was "almost pathologically sensitive about anything concerning the body."

The youthful Hitler, alternately fascinated and repelled, spent time ferreting out the evils of the gaudy city. According to Kubizek, who saw him as a young Werther with a social conscience, he followed an erratic program of self-education, wandering the Meidling section to "research" the housing conditions of the workers; he haunted the Ringstrasse, inspecting it and adjoining areas by the hour, before returning to his dingy hole of a room to redesign large sections of the capital. The youth was as much city planner as architect and, as he strode up and down the narrow passage between door and piano, he forced Kubizek to listen to endless lectures on "conscientious planning." Once he disappeared for three days, returning with the announcement that the "tenements will be demolished," and proceeded to work all night on designs for a model workers' settlement.

Adolf also would sit at the table until late at night, writing in the uncertain glow of their single source of illumination, a smoky kerosene lamp. Curious, Kubizek finally asked what he was doing and Hitler handed over several scribbled sheets:

> Holy Mountain in the background, before it the mighty sacrificial block surrounded by huge oaks; two powerful warriors hold the black bull, and press the beast's mighty head against the hollow in the sacrificial block. Behind them, erect in light-colored robes, stands the priest. He holds the sword with which he will sacrifice the bull. All around, solemn, bearded men, leaning on their shields, their lances ready, are watching the ceremony intently.

Hitler explained to the puzzled Kubizek that it was a play. Excitedly he described the action which took place at the time Christianity was brought to Bavaria; the mountain men would not accept the new faith and were determined to kill the Christian missionaries. This play was probably never finished and others—such as a drama about the painter Murillo—were envisaged and occasionally started, their plots usually lifted from Germanic mythology or history. Adolf would write until dawn, then toss the results on Gustl's bed or read aloud a page or two. Each of these dramas required expensive productions with scenes ranging from heaven to hell, and Gustl suggested that Adolf write something simpler—for example, an "unpretentious" comedy. This adjective infuriated Hitler and he put his mind to an even more ambitious project. It was inspired by a casual remark of Kubizek's that the outline of a music drama about Wieland the Smith had been discovered in Wagner's posthumous papers.

The following day Kubizek returned from lunch to find Hitler at the piano. "I'm going to work up Wieland into a musical drama," he said. Adolf's plan was to compose the music and peck it out on the piano to Gustl, who would "put it on paper, adapt where necessary and finally write the score." A few nights later Hitler played the overture on the piano, then anxiously awaited Gustl's opinion. Kubizek thought it was secondhand Wagner, but the basic themes *were* good and he offered to put the music into proper metric form. While Hitler was never satisfied with his friend's changes, he continued to compose day after day as well as to design the scenery and costumes and sketch the hero in charcoal. Adolf would spend his evenings on the libretto, keeping one eye on Kubizek, and when he fell asleep over the orchestration would shake him awake and then read out, in a soft voice—because of the late hour—from his manuscript. After several weeks, however, Adolf put aside the opera. Perhaps some problem or other had come up that demanded his attention. Or perhaps the fire of creation that had possessed him had burned out. He talked less and less about their unfinished project and finally ceased mentioning it.

The room on the Stumpergasse seemed more dismal than ever to Gustl after the countryside of Linz and he persuaded Hitler to go on excursions in the open country. In the mild spring sunshine they spent several Sundays in the Vienna Woods and took steamer rides down the Danube. Although it was the season when a young man's fancy was supposed to turn to love, sex played little overt part in their lives. On promenades, girls and women would often slyly glance at them. At first Kubizek thought their interest was directed to him, but it soon became apparent that the reserved Adolf was the object; he coldly ignored their silent invitations. If the two did nothing about sex, they spent hours at night discussing women, love and marriage, with Adolf as usual dominating the conversation. Over and over he insisted that he must keep "The Flame of Life" pure. That is, he believed—in accordance with his Catholic upbringing—a man and woman should keep themselves chaste in body and soul until marriage and thus be worthy of producing healthy children for the nation. But the dark side of sex also haunted him and he talked "by the hour" about "depraved [sexual] customs." He railed against prostitution, condemning not only the whores and their customers but society.

Gustl finished his competitive examinations with excellent

grades and conducted the end-of-term concert. Three of his songs were sung and two movements of his sextet for strings performed. In the artists' room, a proud Adolf at his side, he was congratulated not only by the head of the Conductors' School but by the director of the Academy of Music.

It was early July, time for Gustl to return to Linz. He was spending the summer with his parents but insisted on paying his half of the rent until his return in the autumn. Adolf himself was silent about his own plans and, when Gustl vowed to get a position as violinist with the Vienna Symphony Orchestra so he could pay more than his half of their expenses, Hitler's reaction was irritable. The compliant Gustl, inured to his friend's dark moods and still glowing with his own success, took no offense.

Hitler spent the remainder of the month in the stifling, bug-infested room. That his life continued to be dull was indicated in a letter Kubizek received in August. While replete with Hitler's usual self-pity, mistakes in grammar and spelling, it was "a lovely letter" to the uncritical Gustl—"probably the most revealing letter that he ever sent me." Revealing it was, from its emotional greeting, "Good Friend!" First he asked forgiveness for not writing lately. "There were good reasons, or rather, bad ones; I could not think of any news. That I am suddenly writing to you now after all shows merely that I had to search for a very long time, in order to collect a few items of news for you. So here goes." He revealed he had just recovered from "a bad attack of bronchial catarrh" and joked heavily about the weather—"It's lovely pleasant weather with us at the moment, i.e. it is raining heavily and in this year of boiling heat that is truly a blessing from heaven."

Hitler revealed that he was at last quitting Vienna for Spital and would "probably be leaving on Saturday or Sunday." By the end of August he was enjoying the fresh air of that village. There was little else to enjoy. Increased pressure was being brought to abandon his way of life in Vienna, this time by his aunt Johanna. But, recalled Paula, this "last attempt to persuade him to take up the career of an official was in vain." Even Paula was showing signs of crossing her big brother. Now twelve, she resented his advice, including the reading list he prescribed (one item was *Don Quixote*, which he had sent from Vienna). "Naturally he was a great brother for me, but I submitted to his authority only with inner resistance. In fact we were brother and sister, who did frequently quarrel, but were fond of each other, and yet each spoiled each other's pleasure of living together."

As it had been with Angela and Alois, Jr., so it was now with Paula. There was affection but little understanding or common interest. The unpleasantness of Spital that summer marked the end of Hitler's youth. His refusal to consider a more practical profession cut him off from his family; never again would Spital, the scene of so much pleasure in his boyhood, be a refuge. For the fourth time he set off for Vienna, this time truly on his own.

In mid-September Hitler once more applied for admission to the Academy of Art. But the drawings he submitted, the labor of a year's solitary study, were so lowly regarded that he was not allowed to take the test. Along with the crushing blow of a second rejection, Hitler was faced with the problem of survival. His stay at the Stumpergasse room had probably exhausted his patrimony. Even if he had accepted his share of his mother's inheritance—and this is doubtful—it could have amounted to no more than enough to last another year in Vienna. His first economy was a cheaper room. Without leaving a note for Kubizek, who was expected momentarily, he moved to the other side of the Westbahnhof to a gloomy building on the Felberstrasse overlooking the railroad yards.

On November 18 he registered his new address with the police (a regulation in both Austria and Germany whenever one moved), listing his occupation as "student" rather than "artist." Several days later Kubizek arrived in Vienna. Adolf had sent him a picture postcard from Spital with a one-line message: "Best wishes for your esteemed Name Day." Though Kubizek had received no word since, he was accustomed to Adolf's long silences and, upon arriving at the Westbahnhof, he expected to see his friend on the platform. There was no Hitler. Week after week passed without word from Hitler. Kubizek was puzzled. Had he somehow offended Hitler without knowing it? But they had parted the best of friends and Adolf's letters had certainly not been cool.

Adolf had cut himself off from Kubizek, from everything that reminded him of Linz and home. His feeling for Kubizek was not as strong as Gustl's for him; as far as Hitler was concerned their relationship had run its course—at least for the time being. Moreover, Gustl had succeeded and he had failed.

By late summer Hitler had to face another crisis. Except for the twenty-five kronen a month pension he had reached the end of his resources. He moved from the Felberstrasse to a smaller building on the south side of the Westbahnhof. The address was Sechshauserstrasse 58 and he occupied another small room, number 21. On August 22 Hitler registered his change of address at the police station, this time listing himself as "writer." But in less than a month he left his last refuge of respectability and disappeared into the underworld of poverty. He left behind no word, and on his police form there was a blank for "future address," and "unknown" marked the question: "When moved out." Without funds and unable or unwilling to work, he wandered for the next three months, a tramp. He slept in parks and doorways. For a time his home was a bench in the Prater, the famed amusement center on the other side of the Danube; and in rain he found refuge under the arches of the rotunda, using a jacket as pillow. Winter came early that year and by late October 1909 he was forced to find refuge indoors. He slept in bars, in dingy rooms, in cheap flophouses, in a coffeehouse on the Kaiserstrasse, in the crowded "warming room" on Erdbergstrasse established by a Jewish philanthropist. Once he found a strange shelter in a laborers' barracks, a dirty refuge that had to be shared with other homeless people. He could not sleep for the fetid air and the constant noise of crying children or of some drunk beating his wife.

By late fall he had sold most of his clothes, including his black winter overcoat, and so the snow and cold drove him to further humiliation. Huddled in a light jacket late one afternoon just before Christmas, he trudged all the way to Meidling in the outskirts of town. It took two and a half hours to reach his destination, the Asyl für Obdachlose, a shelter for the destitute, and by the time he arrived he was exhausted, his feet sore. Run by a philanthropic society whose principal supporter was the Epstein family, it was originally constructed in 1870 and had been extensively rebuilt and reopened the year before. Here for a modest fee, the homeless—including entire families—were accommodated. Each physically able occupant was expected to help in the housework or tend the grounds. It was a large, modernized structure, sitting alone in a large open field. Its dormitories were spacious and airy with beds lined in military precision, each with its number above a metal clothes rack. The main dining hall, which served a substantial soup with bread, was a model of efficiency yet had a pleasant atmosphere. There were numerous showers, washbowls and toilets—all spotlessly clean.

On that cold December evening Hitler lined up with the other shivering, dejected ones outside the main gate of the Asyl. At last the door opened and the mob of homeless quietly filed in to be segregated by sex, with children accompanying mothers. Hitler got a card entitling him to a week's lodging, and an assignment to one of the large dormitories. To a young man who cherished privacy it must have been a harrowing experience. First he had to endure the humiliation of showering in public and having his bug-ridden clothes disinfected; then his group was trooped like prison inmates to the main dining hall for soup and bread.

It would be difficult for anyone but another recipient of institutionalized charity to understand the shame suffered by a proud young man on his first day within the gates of such an establishment. Entrance into an institution like the Asyl with its efficiency and protectiveness marks an irrevocable enrollment into the bottom rank of the destitute. The inmate has lost the independence of scrounging on his own and becomes, in a sense, a prisoner. The newcomer, overwhelmed by his surrender, is momentarily at a loss. Hitler, too, must have been a picture of dejection that first night in the Asyl, sitting on his neat cot in a large military-like dormitory, surrounded by jabbering comrades, most of whom were veterans of such community living.

A wandering servant in a nearby cot took charge of Hitler. He showed him the ropes: to stay at the Asyl more than the prescribed week, for example, one had only to buy for a few kreuzer the unused portions of admittance cards of those leaving. The servant—his name was Reinhold Hanisch—also had dreams of being an artist and was impressed by Adolf's facile talk. Hitler, in turn, was fascinated by the tales that Hanisch, who had spent several years in Berlin, spun about Germany.

More important, Hanisch taught his student that to survive a winter in the lower depths not a step must be wasted nor an opportunity lost: on mornings they left the Asyl—Adolf in his threadbare jacket, "blue and frostbitten"—early enough to negotiate the long walk to "Kathie's" in time for soup then to a warming room or a hospital for several hours' protection from the bitter cold and a little soup, and back to the Asyl at dusk just as the gate opened. In between the major stops they would occasionally earn a few kreuzer by shoveling snow or carrying baggage at the Westbahnhof. But Hitler was too weak for much physical labor; every step on his sore feet was painful. Once there was a call for ditchdiggers and Hitler wondered if he should apply. Hanisch advised him to forget it. "If you begin such hard work it is very difficult to climb up."

Adolf tried his luck at begging. But he had neither the talent nor the gall for panhandling and became a client of a comrade at the Asyl who made a living by selling addresses of those who were "soft touches." Hitler agreed to split the proceeds fifty-fifty and set off with not only the addresses but specific instructions for each customer; for example, he was to greet an old lady on the Schottenring with a "Praised be Jesus Christ," and then say he was an unemployed church painter or a woodcutter of holy figures. Usually she gave two kronen for such a story, but Hitler only got religious platitudes for his trouble. He had similar bad luck with the other prospects and he again turned to the Church, where he got three meat patties and one kronen from the Mother Superior by greeting her with a "Praised be Jesus Christ," along with a reference to the St. Vincent Association.

Hanisch couldn't understand why a man with such education and talent allowed himself to drift so helplessly and asked what Hitler was waiting for. "I don't know myself," was the listless answer. Hanisch had never seen such apathy in the face of distress and decided to do something about it. His interest was not purely altruistic. Seeing a potential meal ticket in the skinny, woebegone Adolf, he encouraged him to make money painting postcards. Hitler protested that he was too shabbily dressed to sell them on the street or door to door. No problem, said Hanisch; he would do it for fifty per cent commission. But they both might get into trouble with the police without a peddler's license. No problem: Hanisch would sell them in taverns disguised as a blind man or consumptive. Hitler's next argument—that he had sold his painting equipment along with his clothes—was again no problem to the resourceful Hanisch. Didn't Adolf have relatives? Nor was Adolf's final protest that he had no writing materials a deterrent to Hanisch. Together with a salesman from Silesia, Hanisch escorted Adolf to the Café Arthaber, opposite the Meidling station. Following the dictation of the two promoters, and using a borrowed pencil, Hitler wrote a card to a member of his family, probably Aunt Johanna, asking her to send some money General Delivery. A few days later Hitler picked up a letter at the post office. In it was a fifty-kronen bank note ("a nice piece of money in those days"). That evening the exuberant Hitler couldn't resist exhibiting the bill as he stood in line at the Asyl. His crafty companion advised him to keep the money hidden; he'd be robbed or, just as bad, "hit" for a loan.

The first priority was a winter coat for the painter, whose cough was getting worse. Hitler rejected the suggestion that he buy a secondhand coat in the Jewish quarter on the grounds that he had been cheated there when he sold his own. Instead they went to the government pawnshop and found a dark coat for twelve kronen. Hanisch wanted Hitler to start painting at once but he insisted on a week's rest. Moreover, there was no suitable place to work in the Asyl. There were better facilities at the Männerheim, the men's hostel where a man had his own room, tiny to be sure, as well as a common room for hobbies.

On February 9, 1910, he made the long trip to the hostel across the center of Vienna to the other side of the Danube. Hanisch did not accompany him; he had decided to get a job as a servant rather than be a nursemaid to Hitler. The XXth District, Brigittenau, was industrial, with a diverse population, including more Jews than any other section except Leopoldstadt. It was a transient area with many of its inhabitants using it as a stopover on the way up the ladder. The Männerheim, about a half mile from the Danube, was a large building at Meldemannstrasse 25–27 taking up most of a block. It could accommodate five hundred men.

A modern structure, not five years old, its facilities were such that some of Vienna's middle-class citizenry were shocked by its "luxuriousness." On the main floor was a large dining room brightly illuminated by arc lights, the lower half of its walls tiled with a warm shade of green. Food could be picked up at counters and paid for by tokens acquired from a marvel of the day, an automatic machine. The food was cheap but good and the portions generous. Roast pork with one vegetable came to nineteen kreuzer and the complete meal cost an additional four kreuzer.

To those who couldn't afford this much, a dozen or so gas stoves were located in an adjacent room. For no charge any guest could cook up his own modest meal "in the most fantastic cooking utensils." The potato was the basic ingredient; scrambled potato pancakes with or without meat filling was a favorite. Combines were formed; those without jobs stayed at home to do the cooking while others worked and paid for the materials.

Just off this kitchen, up three steps, was a reading room, with a dozen tables. There were a number of other reading rooms and game rooms, as well as a library and a "writing" room where a dozen or so men could carry on private business: a Hungarian cut postcards out of cardboard and sold them in the Prater taverns; one old man copied names of betrothed couples from the newspaper and sold them to stores.

There were several dormitories, as neat as those at the Asyl, but most of the occupants enjoyed privacy in tiny cubicles about five feet wide and some seven feet deep. There was just enough space for a small table, a clothes rack, a mirror, a chamber pot and a narrow iron cot, complete with three-sectional mattress, headrest filled with horsehair, double blanket and, miracle of miracles to any sojourner of the lower depths, two clean white sheets that were changed every week. These were not cheerless cells, for each had its own window in addition to adequate artificial lighting. Every floor had an abundance of washbowls, foot bath troughs and toilets; in the basement were a score of tiled showers. Here too were tailor and barbershops, a shoemaker and a laundry. In addition there were long rows of clean lockers that could be rented by those who needed to store extra clothing or other possessions.

The director was noted as a disciplinarian. He insisted that certain rules be adhered to strictly: the men were to be out of their rooms during the daytime; only chess, checkers and dominoes could be played in the recreational rooms; undue noise, whether argument or enthusiasm, led to expulsion; wine and beer could be consumed on the premises (after all, this was Vienna) but not hard liquor; and city property was to be respected ("There will be no standing on the beds"). There were a few disciplinary problems. A few hopeless tramps did a little stealing but most of the men were sincerely trying to work their way back to respectability.

It was to this snuggery for the homeless that Adolf Hitler came on that chill February day in 1910. He paid his fee—half a crown a day, cheaper by the week—went through another shower and disinfectant routine and was assigned a cubicle. Good as the facilities had been at the Asyl, here, where charity was not so institutionalized, he could feel more like an individual.

In less than a week Hanisch appeared at the Männerheim. Four days as a servant had been enough for him. Again he took charge of Hitler and established his protégé with his art materials in the writing room at a long oak table near a window. Before long Hitler was turning out pictures the size of a postcard. He worked slowly, painstakingly copying photographs or paintings of city scenes. Hanisch had little trouble selling these sketches at Prater taverns and pocketing half the proceeds, but he soon realized there was more money in larger works and so Hitler turned to water-color scenes of Vienna, usually double the size of a postcard, completing about one a day.

Within a few weeks the fruits of this partnership, together with the tolerable conditions at the Männerheim, had rescued the two young men from winter and poverty. No longer did they suffer from the cold or go to bed with growling stomachs. Hitler reveled in the cleanliness of the tile showers and, since he had but one shirt, would launder it every few days as he scrubbed himself. Despite his relative prosperity, he still could not afford new clothes and was a disreputable sight in his tattered, disinfectant-streaked clothing, long hair and beard.

Warmth and food inspired an interest in politics and Adolf did much to turn the writing room into a forum for dispute and discourse. Here the intelligentsia of the Männerheim gathered, fifteen or twenty from the upper and middle class, those with some acquaintance with literature, music and art. A scattering of workers were also tolerated if they "behaved decently." Adolf became a leader of this group, holding forth at length on political corruption just as other down-and-outers in Skid Rows throughout the world were doing.

Adolf became so interested in politics that he spent hours in the magnificent House of Deputies listening entranced to the colorful debates which often degenerated into a babel of multilingual arguments and even brawls. He would return to the writing room and carry on his own harangues, which involved a hodgepodge of Pan-Germanism, along with denunciations of the Social Democrats for their atheism, their attacks on the state and their efforts to seize total power.

Hanisch never heard his friend rail at the Jews during these tempestuous debates or in private, and he remained convinced that Hitler (most of whose favorite actors and singers were Jewish) was by no means anti-Semitic. On the contrary, Adolf would express gratitude for the Jewish charities of which he had been a beneficiary, along with admiration for Jewish resistance to persecutions, and once denied that Jewish capitalists were usurers. Hanisch remembered only one derogatory comment Hitler made when someone wondered why Jews had remained strangers in the land: his answer was that they were "a different race" with "a different smell."

Two of Hitler's closest friends at the Männerheim were Jewish—a one-eyed locksmith named Robinson who often helped him and a part-time Hungarian art dealer, Josef Neumann, who took pity on Adolf's tattered attire and gave him a long frock coat. Hitler "highly esteemed" the latter and once remarked that he was "a very decent man." He also expressed great regard for the three Jewish art dealers who bought most of his work, and more than once told Hanisch, still his agent, that he preferred doing business with Jews "because only they were willing to take chances."

Hitler himself claimed in *Mein Kampf* that he had become a dedicated anti-Semite in Vienna upon his discovery that the Jew was the "cold-hearted, shameless, and calculating director" of prostitution; that the music and art worlds were controlled by Jews; and, most important, that the Social Democrat press was "directed predominantly by Jews." More likely these revelations came much later and his prejudice was little more than that of the average Viennese. Almost every gentile in the Austrian capital was an anti-Semite. Organized groups worked tirelessly to spread hate against Jews and young Hitler became an avid reader of the trash literature which filled the newsstands.

There is evidence that he was a regular reader of such magazines as *Ostara*, the creation of Lanz von Liebenfels, a mystical theorist who shared many of Hitler's own theories and attitudes. The magazine itself was a concoction of the occult and erotic, its editorial policy "the practical application of anthropological research for the purpose of . . . preserving the European master race from destruction by the maintenance of racial purity." Liebenfels' recurring theme was that Aryans must rule the earth by destroying their dark, racially mixed enemies. The latter were damned as inferiors and yet the pages of *Ostara* abounded in lurid illustrations of Aryan women succumbing to the sexual power and allure of these hairy, apelike creatures.

Later Hitler would tell Frau Hanfstaengl that his hatred of Jews was a "personal thing"; and his sister Paula that he was convinced his "failure in painting was only due to the fact that trade in works of art was in Jewish hands." One can only guess at the "personal thing" which Hitler claimed motivated his hatred of all things Jewish: perhaps an art dealer or pawnshop operator; perhaps an official at the Academy of Art; perhaps some combination of these things; or even something which lay dormant in the recesses of his mind. There could have been a dawning hatred of Dr. Bloch, even though Hitler sent him cordial New Year's wishes a year after Klara's death and signed it "Your ever grateful Adolf Hitler." It is not at all uncommon for a bereaved son to blame a doctor, consciously or unconsciously, for the death of a beloved parent. How much more reason in a case involving a Jewish doctor and a dangerous treatment already in disrepute. (Bloch himself later eliminated all mention of iodoform in his accounts of Klara Hitler's treatment.)

By the spring of 1910 Hitler had become so involved with politics and the state of the world that he couldn't fill Hanisch's orders. Reproached, he promised to be more diligent but as soon as Hanisch left the building Adolf would read his newspapers from cover to cover and when he finally sat down to work it wouldn't be long before some discussion lured him from the repetitious painting that was becoming a chore. In desperation, or to get away from Hanisch's nagging, Adolf disappeared on the first day of summer with his Hungarian Jewish friend Neumann. The two had often talked of emigrating together to Germany and so set off in quest of their dream. Somehow they got sidetracked by the wonders of Vienna, particularly Adolf's favorite museums, and never left the city. This spree lasted five days; then, on June 26, with scarcely a kreuzer in his pocket, Hitler returned to the Männerheim. But the brief freedom had its effect. For the next month he worked in spurts, saving only enough to finance another vacation, and before long the partnership with Hanisch ended. Adolf was once more on his own.

In the autumn Hitler made another attempt to enroll in the Academy of Fine Arts. Toting a large portfolio of paintings, he made his way to the office of Professor Ritschel at the Hofmuseum. He requested Ritschel, who was charged with the care and restoration of pictures, to help him get into the Academy. Hitler's work did not impress the professor although he admitted it was executed with remarkable architectural precision. Dejected, Adolf returned to the Männerheim and resumed painting in the writing room. But without Hanisch he found it next to impossible to sell anything. Desperate for money, he appealed to his aunt Johanna, either by mail or on a short trip to Spital. They had parted acrimoniously several summers ago, but Johanna was close to death and apparently had misgivings about her harsh treatment of Adolf. On December 1 she withdrew her entire life savings from the bank. It was a considerable sum, 3800 kronen, and she gave her nephew a substantial part of it.

She died a few months later in early 1911, leaving no will. When Angela Raubal learned that Adolf had received a much larger share of Aunt Johanna's money than anyone else, she immediately applied to the Linz court for her half brother's share of the orphan's pension. It was only fair since she was a recent widow and supported not only her own children but Paula. Either through pressure or shame, Adolf agreed to renounce the twenty-five kronen a month that had been keeping his head above water the past few years. He appeared of his own free will at the district court in Linz to state that he was now "able to maintain himself" and was "agreeable that the full amount of the orphan's pension should be put to use for his sister." The court promptly ordered Herr Mayrhofer henceforth to give Adolf's share of the pension to Paula. The children's guardian had already received a letter from Hitler stating that he no longer wanted any part of the money.

Even without his pension Adolf enjoyed a security undreamed of by a resident of the Männerheim. At the same time he maintained the standards of old, cooking his own meals and continuing to wear the disreputable clothes that kept him in trouble with the management.

Adolf became his own agent and set to work diligently at his corner in the writing room. His comrades respected him because of the artistic air he had acquired. Invariably polite, he never stooped to familiarity though was always ready to help or advise a fellow worker. Yet once politics became a topic, he would toss aside his brush and leap into the fray, shouting and gesturing, his long hair flying. These outbursts made him increasingly unpopular with his fellow lodgers and one day, while preparing his meal in the kitchen, he was roughed up by two big transport workers. He had called them "idiots" for belonging to a Social Democrat labor organization and been rewarded "for his insulting remarks" with a large lump on the head, a bruise on his painting arm and a swollen face.

A new friend, the successor of Kubizek and Hanisch, warned him that he deserved the beating "because you refuse to heed advice and so nobody can help you." Some months previously

Josef Greiner had been attracted to the artist as he hunched over a desk in the writing room daubing at a water color of a church. Greiner was a young man of vivid imagination and he and Adolf would sit for hours discussing economics, religion, astrology and the occult. They also talked at length about the gullibility of people. A case in point was an advertisement currently running in the newspapers. Under the picture of a woman whose hair reached the floor was the text: "I, Anna Csillag, with the very long Lorelei-hair, achieved this beautiful hair with the aid of my secret pomade, which I myself invented. Anyone who wants to have such beautiful hair should write to Anna Csillag and receive free a wonderful prospectus with proof and thank-you letters."

"That is what I call advertising," said Hitler, according to Greiner's account. "Propaganda, propaganda as long as the people believe that this crap helps." The concept excited him. Propaganda, he said, could make believers out of doubters. He was convinced he himself could sell the most preposterous item, such as a salve guaranteed to make windows unbreakable. "Propaganda, only propaganda is necessary. There is no end of stupid people."

During the remainder of 1911 and into the following year Hitler settled into a more stabilized routine. He spent less time in fruitless argument and more at painting. The quality of his work improved. His water color of the Minorite Church of Vienna, for example, was so accurate in every aspect that it could have been traced from a photograph. Technically his pictures were quite professional—surprisingly so for a young man without formal art training. While Hitler was blessed with a natural talent for rendering structures, he had virtually none for the human form. When he introduced figures into a composition, they were poorly drawn and badly out of proportion. A number of his pictures were pleasant to the eye even if they lacked the artistry that separates competence from professionalism. Hitler, in short, was more technician than artist; more architect than painter. It was apparent by 1912 that he could draw competently with pencil, paint well with water colors and even better in oils.

He worked steadily and sold almost everything he completed to Jacob Altenberg and other dealers. Yet Hitler himself no longer boasted of his accomplishments. His comrades in the writing room would cluster around a finished picture and admire it, but he would reply "in a disdainful way that he was only a dilettante and had not yet learned how to paint." His real talent, he thought, was in architecture.

In manner too he had become more circumspect and, while he continued to argue politics, he had received a valuable lesson. "I learned to orate less, but listen more to those with opinions and objections that were boundlessly primitive." He had discovered one does not gain control of other men's minds by antagonizing them.

Nowhere was Hitler's measure of maturity more evident than in the writing room. As a mark of respect, no one thought of occupying his favorite seat at the window. If a newcomer tried to take this place someone would say, "This place is occupied. This is Herr Hitler's place!" One newcomer, Karl Honisch, soon recognized his uniqueness. "We all lived pretty thoughtlessly through the days. . . . I believe that Hitler was the only one among us who had a clear vision of his future way." He told Honisch that although he had been refused admission at the Academy of Fine Arts, he was going to Munich soon to finish his studies there.

Hitler was the nucleus of the intelligentsia in the writing room, recalled Honisch, "because he used to sit in his place day by day with almost no exception and was only absent for a short time when he delivered his work; and because of his peculiar personality. Hitler was, on the whole, a friendly and charming person, who took an interest in the fate of every companion." Friendliness notwithstanding, he kept his distance. "Nobody allowed himself to take liberties with Hitler. But Hitler was not proud or arrogant; on the contrary, he was goodhearted and helpful." If someone needed fifty heller for another night at the hostel he readily contributed his share—"and I saw him several times starting such collections with a hat in his hands."

During ordinary political debates, Hitler kept at work, if occasionally throwing in a phrase or two. But once the key words "Reds" or "Jesuits" came up and someone made a remark that "rubbed him the wrong way," he would leap to his feet and give argument, "not avoiding vulgarisms, in a very impetuous way." Then he would interrupt himself and return to his painting with a gesture of resignation "as if he wanted to say: a pity for every word wasted on you, you won't ever understand."

In a sense Hitler had made peace with Vienna and its lower

depths. He had achieved success and recognition. But the city had little to offer him now. For some months his thoughts had been turning toward Germany, the Fatherland. In a frame over his bed hung a slogan:

We look free and open
We look steadfastly,
We look joyously across
To the German Fatherland!
Heil!

He had spent five and a half years loving and hating the glamorous capital of the Habsburgs and would entitle this chapter of his life "Years of Study and Suffering in Vienna." It was a period of "hardship and misery," "the most miserable time of my life," but one that had molded him more than any university could have done. It was, he thought, "the hardest, though most thorough, school of my life."

On May 24, 1913, carrying all his possessions in a single small battered bag, he stepped for the last time through the double doors of the Männerheim. His mates were sorry to see him leave, Honisch recalled. "We lost a good comrade with him; he understood everyone and helped whenever he could."

Adolf Hitler turned his back on Vienna and looked to Munich for his future. "I had set foot in this town while still half a boy and I left it a man, grown quiet and grave. In it I obtained the foundations for a philosophy in general and a political view in particular which later I only needed to supplement in detail, but which never left me."

Chapter Three

"OVERCOME WITH RAPTUROUS ENTHUSIASM"

MAY 1913–NOVEMBER 1918

1

He stepped off the train from Vienna and climbed the stairs into the hubbub of Munich's Hauptbahnhof. From that first moment almost everything about the capital of Bavaria struck a responsive note. This was home. Even the chatter of the people was pleasing to his ears after the polyglot noise of Vienna. "The city itself was as familiar to me as if I had lived for years within its walls."

It was a pleasant spring day with the sun shining brightly and the air, washed by winds from the nearby Bavarian Alps, seemed much cleaner than that of Vienna. It was a Sunday—May 25—and, except for sightseers, the streets were almost deserted. He gaped at the buildings, the statues, and was seized by a deep love "for this city more than for any other place that I knew, almost from the first hour of my sojourn there. A *German* city!"

After half an hour's enchanted stroll he came to the edge of Schwabing, the student district. Within two blocks he came upon number 34 Schleissheimerstrasse, the Popp Tailor Shop. On its window was stuck a handwritten notice: "Furnished rooms to let to respectable men."

It directed him to the third floor where Frau Popp showed him a room containing a bed, table, sofa and chair. "The young man and I soon came to terms," recalled Frau Popp. "He said it would do him all right, and paid a deposit." She asked him to fill out a registration form and he wrote: "Adolf Hitler, Architectural painter from Vienna."

Hitler had arrived in Munich "full of enthusiasm," intending to study art and architecture for three years, but reality never came up to the dream and he never entered the local Academy of Art. It was even more difficult to make a living as a painter here than in Vienna. The commercial art market was by no means as large and he was forced to undergo the humiliation of peddling his pictures door to door and in beer halls. But he was convinced that despite all obstacles he would in time "achieve the goal I had set myself."

Munich in 1913 with its 600,000 inhabitants was, after Paris, about the liveliest cultural center in Europe, and for some years had been attracting a breed of artists that Hitler himself found decadent: Paul Klee from Switzerland and refugees from the east like Kandinsky, Jawlensky and the Burliuk brothers. Here in Munich his idol had composed *Tristan und Isolde*, *Die Meistersinger*, and *Das Rheingold*, and here resided Germany's leading poets, Stefan George and Rainer Maria Rilke. Here Richard Strauss was writing his operas, Thomas Mann had recently finished a novella of dissolution, *Death in Venice*, and Oswald Spengler, in a room as barren as Hitler's, was scribbling away at the first volume of *The Decline of the West*. At a nearby Schwabing cabaret, the Eleven Executioners, a disreputable genius of *Henkershumor*, Frank Wedekind, was singing his own shocking songs; throughout the country his plays about sex and depravity disgusted and enthralled audiences.

The spirit of bohemianism, in which even the most outrageous and ridiculous theories of art and politics were welcome, had existed in Munich since before the turn of the century and had attracted unconventional souls from all over the world. Another political extremist had spent more than a year of his exile from Russia several blocks up Schleissheimerstrasse, at number 106; registered as Herr Meyer, his given name was Vladimir Ilyich Ulyanov and in the underground he was called Lenin. Here a dozen years earlier he had been writing tracts based on the theories of Marx.

Now Hitler was haunting the same Schwabing cafés and restaurants and luxuriating in the same easy atmosphere of free thought. His rebellious nature and air of feisty independence were not deterrents. In this milieu he was just another eccentric and he could always find someone to listen to his complaints and dreams. Despite his rapport with Schwabing's bohemianism, and in contrast to his own fiery nature and political radicalism, there had been no change in his painting style. His handling of material continued to be academic rather than experimental, daring or even forceful.

His fascination with Marxism, however, was revived in such fertile ground and he spent hours in the libraries studying whatever he could find about "this doctrine of destruction . . . I again immersed myself in the theoretical literature of this new world, attempting to achieve clarity concerning its possible effects, and then compared it with the actual phenomena and events it brings about in political, cultural, and economic life. Now for the first time I turned my attention to the attempts to master this world plague."

At 3:30 P.M. on January 18 Hitler answered a peremptory rap at his door to find a stern-faced officer of the Munich criminal police. The officer—his name was Herle—produced an official document from Austria: a notice for Hitler to "present himself for military service in Linz at Kaiserin Elisabeth Quay 30 on January 20th 1914." If he failed to comply he was liable to prosecution and a fine. More ominous, he was warned that he would be fined heavily and imprisoned up to a year if found guilty of having left Austria "with the object of evading military service."

Adolf was overwhelmed. Three years earlier, while residing at the Männerheim, he had requested permission to report for service in Vienna and had heard nothing since. Officer Herle demanded that Hitler sign a receipt for the induction notice and the young man was so flustered he shakily wrote "Hitler, Adolf." Then Herle arrested him and took him to police headquarters. Next morning he was taken under guard to the Austrian Consulate General. It speaks for Hitler's state that by then the police were sympathetic. The consul general also took pity on the young artist with pinched face, gaunt frame and shabby clothes, and allowed Hitler to send Linz a telegram requesting a postponement until early February. The reply arrived next morning: MUST REPORT ON JANUARY 20. It was already that date and, moved to further compassion by Hitler's alarm, the consul general permitted him to write a letter of explanation to Linz. It was a plea for mercy, replete with grammatical mistakes and misspellings, revealing the fright and desperation of a young man cornered by fate and circumstances. He complained that the summons gave him an "impossible short interval" to settle his affairs, not even enough time to take a bath.

His excuses were flimsy but he so successfully played on the sympathies of the consul general that his letter was dispatched along with a note of the consul's own stating that both he and the Munich police were convinced of Hitler's honesty. Since the young man seemed "extremely deserving of considerate treatment," the consul recommended that he be allowed to report to Salzburg rather than go all the way to Linz. The Linz authorities agreed and on February 5, at the expense of the consulate, Hitler journeyed to Salzburg. He was found "unfit for combatant and auxiliary duties, too weak. Unable to bear arms." His generally run-down condition apparently was sufficient to disqualify him.

Adolf returned to his room on the Schleissheimerstrasse where he continued to eke out a living designing posters and selling pictures but his life as a struggling artist and hopeful architect came to an end on June 28. From his room he heard a hubbub in the streets below. As he started down the stairs Frau Popp exclaimed, "The Austrian heir, Archduke Franz Ferdinand, has been assassinated!" Hitler brushed past her and into the street. He pushed his way through a crowd clustered around a placard to read that the killer of the Archduke and his wife Sophie had been a young Serb terrorist, Gavrilo Princip. Hitler's rooted hatred of all things Slavic, begun at his first visit in Vienna to the House of Deputies, was resurrected.

In Vienna angry mobs were already converging on the Serbian Legation, yet few political experts felt this tragedy would lead to a European crisis. The Kaiser, however, secretly began pressing the Habsburgs to invade Serbia. Germany was ready for war, he told them, and the first country that would rush to Serbia's aid, Russia, was not. Under such pressure Austria declared war on Serbia on July 28. This was followed by a general mobilization of Russia against Austria; whereupon Wilhelm appeared at the balcony of his palace to proclaim "a state of imminent threat of war." An ultimatum was sent to Russia demanding the cessation of mobilization by noon of the following day. There was no answer and at 5 P.M. on the first of August the Kaiser signed the order for Germany's general mobilization against Russia.

The news of war with Russia was received with enthusiasm by a large crowd in front of Munich's Felderrnhalle, the Hall of Field Marshals. Near the front of the crowd stood Adolf Hitler, hatless, neatly dressed, mustached. No one wanted war more than he: "Even today," he wrote in *Mein Kampf*, "I am not ashamed to say that, overcome with rapturous enthusiasm, I fell to my knees and thanked Heaven from an overflowing heart for granting me the good fortune of being allowed to live at this time." To him it meant the realization of the Greater Germany he had dreamed of since youth.

Two days later, on August 3, the day war against France was declared, Hitler submitted a personal petition to Ludwig III, requesting permission to enlist in his army, and that afternoon he stood in the crowd outside the Wittelsbach Palace cheering the old monarch. Finally Ludwig appeared and while he was speaking Hitler was thinking: "If only the King has already read my application and approved it!" The following day he received an answer which he opened with "trembling hands." He was accepted as a volunteer. On August 16 he reported to the barracks of his first choice, the Bavarian King's Own Regiment. A poster outside announced that it was filled; but he was accepted by his second choice, the 1st Bavarian Infantry Regiment.

Two of his most pressing problems were solved: he would never have to join the detested Austrian army nor would he have to endure another hard winter on his own. Besides finding a home with sufficient food, clothing and shelter—he had a purpose. There was no more room for doubt; he knew for the first time in his life exactly where he was going and why. Safe in uniform, his only fear was that the war might end before he saw action.

A few days later he was transferred to the 2nd Bavarian Infantry Regiment and began basic training at the large public school on the Elizabeth Platz. It was a short but intensive course of drilling, route marching and bayonet practice that left the recruits fatigued by the end of the day. Within a week Hitler was permanently assigned to the 16th Bavarian Reserve Infantry Regiment. The training continued in Munich at an accelerated pace. One of Adolf's comrades, Hans Mend, noticed that when he first handled a rifle he "looked at it with the delight that a woman looks at her jewelry which made me laugh secretly."

2

On October 7 Hitler told the Popps his unit was leaving Munich. He shook hands with Herr Popp and asked him to write his sister if he died. Perhaps she would like his few possessions. If not, the Popps were to keep them. Frau Popp burst into tears as Hitler hugged the two children, then "turned tail and ran."

Early next morning the regiment marched out of Munich bound for Camp Lechfeld seventy miles to the west. Carrying packs, the men plodded for almost eleven hours, most of it in the teeming rain. The following day, a Sunday, they marched thirteen hours and bivouacked in the open. It was midafternoon of Monday by the time they finally reached their destination. They were "deathly tired, ready to drop" but marched proudly into the camp under the staring eyes of a group of French prisoners of war.

The first five days at Lechfeld were the most strenuous in his life with "lengthy practice sessions," as well as extra night marches, in connection with brigade maneuvers. This was all part of the amalgamation of their regiment with another to form the 12th Brigade and the recruits were kept so occupied that it was not until October 20 that Hitler found time to write all this to Frau Popp and inform her that they were moving out that evening for the front. "I'm terribly happy," he concluded. "After arrival at our destination I will write immediately and give you my address. I hope we get to England." That night the recruits were loaded onto trains and Adolf Hitler, the archpatriot from Austria, was at last on his way to do battle for the Fatherland.

Eight days later Hitler's company was thrown into battle near Ypres. As the recruits started forward in the morning fog to relieve a hard-pressed unit, English and Belgian shells began dropping into the woods ahead. "Now the first shrapnel hisses over us and explodes at the edge of the forest, splintering trees as if they were straws," he wrote an acquaintance in Munich, Assistant Judge Ernst Hepp. "We watch with curiosity. We have no idea as yet of the danger. None of us is afraid. Everyone is waiting impatiently for the command, 'Forward!' . . . We crawl on our stomachs to the edge of the forest. Above us are howls and hisses, splintered branches and trees surround us.

Then again shells explode at the edge of the forest and hurl clouds of stones, earth and sand into the air, tear the heaviest trees out by their roots, and choke everything in a yellow-green, terribly stinking steam. We cannot lie here forever, and if we have to fall in battle, it's better to be killed outside." Finally it was the Germans' turn to attack. "Four times we advance and have to go back; from my whole batch only one remains, beside me, finally he also falls. A shot tears off my right coat sleeve, but like a miracle I remain safe and alive. At 2 o'clock we finally go forward for the fifth time, and this time we occupy the edge of the forest and the farms."

The battle went on for three more days. The regimental commander was killed and his deputy, a lieutenant colonel, seriously wounded. Under heavy fire Hitler, now a regimental dispatch carrier, found a medic and the two dragged the deputy back to the dressing station. By mid-November the 16th Regiment, according to Hitler, had but thirty officers and less than seven hundred men. Only one in five recruits remained but still came orders to attack. The new commander, Lieutenant Colonel Engelhardt, accompanied by Hitler and another man, ventured far into the front to observe the enemy lines. They were detected and the area was sprayed with machine-gun fire. The two enlisted men leaped in front of their commander, pushed him into a ditch. Without comment Engelhardt shook hands with the two recruits. He intended recommending them both for the Iron Cross but the next afternoon while he was discussing the citations an English shell smashed into the regimental headquarters tent, killing three men and seriously wounding Engelhardt and the other occupants. Moments earlier Hitler and three other enlisted men had been forced to leave the tent to make way for four company commanders. It was the first of a series of narrow escapes verging on the miraculous for Adolf Hitler.

The unsuccessful attempts to take Ypres ended the German offensive and the battle degenerated into static trench warfare. At last Hitler found time to paint. He had brought along some equipment and he finished several water colors, including one of the ruins of a cloister near Messines and another of a trench near the village of Wytschaete. He was called on to do a different kind of painting by Lieutenant Wiedemann, the adjutant of the new regimental commander. The color of the officers' dining room—a small room in a commandeered villa—

clashed with a romanticized painting of a dying soldier lying across barbed wire. Wiedemann asked Sergeant Max Amann to find someone on the staff who could repaint the room. Amann brought back Hitler. Wiedemann wondered if the walls should be painted blue or pink. Hitler observed that the sun gave the picture a light violet tone and suggested blue. He fetched a ladder, paints and a brush and, as he worked, conversed with the lieutenant. "What I noticed first," recalled Wiedemann, "was his unmilitary manner and his slight Austrian accent, and most of all, that he was a serious person who obviously had been through quite a lot in life."

Wiedemann and Sergeant Amann now had time to make up the decoration list. They recommended Hitler for the Iron Cross, 1st Class, but since he was on the staff put his name at the bottom of the list. For this reason alone Hitler was turned down and instead given a 2nd Class award. Even so, Hitler was delighted. He was also promoted to corporal, and no longer was called *Kamerad Schnürschuh* (an insulting Bavarian epithet, "Comrade Laced Boots"). He had earned the respect of his comrades and officers. He belonged.

Despite his lectures on the evils of smoking and drinking, "Adi" was generally liked because of his reliability in a crisis. He never abandoned a wounded comrade or pretended to be sick when it came time for a perilous mission. Moreover, he was a good companion during the long, tedious stretches awaiting action. Being an artist actually drew him closer to his barracks mates. He would draw cartoon sketches on postcards illustrating comical moments of their life. Once, for instance, a man shot a rabbit to take home on leave but left with a parcel containing a brick which someone had exchanged for the animal. Hitler sent the victim of the prank a postcard—with two sketches, one of the soldier unwrapping a brick back home and the other of his friends at the front eating the rabbit.

Unlike the others, Hitler got almost no packages from home and to satisfy his insatiable appetite he was forced to buy extra food from the cooks and kitchen help, thus earning the title of the unit's biggest *Vielfrass* ("glutton"). At the same time he was too proud to share his comrades' packages and would brusquely refuse on the grounds that he couldn't repay the favor.

Late in January Hitler, in a letter to Popp, drew a graphic picture of the static but deadly warfare:

> . . . Because of the constant rain (we do not have winter), the closeness of the ocean, and the low-lying terrain, the meadows and fields are like bottomless morasses, while the streets are covered with slimy mud and through these swamps run the trenches of our infantry, a mass of shelters and trenches with gun emplacements, communication ditches and barbed wire barricades, wolf lairs, land mines, in short, an almost impossible position.

The following month he also wrote Judge Hepp about his battle experiences but then ended the letter, somewhat surprisingly, on a political note:

> I think so often of Munich and each of us has but one wish, that it may soon come to a settling of accounts with the gang, that we'll come to blows, no matter what the cost, and that those among us who have the luck to see our homeland again will find it purer and cleansed from foreign influence, so that by the sacrifice and agony which so many hundreds of thousands of us endure every day, that by the river of blood which flows here daily, against an international world of enemies, not only will Germany's enemies from the outside be smashed, but also our domestic internationalism will be broken up.

Whenever anyone asked where he came from Hitler would reply that his home was the 16th Regiment—not Austria—and after the war he would live in Munich. But first they had to win! On this point he was fanatic and if one of his mates jokingly remarked that the war would never be won he became incensed and would pace back and forth, asserting that England's coming defeat was as certain as the "Amen in the prayer."

As long as his comrades talked of food or women Hitler kept to his reading or painting, but once the conversation turned to serious subjects he would stop and deliver a lecture. His simple comrades were entranced by his fluency and loved to hear him "spout" on art, architecture and the like. His reputation as an intellectual was enhanced by the fact that he "always had a book spread out in front of him." He carried several in his pack, one by Schopenhauer ("I learned a great deal from him"). This philosopher's recurrent affirmation of the strength of blind will, the triumph of that will, must have struck a responsive chord.

By the end of the summer of 1915 Hitler had become indispensable to regimental headquarters. The telephone lines to battalion and company command posts were often knocked out by artillery and only runners could deliver messages. "We found out very soon," recalled Lieutenant Wiedemann, "which messengers we could rely on the most." He was admired by fellow runners as much for his craftiness—he could crawl up front like one of the Indians he had read about in his boyhood—as his exceptional courage. Yet there was something in Hitler that disturbed some of the men. He was too different, his sense of duty excessive.

The tempo of fighting increased in June and July and the constant duty began to tell on Hitler. His face became wan and more sallow. In the dark hours of the morning when an English barrage started he would leap out of bed and, rifle in hand, stride rapidly back and forth, "like a race horse at the starting gate," until everyone was awake. He became even more impatient with his neighbors' gripes. If one complained about the smaller meat ration, he sharply retorted that the French ate rats in 1870.

On September 25 the English pressed their attack and by nightfall the position of the entire 16th Regiment was endangered. Phone communication to the front abruptly ceased. Hitler and another man went forward to find out what had happened and returned "by the skin of their teeth" to report that the lines had been cut. An enemy attack in force was coming. Hitler was sent out to broadcast the warning and somehow survived the deadly barrage once more.

In the past months he had narrowly escaped death an inordinate number of times. It was as if he led a charmed life. "I was eating my dinner in a trench with several comrades," he told an English correspondent, Ward Price, years later. "Suddenly a voice seemed to be saying to me, 'Get up and go over there.' It was so clear and insistent that I obeyed mechanically, as if it had been a military order. I rose at once to my feet and walked twenty yards along the trench, carrying my dinner in its tin-can with me. Then I sat down to go on eating, my mind being once more at rest. Hardly had I done so when a flash and deafening report came from the part of the trench I had just left. A stray shell had burst over the group in which I had been sitting, and every member of it was killed."

In the early summer of 1916 Hitler's regiment moved south, just in time to take part in the crucial battle of the Somme. It began with an English attack so relentless that almost 20,000 Allies were killed or fatally wounded on the first day alone. In the Fromelles sector the enemy barrage on the night of July 14 cut all regimental field telephones. Hitler and another runner were sent out "in the face of almost certain death, peppered with shot and shell every meter of the way." They cowered for shelter in watery shell holes and ditches. The other man collapsed from exhaustion and Hitler had to drag him back to their dugout.

For the next two months the struggle lapsed into dull but deadly trench warfare with advances or retreats measured in yards. It was during this time that Hitler lost a close friend; Hans Mend was transferred to the rear to act as interpreter in a prisoner-of-war camp. But he still had two other comrades, Ernst Schmidt and Ignaz Westenkirchner—and, more important, a pet dog.

After three months the Battle of the Somme still raged. The Allies persistently attacked and, in all, would suffer 614,000 casualties in this one campaign, but it was a useless slaughter, for the German lines did not buckle. For almost a week Hitler continued his charmed life despite a number of dangerous missions. Then on the night of October 7 his luck ended as he slept with the other messengers in sitting position in a narrow tunnel leading to regimental headquarters. A shell exploded near the narrow entrance, knocking the messengers into a heap. Hitler was hit in the thigh but tried to argue Wiedemann into keeping him at the front. "It isn't so bad, Lieutenant, right?" he said anxiously. "I can still stay with you, I mean, stay with the regiment! Can't I?"

3

Hitler was evacuated to a field hospital. His wound, his first, was not serious but in the ward he suffered a curious shock, one that almost made him collapse from "fright." It came as he lay on his cot and suddenly heard the voice of a German woman, a nurse. "For the first time in two years to hear such a sound!" Shortly he was on a hospital train bound for Germany. "The closer our train which was to bring us home approached the border, the more inwardly restless each of us became." At last he recognized the first German house—"by its high gable and beautiful shutters. The Fatherland!"

At a military hospital just southwest of Berlin the comfortable white beds were such a change after trench life that at first "we hardly dared to lie on them properly." He gradually readjusted to such comfort, but not to the spirit of cynicism he found in some men. As soon as he was ambulatory, Hitler got permission to spend the weekend in Berlin. He found hunger and "dire misery"—and "scoundrels" who were agitating for peace.

After two months he was released from the hospital and transferred to a replacement battalion in Munich. Here, according to *Mein Kampf*, he at last found the answer to the collapse of morale. The Jews! They were behind the front line plotting Germany's downfall. "Nearly every clerk was a Jew and nearly every Jew was a clerk. I was amazed at this plethora of warriors from the chosen people and could not help but compare them with their rare representatives at the front." He was also convinced that "Jewish finance" had seized control of Germany's production. "The spider was slowly beginning to suck the blood out of the people's pores." His comrades at the front never heard him talk like this; he appeared to be no more anti-Semitic than they were.

Hitler became disgusted with Munich. He found the mood in the replacement battalion despicable. No one honored a front-line soldier. These recruits had no conception of what Hitler had suffered in the trenches. He longed to be back with his own kind and in January 1917 wrote Lieutenant Wiedemann that he was "again fit for service" and wished "to return to my old regiment and old comrades." On March 1 he was back with the 16th Regiment.

A few days later the regiment entrained for the Arras area to prepare for another spring offensive. But there was leisure time for painting, and Hitler completed more water colors, scenes of former battles that had meaning to him.

Despite long and gallant service Hitler was still a corporal. One reason, according to Wiedemann, was that he lacked "the capacity for leadership." That summer the regiment returned to its first battlefield in Belgium and participated in the third battle for Ypres. It was as deadly as the first. In mid-July they were bombarded for ten days and nights. When it slackened they could hear under them the ominous sound of digging—the enemy was boring tunnels. Overhead came the drone of planes, then the crash of bombs. In addition there was the constant threat of gas and the men sometimes had to keep their suffocating masks on for twenty-four hours at a stretch. On the last day of July the defenders were confronted with a new terror—tanks. Fortunately, torrential rains turned no man's land into a quagmire and the tanks were bogged down.

The unit saw little action for the rest of the year and Hitler had much time for reading. To him novels and magazines were frivolous and he concentrated on history and philosophy. "War forces one to think deeply about human nature," he later told Hans Frank. "Four years of war are equivalent to thirty years university training in regard to life's problems. I hated nothing more than trash literature. When we are concerned with the fate of mankind then one can only read Homer and evangelical works. In the later years of the war I read Schopenhauer and reached for him again and again. [The copy of Schopenhauer's selected works which he kept in his pack was worn out.] Then I was able to do without evangelism—even if Christ was a true fighter. But the turning of both cheeks is not a very good recipe for the front."

At last Berlin made peace with the Soviets at Brest-Litovsk on March 3 but the terms imposed on the young government were so harsh that leftists in Germany claimed the treaty's real purpose was to crush the Russian Revolution. News of the capitulation of the Bolsheviks exhilarated soldiers like Hitler who remained convinced that Germany must win. Now more than ever total victory seemed in their grasp and the majority of troops responded loyally if not eagerly to the high command's order for a massive offensive. In the next four months Hitler's regiment took part in all phases of the massive Ludendorff spring offensives: on the Somme, on the Aisne and finally on the Marne. Hitler's fighting spirit was higher than ever. On one of his trips out front in June he got a glimpse of something in a trench that looked like a French helmet. He crept forward and saw four *poilus*. Hitler pulled out his pistol—messengers had turned in rifles for side arms by then—and began shouting orders in German as though he had a company of soldiers. He delivered his four prisoners to Colonel von Tubeuf personally and was commended. "There was no circumstance or situation," recalled Tubeuf, "that would have prevented him from volunteering for the most difficult, arduous and dangerous tasks and he was always ready to sacrifice life and tranquillity for his Fatherland and for others." On August 4 Hitler was awarded the Iron Cross, 1st Class, but it was for former achievements and not this outstanding feat and simply read, "For personal bravery and general merit." It was presented to him by the battalion adjutant who had initiated the award, First Lieutenant Hugo Gutmann, a Jew.

By this time it was evident that the great Ludendorff offensives which had pushed to within sight of the Eiffel Tower had failed miserably. Defeat on the western front came as a shock, particularly after the historic victories in the East where vast areas extending as far as the Caucasus had been conquered. Consequently there was a serious drop in morale even among the older soldiers. Disorders on troop and leave trains approached rebellion.

In the face of rebellion at home and impending collapse at the front, Hitler became more argumentative and talked at length of the swindle perpetrated by the Reds. But his voice was lost in the chorus of complaints from replacements. At such times, according to Schmidt, Hitler "became furious and shouted in a terrible voice that the pacifists and shirkers were losing the war." One day he attacked a new non-com who said it was stupid to continue fighting. They fought with their fists, and finally, after taking considerable punishment, Hitler beat his opponent. From that day, Schmidt recalled, "the new ones despised him but we old comrades liked him more than ever."

Four years of dehumanizing trench warfare had engendered in Hitler, as in so many other German patriots, an abiding hatred of the pacifists and slackers back home who were "stabbing the Fatherland in the back." He and those like him burned with a zeal to avenge such treachery, and out of all this would come the politics of the future. Hitler was far from the dreamy-eyed volunteer of 1914. Four years in the trenches had given him a sense of belonging along with a degree of self-confidence. Having fought for Germany, he was truly German; and having conducted himself honorably under duress, he had pride in his manhood.

On the morning of October 14 Hitler was blinded by gas near the village of Werwick. He would recover his eyesight only to lose it again November 9, upon learning that Germany was going to surrender. A few days later he would hear voices and see a vision.

4

It is impossible to know how deep Adolf Hitler's fear and hatred of Jews ran on the day he was gassed in Belgium. Within a year, however, hatred of all things Jewish would become an overt and dominant force in his life. Hitler was only one among millions of other patriots who learned to fear Jews and Reds (almost as a single entity) during this period. For in these months the country was engulfed by a terrifying series of Marxist-inspired uprisings that threatened to destroy the fabric of German existence.

Significantly, the revolutions began while Hitler was suffering the depressing aftereffects of mustard gas. On the day he started east in a hospital train—it was October 16—Prince Max of Baden, the new German Chancellor, received a note from President Woodrow Wilson demanding, in effect, the abdication of Wilhelm before America would agree to an armistice. This quickened the disintegration of the German military and within two weeks open revolt broke out when the fleet was ordered to proceed to sea. The crews of six battleships protested. Mutiny broke out in Kiel as sailors pillaged armories and small arms lockers and took over most of the city.

Government after government throughout Germany collapsed as workers' and soldiers' councils took control. Finally, on November 9, the Kaiser reluctantly abdicated, turning power over to the moderate socialists who were led by a former saddlemaker, Friedrich Ebert. It was the end of the German Empire, begun in France on January 18, 1871, when Wilhelm I, King of Prussia and grandfather of Wilhelm II, was proclaimed the first German Emperor in the Hall of Mirrors at the Versailles Palace.

It was also the end of an era. Forty-eight years earlier Bismarck had achieved his dream of unifying Germany and in so doing had created a new image of Germany and Germans. Overnight the foundation on which rested the security of the Junker landowners in East Prussia and the great industrialists crumbled; and overnight the political philosophy on which the majority of Germans had based their conservative and patriotic way of life had apparently disintegrated with the lowering of the imperial flag.

Perhaps the greatest shock to Germans was to find Ebert sitting in the chancellery. In a single day the Hohenzollern regime had evaporated and a man of the people had taken command. How could it possibly have happened? Ebert himself was uneasy in the seat of power. He realized his presence would be an insult to those raised in imperialism. Moreover, he did not even represent the radical spirit of the streets. In fact, whom did he represent?

At 5 A.M. two days later a representative of the Ebert government, Matthias Erzberger, put his signature to the Allied armistice terms in Marshal Foch's private railroad car. Hostilities would cease at 11 A.M. He had insured peace to a shattered nation at the eleventh hour of the eleventh day of the eleventh month of the year, and in so doing innocently gave birth to the myth of the "November criminals"—that it was the socialists who had sold out the nation. It was the Kaiser and the imperial German generals, of course, who had lost the war but President Wilson had refused to make an armistice with them, insisting he could deal only with democratic elements. And by forcing the socialists to assume the blame for something they had not brought about, Wilson gave Adolf Hitler a political tool that he was destined to wield with devastating force.

5

At the end of November 1918 Hitler was discharged from the Pasewalk hospital as "fit for field service" since the patient "no longer complained of anything but a burning of the membrane." Hitler later testified in court that he could only make out the largest headlines in a newspaper and feared he might never read another book. "The medical records at the hospital," he complained, "were made at a time of revolution. Practically no one got personal attention; we were discharged in hordes. For example, I never even received my soldier's pay-book."

He was ordered to report to the replacement battalion of his regiment. This was located in Munich and on his way he must have passed through Berlin, which was in the hands of the Executive Council of the Workers' and Soldiers' Councils—a coalition not only of soldiers and workers but of Majority and Independent Socialists. This conglomeration had already enacted social reforms which would have seemed impossible a few months earlier. It had established the eight-hour day; granted labor the unrestricted right to organize into unions; increased workers' old-age, sick and unemployment benefits; abolished censorship of the press; and released political prisoners.

While Hitler approved the social reforms, he distrusted the

revolutionaries who had effected them: the Executive Council was a tool of the Bolsheviks and the betrayer of the front-line soldiers; and its eventual goal was another Red revolution. When Hitler checked in at the Türkenstrasse barracks of Munich's Schwabing area, he encountered the same spirit of rebellion. There was no discipline; the place was a pigsty. There was no respect for those who had served in the trenches since the first days of the war. Many were there for food and shelter alone. What particularly incensed Hitler was the behavior of the council members. "Their whole activity was so repellent to me that I decided at once to leave again as soon as possible."

Fortunately he found an old comrade, Ernst Schmidt, who experienced the same disgust. Some two weeks later, when guards were sought for a prisoner-of-war camp at Traunstein, sixty miles to the east on the road to Salzburg, Hitler suggested to Schmidt that they volunteer. Their group, comprised mostly of so-called "revolution men," was met at the railroad station by an officer. The men treated his order to fall in as a joke: didn't he know drill had been abolished? The next day the contingent, except for a few who had seen service in the trenches, were shipped back to Munich. Hitler and Schmidt remained.

6

In Berlin the Spartacists, a far leftist group named after the slave who led the rebellion against the Romans, had taken to the streets to make revolution with the help of revolting sailors. This was no *gemütlich* Munich uprising. By Christmas Eve the capital was close to anarchy. Other cities followed suit, if not as dramatically, and throughout Germany the structure of the military and police began to crumble.

With their abdication of authority, a new force made an abrupt appearance—a phenomenon known as the Freikorps, bands of idealistic activists from the armed forces who shared Hitler's passion to defend Germania from the Reds. The Free Corps, spawned from the German generation born in Hitler's time, had been prepared for today's action by two previous experiences. First had come the prewar youth movement, the Wandervögel (Birds of Passage). These youngsters tramped around the land, often wearing colorful costumes, in their search for a new way of life. For the most part from the well-to-do middle class, they despised the liberal bourgeois society they sprang from and were convinced that "parental religion was largely sham, politics boastful and trivial, economics unscrupulous and deceitful, education stereotyped and lifeless, art trashy and sentimental, literature spurious and commercialized, drama tawdry and mechanical." They regarded family life as repressive and insincere. They also were concerned that the relations between the sexes, in and out of marriage, were "shot through with hypocrisy." Their goal was to establish a youth culture for fighting the bourgeois trinity of school, home and church. These young people, thriving on mysticism and impelled by idealism, yearned for action—any kind of action.

They found it in the Great War. Perhaps that is why they were as convinced as Hitler of the righteousness of the Fatherland's cause. Life in the trenches brought officers and men closer together in a brotherhood of suffering and blood. The men worshiped the one who led them into desperate hand-to-hand combat.

These comrades of the front lines, these former Birds of Passage, shared with Hitler the shame of surrender and distrust of a home front degenerating into Bolshevism. Understandably, these veterans responded with enthusiasm to announcements placed by the military in newspapers and on billboards announcing that the Spartacist danger had not yet been removed and calling for soldiers to rise and join the Free Corps to "prevent Germany from becoming the laughingstock of the earth."

While this illegal army was forming, the Spartacists, with the approval of many Berliners, were taking over the capital. They controlled public utilities, transportation, and munitions factories. In desperation, on January 3, 1919, the Ebert government dismissed the chief of police since he was known to sympathize with the Spartacists and had recently supported the sailors' mutiny. In retaliation, the Spartacists, now openly admitting they were Communists, called for revolution. Berlin workers responded with enthusiasm and by midmorning of the sixth, 200,000 workers, carrying weapons and red flags, massed from the Alexanderplatz to the Tiergarten. Nor did the fog and cold dampen the spirit of the crowd. Groups seized the officers of the Social Democrat newspaper, *Vorwärts,* and the Wolff Telegraph Agency. The chancellery itself was surrounded by the angry mob. Inside hid Ebert and his associates.

By the following morning the Communists were ensconced

in the statuary on top of the Brandenburg Gate, their rifles covering the Unter den Linden, the Königstrasse and the Charlottenburger Chaussee. In addition to strategic railroad stations, the Government Printing Office and the Bötzow Brewery were occupied. Within twenty-four hours the government held only a few of the city's major buildings.

Berlin—eventually all of Germany—would probably have gone Communist but for the Free Corps. Within a week units from outside the city marched in and crushed the Red centers of resistance. The Spartacist leaders, including the diminutive Rosa Luxemburg, were hunted down and cruelly murdered.

Four days after the death of "Red Rose" the first national election under the new Republic was held. It was a Sunday, clear and cold. For the first time in German history women were allowed to participate and 30,000,000 citizens out of an electorate of 35,000,000 cast their votes for 423 deputies to the National Assembly. The results, while surprising, should have been predictable. The two rightist parties, which wanted a return of the Hohenzollerns yet pretended they didn't, got about fifteen per cent of the Assembly seats; the two centrist parties, which favored the Republic, won almost forty per cent as did Ebert's Majority Socialists; and the far left Independent Socialists took only seven per cent. The result, as much a victory against revolution as it was for a republic, doomed socialization.

Since strife-torn Berlin was not considered safe, Weimar, some hundred and fifty miles southwest of the capital, was made the home of the National Assembly. Its selection was a cultural as well as geographical choice, for Weimar had been the home of Goethe, Schiller and Liszt. The Assembly met on February 6 in the New National Theater but the convocation lacked the pomp and ceremony of a Hohenzollern event. There were no bands, cavalry escorts or dazzling uniforms.

After five days a working government was organized with Ebert named first President of the Reich by a large majority. He appointed a Chancellor who, in turn, selected his own cabinet. The most significant choice was a strong-willed man named Noske (he called himself the "Bloodhound") as Minister of Defense. It meant that the illegal Free Corps would now operate with the blessing of the infant Weimar Republic and continue to defend the nation from Reds and riot.

7

Hitler, who considered himself born for and destined to politics, was preparing his return to Munich. The prisoner-of-war camp at Traunstein was about to close and he was being reassigned to the 2nd Infantry Regiment barracks in Schwabing along with his comrade Schmidt. Another young man with similar aspirations was already established in Munich. Alfred Rosenberg, a fanatic anti-Semite and anti-Marxist, had come from his native Estonia by way of Russia to find his true home. Like Hitler, he was artist and architect. Like Hitler, he was more Germanic than a native German, and had left his birthplace "to gain a Fatherland for myself." Moreover, he was determined to warn this Fatherland of the Bolshevik terror that had ravaged the old one, and fight to keep it free from Jewish Communism.

Upon learning that there was a German author named Eckart who shared many of his views, Rosenberg decided to make his acquaintance. Dietrich Eckart—poet, playwright, coffeehouse intellectual—was a tall, bald, burly eccentric who spent much of his time in cafés and beer halls giving equal attention to drink and talk. An original, raffish man with a touch of genius (his brilliant translation of *Peer Gynt* was the standard version), he too was a Pan-German and anti-Semite. With his own money he published a weekly paper that had a circulation of some 30,000.

Rosenberg appeared, without introduction, at Eckart's apartment. The poet was impressed by what he saw in the doorway: an intense, dead-serious young man. Rosenberg's first words were: "Can you use a fighter against Jerusalem?" Eckart laughed. "Certainly!" Had he written anything? Rosenberg produced an article on the destructive forces of Judaism and Bolshevism on Russia. It was the beginning of a relationship that would affect the career of Adolf Hitler. Eckart accepted Rosenberg as a "co-warrior against Jerusalem" and soon his articles on Russia began appearing not only in Eckart's paper but in another Munich weekly, *Deutsche Republik*. The theme of these articles was that the Jew stood behind the world's evils: the Zionists had planned the Great War as well as the Red Revolution and were presently plotting with the Masons to take over the world.

8

To many Bavarians Kurt Eisner, an elderly Jew, was the very model of a revolutionary and it was widely believed that his revolution had been financed by Moscow gold. He was, in fact, the antithesis of the ruthless, pragmatic Russian Bolshevik. He ran the Bavarian Socialist Republic as if he were still installed at the *Stammtisch* of his favorite coffeehouse. What Eisner was attempting to establish was not Communism or even socialism but a unique kind of radical democracy. A poet among politicians whose dream of a reign of beauty, illumination and reason was more in keeping with Shelley than Marx, he was already on the path to oblivion; the January elections had brought a resounding victory for the middle-class parties and an overriding demand for his resignation.

Early in the morning of February 21, realizing his cause was hopeless, he wrote out a statement announcing his resignation, but en route to the Landtag to deliver it, he was assassinated by Count Anton Arco-Valley, a young cavalry officer who had been turned down by an anti-Semitic group since his mother was Jewish. Eisner would have been out of office in an hour, his regime replaced by a middle-of-the-road government. The assassination brought about what Arco-Valley most feared, another surge to the left. Eisner became an instant martyr and proletarian saint, and the revolutionary movement was resuscitated. Martial law was declared and a new all-socialist government headed by a former teacher, Adolf Hoffmann, was appointed by the Central Workers' and Soldiers' Council. A general strike was called, a 7 P.M. curfew imposed, and the University of Munich closed since its students were already acclaiming Arco-Valley as their hero.

A fortnight later the congress of the Third International convened in Moscow and the resolution establishing the Communist International (Comintern) was unanimously adopted. In the ensuing victory celebration Lenin called on workers of all countries to force their leaders to withdraw troops from Russia, resume diplomatic and commercial relations, and help rebuild the fledgling nation with an army of engineers and instructors.

Berlin was already responding to the call for world revolution. The previous day, workers, ignoring orders from the Communist Party, had converged on the center of the city to demonstrate and loot. Joined by the Red Soldiers' League and other radical military groups, they seized more than thirty local police stations. Sailors besieged the main police headquarters on the Alexanderplatz which was defended by several companies of Free Corps infantry. The following day 1500 delegates of the Workers' Councils voted overwhelmingly to call a general strike. The capital was immobilized: no electricity, no transportation.

The revolutionaries concentrated on the eastern part of the city, setting up machine guns at key points. To counter them, Defense Minister Noske, using dictatorial powers recently bestowed on him, brought more than 30,000 Free Corps troops into the city on March 5. The rebels were driven back block by block while Berlin's bars, dance halls and cabarets remained open for business as usual.

After four more days of bitter house-to-house fighting with cannon, machine guns and strafing airplanes pitted against rifles and grenades, Noske announced that anyone "who bears arms against government troops will be shot on the spot." Scores of workers were lined up against walls and executed without trial. It was all over by the thirteenth. More than 1500 revolutionaries were dead and at least 10,000 wounded. The spirit of revolt, however, continued to spread throughout the country.

Munich too was on the verge of another revolution, this one inspired by a coup d'état in Budapest. On March 22 news arrived that a popular front of Socialists and Communists had seized control of Hungary in the name of the councils of workers, soldiers and peasants. A Hungarian Soviet Republic was announced under the leadership of an unknown, Béla Kun. A Jew himself, twenty-five of his thirty-two commissars were also Jews, provoking the London *Times* to characterize the regime as "the Jewish Mafia." The triumph of Béla Kun emboldened the leftists in Munich. Early on the evening of April 4 delegates from the councils trudged through streets piled with twenty inches of snow, the heaviest downfall in years. Their destination was the Löwenbräuhaus, only two blocks from Hitler's prewar rooming house. Here a resolution was read aloud: "Elimination of the parties, union of the entire proletariat, proclamation of a Soviet Republic and brotherhood with the Russian and Hungarian proletariat. And then no power on earth will be able to prevent the immediate execution of full socialization."

It was a coffeehouse revolution, an innocent version of the bloody reality. Its spiritual leader was Ernst Toller, the poet, and his platform included a demand for new art forms in drama, painting and architecture so the spirit of mankind could be set free.

The end came abruptly on Palm Sunday, April 13, when the former Minister President, the socialist schoolteacher Hoffmann, attempted to seize Munich by force. His *Putsch* never had a chance despite the exploits of soldiers like Adolf Hitler. Hoffmann was forced to accept help from War Minister Noske's Free Corps units. A tactical plan for the conquest of Munich was drawn up with amazing promptness and executed so effectively that the city was completely encircled by April 27. In vengeful retribution the surrounded Reds hunted down enemies of the Soviet Republic throughout Munich. Sailors captured seven members of the anti-Semitic Thule Society, including its attractive secretary. In all a hundred hostages were imprisoned in the Luitpold high school.

Students slipped through what was left of the Red lines and reported these atrocities to Free Corps commanders who issued orders to march into the city at dawn. The first of May was clear and warm as Free Corps units converged on the city from several directions. They had little difficulty routing scattered revolutionaries despite some opposition in the area surrounding the Hauptbahnhof and in the Schwabing section. On all sides the Free Corps men were cheered by the relieved citizenry.

While Lenin was boasting to a huge May Day crowd in Red Square of the triumphs of Communism, Free Corps troops were ranging through Munich extinguishing nests of resistance and arresting Red leaders. The streets of Munich belonged to the Free Corps and soon they were marching down the Ludwigstrasse, goose-stepping as they passed the Felderrnhalle, with one unit, the Ehrhardt Brigade, wearing swastika-decorated helmets and singing.

By May 3 Munich was secured but at the cost of sixty-eight Free Corps lives. These, of course, had to be avenged. Thirty Catholic workers of the St. Joseph Society were seized at a tavern while making plans to put on a play. They were brought to the cellar of the Wittelsbach Palace where twenty-one of them were shot or bayoneted to death as dangerous Reds. Hundreds were shot under similar circumstances and thousands were "chastised" by cruising Free Corps squads. The repression continued with issuance of a series of harsh edicts, some almost impossible to obey, such as the one to surrender all arms immediately or be shot. In the name of law and order citizens were routed out, insulted, beaten and murdered. The Free Corps had saved Munich from the iron heel of the Soviet Republic and its excesses but these seemed pale compared to the cure.

9

The idealistic youth of the Wandervögel had brought their high hopes into the trenches and now, as Free Corps men, onto the streets of Germany. "This is the New Man, the storm soldier, the elite of Mitteleuropa," wrote their poet laureate, Ernst Jünger.

Jünger could have been speaking for Adolf Hitler, whose slumbering antipathies had been reawakened by the Red regimes in Munich, and shortly after the liberation of Munich came the event that would change his life and turn the course of world history. On June 28, 1919, the victorious Allies signed the Treaty of Versailles. With little delay the German government ratified its terms. These were harsh. Germany was forced to accept sole responsibility for causing the war and required to pay *all* civilian damage caused by the conflict. Great chunks of territory were wrested from the Reich: Alsace-Lorraine went to France, the Malmédy area to Belgium, most of Posen and West Prussia to Poland. Germany also lost her colonies. Danzig was to be a free state; and plebiscites would be held in the Saar, Schleswig and East Prussia. Further, the Allies would occupy the Rhineland for at least fifteen years and a belt thirty miles wide on the right bank of the Rhine was to be demilitarized. The humiliation was made complete by a regulation forbidding the Germans to have submarines or military aircraft and limiting her army to 100,000 men.

This new force, the Reichswehr, almost immediately exercised a power far beyond its size. To keep the ranks free from Bolshevik influence, a bureau was organized to investigate subversive political activities among the troops and to infiltrate workers' organizations. Among the recruits selected by Captain Karl Mayr, the officer in charge of this unit, was Hitler. He was particularly qualified for such a task but Mayr picked him because of his "exemplary" war record and, perhaps, out of pity. "When I first met him he was like a tired stray dog looking for a master." Mayr got the impression that Hitler "was ready to throw in his lot with anyone who would show him kindness" and that he was "totally unconcerned about the German people and their destinies."

In truth, Hitler was in a state of ferment and turmoil because of the epidemic of revolution. Never had he been so concerned for the state of his adopted country. Recently he had been handed a racist pamphlet—perhaps one of Eckart's—and it brought to mind similar pamphlets he had read in Vienna. "Involuntarily I saw thus my own development come to life again before my eyes." His simmering hatred of Jews had been activated by what he himself had witnessed on the streets of Munich.

Before embarking on their duties, he and his fellow political agents were ordered to attend a special indoctrination course at the University of Munich with instructors such as Professor Karl Alexander von Müller, a conservative with right radical leanings. "For me," wrote Hitler, "the value of the whole affair was that I now obtained an opportunity of meeting a few like-minded comrades with whom I could thoroughly discuss the situation of the moment. All of us were more or less firmly convinced that Germany could no longer be saved from the impending collapse by the parties of the November crime, the Center and the Social Democracy, and that the so-called 'bourgeois-national' formations, even with the best of intentions, could never repair what had happened."

During the war Hitler had told Westenkirchner that in peacetime he would become either an artist or go into politics and when his comrade asked him which party he preferred the answer was, "None." His circle at the indoctrination course had also come to the conclusion that only an entirely new movement could answer their needs. They decided to call it the Social Revolutionary Party "because the social views of the new organization did indeed mean a revolution."

Added impetus was given such a movement by one of the lecturers, Gottfried Feder, Professor von Müller's brother-in-law. Founder of the German Fighting League for the Breaking of Interest Slavery, he was an engineer by profession but an economist at heart. He spoke to the political agents about the speculation and economic character of stock exchanges and loan capital. This was a stimulating revelation to Hitler. "Right after listening to Feder's first lecture, the thought ran through my head that I had now found the way to one of the most essential premises for the foundation of a new party." Inspired by Feder's demand to end interest slavery, he restudied Marxism, "and now for the first time really achieved an understanding of the content of the Jew Karl Marx's life effort." At last his *Kapital* was intelligible.

After one of his lectures Professor von Müller noticed a small group in lively discussion. "The men seemed spellbound by one of their number who was haranguing them with increasing vehemence in a strange guttural voice."

"Do you know you have a natural orator among your students?" Müller told Captain Mayr, indicating the pale-faced soldier. Mayr called out, "You, Hitler, come up here." Hitler approached "awkwardly, with a kind of defiant embarrassment." His talent for oratory led to an assignment in a Munich regiment as a lecturer. "I started out with the greatest enthusiasm and love. For all at once I was offered an opportunity of speaking before a larger audience; and the thing that I had always presumed from pure feeling without knowing it was now corroborated: I could 'speak.'" With each speech Hitler grew more confident and his voice developed to such an extent that his words could be understood in every corner of the squad rooms.

Captain Mayr was impressed enough by his abilities as a speaker to send him on a special mission outside Munich; returning German prisoners of war at the Lechfeld transit camp were evidencing Spartacist leanings, and an Enlightenment Detachment was assigned to transform these men into anti-socialist patriots.

The propaganda team left Munich on July 22 and within five days Hitler himself received an education in practical politics. The returnees were bitter and resentful. Cheated of their youth and hope, forced to live like animals in the trenches, they had come home to chaos and hunger. Hitler offered them targets for their hatred as he spoke eloquently of the "Versailles disgrace," the "November criminals" and the "Jewish-Marxist World Plot." His flair for such work was duly noted in a series of commendatory reports. "Herr Hitler, if I might put it this way," commented one observer, "is the born people's speaker, and by his fanaticism and his crowd appeal he clearly compels the attention of his listeners, and makes them think his way."

He returned to Munich and speeches in the squad room. Another duty was to help investigate the fifty or so radical organizations that had recently sprung up in Munich. These included racists, Communists, rabid nationalists, anarchists, and superpatriots, covering the political spectrum from the Bloc of Revolutionary Students and the Society of Communistic Socialists to the Ostara Bund and the New Fatherland.

Early that autumn Hitler was ordered to attend a meeting of a tiny political group calling itself the German Workers' Party. The evening made so little impression on him that he did not mention it in *Mein Kampf*, even though, according to one of the twenty-three participants present, he addressed the gathering in the discussion period and, indeed, "spoke very well." The party's program was a bizarre combination of socialism, nationalism and anti-Semitism. Its background was shrouded in mystery, seeded as it was by a small group called the Political Workers' Circle, the brain child of Rudolf Freiherr von Sebottendorff, himself a man of mystery.

Like Hitler, he believed in the Germanic wave of the future and so threw his considerable energies into the formation of a Bavarian branch of the Teutonic Order. Membership was restricted to Germans who could establish the "purity of their blood" for three generations; and every candidate had to pledge he would join energetically in "the struggle against internationalism and Jewry." The revolutions throughout the country forced Sebottendorff to give his organization the innocent title of Thule Society as a cover. By this time he had decided to implement an idea he had long entertained: to win workers to his *völkisch* cause,* he instructed one of the members of Thule, a down-at-the-heels sports writer, to form a Political Workers' Circle. This man sought out Anton Drexler and they joined forces to found a new political organization. The preliminary meeting of the German Workers' Party was held at a little restaurant, the Fürstenfelder Hof, early that January. Some two dozen workers, most of them railwaymen of Drexler's shop, were on hand to hear Drexler outline the dual purpose of the party: to liberate the workers from Marxist internationalism by ending the divisive class warfare and to make the upper classes aware of their responsibility to the workers. All they really wanted, said Drexler, was "to be ruled by Germans." Drexler suggested calling their group the German National Socialist Party (the same name of a similarly motivated party founded

*Völkisch is impossible to translate in a single word. Literally meaning "folkish," it had overtones of racism; but to translate it simply as "racist" is to ignore its folk-nationalistic implications. Throughout the book it will remain völkisch.

a year earlier in Bohemia, whose emblem, incidentally, was the swastika), but there was objection that the word "socialist" might be misinterpreted.

Painstakingly Drexler penned out notes for a program. The skilled worker should not consider himself to be a proletariat but a middle-class citizen. And the middle class itself had to be enlarged and strengthened "at the cost of big capitalism." The program also included a cautiously anti-Semitic declaration that "religious teachings contrary to the moral and ethical laws of Germany should not be supported by the state" or, in fact, even tolerated. Within two weeks a foundation meeting was held in the Thule headquarters. The seedy sports writer, Karl Harrer, was elected chairman with Drexler as his deputy.

It could hardly be called a party since it consisted of little more than a six-man committee. "Our meetings were private because of this Red threat," recalled Drexler, a serious, undistinguished, sickly man. "We could do little but discuss and study. I embodied my own ideas in a slight brochure called *My Political Awakening*. From the diary of a workingman." His dream was to find someone with energy and nerve who could make something out of his pamphlet "and contrive a real driving force behind us. It would need to be an outstanding personality, anyhow, who could even attempt to do such a thing, a man of intense conviction, single-eyed, and absolutely fearless."

On September 12 Hitler was ordered by a Major Hierl to attend another meeting of the little Workers' Party. A "single-eyed" man of conviction if ever there was one, he walked into the Sterneckerbräu, a little beer hall on the Herrenstrasse, early that evening to find forty or so workers. The main speaker was supposed to be the poet Eckart but he was sick and had been replaced by the economist Feder, whose subject was "How and by what means is capitalism to be eliminated?"

Hitler had heard Feder's lecture at his indoctrination course and so could concentrate on the membership. His impression was neither good nor bad. This was apparently another of those groups which "sprang out of the ground, only to vanish silently after a time." Obviously its founders had no conception of how to make their club into a genuine party. The evening was a bore and he was relieved when Feder finished talking. Hitler started to leave at the announcement of a free discussion period, but something "moved" him to remain. A few minutes later he was on his feet belaboring a professor who had just advocated the separation of Bavaria from Prussia. Hitler talked for fifteen minutes so ably and cuttingly that the professor ". . . left the hall like a wet poodle, even before I was finished."

Drexler was so impressed by Hitler's delivery and logic that he whispered to his secretary, "This one has what it takes, we could use him!" He introduced himself but Hitler didn't get the name of the unprepossessing man with glasses. Like a religious fanatic, Drexler pressed a copy of his booklet, a forty-page pamphlet with a pink cover, into Hitler's hand and mumbled that he must read it and please come again.

Hitler returned to his little room on the upper floor of the barracks. As usual he had trouble sleeping and set out crusts of bread and leftovers on the floor for the mice. He had gotten into the habit of passing the hours before dawn "watching the droll little beasts chasing around after these choice morsels. I had known so much poverty in my life that I was well able to imagine the hunger, and hence also the pleasure, of the little creatures."

At about five that morning he was still awake on his cot following the antics of the mice when he remembered the pamphlet that Drexler had forced upon him. Hitler was surprised to find himself enthralled from the first page. "Involuntarily I saw my own development come to life before my eyes." The ideas and phrases of the little book kept intruding into his thoughts the following day. He was struck by the phrases "National Socialism" and "new world order," as well as the prediction that a new political party would capture the disillusioned and disinherited among not only the workers but civil servants and the solid lower middle class.

But his interest waned quickly and he was surprised to receive a postcard informing him that he had been accepted as a member of the German Workers' Party. He was requested to attend a committee meeting the following Wednesday. He had no intention of joining a ready-made party since he wanted to found his own and he was about to send off an indignant refusal when "curiosity won out" and he decided to have another look at the queer little group. The minutes of the previous meeting were read and the treasurer reported there were seven marks fifty pfennig on hand. Letters were read and discussed at intolerable length. It was worse than Hitler had imagined. "Terrible, terrible! This was club life of the worst manner and sort. Was I to join this organization?" When they began to discuss new membership, Hitler asked a number of questions about the practical aspects of organization. He learned there was no program, not a leaflet, not even a rubber stamp, only good intentions. He quickly glanced through their few directives. They were unclear or vague.

He left depressed by what he had seen but still undecided whether to join or not. It was the "hardest question" of his life and he debated with himself for the next two days. Reason told him to decline but his feeling argued for acceptance. He had vowed to enter politics and this absurd little club had one transcendent advantage—it had not "frozen into an 'organization,' but left the individual an opportunity for real personal activity." Being so small, it could also be more easily shaped to his needs.

Hitler had already reported his findings to Captain Mayr, who passed them on to a group of high-ranking officers and capitalists who met once a week at the Hotel Four Seasons to discuss means of rebuilding Germany's military power. They had come to the conclusion that this could only be achieved with the support of the workers. The little German Workers' Party could be a start and, according to Mayr, General Ludendorff himself appeared at Mayr's office one day with a request that Hitler be allowed to join the organization and build it up.

It was illegal for members of the new army to join political parties but "to please Ludendorff, whose wishes were still respected in the army, I ordered Hitler to join the Workers' Party and help foster its growth. He was allowed at first the equivalent of twenty gold marks in the current inflation money weekly for this purpose." So, in a sense, Hitler was ordered to do what he had already decided to do. He registered as a member of the DAP and was given a membership card.

Hitler's plunge into practical politics was accompanied by an equally important ideological development which also came to fruition as the result of an order of Captain Mayr. Hitler was instructed to answer a letter from a fellow trainee in the education unit requesting information on the Jewish menace. His lengthy answer revealed a surprising progression in his own solution of the Jewish question. It was replete with denunciations of Jews that would become all too familiar: "He burrows into the democracies sucking the good will of the masses, crawls before the majesty of the people but knows only the majesty of money. . . . His activities result in racial tuberculosis of the people." The anti-Semitic program, he concluded, should start with legal attempts to deprive Jews of certain privileges on the grounds that they were a foreign race. "But the final aim must unquestionably be the irrevocable *Entfernung* of the Jews." This word could be translated as "removal" and merely mean expulsion from Germany but it is more likely he meant "amputation," that is, liquidation of Jewry.

This was Hitler's first known political document and for the first time he had succeeded in transforming his hatred of the Jews into a positive political program.

PART 2

IN THE BEGINNING WAS THE WORD

Chapter Four

BIRTH OF A PARTY

1919–1922

1

Hitler's first task was to turn what was essentially a debating society into a political organization. The light at their meeting in the back room of the Rosenbad was a single gas flame that burned poorly. "When we were assembled . . . how did we look? Forbidding. Military pants, dyed coats, hats of undefinable shapes but shiny from wear, our feet in remodeled war boots, and a thick cudgel in our hands as a 'walking stick.'" In those days it was a sign of distinction, a proof that one belonged to the people.

"We were always the same faces. . . . First we received the brotherly greetings, and we were informed that the 'seeds' had been planted in respective places, or even established and we were asked if we could make such a report also, and the necessity was stressed to act as a unit." The treasury was usually about five marks and once it reached the high point of seventeen.

Hitler finally persuaded the committee to increase membership by holding larger meetings. At the barracks he personally typed out on the company typewriter some of the invitations to the first public meeting, others he wrote by hand. On the night of the first meeting the committee of seven waited "for the masses who were expected to appear." An hour passed but no one came. "We were again seven men, the old seven." Hitler changed his tactics. The next invitations were mimeographed and this time a few came. The number rose slowly from eleven to thirteen and finally to thirty-four.

The pittance collected from these meetings was invested in an advertisement in the *Münchener Beobachter*, a völkisch, anti-Semitic newspaper, for a mass meeting in the cellar room of the Hofbräuhaus on October 16.

If only the usual number turned up, the expenses would bankrupt the party. By 7 P.M. seventy people had collected in the smoky room. There is no record of the reception given the main speaker but almost from the moment Adolf Hitler stepped behind the crude lectern placed atop the head table the audience was "electrified." He was supposed to speak for twenty minutes but went on for half an hour, spilling out a stream of denunciations, threats and promises. Abandoning all restraint, he let emotion take over and by the time he sat down to loud applause sweat covered his face. He was exhausted but elated "and what before I had simply felt deep down in my heart, without being able to put it to the test, proved to be true; I could speak!"

It was a turning point not only in his career but in that of the German Workers' Party. Three hundred marks had been donated by the enthusiastic listeners; now the organization had funds to advertise more extensively and print slogans and leaflets. On November 13 a second mass meeting was held, this time in another beer hall, the Eberlbräu. More than 130 men (mostly students, shopkeepers and army officers) paid an admission fee of fifty pfennigs, something new in local politics, to hear four speakers. The main attraction was Hitler. In the middle of his speech hecklers began to shout out but he had alerted his military friends and within minutes the agitators "flew down the stairs with gashed heads." The interruption only spurred Hitler to greater rhetorical heights as he closed with an exhortation to stand up and resist. "The misery of Germany must be broken by Germany's steel. That time must come."

Once more he carried the audience with him. He spoke with a primitive force and unabashed emotion that set him apart from the intellectuals who appealed to reason. A police observer, after describing Hitler as a merchant, reported that he had "held forth in an outstanding manner" and was destined to become "a professional propaganda speaker." His appeals were visceral—love of country and hatred of Jews for bringing about the defeat of 1918. By his manner and use of the language of the streets and the trenches, war veterans recognized that he had shared the democracy of the machine gun, barbed wire and muck and thus represented the sacred comradeship of the front lines.

Hitler's ascendancy deeply concerned some of the other members, who objected to his volcanic, mercurial style. Moreover, he was changing the entire face of the organization with the influx of his rough-mannered army friends, and they feared it would all end in ruin. While Drexler was equally distressed, he was so convinced that Hitler was the hope of the party that he supported the move to make him the new chief of propaganda. Promotion only made Hitler more critical of the inefficiency of the party's business procedures. How could one administer properly without an office and equipment? On his own he found an office at the Sterneckerbräu, scene of his introduction to the party. It was small and had once been a taproom. The rent was so little, fifty marks a month, that the committee didn't even complain when the landlord removed the wood paneling and left the room looking more like "a funeral vault than an office." Using funds he got from Captain Mayr as well as those from the party treasury, he had an electric light installed along with a telephone, a table, a few borrowed chairs, an open bookcase and two cupboards. Hitler's next step was to insist on a paid business manager who would work full time. He found one in his barracks, a sergeant "upright and absolutely honest," who also brought along his small Adler typewriter.

That December Hitler called for a complete reform of the party's organization from a debating society to a genuine political party. A majority of committee members, content to remain just another extreme rightist group, opposed these changes. They could not see, as Hitler clearly did, that propaganda was not an end in itself, only a means to overthrow the Weimar Republic.

One evening in the last days of 1919 Hitler arrived at the Drexlers' "armed with a sheaf of manuscript" on which he had roughly sketched out the official party program. They worked for hours "boiling it down" to make it as pithy as possible. "We cracked our brains over it, I can tell you!" recalled Drexler. By the time they finished it was morning. Then Hitler sprang up and banged his fist on the table. "These points of ours," he exclaimed, "are going to rival Luther's placard on the doors of Wittenberg!"

There were twenty-five points to the program and Hitler wanted to present them to the public at a mass meeting. Predictably there were objections from the committee, not only to a number of the points but to an open meeting. At first dubious, Drexler was finally carried away by the idea and at the next meeting gave Hitler his full support. Those who objected were overruled and a date was set: February 24, 1920.

Leaflets and posters printed in bright red were plastered all over Munich but by this time Hitler himself began to fear he might be speaking to "a yawning hall." The meeting was to start at 7:30 P.M. and when Hitler entered the great Festsaal of the Hofbräuhaus at seven-fifteen he found it jammed with almost 2000 people. His heart "burst with joy." What particularly pleased him was that more than half the crowd appeared to be Communists or Independent Socialists. He was confident that the true idealists among this hostile group would swing over to his side and he welcomed any disturbance they might provoke.

The meeting opened quietly with the main address by an experienced völkisch speaker named Dingfelder. He attacked Jews but did so obliquely. He quoted Shakespeare and Schiller and was so bland that even the Communists weren't offended by anything he had to say. Then Hitler got to his feet. There were no catcalls. He looked anything but an orator in his worn, old-fashioned blue suit. He opened quietly, without emphasis, outlining the history of the past ten years. But as he told of the postwar revolutions that swept through Germany, passion crept into his voice; he began to gesture, his eyes flashed. Angry shouts came from all parts of the large hall. Beer mugs flew through the air. Hitler's army supporters—"swift as greyhounds, tough as leather, and hard as Krupp steel"—eagerly went into battle armed with rubber truncheons and riding whips. Troublemakers were hustled outside. At last some degree of order was restored and Hitler resumed speaking, undismayed by the continuing chorus of derisive shouts.

Unaccustomed to speaking to such a large audience, his voice would be loud one moment, weak the next. But even his inexperience was appealing. A twenty-year-old law student named Hans Frank was struck by his obvious sincerity. "The first thing you felt was that there was a man who spoke honestly about how he felt and was not trying to put something across of which he himself was not absolutely convinced." After the polished phrases of the first speaker his words had an explosive effect. They were often crude, always expressive. And even those who had come to hoot him were compelled to listen. He spoke simply and so clearly that those at the farthest tables could hear. What particularly impressed young Frank was that he "made things understandable even to the foggiest brain . . . and went to the core of things."

Finally he submitted to the audience the twenty-five theses of the program, asking them to "pronounce judgment" on them point by point. There was something for almost everyone but Jews. For the patriotic, union of all Germans in a Greater Reich; colonies for excess population; equality for Germany among nations; revocation of the Versailles Treaty; creation of a people's army; and a "ruthless battle" against criminals to ensure law and order. For the workers, abolition of all income unearned by work; confiscation of war profits; expropriation of land without compensation for communal purposes; and profit sharing in large industrial enterprises. For the middle class, the immediate socialization of the great department stores and their lease, at low rates, to small tradesmen; "generous development" of old-age national health standards. For the völkisch-minded, the demand that Jews be treated as aliens, denied the right to hold any public office, deported if the state found it impossible to feed its entire population, and expelled immediately if they had emigrated after August 2, 1914.

After each point Hitler would pause to ask if everyone understood and agreed. The majority shouted out raucous approval but there were organized cries of derision and some protesters jumped up on chairs and tables. Again and again the truncheon and whip brigade went into action and by the end of Hitler's two-and-a-half-hour tirade there was almost unanimous support for every word he uttered. The final applause was tumultuous and young Frank was fully convinced that "if anyone could master the fate of Germany, Hitler was that man."

To Hitler the evening, including its riotous objections, had been an unalloyed triumph, and as the crowd filed out he felt that the door to his future had at last opened. "When I closed the meeting, I was not alone in thinking that now a wolf had been born, destined to burst in upon the herd of seducers of the people." He was living up to his own name, for Adolf was derived from the Teutonic word meaning "fortunate wolf." And from that day on "wolf" would have a special meaning for him—as nickname among close friends; as a pseudonym for himself and his sister Paula; and as a name for most of his military headquarters.

There was little notice of Hitler's emergence in the Munich newspapers, but the meeting meant the first major step forward for the German Workers' Party. A hundred new members were enrolled. At Hitler's insistence a list of members had already been drawn up and proper membership cards issued. To give the impression of size the first card was numbered 501, with the members listed in alphabetical order. Hitler, painter, was number 555.

2

He began a new life, mixing with an enlarged circle of colorful characters whose common denominator was a love of things German and a fear of Marxism. There was a Munich physician, a believer in the sidereal pendulum, who claimed this gave him the power to detect the presence of a Jew in any group of people. Of far more importance was a former company commander, Captain Ernst Röhm, a homosexual. Röhm was an exemplary officer, a comrade to be trusted in peril. He was short and stocky with closely cropped hair and an engaging smile. He was a walking monument to the war; the upper part of his nose had been shot away and a bullet had left a deep scar in one cheek. From the moment the two met at a secret meeting of a nationalist group called the Iron Fist, Röhm was convinced that the dedicated corporal was just the man to head the German Workers' Party. Röhm had already changed the working-class character of the Drexler-Harrer organization by bringing in so many soldiers. They were the ones who kept order at rowdy meetings. Between Hitler and Röhm were bonds of blood and suffering since both belonged to the brotherhood of the front-line fighter, and though Röhm had recently replaced Captain Mayr as Hitler's commander he insisted that his subordinate use the familiar *du*, a familiarity which was leading to Hitler's acceptance by other officers.

An even closer acquaintance was the writer Dietrich Eckart, who had once remarked that the new breed of political leader must be able to stand the noise of a machine gun. "I prefer a vain monkey who is able to give the Reds a salty reply, and doesn't run away when people begin swinging table legs, to a dozen learned professors."

Eckart, a born romantic revolutionary, was a master of coffeehouse polemics. A sentimental cynic, a sincere charlatan, constantly on stage, lecturing brilliantly if given the slightest opportunity be it at his own apartment, on the street or in a café. A drug addict and drunkard, his vulgarity was tempered by vestiges of his social background. Hitler reveled in the company of this warm and voluble intellectual buccaneer who was playing Falstaff to Hitler's Prince Hal in Munich's ribald night world. Eckart became the younger man's mentor. He gave Hitler a trench coat, corrected his grammar, took him to better-class restaurants and cafés and introduced him to influential citizens ("This is the man who will one day liberate Germany"). The two spent hours discussing music, art and literature as well as politics and the association with the tempestuous writer left a lasting mark on Hitler.

Several weeks after the Hofbräuhaus meeting the two men set off together on an adventure in Berlin. Elite Free Corps troops under General Walther von Lüttwitz, ordered to disband by the socialist Weimar government, had instead marched on the capital where they seized control of the city and installed their own Chancellor, a minor civil servant named Kapp. Both Hitler and Eckart saw the potentialities of the right-wing Kapp Putsch and volunteered to go to Berlin and determine whether there was any possibility for joint revolutionary action in Bavaria. Captain Röhm approved the project and they were sent off in an open sports plane. It was Hitler's first flight and the pilot—a young war ace, Lieutenant Robert Ritter von Greim, winner of the Pour le Mérite—would become the last Luftwaffe commander. The weather was so turbulent that despite Greim's skill Hitler kept vomiting. For a time it appeared as if the mission was aborted since the airport at their interim stop was occupied by striking workers, but Hitler snapped on a fake goatee and Eckart posed as a paper dealer, and the party was permitted to proceed to Berlin. When they touched down at Berlin the wan Hitler vowed that he would never, never fly again.

Although Berlin had surrendered to the Free Corps on March 13 without a shot being fired, theirs was a hollow victory. No one of stature would accept a position in "Chancellor" Kapp's cabinet. From the beginning his hastily planned Putsch was a fiasco and what brought it down was not a counterattack or acts of sabotage. Berliners, joining the rest of the nation in a wave of anti-militarist feeling, had apparently concluded that another revolution was too much, and when a general strike was called by the Ebert government the workers responded so wholeheartedly that it was impossible for the Kapp regime to function. Electricity was shut off; trolley cars and subways stopped. There was no water; garbage rotted in the streets; shops and offices were closed.

Only Berlin's night life went on unimpeded, in darkness or candlelight. It was corruption out of an overdone movie with heavily rouged girl prostitutes of eleven competing with whip-toting Amazons in high lacquered boots. There were cafés for every taste and perversion—homosexuals, lesbians, exhibitionists, sadists, masochists.

The general strike of the Ebert government turned into a Frankenstein monster. By crushing the Kapp forces so successfully, it opened the way for another wave of leftist revolt. The Communists stirred up disorders throughout Germany to such a degree that President Ebert was forced to beg General von Seeckt, who had walked out on the government a few days earlier, to accept command of all military forces and crush the Red revolt. His first act was to recommission all the Free Corps troops which had just been disbanded.

The task facing the reorganized Free Corps was formidable. In Saxony a Soviet republic had already seized power and by March 20 a Red Army of 50,000 workers had already occupied most of the Ruhr. On April 3 the Free Corps troops swept through the Ruhr, wiping out Red strongholds and dealing ruthlessly with any survivors.

Hitler returned to Munich on March 31. That same day he became a private citizen, perhaps of his own accord, more likely because he was ordered to do so. He packed his belongings, received his demobilization pay of fifty marks along with a coat, cap, jacket, pants, a suit of underwear, a shirt, socks and shoes. He sublet a small back room at Thierschstrasse 41, a middle-class district near the Isar River dominated by three- and four-story buildings with shops and offices on the ground floor and small apartments and rooms above.

It was no accident that Hitler had chosen a room a few doors from the offices of the *Münchener Beobachter*. It had a new name, the *Völkischer Beobachter*; and continued to be the mouthpiece for anti-Semitic and anti-Marxist sentiments.

The Russian exiles who wrote about the peril of Bolshevism were having an increasing effect on Hitler. The most persuasive of these apostles of doom from the East was Alfred Rosenberg, the young architect-artist from Estonia. At their first meeting, neither was much impressed by the other. "I would be lying if I said I was overwhelmed by him," recalled Rosenberg. It was only when he heard Hitler speak in public that he became entralled. "Here I saw a German front-line soldier embarking on this struggle in a manner as clear as it was convincing, counting on himself alone with the courage of a free man. That was what drew me to Adolf Hitler after the first fifteen minutes."

The attraction and admiration became mutual in the next few months with the appearance of Rosenberg's articles in Eckart's weekly paper and other nationalist-racist publications. What particularly impressed Hitler was Rosenberg's revelations that Bolshevism was but the first step in a vast global Jewish plot to conquer the world.

Hitler's hatred of Jews had come primarily from his own observation in the last days of the war and during the revolutions that followed. What he learned from Rosenberg, the Thule Society, or from Gobineau, Luther and other famous anti-Semites merely buttressed his own conclusions. He borrowed only what he wanted from such sources. He probably had been much more influenced by pamphlets and freakish right-wing newspapers that breathed venomous anti-Semitism. Since his early days in Vienna he had devoured such gutter literature and its seed came to fruition on Friday the thirteenth of August 1920, at a mass meeting in Munich's famous Hofbräuhaus.

For two hours he expounded on the subject of "Why We Are Against the Jews," and from the beginning made it clear that his party alone "will free you from the power of the Jew!" In great detail he told how the Jews had polluted society since medieval days. While distinguished by neither originality nor rhetoric, his speech was a marvel of propaganda. Although his own anti-Semitism was personal rather than historical, Hitler demonstrated a genius for amalgamating facts with events of the day in a manner calculated to inspire resentment and hate. He was often interrupted by shouts of approval and laughter. Eighteen times the audience burst into loud applause and the reaction was particularly boisterous when he referred to the Jew as a nomad involved in "highway robbery."

His earlier attacks on Jews had been low key in comparison to this carefully prepared denunciation. For the first time in public he charged that the Jewish conspiracy was international and that their advocacy of equality of all peoples and international solidarity was only a scheme to denationalize other races. Previously he had called the Jew despicable, immoral and parasitic; tonight the Jew was a destroyer, a robber, a pest with the power to "undermine entire nations." Hitler called for an all-out struggle to the death. There was no difference between the East and West Jews, the good or bad ones, the rich or poor ones, it was a battle against the entire Jewish race. The slogan "Proletarians of the world, unite" no longer applied. "The battle cry must be 'Anti-Semites of the world, unite.' People of Europe, free yourselves!" Hitler demanded, in short, a "thorough" solution which he vaguely but ominously described as "the removal of Jews from the midst of our people."

Scribbled outlines of other speeches delivered by Hitler during this period indicate the depth of his obsession: "The bloody Jew. Butchering of spiritual leadership of people The Russian funeral parlor." "The Jew as dictator and today's Germany? Battle between democracy and Dictatorship—No. Between Jew and Germanic. Who understands this?" "Hunger in peace (inflation) through stock market and speculation? Need for luxuries etc. who profits? The Jews . . . Genocide Preparation for this mass insanity—can be proven through mass need—hunger—Hunger as a weapon at all times. Hunger to serve the Jews." "The world revolution means subjugation of the entire world under the dictatorship of the world exchange and its Masters, Judai."

As can be seen from these excerpts, Hitler's obsessive hatred was developing into an encompassing political philosophy. At the same time his hitherto obscure concept of foreign policy was taking shape. By September of that year he had reached the point where he told one audience, "We are tied and gagged. But even though we are defenseless, we do not fear a war with France." In addition he was considering the possibility of a foreign ally and recently had declared, "For us the enemy sits on the other side of the Rhine, not in Italy or elsewhere." Also for the first time Hitler publicly assailed the Jews for their internationalism. His equation of Jews and internationalism and his selection of Italy as an ally against France were still tentative concepts but did indicate his striving for a logical and practical foreign policy.

Adolf Hitler was advancing faster in the field of practical politics. Almost singlehandedly he had broadened the base of the party which now bore the name of *Nationalsozialistische Deutsche Arbeiterpartei* (NSDAP)—the National Socialist German Workers' Party. It was a name he hoped would inspire and incite, that would scare off the timid and attract those willing to bleed for their dreams.

In this same spirit, Hitler insisted upon a party flag that could compete with the flaming red Communist banner. "We wanted something red enough to out-Herod Herod," recalled Drexler, something to outdo the Reds but "quite different." Finally a dentist from Starnberg submitted a flag which had been used at the founding meeting of his own party local: a swastika against a black-white-red background. The swastika—originally a Sanskrit word meaning "all is all"—long a symbol of the Teutonic Knights, had been used by Lanz von Liebenfels, the Thule Society and a number of Free Corps units. For centuries it had represented not only for Europeans but also for certain North American Indian tribes the wheel of the sun or the cycle of life. From now on, and perhaps forevermore, the swastika would have a sinister connotation.

3

On January 22, 1921, the first national congress of the NSDAP was held in Munich. In little more than a year the party had become a respected force in Bavarian right-wing politics largely because of Hitler's magnetic personality and obsessive drive. His abilities as an orator, moreover, had turned the original organization from discussion to action. Most of the founders, including Drexler, viewed this transformation with growing concern. While they appreciated the vitality Hitler brought to their lethargic group, they were beginning to wonder if it was worth it. In a remarkably short period of time Hitler had become the dominant force, backed by his fervently faithful entourage. These followers—Röhm, the bothers Otto and Gregor Strasser, who were seeking a German-oriented socialism, and Rosenberg—brought with them the undeniable aura of violence.

The first congress would seem to have been the logical place for Hitler to stage a revolt and openly seize power that seemed his for the asking. But he restrained himself since only 411 members answered the call to Munich. Nor was the widening split in policy and tactics yet well enough known to rank-and-file members. On the surface there was unity at the congress, obvious as it was to insiders that a confrontation was in the offing, and everyone joined in the effort to make Hitler's first appearance twelve days later at the Zirkus Krone a success.

The winter had been a severe one with food riots rampant throughout Germany. These public disorders were heightened by a demand of the Allied Supreme War Council in Paris for exorbitant war reparations. Germany, close to bankruptcy, was expected to pay 134 billion gold marks. A large segment of the population already lived with little or no heat and went to bed hungry, and the annual payment was believed to hold out a bare subsistence for the workers as well as hardships for the middle class.

The spirit of indignation was so general that all the major political parties considered holding a common protest demonstration on the Königsplatz. This was canceled lest it be broken up by the Reds. On February 1 Hitler demanded a final decision. The inappropriately named action committee put him off until the following day, and he was informed they "intended" to hold the meeting in a week. "With this the cord of my patience snapped and I decided to carry through the protest demonstration alone." That noon Hitler reserved the Zirkus Krone for the following evening—the manager was a party member and he reportedly charged Hitler little or nothing—and then dictated copy for a flashy poster. Many of the party faithful had qualms. The circus arena could accommodate an audience of 6000 and it seemed impossible that even a moderate number could be induced to attend at such short notice.

The posters were not put up until Thursday morning. Moreover, a cold rain mixed with snow was falling. Hitler himself was so concerned that he hastily dictated leaflets and sent them off to the printer. That afternoon two hired trucks covered with red festoons and flying large swastika flags cruised the city. Each vehicle was manned by a score of party members who tossed out the leaflets and shouted slogans. It was the first time that propaganda trucks had been used by non-Marxists in Munich streets and in some working-class sections they were greeted with raised fists and angry shouts.

By seven that night Hitler got a depressing telephone report from the Zirkus Krone: the auditorium was far from filled. Ten minutes later came a more favorable report and at seven forty-five he was informed that three quarters of the seats were occupied with long lines queuing at the box office windows.

As he entered the building "the same joy" seized him as it had a year before at the Hofbräuhaus.

"Future or Ruin" was his theme, and his heart rejoiced in the conviction that down there before him lay his own future. After the first half hour he had the feeling that contact had been established and the audience was his. Applause began to interrupt him "in greater and greater spontaneous outbursts." This was finally succeeded by a remarkable hush, a solemn stillness. The man who had released this flood of emotion was himself intoxicated, and he remained on the platform for twenty minutes watching the arena empty. Then, "overjoyed," he went out into the sleet to his dingy, unheated little room on the Thiersch-strasse.

Hitler's performance at the Zirkus Krone was pilloried and praised in the Munich press and he was as pleased by the vituperation as by the approbation. It was not only that he thrived on opposition but that the violence of the attacks against him showed he was rousing visceral feelings. Despite the turbulence he generated, Hitler was becoming the darling of the respectable nationalist forces then making Munich their capital and receiving considerable secret support from the police president and his subordinate, who headed the department's Political Division.

The Bavarian government also gave him a measure of official recognition. Hitler and other party leaders were received by Gustav Ritter von Kahr, the right-wing Minister President, who was devoted to the preservation of Bavaria's peculiar status against encroachment by the Weimar regime. Bavaria still retained much of its autonomy, such as its own postal service, and its citizens continued to resent any directives from benighted northerners. Upon this issue Hitler and Kahr found common ground and although the Minister President disagreed with the "raging Austrian" on many points he felt the leader of the NSDAP could be useful as a propagandist in his own battle with Weimar.

Kahr's friendly reception gave public notice that Hitler was now a political force. Such recognition was welcome since his differences with the old guard in the party were coming to a head. Hitler's transformation into a personality because of his magnetism and crowd appeal indicated that he had not only altered the original purposes of the party but intended to seize complete control. His adversaries, therefore, took advantage of his absence in Berlin (where he was consolidating ties in that area with conservatives, nationalists and right-wing radicals) to engineer an alliance with a group of socialists from Augsburg. It seemed innocent but Hitler realized this was a sly tactical move to weaken his influence. He hastened back home and launched a startling counterattack. On July 11 he announced his resignation from the party. Three days later he put his cause before the general membership in an ultimatum. He would not return to the party unless he was made first chairman and given dictatorial powers. It was the first manifest appearance of the concept Adolf Hitler had brought from the war—the *Führerprinzip*, the leadership principle, absolute obedience to the commander.

Hitler gave the committee eight days to act but Drexler was so incensed that he refused to compromise. The eight-day deadline passed. Still Drexler and the committee refused to act. It looked as if Hitler's bluff had failed but in a last-hour secret session Eckart persuaded Drexler to compromise. He, in turn, brought around the rest of the executive committee on the grounds that they would still be a minor group but for Hitler.

With Hitler and his "armed Bohemians" now in absolute control of the NSDAP, all the traditions of the German Workers' Party were dumped overboard, since the elitists were dedicated to the proposition that a new order could not be built on old foundations. There would be no more parliamentary debate and democratic procedures. Henceforth, they would follow the Führer principle.

At the same time Hitler did his best to placate the old guard by making no display of power. He issued no general orders and refrained from enforcing the strict discipline he might have. Instead he spent the summer consolidating inner-party support in Munich and quietly expanding the rough-and-ready group which kept order at political meetings into a cohesive uniformed, paramilitary unit. It was given a more descriptive name: *Sturmabteilung* (Storm Detachment). To Hitler the SA was merely a political weapon to keep order and to march around in uniform to impress the discipline-loving burghers. But its leader, Captain Röhm, regarded it as a genuine armed force, his private army.

With the establishment of a private army and the party apparatus under his complete control, Adolf Hitler was now ready to set the NSDAP on a new, more revolutionary course. In the next months he instigated a series of public provocations. The campaign opened with apparently random acts: the assault of a Jew in the street, illegal display of flags and distribution of pamphlets, and a number of minor public brawls. These petty disturbances of the peace were succeeded, on the evening of September 14, 1921, by one of significance. The occasion was a meeting at the Löwenbräukeller of the Bavarian League, a federalist organization which accepted the social program of the Weimar Constitution while deploring its centralism. Its leader, an engineer named Ballerstedt, was preparing to address the crowd just as Hitler, who regarded him as "my most dangerous opponent," marched in. Scores of SA troops sans uniform had been planted in the audience near the podium and they leaped to their feet to give Hitler a raucous demonstration. Hundreds of other party adherents planted throughout the audience joined in. Then Hermann Esser, a left-wing Bavarian who had become one of the Führer's closest advisers, climbed on a chair, shouting that Bavaria was in its present low state because of the Jews. This brought a chorus of demands that Ballerstedt "give the floor" to Hitler. Someone threw the light switches in an effort to prevent a brawl. It only created tumult. When the lights went on again the SA flooded onto the stage, engulfing Ballerstedt. After beating him up, the SA group shoved him off the stage into the audience.

At an examination by the police commission investigating the fracas, Hitler expressed no regrets. "It's all right," was his dogged comment. "We got what we wanted. Ballerstedt did not speak." The matter did not end with an inquiry. Hitler and Esser were both informed they would be tried for violating the peace. The impending trial only inspired violence which erupted on the evening of November 4, during a Hitler speech at Munich's Hofbräuhaus. By the time he entered the vestibule at 7:45 P.M. the hall was overflowing with more than eight hundred occupants. The women were told to take seats near the front, as far from the doors as possible. The warning didn't faze Frau Magdalena Schweyer, proprietor of a vegetable and fruit shop opposite Hitler's dwelling and his faithful adherent. "I was too excited really to be frightened. It was plain there'd be some trouble: half the people in the place belonged to the Reds."

When Hitler saw that the Social Democrats had come early and taken most of the places, he ordered the doors closed. He told the SA bodyguard—there were less than fifty on hand—that this was their chance to show loyalty to the movement "and that not a man of us must leave the hall unless we were carried out dead." They were to attack at the first sign of violence on the theory that the best defense was a good offense.

"The answer was a threefold *Heil* that sounded rougher and hoarser than usual."

As Hitler started toward the speaker's platform, workers shouted threats. Hitler ignored them and pushed forward. Hermann Esser was now standing on the front table, calling the meeting to order. He jumped down and Hitler took his place. At first there were boos but even those who had come to jeer listened to his arguments and he was able to talk for more than an hour without interruption. But his opponents were only biding their time as they downed numerous mugs of beer, storing the empty ones under the tables for ammunition.

All at once someone interrupted Hitler and he shouted a retort. There were isolated angry shouts throughout the room. A man jumped on his chair and yelled, "*Freiheit* [Freedom]!" A beer stein hurtled at Hitler's head. Then half a dozen more. "Duck down!" the young monitors up front shouted to the women. Frau Schweyer obeyed. "One heard nothing but yells, crashing beer mugs, stamping and struggling, the overturning of heavy oaken tables, and the smashing of wooden chairs. A regular battle raged in the room." Curious, she looked up to see Hitler still standing atop a table despite the barrage of heavy mugs flying past his head. The outnumbered SA fought so ferociously that within half an hour the enemy had been driven down the stairs. It looked as if a shell had exploded in the hall demolishing chairs, tables and beer mugs. Finally above the din came the voice of Hermann Esser: "The meeting goes on. The speaker has the floor."

Hitler resumed his speech even as his storm troopers were bandaged or carried out of the room. He finished to an outburst of applause, moments before an excited police officer entered and shouted, "The meeting is dismissed!"

4

Out of the controversy over the Law for the Protection of the Republic, which was designed to halt radical right terrorism, and the widening split between Weimar and Bavaria came plans for another coup d'état. Its instigator was an obscure Munich public health official, Dr. Otto Pittinger, who planned to overthrow the Bavarian government with the support of the NSDAP and other nationalist organizations and replace it with a dictatorship under former Minister President von Kahr.

Hitler's new convert, Kurt Lüdecke, an ardent nationalist who was seeing Hitler for the first time, was given the task of relaying final instructions to possible co-conspirators in the Berlin area. He ranged through North Germany, envisaging himself as the "German Paul Revere" rousing nationalists from bed, until he learned that nothing at all was happening in Bavaria itself. He took the train back to Munich—it was late September 1922—and drove at once to Pittinger's headquarters where the doctor was just emerging. "Is this the coup d'état?" said Lüdecke accusingly. But Pittinger, looking "very haughty in his goggles," ignored him and sped off in a Mercedes for a vacation in the Alps. His uprising had fizzled out. Only the National Socialists were ready to march, and their leader had been forced to go into hiding.

Lüdecke found Hitler in a shabby attic room, his only companions a large dog and Ulrich Graf, his personal bodyguard and a former butcher. "I was ready—my men were ready!" he angrily told Lüdecke. "From now on I go my way alone." Even if not a soul followed he would go it alone. "No more Pittingers, no more Fatherland societies! One party. One single party. These *gentlemen*, these counts and generals—they won't do anything. I shall. I *alone*."

The lesson learned in the ignominious Pittinger Putsch convinced Hitler that he must act alone as Führer. It was a concept that excited Lüdecke and he suggested the party copy the technique of Benito Mussolini, who was striving to be the leader of Italy. His Fascist movement was nationalistic, socialistic and anti-Bolshevik; his Blackshirts had recently occupied Ravenna and other Italian cities. Lüdecke volunteered to go to Italy as Hitler's representative to see if Mussolini might prove to be a valuable ally.

In Milan Il Duce received Lüdecke graciously even though he had never heard of Hitler. He agreed with Hitler's views on the Versailles Treaty and international finance but was evasive about the measures that should be used against Jews. What impressed Lüdecke most was Mussolini's supreme assurance when asked if he would resort to force in case the Italian government did not yield to his demands. "We shall *be* the State," he said as if he were royalty, "because it is our will."

Lüdecke's report to Hitler was enthusiastic. Mussolini, he said, would probably seize control of Italy within months. He also confirmed that there were remarkable similarities between

Fascism and National Socialism. Both were ardently nationalistic, anti-Marxist and anti-parliamentarian, both were dedicated to a radical new order. In addition, the two leaders were alike. Both came from the people and were war veterans.

Hitler was particularly interested in Mussolini's use of brute force to gain political power. "His eyes grew thoughtful," recalled Lüdecke, "when he heard how the Blackshirts marched into Bolshevized towns and took possession, while the garrisons kept benevolently neutral or, in some cases, even quartered the Fascisti." It only proved what could be achieved by nerve.

Inspired by Mussolini's success and reassured by his own growing support throughout Bavaria, Hitler decided to make his show of force that autumn. He selected Coburg, a town in Upper Bavaria more than a hundred and sixty miles north of Munich. The occasion was a "German Day" celebration which had been organized by a group of völkisch societies. The guests of honor were to be the Grand Duke and Duchess of Coburg. Both were openly nationalistic and she was a relative of the late Czar.

Hitler was invited to attend and to "bring some escort." Choosing to interpret this invitation broadly, he left Munich in a special train on Saturday morning, October 14, 1922, with some 600 SA men, many of whom were paying their own expenses. There was a festive air as the storm troopers, equipped with rations for two days, piled into the special train to the music of their forty-two-piece brass band.

With Hitler were seven men, the brains and brawn of the inner circle: a former sergeant (Max Amann), a wrestler (Graf), a horse trader and ex-barroom bouncer (Christian Weber), a pamphleteer and ex-Communist (Esser), an architect (Rosenberg), an author (Eckart) and a self-styled sophisticate (Lüdecke). To the last-mentioned, the two most interesting were the ebullient Eckart, who "outshone all the others with his wit and common sense," and Rosenberg, a "block of ice!" who gazed toward him with pale lackluster eyes as though he weren't there.

The train stopped for half an hour in Nuremberg to pick up more adherents. The band struck up again and the men shouted as they waved swastika flags from the windows. Curious bystanders gathered to see what kind of a circus train it was. Jews in another halted train jeered at the swastika flags until Julius Schreck, who would later become Hitler's chauffeur, "leapt into the midst of them and started laying about him."

By the time the train pulled into the Coburg station there were 800 storm troopers. Grim-faced, Hitler stepped out to the platform. He had chosen Coburg as a battleground because of its preponderance of socialists and Communists. He would emulate Mussolini and drive them from their own stronghold. The people of Coburg, Bavarians for only two years, were taken aback by the noisy group that piled out behind Hitler onto the platform with their large band and red banners. The brass band struck up a march and then, with military precision, the SA paraded into town. In the van were eight husky Bavarians in leather shorts carrying alpenstocks. Just behind a row of men carrying large red and black flags came Hitler and his entourage of seven, followed by 800 men armed with rubber bludgeons or knives. Some wore faded and mended field-gray uniforms, some their Sunday best; their only common distinction was a swastika band on the left arm. Hitler himself was the epitome of the common man in his belted trench coat, slouch hat and ridiculous calf-high boots.

A mob of workers pressed from both sides shouting "Murderers! Bandits! Robbers! Criminals!" The National Socialists ignored the epithets, never breaking step. Local police guided the line of march to the Hofbräuhauskeller in the very center of town, then locked the gates, but Hitler insisted on quartering his men in a shooting gallery. To the beat of drums the storm troopers marched back through the hostile mob toward the outskirts of town. As cobblestones began to fly at the columns, Hitler signaled with a wave of his whip, and his men turned on the attackers with their bludgeons. The crowd fell back and the storm troopers continued their march, strutting like soldiers after their first battle. One of the proudest was the bon vivant Lüdecke, who felt as if he had been finally accepted by the rank and file. "Seeing that one brawls as well in an English suit as in shoddy clothes, they forgave me my tailor."

The following morning, Sunday, the leftists called a mass demonstration "to throw out the Nazis." Ten thousand protesters were expected to collect at the square but the size of the opposition only spurred Hitler to defiance. Resolved "to dispose of the Red terror for good," he ordered the SA, whose ranks had grown to almost 1500, to march on the Fortress of Coburg by way of the square. At noon the storm troopers with Hitler in the lead paraded into the center of the city but there were only a few hundred demonstrators at the square. Yesterday the citizens had stood on the sidewalks watching the SA pass by with silent disapproval. Today hundreds of imperial flags hung from the windows and friendly crowds lined the way, cheering the National Socialists with their strange emblem. Today they were heroes. They had ended Red domination of the Coburg alleys and streets. "That's typical of your bourgeois world," Hitler remarked to the men marching at his side. "Cowards at the moment of danger, boasters afterwards."

Coburg proved to Hitler that he and his SA could emulate Mussolini. In little more than two weeks the latter set another example. On October 28 Il Duce's Blackshirts marched into Rome (he took the train) and seized control of Italy.

Four days later Esser, in his usual role as introducer of the Führer, dramatically announced at the banquet hall of the Hofbräuhaus: "Germany's Mussolini is called Hitler!"

Chapter Five

"SUCH A LOGICAL AND FANATICAL MAN"

1922–1923

1

By 1922 Adolf Hitler had surrounded himself with a diverse group from every class which embraced a wide spectrum of cultures and occupations. All shared, to varying degrees, his nationalism and fear of Marxism. Two aviators were among them: Hermann Göring, a fighter ace and last commander of the famed Richthofen Flying Circus; and Rudolf Hess, who had started the war as an infantry officer in Hitler's regiment and ended it as a pilot. Although both were convinced Hitler was the answer to Germany's future and both came from well-to-do families, they differed strikingly in appearance, character and temperament.

Göring was buoyant, theatrical, an extrovert, who made friends easily and nearly always dominated them. His father had been a district judge before accepting an appointment from Bismarck as Reichs Commissar for Southwest Africa. He was married twice and had eight children. Hermann, the next to youngest, was an indifferent scholar whose dream was to serve his country in battle. Through the offices of his godfather he was admitted to the Royal Prussian Cadet Corps. He distinguished himself in the war and, after his twentieth air victory, was awarded the highest military decoration, the Pour le Mérite order. After the armistice he became a pilot for the Swedish airline and got engaged to a married woman, Carin von Kantzow, whose father was a member of the Swedish nobility and whose mother came from a family of Irish brewers. They were to get married as soon as her divorce was final.

Göring could have enjoyed a life of comparative ease in Sweden but he felt the urge to return to Germany and help "wipe out the disgrace of Versailles—the shame of defeat, the corridor right through the heart of Prussia." He enrolled at the University of Munich to study history and political science but was more interested in practical politics and once tried unsuccessfully to form his own revolutionary party among officer veterans. In 1922 he attended a meeting at the Königsplatz protesting Allied demands to hand over alleged war criminals. A series of speakers from various parties took the platform. Then the crowd began calling out, "Hitler!" By chance he was standing near Göring and Carin, who had been married early that year, and they overheard him remark that he wouldn't think of addressing "these tame bourgeois pirates." Something about the man in the belted trench coat impressed Göring so much that he went to a party meeting at the Café Neumann. "I just sat unobtrusively in the background. I remember Rosenberg was there. Hitler explained why he hadn't spoken. No Frenchman is going to lose sleep over that kind of harmless talk, he said. You've got to have bayonets to back up your threats. Well, *that* was what I wanted to hear. He wanted to build up a party that would make Germany strong and smash the Treaty of Versailles. 'Well,' I said to myself, *'that's* the party for me! *Down with the Treaty of Versailles,* God damn it! That's my meat!'"

At party headquarters he filled out a membership application. The appearance of such a war hero in the shabby office must have caused a stir. "Anyway," he recalled, "somebody tells me that Hitler would like to see me immediately." One look at the imposing Göring was enough for Hitler. Here was the ideal Nordic: luminous blue eyes, straight features and pink and white complexion. "He told me that it was a stroke of fate that I should come to him just as he was looking for somebody to take charge of the SA." They agreed to postpone the announcement a month, but Göring immediately began training the SA as a military organization. "Military! I'll tell the world it was military!"

He may have looked the perfect Germanic type but he was no racist by Hitler's standards and, in fact, had a number of

Jewish friends. Göring had joined the NSDAP "precisely because it *was* revolutionary, not because of the ideological stuff. Other parties had made revolution, so I figured I could get in on one too!" A man of action, he was drawn to an organization dedicated to action and he was just the man Hitler needed at that moment. He had invaluable connections with Junker officers and members of society, and was a display piece for parades and meetings. Nor was he squeamish about bashing in a few heads if necessary.

Compared to Göring, Rudolf Hess was colorless. Born in Alexandria, Egypt, he was sired by a well-to-do wholesaler and exporter who persuaded him to enter the family business, although he would have preferred to become a scholar. He attended boarding school in Bad Godesberg before enrolling at the École Supérieure du Commerce in Switzerland. His studies were interrupted by the war, and when it ended he could not bring himself to continue a business career. Like Göring, he entered the University of Munich, reading history, economics and geopolitics. He too felt betrayed by the "November criminals" but, instead of trying to make a revolution of his own, joined the Thule Society. He took part in demonstrations, spoke on street corners (despite his painful self-consciousiness), and as a member of a Free Corps unit helped overthrow the Bavarian Soviet regime.

He too was searching for a leader and had won a prize at the university for writing an essay on the theme "How must the man be constituted who will lead Germany back to her old heights?"
to the use of slogans, street parades and demagoguery. He must be a man of the people yet have nothing in common with the mass. Like every great man, he must be "all personality," and one who "does not shrink from bloodshed. Great questions are always decided by blood and iron." To reach his goal, he must be prepared "to trample on his closest friends," dispense law "with terrible hardness" and deal with people and nations "with cautious and sensitive fingers" or if need be "trample on them with the boots of a grenadier."

Hess found his ideal in Hitler and for more than a year had served as his trusted lieutenant and confidant. At the same time he also gave allegiance to a man married to a Jew. General Karl Haushofer returned to Germany in 1911 after three years in Tokyo as military attaché, speaking fluent Japanese. He brought back an abiding interest in Asian affairs along with a conviction that a nation's existence depended on the space it controlled. The war was proof to him of his theory. An encircled and suffocated Germany had gone down to humiliating defeat because she lacked *Lebensraum* (living space). After the armistice he became professor of geopolitics at the University of Munich, teaching his students that national salvation lay in selfsufficiency and for this Germany must have not only autarchy (national economic independence) but Lebensraum. Hess was almost as enthralled by Professor Haushofer as he was by Hitler and his hope was to bring the two together. One impediment was Frau Haushofer, whose father was a Jewish merchant. And while Hess followed the letter of racist doctrine, he was a man of sentiment as devoted to her as he was to the Herr Professor.

Hess was a retiring man, modest and unassertive. Although he had fought well on the battlefield and in the streets and his prize-winning essay breathed blood and iron, he was far from bloodthirsty. Yet while he preferred books and music to brawling, he was never found wanting in beer-hall battles and had won Hitler's affection by his action in the bloody fracas at the Hofbräuhaus. With his solid square face, bushy black eyebrows, intense and clenched lips, he was the picture of a man "prepared to trample on his closest friends." Only when he broke into a smile was the true Hess revealed—an ingenuous, bucktoothed young idealist.

Another blind follower was Julius Streicher. Where Hess and Göring lagged far behind their leader in anti-Semitism, Streicher surpassed Hitler in the virulence of his language. A stocky, primitive man with bald head and gross features, he gave off an aura of raw energy. He had excessive appetites alike at table and in bed. He could be bluffly jovial or blatantly brutal, shifting effortlessly from maudlin sentimentality to ruthlessness. Like Hitler, he was rarely seen in public without a whip but where the former draped his from the wrist like a dog leash, Streicher flaunted his as a weapon. In younger days he had "restlessly wandered from place to place with a rucksack full of anti-Semitic books and pamphlets." His speech was glutted with sadistic imagery and he relished attacking personal enemies in the foulest terms. Convinced that the Jew was plotting against the Aryan world, he had an endless catalogue of abuse at the tip of his tongue.

He was made for the NSDAP and, soon after founding the Nuremberg branch of the party in 1922, he spawned a newspaper dedicated to the damnation of Jews. *Der Stürmer* went a long step beyond *Ostara*, the Viennese magazine that exercised such influence on the youthful Hitler, in filth and virulence and was already a source of dismay to many of those close to Hitler. The Führer himself was repelled by pornography, disapproved of Streicher's sexual activities, and was concerned by the incessant intraparty quarrels this erratic disciple instigated. Yet at the same time he admired Streicher's boundless energy and fanatic loyalty.

Such were the men close to Hitler. His movement cut across all social classes and so all types were drawn to him—the intellectual, the street fighter, the fanatic, the idealist, the hooligan, the condottiere, the principled and the unprincipled, laborers and noblemen. There were gentle souls and the ruthless, rascals and men of good will; writers, painters, day laborers, storekeepers, dentists, students, soldiers and priests. His appeal was broad and he was broad-minded enough to accept a drug addict like Eckart or a homosexual like Captain Röhm.

2

In the fall of 1922 the activities of Adolf Hitler began to interest the Allies. At the suggestion of the American ambassador, Captain Truman Smith—Yale man, West Pointer, and now assistant military attaché in Berlin—was dispatched to Munich "to assess the reported developing strength of the National Socialist movement." Smith was instructed to meet Hitler and "form an estimate of his character, personality, abilities, and weaknesses." He was also to investigate the NSDAP's strength and potentialities. Specifically Smith was to find the answer to these questions: "Was there danger that Bavaria would declare itself independent of Germany? Did there exist in Munich danger of a renewed Communist revolt? Did the possibility exist that Hitler's National Socialists were strong enough to seize power in Bavaria? Was the 7th Divison of the Reichswehr, which was garrisoned in Bavaria, loyal to the Reich or was its loyalty divided between Berlin and Munich? Could it be depended upon to put down disorders or revolts whether staged by the right or left?"

Smith talked with generals, civil officials, Crown Prince Rupprecht, a liberal newspaper editor, and Max Erwin von Scheubner-Richter, a refugee of German origin from a Baltic state, who had borrowed his wife's title. The last, a close friend of Rosenberg's, was beginning to exert considerable influence on Hitler. Scheubner-Richter assured Smith that the party's anti-Semitism was "purely for propaganda," and then invited him to attend a review of storm troopers before the new National Socialist headquarters.

"A remarkable sight indeed," Smith noted. "Twelve hundred of the toughest roughnecks I have ever seen in my life pass in review before Hitler at the goosestep under the old Reichflag wearing red arm bands with Hakenkreuzen. Hitler, following the review, makes a speech . . . then shouts, 'Death to the Jews' etc. and etc. There was frantic cheering. I never saw such a sight in my life."

Smith spoke with Ludendorff at his home. The general confessed that he had "formerly believed that Bolshevism had first to be stamped out in Russia before it could be crushed in Germany. He has now changed his mind, and thinks that Bolshevism must first be crushed in Germany." He asserted that the Allies "*must* support a strong German government capable of combatting Marxism" and that such a government will never "develop out of the existing chaotic parliamentary conditions" but "can only be formed by patriotic men." He was convinced that the "Fascist movement was the beginning of a reactionary awakening in Europe," and that Mussolini had "real sympathy for the national cause in Germany."

Smith also met Hitler. The room was "drab and dreary beyond belief; akin to a back bedroom in a decaying New York tenement." The first words Smith wrote down in his notebook after the meeting were: "A marvelous demagogue. I have rarely listened to such a logical and fanatical man. His power over the mob must be immense." Hitler described his movement as a "union of Hand and Brain workers to oppose Marxism," and said that the "present abuses of capital must be done away with, if Bolshevism is to be put down." The parliamentary system had to be replaced. "Only a dictatorship can bring Germany to its feet." He stated that it was "much better for America and England that the decisive struggle between our civilization and Marxism be fought out on German soil rather than on American and English soil. If we (America) do not help German Nationalism, Bolshevism will conquer Germany. Then there will be no more reparations and Russia and German Bolshevism, out of motives of self preservation must attack the western nations."

He discoursed on other subjects but did not even mention Jews until Smith queried him point-blank about anti-Semitism; and then Hitler replied disarmingly that he merely "favored the withdrawal of citizenship and their exclusion from public affairs." By the time Smith left the dingy room he was convinced Hitler would be an important factor in German politics. He accepted a ticket for Hitler's next speech on November 22 and, upon being unexpectedly summoned back to Berlin, passed it on to Ernst Hanfstaengl, a towering lantern-jawed eccentric who had graduated from Harvard. Would Hanfstaengl be kind enough to take a look at this fellow Hitler and pass on his conclusions? "I have the impression he's going to play a big part," said Smith, "and whether you like him or not he certainly knows what he wants."

He was relying on Hanfstaengl's judgment because of the latter's unusual background. His mother came from a well-known New England family, the Sedgwicks; two of his ancestors were Civil War generals, one of whom helped carry Lincoln's coffin. Two generations of Hanfstaengls had served as privy councilors to the Dukes of Saxe-Coburg-Gotha and were connoisseurs and patrons of the arts. The family owned an art publishing house in Munich well known for its excellent reproductions. Hanfstaengl had been brought up in an atmosphere of art and music. His nickname was Putzi (little fellow).

On the twenty-second Hanfstaengl took a streetcar to the Kindlkeller, a large L-shaped beer hall filled with a conglomerate audience. There were a few ex-officers and minor civil servants, some small shopkeepers and numerous young people and workers. Many wore the Bavarian national costume. From the press table Hanfstaengl searched in vain for someone he knew. He wondered where Hitler was and a journalist pointed to a trio on the platform. The short one was Max Amann, the one with the glasses was Anton Drexler, and the third was Hitler. He wore clumsy ankle-high shoes, a dark suit. His white collar was starched and he reminded Hanfstaengl of a waiter in a railway station restaurant. But after Drexler introduced him to the audience and Hitler strode swiftly and confidently past the press table he was "the unmistakable soldier in mufti."

The applause was deafening. Hitler stood like a sentry, legs firmly stretched, hands folded behind his back, as he began reviewing the events of the past few years in a quiet, reserved voice. Methodically he built up his case against the government, never stooping to histrionics or vulgarisms. He spoke carefully in literary High German, occasionally allowing a Viennese accent to creep in. Hanfstaengl, not a dozen feet away, was particularly impressed with the speaker's clear blue, guileless eyes. "There was honesty, there was sincerity, there was suffering and the dignity of mute entreaty." After about ten minutes Hitler had the audience's complete attention. Now he relaxed his position and used his hands and arms like a trained actor. He began to insinuate with sly malice in Viennese coffeehouse style, and Hanfstaengl noticed that the women nearby were enjoying the performance enormously. Finally one of them called out, "That's right, bravo!" and, as if in acknowledgment, Hitler raised his voice and with a sweeping gesture began condemning war profiteers. There was a roar of applause.

Hitler wiped the sweat from his brow and took a mug of beer from a man with a dark mustache. It was a telling touch of theater for the beer-drinking Müncheners. When he resumed speaking his gestures became more sweeping. Every so often someone would shout out an insult and he would calmly raise his right hand slightly as if catching a ball or fold his arms and spit out a brief rejoinder that would crush the heckler. "His technique resembled the thrusts and parries of a fencer, or the perfect balance of a tightrope-walker. Sometimes he reminded me of a skilled violinist, who, never coming to the end of his bow, always left just the faint anticipation of a tone—a thought spared the indelicacy of utterance." Gone was all caution as he stormed at his favorite enemies—the Jews and Reds.

As Hanfstaengl emerged from his fascination, he looked around and noted with astonishment how the audience's behavior had changed. "The muffled restlessness of the masses who, an hour ago, had shoved against me and uttered all manner of nasty remarks, had become a deeply moved community. People were sitting listening breathlessly, who had long since forgotten to reach for their beer mugs and instead were drinking in the speaker's every word."

On the spur of the moment, Hanfstaengl approached the committee table where Hitler was receiving compliments with a self-assured smile free of any arrogance. "Captain Truman Smith asked me to give you his best wishes," said Hanfstaengl. Smith's name piqued Hitler's interest and he asked how Hanfstaengl liked the speech. "Well, I agree with you," he said careful not to hurt Hitler's feelings. "About ninety-five per cent of what you said I can set my name to, and five per cent we will have to talk about that." What he particularly objected to was Hitler's blatant anti-Semitism.

"I am sure we shall not have to quarrel about the odd five per cent," said Hitler affably. He seemed modest and friendly as he stood dabbing at his face with a crumpled handkerchief. He cleared his throat, coughed, then held out a hand. It felt "hardboned, rough," like the "grip of a front-line soldier."

That night Hanfstaengl could not fall asleep. "My mind still raced with the impressions of the evening. Where all our conservative politicians and speakers were failing abysmally to establish any contact with the ordinary people, this self-made man, Hitler, was clearly succeeding in presenting a non-Communist program to exactly those people whose support we needed." Hanfstaengl decided to help him.

In Berlin Captain Smith turned in a long detailed report on his visit to Munich and, on December 5, Embassy Counselor Robbins dispatched a personal message to the Under Secretary of State: "My own prognostication on the general attitude of the Bavarian outfit is that sooner or later a serious break is going to come from here. Hitler, the young Austrian Sergeant, who fought in the German army during the war, and who is now leading a Fascist movement, known as the 'Grey shirts,' is working very slowly and I should say efficiently along the same lines as Mussolini. I am told by some of our men who have been down there, that he is an extraordinary orator and though not of the highest moral standing, a great leader of men. He is obtaining a greal deal of money from the manufacturers just as Mussolini did and is going very slowly. He told Truman Smith, our Assistant Military Attaché, who was down there, that he had no intention of starting any big movement for the next month or so, and probably not before two months, that he is collecting funds and equipment, and that all was going well."

The report caused little stir in the State Department, which was concerned with more pressing matters, and was filed away. But in Germany there was growing concern over the increase in membership in the NDSAP and its private army. In mid-December a police official of the Bavarian State Ministry of the Interior filed a disturbing report charging that the Hitler movement was "without a doubt dangerous to the government, not only for the present form of government, but for any political system at all, because if they really achieve their dark ideas in regard to the Jews, Social Democrats, and Bank-capitalists, then there will be much blood and disorder."

3

In the first days of 1923 a quarrel between the French and British at the Reparations Commission resulted in the withdrawal of the latter's delegation. This gave France the opportunity to solve the reparations problem by force. On January 11 French and Belgian troops marched into the Ruhr on the excuse that Germany had failed to fulfill her obligations. This act not only inflamed nationalist spirit throughout Germany but quickened the descent of the mark.

The invasion of the Ruhr, along with inflation and increased unemployment, broadened the base of nationalism and brought Hitler more adherents. Disdaining co-operation with other groups, including the Majority Socialists, he organized protest meetings of his own and announced that twelve public rallies would be held on January 27, the First Party Day of the NSDAP.

Although the Bavarian police president informed Hitler that these demonstrations were banned, he defiantly shouted that the police could shoot if they wished but he himself would be in the first row. He was as good as his word and on the assigned day hurried from one rally to another by car. "Neither during the war nor during the revolution have I experienced such hypnotic mass-excitement," recalled historian Karl Alexander von Müller, who attended the rally at the Löwenbräukeller. The audience rose as one man, with shouts of "Heil!" as Hitler strode down the aisle. "I was very close when he marched through and I saw that this was different from the man I had met here and there in private houses: his small pale face expressed an inner fanaticism."

The following day, again flouting a police ban, the trooping of SA colors took place on the Marsfeld with 6000 storm troopers shivering in the snow. Some wore a uniform of ski cap, brown jacket and leggings while others were in business suits. There was a varied array of flags with swastikas of various sizes. It was a motley group but, once called to attention, the men stood as rigidly as if they were elite troops of the Kaiser. Although the police were ready for trouble there were no disorders. In fact the two-day affair turned out to be anticlimax.

There was no Putsch, no public disturbance. Only its repercussions were of import. Hitler's defiance of the police brought a number of middle-of-the-road leaders to his side and drove the University of Munich students down a much more radical path. More significantly, it lowered the prestige of the Bavarian government itself. In his first serious confrontation with the establishment Hitler had come out the victor.

By his own admission, Hitler was a recluse in his youth and had little need of society, but after the war he confessed that he could no "longer bear solitude." Though his room was a lonely refuge and prison, he lived a second existence in the cafés, salons, coffeehouses, and beer halls of Munich. Every Monday he would meet with intimates at the Café Neumaier, an old-fashioned coffeehouse.

Other evenings were spent at Dietrich Eckart's apartment on the Franz Josef Strasse. Perhaps Hitler's most constant companion these days was his new acolyte, Hanfstaengl, who introduced him to important people such as William Bayard Hale, classmate of President Wilson at Princeton and leading European correspondent for the Hearst papers, and Wilhelm Funk, whose salon attracted wealthy nationalist businessmen. Together Hitler and Hanfstaengl often attended the soirées of Frau Elsa Bruckmann, the wife of a publisher and born a Hungarian noblewoman, who was greatly impressed by the new political leader. Hitler was dazzled by life at this level. After one visit to the suite of Helene Bechstein and her husband, the piano manufacturer, in a Munich hotel he told Hanfstaengl that he had felt embarrassed in his blue suit. Herr Bechstein had worn a dinner jacket, the servants were in livery and nothing but champagne was served before the meal. "And you should have seen the bathroom, you can even regulate the heat of the water."

Hanfstaengl became a frequent visitor to the little room on the Thierschstrasse and one day Hitler asked him to play something on the piano in the hallway "to calm him." Hanfstaengl found the old upright badly out of tune but played a Bach fugue. Nodding, Hitler listened absently. Then Hanfstaengl began the prelude to *Die Meistersinger*, hoping the old piano wouldn't fall to pieces under his assault. He played "with plenty of Lisztian *fioriture* and a fine romantic swing," and Hitler became so excited that he strode up and down the narrow hallway gesticulating as if conducting an orchestra. "This music affected him physically and by the time I had crashed through the finale he was in splendid spirits, all his worries gone."

Infatuated with Hanfstaengl's style, Hitler would introduce him to all his social circles as a showpiece. "Whereas he otherwise kept the different groups in watertight compartments and told no one where he was going or whom he had been talking to," recalled Hanfstaengl in his unpublished memoirs, "he dragged me around from house to house as his resident musician, and had me sit down at the piano to perform." Once at the home of the photographer Heinrich Hoffmann he began playing Harvard football marches. Whereupon Hanfstaengl demonstrated on the piano how German marches could be adapted to the buoyant American beat. "That is it," exclaimed Hitler, and paraded up and down like a drum major, "that is what we need for the movement, marvelous." Hanfstaengl wrote several marches in this style for the SA band but his most significant contribution was the transference of the Harvard "Fight, Fight, Fight" to "Sieg Heil, Sieg Heil!"

Hitler often visited the small Hanfstaengl apartment in Schwabing across from the large school where he had done his basic training in 1914. Probably the greatest attraction was Hanfstaengl's wife, Helene, an American of German descent who was tall, brunette and strikingly attractive. He came in his best suit, the shiny blue serge. "He was respectful, even diffident," recalled Hanfstaengl, "and very careful to adhere to the forms of address still *de rigueur* in Germany between people of lower rank when speaking to those of better education, title, or academic attainment." From the first it was obvious he was physically attracted to Helene, as much by her warm, quiet charm as by her looks, and he treated her with a respect bordering on worship. In her unpublished memoirs written ten years later, she describes their first meeting on a Munich street in early 1923: "He was at the time a slim, shy young man, with a far-away look in his very blue eyes. He was dressed almost shabbily—a cheap white shirt, black tie, a worn dark blue suit, with which he wore an incongruous dark brown leather vest, a beige-colored trench coat, much the worse for wear, cheap black shoes and a soft, old greyish hat. His appearance was quite pathetic."

By spring Hitler felt so at ease with the Hanfstaengls that he would amuse them with imitations of other followers (such as the affectionate Görings) and play on the floor with their two-year-old son Egon. For hours he could idly gossip as he consumed a cup of coffee sweetened with squares of chocolate or, on occasion, sip a glass of the best dry Johannisberger wine after improving it with "a heaping spoonful of castor-sugar."

The Hanfstaengls discussed Hitler's private life at length. What, for example, was his true relationship with women? One day he told them, "The mass, the people, to me is a woman," and likened his audiences to a woman. "Someone who does not understand the intrinsically feminine character of the mass will never be an effective speaker. Ask yourself what does a woman expect from a man? Clearness, decision, power, action. . . . If she is talked to properly she will be proud to sacrifice, because no woman will ever feel that her life's sacrifices have received their due fulfillment." Another time he asserted that he would never marry. "My only bride is my Motherland," he said, referring to a nation commonly known as the Fatherland. In that case, Hanfstaengl jokingly replied, why not take a mistress? "Politics is a woman," replied Hitler. "Love her unhappily and she will bite off your head."

4

The spring of 1923 was a busy season for Hitler. The most pressing need was money and he set out on a series of tours to raise funds for the party. In Berlin he and Hanfstaengl not only begged money but spent a Sunday visiting the War Museum and the National Gallery. At the latter Hitler stopped in front of Rembrandt's "Man in a Golden Helmet" and drew attention to the heroic, soldierlike expression. It proved, he said, that the great painter, "in spite of the many pictures he painted in Amsterdam's Jewish quarter, was at heart a true Aryan and German!" Afterward they watched the women boxers in Luna Park. Hitler looked on without expression but insisted on staying for several matches, remarking that "at least it was better than this duelling with sabres that goes on in Germany."

Upon return to Munich, Hitler embarked on a campaign attacking France's occupation of the Ruhr but often did so obliquely, as if more interested in rousing his audiences against Jews. On April 13, for instance, he blamed them directly for the Ruhr takeover as well as the loss of the war and inflation. He charged that "so-called World Pacifism" was a Jewish invention; that the leaders of the proletariat were Jews ("Jews again!"); that the Freemasons were tools of the Jews ("Once more the Jews!"); and that, in fact, the Jews were conspiring to conquer the world!

In his obsessive hatred of Jews, Hitler had gone over the edge of reality. His anti-Semitism, though expressed in logical terms, had passed all boundaries of logic. He had turned the world upside down: France, England and America had really lost the war. Germany was the eventual winner since she was freeing herself from the Jews. If Hitler was deceiving himself, he also had succeeded in deceiving his listeners. Hitler skillfully appealed to primitive emotions and when audiences left meetings they remembered few details, only that they must join Hitler's crusade to save Germany; that France must be driven out of the Ruhr and, most important, that the Jews must be put in their place.

In the past year Hitler's platform technique had improved markedly. His gestures had become as varied and flexible as his arguments. Hanfstaengl was particularly impressed by a soaring upward movement of the arm. "It had something of the quality of a great orchestral conductor who instead of just hammering out the downward beat, suggests the existence of hidden rhythms and meaning with the upward flick of his baton." Utilizing his knowledge and feeling for music, Hitler's speeches became musical in tempo. The first two thirds were "in march time," quickening until the last third became "primarily rhapsodic." His power of mimicry was also put to adroit use. He would impersonate an imaginary opponent, "often interrupting himself with a counter-argument and then returning to his original line of thought after completely annihilating his supposed adversary."

Despite the complicated structure of his speeches, they were easy to follow, being designed primarily for emotional appeal. Thus he could switch from subject to subject without losing his listeners because the bridge between topics was an appeal to some emotion—indignation, fear, love or hate. Despite twistings and turnings, he drew along the listeners as an accomplished actor will guide his audience through some complicated progression in a play.

Hitler also had the rare ability to involve his listeners in the proceedings. "When I talk to people," he told Hanfstaengl, "especially those who are not yet Party members, or who are about to break away for some reason or other, I always talk as if the fate of the nation was bound up in their decision."

Audiences were always properly prepared for his virtuoso

displays by pagan-military pageantry. In addition to stirring music and flying banners, new features had been added—Roman-type standards that Hitler had designed himself and a Roman-style salute. Perhaps he had borrowed both from Caesar by way of Mussolini but he claimed that the stiff-arm salute at least was German. "I'd read the description of the sitting of the Diet of Worms, in the course of which Luther was greeted with the German salute. It was to show him that he was not being confronted with arms, but with peaceful intentions. . . . It was in the Rathskeller at Bremen, about the year 1921, that I first saw this style of salute." Whatever source, the salute, the vibrant "Heils!" together with the music and banners did much to assure the audience that the man they were about to hear was the true voice of Germany.

Hitler staged another confrontation with the Bavarian government. He called upon the Minister President and brought along with him a former military officer who was the commander of a private army of the *Arbeitsgemeinschaft der Kampfverbände* (Working Group of Combat Organizations), a conglomeration of radical right-wing groups. The two delivered an ultimatum, demanding that the Bavarian government itself demand nullification of the Law for the Defense of the Republic. If Weimar refused to comply, then Bavaria must defy the law.

The Minister President finally gave his answer to Hitler: he personally objected to the edict for the Defense of the Republic but since it was the law of the land he was obliged to enforce it. In protest Hitler called for a mass demonstration on May 1. The possibilities were explosive since the day was not only a sacred holiday to labor and Marxists but the anniversary of Munich's liberation from the Soviet Republic. On the evening of April 30 the forces of the radical right wing began converging on the Oberwiesenfeld, a military training area several miles north of Munich's main railroad station. By dawn there were 1000 men on hand. Guards were mounted in expectation of leftist attacks but hour after hour passed without action. "At six o'clock," recalled Hitler, "gangs of Reds gathered to meet us. I sent some men to provoke them but they didn't react."

By nine all detachments from outside the city had arrived, swelling the Hitler forces to some 1300. They stood in the warm sun leaning on rifles, waiting with mixed boredom and anxiety, while a disgusted Hitler strode around carrying a steel helmet by its chin straps and asking, "Where are the Reds?" Just before noon a detachment of army troops and green-uniformed police appeared and rapidly surrounded the armed demonstrators. With them was a chagrined Captain Röhm. He told Hitler that he had just come from the commanding general of the area who demanded that the arms be turned over immediately or Hitler would have to take the consequences.

Hitler was incensed but still withstood the pleas of Gregor Strasser and others to defy the government and charge the troops. The decision to turn over arms must have been a bitter one. But if Hitler had attacked, his forces would certainly have been repelled and the fruitless carnage might have meant his end as a political leader, perhaps even as a man.

5

When Hanfstaengl heard that a number of patriotic organizations were going to stage a protest demonstration in the Königsplatz the following week, he felt that Hitler should return from his holiday in the mountains and participate. He took the train to Berchtesgaden, a beautiful resort town on the border of Germany and Austria near Salzburg where he found Hitler ("I had fallen in love with the landscape") registered under the name of Herr Wolf at the Pension Moritz on a steep hill known as the Obersalzberg. At first Hitler was not enthusiastic about addressing a demonstration with so many diverse speakers, but Hanfstaengl persisted and the two began blocking out a speech.

That night Eckart, who shared Hanfstaengl's bedroom, complained that Hitler would parade around swinging his rhinoceros-hide whip in a swashbuckling manner to impress the wife of the pension manager. "The way Adolf is carrying on now goes beyond me," he said. "The man is plain crazy." He told of overhearing Hitler show off to the lady in question by denouncing Berlin in extravagant terms: ". . . the luxury, the perversion, the iniquity, the wanton display and the Jewish materialism disgusted me so thoroughly that I was almost beside myself. I nearly imagined myself to be Jesus Christ when he came to his Father's Temple and found the money changers." Whereupon, claimed Eckart, Hitler brandished his whip and exclaimed that it was his mission to descend upon the capital like a Christ and scourge the corrupt.

The following day Hitler accompanied Hanfstaengl to the station and, as they descended the Obersalzberg, remarked that Eckart, whom he had recently replaced as editor of the party newspaper, had become "an old pessimist, a senile weakling."

Anton Drexler and his wife also disapproved of Hitler's play-acting on the Obersalzberg. They were equally disconcerted by his growing enthusiasm for revolutionary action. Their alarm was shared by others who objected to his associating with industrialists, wealthy socialites and bankers rather than building a solid base of genuine socialists from the working class. Hitler must have been aware that he faced another revolt within the party, one born of discontent and dismay among those who first held highest hopes for him as leader of Germany's renaissance.

Early that September Hitler attempted to bolster his slipping prestige by a public appearance. The occasion was the German Day celebration in Nuremberg which took place the first two days of September, the anniversary of the Battle of Sedan. More than 100,000 nationalists swarmed into the ancient city, parading through the streets and, according to a state police report, generating "such enthusiasm as had not been seen in Nuremberg since 1914." The streets were a sea of Nazi and Bavarian flags as the crowd roared "Heil!" waved handkerchiefs and tossed flowers and wreaths at Ludendorff and the marching units.

The largest number of marchers came from the NSDAP and after the opening parade Hitler spoke at one of the meetings. He looked more groomed than he had at Coburg, with pressed suit, low-cut shoes and neatly slicked-down hair. "In a few weeks the dice will roll," he declared prophetically. "What is in the making today will be greater than the World War. It will be fought out on German soil for the whole world."

On the second day the German Battle League was formed. Outwardly an association of nationalists, it was a creature of the NSDAP: its secretary-general was Scheubner-Richter, its military leader was another Hitler man, one of its main organizations (the *Reichsflagge*) was dominated by Röhm; and its initial proclamation (written by Feder) sounded as if it came out of Hitler's mouth. It declared opposition to parliamentarianism, international capital, the class struggle, pacifism, Marxism and the Jews.

German Day at Nuremberg and the founding of the German Battle League marked Hitler's public return to revolutionary tactics. This became more apparent a month later when he was officially made political leader of the new organization. Its "action program" called openly for seizure of power in Bavaria and the rumor spread that Hitler was preparing a revolution. He did, in fact, announce openly that he intended to act rather than allow the Reds to seize power again. "The task of our movement, as always is . . . to prepare for the coming collapse of the Reich, so that when the old trunk falls the young fir tree may be already standing."

Although the Minister President of Bavaria, Eugen von Knilling, shared some of Hitler's beliefs, he had been pushed to the edge of patience by his rabble-rousing tactics. On September 26 Knilling told his Cabinet that the emergency was so grave that a state commissar general should be appointed who, while subordinate to the Cabinet, "would have a free hand in the exercise of the executive power." He proposed former Minister President von Kahr, who had the support of several nationalist groups and was held in esteem by both conservative monarchists and the Catholic Church.

In the name of law and order Kahr accepted this onerous position and his first act was to ban fourteen mass meetings the Nazis had planned for the morrow. This action was both a threat and an opportunity for Adolf Hitler, who had just returned from a trip to Switzerland to solicit funds. If he submitted it could mean ruin. If he successfully resisted, he could become a politician of national importance. He was cautioned to retreat and fight another day; the movement was not yet strong enough for action. But those close to the rank and file urged him to act.

These were the urgings Hitler needed. This impulse for action set him on the road to revolution and he began searching Munich and its environs for activist allies. His days were filled with interviews and visits to a variety of influential men: military figures, politicians, industrialists and officials. He talked to the party faithful as well as those who wavered—promising, threatening and cajoling. The one sentence he continuously used was "We must compromise these people so that they have to march with us."

"Absolutely no one could ever persuade him to change his mind, once it was made up," recalled Helene Hanfstaengl. "On a number of occasions when his followers tried to coerce him I noticed the faraway, unheeding expression in his eyes; it was as though he had closed his mind to all ideas but his own."

That autumn the faraway, unheeding expression in his eyes had a specific meaning. He saw himself emulating Mussolini—and his march would be to Berlin. Nor was this a vision he revealed only to intimates. In a conference with right-wing military men he called for an attack on Berlin with all Bavaria's forces. "Hitler now had definite Napoleonic and Messianic ideas," recalled one of those present. "He declared that he felt the call within himself to save Germany and that this role would fall to him, if not now then later. He then drew a number of parallels with Napoleon, especially with the return of Napoleon from Elba to Paris."

Chapter Six

THE BEER HALL PUTSCH

1923

1

On the last day of September 1923 Hitler received an unsettling letter from "an old member and fanatic member of your movement," who pointed out a startling prediction in the current yearbook of the well-known astrologer, Frau Elsbeth Ebertin. "A man of action born on 20 April 1889," it said, "can expose himself to personal danger by excessively uncautious action and very likely trigger off an uncontrollable crisis." The stars showed that this man was "to be taken very seriously indeed; he is destined to play a 'Führer-role' in future battles." He was destined to "*sacrifice himself for the German nation.*"

Although no name was mentioned, it was apparent that Frau Ebertin was referring to Hitler, and while she did not specify any particular date, she warned that acting rashly in the near future would endanger his life. Another astrologer, Wilhelm Wulff (years later he would advise Himmler's SS on astrological matters), also cast Hitler's horoscope late that summer and *was* definite about a date. His prediction was also ominous: "violence with a disastrous outcome" for the subject during the period of November 8–9, 1923.

Whether he believed in astrology or not, Hitler was convinced that his own destiny would eventually lead him to success; and, as Helene Hanfstaengl had noticed, he tuned out all but affirmative voices. By coincidence he found one of them the same day he received Frau Ebertin's astrological warning. It came in Bayreuth at the Villa Wahnfried, Wagner's home, where he was paying homage to Cosima, the eighty-six-year-old widow of the master. Winifred Wagner, the English wife of Wagner's son Siegfried, was already entranced by Hitler and his movement. She welcomed him warmly; her six-year-old daughter Friedelind thought he looked funny in his Bavarian leather shorts, thick woolen socks, red and blue checked shirt and baggy blue jacket.

Ill at ease, Hitler walked shyly, awkwardly around the music room and library, tiptoeing as if he were in a cathedral. But later in the garden, as he told the Wagners of his plans for the near future, "his voice took on tone and color and grew deeper and deeper until we sat like a circle of little charmed birds listening to the music although we didn't pay any attention to a word he said." After he left, Frau Wagner said, "Don't you feel that he is destined to be the savior of Germany?" Siegfried laughed indulgently. So far as he was concerned, Hitler was an obvious "fraud" as well as an upstart.

Hitler was across the street, making a pilgrimage to the home of the aged Houston Stewart Chamberlain, paralyzed in his wheel chair. This son of an English admiral had been drawn to Germany, seeing in her people the master race. He was talented and neurotic, and widely regarded as one of the leading men of culture of his day. A worshiper of Wagner, he had married his daughter Eva. The English prophet of racism was so taken by Hitler that he had a "longer and more refreshing sleep" that night than any since he had been stricken in August 1914.

2

Another aspect of fate, in the guise of the inflation, also appeared to be working in favor of Hitler and his march on Berlin. By the beginning of October it took 6,014,300 marks to equal a single prewar mark. The price of one egg equaled that of 30,000,000 in 1913. Many municipalities and industrial firms took to printing their own "emergency money" to meet expenses. The Reichsbank could not refuse to accept this emergency money or to treat it as of equal value with their own notes. The printing of government money itself became farcical: a thousand-mark note issued in Berlin the previous December was now stamped over in red: *Ein Milliarde Mark*; and a 500,000,000-mark note printed by the Bavarian State Bank a few weeks earlier was stamped: *Zwanzig Milliarden Mark*. This 20-billion-mark note presumably could be exchanged for more than $800 but by the time the holder of the modest-looking little note with the astronomical figure got to the cashier it would be worth a fraction of that—provided any cashier was willing to surrender hard foreign currency for it. People were frantic. They dared not hold currency for an hour. A missed trolley car to the bank could mean a man's monthly salary was reduced to a quarter or less.

The burden of inflation naturally fell on those who could not pay with notes—the workers and the elderly. The first were reduced to a near starvation diet and the latter were brought to poverty level overnight. Pensioners and those who lived on interest from bonds and life insurance found themselves destitute. Securities bought with gold marks were paid off in paper money that deteriorated in value in one's hand. In America only Southerners, whose families had suffered a similar fate after the Civil War days, would have understood.

About the sole ones who rejoiced were those deeply in debt who could pay off their obligations with worthless paper. But the greatest beneficiaries were the exchange barons, the profiteers and opportunistic foreigners who bought up jewelry and real estate at ridiculously low prices. Large estates and buildings went to these vultures for a few hundred dollars. Family heirlooms were exchanged for enough to feed a family a few weeks. There were scenes beyond belief: a woman who had left a basketful of money on the street, returning a moment later to find the money dumped in the gutter and the basket stolen; a worker with a salary of two billion marks a week able to buy his family only potatoes. And when distribution of the most basic food broke down, raids on potato fields in law-abiding Germany became commonplace.

By mid-October Hitler, after drawing almost 35,000 new members into the party since January, was more than ever convinced that the people were ready for revolution. "I can only take action," he told a Nuremberg audience, "where my fanatical belief and love for the entire German people lead me."

In Bavaria the pressure exerted by such rousing, hypnotic speeches made Commissar von Kahr's task, despite his dictatorial power, an impossible one. Called upon to restrain Hitlerian violence, he was under pressure from a large segment of the Bavarian leadership to go easy on him. The temper of Bavaria was conservative and nationalistic and, while many regretted Hitler's crude tactics and violent language, they shared his dream of a strong, rejuvenated Germany. Because of this attitude Bavarian police authorities, aggravated as they were, did little to restrain Hitlerian violence. The head of the army in Bavaria, General Otto von Lossow, was also resisting demands from Berlin to curb Hitler and to ban his newspaper. In the face of Lossow's continued defiance, he was dismissed, an act so infuriating to the Bavarian government that it assumed command of all Reichswehr units in the state.

This defiance, tantamount to revolt, was repeated the next day by army men stationed throughout Bavaria. They renounced the Weimar Republic by taking an oath to the Bavarian government "until an adjustment between Bavaria and the Reich has been arrived at, and I renew my obligation to obey my superior officers." It was mutiny, executed legalistically, formally and without violence—but mutiny nonetheless.

A few days later General von Lossow—still in command of his troops despite dismissal by the Weimar Republic—was reported to have made a speech declaring that there were only three possibilities: going on as usual "in the old jogtrot way," seceding Bavaria from the Reich, or marching on Berlin to proclaim a national dictatorship. Hitler was dedicated to the last proposal. The secession of Bavaria from the federal government was as distasteful to him as a return to a monarchist government with Crown Prince Rupprecht, the pretender, as King. Yet could he force Commissar von Kahr and General von Lossow to join him in a march on Berlin without declaring Bavarian independence? The answer was supplied by Rosenberg and Scheubner-Richter. Their plan was to kidnap Prince Rupprecht and Kahr at the ceremony on November 4 celebrating German Memorial Day. Several hundred storm troopers would seal off the alley near the Feldherrnhalle where the dignitaries would assemble. Hitler would then politely inform the prisoners that he had seized the government to prevent a Red takeover and prevent the separation of Bavaria from the Reich. The Putsch would be, according to Rosenberg, "both short and painless," since Kahr and Rupprecht would be impelled to co-operate.

Hanfstaengl thought it was a "crazy plan," arguing that any

attack on the Crown Prince would surely force the army to retaliate. Emphasizing the impracticability and senselessness of the operation, Hanfstaengl turned his warning into a personal attack on Rosenberg. If Hitler kept listening to these Baltic plotters, he said, it would mean the ruin of the movement. Hitler agreed to veto the kidnaping but would make no immediate promises concerning Rosenberg.

3

By now the Bavarian government was run, under the supervision of Minister President von Knilling, by a triumvirate of "vons": Kahr, Lossow and Colonel Hans Ritter von Seisser, chief of the Bavarian state police, who had gathered together a group of bright young officers too young to challenge his position. The triumvirate resembled a dictatorship in the old Roman caretaker sense and, though the three men represented a variety of ultraconservative and right radical values, they agreed that Hitler's revolutionary tactics were not pro bono publico and should either be channeled properly or outlawed. The breaking point was reached on October 30 when Hitler made it clear to a wildly receptive audience at the Zirkus Krone that he was ready to march on Berlin. "The German problem will be solved for me only after the black-white-red swastika banner floats on the Berlin Palace!" he shouted.

In an effort to split the triumvirate, Hitler requested an interview with Colonel von Seisser. They met privately on November 1. Hitler tried to persuade Seisser that Kahr was unfit and only a pawn of the Bavarian government, then proposed, as he had a week earlier, that Seisser and Lossow align themselves with himself and Ludendorff. But Seisser again declared he would have nothing to do with the World War idol, nor would the top officers in the army. Hitler admitted that, while the generals would be against Ludendorff, majors and lower-grade officers would support him in defiance of their own commanders. It was "high time" to take action, warned Hitler. "Our people are under such economic pressure that we must either act or they will swing to the Communists."

While Seisser privately agreed with Kahr that the Nazis were "trash," both did act. On November 6 the triumvirate conferred with representatives of the nationalist organizations. Their most urgent task, said Kahr, was the establishment of a new national regime. They all agreed that the Weimar government had to be overthrown but it must be done in concert and not independently as certain nationalist organizations were planning. He didn't mention any name but everyone knew he was referring to Hitler. It was questionable, said Kahr, if Chancellor Stresemann could be ousted in the normal way.

The next speaker, Lossow, supported Kahr and his determination to crush any Putsch by force of arms. "I am ready to support a rightist dictatorship if the affair is likely to succeed," said the general. He would participate if there was a fifty-one per cent chance for success. "But if we are merely to be harrassed into a Putsch, which will come to a sorry end in five or six days, I will not cooperate." In conclusion, both he and Colonel von Seisser underlined their warnings to members of the Battle League to co-operate—or else.

That evening Hitler met with his advisers in the apartment of Scheubner-Richter to draft their own plan of action. They agreed to stage a full-fledged Putsch on the following Sunday, November 11. There were two reasons for this date, one historical, one practical. This would be the fifth anniversary of Germany's surrender. It would also be a holiday with all offices deserted and police and military at low strength. The streets would be relatively free of traffic and the storm troopers could march unimpeded.

The next morning the conspirators met again, this time with the senior leader of the Battle League. Probably Ludendorff was present though he later denied it, but Hitler certainly was there and so were Göring and Scheubner-Richter. Final arrangements for the Putsch were adopted: the major towns and cities of Bavaria would be controlled with the seizure of railroad stations, telegraph offices, telephone offices, radio stations, public utilities, town halls and police headquarters; Communist and socialist leaders among the trade union heads and shop stewards were to be arrested. Numerically Hitler's forces in Munich would have superiority with 4000 armed Putschists facing perhaps 2600 state police and army troops.

Early that same evening Hitler called a second meeting, this time with two additional members, ex-Police President Pöhner, and his former assistant, Wilhelm Frick, who had remained with the police and was still protecting Hitler and his followers. The conspirators discussed a development that called for a drastic change in plan. Commissar von Kahr had unexpectedly announced he was holding a mass "patriotic demonstration" at the Bürgerbräukeller the next night. The outward purpose was to outline the aims of his regime but it was probably an attempt to forestall any display of unified action by the National Socialists among leading government officials, military leaders and prestigious civilians. Hitler was asked to attend but it seemed obvious that the invitation was a trap. Perhaps the triumvirate was going to announce Bavaria's break with Berlin and the restoration of the Wittelsbach monarchy.

Hitler argued that it was a heaven-sent opportunity. The triumvirate as well as Minister President von Knilling and other government officials would be on the same platform. Why not simply escort them to a private room and either convince them to go along with a coup d'état or, if they were adamant, imprison them? Hitler was undoubtedly talking for effect. He knew very well that he could not mount a successful Putsch without the full co-operation of the triumvirate. He had no real intention of seizing the government of Bavaria, only of attempting to arouse the Bavarians by dramatics and thus successfully defy Berlin. He actually had no long-range program and was willing to trust luck and fate.

November 8 dawned bitter and windy. On the most important day of Hitler's life he had a headache and a throbbing toothache. Late that morning orders were issued to SA leaders by phone, letter or in person to alert their men for action. There were no details, no explanations. Moreover, many of those closest to Hitler still had no idea there was a change in plans. Just before noon, in his little whitewashed office, Rosenberg (sporting a violet shirt and scarlet tie) was discussing the morning's *Völkischer Beobachter* with Hanfstaengl. They heard stamping outside and a hoarse voice: "Where is Captain Göring?" The door was flung open and Hitler, wearing his tightly belted trench coat and gripping his whip, burst in "pallid with excitement."

"Swear you will not mention this to a living soul," he said with suppressed urgency. "The hour has come. Tonight we act!" He asked them both to be part of his personal escort. They were to bring pistols and rendezvous outside the beer hall at seven o'clock. Hanfstaengl hurried home to tell his wife to take their son Egon to the villa they had just built in the country, then informed a number of international journalists, including

H. R. Knickerbocker, that they "must under no circumstances" miss the meeting that evening.

By afternoon Hitler had controlled his excitement and was gossiping at the Café Heck with Heinrich Hoffmann, his photographer crony, as though this was just another ordinary day. Suddenly Hitler suggested they visit Esser, who was laid up with jaundice. While Hoffmann waited outside, Hitler revealed to Esser that he was going to announce the national revolution that evening. He needed help. At exactly 9:30 P.M. Esser, carrying a flag, was to rush up to the podium of the Löwenbräukeller, where a nationalist meeting was to be held, and announce the National Socialist revolution.

By now the SA men were getting out of their work clothes and putting on uniforms which consisted of field-gray windbreakers with swastika armbands, field-gray ski cap, and revolver belt. They were bound for various rendezvous. Karl Kessler of the 2nd Company, was instructed to report to the Arzbergerkeller while shoemaker Josef Richter was sent to the Hofbräuhaus. Members of the Bund Oberland were also on the move. Instead of a swastika they wore a sprig of edelweiss and were equipped with steel helmets. One of the key units, the Führer's special hundred-man bodyguard, gathered at the Torbräu. Their leader, a tobacconist, was haranguing them. "Any one of you who isn't going into this heart and soul had better get out right now." It was their task, he said, to bear the brunt of whatever happened that night at the Bürgerbräukeller. "We're going to run the government out."

It was dark when a car stopped in front of Scheubner-Richter's apartment house and General Ludendorff got out. He talked a few minutes with Scheubner-Richter, then left. Moments later Scheubner-Richter and his servant also drove off at top speed. "Hansl," Scheubner-Richter said, "if things don't go right today, we will all be in jail tomorrow." At party headquarters they met Hitler and other leaders. After some discussion the group headed for the Bürgerbräukeller in two cars. It was almost 8 P.M. The beer hall was about half a mile from the center of Munich on the other side of the Isar River. It was a large rambling building, flanked by gardens and containing a number of dining rooms and bars. The main hall, the largest in the city, except for the Zirkus Krone, could hold 3000 at its sturdy round wooden tables. Officials knew there might be trouble and there were on hand 125 municipal policemen to control the crowd. In addition there was a mounted detachment as well as a number of officers scattered in the audience. In case of an emergency, a company of green-uniformed state police had been installed in a barracks only a quarter of a mile away.

By the time the Hitler caravan crossed the Isar River the hall was closed to all but important personages. Every seat was taken and Hanfstaengl wasn't able to bring in his little group of international journalists. A few minutes past eight Hitler's red Mercedes, followed by Scheubner-Richter's car, approached the beer hall. Hitler was disturbed by the milling crowds. Would his trucks be able to get through this mob? The two cars slowly pushed their way to the front entrance, which was blocked by a phalanx of policemen. Hitler persuaded the police to leave and make room for his troops, which were expected shortly, then led the way through the beer-hall door which Hess held open.

Hanfstaengl figured that Hitler would fit more naturally into the scene if he too had a beer and so bought three at the serving counter for three billion marks. Hitler occasionally sipped his as he waited impatiently for the special Brownshirt bodyguard unit. Trucks filled with other storm troopers were already outside but they stayed in place until a few minutes after 8:30 P.M. when his helmeted bodyguard finally arrived. This was the signal for action. The trucks emptied and the armed Nazis surrounded the building. Bewildered and outnumbered the municipal police—unprepared for a political battle—did nothing.

Hitler set aside the beer he had been nursing, pulled out his Browning pistol and, as the storm troopers shouted, "Heil Hitler!" he started into the hall with ex-butcher Graf, Scheubner-Richter and his faithful servant, Harvard-graduate Hanfstaengl, an ex-police spy, business manager Max Amann, and the idealist-activist student of geopolitics, Rudolf Hess. Brandishing weapons, this motley band began pushing its way through the packed humanity toward the platform. By this time one group of Brownshirts had blocked the exit while another group set up a machine gun positioned to rake the audience. Tables overturned in the uproar. A cabinet member scrambled for cover under his table. Some made for the exits in consternation but were warned back, and if they resisted, were beaten or kicked.

The Hitler phalanx was blocked and, amidst the uproar, he climbed onto a chair waving his pistol. "Quiet!" he shouted and when the tumult continued he fired a round into the ceiling. In the shocked silence Hitler said, "The national revolution has broken out! The hall is surrounded!" No one was to leave the hall. Sweat poured down his pale face. He looked insane or drunk to some but a few were struck by the ridiculous sight of a pistol-brandishing revolutionary in such a badly cut morning suit. Comic as he looked, Hitler was dead serious. He ordered the triumvirate to follow him into an adjoining room, guaranteeing their security. But the three men did not move. Finally Kahr took a backward step as Hitler began clambering over a table toward the speakers' platform. Seisser's aide, a major, came forward, hand in pocket as if about to draw his pistol. Hitler jammed his own pistol against the major's forehead and said, "Take your hand out."

Hitler assured the triumvirate and the audience that everything could be settled in ten minutes. This time the three men and two aides followed Hitler to the side room. "*Komödie spielen* [Put on an act]," whispered Lossow to his colleagues. In the private room Hitler was more agitated than ever. "Please forgive me for proceeding in this manner," he said, "but I had no other means." He answered Seisser's accusations of breaking his word not to make a Putsch with an apology: he did it for the good of Germany. He told them that ex-Police President Pöhner was going to be the new Bavarian Minister President and Ludendorff would assume command of the new national army based on the radical right Battle League, and lead the march on Berlin. After the Putschists seized power, Hitler promised, the triumvirate would have even greater powers; Kahr would be made Regent of Bavaria; Lossow Reich Army Minister; and Seisser Reich Police Minister.

When the three failed to respond Hitler drew out his pistol (all in jest, he later testified). "There are five rounds in it," he said hoarsely, "four for the traitors, and if it fails one for me." He handed over the weapon to Graf, who already was armed with a machine pistol. Under such circumstances to die or not to die was meaningless, replied Kahr coolly. What interested him was General Ludendorff's position in the matter. Hitler didn't seem to know what to do. He took several quick swallows of beer, apologized to Kahr, then charged out of the room. The audience outside was getting out of hand.

The uproar did not faze Hitler. He pushed his way up to the platform ignoring the catcalls and insults. He raised his pistol. The din continued and he shouted angrily, "If silence is not restored, I will order a machine gun placed in the gallery!" All of a sudden he was no longer the figure of fun. "What followed then," recalled Professor von Müller, the conservative historian, "was an oratorical masterpiece, which any actor might well envy. He began quietly, without any pathos." He made it appear as if the triumvirate was about to come around as he assured the audience that Kahr had his full trust and would be Regent of Bavaria. He promised that Ludendorff would assume leadership of the army; that Lossow would be Army Minister and Seisser Police Minister. "The task of the provisional German National Government is to organize the march on that sinful Babel, Berlin, and save the German people!"

From the first words, recalled Hanfstaengl, the insignificant man in the comical cutaway, who resembled a nervous "provincial bridegroom" on display in the dusty window of a Bavarian village photographer, became a superman. "It was like the difference between a Stradivarius lying in its case, just a few bits of wood and length of catgut, and the same violin being played by a master." Professor von Müller couldn't remember in his entire life "such a change of attitude of a crowd in a few minutes, almost a few seconds. There were certainly many who were not yet converted. But the sense of the majority had fully reversed itself. Hitler had turned them inside out, as one turns a glove inside out, with a few sentences. It had almost something of hocus-pocus, or magic about it. Loud approval roared forth, no further opposition was to be heard."

"Outside are Kahr, Lossow and Seisser," Hitler said earnestly. "They are struggling hard to reach a decision. May I say to them that you will stand behind them?"

"Ja! Ja!" roared the crowd.

"In a free Germany," shouted the impassioned Hitler, "there is also room for an autonomous Bavaria! I can say this to you: either the German revolution begins tonight or we will all be dead by dawn!" The crowd his, he headed back for the private room to bring the triumvirate to heel.

The man who could decide the matter was already approaching the Bürgerbräukeller in Hitler's Mercedes. General Ludendorff was in the back seat with his stepson (an ardent Putschist) and Scheubner-Richter. The sight of the general at the entrance of the beer hall brought a chorus of Heils! But Ludendorff, seeing how far things had gone, was "amazed and far from pleased." Hitler hurried out of the anteroom to shake hands with him. They conversed briefly and the scowling Ludendorff agreed to help convince the triumvirate. They disappeared into the side room.

Irritated as he was by Hitler's unilateral action, Ludendorff applied the force of his rank and personality on his two fellow officers. "All right, gentlemen," he told them, "come along with us, and give me your hand on it." It was the general who responded first. Lossow extended his hand and said, "Good." Then the colonel gave his hand to Ludendorff. The civilian, Kahr, was the last to submit but the first to speak once the entire group returned to the platform. Ramrod stiff, his face a mask, the commissar declared that he would serve Bavaria as Regent for the monarchy.

As he surveyed the enthusiastic audience, Hitler was in a state of ecstasy. "I am going," he said emotionally, "to fulfill the vow I made to myself five years ago when I was a blind cripple in the military hospital: to know neither rest nor peace until the November criminals had been overthrown, until on the ruins of the wretched Germany of today there should have arisen once more a Germany of power and greatness, of freedom and splendor."

The crowd stood and roared out "Deutschland über Alles." Tears streamed down many a cheek and some people were so emotionally wrought they could not even sing. But someone next to a state police official turned and said, "The only thing missing is the psychiatrist."

4

There was also high emotion across the Isar at the Löwenbräukeller. The main hall, resounding with the blast of two brass bands, was jammed with more than 2000 members of the Battle League and SA. Only a small part of the audience was made up of the scar-faced Captain Röhm's fanatic followers, but he was the main attraction. He called "for revenge and retaliation against the traitors and the despoilers of our people. . . ."

Then Esser, who had dragged himself from a sickbed, mounted the podium. The plan had been changed somewhat and he did not charge up the aisle carrying a flag or immediately announce the revolution. He was to wait for word that Hitler's coup had succeeded. In the middle of his speech, at 8:40 P.M., a cryptic telephone message was received from the Bürgerbräukeller: "Safely delivered!" Röhm purposefully strode up to the platform and interrupted Esser. The Kahr government, he shouted, had been deposed and Adolf Hitler had declared a national revolution. Reichswehr soldiers tore off the Republic cockades from their hats, leaped onto tables and chairs shouting. Storm troopers embraced each other. Röhm shouted for everyone to march on the Bürgerbräukeller. The men piled out of the Löwenbräukeller as if it were on fire and formed up. With shouting and cheers the raucous army started down the street toward the Isar River. A motorcycle courier stopped the procession with new marching orders from Hitler: Röhm's men were to turn toward the university and occupy General von Lossow's headquarters on the Schönfeldstrasse; the storm troopers were to proceed to St. Annaplatz, pick up a cache of 3000 rifles in the basement of the monastery, then take up positions at Giessing. Only the Bund Oberland was to continue on to the Bürgerbräukeller.

As Röhm's force marched down the Briennerstrasse followed by one of the brass bands, gathering crowds cheered them on. Near the head of the column, proudly holding an imperial war flag, was a fervent young nationalist, there because of allegiance to Röhm and Strasser, not Hitler. His name was Heinrich Himmler. The enthusiasm of jubilant onlookers was heady and the men continued like conquerors up the broad Ludwigstrasse to the entrance of the military district building. Röhm halted his troops outside the gates and strode into the building where he had worked for so many years. The guards threatened to shoot but Röhm outfaced them. He marched up to the second floor to the office of the duty officer, who declared that he was bowing only to force, and then gave the order to open the gates to the rioters. Röhm posted guards, emplaced machine guns at windows and strung barbed wire around the building. He did just about everything except take over the telephone switchboard. This, incredibly, he left in charge of the duty officer, who had no revolutionary leanings.

The man principally responsible for the first successes of the Putschists was Frick of the Munich Police Presidium. He persuaded his colleagues on duty not to launch any counterattack against the Putschists, then hovered near a phone to calm bewildered police officials who called in for information. His advice always was to wait and do nothing.

At the Bürgerbräukeller Hitler was in a state of euphoria with the police under control and district headquarters occupied by Röhm. Then came a report from the engineer barracks: the Putschists were having an argument with the engineers. Hitler made a snap decision to leave his command post to straighten out the matter in person. It was a grave tactical error, followed by a second: placing General Ludendorff in charge. No sooner had Hitler left the building than General von Lossow said he had to go to his office and issue orders. This seemed reasonable to Ludendorff, who allowed Lossow to march out of the beer hall with Kahr and Seisser not far behind. Hitler did no good at the engineer barracks, being turned away at the gate. He returned half an hour later and was appalled to find that the triumvirate had been allowed to escape.

Hitler's spirits were raised at 11 P.M. by the arrival of a thousand-man military unit. It was almost the entire complement of the Infantry School, an elite group of cadets. Except for a handful of dissidents, they had been persuaded to join the uprising en masse by Lieutenant Gerhard Rossbach, a veteran of the Free Corps movement. The cadets had placed their own commander under house arrest and accepted the flamboyant Rossbach (like Röhm, a homosexual and gallant fighter) as their new leader. The cadets marched off to occupy the offices of Commissar von Kahr while the leaders of the Putsch set off in their cars for military district headquarters. At Röhm's command post—the office of General von Lossow—the group began discussing the future course of the revolution. Ensconcing himself in an easy chair, Ludendorff demanded that someone get hold of Lossow or Seisser on the phone. A number of calls were made but neither could be reached. Scheubner-Richter expressed the feeling that something was wrong. Lossow had said he was coming here to his own office. Where was he? And where were Kahr and Seisser? Ludendorff again protested that these three gentlemen had given their oath in full view and sound of thousands. They could not possibly have changed their minds.

Major Max Schwandner, an officer on the staff of the commander of army units in Bavaria, was just entering the building. He had heard rumors of a Putsch and sought out the duty officer, who could only say that "the affair was extremely unclean and fishy." Schwandner recalled, "I immediately told Röhm that this Putsch was in clear violation of yesterday's understanding with von Lossow. Röhm replied in a voice vibrant with sincerity that everything was all right. Von Lossow, Kahr and von Seisser had all declared themselves in accord with everything and would soon come to Hitler in the military district headquarters. I said only that that was something different."

A little later a call came through the still unmonitored switchboard. It was from Lossow at his new command post, safe in the center of the regimental barracks complex. He ordered a counterattack on the Putschists he had recently pledged to support; loyal army battalions in Augsburg, Ingolstadt, Regensburg, Landshut and other surrounding localities were to be transported to Munich by rail. Schwandner promptly called the transport officer, passed on Lossow's orders and agreed to phone instructions to half of the battalions himself. The Putsch was being planned in one room and sabotaged in the one next to it.

Despite the marching troops, the bands and the excitement, most Müncheners had no idea revolution once more had come to their city. It was a night of terror for those opponents of the coup who were dragged from their homes and held hostage; and for some picked out of the phone book if their names sounded Jewish, who were corralled by the Brownshirts.

At military district headquarters it was becoming increasingly evident that the triumvirate had broken their word (no one seemed to recall that it had been made under duress) and that events were getting out of hand. Things were also not going well for the Putschists at the headquarters of Commissar von Kahr. He had gone there after his escape from the beer hall to find that machinery had already been set in motion to crush the Putsch. Understandably, he did nothing to stop these measures and was helping direct the defense of his building against the lively threat of Lieutenant Rossbach and his thousand cadets from the Infantry School. It should have been easy for the revolutionists to carry out Ludendorff's order to take the building "whatever the cost," and it would have been an important victory but it turned into a standoff with cadets and police facing each other at bayonet point, each group waiting for the other to fire the first shot. No one wanted bloodshed. The battle that might have swung the decision was lost by default, primarily because the Hitler forces were reluctant to fire upon men they wanted as allies.

General von Lossow had sent out this message "to all German wireless stations" at 2:55 A.M.:

> State Commissar General v. Kahr, Col. v. Seisser and General v. Lossow repudiate the Hitler Putsch. Expressions of support extracted by gunpoint invalid. Caution is urged against misuse of the above names.
>
> *v. Lossow*

It was not until 5 A.M. that confirmation of the repudiation of the Putsch by the triumvirate reached military district headquarters. The informant was the deposed commandant of the Infantry School. He regretfully informed Hitler that the triumvirate did not feel honor bound to their oaths since they were made at pistol point. General von Lossow was going to put down the Putsch with force. If Hitler was stunned, he did not show it. He made a long speech to his fellow conspirators, ending with the declaration that, if need be, he was determined to fight and die for his cause.

5

It was a dull, overcast dawn with a biting damp chill. The cold wet snow continued to fall spasmodically. The rank and file of Putschists were gathered glumly in the smoke-filled, dank main hall of the Bürgerbräukeller. Unshaven and unwashed, they were eating a breakfast of coffee, cheese and bread. The excitement and exaltation of last night had evaporated. Then someone announced that the triumvirate had publicly denounced the revolution and the army would not participate. Someone else mounted the speakers' platform, recent scene of such high drama, and began raging against all the traitors—the bourgeois and the generals. "March to Berlin!" he shouted. There was some applause but the suggestion struck Hitler's lawyer, Hans Frank, as "highly romantic and very unpolitical."

The leaders were in a private room upstairs where Ludendorff sat "stony-faced and frightening in his unperturbed calm," as he sipped red wine for breakfast. In his old tweed shooting jacket he was still an impressive figure. But his show of confidence cracked upon getting the information that Lossow had publicly denounced the new government. "I will never again trust the word of a German officer," he exclaimed and retreated into glum silence.

The Putsch was marked by confusion and hesitation on both

sides. In some parts of the city the municipal police were pulling down Putschist posters and arresting rebels while in the inner city rebels were arresting police for attempting to put up government posters repudiating the Putsch and dissolving the NSDAP. Hitler's men held most of the major downtown bridges over the Isar River, including the most important, the Ludwigsbrücke, connecting the beer hall with the center of the city. At the Museum bridge citizens were chiding the youthful Putschists. "Do you have your mother's permission to play with such dangerous things in the street?" called out one worker. The little ten-man detachment returned sheepishly to the beer hall.

At the beer hall the rebel leaders were in dispute. Colonel Hermann Kriebel, who had served in the war on Ludendorff's staff, wanted to withdraw to Rosenheim on the Austrian border where they might win over the local right radicals. Göring seconded this. It was his home town and he assured everyone it was strongly pro-Hitler. Here they could assemble reinforcements and regroup. "The movement cannot end in the ditch of some obscure country lane," was Ludendorff's sarcastic retort. It was up to Hitler. He hesitated briefly but he was a born gambler and the prospect of a lengthy guerrilla campaign was not appealing. He wanted to win or lose on one throw of the dice and he vetoed the Kriebel plan.

The discussion dragged on until late morning while the situation on the streets deteriorated. At military district headquarters Captain Röhm and his men were under siege by army and state police troops. While the older members of the Battle League were not all eager to face such overwhelming odds, the 150 men of Röhm's own group were ready for combat.

Word of the government attack against Röhm brought arguments at the Bürgerbräukeller to a halt. It was evident that the Putschists had to act now or surrender ignominiously. According to Ludendorff, it was he who first thought of marching in force into the heart of Munich to rescue Röhm. "We march!" he said. If it was Ludendorff's idea, it was carried out in Hitler fashion—as a propaganda parade, a display of power designed to arouse support for the Putsch from the citizenry.

Ludendorff was convinced that army troops would not impede the march, and recently had assured a friend: "The heavens will fall before the Bavarian Reichswehr turns against me." Hitler was just as confident that neither army nor state police would fire on a war hero like Ludendorff, who would be in the front row. Hitler's decision ("the most desperately daring decision of my life") was made and orders were hurriedly dispatched to units manning the bridges.

The parade formed quickly. There was no band to lead off since the musicians who had reported to the beer hall that morning got neither breakfast nor pay and marched off after playing a dutiful chorus of the "Badenweiler," the march of Hitler's regiment in the war. In the van were picked skirmishers and eight men carrying the swastika and the black-white-red flags. Next came the leaders: Hitler with Scheubner-Richter on his right and Ludendorff on his left. Alongside were Colonel Kriebel, personal bodyguard Graf, the commander of the Munich storm troopers, and Captain Hermann Göring romantically militant with steel helmet decorated with a large white swastika and wearing a smart black leather coat open enough so that his Pour le Mérite could be seen. He was somewhat ruffled because his idea to bring along the captured councilors as hostages had been vetoed. But the Führer had curtly rejected the scheme; he wanted no martyrs.

Behind the leaders were three units marching abreast in columns of four. On the left was Hitler's hundred-man bodyguard, steel-helmeted and armed with carbines and potato masher grenades; on the right the Bund Oberland; and in the middle the battle-seasoned Munich SA Regiment. There followed a motley collection of men, some in uniform or parts of tattered World War uniforms, some wearing work clothes or business suits. The cadets from Infantry School, smart and ultramilitary, were sandwiched between students, shopkeepers, middle-aged businessmen and hard-faced freebooters. The only common mark was a swastika brassard on the left arm. Most of them had rifles and many had fixed bayonets. Others, particularly the SA, held pistols in chilled hands.

It was almost noon when the straggling column moved off. In fifteen minutes the 2000 men reached the Ludwig bridge and a small force of state police. The police commander stepped forward as the Putschist skirmishers slowly advanced, called out to halt or be fired upon, then turned to his men and told them to load with live ammunition. As he spoke a bugle blasted, and selected Putschists suddenly converged on the police with bayonets leveled, shouting, "Don't shoot at your comrades!" The police hesitated and before a shot could be fired were overrun. The column continued across the bridge and marched straight ahead. The Zweibückenstrasse was lined with people, many cheering enthusiastically and waving swastika flags. Bystanders began joining the parade.

The chilled men, their exhalations visible in the cold, continued unimpeded and in another fifteen minutes flowed into the Marienplatz, still festooned with swastika banners from the rallies. The Nazi flag still waved atop the City Hall and a large crowd was singing patriotic songs. At this point there was confusion among the marchers. Some were under the impression they were to turn around and return to the beer hall, while others assumed they would continue into the city and rescue Röhm. Colonel Kriebel was surprised when Ludendorff led the way to the right into the Weinstrasse and toward the Odeonsplatz but said to himself, "If Ludendorff is marching that way, naturally we'll go with him." The general himself had not planned this move. "At certain moments in life one acts instinctively and doesn't know why. . . . We just wanted to get to Röhm and bring him back."

The impulsive turn to the right by the heavy-set man in the dark brown overcoat was bringing the Putschists face to face with government forces. The state police jogged forward but the Putschists did not break, standing off the enemy with leveled bayonets and pistols. Both opened fire and panic broke out as marchers and bystanders scrambled for safety. One of the first to fall was Scheubner-Richter—shot in the lungs. Another was Graf, who had leaped in front of Hitler to take the half dozen bullets meant for him. In falling, the personal bodyguard clutched Hitler, yanking him down so sharply that his left arm was dislocated. On the other side Scheubner-Richter also helped drag Hitler to the pavement. Ludendorff's faithful servant, who had been ordered to go home, was bleeding on the asphalt.

As Hitler sprawled on the ground thinking he had been shot in the left side, comrades tried to shield him. Eighteen men lay dead in the street: fourteen followers of Hitler and four state police, all, incidentally, more or less sympathetic with National Socialism. Those in the front of the marching column alone knew what had happened. The crowd jammed up behind only heard firecracker explosions ahead, then a rumor that both Hitler and Ludendorff were killed. The Putschists scrambled to the rear.

Ludendorff marched through the police cordon and into the arms of a lieutenant who placed him under arrest and escorted him to the Residenz. Once inside, the man who moments before had acted like a hero in fiction began behaving like a spoiled child. He petulantly refused an offer by a police colonel to inform his family of his safety and forbade the colonel to call him "Excellency." From now on he was "Herr Ludendorff" and he would never don uniform as long as the offending police officer wore one.

Hitler painfully struggled to his feet, cradling his injured arm. He was in agony as he slowly moved away from the battleground, face pale, hair falling over his face. He was accompanied by Dr. Walter Schultze, chief of the Munich SA medical corps, a towering young man. At Max Joseph Platz they finally reached Hitler's old gray Selve, which had been loaded with medical supplies. Hitler told the driver to head for the Bürgerbräukeller so he could find out what was going on. But at the Marienplatz they came under heavy machine-gun fire and had to change directions several times. Since it was impossible to get back to the beer hall, there was nothing to do but keep driving south toward Salzburg.

Göring's display of his Pour le Mérite decoration had not saved him and he lay on the pavement with a bullet in his upper thigh. Frau Ilse Ballin, who had rushed from her home to help the wounded, found him bleeding profusely. With the help of her sister, she dragged the heavy burden indoors. The sisters dressed Göring's wound and were about to summon an ambulance when he weakly asked them to help him get to a private clinic. He could not bear the indignity of arrest. Frau Ballin, the wife of a Jewish merchant, had pity on him and thus he escaped prison.

6

What had started as a battle ended in a frenzied scramble for refuge as if some natural disaster had struck the Marienplatz. One group of Putschists got inside a young ladies' academy and were allowed to hide under beds and in closets. Others burst into a *Konditorei* and hid their arms under ovens, in flour sacks and coffee machines. The state police rounded up hundreds, disarming them on the street. Those left behind at the beer hall to hold the command post were so unstrung by the catastrophe they surrendered without resistance to green and blue police. They stacked arms and went home to brood.

At military district headquarters Captain Röhm also surrendered, realizing there was nothing to be gained by further resistance. The Putsch was over but victorious state police marching away from the beer hall were abused by indignant citizens with cries of "Pfui! Jew defenders! Betrayers of the Fatherland! Bloodhounds! Heil Hitler—Down with Kahr!"

Hanfstaengl missed all the action. He was at his apartment when his sister phoned to say that Putschists were marching into the center of Munich. In the street he encountered an SA acquaintance in a state of collapse who told him that Hitler, Ludendorff and Göring were dead and it was the end of Germany. As Hanfstaengl headed back home to prepare for flight an open car screeched to a halt beside him. Inside were Amann, Esser, Eckart and Hoffmann. He went with them to the photographer's apartment where it was agreed to escape singly to Austria.

Hanfstaengl never thought of hiding in his country home at Uffing but a mishap would force Hitler to do so. His car was some ten miles from Munich when he broke a long silence to announce abruptly that he must have been shot in the arm. "Is it warm?" asked Dr. Schultze. It was not. Perhaps a bullet was there or something was broken. They parked in the woods and with difficulty the doctor began removing Hitler's leather jacket, two sweaters, necktie and shirt. Schultze discovered that the left arm was severely dislocated but it would be impossible to set it properly in a car without assistance. He fastened Hitler's injured arm to his body with a kerchief, then suggested they flee to Austria. Hitler vetoed this and they kept driving south. On nearing Murnau Hitler remembered that the Hanfstaengl villa in Uffing was only a few miles away. He ordered the driver to hide the Selve, then started on foot with the doctor and first-aid man toward Uffing.

They arrived at the Hanfstaengl villa, a small stone structure near the village church, about 4 P.M. Without comment Helene led the three exhausted men up to her sitting room. Hitler began to lament the death of Ludendorff and his faithful Graf, both of whom he had seen drop. He became more and more excited. It was Ludendorff's trustfulness, he said, which had cost him his life, and Graf's faithfulness which had robbed Hitler of a perfect adjutant. He began criticizing and condemning the triumvirate for their treachery "and swore he would go on fighting for his ideals as long as breath was in him."

7

It had been a restless, anxious night at Uffing. Hanfstaengl had not come home and Hitler, rolled up tightly in his host's English traveling rug to ease the pain, had been unable to sleep. Hitler sent for Helene Hanfstaengl and told her the aid man was being dispatched to Munich in hopes of persuading the Bechsteins to send out their closed car to take him to Austria.

Hitler tried to reassure his hostess that her husband was safe, then fretted about what might have happened to his comrades. He grew restless and began pacing up and down the sitting room. He became increasingly impatient concerning the Bechstein car. Why the delay? It was only a matter of hours, perhaps minutes, he fretted, before he would be traced to Uffing. At dusk he asked Helene to close the shutters and draw the curtains, then resumed his moody pacing. Just after 5 P.M. the phone rang. It was Helene's mother-in-law, who had a villa nearby, and as the elder Frau Hanfstaengl began to relate that her house was being searched by police, she was abruptly interrupted by some official who firmly but courteously forbade her to speak. Then he spoke directly to Helene: he and his men would soon be at her villa.

She walked slowly upstairs. Hitler, in his host's outsized bathrobe, was standing expectantly in the doorway. She quietly told him the police were coming. "He completely lost his nerve for the moment and exclaimed 'Now all is lost—no use going on!'" He snatched his revolver from a cabinet.

"What do you think you're doing?" said Helene. She grasped his hand and took the weapon from him without a struggle. "How can you give up at the first reverses?" she scolded. "Think of all your followers who believe in you, and who will lose all faith if you desert them now."

She told him that the party had to know what to do while he was in prison and offered to write down instructions to each of his closest followers. All he had to do was sign a number of blank sheets which she could fill in later and deliver to his lawyer. Hitler thanked her for helping him remember his duty and began dictating instructions. First he requested that Amann keep business matters and finances in order, then Rosenberg was to "watch over" the party newspaper and—countermanding earlier instructions to Dr. Schultze—"lead the movement from now on." Hanfstaengl was to help build up the *Völkischer Beobachter* through his foreign connections. Esser and others were to carry on the political end. After all instructions were written and signed, Helene hid the papers in the flour bin.

Moments later came the sound of cars, followed by crisp commands and, most startling of all, the yelp of police dogs. After a wait of several moments there was a knock. It was a diffident young state police lieutenant accompanied by two other officers. The lieutenant politely introduced himself and apologetically wondered if he might search the house. Helene led the officers up the stairs and opened the door to the sitting room. There stood Hitler still in pajamas and bathrobe. The unexpected apparition startled the officers and they stopped. She beckoned them on and once everyone was in the room Hitler not only regained his composure but "broke forth in a tirade against the government, its officials, raising his voice more and more." Completely shattered a moment ago, Hitler now was master of himself. Abruptly he cut himself off and curtly asked the lieutenant to waste no time. He shook hands with the young man and said he was prepared to leave.

It was bitterly cold and he had no overcoat but he refused to put on one of Hanfstaengl's outsize garments, instead draped his trench coat over the blue bathrobe. He was allowed to pin his Iron Cross on the coat.

He was formally arraigned at the district office in Weilkeim before being hustled to the prison at Landsberg, some forty miles west of Munich. By this time it was raining hard and gusts of wind occasionally rocked the car. Throughout the tiring trip over winding, deserted roads Hitler was depressed and sullen. Except for a single question concerning the fate of Ludendorff (who in fact was now free after assuring authorities he was little more than an innocent bystander), he remained silent.

At Landsberg prison the chief warden was preparing for a possible attempt by Putschists to free Hitler. An army detachment was on its way to stand guard but had not arrived by the time the great nail-studded, iron entrance gate creaked open to admit Hitler. He was brought to the fortress section of the prison and put into Cell 7, the only one with an anteroom large enough for a military guard.

Hitler was left in the charge of Franz Hemmrich, who helped him undress. "He refused a bite or soup, but lay down on the cot. I went away after securely locking him in." From one lonely bunk in northern Germany where he had lain blind until a vision restored his sight, Hitler had come full circle to another in the south, with only the bare walls and ceiling for company.

In his youth Hitler suffered two major depressions: rejection by the Vienna Academy of Art and the death of his mother. Later he underwent two more crises: the surrender of Germany while he lay gassed and the catastrophe at the Feldherrnhalle. It would take a man of extraordinary will to rise above this last shock and, profiting by his own mistakes, resume his ordained path. In the past few months Hitler, the drummer, had given way to Hitler, the Führer.

PART 3

A MIND IN THE MAKING

Chapter Seven

IN LANDSBERG PRISON

1923–1924

1

The small town of Landsberg had not changed outwardly in five hundred years. Nestling in the valley of the Lech River, it was hemmed on both sides by steep and wooded heights. A bulwark against Swabian invasion since the Middle Ages, it was surrounded by ancient walls pierced by watchtowers. To get to the prison from the Munich side, one crossed an old wooden bridge over the Lech, which was scarcely more than a gushing stream. On the hill ahead was the Gefangenenanstalt und Festungshaftanstalt Landsberg, a complex of grayish-white buildings encircled by high stone walls. The prison was divided into two sections, one for ordinary criminals and one for political prisoners.

In the Festung section the man in Cell 7 refused to eat. Hitler brooded in his room but not because of its smallness and discomfort. His room at the Männerheim had been only half the size and the room on the Thierschstrasse was far gloomier. The narrow white iron bed was comfortable by his monkish standards, and the double barred window not only flooded the room with daylight but looked out on trees and shrubbery to a far pleasanter prospect than that in Munich.

The pain in Hitler's arm was so excruciating he could get little sleep. The house doctor, Brinsteiner, had discovered that he "suffered from a dislocation of the left shoulder with a break in the upper arm and, as a result, a very painful traumatic neurosis." He remained under constant medical treatment and would, in Dr. Brinsteiner's opinion, "most likely suffer permanently a partial rigidity and pain in the left shoulder."

But it was not pain alone that accounted for his utter dejection, or even the realization that his hopes for a march on Berlin had ended in disaster. What hurt as much was the feeling that he had been betrayed—by the triumvirate, by the army, by Fate itself. Moreover, the debacle at the Feldherrnhalle was being ridiculed in the newspapers as a "miniature beer hall revolution" and a Redskin raid schoolboy-style. Foreign correspondents were describing him as "Ludendorff's noisy lieutenant," a pawn in a royalist coup d'état, and the New York *Times* printed his political obituary on the front page: "The Munich putsch definitely eliminates Hitler and his National Socialist followers." Ridicule had always cut Adolf Hitler deeply. Beatings and hunger could be endured but not derision.

Even after Hitler broke his fast he would not give evidence for his trial. At first he insisted on being questioned but as soon as interrogators arrived he refused to say a word. In desperation, the chief prosecutor dispatched his assistant, Hans Ehard, to Landsberg to "see if he would get anything out of Hitler." Ehard's efforts were as fruitless as his predecessors' but he patiently continued speaking across a table in a "friendly voice as if to a sick horse." Hitler sat in sullen silence "staring blankly like a sheep," then abruptly indicated a pile of reports on the table and sarcastically said that all those official records would certainly not "hinder my future political work!"

"Well, Herr Hitler," replied Ehard after some thought, "you're probably annoyed by the presence of a stenographer." He ordered the secretary, a prison employee, to leave and take with him the offending papers. Once they were alone, Ehard tried a new tack, pointing out that he was only doing his job. Wouldn't Hitler please discuss the matter? Taken off guard by Ehard's unofficial approach, Hitler suddenly poured out words in a torrent. He not only gave details of how the Putsch was planned and executed but why he had been forced to take such drastic action. His voice rose and his face turned bluish. It was, thought Ehard, as if he were addressing a vast audience. Occasionally the assistant prosecutor would insert a question. If it was an embarrassing one, Hitler would subside into sullen silence, almost immediately broken by another eruption of words. Ehard returned to Munich and turned over his report to his superior and to Georg Neithardt, who would be the presiding judge at the trial.

The resurrection of Adolf Hitler was confirmed early the following month by his half sister Angela. She came to the prison "on a cloudy foggy December evening" expecting to find him despondent. "Never in my life will I forget this hour," she wrote their brother, Alois Hitler, Jr. "I spoke with him for half an hour. His spirit and soul were again at a high level. Physically he is quite well. His arm still gives him trouble, but they think it is almost healed. How moving is the loyalty he is accorded these days. Just before me, for example, a count visited him and brought a Christmas package from the Villa Wahnfried from B. That which he has accomplished is as solid as a rock. The goal and the victory is only a question of time. God grant it be soon." The package had come from the Wagner home in Bayreuth and several days later Winifred Wagner sent another containing a book of poetry. Frau Wagner had lost none of her faith in Hitler. "Believe me," she reportedly told one audience, "Hitler is the coming man in spite of everything, and for all that he will pull the sword out of the German oak."

His racist allies remained confident of eventual triumph and were re-forming their ranks under such innocuous titles as "Völkischer Singing Club," "Völkischer Pathfinder Detachment," "League of True German Women," and "German Rifle and Hiking League." The old Battle League was also resuscitated under a new name, Frontring, by Captain Röhm, who was in Stadelheim prison with another group of Putschists; it was designed as an "umbrella organization" for all paramilitary groups recognizing the leadership of both Hitler and Ludendorff in the racist movement. Hitler disliked the idea but Röhm, still regarding himself as Corporal Hitler's superior officer, ignored his protests.

Hitler's party, although disbanded by law, began covert political operations. The underground center was Munich where Rosenberg set up a committee to continue the NSDAP. But progress was impeded by personal squabbles and ideological feuds. While Rosenberg considered himself Hitler's temporary political heir, an exiled group in Salzburg—Esser, Streicher, Amann and Hanfstaengl—regarded him as an impostor. They neither liked nor respected Rosenberg. But perhaps that was exactly why he was chosen. He was not the type to attempt to take permanent control of the party, nor did he have followers. Moreover no one else was available. Göring was also hiding in Austria, slowly recuperating from his painful wound; Scheubner-Richter was dead; Eckart, released from Landsberg, was dying in Berchtesgaden; and Drexler disapproved of the direction in which Hitler was taking the party. Of one thing Hitler could be sure: Rosenberg was loyal.

In Munich Hitler was still taken seriously. That Christmas a group of Schwabing artists in the movement celebrated the holiday season in the Blute Café with a living tableau, "Adolf Hitler in Prison." The curtain rose on a cell. Snowflakes were falling outside a small barred window. A man sat at a desk, face buried in hands, and an invisible male chorus was singing "Silent Night, Holy Night." Then an angel placed an illuminated Christmas tree on the table. Slowly the man turned and revealed his face. "Many thought it was indeed Hitler himself," remembered Heinrich Hoffmann, who had provided the *Doppelgänger*, "and a half-sob went through the hall." When the lights went up the photographer noticed moist-eyed men and women hurriedly putting away handkerchiefs.

On New Year's Day, 1924, the financial fate of Germany was settled in London at a meeting between Hjalmar Schacht, the new Reich Commissioner for National Currency, and Montagu Norman, governor of the Bank of England. Schacht, who had already abolished emergency money, began with a frank disclosure of Germany's desperate financial situation. Once the Ruhr crisis was settled, he said, it would be "necessary to set German industry going again," and this could only be done with the assistance of foreign credit and the founding of "a second credit bank in addition to the Reichsbank, a bank based entirely on gold." He thought he could raise half of the capital for this *Golddiskontbank* in foreign currency within Germany itself. "The remaining half I should like to borrow from the Bank of England."

Norman, so wrote Schacht in a memoir characteristically entitled *The Old Wizard*, was not impressed until Schacht announced that the new bank would issue bank notes based on its gold capital of two hundred million marks.

Within forty-eight hours Norman not only formally approved the loan at the exceptionally low interest of a flat five per cent but convinced a group of London bankers to accept bills far exceeding the loan, "provided they are endorsed by the Golddiskontbank." With a few bold strokes, the self-styled Old Wizard had deprived Adolf Hitler of one of his most potent political weapons—economic disaster.

2

That Hitler was physically able to stand trial was attested by the prison physician, Dr. Brinsteiner, who also stated categorically in a special report to the warden on January 8 that his patient had no symptoms of psychic disorders or psychopathic tendencies. The doctor, who seems to have had some psychiatric training, concluded that "Hitler was at all times in control of himself, and his will and his mental capacity were not impaired by any illness even if the aims and purposes of the Putsch are interpreted as being faulty."

Hitler had profited by brief imprisonment in Stadelheim prison two years earlier. Similarly the enforced confinement at Landsberg obliged him to re-evaluate his past. In the quiet of his little cell he had come to recognize some of his own mistakes. He had intended the Putsch, for example, to be the beginning of a march on Berlin and the abrupt seizure of power after Mussolini's example. "From its failure I learned the lesson that each country must evolve its own type and methods of national regeneration."

He was able to convince himself that Fate had come to his rescue in the guise of crushing defeat. "It was the greatest good fortune for us National Socialists that this Putsch collapsed," he later wrote and listed three reasons: it would have been "absolutely impossible" to co-operate with Ludendorff; the abrupt takeover of power throughout Germany would have led to the "greatest difficulties" since the party had not begun to make the proper preparations; and the "blood sacrifice" of fourteen comrades at the Feldherrnhalle eventually proved to be "the most effective propaganda for National Socialism."

In ten weeks Hitler had raised himself from the depths of despair. Confident that he would be the leader of Germany, he spent long hours worrying over the nation's economic problems and even evolved a clever way of putting many unemployed back to work: he would construct a system of highways binding the nation closer together and would then mass-manufacture a small economical car that the little man could afford. On February 22, when he and his companions were escorted through the prison gates and driven to detention quarters in Munich, he was mentally and physically prepared for the trial that would determine his future. It would begin in four days.

By chance Frau Ebertin, who had predicted failure of his Putsch, was also in Munich writing an astrological tract. She had a new prophecy for Hitler: he would not be crushed by his humiliating defeat but rise as a phoenix. "It will turn out that recent events will not only give this [Hitler] movement inner strength, but external strength as well, so that it will give a mighty impetus to the pendulum of world history."

All Germany, if not the world, was watching Munich on the morning of February 26, for the political significance of the treason charges against Hitler, Ludendorff and eight co-defendants went far beyond their personal fate. The new republic and democracy were as much on trial as one of Germany's most respected war heroes and a fanatic from Austria.

General Ludendorff was the first defendant named in the accusation but it was obvious from the beginning that Hitler was to be the center of attention. He was first to be called to the stand and his opening words made it obvious that he intended to be the hammer. He had come not as defendant but as accuser. In a strong baritone voice he described to the court, much as he had to Ehard in prison, what impelled him to launch the Putsch. He spoke of the march, the bloody assault, his escape to Uffing and his admittance to Landsberg prison. He had but one regret—that he too had not suffered the same fate as his dear slaughtered comrades.

He assumed all responsibility for what had happened ("The other gentlemen have only co-operated with me") and then denied that he was a criminal. How could he be treated as one when his mission in life was to lead Germany back to honor, to its proper position in the world? The effect of his words, delivered with the conviction of the true believer, could be seen on the faces of the little presiding judge and the chief prosecutor. Neither protested Hitler's accusatory manner or attempted in any way to control his rhetoric.

As the trial proceeded Hitler continued to dominate the judges and the courtroom with his oratory and shrewd tactics. At the same time Ludendorff had become a minor character in the drama. Moreover his resentment against the principal codefendant was becoming obvious. "Hitler misled me," he complained to Hans Frank after the trial. "He lied to me. He told me on the evening of his mad Putsch that the army was behind it to a man. . . . He is only a speech maker and an adventurer." Perhaps he resented that the speech maker and adventurer, the despised corporal, was acting more like the traditional officer of honor than the general. While Hitler accepted responsibility Ludendorff consistently avoided it. He conducted himself with arrogance, snapping at the attorneys and judges as if it were a court-martial and he the presiding officer.

Hitler surpassed himself at the closed sessions of March 11 and 14. These were the days when the defendant was allowed by the law, unlike the English adversary system, to go on at length and freely interrogate the witnesses. And so Hitler treated the triumvirate as if they were the guilty parties. When General von Lossow took the stand Hitler jumped to his feet, shouting out questions. The towering, shaven-headed general bellowed back and pointed a long forefinger at the ex-corporal as if it were a pistol. Hitler sank back into his seat, momentarily subdued, but in a minute was on his feet again attacking the three men who had promised to join him.

General von Lossow's contemptuous declaration that Hitler was only fit to play the role of a political drummer brought such rowdy insults that the defendant was cautioned by the judge to lower his voice. He did so, but only until Lossow described him as part sentimental, part brutal. This time Hitler sprang out of his chair like a jack-in-the-box. "And where is your word of honor! Was this the sentimental and brutal Hitler?"

No, replied Lossow coolly, staring down his nose at the defendant, it was Hitler with the bad conscience. This brought a fresh barrage of insults and Lossow turned to the presiding judge. When no rebuke to Hitler was forthcoming, the general bowed and left the courtroom. Only then did presiding Judge Neithardt, an ardent nationalist, tardily announce that Hitler's behavior was a personal insult not to be tolerated. "I accept the reprimand," was Hitler's ironic retort.

"I never can think without melancholy and bitterness about this monstrous trial," recalled one German journalist. "What went on there reminded me of a Munich political carnival. A court which time after time gave the accused the opportunity to make lengthy propaganda speeches; a lay judge who, after

Hitler's first speech, declared (I heard it myself): 'But he's a colossal fellow, this man Hitler'; a presiding judge who let one man [Hitler] ridicule the highest officials in the Reich, as 'His Highness, Herr Fritz Ebert': . . . an officer who shouted to an American journalist who was chatting in English with a colleague, 'Speak German in my presence!'; a presiding judge who banished a newspaper cartoonist from the courtroom because one of the accused felt he had been the subject of a cartoon—doesn't all this belong in the Munich picture book of a great political carnival?"

The *Fasching* spirit continued to the end with Hitler's oratory reaching its peak in his final speech. One part lecture, another part exhortation, and a third part invective, it was always compelling and particularly effective since, under German law, the defendant had the last word. Hitler stoutly denied that he was only fit to be the drummer of the nationalist movement and that he was motivated by ambition alone. Hitler revealed his innermost intention. "The man who is born to be a dictator is not compelled; he wills; he is not driven forward; he drives himself forward; there is nothing immodest about this . . . The man who feels called upon to govern a people has no right to say: If you want me or summon me, I will cooperate. No, it is his duty to step forward."

He told the members of the court that, despite the failure of the November Putsch, they must honor him as the future power in Germany. For it was destined that the army and those who supported the ideas of the Putschists would be reconciled. "I believe that the hour will have come when the masses, who today stand on the street with our swastika banner, will unite with those who fired upon them. I believe that this blood will not always separate us. When I learned that it was the municipal police which fired, I had the happy feeling that at least it was not the Reichswehr; the army stands as untarnished as before. One day the hour will come when the army will stand at our side, officers and men."

"Herr Hitler," protested Judge Neithardt, "you say that the municipal police was stained. I cannot permit that."

Hitler ignored the gentle rebuke and without breaking his rhythm boomed out his final words: "The army which we have formed grows from day to day; from hour to hour it grows more rapidly. Even now I have the proud hope that one day the hour is coming when these raw recruits will become battalions, when the battalions will become regiments and the regiments divisions, when the old cockade will be raised from the mire, when the old banners will once again wave before us; and then reconciliation will come in that eternal last Court of Judgment—the Court of God—before which we are ready to take our stand. Then from our bones, from our graves will sound the voice of that tribunal which alone has the right to sit in judgment upon us. For, gentlemen, it is not you who pronounce judgment upon us, it is the eternal court of history which will make its pronouncement upon the charge which is brought against us."

It took almost an hour to read out the sentence and there was no outburst when Hitler (along with Pöhner, Kriebel and Weber) was sentenced to five years in Landsberg prison. Six months were deducted because of the pretrial detention. Ludendorff was set free.

Even in guilt Hitler was honored by the court. It refused to deport him to Austria as an undesirable alien. "Hitler is German-Austrian. In the opinion of the court a man who thinks and feels as German as Hitler, a man who voluntarily served 4½ years in the German army during the war, who earned high war decorations for bravery in the face of the enemy, who was wounded and whose health was impaired . . . should not be subjected to the Republic Protection Law." The court saved its scorn for Hitler's three enemies, declaring that the tragedy could have been prevented if Kahr, Lossow and Seisser "had clearly said 'no' to Hitler's demands for participation [in the Putsch] or if the repeated attempts by the accused on the night of November 8 to clarify the situation had met with a measure of cooperation."

Hitler's sentence was the first announced. While the others were being read out, he was hurried outside to a waiting car to prevent any demonstration. By late afternoon Hitler was back in Cell 7. It had been refurnished in his absence and looked much more inviting. But his earlier confidence was gone and jailer Franz Hemmrich noticed that he "looked more wretched than ever." This depression soon passed. Before long he opened his leather briefcase and brought out an empty diary. On the frontispiece in the upper right-hand corner he wrote: "Motto: When a world comes to an end, then entire parts of the earth can be convulsed, but not the belief in a just cause." Below this he inscribed these words:

> The trial of common narrow-mindedness and personal spite is over—and today starts
>
> MY STRUGGLE (Mein Kampf)
>
> Landsberg on 1 April 1924

The trial that only the Putschists wanted was over and, although Hitler had won the battle of propaganda, he was back in prison. For all he knew, he would remain there four and a half years. To a large segment of the German public and to the Western world in general, the sentence was ridiculously mild for treason and armed uprising. "The trial," commented the London *Times*, "has at any rate proved that a plot against the Constitution of the Reich is not considered a serious crime in Bavaria."

3

Hitler had two comrades on the upper floor of the Festung. Colonel Kriebel was in Cell 8 and the leader of the Bund Oberland, Dr. Weber the veterinary, was in number 9. Although Hitler complained daily about the barred windows, life at the fortress was passable. At 6 A.M. the two night warders went off duty and the cell doors would be opened. Invariably Hitler was dressed, washed and waiting ("He took a good deal of care of his teeth and mouth. That came of his having been gassed in the war"). An hour later convict trustees served the political prisoners a breakfast of coffee and bread or porridge in their common room. At eight the doors to the court and garden were opened and the men were allowed to wrestle, box or exercise on the parallel bars and vaulting horse. Because of his injured arm Hitler "had to content himself with the job of referee."

After half an hour the prisoners strolled in the long narrow garden, bordered on one side by the prison building and the other by a twenty-foot wall. A gravel path was Hitler's favorite promenade and here he would stroll back and forth, usually with Emil Maurice, his chauffeur, voicing the political theorems he had jotted down in his diary. "Sometimes," recalled Hemmrich, "those who had formerly belonged to the Storm

Troops would start singing party songs as they stamped along. At first we took no notice, or at least we raised no objection to this, but when the convicts on their side took to yelling in unison and disturbed the peace of the whole neighborhood, we put a stop to it."

At about 10 A.M. the men were brought in from their exercise and mail was distributed. Numerous food packages arrived from nationalist organizations and private admirers.

Just before noon the political prisoners were served dinner—usually a one-pot meal—in the common room. The others waited behind their chairs until Hitler strode in, then someone called out, "Attention!" He stood at the head of the table "until every man in turn came forward with his table-greeting." Politics was rarely discussed. Hitler usually chatted about theater, art or automobiles. After the meal they would smoke and gossip for a quarter of an hour while the table was cleared, and then the Chief would retreat to his cell on the top floor to read, write in his diary or try to catch up on his correspondence. This period was interrupted at about four o'clock for tea or coffee, which was brewed in the common room. At four forty-five the gates to the garden were unlocked again and Hitler would walk alone, or with Maurice, for more than an hour. At six each man had supper in his own cell—a herring or sausage and salad. Those who wanted could buy half a liter of beer or wine. After another hour of sport or exercise the men assembled in the common room before returning to their cells. At ten lights went out.

Occasionally Hitler varied his schedule, retreating to his cell as soon as breakfast was over to study or receive visitors. According to Hemmrich, who soon became his enthusiastic admirer, he exercised a great influence over his comrades. Because of his "sense of soldierly discipline," there were none of the usual outbursts of temper of men penned up together. "He was always at their command to be of help or service."

Usually he was "singularly cheerful" but bad news made him "a trifle thoughtful and anxious." He was particularly disturbed by the rancor of party feuds. It was becoming increasingly obvious that the NSDAP was being split in two and that the schism was due in large part to his own vague instructions to his proxy. Rosenberg had joined with Strasser and others to support the völkisch bloc in the Bavarian state elections; more significant, these two, with the help of Ludendorff, had not only formed the National Socialist Freedom Movement but entered a slate of thirty-four candidates in the national elections.

The Bavarian election came first, in April, and the ill-assorted völkisch bloc scored an unexpected triumph, winning 191,862 votes, and finished second to the Bavarian People's Party. The Görings were delighted with the triumph. "Also," Carin wrote her father from Austria, "it means pardon for all of us living in foreign countries."

The national election a month later proved to be as successful as predicted, with the newly formed National Socialist Freedom Movement polling almost two million votes. Thirty-two of the thirty-four candidates—including Strasser, Röhm, Feder, Frick and Ludendorff—were elected. It was ironic that Hitler, who had opposed the basic idea, was responsible in large part for their victory. His oratory at the trial had introduced National Socialism to many voters who were impressed by its leader's forceful manner and his effectively enunciated ideas. But other more profound and lasting forces also contributed to the triumph. The tandem appeal of patriotism and racism was growing throughout the nation. Moreover, even though inflation had been ended by the drastic national currency reform, those in the middle class who had lost homes and property were expressing displeasure at the polls along with those in the working class who were still unemployed.

Understandably, Hitler was not overjoyed by the elections. Ludendorff was claiming credit for the victory and, being free, was in a position to capitalize on his claim. Hitler was forced to join in the applause while fearing that the new group might swallow up his outlawed party. Nor was his apprehension groundless. The threat to his political power was illustrated by circulation of a pamphlet to völkisch groups which admitted that the National Socialists were "pioneers and forerunners" of the völkisch movement, then sarcastically declared that "they are not [its] savior." The whole affair was a painful but valuable lesson to Hitler. Never again, he vowed, would he take a stand unless he was sure he had the power to enforce it.

Hitler was being attacked from his own stronghold. At the offices of the *Völkischer Beobachter*, which had been closed down after the Putsch, Drexler and Feder were conducting a campaign against him. "They called Hitler a dictator and a prima donna and proclaimed that he must be brought under greater control if the party was ever to be built up again," recalled Hanfstaengl.

That May Kurt Lüdecke returned from his money-raising

trip abroad to find confusion in the ranks of the underground NSDAP. "The various groups quarreled internally and with each other. Nor were their antagonisms private scandals—enemies clawed each other in public regardless both of the spectacle they were giving the shocked onlookers and of the damage they were doing to themselves." From Hanfstaengl, Amann and Esser he learned that Rosenberg was the cause of party deterioration. But Rosenberg told him a different story. "They attack me," he said, "because I represent Hitler, whom they dare not attack, helpless though he is. If they eliminate me, they move one step nearer the top."

Lüdecke decided to travel to Landsberg to find out from Hitler how the danger could best be dispelled. According to Lüdecke's account, Hitler declared that the party must pursue a new line of action. Its future lay not in armed coups but the ballot box. "I am convinced this is our best line of action, now that conditions in the country have changed so radically." Hitler appeared to be not at all downcast by the party squabbles. "Indeed, he was so confident of final victory that my own misgivings were dispelled, for his mood was contagious." But the party split continued to widen. A few weeks later Strasser joined with Ludendorff in proposing the foundation of the National Socialist Freedom Party, thus creating a single völkisch party of which the NSDAP would be but a part. This raised the intensity of interparty rancor which, in turn, forced Hitler into making a radical decision. On July 7 *Der Völkische Kurier* announced that he had "laid down the leadership of the National Socialist movement, and that he will refrain from all political activity during his term of detention. He requested his adherents not to visit him in prison since he had so much work and was also engaged in writing a book."

In some circles it was deduced that Hitler was pretending to write as an excuse to avoid the internecine political battle. But even before his arrest he had been seriously thinking of composing a history of the Jews. Now he had a better idea, which obsessed him to such a degree that he welcomed a vacation from politics so he could get it down on paper. In addition to jotting down ideas in his diary, he dictated to Maurice. Then, in the privacy of his cell, he would laboriously type out the manuscript with two fingers on the typewriter loaned to him by the warden.

Guard Hemmrich recalled: "As he finished one section of the book after another he would read it aloud to the others in their evening assemblies." The book was not always written under favorable conditions. The window, for instance, leaked during a heavy rain. One day while mopping the floor Hitler burst into laughter. There was the prison cat "perched on top of a stool in the middle of the mess and puddle and licking at it after her own finicky fashion." His most helpful assistant was a newcomer to the top floor. After Hitler's sentence Rudolf Hess had taken Professor Haushofer's advice to surrender. Hess helped Hitler formulate ideas, took dictation and relieved him of typing chores. Frau Wagner also helped by providing quantities of bond paper, carbon paper, pencils, ink and erasers.

At first the book was to have been a general history but the first volume—under the ponderous working title *Four and a Half Years of Struggle Against Lies, Stupidity and Cowardice*—now included an autobiographical account of Hitler's childhood, his years in Vienna, the war, the Red revolution and the beginnings of the party in Munich. It turned out to be the story of a poor boy's political education and gave him the opportunity to discourse not only on his three favorite subjects—Jews, Marxism and racism—but the futility of parliamentary government, syphilis, the decline of the theater, the monarchy, and responsibility for loss of the war.

Writing down his political theories was in itself a process of self-education. "During my imprisonment I had time to provide my philosophy with a natural, historical foundation." The authorities had made a mistake by imprisoning him. "They would have been far wiser to let me make speeches all the time, without giving me respite!"

It was remarkable how Hitler had gained ascendancy over his jailers. He had already converted a majority of the staff to National Socialism and even the warden became so impressed that he permitted Hitler's lights to stay on until midnight. Surveillance was so lax that the prisoners established their own underground newspaper, which was typed and then hectographed. One section was comic, the other serious. Hitler usually wrote the leading article and would often contribute caricatures. The existence of the paper was not discovered until one man thoughtlessly wrote home about it but by the time Hemmrich raided the editorial office in Cell 1 nothing could be found. be found.

It was also Hemmrich's duty to spy on the evening get-togethers in the common room to make sure no revolution was being plotted. But the eavesdropper became propagandized by

Hitler's words and soon fell almost completely under his spell. He and his assistants would gather outside the door "all ears, alert for what he was saying about things that concerned our own interests. We were immensely struck by his speaking."

4

Throughout the summer Hitler luxuriated in his pleasant quarters, preparing himself for the battle to come. He confined most of his efforts to the book, secure in the expectation of an early parole. It seemed to be assured on September 18 when Warden Leybold dispatched an extremely favorable report to the Bavarian Ministry of Justice. It declared that during his months of imprisonment Hitler had "proved himself to be a man of strict discipline and order," who was "at all times co-operative, modest and courteous to everyone, particularly to the officials of the institution." Leybold concluded with a prediction that Hitler, upon release, would not resort to any violence or illegality. "There is no doubt that he has become a much more quiet, more mature and thoughtful individual during his imprisonment than he was before and does not contemplate acting against existing authority."

At first it seemed certain that Leybold's strong recommendation would bring about Hitler's release in early fall, but on September 22 the Bavarian state police sent a confidential report to the Ministry of the Interior recommending that Hitler not be released on October 1; and if this came about "unexpectedly" he should be deported as a security measure. The moment he was set free, Hitler would generate riots "because of his energy." Penal Chamber I ignored this recommendation and declared Hitler eligible for parole but an appeal from the Minister of Justice on the grounds that the prisoner had flagrantly violated visiting privileges was upheld. Parole was denied.

Hitler's frustration was complete but, as he had done before, he lifted himself out of this depression and returned to work on his book. "All day long," recalled Hemmrich, "and late into the night one could hear the typewriter going in his room, and his voice dictating to Hess." Nor did he neglect his duty as Führer. On the first anniversary of the Munich Putsch he spoke "with deep emotion" to the political prisoners gathered in the common room. While charging himself "with the entire responsibility for the whole affair," he demonstrated how it had failed for historical reasons. "His hearers were profoundly impressed with the Leader's sincerity and deep morality."

November passed and though there was still no indication that parole was at hand, he remained stoic.

In the meantime one of his most prestigious followers, Göring, was in a Venice hotel attempting to negotiate a badly needed loan from Benito Mussolini. Although still recuperating from his painful wound, which required heavy drug dosage, the former war ace was exerting himself in the Führer's service.

But apparently the Fascists doubted they would get their money's worth from a party whose attempt to emulate the March on Rome had ended so disastrously, and Göring's pleading became shrill. "The Fascists were at one time small and laughed at," he argued. "One should not believe that National Socialists have no future." In a few years they would be in power. He enlarged upon the embarrassment the NSDAP would face because of its support of such an unpopular cause as the South Tyrol; and pointed out what a bargain Mussolini was getting for a mere two million lire. "For this you would have in our press an important speaking-trumpet. Besides you will get your two million back at the *latest* in five years."

But the month of November slipped by with Mussolini still refusing to commit himself (nor is it likely that he ever did loan the two million lire) and the Führer still in prison. A few of his comrades were released by mid-December. "Hitler bore these repeated disappointments about his own return to freedom with equanimity and philosophy," remembered Hemmrich. "The remainder prepared to celebrate the season at Landsberg as best as they could." They put up holiday decorations and set up a Christmas tree in the common room. But before they could decorate it the efforts of the state cabinet to prevent Hitler's parole finally ended. On December 19 the Bavarian Supreme Court—perhaps influenced by a threat from the three lay judges of the Hitler trial to make a public appeal—ordered his immediate release.

Warden Leybold himself brought the news to Hitler, and early the following afternoon, after spending more than a year in prison, Hitler bade farewell to his comrades, gave them all his money (282 marks), then shook hands with Hemmrich and thanked him for all he had done. There followed a tearful parting with Leybold. "When I left Landsberg," recalled Hitler, "everyone wept (the warden and the other members of the prison staff)—but not I! We'd won them all to our cause."

It was a raw, gray day. Hitler tersely greeted the two who had come to take him home, his printer, Adolf Müller, and Hoffmann, the photographer, before stepping briskly into the touring car, its canvas top raised as protection against the cold. He turned to Hoffmann, who had not been allowed to take photographs in the prison, and told him to get his picture. After one was taken at the ancient city gate, which had a fortress atmosphere, Hoffmann wanted to know what Hitler intended to do now. "I shall start again, from the beginning," he said. As they sped toward Munich Hitler reveled in the experience. ("What a joy it was for me to be in a car again!") He asked Müller to go faster. "No," was the reply. "It's my firm intention to go on living for another twenty-five years."

At Pasing they were met by a group of Nazi motorcyclists who accompanied them into the city. Party faithfuls were waiting outside his apartment house. At the top of the stairs, Hitler was almost bowled over by his exuberant dog. He found his room filled with flowers and laurel wreaths. Neighbors had covered the table with food and drink, including a bottle of wine. Prison had not marked him with self-pity. Far from regretting his months in Landsberg, he professed they had been essential for his development. From now on he would be a true Führer, shaping his own program in his own way toward long-range goals.

His first task was to assess the political situation. The National Socialist bloc had lost more than half its seats in the December elections. Moreover the NSDAP itself was still illegal and he would have to operate underground. On the positive side, he was not only free but deportation proceedings against him had been quashed by the man who had recently fought his parole; Justice Minister Gürtner had undoubtedly been influenced by Austrian refusal to take Hitler back. He had come out of prison as a martyred saint to all völkisch groups, and this racist movement, despite the evidence of the December elections, was burgeoning. This growth, ironically, had been unleashed by the Putsch; many people who had wavered between the moderate and radical wings of the patriotic movement swung to extremism as a result of their emotional involvement in the abortive uprising.

In a sense the NSDAP had a stronger base than ever and, while its two warring groups were wide apart, Hitler was confident he could somehow induce both factions to place loyalty to him above their differences. He was to be the program and his followers would have to equate völkisch aims with his personal political success. The image of Adolf Hitler, the national martyr, would become the personalization of flag, freedom and racial purity.

What had been thought out carefully in the peace and solitude of his cell was quite another thing in the unaccustomed freedom of Munich. On that first evening of liberty he didn't know what to do with himself. "I had the impression that any moment a hand would be laid on my shoulder, and I remained obsessed by the idea that I'd have to ask leave for anything I wanted to do!" Shrewd enough to realize that only time would enable him to regain "contact with reality," he decided to remain quiet for several weeks before embarking on the task of "reconciling the enemy brothers."

One of the first steps in his project to regain civilian composure was a visit to the Hanfstaengls on a snowy Christmas Eve. They had moved from their cramped apartment to a spacious house across the Isar River, a pleasant sector near Herzog Park boasting such prestigious neighbors as Thomas Mann. As Hitler entered the studio he looked around nervously, then said, almostpleadingly, "Hanfstaengl, play me the 'Liebestod.'" After Hanfstaengl "hammered out this tremendous thing from *Tristan und Isolde*, with Lisztian embellishments," Hitler began to relax.

Before he left, Hitler managed to have a few moments of privacy with Helene in the studio. She was seated on the large sofa and all at once he dropped to his knees and put his head in her lap. "If only I had someone to take care of me," he said.

"Look, this won't do," said Helene and asked him why he didn't get married. "I can never marry because my life is dedicated to my country." She thought he was acting like a little boy, and perhaps he was. Seventeen years ago, almost to the day, his mother had died. "It would have been awful if someone had come in," recalled Helene. "Humiliating to him. He was taking a chance, he really was. That was the end of it and I passed it off as if it simply had not happened."

Chapter Eight

HITLER'S SECRET BOOK

1925–1928

1

Hitler was invited to spend New Year's Eve at Hoffmann's home. He refused but when the party was under way a girl urged the photographer to phone the Führer and try again. To Hoffmann's surprise Hitler said he would come "but only for half an hour." His arrival was eagerly awaited, particularly by the ladies, none of whom had met him. Nor were they disappointed. "In his cutaway coat he looked very smart," wrote Hoffmann. "He had not yet started to wear the lock of hair hanging from his forehead, and his air of modest reserve only served to enhance his charm." The women were particularly entranced by his little mustache.

One pretty girl maneuvered Hitler under the mistletoe and kissed him. "I shall never forget the look of astonishment and horror on Hitler's face! The wicked siren, too, felt that she had committed a faux pas, and an uncomfortable silence reigned. Bewildered and helpless as a child, Hitler stood there, biting his lip in an effort to master his anger. The atmosphere, which after his arrival had shown a tendency to become more formal, now became almost glacial."

Ever since release from Landsberg, Hitler had lived in semi-solitude. He was finding it difficult to adjust politically as well as socially. Determined to confine his activities to behind-the-scenes discussions with Esser and Pöhner, he refused to reveal his new plans and put off worshipful delegations who sought his advice and blessing. At the same time he did not make the mistake of discouraging the adulation of rank-and-file followers, and his silence made them more eager than ever to hear his first speech.

Hitler needed this concentrated solitude to become familiar with recent drastic political and economic developments. The regime in France which had been demanding occupation of the Ruhr had been replaced by a more conciliatory group, and a more equitable payment by Germany of war reparations had been recently instituted by the Allies. On the economic front the establishment of a stable mark had stemmed the toboggan slide to economic chaos. The dual prospect of a peaceable settlement with France and economic recovery meant that Hitler had been deprived of political assets.

On the other hand, a social change had come about which now offered him the chance to re-enter politics on a national scale. Rapid technical developments, urbanization, dispersal of the population and the industrialization of the past decade had upended the middle class. The small merchant, the independent businessman and the farmer were in a state of uncertainty and fear. It was the middle class that had suffered most during the inflation. The margin of affluence which had set these people above the working class had been wiped out along with their savings and capital. Many blamed their misfortunes on the Reds and Jews and their bitterness was already turning into hatred, making them receptive to Hitler's message of anti-Semitism.

The new year presented as many opportunities as difficulties and his political future would depend on ability to cope with both. He made his first move on the fourth day of 1925 in the form of a gesture of truce to the new Minister President of Bavaria, Heinrich Held. He spent half an hour alone with Held, pledging his loyalty and offering to co-operate in the fight against the Reds. He promised to confine himself to legal means in his future political struggles and made such a favorable impression that Held reportedly remarked that evening, "This wild beast is checked. We can afford to loosen the chain."

On February 16 the Bavarian government canceled the state of emergency and removed its restrictions on the NSDAP. Ten days later the *Völkischer Beobachter* was back on the stands with a lengthy editorial by Hitler entitled "A New Beginning." He promised to confine himself henceforth to organization and policy, not personal and religious differences, and called for peace among all völkisch elements within the party. They must unite, he said, to defeat the common enemy, Jewish Marxism. It was the new Adolf Hitler in action, determined to operate legally and willing to compromise for the sake of a party unity. At the same time he was going to run the party *his* way, and despite a pledge to work within the government framework, he had not tempered his attack on his primal enemy—the Jew.

On the following day, February 27, Hitler made his eagerly awaited return to public life at a party convention in the Bürgerbräukeller where he had launched the Putsch. National Socialists from all over the nation were on hand—with three important exceptions: Röhm, Strasser and Rosenberg. "I won't take part in that comedy," the latter told Lüdecke that afternoon. "I know the sort of brother-kissing Hitler intends to call for." Rosenberg was proud and refused to shake hands with a man he felt had forsaken him.

There was almost as much excitement in the hall as there had been on the night of the Putsch, and as Hitler marched down the aisle wildly enthusiastic adherents waved beer mugs, cheered and hugged each other. Lifting his eyes above the party leaders, he appealed to the multitude beyond. While his words were fervent, they were not designed to antagonize either faction. He didn't make the mistake of going into the details of the squabbles of 1924; he ignored them. He called Ludendorff "the most loyal and selfless friend" of the movement and urged all those who "in their hearts remained old National Socialists" to join together behind the swastika flag and crush their two greatest enemies: Marxism and Jews. The first was an appeal to revolutionaries like Esser, the second to Drexler and his more conservative völkisch followers.

After an inspirational appeal for national regeneration ("It is madness to believe that a great people of sixty or seventy million cannot be destroyed. It perishes as soon as it loses its drive for self-preservation") he turned his attention to the party officials at the front tables. He neither asked for their loyalty and support nor offered any compromise. He ordered them to join the crusade or get out. "If anyone comes and puts conditions to me, then I say to him: 'My friend, wait and see what conditions I will put to you.' I am not out to get the great masses. After a year you can judge, my party comrades, if I have acted correctly and that it is good; if I have not acted correctly, then I will place my office back in your hands. Until that moment, however, I alone lead the movement and no one makes conditions for me so long as I personally assume all responsibility. And I unconditionally assume responsibility for everything that happens in the movement."

The frenzy in his manner was communicated to the audience. Cries of "Heil!" rang out. Women wept as the crowd pressed from the rear, climbing onto chairs and tables. Men who had been bitter enemies surged to the platform and shook hands, some of them unable to restrain tears. Then Max Amann shouted, "The wrangling must stop! Everyone for Hitler!" Rudolf Buttmann of the German Nationalist Party came forward to make an emotional announcement that all his doubts had suddenly "melted away within me as the Führer spoke." Buttmann's use of this title, hitherto uttered only in private, underlined Hitler's overwhelming success. From now on he would be the Führer in public. He had not only unified the NSDAP but established the leadership principle, the unquestioned rule of one man.

The resurrection of Hitler was followed the very next day by a political development of significance. In the national elections occasioned by the death of Ebert, seventy-eight-year-old Field Marshal von Hindenburg became the second President of the Republic. It was obvious that the sympathies of this hero of the right did not lie with the Republic and, while he attempted to remain neutral, he did little to strengthen the republican forces. There continued to be frequent cabinet crises, often over trivial issues such as the conservative proposition to award a large financial indemnity to the Hohenzollerns. When this was carried over vigorous socialist protest, a new bill was introduced to indemnify all dispossessed princes.

It seemed inevitable that this change in national politics should add impetus to Hitler's rise in power. But his return to the politics of the beer hall had been too sudden and triumphant to suit the Bavarian government. It only proved how dangerous his gift of oratory was to the state. He had injected new life into the party too fast, too excessively and the police forbade him to address five mass meetings set for early March on the grounds that he had inflamed the Bürgerbräu audience with such violent phrases as "Fight Marxism and Judaism not according to middle-class standards but over corpses!"

Hitler protested the ban in person. "Those who want to have a fight with us can have one," he told police officials. "Whoever attacks us will be stabbed from all sides. I will successfully lead the German people in their fight for freedom, if not peacefully, then with force. This sentence I repeat emphatically for the benefit of police spies so that no erroneous reports will be circulated." These were strong words for a man on parole and the end result was a ban on speaking in public throughout Bavaria. Open NSDAP meetings could be held, but not if their Führer spoke. Before long the proscription extended to almost every German state; Hitler had been deprived of his major political weapon.

The ban obliged Hitler to confine himself to rebuilding the party and he tirelessly went from one closed meeting to another in Munich, exhorting audiences much as he had done in the Bürgerbräukeller. By grass-roots technique—shaking hands with men, kissing the hands of women and holding innumerable intimate conversations—he came into contact with the entire metropolitan membership. He succeeded not only in solidfying his magnetic attractions to the commonalty but in winning complete organizational control of the city party. At the same time Esser and Streicher roamed Bavaria duplicating Hitler's tactics as they rallied local organizations behind the Führer.

By the end of March Hitler controlled almost all Bavarian locals but he was forced to turn over the fate of the party in North Germany to Gregor and Otto Strasser. The first was a good organizer and a gifted speaker and could, as a delegate to the Reichstag, travel free on railroads. After the inspiring speech in the Bürgerbräu, he pledged his allegiance to Hitler but Otto, already a clever journalist despite his youth, had reservations. How long, he wondered, would the honeymoon with Hitler last?

Hitler accepted his enforced retirement from public life much as he had his imprisonment and took advantage of its opportunities. He utilized his free time to establish a solid party apparatus with the help of two colorless but efficient bureaucrats: Philipp Bouhler and Franz Xaver Schwarz. The first became executive secretary of the party. An owlish-looking individual who invariably bowed to Hitler before addressing him, he was obsessed with details. Schwarz, formerly an accountant at the Munich City Hall, was party treasurer. He brought to his job the talents of an adding machine and the spirit of a miser. Together the two men, by subordinating themselves completely to the Führer, became indispensable to the party machinery.

The efficient depersonalization of the party's internal organization by Bouhler and Schwarz enabled Hitler to concentrate on long-range political strategy, write articles and travel extensively in the north to make personal appearances at closed party meetings. He also had the leisure to repair broken friendships, chastise recalcitrants, bring opponents together and attend to personal problems. He reinstated Rosenberg as editor of the refounded *Völkischer Beobachter*, then wrote him a letter praising his integrity and calling him "a most valuable collaborator."

A few days later Hitler wrote another letter and solved a nagging personal problem—deportation to Austria—by facing it directly. He requested the city officials in Linz to cancel his Austrian citizenship since he intended to become a citizen of Germany. Three days later the provincial government of Upper Austria issued an emigration permit absolving him "from allegiance to the Austrian State." For a fee of 7.5 schillings Hitler was freed of the threat of deportation. And though he was not yet a German citizen, and consequently unable to vote or hold elective office, he was confident that this matter could be resolved when it became necessary.

Of more immediate concern were the rebellious actions of the contumacious and egocentric Captain Röhm. From the beginning he had attempted to make the SA his private army rather than Hitler's political instrument, and while the Führer was in prison he had formed a new organization from storm troop remnants under the name of Frontbann. Convinced that everything he had been working for since the Putsch would be lost if he subordinated the Frontbann to the party, Röhm presented Hitler with a memorandum on April 16 that the 30,000 men of the Frontbann could be the foundation of a national political organization but it must be under Röhm's absolute authority. His request was accompanied by appeals to their past friendship and a vow of personal loyalty.

Hitler had learned how disastrous it was to be dependent on an organization he did not control. Determined to make the new SA solely his instrument, he demanded that the Frontbann accept his personal authority at once. In an apparent effort to apply pressure, Röhm tendered his resignation from the Frontbann and requested a written acknowledgment of this action from the Führer. After waiting for an answer in vain he again wrote Hitler on the last day of April. "I take this opportunity," he concluded, "in memory of the fine and difficult days we have lived through together, to thank you [he used the familiar *Dir*] for your comradeship and to beg you not to exclude me from your personal friendship." There was still no reply and the following day Röhm announced formal resignation of his offices and withdrawal from politics. By maintaining silence, Hitler had forced Röhm to become a man without party or a Frontbann, and was himself free to set up a revitalized SA tailored for his own purposes.

2

That spring at least two of Hitler's personal dreams were realized. First, he managed somehow to acquire a new red Mercedes in which he spent many pleasant hours touring the Bavarian countryside with his bosom companions. He also established an auxiliary headquarters in the mountain village of Berchtesgaden. In this breath-taking scenic area he always found refreshment and mental stimulation.

Hanfstaengl offered to teach him English so he could read British and American newspapers and understand something of the broader world outside Germany. While never refusing the offer, Hitler could never make up his mind to accept it. And even the influence of Helene Hanfstaengl was waning. In hopes of instilling in him some of the social graces, she suggested he learn to waltz. He refused on the grounds that it was an unworthy preoccupation for a statesman and, after her husband noted that Washington, Napoleon and Frederick the Great all enjoyed dancing, retorted that it was "a stupid waste of time and these Viennese waltzes are too effeminate for a man to dance. This craze is by no means the least factor in the decline of their Empire. That is what I hate about Vienna."

Perhaps this rejection of Helene had something to do with her rejection of him the previous Christmas Eve. He was turning to other women for solace. Just across the street from his new rooming house in the town of Berchtesgaden was a boutique run by the Reiter girls, Anni and Mitzi. If one can believe Maurice, Mitzi caught the Führer's eye while he was walking his Alsatian in the Kurpark. A friendship between Prinz and Mitzi's police dog led to a flirtation between the owners. Hitler invited Mitzi to a concert, but her older sister protested on the grounds that Hitler was twenty years older than her sixteen-year-old sister. Hitler left in mortification but soon returned with an invitation to both sisters to attend a party meeting. Years later Mitzi claimed that Hitler went beyond flirtation: he called her Mitzerl, compared her beautiful eyes to his mother's and asked for a kiss. When she refused the Führer declared that they must not see each other again. But before long he was walking her around the lake. At a secluded spot he put his hands on her shoulders and suddenly kissed her. "He said, 'I want to crush you.' He was full of wild passion." Before long they were lovers; and while she had visions of marriage, he only talked of renting an apartment in Munich where they could live together.

Hitler found feminine stimulation of a different nature from Winifred Wagner, who accepted him uncritically. He became a hero in the household and delighted in playing the role of the mysterious figure fleeing from enemies bent on assassinating him. In the dead of night he would steal into the Villa Wahnfried. "Late as it was," recalled Friedelind Wagner, "he never failed to come into the nursery and tell us gruesome tales of his adventures. We . . . listened while he made our flesh creep, showing us his pistol which, of course, he carried illegally—a small one that he could hide in his palm, but it held twenty bullets." Then it was that he told the children that the bags under his eyes had been caused by poison gas in the war.

At Wahnfried he was called Wolf. Everybody liked him, even the new schnauzer, which snarled at strangers, but the children were particularly attracted to him. "He drew them quite effortlessly with his hypnotic power. . . . His life was fascinating to us, because it was completely unlike ours—it all had a story-book quality."

On July 18 the first volume of his book was published in Munich by Eher. At Amann's suggestion the title had been changed to *Mein Kampf*, the name he had given his diary. Sales were good, a little under 10,000 by the end of 1925, but it was criticized then and later as abominably written, pompous and turgid. It read like a Horatio Alger novel grafted onto a political tract. Even its subtitle, *A Reckoning*, was novelistic. Even so, the detailed subjective portrayal (self-serving as it was) of the development of a young man's personal and political convictions gave insight into the nationalistic völkisch wave sweeping across Germany.

3

Hitler must have known that giving Gregor Strasser full power to reorganize the NSDAP in North Germany would be risky and the more successful he became the more dangerous he would be as a political rival. While anti-Semitic, Strasser was no reactionary. His political philosophy could be traced to Spengler and the front-line socialism of the war, based on the elitist principle that leadership of the proletarians must come from the military. He was a typical left-wing National Socialist and this made him particularly useful in bringing party revolutionaries back into line. A husky, outgoing man, he would move crowds as well as individuals and by late summer helped bring more prosperity to the cause than Hitler had expected. The number of cells in some sections doubled and even tripled. This increase came largely through Strasser's appeal to the working class and his freedom from the autocratic control of the Munich leadership.

In early September the struggle against the south became an open issue at a party conference in Hagen. Gregor Strasser had called the meeting to form a coalition against Munich bureaucracy. The conferees naïvely hoped to pry the Führer from his reactionary Bavarian advisers so he could lead Germany toward a revolutionary völkisch millennium. Strasser's program was endorsed. The delegates voted to unite for greater efficiency in organization and propaganda, and approved publication of a series of articles expressing programmatic policies that included economic reforms verging on national Bolshevism. Their editor was to be a brilliant twenty-nine-year-old who had replaced the methodical Himmler as Strasser's secretary. Josef Goebbels was just over five feet tall and weighed not much more than a hundred pounds. Moreover, his small frame had been wracked by infantile paralysis, leaving him with a deformed foot. Goebbels was compensated by a variety of talents: he was a facile writer and, despite an appearance of frailty, was a commanding figure on a platform with his magnetic baritone voice, expressive hands and appealing dark eyes.

Son of a Rhenish petty bourgeois Catholic family, he was molded by academia rather than home or church. His character was most significantly shaped by the University of Munich to which hundreds of disillusioned soldiers had flocked after the armistice. He had been exempted from service because of his clubfoot, but his hero was a tall, strikingly handsome veteran named Richard Flisges—pacifist and anarchist—who instilled in him ideals that would color the rest of his life. Flisges also introduced him to Dostoevski, whose emotional mysticism inspired young Goebbels.

He transferred to Heidelberg and left in 1921 with a Ph.D. in literature. The next few years he spent writing a romantic autobiographical novel entitled *Michael*, several plays and numerous lyric poems. To support himself he worked at a bank, as floorman of the Cologne stock exchange, as tutor, as part-time bookkeeper. It was during this frustrating period that he split with Flisges, for he had come to loathe the internationalism of Marxism. He moved to a völkisch socialism and in Hitler ("incarnation of our faith and idea") he found a second Flisges to worship. At the same time he was bound to Gregor Strasser. It was this split fealty and its inevitable denouement that helped determine the course of the NSDAP.

This struggle was complicated by an ideological dilemma. In many respects Goebbels was still a Marxist and he persistently attempted to convert Communists to National Socialism. He was determined to evolve a theory which would erect "the bridge from left to right over which those willing to sacrifice came together." He, along with Gregor Strasser, believed that the party should champion the cause of workers in general and trade unionism in particular. This was one of the main points of difference between Hitler and Goebbels.

At last on November 4 the two met in Braunschweig, and when Hitler shook his hand Goebbels was in ecstasy. "Like an old friend," he wrote in his diary. "And those big blue eyes. Like stars. He is glad to see me. I am in heaven." The personal encounter was the beginning of Goebbels' enchantment with the Führer, an enthrallment intensified at a second meeting several weeks later in Plauen. "Great joy! He greets me like an old friend. And looks after me. How I love him!"

Yet within twenty-four hours Goebbels was participating in an open revolt against the central party organization at a meeting of northern Gauleiters. He had been delegated to help Strasser draft a new party program aimed at liberating the Führer from the "reactionary" Munich group and turning him to the left. This program called for state ownership of all land, division of large agricultural estates among landless farmers and nationalization of corporations. It was presented to the Gauleiters at a two-day conference in Hannover on January 24–25, 1926. The sessions were stormy, largely due to the surprise appearance of Gottfried Feder, Hitler's proxy. Feder, who had objected to almost everything, said, "Neither Hitler nor I will accept this program." He was reminded that he was only a guest but he persisted. As he was announcing that Hitler opposed the Marxists' request for confiscation of crown property as a "Jewish swindle," he was shouted down. Goebbels leaped to his feet, furiously attacking the Munich leadership. He demanded Hitler's expulsion from the party unless he freed himself from their influence. This ultimatum seemed strange coming from someone who had recently written, "How I love him!" but it could have been a product of that adoration, since he was convinced that the Munich bureaucrats were leading Hitler to ruin.

Whatever the case, Feder's report of the fractious meeting finally roused Hitler to action. He summoned all party leaders to Bamberg on Sunday, February 14. He did not make the mistake of assaulting either Strasser of Goebbels. Perhaps his intuition told him the truth—that both really were loyal to him and merely wanted to guide him away from the likes of Streicher and Esser. He had come to Bamberg not to humiliate the northerners but to bring them back into the fold. He launched his oblique attack on the leftists in purely leftist rhetoric, then offered as an alternative to the two conflicting views a new concept. He took the party out of politics and into the mythology of the leader.

The unexpected thrust of his speech took the northerners completely by surprise. Goebbels had come to Bamberg confident that Hitler could be wooed to the left yet he neither endorsed their position nor debated the issues. Rather he faced the party leadership with a choice: to reject or accept him as the Führer. To have denied him would have meant the end of the party. Strasser replied briefly and nervously. He was a beaten man. And Goebbels, except for shouting out several slogans, remained silent, except in his diary: "My heart aches!"

4

By mid-spring of 1926 Hitler had gained complete control of the NSDAP with establishment of the principle that the Munich local was the hub of the entire movement and should provide the leadership of the national party. This was confirmed at a general membership meeting at the Bürgerbräu on May 22. Here, as supreme Führer, Hitler was invested with the power to select and dismiss any Gauleiter or subleader. This meant the termination of all democratic procedures and complete subservience to the Führer principle. As a final precaution, Hitler insisted that the twenty-five points of the original party program be declared unalterable. He got his way—and was now in sole charge of the party's ideology.

In his heart Goebbels had already gone completely over to Hitler but he kept up the façade of loyalty to Strasser, who still had doubts about the Führer. On June 10 Goebbels assured his diary that he would only go to Berlin as Hitler's representative if he could remain "absolutely independent" but two days later was eager to accept any invitation. "Then I would be away from all the muck. Now all depends on his decision. Does he want me?" By the time they met again Goebbels had worked himself into a state of exultant hero-worship.

> Hitler is the same dear comrade. You cannot help liking him as a man. And on top of it that overriding mind. You always discover something new in that self-willed head. As a speaker he has developed a wonderful harmony of gesture, histrionics and spoken word. The born whipper-up! Together with him you can conquer the world. Give him his head and he will shake the corrupt Republic to its foundations. His best epigram yesterday: "For our struggle God gave us His abundant blessing. His most beautiful gift was the hate of our enemies whom we too hate with all our heart."

Early the next month Hitler all but conciliated the warring factions at the party congress in Weimar. The site had been chosen because Thuringia was one of the few states where Hitler was allowed to speak in public. His major address on the last day of the congress, July 4, was more emotional than political. "Deep and mystical," wrote Goebbels. "Almost like the Gospels. Shuddering we pass together with him along the edge of life's abyss. Everything is being said. I thank providence for having given us this man!" As Hitler walked off the stage the audience exploded into applause and the cheers continued for several minutes. Later Hitler, wearing an ill-fitting field jacket and puttees, stood in the back seat of an open car to review 3500 (the enthusiastic Goebbels put the number at 15,000) storm troopers who marched past, a bit out of step, with right arms raised in salute.

It was an impressive end to a memorable congress despite complaints that there were still fewer than 40,000 members in the NSDAP. Numbers did not concern Hitler at the moment. The party was one of the smallest in Germany but it was an iron fist, his iron fist. He returned to Berchtesgaden to complete the second volume of *Mein Kampf* and to recharge himself for the final task in the reconstruction of the party: conversion of the spell he had cast at Weimar into bureaucratic control of all party locals.

There were almost 50,000 party members by the end of the year, as well as an efficient party directorate with Hess as secretary, Schwarz as treasurer and Bouhler as secretary-general.* The directorate had started with three automobiles and a staff of twenty-five but was growing rapidly. It was a quasi state within a state with departments for foreign policy, labor, industry, agriculture, economy, interior, justice, science and press. Party auxiliaries were either formed or envisioned: a Hitler Youth and leagues for women, teachers, law officers and physicians.

The most important arm of the party was the SA. Eight new units had been installed at the Weimar party congress as demonstrable proof that they were an integral part of the NSDAP. At the same time local and regional storm troop units were coordinated with the Führer in direct control.

The end of 1926 was also marked by publication of the second volume of *Mein Kampf*. Subtitled *The National Socialist Movement*, it was based on the history of the party from the day the twenty-five points of the program were presented

*The official membership figures for this period are unreliable. Schwarz deliberately numbered all members consecutively to obscure losses caused by resignations or expulsion. Moreover, Gauleiters and local leaders consistently turned in misleading reports so they wouldn't have to send headquarters its full share of the dues.

to the Munich Putsch. History of a sort had replaced autobiography. Since Machiavelli there had rarely appeared such pragmatic instructions on politics, and Hitler's precepts on propaganda and organization were practical for those operating on street level. His analysis of crowd psychology indicated he had read Freud's *Group Psychology and the Analysis of the Ego*, published a few years earlier in Germany. "A group is extraordinarily credulous," wrote Freud, "and open to influence; it has no critical faculty, and the improbable does not exist for it. The feelings of a group are always very simple and very exaggerated, so that it knows neither doubt nor uncertainty." Ironically it took a Viennese Jew to instruct Hitler that the orator who wished to sway a crowd "must exaggerate, and he must repeat the same thing again and again." And it was Freud too who pointed out that the mass was "intolerant but obedient to authority. . . . What it demands of its heroes is strength or even violence. It wants to be ruled and oppressed and to fear its masters." Typically Hitler took what he wanted from his compatriot, combining Freudian theory with his own ideas to forge a formidable weapon.

The book also indicated that Hitler had drastically altered his foreign policy. He had come out of the war convinced that France was Germany's chief foe and in a speech in July 1920 even considered the possibility of an alliance with the Soviet Union once their Jews were expelled. Now, six years later, in the next to the last chapter of this second volume, he admitted it had been a mistake to look upon France as the main enemy, and completely rejected a war of revision. National Socialist foreign policy must be altered, he said, namely (and the stress is his), "*to secure for the German people the land and soil to which they are entitled on this earth*." Several pages later he was more explicit. "*We take up where we broke off six hundred years ago. We stop the endless German movement to the south and west, and turn our gaze upward toward the land in the east*." And by the east he meant primarily Russia which, he charged, had fallen under "the yoke of the Jew." And Fate had chosen Germany to help bring about conquest of this vast Jew-ridden territory.

A few days after publication of the second volume Hitler turned a Nazi Christmas celebration at the Hofbräuhaus into another virulent attack on Jews. "Christ," he said, "was the greatest early fighter in the battle against the world enemy, the

Jews."* He was not the apostle of peace. His life's purpose and life's teaching was the battle against the power of capitalism, and for this he was crucified on the cross by his archenemy, the Jews. "The work that Christ started but could not finish, I—Adolf Hitler—will conclude."

A few months later the self-proclaimed Messiah's greatest political weapon was restored. The public-speaking ban in Bavaria was lifted on March 5, 1927. Four nights later he addressed a large, excited throng at the Zirkus Krone. At 8:30 P.M. there was a shout from outside of "Heil Hitler!" and the band struck up a rousing march. Hitler entered, wrapped in trench coat, followed by his entourage. He quickly strode down the aisle as the audience cheered, feet stamped. Once Hitler reached the platform there was abrupt silence. Then 200 Brownshirts marched in preceded by two drummers and the flag. The audience broke into thundering Heils and held out arms in Fascist salute. On the stage, Hitler stood stern-faced, his right arm out. The music mounted, flags passed by the stage, glittering standards with swastikas in wreaths with eagles, patterned after the banners of the Roman legions. The SA men took position below the stage except for flag- and standard-bearers riveted at attention behind the speakers.

At first Hitler spoke slowly, deliberately, then the words began tumbling out in a torrent. According to one police reporter, his gesticulations as he jumped excitedly back and forth fascinated "the spell-bound thousand-headed audience. When he is interrupted by applause, he extends his hands theatrically. The word 'no,' which appears repeatedly in the latter part of the speech, is deliberately and theatrically emphasized."

During a major speech such as this Hitler would drink as many as twenty small bottles of mineral water and his shirt would be wringing wet. Sometimes, especially in warm weather, he also insisted on having a piece of ice on the rostrum so he could keep his hands cool. After a speech he would leave at once for a nearby room—provided by the sponsors of the meeting—and take a bath.

*Hitler did not consider Jesus a Jew but a *Mischling* (a half Jew who did not adhere to the Jewish religion and therefore was free of the Jewish virus) on the grounds that, with immaculate conception, he only had two Jewish grandparents.

5

In this and subsequent orations Hitler seemed to be following the socialist line of Gregor Strasser; he even used the terminology of the leftists in attacks on capitalism and the decadent bourgeoisie. But the brunt of the battle to win urban workers over to National Socialism he left to someone more qualified. Josef Goebbels had set off for Berlin in a third-class railroad compartment with a worn satchel containing two suits, several shirts, a few books and a pile of manuscripts. He arrived to find the Berlin Gau in complete disarray and later would write that "what went as the party in Berlin in those days in no way deserved that description. It was a widely mixed collection of a few hundred people with National Socialist ideas."

Goebbels was faced with an apparently impossible task. Besides being at odds with one another, the thousand party members under his jurisdiction were opposed on the streets by overwhelming numbers of Communists and Social Democrats. "The finances were a mess. The Berlin Gau then possessed nothing but debts." This state of affairs inspired rather than depressed Goebbels. He moved his headquarters to a better area, set up regular office hours and established a sound accounting system under his personal control. By February 1927 the Gau owed nothing while owning almost 10,000 marks' worth of office equipment as well as a used car.

Goebbels decided it was now time to broaden the base of membership and to do what he had to attract the attention of a jaded public. "Berlin needs its sensations as a fish needs water," he wrote, "this city lives on it, and any political propaganda not recognizing this will miss the mark." His speeches and articles took on a crisp, graphic style attuned to the Berliner; his SA troops deliberately sought physical combat with the Reds—preferably when the odds were in their own favor—on his theory that "He who can conquer the streets can also conquer the masses; and he who has conquered the masses has thereby conquered the state."

He rehearsed his speeches before a full-length mirror and, according to his landlady, would practice body movements by the hour. Once on the podium he was a brilliant improviser, and soon perfected a variety of styles. Before a meeting he would ask what audience he would face. "What record must I use—the national, the social or the sentimental? Of course, I have them all in my suitcase."

He appealed directly to the masses in graphic, aggressive language. A consummate actor, he could switch from humor to sentiment and then to invective. Often he deliberately provoked the Reds into vocal protests which he would twist to his own advantage. "Making noise," he once said, "is an effective means of opposition." To him propaganda was an art and he was, by all accounts, including his own, a genius at it—and he sold National Socialism with American-style showmanship as if it were the best soap in the world.

The problem of Berlin, aggravated by the bitter feud between Goebbels and Strasser, created an atmosphere of sober realism at the annual party meeting in Munich late that July. The expected rate of growth in the urban areas was disappointing. Rather than address the meeting on this crisis, Hitler spoke only in generalities, his heat directed at a target no one in the Bürgerbräu would defend—the Jew.

It was almost as if he were not concerned with the party doldrums and had more important things on his mind. His speeches of the last few months indicated that he was obsessed with his personal ideology, his Weltanschauung. Again and again he hammered at race and the fact that Germany's future lay in conquest of eastern territories.

This program was carried a step forward at the third Party Day in Nuremberg. Almost 20,000 members, 8500 of them in uniform, flooded into the ancient city and there was the usual pageantry—a march with flags and standards to the strains of rousing military airs. It was on the last day of the celebration, Sunday, August 21, that Hitler connected the concept of Lebensraum with anti-Semitism but few realized the significance of this misbegotten marriage, for his terms were too vague. He reiterated his demand for more living space for the German people, then pointed out that power and power alone was the basis for acquisition of new territory. But, he said, Germany had been robbed of her power factors by three abominations: internationalism, democracy and pacifism. Hitler then linked this evil trinity with racism. Were not internationalism, democracy and pacifism all creations of the Jew? Surely if obscurely Hitler had joined Lebensraum with anti-Semitism. His unsystematic search for a Weltanschauung was close to realization.

Hitler was still living at his little room on the Thierschstrasse, and although he was received as a hero in some of the best homes in Germany, his standard of living remained monastic. It was common talk in the neighborhood that he even shared some of his short supply of shirts and socks with the needy. In his modest room he received admirers rich and poor, from all over Germany, exhibiting a willingness and aptitude for making himself agreeable. Many a hand-kiss insured lifelong devotion from women; men were reassured by his firm handshake, his down-to-earth, man-to-man approach.

He was learning how to appeal to the basic needs of the average German. No longer was he the völkisch fanatic, the frightening revolutionary of the Munich Putsch, but a reasonable man who sought only the welfare of the Fatherland. His "basic values and aims" were as reassuring as they were acceptable. His listeners could not possibly know that the "reasonable" words were a mask for one of the most radical programs in the history of mankind, a program that would alter the map of Europe and affect the lives, in one way or another, of most of the people on earth.

6

By the end of 1927 Hitler had demonstrated that he could handle people as individuals and in groups. It was also evident that his interest in rebuilding the party was long-range. Further, he realized something his advisers did not: before launching an all-out campaign to broaden the base of the movement he must have a burning public issue on which he could mobilize support from worker and burgher alike. Just as important, he would need a clearly defined world outlook to give him direction. This Weltanschauung would come in a year but the issue would not arise for two years and would originate in New York City's Wall Street.

The spring of the new year brought a revocation of the ban against the party in Berlin, followed by a burst of political energy on the part of Goebbels in an effort to win substantial gains in the Reichstag during the coming elections. While his appeal was directed largely at the worker, he called on nationalists and socialists to bury their differences. "Socialism and nationalism are things which supplement, not contradict, each other. Against each other they are destructive; with each other they are revolutionary and progressive."

The national elections of May 20 were a personal triumph for Goebbels, who was sent to the Reichstag, but defeat for the Führer since the party elected only eleven other delegates. The Nazis had lost 100,000 votes and two seats over the past two years. The loss could be laid neither to Hitler nor to poor organization but to the healthy state of the economy and the absence of a crucial issue. No longer could mere mention of the Versailles Treaty and the "November criminals" win a voter. Politicians are often the last to sense a new trend and the Nazi elite who had gathered at party headquarters in Munich that evening to celebrate a major political breakthrough were deep in gloom at the succession of dismal returns brought in by messengers on bicycles.

Hitler arrived about midnight. Ignoring the atmosphere of dejection, he surprised his followers with a philosophical, almost detached speech. The old politicians expected the usual remarks of a defeated leader. But Hitler dwelt mostly on the healthy gains made by the two working-class parties—the Social Democratic and the Communist. He neither minimized their victory nor treated it as a National Socialist defeat and, in fact, seemed curiously pleased that the two "enemy" parties had defeated the German moderate middle and rightist parties. Unlike his comrades, the Führer felt that a bright political future lay ahead.

After the election Hitler returned to Berchtesgaden, his fount of inspiration. At last he had a place of his own, the Haus Wachenfeld on the Obersalzberg. It was a simple country house in Upper Bavarian mountain style, surrounded by a wooden veranda, with heavy rocks on the pitched roof to prevent the shingles from being ripped off in a storm. The first time he looked through the villa he had been "completely captivated." Luckily for him the owner, the widow of an industrialist, was a party member and she rented it to him for a hundred marks a month. "I immediately rang up my sister in Vienna with the news and begged her to be so good as to take over the part of mistress of the house." Angela brought along her two daughters, Friedl and Angela Maria. The latter, usually called Geli, was a twenty-year-old vivacious girl with light brown hair. "It was not that she was so very pretty," recalled Ilse Pröhl, who had recently married Hess, "as that she had the famous Viennese charm." There were a few critics, including Hanfstaengl, who characterized her as "an empty-headed little slut, with the coarse bloom of a servant-girl, without either brains or character," but most people liked Geli, including Helene Hanfstaengl, who considered her "a nice, rather serious girl," by no means a flirt. Henriette Hoffmann considered her "coarse, provocative and a little quarrelsome." At the same time, Henriette was convinced that the "irresistibly charming" Geli was the Führer's only true love.

Their difference in age, nineteen years, was about the same as that between Hitler and Mitzi Reiter, the former object of his affection. By her own account, Mitzi in a fit of jealousy had tried to commit suicide the previous summer. In a bizarre attempt to choke herself, she tied one end of a clothesline on a door, the other around her neck, but her brother-in-law freed her after she lost consciousness.

In the discreet love affair with Geli (which most likely was never consummated), it was Hitler who was the jealous partner. One day, recalled Frau Hess, Geli sketched the costume she wanted to wear at the next Fasching carnival and showed it to him. "You might as well go naked if you want something like that," he said indignantly and sketched his idea of a proper costume. "Then she got angrier, much angrier than he had been. She picked up her drawing and ran out the door, slamming it shut. And Hitler was so contrite that within half an hour he was looking for her."

His frustrated love life was overshadowed by a new book which embodied a philosophy of life, a unification of his political and personal convictions. While outwardly unsystematic, his intuition had its own relentless symmetry; and for the past four years, as seen from his speeches and private conversations, he had been methodically chopping a path through the jungle of his mind in search of the idea.

From the first words he dicated to Max Amann ("Politics is history in the making") it was obvious that he was embarked on a venture of significance. An essential of Hitler's conclusions in this book was the conviction drawn from Darwin that might makes right. It led to a vital link between self-preservation and Lebensaum. "The compulsion to engage in the struggle for existence lies in the limitation of the living space; but in the life-struggle for this living space lies also the basis for evolution." The consequence was an eternal battle between nations which could only be won by a people dedicated to strict racial, folk and blood values. Once standards were lowered and pure blood was mixed with inferior blood the end was in sight.

In *Mein Kampf* he had simply drawn up charges against Jews as enemies of the world and effectively stated the case for a drive to the East to attain living space. Now at last he was ready to bring all the threads of his political and personal convictions together into a consistent (if twisted and paranoid) Weltanschauung, and he waited until the last few pages of his new book to do it. "It is not my task here to enter into a discussion of the Jewish question as such," he began tentatively. Jewry had "special intrinsic characteristics which separate it from all other peoples living on the globe"; it was not a religious community with a "territorially bounded state"; and it was parasitical rather than productive. He had stated all this many times before in far stronger terms but at this point he abruptly explored a new idea. "Just as every people as a basic tendency of all its earthly actions possesses a mania for self-preservation as its driving force, likewise is it exactly so with Jewry too."

Hitler's continued use of non-polemic language was surprising. The Jew, he wrote, was merely impelled by the same motives as everyone else in this deadly struggle for life; the only difference was a different purpose. But then Hitler abruptly turned shrill. "His ultimate goal is the denationalization, the promiscuous bastardization of other peoples, the lowering of the racial level of the highest peoples as well as the domination of his racial mishmash through the extirpation of the folkish intelligentsia and its replacement by the members of his own people." This different goal, expressed in such comparatively calm terms, was what made the Jews the threat of mankind. And since their ultimate aim was conquest of the entire world, Hitler's battle against the Jews was for the good not only of Germany but of the entire world.

By the end of the summer of 1928 Hitler had finally come to the realization that his two most urgent convictions—danger from Jews and Germany's need for sufficient living space—were entwined. If the Reich failed to acquire essential living space it would perish. If the Jewish menace were not stemmed there could be no struggle for Lebensraum, no culture, and the nation would decay. This, in all likelihood, marked Hitler's point of no return and was the essence of his Weltanschauung.

He himself forbade publication of what became known as *Hitler's Secret Book* and appeared for the first time thirty-two years later. Perhaps he feared it was too philosophically heavy for his adherents, too flimsily transparent for the more sophisticated; perhaps he did not want to reveal the ultimate mass-murder plan that hid behind its terminology. Within the pages also lay clues to his motivation for genocide. They were replete with revealing references: the Jew was a "master of international poisoning and race corruption," as well as the instigator of the "evil pacifist liquid manure [which] poisons the mentality favoring bold self-preservation." He referred to the flood of "disease bacilli" now breeding in Russia; and called the crowded working-class districts of Germany (the result of inadequate Lebensraum) "abscesses in the national body" as well as "breeding grounds of blood mixing and bastardization, and of race lowering, thus resulting in those purulent infection centers in which the international Jewish racial-maggots thrive and finally effect further destruction."

Fear that his father may have been part Jewish (which could be a substantial part of why he wanted no children); anguish, anger and guilt at his mother's painful death from cancer along with mixed feelings about the Jewish doctor who, with Hitler's consent, treated her *drastically* with iodoform—all this would seem to permeate *Hitler's Secret Book*. And perhaps it was no coincidence that shortly after finishing this work he made a voluntary visit to a psychiatrist. He sought help from a party member in Munich, Dr. Alfred Schwenninger, to allay a "fear of cancer." There is no record of the treatment but it was soon evident that the psychiatrist missed a golden opportunity to turn Hitler from his awful goal; Dr. Schwenninger also failed to remove his patient's fear of cancer which, along with the obsession to eliminate all Jews, would persist to the last day of his life.

Chapter Nine

A DEATH IN THE FAMILY

1928-1931

1

Hitler's first efforts to implement his Weltanschauung were made by proxy. In Berlin Josef Goebbels was doing his utmost to rejuvenate the party after defeat at the recent elections. During the summer of 1928 he wrote three articles for his weekly paper, *Der Angriff*, (*The Assault)* in an attempt to woo those workers who had voted leftist. In language that could have come from a Communist, he charged that the worker in the capitalist state was "no longer a living human being, not an originator, not a creator. He is changed into a machine. A number, a robot in a factory without sensibility or goal." Only National Socialism would bring him dignity and make his life meaningful. In a surprisingly short period Goebbels had replaced Strasser as the chief recruiter of workers in the north, and in so doing apparently removed him as a political rival to the Führer. That Hitler was pleased with Goebbels and approved his socialist line became clear when he permitted *Der Angriff* to become a biweekly and made its editor propaganda chief of the party.

In politics Hitler could be forgiving. If a former opponent was contrite the Führer was likely to reward him. It was his way of turning a liability into an asset. After crushing Gregor Strasser's attempt to change the direction of National Socialism, he had put him in charge of reorganizing the party; and

Strasser had so successfully centralized administration that he was becoming one of the most powerful men in the NSDAP. Due primarily to his and Goebbels' efforts party membership rose to some 100,000 by the end of the year.

To solidify his gains in the north, Hitler came to Berlin on November 16, 1928, to speak at the huge Sportpalast on racial and national regeneration. Since it was likely Reds would try to break up the meeting, Hitler's personal bodyguard was present in force. This was a small select group of young men, ranging in age from eighteen to twenty, pledged to protect the Führer with their own lives. They called themselves *Schutzstaffel* (guard detachment) or SS for short. Most of the audience of more than 10,000 had never before heard Hitler and his first words made little impact. The problem was the new loudspeaker system. Standing at the back of the hall, the British journalist Sefton Delmer had trouble making out what Hitler was saying. Delmer did hear him urge Germans not to eat oranges and, putting him down as a "crackpot," left the hall. The cacophony was such that Hitler himself turned off the microphones and shouted. In a few minutes he quieted the Red hecklers and completely dominated the vast audience. "Whoever shows his fist to the German people, we will force to be our brother," he said and then raised the bogy of racial degeneration. "The bastardization of great states has begun. The negroization of culture, of customs—not only of blood—strides forward. The world becomes democratized. The value of the individual declines. The masses apparently are gaining the victory over the idea of the great leader. Numbers are chosen as the new God."

2

Hitler's personal approach would have been ineffective without an efficient party organization, and while the 1929 party congress in Nuremberg was outwardly a rally, an emotional testimony of dedication to the Führer and his ideals, the organization of the party was being buttressed in the working sessions. By the end of that summer Hitler had succeeded in setting up a functionary corps in line with an appeal to the German middle class by admitting university graduates and other representatives of the bourgeoisie into the party bureaucracy. While allowing Goebbels and Strasser to win over the workers, he directed his opening campaign primarily to militant veterans and capitalistic businessmen, for he realized he would never get into power without them.

In the meantime he and the party were enjoying the financial benefits of their *mariage de convenance* with industry. Hitler bought the Barlow Palace, a three-story building on the Briennerstrasse, as national party headquarters; then early that September moved from his monastic room to one of the most fashionable sections of Munich across the Isar, where he took a nine-room apartment covering the entire second floor of 16 Prinzregentenplatz. He brought along Frau Reichert, his landlady from the Thierschstrasse, and her mother, Frau Dachs.

His sister Angela remained in charge of the Berchtesgaden villa (now his property), but she allowed her daughter Geli, now twenty-one, to take a room in Uncle Alf's new apartment while pursuing her medical studies in Munich. His feelings for her had not altered but their relationship changed. While maintaining the role of uncle, Hitler began overtly, if discreetly, to act more like a suitor. They were occasionally seen together in public at the theater or at his favorite table in the garden of the Café Heck where he often held court late in the afternoon.

Hitler was so enthralled, according to Hanfstaengl, that "he hovered at her elbow with a moon-calf look in his eyes in a very plausible imitation of adolescent infatuation." She inveigled him into going shopping even though he confessed to Hoffmann "how he hated it when Geli tried on hats or shoes, or inspected bale after bale of material, engaging the shopgirl in earnest conversation for half an hour or more, and then, finding nothing that suited her, walked out of the shop." Hitler knew that this would happen on every shopping expedition—yet "always followed her like a faithful lamb."

At the same time Hitler remained the stern uncle, restricting the high-spirited girl's social life to restaurants, cafés and an occasional visit to the theater. Even when she nagged him into letting her go to a Shrovetide ball it was under rigid conditions: her escorts were Max Amann and Hoffmann and they were instructed to bring her back at 11 P.M. Hoffmann warned that these restraints were making her extremely unhappy but the Führer replied that he felt bound to watch over his niece. "I love Geli, and I could marry her." At the same time he was determined to remain a bachelor. What Geli regarded as restraint, he said, was wisdom. "I am quite determined to see that she does not fall into the hands of some unworthy adventurer or swindler."

That Hitler was sexually frustrated seems borne out by an inept attempt to kiss the seventeen-year-old daughter of Heinrich Hoffmann. One day he found Henriette alone at home. "Won't you kiss me?" he said quite seriously, according to her account. Usually he addressed her with the familiar "thou." Today it was "you." ("I liked him because he always was considerate, he always helped me when I wanted something from Father, money for tennis lessons, for instance, or for skiing expeditions. . . . But kissing him?") She politely refused and after a moment's silence Hitler struck the palm of his hand with his whip and slowly walked away.

Of more significance was his meeting with another pretty seventeen-year-old who worked in Hoffmann's photo shop. Eva Braun, the daughter of a teacher and the product of a convent, was—like Geli—a modern girl, athletic and lively. She preferred jazz to opera and American musical comedies to the dramas of Kaiser and Wedekind. Unlike Geli, she was on the plump side and had fair hair. "She was a terror, it's true, the troublemaker of the class," recalled a teacher, Fräulein von Heidenaber, "but she was intelligent and quick to seize the essential aspects of a subject, and she was capable of independent thought."

They met late on a Friday afternoon in early October. Eva had stayed in the shop to catch up on filing and was on a ladder reaching for the files on the top of a cupboard. "At that moment," she later told her sister, "the boss came in accompanied by a man with a funny mustache, a light-colored English-style overcoat and a big felt hat in his hand. They both sat down on the other side of the room, opposite me." She sensed that the newcomer was examining her legs. "That very day I had shortened my skirt and I felt slightly embarrassed because I wasn't sure I'd got the hem even."

After she climbed down Hoffmann introduced her to the stranger. "Herr Wolf. Our good little Fräulein Eva." A few minutes later they were all sitting down to beer and sausages. "I was starving. I gobbled my sausage and had a sip of beer for politeness' sake. The elderly gentleman was paying me compliments. We talked about music and a play at the Staatstheater, as I remember, with him devouring me with his eyes all the time. Then, as it was getting late, I rushed off. I refused his offer of a lift in his Mercedes. Just think what Papa's reaction would have been!" But before she left, Hoffmann took her aside and asked, "Haven't you guessed who that gentleman is? It's Hitler! Adolf Hitler!" "Oh?" replied Eva.

In the days to come Hitler would quite often drop in at the studio with flowers and candy for "my lovely siren from Hoffmann's." On the rare times he took her out, he avoided his usual haunts for tea in an obscure corner of the Carlton Café or a movie in Schwabing. But by the end of the year his visits to Hoffmann's studio had become a rarity. Perhaps it was because of Eva's boast to several fellow employees that she was Hitler's mistress and he was going to marry her. Hoffmann, who was sure she had never even visited Hitler's apartment, summoned her to his office. Eva broke into tears, confessing she had lied and he threatened to fire her if she repeated the story.

3

Hitler was thinking of victory in the 1930 national elections and felt it was possible if he could win new workers to his cause. To do this, there must be a dramatic new propaganda ploy. The opportunity came early in 1930, with the death of a law student in Berlin. Horst Wessel, the twenty-one-year-old son of a preacher and a Freemason, had rebelled against his bourgeois upbringing to become a dedicated Brownshirt in the bloody street battles against the Reds. He wrote a poem, "Raise High the Flag!" immortalizing comrades who had sacrificed their lives—"shot dead by Red Front and Reaction," which was published in *Der Angriff* and later set to music. Wessel fell in love with a onetime prostitute named Erna and moved in with her. In an effort to eject the couple her landlady sought help from the Communists. A Red gang burst into the lovers' room. Their leader, an intimate of Erna's, reportedly shouted, "You know what that's for!" and shot Wessel. In an attempt to make political capital out of the sorry affair, the Communists called Wessel a pimp, which he was not. On his part Goebbels publicly transfigured the lover into a working-class Jesus, which he was not. "Leaving home and mother," wrote Goebbels, the novelist manqué, "he took to living among those who scorned and spit on him. Out there, in a proletarian section, in a tenement attic he proceeded to build his youthful, modest life. A socialist Christ! One who appealed to others through his deeds."

While Wessel lay dying in a hospital, Goebbels turned a private feud into political assassination by having Wessel's song sung at the conclusion of a meeting in the Sportpalast: "The banners flutter, the drums roll, the fifes rejoice, and from millions of throats resounds the hymn of the German revolution, Raise high the flag!" At last, on February 23, Wessel died. "His spirit has risen in order to live on in all of us," wrote Goebbels. He is "marching within our ranks." To cap the propaganda campaign Goebbels decided to stage an extravagant funeral with Hitler delivering the final oration. But the Führer had reservations about such showmanship. So did Göring, who had returned from Sweden after a cure for drug addiction to win election to the Reichstag. The situation in Berlin, he argued, was already tense enough and the Führer's safety could not be guaranteed. "If anything goes wrong," he said, according to Hanfstaengl's recollection, "it would be a catastrophe. After all, there are only twelve of us in the Reichstag, and we simply haven't enough strength to make capital out of this. If Hitler comes to Berlin it will be a red rag to the Communist bulls and we cannot afford to take the consequences."

Hitler pleaded illness and the funeral had to proceed without him. Göring was right. The procession turned into a battle march with the Reds assaulting the mourners, and even as Goebbels stood at the graveside and dramatically called the roll: "Horst Wessel?" and the storm troopers shouted back "Present!" stones flew over the cemetery wall into the grave. Nothing could have pleased propagandist Goebbels more. "As the coffin came to rest in the cool ground," he wrote, "there went up outside the gates the depraved cry of the subhuman. . . . The departed, still with us, raised his weary hand and beckoned into the shimmering distance: Forward over the graves! At the end of the road lies Germany!"

From such words one would never guess at the true relationship between ordinary Reds and Nazis. While they fought each other relentlessly, they felt a unique comradeship, and it was no rarity for them to unite if one of their brawls in a bar or beer hall was interrupted by the police. Both groups were driven by fervor for a cause, both believed that the end justified the means. They shared similar socialist goals and had the same contempt for parliamentary procedures.

4

Hitler offered something to almost every German voter in 1930—the farmer, the worker, the student, the patriot, the racist and the middle-class burgher. The common denominator of his wide appeal was the world depression which had followed the Wall Street crash of 1929 and abruptly ended Germany's remarkable recovery. By late summer there were almost three million unemployed in the nation and Chancellor Brüning's policy of economic retrenchment was making matters worse. Here at last was the burning issue that could bring him political control of Germany, thought Hitler. His appeal to workers was couched in Communist terminology. "Working Germany, awake! Break your chains in two!" proclaimed Goebbels' *Der Angriff*. To farmers, whose recent profits were being wiped out by the world-wide decline of agricultural prices, Hitler offered tax adjustments and import duties. The lower middle class, with no trade unions to fight for them, were offered hope; to those just above them in the social hierarchy to whom poverty was a stigma—self-respect; and to the young idealists in and out of universities—an idealistic new world.

This last group was not large but it provided Hitler with a militant, dedicated cadre for the future. They listened entranced as he preached against materialism and selfishness, promised to establish social harmony and a front rank in his crusade for social justice and a revitalized Germany. Convinced that Hitler would create a genuine socialist regime, these young people roamed the streets of the large cities chanting the slogan they shared with their Communist adversaries, "Freedom, Work and Bread!" The rising generation "felt something was moving and the terrible stagnation was over," recalled one follower. "You had to live through it to really understand it." It was a chance to serve that attracted most of these young idealists and Hitler was the only politician of his day who understood the power of such an appeal.

A number of intellectuals, the social elite and royalty itself were also drawn to him. That spring the Kaiser's young son, August Wilhelm ("Auwi"), wrote his dear battle comrade Hitler that it was his "heart's desire" to inform him personally that he had just been admitted to the party. "It was for me a very emotional moment and my thoughts turned to you in loyalty." The Prince feared the spread of Communism and his conversion influenced Prince Philip von Hessen, a nephew of the Kaiser and grandson of Queen Victoria, to join in support of Hitler.

In 1930 he was offering Germans something new—a feeling of unity. He welcomed everyone to join in the crusade. There was no class distinction; the only requirement was willingness to follow Hitler without hesitation in his fight to the death against the Jews and the Reds, in his struggle for Lebensraum and the glory and the good of Germany. "What we felt," wrote an early party member, "what our hearts compelled us to think, was this—Hitler, you're our man. You talk like a human being who's been at the front, who's been through the same mess we were, and not in some soft berth, but like us an unknown soldier." It was these transcendental appeals which roused the emotions of such divergent voters. Nor did Hitler press his anti-Semitism—particularly the "removal" of Jews—except with völkisch groups and the workers. To the more educated and the idealistic this issue was discussed either in whispers or an offhand manner.

That summer Hitler campaigned tirelessly with his omnibus program, delivering twenty major speeches in the final six weeks. A born politician, he found it not only natural but inspiring to mix with crowds, shaking hands, kissing babies and bowing to women. He would eat with the working-class and middle-class adherents more often than with the elite, and his man-to-man approach appealed to the clerk and small businessman as well as the laborer.

Although he approached each group with a separate message, Hitler never forgot the lesson he had learned in Landsberg: that he must win the masses. Consequently he never allowed himself to take an aggressive stand on issues. Over and over he hammered at the money barons, the Reds, the Marxists and the "system" that had brought unemployment, lowered farm prices and wiped out the savings of the middle class. He did not pit class against class. He could embrace them all.

Never had Germany—or the world for that matter—been subjected to such persuasion. Goebbels organized six thousand meetings—in large halls, in tents that could hold ten thousand, in the open air. There were torchlight parades; towns, cities and villages were plastered with glaring red posters. The entire Nazi press blanketed the country with special campaign editions that ran into millions of copies, and those that couldn't be sold were given away.

In a final admonition to party workers on the morning of the election Goebbels gave them cynical but practical advice on how to electioneer. "Do it jokingly, do it seriously! Treat your dear fellow creatures as they are used to being treated. Stimulate their rage and their fury, direct them to the proper course." That day long lines queued up at polling places throughout the country. A record 35,000,000 ballots were cast, 4,000,000 more than in 1928. Officials checked and rechecked for errors before announcing that the Nazis had won 6,371,000 votes, more than eighteen per cent of the total vote. In two years the Hitler movement had risen from 810,000 votes to become the second largest party in the Reich. After pronouncing Hitler dead politically, the Social Democrats had made the mistake of concentrating their attacks on the Reds.

The Communists also made a substantial gain of 1,326,000 votes and the Social Democrats lost fewer than 60,000 votes, an indication that Hitler's gains had come mainly at the expense of the middle-class parties. The most sensational Nazi increase was among the farmers and lower middle class in the rural and Protestant areas in the northern half of the country, but considerable gains were also made among Catholics. In the days before the Beer Hall Putsch Hitler had sought almost exclusively for the dissident, disenchanted, desperation vote. Now he had received support from people who expected him to bring them better lives. It was Hitler's elastic appeal and forceful oratory which had attracted the new voters but it was the tireless work of thousands of cell leaders and cell foremen in the party's efficient vertical organization that got them to the polls.

5

1931 augured well for Adolf Hitler. He had suddenly become a best-selling author. *Mein Kampf* had sold an average of little more than 6000 copies annually until the last year when the amount rose to 54,086. This got him a respectable personal income which promised to continue indefinitely. Furthermore, the Brown House, the new party headquarters, was opened on the first of the year. Purchased and renovated by special contributions, profits from Hitler rallies, gifts and dues, it represented the substance and reliability of the NSDAP as a party. On the second floor were the offices of Hitler, Hess, Goebbels, Strasser and the SA. The Führer's office was large and attractively decorated in reddish brown. Ceiling-high windows overlooked the Königsplatz. There was a large bust of Mussolini, and among the pictures on the wall were a painting of Frederick the Great and another of the first attack of the Führer's old regiment in Flanders. "Hitler was not often there," recalled Frank. His method of working was totally unsystematic. He would "breeze in" but before he could be pinned down "just breeze out again." Once cornered, he would hastily finish the business, then launch into "an hour-long monologue."

He preferred to spend his time downstairs in the small refreshment room where he would sit in a corner of the "Führer" table over which hung a picture of Dietrich Eckart. But even this soon palled. The sedentary existence of the Brown House was not for him. He was driven by an urge to move, to win mass support for himself and the party among the people, or to hold high-level conversations with those who could give him either political or financial assistance. The problems he faced at the beginning of 1931 were truly formidable, largely due to the NSDAP's phenomenal membership growth which, in turn, brought an expansion of bureaucracy in every department of the party with the resultant frictions and jealousies.

Most troublesome was the SA, many of whose members refused to take Hitler's avowals of legality seriously. The storm troopers had always boasted of their tradition of violence and saw no reason why they should knuckle under to the civilian leaders in Munich. These men were among the most idealistic and many were socialists at heart, sharing with their Communist rivals a revolutionary zeal that was becoming an embarrassment to the Führer. From the first he had trouble with its leaders, who wanted to make the SA the military arm of the party, whereas he had insisted that its main function was to protect rallies and mobilize political loyalty. First had been Captain Röhm, whose violent disagreement with Hitler led to voluntary exile in South America; then came Pfeffer von Salomon, whose similar demands for a stronger SA had led to his recent resignation.

The dissatisfaction of the leaders was shared by their men. Recently dissident Brownshirts in Berlin had revolted on the grounds that they were hungry, overworked and constantly exposed to injuries as well as arrest in their battles with the police and Reds. They refused to act as mere bodyguards for party rallies and, after their seven demands, including a reasonable one for more funds, were turned down by Goebbels, one troop went berserk and raided a local party headquarters guarded by the SS. It took Hitler's personal intervention to put down the revolt. He toured the various SA meeting places, accompanied by armed SS troops, calling for reconciliation. Like a patient and forbearing father, he pleaded, promised and scolded. He spoke little about the seven Brownshirt demands but kept the matter on a personal level, calling for allegiance to himself. Then he announced that he himself would become the new commander of the SA. The wild cheers that followed signaled an end to the brief rebellion and Hitler could return to the election trail.

His promise to head the SA personally was an empty one. He had neither the time nor the inclination to take on such an assignment and by the beginning of 1931 the Brownshirts were still without effective leadership. Then on January 4 it was announced that Captain Röhm (recently recalled from Bolivia where he had helped the Republic fight one of its wars with Paraguay) would become the new chief of staff of the SA. What attracted Röhm back to Germany was Hitler's willingness to give him a fairly free hand in the internal structure of the 60,000-man organization. Resigned to keeping the storm troopers as a disciplined marching unit for the time being, this capable organizer and inspiring leader began reshaping the SA in his own image.

But efficiency was no cure for the deep-seated complaints within the organization, and it soon became evident that another serious revolt was brewing in the capital. The basic grievances of the Berlin Brownshirts remained. Their leader, Captain Walter Stennes, was incensed by the inequities within the organization, and once more demanded a system based on "what you know," not "who you know." He openly complained that Hitler "changed his mind every few months with new orders" and that it was impossible to operate under such conditions. Stennes' men were perplexed and perturbed. While agreeing with him, they felt irresistibly drawn to the Führer.

The issue surfaced on February 20, 1931, after Hitler issued orders to both the SA and SS to cease fighting the Reds and Jews in the streets. "I understand your distress and rage," he told the Brownshirts, "but you must not bear arms." They grumbled but did nothing until late the following month when the Führer bowed to a Weimar government decree requiring all potential rallies to be approved by the police. The indignant Stennes denounced this capitulation to the establishment, then called a secret conference of SA leaders at midnight of March 31. All those present declared themselves in favor of Stennes and against Hitler.

In an attempt to settle the matter without bloodshed and publicity, the Führer ordered Stennes to report to Munich for a desk job at the Brown House. Stennes refused and Hitler loosed the SS on the rebels. Open resistance ended within twenty-four hours. It had been a puny rebellion. All Stennes wanted was to bring about pure National Socialism, to serve a party, not an individual. "Whoever goes with me has a hard road," he told his men in a farewell speech. "I recommend, however, that you stay with Hitler for the sake of the National Socialist idea which we do not want to destroy."

Hitler rushed to the capital in his role as conciliator and middle-of-the-road revolutionary. This time he took along Hanfstaengl, who wrote: "Hitler had to go around from suburb to suburb and beseech them with tears in his eyes to rely on him to see that their interests were protected." He managed to restore order and spent the next day in a commercial travelers' hotel with Stennes. The latter impressed Hanfstaengl as more the victim than the leader of the revolt. "I found him a very decent fellow, a nephew of Cardinal Schulte of Cologne, and he took me over to one of the open windows, where our conversation was drowned by the noise of traffic, and said: 'Does Hitler realize that the real instigator of this revolt is standing by him?'—and that was Goebbels. 'He has been egging them on to demonstrate in the streets in spite of Hitler's orders that we were not to get into fights, and now they blame it all on me.'"

As usual the appearance of Hitler (backed up by his faithful SS force) brought unity to the SA and this time it was lasting. The dismissal of Stennes and a handful of followers caused no reverberations. Goebbels managed to emerge safely from the farrago, even though many besides Stennes felt he had played an insidious part in the revolt. The Führer himself had suspicions and at an informal gathering of Gauleiters a little later made allusion to them. "When a mother has many children and one of them goes astray," he said, "it is the wise mother who takes the child by the hand and holds on to him."

Hitler also realized that it had taken the force of the SS to bring his straying children back into the fold and, recognizing this, he replaced Stennes as leader of the Berlin-run SA with an SS man. The SS was exultant with its expanded role as protector of the Führer principle. "We were not loved everywhere," their chief, Heinrich Himmler, told a conference of SS leaders a few weeks later. "When we have done our duty we may be stood in the corner; we should expect no thanks. But our Führer knows the value of the SS. We are his favorite and most valuable organization because we have never let him down."

At the same time Hitler the mediator was ready to welcome back into the fold all those storm troopers who had strayed or hesitated—with the exception of those too independent spirits who had to be purged and replaced by loyal adherents. The response to Hitler's gesture of amnesty was almost unanimous. While many Brownshirts were disappointed in Hitler and his insistence on legality, such logic dissolved before his nearly Christlike declaration: "I am the SA and SS and you are members of the SA and SS as I am within you in the SA and SS."

No sooner had the SA been brought into line than their leader, Captain Röhm, came under heavy attack for alleged homosexuality. Earlier Hitler had brushed aside similar charges, "The SA is a collection of men for a particular political goal. It is not a moral institution for raising young girls, but an association of rough fighters." A man's private life, he added, was his own so long as it did not interfere with the National Socialist mission.

6

Hitler spent the summer of 1931 in consolidating the party and revamping the SA in light of the weaknesses made evident by the Stennes revolt. At the same time he was profoundly disturbed by a personal crisis. He learned that his chauffeur and companion, Maurice, had become secretly engaged to his niece Geli, who had been living a restricted life in the Prinzregentenplatz apartment. Ironically it was the Führer himself, the perpetual matchmaker, who had given the idea to Maurice. "I'll come and have supper with you every evening when you are married," he urged the young man. "Following his advice,"

Maurice told an interviewer, "I decided to become engaged to Geli, with whom I was madly in love, like everybody else. She gladly accepted my proposal." For some time the inner circle had known they were lovers; Maurice had openly lamented about "his unhappy love" to Goebbels. Finally he steeled himself to confess. Hitler flew into a rage, accused Maurice of disloyalty and dismissed him as chauffeur.

Some of those close to the Führer were convinced he was only a concerned relative. "His affection was that of a father," Frau Anny Winter, the housekeeper, insisted years later. "He was concerned only with her welfare. Geli was a flighty girl who tried to seduce everybody, including Hitler, and he merely wanted to protect her." In a sense Geli had become a captive. Hitler gave her everything she wanted except freedom and insisted that she have an escort he trusted even when she went to her singing lessons.

One evening the Hanfstaengls met the couple at the Residenz Theater and they all had late supper at the Schwarzwälder Café. Hanfstaengl noticed that Geli "seemed bored, looking over her shoulder at the other tables, and could not help feeling that her share in the relationship was under compulsion." Frau Hanfstaengl also got the feeling that the girl was repressed, as if "she couldn't do with her life what she wanted." But Frau Winter persisted in her belief that it was Geli who was the chaser. "Naturally she wanted to become Gnädige Frau Hitler. He was highly eligible . . . but she flirted with everybody, she was not a serious girl."

There was no doubt that Geli was impressed by her uncle's fame. Every time they had tea at the Café Heck their table would be besieged by admirers, many of them women who kissed his hand and begged for souvenirs. It was equally evident that the Führer's fondness for her went far beyond that of an uncle. "He loved her," averred Maurice, "but it was a strange affection that did not dare to show itself, for he was too proud to admit to the weaknesses of an infatuation."

There were others who claimed that the two were having a love affair, and Otto Strasser publicized a sensational hearsay story of their aberrant sexual relations that was given credence only by those who wanted to believe the worst of Hitler. He deeply loved his niece but it was unlikely that they had sexual relations. He was too reserved to openly court any woman and too cautious to ruin his political career by taking a mistress into his own apartment—particularly the daughter of a half sister.

By September Geli was involved with another young man, an artist from Austria who had become so enamored on first sight, according to Christa Schröder (Hitler's secretary), that he proposed to her. Once she started to tell Frau Hoffmann of the unhappy romance but, after admitting she was in love with an artist from Vienna and was miserable, cut herself off with: "Well, that's that! And there's nothing you or I can do about it. So let's talk about something else." As soon as Hitler learned of the liaison he forced her to break with the artist, apparently with the connivance of his half sister Angela.

In mid-September Geli phoned her voice teacher that she was taking no more lessons and was leaving for Vienna, then set out for Berchtesgaden to see her mother. No sooner had she arrived than she got a phone call from Uncle Alf urgently requesting her to return to Munich at once. She felt obliged to do so but, upon learning that he was about to leave Munich to attend a meeting of Gauleiters and major SA leaders, she "reproached him for having made her come for nothing." Her indignation turned to fury when he forbade her to leave for Vienna during his absence. The argument continued at a spaghetti lunch for two on September 17. From the kitchen Frau Winter heard their voices loudly raised in argument and, as Geli rushed out of the dining room, the cook noticed her face was flushed.

Geli stayed in her room until she heard her uncle start down the stairs to join Hoffmann, who was accompanying him on the trip, then she followed Hitler to the hallway. She held something in her left hand but Frau Reichert couldn't see what it was. "*Servus*, Uncle Alf!" she called down. "*Servus*, Herr Hoffmann!"

At the outside door Hitler stopped, looked back, and mounted the stairs. He fondly stroked Geli's cheek and whispered something. But Geli remained stiff, resentful. "Really," she told the housekeeper moments later, "I have nothing at all in common with my uncle."

As the new chauffeur, Julius Schreck, drove the Mercedes along Prinzregentenstrasse, Hitler was silent. Suddenly he turned to Hoffmann. "I don't know why," he said, "but I have a most uneasy feeling." Hoffmann, whose unofficial duty was to amuse and cheer up the Führer, told him it was probably just the

Föhn, a south wind peculiar to the Alps which caused a strange depression. Hitler didn't answer and they drove on toward Nuremberg.

From the kitchen of the apartment, Frau Reichert heard something smash and remarked to her mother, "Geli must have picked up a perfume bottle from her dressing table and broken it." This may have been when she rummaged in the pockets of Hitler's jackets and found a letter written on blue paper. It was from Eva Braun. Hitler had renewed his liaison with her some months previously but so discreetly that Geli had not known about it. Later in the day Anny Winter saw Geli angrily tear this letter in four parts. The prying housekeeper pieced them together and read something like this:

> Dear Herr Hitler,
>
> Thank you again for the wonderful invitation to the theater. It was a memorable evening. I am most grateful to you for your kindness. I am counting the hours until I may have the joy of another meeting.
>
> Yours,
> Eva

Geli locked herself in her room with instructions not to be disturbed. But her show of temper did not disturb Frau Winter and so the housekeeper left the apartment as usual that evening and went home. Frau Reichert and her daughter slept in and they both heard a dull sound during the night but thought nothing of it. They too were used to the "capricious" girl.

But next morning Frau Reichert became alarmed when she found Geli's door still locked. She phoned Max Amann and Franz Schwarz. These two summoned a locksmith. Geli was lying on the floor next to a couch, a 6.34-caliber pistol beside her. She was shot in the heart.

That morning Hitler and Hoffmann left the Deutscher Hof Hotel in Nuremberg to continue their journey to Hamburg. As the Mercedes left the city Hitler noticed a car was following them. Fearing this might be an attack, he was about to tell Schreck to speed up. Then he realized the other vehicle was a taxi and a pageboy from the Deutscher Hof, who sat next to the driver, was gesticulating to stop. Upon learning from the boy that Herr Hess had telephoned from Munich and was holding the line, Hitler rushed back to the hotel, flung hat and whip onto a chair and went into a phone booth. He left the door open and Hoffmann could hear him say, "Hitler here. Has something happened?" After a short pause he cried out, "Oh, God, how awful!" Then his voice rose almost to a scream. "Hess, answer me—yes or no—is she still alive?" Apparently the line was cut or Hess had hung up.

"Hitler's frenzy was contagious," recalled Hoffmann. "With its accelerator jammed to the floor boards the great car screamed its way back to Munich. In the driving mirror I could see the relection of Hitler's face. He sat with compressed lips, staring with unseeing eyes through the windscreen." By the time they reached the apartment Geli's body had been removed. Since it was Saturday the newspapers didn't carry the story until the following Monday. There were innuendoes that the Führer himself had done away with his niece and allegations that Minister of Justice Gürtner had destroyed the evidence. The Munich *Post*, a socialist daily, gave a long account filled with circumstantial detail about the frequent arguments between Geli and Hitler. It also alleged the bridge of her nose had been broken and there were other signs of maltreatment.*

Depressed and humiliated, Hitler told Frank that "he could not look at a paper any more since the terrible smear campaign would kill him. He wanted to step out of politics altogether and not appear in public any more." In desperation, he fled with Hoffmann to the empty country house of his printer, Adolf Müller, on the Tegernsee. Upon arrival their driver, Schreck, whispered to Hoffmann that he had hidden the Führer's gun, fearing he might use it on himself. The moment Hitler got to his room he clasped hands behind his back and began pacing. Hoffmann asked what he would like to eat. Hitler shook his head. Hour after hour he paced without pause. It went on all night. At dawn Hoffmann knocked softly at the door. There was no answer. He entered but Hitler continued pacing, hands still clasped behind his back, staring into the distance.

Hoffmann phoned home and got a recipe for spaghetti, a favorite dish of Hitler's. But he still refused to eat. He paced

*Hitler could not have killed Geli since he was in Nuremberg nor is it likely that he or one of his associates ordered her done away with to prevent scandal. If that had been the case, murder would certainly have been committed somewhere else than in the Führer's own apartment. Some of Hitler's adherents claimed that the death was accidental: she was probably frightened by some noise and shot herself in fright. There was also the theory that she was playing theater with the gun and it went off. From the evidence, however, the most logical conclusion is that she shot herself—perhaps in desperation, perhaps in jealousy, perhaps for an unknown reason.

relentlessly two more days without food. Once he came to the phone to hear that Frank had taken the necessary legal steps to stop the scurrilous press campaign. In a tired and weak voice he said, "I thank you. I will get myself back together again. I will never forget you for this."

At last word reached the Müller villa that Geli had been buried in Vienna; present at the ceremony in the Central Cemetery were Röhm, Müller, Himmler and young Alfred Frauenfeld, the self-appointed National Socialist Gauleiter of Vienna. Although Hitler was banned from entering his homeland because of his politics, he decided to risk arrest and that night he got into the front seat of the Mercedes next to Schreck. Hoffmann sat alone in the back as they drove silently to the Austrian border, followed by bodyguards in another large car. By the time they arrived it was dawn.

Outside of Vienna Frauenfeld was waiting for Hitler in a small car since the Mercedes would have been too noticeable. They drove without a word to the Central Cemetery. Hitler placed flowers on the grave. On the marble slab was this inscription:

Here Sleeps Our Beloved Child
Geli
She was Our Ray of Sunshine
Born 4 June 1908—died 18 September 1931
The Raubal Family

While en route to Frauenfeld's apartment, Hitler suddenly broke his long silence. He asked if, by chance, they passed the Opera. Frauenfeld said it would take a slight detour. "Ach, please do so," said Hitler. "At least drive by even though I cannot go in." At Frauenfeld's Hitler ate a good breakfast, then began speaking quietly, not of the tragedy, but of the political future of Germany and himself. His voice was firm and confident as he assured Frauenfeld that he would take over power in Germany by 1933 at the latest, before the Poles seized Danzig. Once back in his own car, Hitler gazed fixedly ahead. Finally he said, as if thinking aloud, "So. Now let the struggle begin—the struggle which must and shall be crowned with success."

A day or two later he drove north to attend the Gauleiter conference. The party stopped at an inn overnight and at breakfast the following morning he refused to eat a piece of ham.

"It is like eating a corpse!" he told Göring. Nothing on earth would make him eat meat again.

In Hamburg he addressed a large, sympathetic audience. He spoke as forcefully and brilliantly as ever. Twice before—at the hospital in Pasewalk and in Landsberg prison—he had emerged from suicidal depressions. Perhaps these were a form of regeneration, for each time he had bounced back from the depths with renewed vigor and a new sense of direction. This was his third resurrection.

PART 4

THE BROWN REVOLUTION

Chapter Ten

"IT IS ALMOST LIKE A DREAM"

1931–JANUARY 30, 1933

1

Hitler recovered sufficiently from the death of Geli to attend the leadership meeting in the north that was already in session. It was of such import that only Gauleiters and major SA leaders were present and so successful that it marked the end of the party's reorganization. "The movement," he said a few days later, "is today so united that the Gauleiters and political leaders instinctively make the right decisions." As a result, there followed purges of "all lazy, rotten, useless" elements and a thinning of ranks that strengthened the party structure and buttressed Hitler's personal control.

With his own house in order, Hitler felt free to re-enter national politics. On October 14, 1931, an interview was arranged with President von Hindenburg through General Kurt von Schleicher, who had been one of the Old Gentleman's closest advisers. Hitler was visibly ill at ease in the presence of Hindenburg, an overwhelming figure with his six-foot-five-inch height and deep, booming voice. Hitler's lengthy remarks irritated the field marshal, who later reportedly complained to Schleicher that Hitler was a queer fellow who would never become Chancellor; the best he could hope for was to head the Postal Department. Disappointing as the meeting was, Schleicher still had hopes for Hitler; he had been impressed not only by the Führer's success at the last elections but by his nationalistic program. "An interesting man with exceptional speaking abilities," was his judgment. "In his plans he soars in the clouds. You then have to hold him by the coattails in order to keep him on the ground." Schleicher, whose name in German meant "intriguer," was a brilliant improviser but impetuosity tended to lead him into dangerous waters. Privately he felt quite able to handle any former corporal.

Hitler was used to being underestimated. For the next few months he contented himself with building a base of mass support among those Germans who had become disillusioned with the government's failure to cope with rising unemployment. He also made an unprecedented attempt to win foreign approval by talking directly to the American people. He was scheduled to make a radio broadcast on Friday night, December 11, over CBS to explain the "course, meaning and aims" of his party. The German government canceled the speech at the last moment but a translation was published in the Hearst newspapers which were noted for their extreme anti-Communist policy. In it Hitler expressed the hope that Americans, out of an inner impulse for self-preservation, would join him in the "struggle against this world pest" known as Bolshevism.

On the first day of 1932 Hitler told a Munich audience that God was on his side in the battle for a better world. Didn't the Bible say that the lukewarm was condemned to be spewed out? A victory of sorts seemed to offer itself almost immediately in the form of an invitation to Berlin from Hindenburg's advisers. They urged him to help prolong the field marshal's presidency but this went against Hitler's scruples, he said, since it would more or less force him to support Chancellor Brüning's policies. The refusal indicated that Hitler might be prepared to risk his entire political future in a presidential election even though an open contest with Hindenburg was a gamble. The Old Gentleman was a legend. His conservatism would draw many votes from the right and his defense of the Weimar Republic against an extremist like Hitler was sure to attract moderates and democrats alike.

Goebbels wrote in his diary, ". . . the chess game for power begins," and urged Hitler to take the chance. His chief concern was getting enough money to run a campaign. Hitler helped solve this particular problem with a single speech at the Park Hotel in Düsseldorf, center of the German steel industry. In line with a recent decision "to work systematically on the influential personalities of business," and under the auspices of Fritz Thyssen, a leading steel industrialist, he addressed an influential group at the Industry Club on January 17.

In confidential conversations prior to the Düsseldorf speech, Hitler had already drastically revised his economic program. He was now for elimination of unions and for managerial freedom as well as a program of public works and rearmament to be directed by the leaders of big business in the interest of economic recovery. Within an hour he had the rapt attention of his audience, for he spoke of matters that directly concerned these hardheaded businessmen. He asserted, for example, that private property was justified and then drew a frightening picture of the growth of Communism. "Bolshevism, if unchecked, will change the world as completely as Christianity once did. . . . If this movement continues to develop, three hundred years from now Lenin will be regarded not only as one of the revolutionaries of 1917, but as the founder of a new world doctrine and he will be worshiped as much perhaps as Buddha." Millions of unemployed and deprived Germans made desperate by the depression, he said, were already looking to Communism for the answer to their distress. That was Germany's most pressing problem of the day and it could be solved not by economic decrees but by political power. The NSDAP alone was prepared and willing to stem the Red tide. Without National Socialism there would no longer be a middle class in Germany, and only with it could the nation be united and revitalized.

Rarely had Hitler spoken so effectively, alternating between emotion and logic. In one moment he shook his listeners with terrible visions of Bolshevism and the end of the system that had brought them security; in the next he appealed to their selfishness: if they wanted their industrial complex to survive and expand they would need a dictator at the helm of government, one who would eventually lead Germany back to its position as a world power. His listeners could visualize fifty years of accomplishment and wealth dissipating and many went home prepared to contribute considerable sums to the man who promised to save them.

2

In mid-February Hindenburg announced he would stand again for President. This forced Hitler to make his own decision. It was apparent that the NSDAP had to run a presidential candidate and no one but Hitler had a realistic chance. Even so he hesitated. "I know that I shall come to power, all others will fail," he once told Frank. "I see myself as Chancellor and I will be Chancellor. I do not see myself as President, and I know I will never be President." His reluctance was genuine and he wavered for almost two weeks before Goebbels finally persuaded him to run. Then he acted with dispatch to make himself eligible. He hastily became a citizen of Germany through the machinations of the Nazi Minister of Interior in Braunschweig, who made him a councilor of that state. The following day, February 27, Hitler formally announced his candidacy for elections to take place in fifteen days.

Hate scourged the land as the victims of the depression turned on those more fortunate than themselves. Shopkeepers driven out of business cursed the great department stores; the millions of unemployed envied those with jobs and hated the "bosses"; thousands of university graduates found the future barred to them and turned their despair on the establishment. The depression had hit almost every level. Peasants, burdened with taxes and faced with low prices, despised city people while the masses of white-collar unemployed envied the peasants their crops. Those without work camped in hordes on the outskirts of the larger cities. Beggars haunted every street corner and by the time of the election campaign there were six million registered unemployed in the land—with millions of others working only part time or too proud to register as jobless.

To multitudes of these casualties of economic collapse Adolf Hitler was the answer. They cared little about the rumors of his deals with industrialists since he had never compromised with the Weimar government and had remained outspoken in his opposition to the Versailles Treaty and the Red menace. His call was simple: "For Freedom and Bread." Amid the confusion of the nation he seemed to stand like a rock, insisting only on what was best for Germany. Hindenburg countered with posters urging voters to remember his past services: "He hath kept faith with you; be ye faithful unto him." Goebbels answered with: "Honor Hindenburg: Vote for Hitler."

The Führer's appeal was to both the defeated middle-aged and the idealistic youth, and as he toured the country speaking tirelessly he called upon both to join him in his battle against the establishment. The campaign, masterminded by Goebbels, was a marvel of inventiveness. It was the rare wall in the nation that wasn't plastered with glaring red Nazi posters; leaflets were showered on the populace from planes. Fifty thousand small propaganda records were mailed to those well enough off to own a phonograph; "talking pictures" of speeches by Hitler and Goebbels were projected at night in public squares. The heart of the program, however, was a backbreaking speaking schedule. In the first eleven days of March Hitler and Goebbels each made at least one major speech daily and usually two or three.

In the meantime the Hindenburg camp was disordered. Split from the beginning, it was staggered by a whispering campaign alleging that the President's son Oskar had secretly become both a Catholic and a member of the Social Democratic Party. Even more ridiculous was the charge that Hindenburg's two middle-aged daughters were leaders in the Socialist Students League. More time was spent in denying rumors than in attacking Hitler's policies and each denial helped give the fiction more of an appearance of fact. Hindenburg's supporters began arguing and he did little himself to get votes. He made but one public appearance, three days before the election, when he asserted that he had consented to run only because so many Germans of all political hues urged him to stay in office to prevent a takeover by either left or right.

By early evening of election day, March 13, the results showed that Hindenburg was pulling ahead of Hitler. The party militants like Goebbels had been confident that he would sweep into the presidency and, as the returns widened the margin, they grew despondent. An hour after midnight there was no doubt that Hindenburg was winning by more than 7,000,000 votes and was only about 350,000 votes short of the necessary majority. Though there would have to be a runoff election between the two leaders, Goebbels for one was sure that "the dream of power was temporarily over."

Not so Hitler, who had waited stoically at the Café Heck with intimates. He hurried to the Brown House and dictated a statement exhorting the party to begin the battle for the runoff without delay. "The first election is over, the second begins today. I will also lead this one personally!" In the space of a week he and Goebbels, roused from his depression, addressed meetings of Gauleiters, Reichstag deputies and party editors so inspirationally that those present were convinced that Hitler would win next time.

* * *

Success in the runoff election was suddenly threatened by publication in the Social Democratic *Münchener Post* of incriminating letters between Röhm and a doctor specializing in psychology. It seemed they shared two interests—homosexuality and astrology. When Hans Frank, after reviewing the evidence, refused to handle a libel suit against the paper, Röhm—with much embarrassed twisting and turning—confessed he was a "bisexual." Hitler's lawyer was flabbergasted, for he had always thought homosexuals were effeminate thrill seekers. "And here," recalled Frank, "was actually the prototype of a brave, aggressive soldier, who gave the impression outwardly, with his scarred face, his upright soldierly posture, that he was very much the whole man."

Hitler had long tolerated Röhm's homosexuality—a remarkable attitude for those days—but his first reaction upon reading the documentary evidence was to lose his temper. Finally he calmed down. "This is a terrible blow," he told Frank. "Such a horrible mess! It's not human, it's bestial, worse, even animals would not do such a thing." He asked if Röhm had "abused" young men or boys. There was nothing in the records to indicate this, said the lawyer, and Hitler became calmer. "That would be utterly intolerable. As long as it is between grown men—what Röhm does. Children are not his victims?" Frank assured him that there was not a single instance. "Well, then we can at least consider whether to keep him or not, but God help him if he abuses young boys! Then he must go!"

If the Röhm scandal distracted Hitler, he certainly had put it behind him by the time the runoff campaign began. He was full of his usual vigor and optimism. This time there was only a week to campaign and Hitler decided to use an airplane so he could make three to four speeches daily.

While Hitler gave the public a picture of youthful energy, the Hindenburg forces ran another desultory campaign. This time Hindenburg did not make a single speech, spurring rumors that he was dying. There were also whispers that pensions and salaries would be cut and unemployment relief would be ended if he won re-election. By election eve it appeared that Hitler would win. Even Spengler, who had been deriding him, decided to vote National Socialist on the grounds that "Hitler is a fool but one must support the movement." On Sunday, April 10, Hitler got an additional 2,000,000 votes, raising his total to 13,418,051. The old field marshal increased his total by less than 700,000, yet this gave him a solid majority, fifty-three per cent. The Communist vote had slipped badly. More than a quarter of their voters had either listened to Goebbels' appeals or gone over to Hindenburg to keep Hitler out of the presidential palace.

In London, the *Daily Telegraph* predicted the end of Adolf Hitler while in Munich the iconoclastic Spengler and his sister hung swastika flags out of their windows. "When one has a chance to annoy people," he said, "one should do so."

3

A few days after the election Brüning was persuaded to enact a decree outlawing the SA and SS. The effect of this act was to ruin the politically naïve Chancellor, for it was not only ineffective but brought a concerted storm of protest from the right. This was the opportunity that the politically ambitious General von Schleicher had been waiting for. His dream was to establish a government of the right that would include the Nazis but not give them control. After all, Corporal Hitler and his people were, in Schleicher's words, "merely little children who had to be led by the hand."

He met secretly with the Führer that May and promised to remove the ban on the SA and SS if Hitler agreed not to attack the new rightist government. The deal was made and late that month Schleicher chose as figurehead Chancellor for his regime a wealthy, polished gentleman jockey, Franz von Papen. An ex-General Staff officer, he was also a member of the Prussian Landtag. The astounded Papen's first reaction was "I very much doubt if I am the right man," but it took only a few minutes to persuade him that he might be. Before Papen knew it he was standing, somewhat dazed, before Hindenburg.

"Well, my dear Papen," said the field marshal with paternal kindliness, "I hope you are going to help me out of this difficult situation." He knew only that Papen was a former cavalry officer, financially independent, well known on the racecourses, and had some experience in foreign affairs. But he was pleased with his military bearing and gentlemanly appearance. Again Papen protested that he was not the right man but this time was persuaded in even shorter order by Hindenburg's words: "You have been a soldier and done your duty in the war. When the Fatherland calls, Prussia knows only one response—obedience."

Hitler was spending the weekend at Mecklenburg when Goebbels phoned that Hindenburg wanted to see him that same afternoon. The Führer hastened back to the capital where he was informed by the President that he was going to appoint Papen (no news to the Führer thanks to Schleicher) and asked if Hitler was going to support him. "Yes," was the answer and the brief interview was over.

Undoubtedly Schleicher thought he was acting in the best interest of the people. Convinced that Brüning was too weak to handle Hitler, he was confident, like so many other military men, that the army itself could deal properly with such a radical—and utilize him to help establish a strong nationalist Germany. Schleicher had at last achieved his first aim but as so often happens with those attempting to outdo Machiavelli he was too clever for his own good. He soon learned that Hitler's pledge to support the new government was provisional. He could not consider the matter, he said, until Papen showed his good faith by dissolving the Reichstag and abolishing the repressive measures against the National Socialist movement. Papen did so but Hitler still withheld his support. Instead he sanctioned resumption of street battles with the Reds. A new wave of violence swept over Germany. In July alone eighty-six died in the fighting, including thirty Reds and thirty-eight Nazis.

Papen invoked the President's emergency powers—Article 48 of the Weimar constitution. This article had already been invoked a number of times, by Ebert in the economic crisis of 1923 to abolish the eight-hour day, and several times by Brüning to suspend newspapers. Using the argument that the Prussian government could no longer deal with the Reds, Papen made himself Reichs Commissioner of Prussia. This meant the end of parliamentary government in that state and foreshadowed what could be done in every state by a man resolute enough to use the emergency authority granted by the constitution.

4

Elections for the Reichstag were set for the last day of July. It was another whirlwind campaign and Hitler's second "Flight over Germany." Once more Hitler chartered a plane and the same pilot. Hans Baur had proved so competent in all kinds of weather—several times they had made forced landings in storms and fog—that Hitler now refused to fly with anyone else. He also had a second private chauffeur, twenty-one-year-old Erich Kempka. He would meet Hitler's plane in the western part of Germany while Schreck would be on hand in the east. In this election the two drivers covered more than fifty thousand kilometers, most of it over unpaved highways. Hitler treated Kempka as a member of the family. He was equally familiar with Baur.

During the campaign anti-Semitism never was an issue. It was well known that Hitler detested Jews but many voters were ready to overlook this as long as he kept his prejudice on a sensible level. The majority of Germans agreed that there were too many Jewish lawyers and objected to their monopoly of department stores and the entertainment industry. Many Jews themselves deplored the postwar flood of Jews from the East who brought with them the costumes and customs of the ghettos. Two well-known Jewish bankers, in fact, had already requested the new Minister of Labor, Friedrich Syrup, to stop further immigration of these Eastern Jews since their presence increased latent anti-Semitism. Jews regarded themselves as Germans first and then Jews. They had become so integrated into the German economy that they were willing to overlook the social prejudice that remained. After all, even in enlightened Britain and America Jews were excluded from the best clubs and hotels. Nor was toleration of National Socialism confined to German Jews. A group of Palestinian extremists had recently announced that, except for Hitler's anti-Semitism, the NSDAP movement was acceptable and would save Germany.

On July 31 the Nazis won 13,732,779 votes, half a million more than the combined total of their closest rivals—the Social Democrats and Communists. Encouraged by a victory giving him 37.3 per cent of all the votes, Hitler proposed to his own party that he run for Chancellor.

Göring protested. So did Strasser, for it wrecked his entire policy of seizing power by a coalition with other right-wing parties. But Hitler was too impatient for power to be dissuaded. A messenger immediately was dispatched to Berlin informing Schleicher of Hitler's demand. The general could not take it seriously, so sure was he that Hindenburg would balk at bestowing such an honor on an ex-Gefreiter. He invited Hitler to a meeting in Mecklenburg under the illusion that he could "talk him out of his plans." The two met on August 5 at the Fürstenberg barracks near the capital, and Hitler demanded not only the chancellorship but passage of an enabling bill which would give him power to govern the nation by decree—in effect, to establish a dictatorship. The meeting went so well that Hitler was convinced Hindenburg would also be brought around and, in elation, he proposed that a tablet be fastened to the wall in commemoration of such a historic conference.

Although he brought his euphoria back to the Obersalzberg it was not shared by Goebbels, who doubted they would gain power so easily. He was all for action, not dubious compromises, and his zeal permeated the Nazi ranks. "The whole party is ready to take over power," he wrote in his diary on August 8. "The SA men are leaving their places of work in order to make themselves ready." By August 10, when Hindenburg left his own country home for Berlin, the capital was in a state of semi-siege. To end the crisis Papen offered to resign but Hindenburg was enraged at the thought of making Hitler Chancellor. The upstart Austrian had already broken his promises to Schleicher; besides, Hitler had no governmental experience and couldn't even control the hotheads in his own party. The President even refused to invite him to a meeting.

On August 13 Hitler saw Schleicher, who informed him that Hindenburg could only offer him the vice-chancellorship. Understandably irate, Hitler attacked the general for breaking his promise and stormed out. Moments later he was in Chancellor Papen's office berating the administration for its leniency with the old system. Papen was taken aback by his caller's aggressive attitude. "The President is not prepared to offer you the post of Chancellor," he said, "as he feels he does not yet know you well enough." Hitler was in no mood for half a loaf. He had dedicated himself to wiping out the Marxist parties, he said, and this could not be done unless he took over the government and ran things his own way. One could not shy away from bloodshed, he added ominously. That was a lesson of history. Had the King of Italy offered Mussolini a vice-chancellorship after the march on Rome?

He left the chancellery in a black mood, driving directly to Goebbels' apartment. Here he waited, irritated and frustrated, for a summons from Hindenburg. At last, at three in the afternoon, Papen's state secretary phoned. Hitler was interested in but one thing: was Hindenburg making him Chancellor? The state secretary would only reply that the President wished to speak with the Führer. The meeting in the study of the presidential palace was short and formal. Hindenburg had made up his mind not to appoint a man like Hitler to such a responsible post but would "make one more appeal to his patriotism" to co-operate with Papen. He opened cautiously by stating that he welcomed the participation of the National Socialists in the government. Hitler just as politely replied that this was out of the question; as head of the largest party in the nation, he would have to insist on a new cabinet with himself as Chancellor.

"Nein!" exclaimed Hindenburg. Never could he "before God, his conscience, and the Fatherland bear the responsibility of entrusting all governmental authority to a single party." Hitler regretted that he could accept no other alternative. "You are going into opposition, then?" "I have no other choice," said the Führer.

With some feeling, Hindenburg complained of the recent clashes between the Nazis and the police. Such incidents, he said, strengthened his conviction that there were wild uncontrollable elements in the NSDAP. He was ready, however, to accept Hitler in a coalition government. The invitation was followed by a lofty rebuke, from field marshal to corporal. "Then I must warn you to carry on your opposition in a chivalrous manner and to remain conscious of your responsibility and duty toward the Fatherland. I do not doubt at all your love for the Fatherland. But I am going to proceed very harshly against any acts of terror or force, such as have been regrettably perpetrated by members of the SA."

The severity of this lecture was somewhat mitigated by Hindenburg's closing words: "We are both old fellow soldiers and want to remain so since our paths may be crossing again. Thus I extend my hand to you as a comrade-in-arms." Hitler emerged from the study overwhelmed by the personality of the marshal but, once the door closed, he turned on Papen for maneuvering him into such a humiliating scene. Out of all this, warned Hitler, would possibly come the downfall of the President. He would not be responsible for what happened next.

Newsboys in the street were shouting out headlines from extras: SHOCKING PRETENSION—HITLER'S BREACH OF FAITH—HITLER REPRIMANDED BY THE REICH PRESIDENT. The stories, which stated that Hitler had demanded complete power, were based on a government communiqué issued so soon after the interview that it must have been prepared ahead of time. This infuriated Hitler. He felt he had been "deceived" by the military and the politicians.

Schleicher was almost as dismayed by the Papen communiqué as Hitler, since he was still convinced that the best solution was to get the Nazis into the government. He hastily sent word to the Führer that there was still a chance to work out an agreement and asked for a meeting. Hitler's brusque refusal to see him sent the ordinarily self-possessed general into a state of shock. That evening a friend found Schleicher pale and frightened, incoherently muttering to himself. Finally his words could be made out: "The decision was right, one could not have given the power to Adolf Hitler."

Throughout the city embittered Brownshirts, long held in check by party leadership, were clamoring for action. By this time Hitler had regained his composure. He summoned SA commanders to the Goebbels apartment and such were his powers of persuasion that they accepted his argument that it was not yet time to seize power, and that a Putsch at this time would be disastrous. All units were sent on a two-week furlough.

5

At the opening session of the new Reichstag the National Socialist delegates behaved correctly, sitting in silence during opponents' speeches and co-operating in the election of parliamentary officers. Such exemplary conduct was rewarded by support of the Center Party for Göring as president of the Reichstag. Several days passed in peaceful and constructive activity. Political stability had at last returned to Germany—thanks to Adolf Hitler. But within a week he abruptly changed course, apparently on the spur of the moment. He ordered his delegates to make no objections to a Communist motion of no confidence in the Papen government.

The session erupted into a wild shouting match and when Papen, who had rushed out to get Hindenburg's signature on a document to dissolve parliament, tried to get the floor, President Göring pretended not to see him. Ignoring the decree which the infuriated Papen had flung onto the presidential desk, Göring called for a vote. It was an overwhelming defeat for Papen—512 to 42. Hitler was elated by the success of his unexpected coup and prepared for the national election with confidence.

Despite Hitler's crowd appeal, his campaign was sluggish since the financial and physical resources of the party had been severely strained to the breaking point. Too, Germany had been emotionally drained by the seemingly endless elections. Goebbels could not stir up the enthusiasm of the previous campaign and attendance at rallies and meetings slacked off.

In the midst of Hitler's attempts to generate life in the campaign he was once more beset by personal misfortune. On the first of November Eva Braun, his mistress of some months, shot herself with a pistol as Geli Raubal had done. While she had fallen desperately in love, he had become so involved with elections that he could spend little time with her. He would send her brief messages and even these became less frequent as the political situation intensified. To add to her misery, at least one malicious rival for the Führer's affections showed her photographs of the electioneering Hitler posing with beautiful women.

A little after midnight on All Saints' Day she wrote a letter of farewell to Hitler, then shot herself in the neck, severing an artery. She got to the phone and gasped out to a surgeon, Dr. Plate, that she had shot herself through the heart.

Hitler left the campaign trail and, carrying a bunch of flowers, hastened to the private clinic where she was recovering. "Do you think," he asked Dr. Plate, "that Fräulein Braun shot herself simply with the object of becoming an interesting patient and of drawing my attention to herself?" The surgeon assured the Führer that it appeared to be a genuine case of attempted suicide. She had felt so neglected that she wanted to end it all. When the doctor left, Hitler turned to his companion, Hoffmann. "You hear," he said, "the girl did it for love of me. But I have given her no cause which could possibly justify such a deed." As he paced in agitation he muttered, "Obviously I must now look after the girl." Hoffmann objected. Who could possibly blame him for what happened? "And who, do you think, would believe that?" said Hitler, who knew more about human nature. Nor was there any guarantee that she might not try again.

This incident distracted Hitler from a campaign that was showing signs of deteriorating, and two days later he was presented with another embarrassing problem. On his own, Goebbels joined the Reds in a wildcat strike of Berlin transport workers asking for a pfennig or so an hour increase in pay. It was not the first time that the two parties, with many goals in common, had fought together; and for the next few wet, raw days the Communists and the National Socialists ate communally on the picket line. Side by side they pelted rocks at strikebreakers, tore up streetcar tracks and built barricades. Hitler could not publicly disavow the actions of his impetuous disciple but he was privately angry at alienating so many middle-class voters and sent orders to end the strike.

Goebbels' impetuous act also put a crimp in the flow of bourgeois money for the campaign and on Sunday, November 6, Hitler lost more than two million votes along with thirty-four seats in the Reichstag. No longer could a simple alignment with the Center Party give him a majority. More significant, it indicated that the Hitler flood tide had ebbed and the strategy of gaining power through the ballot box had reached a dead end.

6

Hitler's defeat was of little consolation to Papen, who was still badly outnumbered in the Reichstag. Putting personal distaste aside, he wrote Hitler that the recent elections provided a new opportunity for uniting the country. "We must endeavor to put aside the bitterness of the election campaign and place the good of the country, which we both seek to serve, above all considerations." The memory of their August meetings was too bitter and the response was a letter of accusation. The Führer refused the Chancellor's invitation to a conference on the grounds that discussions led to misconceptions. After their last conference hadn't Papen publicly announced that Hitler demanded total power when he had only requested leadership? Moreover, he was not ready "under any circumstances to repeat the proceedings of August 13" when Papen had insisted on sharing responsibility with Hindenburg. "Unfortunately you could not be persuaded to assume your part of this responsibility. I assumed mine. Instead your chancellery, through trickery—against my wishes and my explanations—successfully lured me into a colloquy with the Reich president. . . . I do not want to have a repetition of this game."

Thwarted, Papen reported to Hindenburg on the afternoon of November 17 that he was unable to negotiate with other

parties and that any coalition under his leadership was impossible. The President accepted his resignation and the following day asked Alfred Hugenberg, the nation's leading film and press lord and head of the völkish right-wing German National People's Party, what he thought of Hitler as Chancellor. The latter no longer trusted the Führer. "His entire manner of handling political affairs makes it very difficult, in my opinion, to give him leadership. At any rate, I have grave doubts." The marshal then turned to his adviser, State Secretary Otto Meissner, and wondered if it was true that Hitler had been a house painter in Munich. Without waiting for an answer he turned back to the gray-haired Hugenberg. "My dear young friend, you have spoken out of my own heart!" he said and proceeded to help perpetuate the myth that persists to this day. "One can't put a house painter in Bismarck's chair."
his visitor for the rude behavior of youthful Nazis in East Prussia. "Not long ago, at Tannenberg, they shouted out so that I could hear: 'Wake up, wake up!' And yet I'm not asleep!" Hitler explained that his followers had not meant to be offensive; they were merely chanting the National Socialist slogan, "Germany, awake!"

After about an hour Meissner entered and the talk became more pointed. Hitler refused to join a non-partisan cabinet unless he was made Chancellor. "In the interest of the Fatherland," he said, "my movement must be preserved and this means that I must have the leadership." Why then did the Nazis join the Reds in the recent transportation strike? "If I had tried to restrain my people," explained Hitler frankly, "the strike would have taken place nonetheless, but I would have lost my following among the workers; this would not have been in Germany's interest."

Much as he distrusted the "house painter," Hindenburg did his utmost to gain his co-operation. "I can only repeat my request: Give me your help." It was an open call for personal allegiance. "I do appreciate the great idea which inspires you and your movement, and I would like to see you and your movement join the government." At the same time he could not give Hitler the chancellorship. Of course, Hitler was free to form a National Socialist government once he had a majority.

With clenched fists on knees, Hitler exclaimed, "Herr Feldmarschall! In order to negotiate with other parties it is only logical, Herr Feldmarschall, that I first have a mandate from you!" He could not conceal his irritation.

Hindenburg smiled ironically.

There was an awkward pause. "Herr Feldmarschall," Hitler finally said, "I have no intention of ruling as dictatorially as the Feldmarschall seems to assume. If you insist that I produce a Reichstag majority, then I cannot desist from putting before the Reichstag a kind of enabling act for special and urgent matters." He alone could get passage of such a decree and that would solve the problem.

This was unacceptable to Hindenburg and once more he tried the personal approach, appealing to Hitler's sense of duty as a soldier. It invoked the "old comradeship-in-arms" which had brought them together in the war. "Meet me half-way in this matter so that we can work together." Hitler departed, intransigent as ever.

Petitions for Hitler's appointment as Chancellor deluged Hindenburg and two days later he felt compelled to see him once more. This time Hitler brought with him a carefully prepared statement. Parliamentary government, it read, had failed and was not an expression of the will of the people. The National Socialists alone could prevent Communism and he requested Hindenburg to appoint him leader of a presidential cabinet.

Hindenburg would only repeat his suggestion that Hitler find a majority in the Reichstag to support his chancellorship. Hitler's response was visibly cool but the President ended the ten-minute talk with another offer of friendship.

Late that November, thirty-nine prominent businessmen (including Hjalmar Schacht, former Chancellor Cuno, and tycoons like Krupp, Siemens, Thyssen, Bosch, Wörmann and Vögler) signed a letter petitioning Hindenburg to appoint Hitler Chancellor of Germany. These pragmatic men were placing a bet on the NSDAP. They were confident Hitler's socialism was a fraud and that, once in power, he would be the tool of capitalism.

The machinery of parliamentary government had brought Germany to a political standstill. Hindenburg was finding it impossible to form a new cabinet which could operate with a deadlocked Reichstag. Frustrated on all sides, Hindenburg summoned Papen and Schleicher, the new Minister of Defense, to his office on the first day of December. Papen pointed out that Hitler would accept responsibility only as head of another presidential cabinet, and suggested that his government remain in office for the time being. He realized he would not get the support of the Reichstag and that body would have to be suspended for a short period. This procedure involved a breach of the constitution by the President but the situation was grave enough to warrant such action. Then if the police could not keep order the army could step in.

Papen's plan would not work, said the Minister of Defense, and suggested one that would: replacement of Papen as Chancellor by himself. This would split the Nazis into two factions and he would get a majority in the Reichstag. He would simply offer Gregor Strasser and one or two of his close supporters posts in the new government and thereby get the votes of sixty Nazi delegates. Other support would come from the Social Democrats and bourgeois parties.

For weeks Papen had noticed that Schleicher was "no longer as frank and open" as previously and their "relationship had become distinctly cool." Even so the Chancellor was amazed that the general who had helped him into office was now proposing to get rid of him. Resentfully, Papen argued that his Minister of Defense's scheme meant the abandonment of the President's long-range policy of striving for a more satisfactory relationship between administration and parliament.

Exhausted by almost uninterrupted discussions since early morning, Hindenburg sat in silence until the argument finally ended. Then he rose and turned to Papen. "Herr Reichskanzler," he said, "I desire you to undertake immediately the necessary discussions to form a government, to which I shall entrust the carrying out of your plan."

Schleicher was dumfounded. As he left the office with Papen the latter suggested staying in office for a few months until the constitution was amended and parliamentary peace restored. "Then I can resign and you will be able to take over the government with every hope of a good start."

Schleicher's icy retort was that made to Luther as he was leaving the Diet of Worms: "'Little monk, little monk, you have chosen a difficult path.'"

This was painfully apparent the next morning at a cabinet meeting. After Papen had given an account of the previous night's conference with the President he called upon Schleicher, who got to his feet and declared that any attempt to form a new government under Papen would reduce the country to chaos. Nor could the police and the armed services ensure law and order in the event of civil war. After a study of the matter, he said, the General Staff had concluded that local units such as the police and the technical emergency service were so infiltrated with Nazis that the army could not control a Hitler Putsch.

When no minister challenged the army study, Papen hastened to the President's office. Hindenburg, drained by the events of the past day, listened to his complaints in silence. "My dear Papen," he said in a voice that had lost its confident ring, "you'll consider me a cad if I change my mind now. But I am now too old, at the end of my life, to take the responsibility for a civil war. We'll have to let Herr von Schleicher try his luck in God's name."

And so on December 2, 1932, Kurt von Schleicher became the first general to be appointed Chancellor since the man who replaced Bismarck in 1890. One of his first acts was to invite Gregor Strasser to his home and offer to make him Vice-Chancellor and Minister President of Prussia. The proposition appealed to Strasser but he was loyal to Hitler and said he must first check with his chief. What he didn't add was that the problem was getting through the protective circle of sycophants and adulators which had formed around the Führer and seemed to control him. "Along comes Hindenburg," Strasser had recently complained, "a man of honor, who honestly and decently offers him a place in the government, and there stands the '*wahnfriedische*' Lohengrin-Hitler with his darkly menacing boys. Frank, I see black: Göring is a brutal egotist who cares nothing for Germany as long as he becomes something. Goebbels is a limping devil and basically two-faced, Röhm is a pig. This is the Old Guard of the Führer. It is terrible!"

Someone in Papen's office learned about the secret Schleicher-Strasser meeting and told a correspondent, who informed Hanfstaengl, who in turn passed the story on to Hitler. Thus Papen—or a Papen associate—paid back Schleicher in his own coin. The immediate victim, however, was Strasser, who had been dealing with Schleicher in good faith on the Führer's behalf, with the conviction that the best way to keep the party from disintegrating was to get into power at once—even at the price of coalition.

While Hitler, whose suspicions of Strasser had been inflamed by Goebbels, understandably took it as a betrayal, more moderate advisers were inclined to consider Schleicher's latest offer—this time of the vice-chancellorship to the Führer. At a stormy conference of party leaders at the Kaiserhof on December 5 Strasser begged Hitler to accept. But Goebbels and Göring vehemently opposed such a deal and Hitler went along with them. Strasser gave warning that Schleicher would merely dissolve the Reichstag if NSDAP support was not forthcoming. But Hitler, still rankled by Strasser's "betrayal," refused to discuss the matter further.

Two days later Strasser again saw the Führer at the Kaiserhof. This time Hitler openly accused him of treason. Too angry to find the right phrase, Strasser turned, slammed the door and took a taxi to the Hotel Excelsior. Alone in his room he fumed with indignation but he waited until the next morning, December 8, to pen a letter resigning his party offices on the grounds that the Führer no longer trusted him. No call for open revolt, it urged all party officials to remain in their posts. Strasser could not bring himself to deliver the message to Hitler in person but sent it by mail, then waited next to the telephone for a call.

The letter landed at the Kaiserhof, in Goebbels' words, "like a bombshell." Hitler went into such shock that he was momentarily unable to make any decisions.

Finally someone suggested that the most sensible course was to summon Strasser and patch up the quarrel. Whereupon Hitler ordered his chauffeur, Schreck, to find Strasser "at any price." But he was already at his apartment in Munich, hastily packing to leave for a holiday in Italy. To a friend, who happened to drop by, Strasser said in a resigned voice: "I am a man marked by death." He warned his friend to stay away from the apartment. "Whatever happens, mark what I say: From now on Germany is in the hands of an Austrian, who is a congenital liar, a former officer, who is a pervert, and a clubfoot. And I tell you the last is the worst of them all. This is Satan in human form." Although it was at least the second time Strasser had used such words to damn the Hitler inner circle, he still revered the Führer.

That same day party leaders and Gauleiters assembled in the palace of the president of the Reichstag to hear a declaration attacking Strasser. Still in an emotional state, Hitler stammered with a sob that he had been shocked by Strasser's treachery.

Strasser's drastic action was no revolt, only a personal attempt to save the Führer from men such as Goebbels. He represented no faction and no important party member followed him into oblivion. Nor was any purge necessary. Hitler merely announced that Strasser had started an authorized three-week sick leave, and once it was known that the Führer had withdrawn his confidence in the traitor the general membership withdrew theirs.

While the Führer had regained control of the party, the membership remained uneasy and demoralized. Their political future was bleak. "It is hard to hold the SA and the party officials to a clear course," Goebbels confided to his diary on December 15, and on the twenty-fourth, "I sit here all alone and worry about many things. The past is difficult and the future is cloudy and dark. The terrible loneliness overwhelms me with hopelessness. All possibilities and hopes have disappeared."

Hitler too had fallen into a depression that was undoubtedly intensified by his usual Christmas season despondency. (Later Hitler confided to his valet that he could not abide Yuletide decorations. His mother, he explained, had died near a lighted Christmas tree.) "I have given up all hope," he wrote to Frau Wagner after thanking her for a present. "Nothing will ever come of my dreams." He had no hope left, his opponents were too powerful. "As soon as I am sure that everything is lost you know what I'll do. I was always determined to do it. I cannot accept defeat. I will stick to my word and end my life with a bullet."

Enemies were already celebrating his political demise on the assumption that he had at last overreached himself. "Hitler is finished—not as an agitator or as a leader of an aggressive minority, but as a possible dictator." So wrote William Bullitt in an eleven-page report to President-elect Franklin Roosevelt.

7

Hitler's meeting with Papen at Baron Kurt von Schröder's home in Cologne took place as scheduled on January 4. It was supposed to be secret but despite elaborate precautions by all parties a reporter from a Berlin newspaper (he had bribed a member of Hitler's bodyguard) was on hand to take pictures of Hitler and Papen separately entering the Schröder mansion. At the outset of the two-hour conference the latter suggested that the Schleicher regime be replaced by a Hitler-Papen government in which both would be equal. Hitler replied to this startling proposition at length: If he were made Chancellor he would have to be the actual head of government; he would accept some Papen men as ministers but only if they agreed to his policy of eliminating Social Democrats, Communists and Jews from leading positions in the nation. The two men, according to Schröder, "reached agreement in principle" and while leaving the house cordially shook hands.

When Schleicher was shown a picture of his handclasp he stormed to the presidential palace to charge Papen with treachery. He asked Hindenburg never to receive the former Chancellor again except in his presence. But the Old Gentleman was too fond of the dashing ex-cavalryman to believe him capable of deceit. Instead he authorized Papen to continue to meet with Hitler informally while instructing his secretary to keep these negotiations secret from Chancellor von Schleicher.

With each day Schleicher's position was becoming more untenable and by January 20 he had succeeded in antagonizing almost every party from right to left. His extremity was Papen's opportunity. Ever since his resignation the ex-Chancellor had regularly visited his neighbors—Hindenburg and son—bringing gaiety and frivolity into their dour household. But today he took the short walk through the snowy gardens of the chancellery for a definite purpose. Instead of amusing the President he informed him in detail of the meetings with Hitler and the possible amalgamation of conservative parties. Why not, he suggested persuasively, make Hitler Chancellor—so long as policies were dictated by himself?

The greatest obstacle to this was not the President but his son, who openly disliked the Führer. But Oskar's feelings were apparently based more on snobbery than ideology and he accepted an invitation to discuss their differences at the luxurious Ribbentrop villa on Sunday evening, January 22.

It was decided that Oskar should bring along his father's state secretary, Meissner, and to keep the parley secret from Chancellor von Schleicher, these two started the evening in a box at the Prussian State Opera House where an early work of Wagner's, *Das Liebesverbot*, was being performed. An icy wind was blowing down the Unter den Linden as the party arrived at the theater. One of the main topics of conversation before the curtain went up was the Nazi demonstration held a few hours earlier in front of Communist headquarters. Schleicher had permitted a parade of 20,000 Brownshirts while banning a counterdemonstration by the Reds, and then was forced to send out police to protect the marchers with armored cars and machine guns.

During the intermission Oskar and his wife made themselves conspicuous by greeting many acquaintances. But when the lights went down for the final act Hindenburg and Meissner left by a side entrance, leaving their wives behind. They hailed a taxi, giving their destination only when inside. They saw no car following them and assumed they had tricked Schleicher's spies but to be on the safe side they got out some distance from the Ribbentrop home and trudged through the snow. After some difficulty they located the Ribbentrop gate.

In the salon they found Papen, Hitler, Göring and Frick. The atmosphere was stiff and, after some awkward small talk, Hitler abruptly suggested to Oskar that they retire into the next room. Before Meissner could say anything the two were out of the room and Ribbentrop had closed the door behind them. According to young Hindenburg, Hitler dominated the conversation: he alone could save Germany from the Reds; he alone could be a strong Chancellor since no other government could operate without National Socialist support.

After an hour the two men returned, solemn-faced and the entire company moved into the dining room where a simple one-pot meal of peas and bacon was served from a silver bowl by a gloved servant. Hitler drank mineral water, the others champagne. Hindenburg and Meissner, the last to come, were the first to go and as their taxi plunged into the swirling snow Meissner noticed that his companion was "extremely silent, and the only remark which he made was that it could not be helped—the Nazis had to be taken into the government. My impression was that Hitler succeeded in getting him under his spell." It may have been simpler than that. Hitler could have threatened to make a public scandal of an open secret in high places: the Eastern Aid Fund had been put into effect six years earlier to help the Junkers retain their properties. President von Hindenburg had not only profited handsomely by this act (one reported figure was 620,000 marks) but had already turned over his estate to Oskar to avoid death duties. Nor had conveyance fees been paid. These were grounds for impeachment, and even if no conviction ensued, the name of Hindenburg would be besmirched.

Papen had noticed the impression Hitler had made on Oskar and after the latter's departure pledged his allegiance to the Führer. He promised to support him for Chancellor, vowing he would under no circumstance accept the appointment himself. The clandestine meeting ended with the Hitler party furtively disappearing into the garage. But Schleicher's spies had not been fooled. The next morning the Chancellor phoned Meissner with a sarcastic question: how had he liked last night's one-pot supper? Being a master of intrigue, the general knew he must act quickly. He told Hindenburg that he needed a "military dictatorship" to control the Nazis and tried to persuade him to dissolve the Reichstag and suspend elections. But Hindenburg, weary of Schleicher's interminable schemes, refused to authorize any such emergency measures.

When the word of the proposed military dictatorship leaked out, both the Social Democrat and Center parties branded Schleicher as an enemy of the people. His plan was not only unconstitutional but "open high treason."

The sudden turn of events in Hitler's favor brought him back to Berlin on January 27, but then almost immediately he became so frustrated by the intrigues in the capital that he told Ribbentrop he was going to leave.

That evening Ribbentrop somehow convinced Papen that a Hitler chancellorship was the only solution; and the next morning Papen passed on this conviction to Hindenburg. The field marshal wavered. For months he had been inundated with requests to appoint Hitler, and lately his own son had come to the same conclusion. Though his own distaste for the "Czech corporal," as he persisted in calling him, was as strong as ever, it was apparent that the Old Gentleman was at last in the mood to accept Hitler.

At the moment Schleicher was convening with his cabinet members: he told them that he proposed asking Hindenburg once more for an order to dissolve the Reichstag and if this failed he would be forced to resign. He temporarily adjourned the meeting to see the President. It was a short interview. Would Hindenburg grant a dissolution decree? "Nein!" In that case, said Schleicher, the only alternative was a Hitler government. Hindenburg muttered that the Schleicher government hadn't been able to win a majority but perhaps he himself could find one that could stabilize Germany. He accepted the resignation of the cabinet and, in an exasperated aside, muttered that he didn't want to argue any more about it.

Hindenburg's mind seemed to be wandering. "Whether what I am going to do now is right, my dear Schleicher," he said, "I don't know; but I shall know soon enough when I am up there." He pointed heavenward. "I already have one foot in the grave and I am not sure that I shall not regret this action in heaven later on."

"After this breach of trust, sir," was the bitter answer, "I am not sure that you will go to heaven."

The next morning, a Sunday, Papen saw Hitler. He was agreeable—but had his own demands: new general elections and an enabling law which would give him as Chancellor authority exceeding that of a former Kaiser. It was early afternoon by the time Papen finally reported to Hindenburg that all parties were agreed on the new government. Only then did he mention Hitler's demand for new elections and he made it sound reasonable. He clinched the point with Hitler's promise that these would indeed be the *last elections*. Out of relief that the constitutional crisis was at last ending, neither the President nor his protégé was at all struck by the implications of this promise.

The rumor of a military coup spread rapidly through government circles, causing considerable panic in the capital throughout the night. The next morning—Monday, January 30—panic was succeeded by a monumental argument in Papen's residence. Hugenberg, the Nationalist Party leader, violently objected to Hitler's demand for new elections and it appeared as if the new government was already doomed. Hugenberg wrangled on at such length that Papen finally exclaimed in desperation, "If the new government is not formed by eleven o'clock, the army is going to march. Schleicher may establish a military dictatorship."

Just then there was a loud cry of "Heil!" from the crowd outside the Papen villa and Hitler entered with Göring. It was 10:35 A.M. and Papen suggested they all follow him to the chancellery. They paraded through the snow-covered chancellery garden and up to Meissner's office. Here they met other ministerial candidates and while they all were waiting to be brought into the President's office Papen raised the question of elections.

"Elections?" Hugenberg testily declared that he thought the question had been settled. Hitler drew him aside but the Führer's considerable powers of persuasion only provoked Hugenberg to vociferous objections. Hitler tried to pacify the old man by seizing his hand and promising to make no changes in the cabinet no matter how the elections came out. The answer was still no.

At that moment Meissner appeared. "Gentlemen, it is five

minutes past the appointed time," he said. "The President likes punctuality." Papen saw his coalition breaking up at the threshold of success.

Hugenburg continued to argue bitterly until the harried Meissner rushed out again, watch in hand. "The President requests you not to keep him waiting any longer," he announced. "It is now eleven-fifteen. The Old Gentleman may retire at any moment!"

Once more Hitler seized Hugenberg's hand and this time promised to consult the Center and Bavarian People's parties to ensure the widest possible basis for parliamentary majority. The threat of Meissner's watch probably helped induce Hugenberg to say that he would leave the decision to Hindenburg. Hitler hastily agreed to this and Göring boomed out, "Now, everything is in order!" and they all filed into the President's office.

Hindenburg was so irked he didn't personally offer the post of Chancellor to Hitler—the only Chancellor so slighted. Nor did he greet the new cabinet with a welcoming speech or even outline what tasks lay before them. The swearing-in ceremony was finished rapidly in the style of a shotgun wedding. But Hitler could not let such a historical moment pass in silence and, to everyone's surprise, began a speech. After solemnly vowing he would observe the Weimar constitution, he promised to find a majority in the parliament so that the President would no longer have to sign emergency decrees. Further, he would solve the economic crisis and unite a Germany torn by bitterness and debate. There was a pause for an appropriate response from Hindenburg but the field marshal would only say, as if dismissing the troops, "And now, gentlemen, forward with God!"

On New Year's Day, Erik Jan Hanussen, one of the most renowned seers and astrologists in Europe, had presented to the Führer a rhymed prediction that Hitler's rise to power would begin on January 30. Now Hanussen's prediction, if it was one, had come true. The man who had failed to graduate from high school, who had been refused admission to the Academy of Fine Arts and who had lived as a tramp on the streets of Vienna was Chancellor of Germany on the thirtieth day of January 1933.

The news was received throughout Germany with mixed feelings. The liberals were horrified but to the average German anything was better than the parliamentary shambles of the past year. And for many young idealists, the dispossessed, the embittered patriots and the racists there was unrestrained joy. Their dreams were coming true.

No group was more surprised at the sudden ascension of Adolf Hitler than the Berlin Brownshirts. They had been living in poverty for years, risking their lives on the streets of the capital, often in opposition to their Führer's wishes. Now at one stroke their dream was realized but it was only through the newspapers that most of them learned there would be a torchlight parade that evening.

Every able-bodied SA and SS man was out in uniform. Those who expected the usual trouble with the police were surprised by smiles from their old enemies, some of whom now wore swastikas. Carrying torches, the storm troopers started from the Tiergarten at dusk, joined by thousands of Stahlhelm men, and passed under the Brandenburg Gate in disciplined columns to the blare of martial music. Hour after hour they marched down the Wilhelmstrasse shouting the "Horst Wessel Lied" and other fighting songs. First they paid homage to Hindenburg, who stood at a window of the presidential palace and, moments later, to Hitler, who looked down fondly from a window of the chancellery.

Young men perched in trees along the Wilhelmstrasse; boys clung to the iron fences like "bunches of grapes." The excitement was intensified by the winter darkness as the stream of flares glowed hypnotically and the drums beat thunderously. It had all been staged by the master showman, Goebbels, and Hitler himself was so impressed that he turned and asked, "How on earth did he conjure up all these thousands of torches in the space of a few hours?" The little doctor had also managed to take over the radio stations and the country was being treated to a running eyewitness account of the procession.

Papen watched the marchers over Hitler's shoulder. He noticed that as they approached Hindenburg there were respectful shouts but the sight of Hitler brought frantic acclaim. "The contrast was most marked and seemed to emphasize the transition from a moribund regime to the new revolutionary forces. . . . It was an extraordinary experience, and the endless repetition of the triumphal cry: 'Heil, Heil, Sieg Heil!' rang in my ears like a tocsin." As Hitler turned to speak to Papen, his voice was choked. "What an immense task we have set ourselves, Herr von Papen—we must never part until our work is accomplished."

Hitler had a late supper with Hess, Göring, Goebbels, Röhm

and Frank in a small private room. Compulsively he talked on and on. "Some foreign source today called me 'anti-Christ,'" he said. "The only kind of anti I am is anti-Lenin." According to Frank, Hitler went on to say he hoped Hindenburg could be won over to his side. "The Old Gentleman liked it very much when I said to him today that I would serve him as Chancellor as loyally as in the days as a soldier when he was my hero."

That night an exultant Goebbels wrote in his diary: "It is almost like a dream . . . a fairy tale. . . . The new Reich has been born. Fourteen years of work have been crowned with victory. The German revolution has begun!" Few Germans that evening realized this, and perhaps none recalled the prophetic words written by Heinrich Heine, a Jew, not quite a century earlier: "German thunder is truly German; it takes its time. But it will come, and when it crashes it will crash as nothing in history crashed before. The hour will come. . . . A drama will be performed which will make the French Revolution seem like a pretty idyll. . . . Never doubt it; the hour will come."

Chapter Eleven

AN UNGUARDED HOUR

1933–JUNE 1934

> "Neither a nation nor a woman is forgiven for *an unguarded hour* in which the first adventurer who comes along can sweep them off their feet and possess them."
>
> KARL MARX

1

The next morning Frau Goebbels brought flowers to Hitler. He was looking out the window of his room in the Kaiserhof. Slowly he turned and, "with an almost solemn gesture," took the bouquet. "These are the first flowers, and you are the first woman to congratulate me," he murmured, according to her reverent account. After moments of silence he said as if continuing a monologue, "Now the world must realize why I couldn't be Vice-Chancellor. How long my own party members did not understand me!" After another long silence she started for the door. "Yes," she heard him softly exclaim, "now I must remain by myself for some time."

He regarded what had happened as fate, another step on a path long since mapped out. But those who had put him in power were convinced he was merely their dupe. Papen, for one, boasted to his circle: "We have hired him for ourselves," and then reassured a critical friend: "What do you want? I have Hindenburg's confidence. Within two months we will have pushed Hitler so far in the corner that he'll squeak."

The Junkers, as embodied by Papen, thought they had bought a restitution of authoritarian rule but Hitler had no intention of being their puppet and at once began laying the foundation for a dictatorship. First he dismissed out of hand a list of questions and demands submitted by the Center Party with the comment that, since negotiations with that party had failed, new elections were necessary. Then, through Papen, he persuaded Hindenburg to dissolve the parliament.

Few realized the import of these first steps. Editorials in the liberal bourgeois papers foresaw no revolutionary changes. After all there were only two other Nazis in Hitler's cabinet—Göring and Frick. Even the Social Democrats were not alarmed since it was widely believed that Hitler could never get the two-thirds majority to change the Weimar constitution. A similar view was held by the New York *Times*: "The composition of the Cabinet leaves Herr Hitler no scope for the gratification of his dictatorial ambition."

While all these observers were assuring the world of Hitler's impotence, he was hiding his revolutionary intentions behind a flow of inspirational but conservative phrases in a radio address to the voters on the first of February. He made it clear that he wanted only a return to the old virtues of the past. He said nothing of his plans for the Jews, said nothing, in fact, that offended or alarmed the average citizen.

During the speech the American chargé d'affaires in Berlin was dining with one of those kingmakers who had helped put Hitler in power. Hjalmar Schacht, president of the Reichsbank, revealed that he was the Führer's court financial and economic adviser, and then assured the American that the Nazis would "make no attempt to carry out their well-known demagogic reforms" and that consequently "all big business viewed the new regime with sympathy."

While the last remark was an exaggeration, Hitler would not have been Chancellor without the support of industrialists and the military. The majority in the officer corps agreed with Karl Dönitz, a rising man in the navy, who felt it was simply a choice between Hitler and the Reds. The support of the military was as self-serving as that of the industrialists, and Hitler knew it. His opinion of generals was not high. But now that he was in power he was determined to make his peace with the military and enlist them in the regeneration of Germany.

He took the first step on the evening of his fourth day as Chancellor by accepting an invitation to dine at the home of General von Hammerstein, who had been outspoken in his contempt for the Nazis. The party had been arranged by the new Minister of Defense, General von Blomberg, and its purpose was to introduce the Führer to leaders in the armed forces. After dinner he rose to speak. At first he was stiff before such company, as he told of the disastrous economic problems facing the nation. The answer was not a renewed export drive since production exceeded demand throughout the world and Germany's former customers had developed their own markets. Unemployment and depression, he concluded, would continue until Germany recovered her former position in the world.

Interest in the room was aroused. It was a solution most of them cherished. Hitler went on to say that pacifism, Marxism and that "cancerous growth, democracy," must be eradicated. Rearmament was the first requirement for a resurgent Germany and once the Fatherland had regained its power there would come "the conquest of the land in the East and its ruthless Germanization." Lest this revelation of his blueprint for the future cause apprehension, Hitler promised that his listeners need not concern themselves over the domestic or foreign policy. The army would not be used to deal with unrest at home and should devote itself for the next few years "to the operation of its main objective, training for the defense of the Fatherland in the case of aggression." As reassurance regarding the SA, he added that the army would be "the sole bearer of arms, and its structure would remain unaltered."

The response was mixed, but Hitler had won over a number of new adherents. Those who hoped to transform the new government into a military dictatorship as the first step to a restored monarchy were ready to sanction the National Socialist reforms and many of those with qualms were inclined to go along out of respect for Field Marshal von Hindenburg.

Using the emergency powers of the constitution that had once felt his scorn, Hitler next pushed through a decree, "for the protection of the German people," controlling political meetings and restricting the press. Neither Papen nor any of his colleagues in the cabinet protested regulations that enabled Hitler to paralyze rival parties and to control public opinion. Faced by such unanimity, Hindenburg also succumbed and signed the decree. This was followed shortly by an emergency decree replacing the political regime in Prussia with one of his own choice. The first protests were answered by reason—Papen as the newly appointed Prussian Minister President could surely control the new Minister of the Interior, Göring—but the fact remained that Hitler had accomplished his second step toward dictatorship.

There was a new elite in Germany. The borough president of Hamburg came from a notions shop, one of hundreds who had risen overnight from the lower middle class. Teachers, lawyers and businessmen were also among the leaders. Never before had so many men of modest means been thrust into political prominence. These were the old Nazi fighters whose dedication to the movement and Hitler was now drawing dividends.

Perhaps no other German Chancellor had been so well prepared for assumption of leadership as Hitler, who had regarded himself as Führer for some time. The same could not be said for the party. It had been held together by his magnetism and the dream of power and jobs. This new elite did manage to carry out a National Socialist revolution on the local level but only because of the complacency of the conservatives and the confusion among liberal and leftist opponents.

2

Despite Hitler's personal success, the fate of the Brown Revolution was still in doubt at the end of the first six weeks of power. The emergency deposition of the Prussian government was causing grave concern in other states. By the middle of February Göring had drastically purged the Prussian police of men he could not rely on and issued an order instructing his police force "to avoid at all costs anything suggestive of hostility to the SA, SS and Stahlhelm, as these organizations contain the most constructive national elements. . . . It is the business of the police to abet every form of national propaganda." This was followed by an ominous note to the effect that the police should act decisively against "organizations hostile to the state" and should not hesitate to use their firearms. On the contrary, they would be punished if they failed "in their duty." He was declaring open season on Communists, Marxists and their sympathizers.

Seven of the smaller states were already as hamstrung politically as Prussia, but the larger states—including Bavaria, the home of National Socialism—refused to bow to the Hitler government. This rebellion was accompanied by a Communist campaign calling for resistance to the Nazis.

Göring raided the Karl Liebknecht House in Berlin on February 24. An official announcement proclaimed that the police had discovered plans for a Communist uprising. On the evening of February 26 Hanussen predicted that this revolution would soon literally burst into flames. At a séance attended by some of the most influential people in the capital he claimed to see smoke . . . an eagle rising from flames . . . and then a large Berlin building engulfed in fire. Those of his listeners who were aware that there had been three attempts the previous day to set fire to governmental buildings must have been particularly impressed.

The arsonist, a twenty-four-year-old native of Holland, Marinus van der Lubbe, had in fact also made up his mind to burn down the Reichstag. A strong, lumpish young man, his protest against capitalism was setting buildings on fire. Four years earlier he had resigned in disgust from the Communist Party to join International Communists, a tiny splinter group which opposed Moscow policies. He had come to Berlin a week earlier under the impression that great things were about to happen there. But attendance at Social Democratic and Communist demonstrations convinced him that the German workers would start a revolution only under the impetus of some startling event. He hoped the sight of governmental strongholds going up in flames would inspire the lethargic German masses to revolt.

Not discouraged by the three abortive fires, on Monday noon—it was February 27—he bought four packages of fire lighters at a shop on the Müllerstrasse and then set off on foot for the Reichstag. The western approach was deserted and in moments he had scaled the wall and was on the balcony of the first floor.

At 9:30 P.M. a theology student on his way home heard breaking glass inside the parliament building. He saw a figure with a burning object in his hand and ran to alert a police sergeant at the northwestern corner of the Reichstag. The sergeant found the broken window and a glow behind it but watched in astonishment and it was some minutes before he summoned the fire brigade. The first engines arrived just before ten and by then the Session Chamber was in flames.

At his Berlin quarters opposite the Reichstag, Hanfstaengl was awakened from a sickbed by the screams of the housekeeper. He looked out the window at the fire and telephoned the Goebbels apartment where a party for the Führer was in mid-career. When Goebbels heard the news he thought it was a joke. "If you think that, come down here and see for yourself," retorted Hanfstaengl and hung up. A moment later his phone rang. It was Goebbels. "I have just talked to the Führer and he wants to know what's really happening. No more of your jokes now." The annoyance and suspicion in Goebbels' voice seemed genuine and Hanfstaengl lost his temper. He said the place was in flames and the fire brigades were already there. He was going back to bed to nurse his fever.

After Hitler saw the red sky above the Tiergarten he shouted, "It's the Communists!" and set off with Goebbels for the scene of the fire. They found Göring inside the burning building, brown hat turned up in front and looking immense in a camel-hair coat. He had been one of the first to reach the conflagration, and his first order was characteristic: "Save the tapestries!"

The party began a tour of the destroyed area across pools of water and charred debris. After they had climbed the stairs to the next floor they were approached by Papen, who had rushed from a dinner at the Herrenklub in honor of Hindenburg and was immaculate in gray tweed overcoat and black Homburg. "This is a God-given signal, Herr Vice-Chancellor!" Hitler exclaimed. "If this fire, as I believe, is the work of the Communists, then we must crush out this murderous pest with an iron fist!" Papen was relieved that the Gobelin tapestries had been saved and the library was untouched and, when Hitler invited him to attend a conference in Göring's office to decide on what should be done, politely but pointedly declined. He thought he should first report to Hindenburg.

The stimulation of that night emboldened Hitler to throw off his last inhibitions, for late the next morning he flung himself into an open battle for power. It started incongruously at a cabinet meeting as the Chancellor politely greeted each minister according to rank. After this traditional beginning he took over in dictatorial fashion. The crisis was such, he said, as to warrant "a ruthless settling of accounts" with the Communists which "must not be dependent on legal considerations." He proposed, therefore, an emergency decree to protect the nation from the Reds but made it sound purely defensive and innocuous, referring almost casually to a "special measure to safeguard all the cultural documents of the German people." But when Frick read off his draft it should have been obvious that the decree canceled most rights expected by a democratic society. First it suspended the civil liberties granted by the Weimar constitution—free speech, free press, sanctity of the home, secrecy of mail and telephone conversations, freedom to assemble or form organizations and inviolability of private property. Next it authorized the Reich Minister of Interior to seize control temporarily of any state government unable to maintain order. Not a single minister opposed the deprivation of civil rights but Papen did protest that the threat to intervene with states would be deeply resented, particularly in Bavaria. Papen's dissent was short-lived; he approved a minor change that was a modification in name only. That evening Hitler and he reported to Hindenburg. The Führer argued that the decree was necessary to put down the Red revolution and, when neither Papen nor Meissner expressed disapproval, the President signed without comment.

A civil state of emergency had been substituted for the military measure sought by the conservatives, with the cabinet holding those powers usually bestowed on the commander-in-chief in a military dictatorship. On the surface such power was not so ominous since the cabinet was still overwhelmingly non-National Socialist. The decree was passed so hastily and under such emotional circumstances that no one was sure exactly who had originated the idea to abolish civil rights rather than curtail them as previous chancellors had done. Possibly it was not an underhanded plot of Hitler's in his avowed move toward dictatorship but an accident of history. The fire had obviously brought Hitler to the edge of hysteria and he truly feared a Red revolution. Certainly his erratic actions as well as those of Göring and others close to him were not those of conspirators with a levelheaded plan. Nor did Hitler react so much in panic as in utter faith in his mission. So far as he was concerned the fire was proof of all he had been saying about Reds and Jews for years.

The emergency measures that followed, designed primarily to put down a non-existent revolt, turned out to be a leap forward in Hitler's drive for total power. Truckloads of SA and SS men hastily sworn in as auxiliaries were helping the police enforce the decree. They descended on the rooms and taverns of known Reds and carted them off to prison or interrogation cellars. More than three thousand Communists and Social Democrats were taken into protective custody by the regular police. Airdromes and ports were under strict surveillance while trains were searched at frontiers.

Göring was in his glory and the following day, as Prussian Minister of Interior, he spoke to the nation by radio about the insidious plans of the Reds, groups of whom planned to don Brownshirt and Stahlhelm uniforms and carry out terrorist acts in an effort to destroy the unity of the nation. The burning of the Reichstag, he predicted, was only the first of many other fires that would distract the police and leave the people at the mercy of the revolutionaries. But, he concluded, the nation need not fear. "I may say to the Communists that my nerves have not yet collapsed, and I feel myself strong enough to give the knockout blow to their criminal plans!"

While his explanation was widely accepted in Germany, the outside world was not so gullible. "The assertion that German Communists had any association with the fire is simply a piece of stupidity," stated the London *News Chronicle* and this view was generally shared in diplomatic and foreign press circles. There was a growing feeling that it was the Nazis themselves who had burned the Reichstag as a pretext for crushing the Communists.

3

The short-term advantages of the fire did work to the Führer's advantage. Coming so close to the elections, it played on the fears of revolution shared by most Germans. Few objected when squads of Brownshirts ripped down the Red election posters and replaced them with their own. Hitler did not make the political mistake of outlawing the Communist Party but decided to wait until after the elections lest the working-class vote swing over to the Social Democrats. Göring was blunt: "Fellow Germans, my measures will not be crippled by any judicial thinking," he told a Frankfurt audience on March 3, just two days before the elections. "My measures will not be crippled by any bureaucracy. I won't have to worry about justice, my mission is only to destroy and exterminate. This struggle will be a struggle against chaos, and I shall not conduct it with police power. A bourgeois state might have done that. Certainly I shall use the power of the state and the police to the utmost, my dear Communists, so don't draw any false conclusions; but I shall lead the Brownshirts in this struggle to the death and my claws will grasp your necks!"

It was a confession that brute force would be applied outside the law, and it could have been made only in the charged atmosphere of the Reichstag fire. Fortunately for the Nazis, the Papens, Hindenburgs and industrialists were not at all concerned by alarming words and gave substantial, if occasionally tacit, support to the Hitler campaign.

The industrialists were so sure of their ability to handle Hitler that some twenty-five of them had decided at a recent meeting to underwrite the election financially. After Krupp von Bohlen expressed the unanimous feeling of the industrialists in support of Hitler, Göring made an appeal for funds: "The sacrifice we ask is easier to bear if you realize that the elections will certainly be the last for the next ten years, probably for the next hundred years." This threat of an end to democratic procedures was taken as a promise by banker Schacht, who said: "And now, gentlemen, cash on the counter." The industrialists conferred in whispers. The elder Krupp pledged 1,000,000 marks (about $250,000) for the Ruhr combine and the representative of I. G. Farben promised 400,000 marks. Other contributions brought the total up to 3,000,000.

With all this money at their disposal, the National Socialists and their two coalition partners were able to blanket the nation with publicity. All major party speeches were broadcast and, to those without radios, loudspeakers on streets and squares blared out the promises and threats of the new government. Hitler made frequent use of Hindenburg's name as proof of his own legitimacy. Months earlier the same speakers had pictured the old man as a senile fool; now he was transformed into a heroic figure of towering strength.

In his speeches Hitler criticized opponents for having no program yet presented none of his own. All he wanted was four years in office to prove himself. Election eve was turned into a semi-holiday by Goebbels, who labeled it "Day of the Awakening Nation." It seemed that almost everyone was for Hitler. He was the hope of the young idealists and carried the same banner as the patriots. Those who feared a Moscow-inspired revolution saw only two alternatives, a Red or Brown Germany, and the latter seemed more palatable.

Despite outer appearances and the vast amounts of money

and energy expended on the campaign, the National Socialists received only 43.9 per cent of the votes, and it took those of his nationalist allies to give him a bare majority in the parliament. Narrow as was the margin of victory, it was enough for Hitler to claim a clear mandate from the people and resume his attempt to take control of those states not under his rule.

Many foreigners erroneously believed that Hitler had already consolidated control throughout Germany. Consummate politician that he was, he was assuming power gradually and with the people's consent. "Authority," he remarked to Frank, "is only a springboard, a step to the next step," consequently conciliation with all levels of German society was his present byword. Out of respect for both the Hohenzollerns and Hindenburg, he selected the Potsdam garrison church for the opening of the new Reichstag on March 21. The ancient town, founded by Frederick Wilhelm I and containing the grave of Frederick the Great, was also steeped in Prussian military tradition. It was gaily decorated with swastika banners and the black-white-red flags of the former empire. Guns boomed. Army, Stahlhelm and SA troops formed ranks. Bells pealed out as the official motor caravan headed down the road to the little church in the bright spring sunlight.

Once the towering form of Hindenburg appeared in the field-gray uniform of a Prussian field marshal, the audience rose. Leaning with one hand on his cane and carrying his field marshal's baton in the other, he advanced slowly with dignity. At the imperial gallery he turned, raised his baton and saluted the empty seat of the Kaiser and the royalty lined up behind it. The marshal completely dominated the much smaller man beside him. Ill at ease in his cutaway, Hitler looked to French Ambassador André François-Poncet "like a timid newcomer being introduced by an important protector into a company to which he does not belong."

The two sat down facing each other. Then Hindenburg took out a pair of tortoise-shell glasses and began to read his speech. The tasks facing the new government, he said, were varied and difficult and he called for a revival of the disciplined and patriotic spirit of old Prussia.

Hitler's speech was directed to those in the crowded church rather than to the people at home listening to their radios. The war had been forced on the Kaiser and Germany, he said and summarized the legacy of economic depression and unemployment he had inherited. After outlining a program for the future he turned to Hindenburg as if he were still his commander and paid him extravagant homage as military and civilian leader. "We consider it a blessing to have your consent to the work of the German rising."

Hitler walked to Hindenburg's chair, bent low to grasp his hand. The old man, visibly moved, slowly descended into the crypt of Frederick the Great and Frederick Wilhelm I, followed by his son and an adjutant who laid wreaths on the two tombs, to the well-timed accompaniment of cannon salutes.

The ceremony, stage-managed by Goebbels, made its expected impression. All those present—the military, the Junkers and the monarchists—were convinced Hitler was subservient to Hindenburg and would follow the Prussian ideal. But two days later Hitler made it clear to any objective observer that he was subservient to no man. The setting was different—Berlin's Kroll Opera House, temporary site of the Reichstag—and so was the atmosphere: SA and SS men patrolled the corridors and behind the stage hung a huge swastika flag as a reminder of who was going to be master of Germany. At 2:05 P.M. President Göring opened the session. After a brief speech, including recitation of the song "Germany, Awake!," he turned over the floor to Hitler, who had entered in the simple uniform of a Brownshirt.

There was a momentary silence, followed by a single shout of "Sieg Heil! Sieg Heil!" This set off wild applause as the Führer strode up to the podium through a forest of raised arms. It was his first appearance before parliament and he began reading off a speech that was remarkable for its prudence and moderation. He vowed to respect private property and individual initiative; promised aid to peasants and middle class alike. He would end unemployment and promote peace with France, Britain and even the Soviet Union. But to do all this he needed enactment of the Law for Alleviating the Distress of People and Reich. This so-called enabling act gave him overriding if temporary authority in the land but he made it sound moderate and promised to use its emergency powers "only in so far as they are essential for carrying out vitally necessary measures."

After giving reassurance to parliament, President, the states and the Church that none of their rights would be infringed, Hitler concluded on a firm note that should have canceled out

Birth certificate of Adolfus Hitler. HOFFMANN

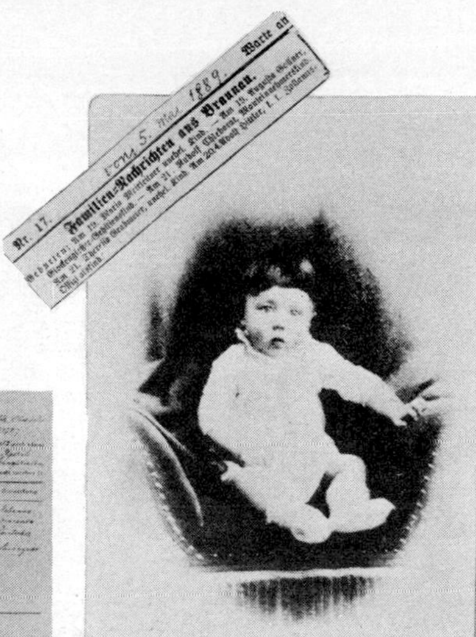

Baby Adolf. BUNDESARCHIV

Hitler's mother. LIBRARY OF CONGRESS

Hitler's father. LIBRARY OF CONGRESS

Alois Hitler with son Alois, Jr.
HANS HITLER

Angela (Hitler) Raubal and son Leo. HANS HITLER

Angela, Hitler's half sister, and Alois, his half brother, with Granny. HANS HITLER

Top picture, choir school at Lambach monastery about 1899, Hitler top row, second from right. HARRY SCHULZE-WILDE

Above, Hitler, the leader of his class in a village school. Leonding, 1900. HARRY SCHULZE-WILDE

Right, Hitler, the failure in a city school. Linz, 1901. LIBRARY OF CONGRESS

Paula, Hitler's younger sister, studying family album about 1950. HANS HITLER

Alois Hitler, Jr., about 1950. HANS HITLER

Hitler's best boyhood friend, August Kubizek. HARRY SCHULZE-WILDE

Kubizek about 1960. His doctor is on the right. HARRY SCHULZE-WILDE

Above, Hitler at sixteen as sketched by F. Sturmberger, a schoolmate from Steyr who presently resides in Linz. LIBRARY OF CONGRESS

Below, Dr. Bloch, who treated Hitler's mother for cancer, in his office at Linz. This picture was taken in 1938 by order of Bormann for the Führer's "personal film cassette." The inscription read: "The Führer often sat on the chair beside the desk." BUNDESARCHIV

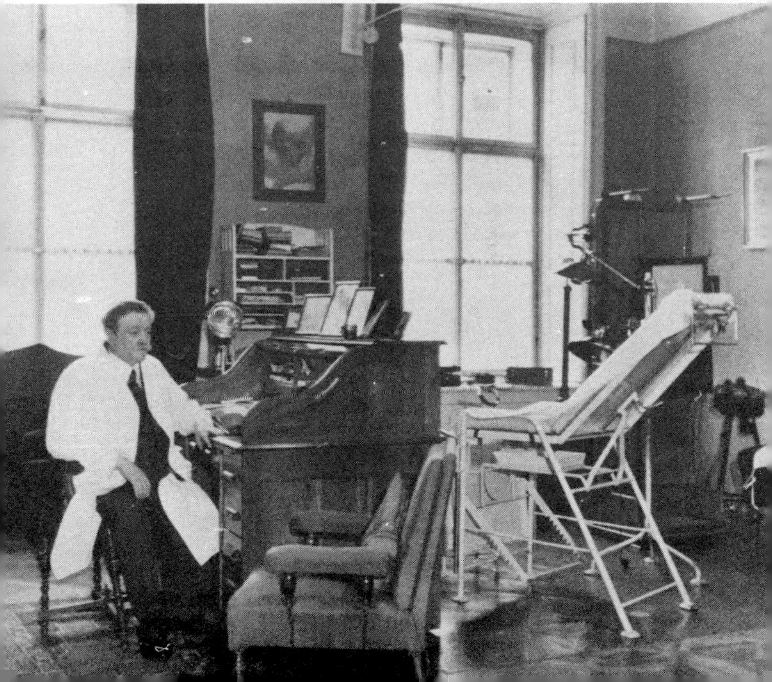

Water color of old Vienna by Hitler in 1911-12. U.S. ARMY

Auersberg Palace, Vienna, 1911-12. Architecturally accurate but the figures are far out of proportion. U.S. ARMY

Ruins of Becelaere, Belgium. 1917. U.S. ARMY

Above, Hitler, extreme left, in trenches. HOFFMANN

Below, l. to r., two World War I comrades—Ernst Schmidt and Sergeant Max Amann—with Hitler and his dog Fuchsl. HARRY SCHULZE-WILDE

Above, Hitler decorated with the Iron Cross. U.S. ARMY

Below, Dr. Edmund Forster, the first psychiatrist to treat Hitler, October–November 1918. FESTSCHRIFT ZUR 500-JAHRFEIER DER UNIVERSITAT GRIEFSWALD 17.10.1956, 11.411

"In the Beginning Was the Word," a painting by H. O. Hoyer. U.S. ARMY

Hitler making speech on the Marsfeld in Munich on January 28, 1933. IMPERIAL WAR MUSEUM

Sterneckerbräu in Munich where NSDAP was founded in 1920. HOFFMANN

Early picture of Hitler in full SA (Brownshirt) uniform. LIBRARY OF CONGRESS

Early party meeting at Hofbräuhaus in Munich. Gregor Strasser is at Hitler's right. To his left, Franz Xavier Schwarz, party treasurer, Max Amann, the party's publisher and the Führer's former sergeant; and Ulrich Graf, the bodyguard. STADTARCHIV, MUNICH

Leaving party meeting, circa 1922. IMPERIAL WAR MUSEUM

The Beer Hall Putsch, November 9, 1923. LIBRARY OF CONGRESS

The Beer Hall Putsch, November 9, 1923. STADTARCHIV, MUNICH

Julius Streicher addresses crowd in the Marienplatz, November 9, 1923. STADTARCHIV, MUNICH

Left, Hitler's cell at Landsberg prison. STADTARCHIV, MUNICH

Right, Hitler returns fifteen years later and tells Max Wünsche, his ordnance officer (who took picture), that his time in prison gave him the opportunity to write *Mein Kampf*. Over the cell door was a large plaque: "In this room lived Adolf Hitler from 11 November 1923 to 20 December 1924." MAX WÜNSCHE

Two previously unpublished letters. Left, Winifred Wagner encloses a book of poetry which she hopes will help Hitler over the long hours. "The poetry is to be interpreted in the frame of reference of Richard Wagner as a drama that can only be understood in connection with the music." EDWARD WHALEN

Below, Hitler's half sister Angela writes their brother about her visit to Adolf in prison and ends the myth that his family did not enthusiastically support his political career. "His spirit and soul were again at a high level. . . . The goal and victory is only a question of time. God grant it be soon." HANS HITLER

Common room of Nazi prisoners at Landsberg. Behind Hitler, Emil Maurice, early companion and chauffeur. To left, Colonel Hermann Kriebel, military leader of the Putsch. Ilse Pröhl, later Frau Hess, smuggled in the camera that took this and other prison pictures. LIBRARY OF CONGRESS

Hitler in prison with Maurice, Kriebel, Hess and Dr. Friedrich Weber of Bund Oberland. IMPERIAL WAR MUSEUM

Release from prison, 1924. LIBRARY OF CONGRESS

Hitler and two friends outside Haus Wachenfeld, the modest villa he bought on the Obersalzberg which grew into the Berghof.
HANS HITLER

Hitler confers with Captain Pfeffer von Salomon, head of the Brownshirts, prior to his replacement by Röhm in 1931. Alfred Rosenberg, who introduced "The Protocols of Zion" to the Führer, on right. LIBRARY OF CONGRESS

The depression. One-man demonstration in Berlin, August 1930.
BUNDESARCHIV

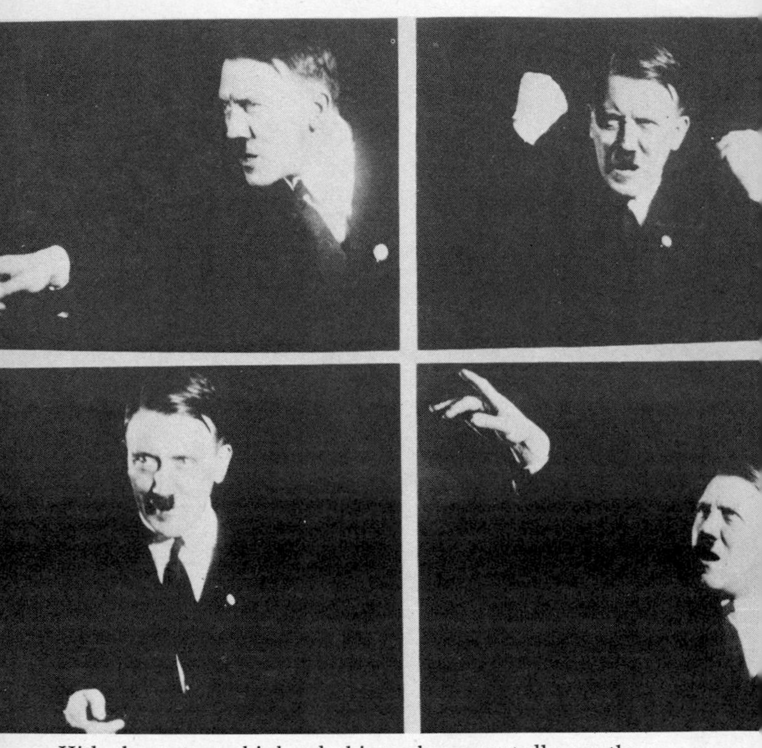

Hitler learns to use his hands; his teacher, reportedly, was the famous seer Hanussen. BUNDESARCHIV

Geli Raubal, the only true love of Hitler, commits suicide in his Munich apartment during the 1931 presidential campaign.
HANS HITLER

Geli with mother, left, and Paula Hitler. TOLAND COLLECTION

Hitler in February 1932, autographed to Egon Hanfstaengl.
EGON HANFSTAENGL

Tenant strike in Berlin. Reds join Nazis. BUNDESARCHIV

Chancellor Hitler with President von Hindenburg and his son Oskar. NATIONAL ARCHIVES

Hitler campaigns for electoral approval of his policies in 1933. Ernst Hanfstaengl, his foreign press officer, is at the extreme right, mostly obscured.
BUNDESARCHIV

Propaganda poster. The grandparents: "That we should live to see this!" The grandchildren: "When will I see the Führer?"
BUNDESARCHIV

Above, a Brownshirt points to the Führer's pistol shot in the ceiling. STADTARCHIV, MUNICH

Right, re-enactment of the march, November 9, 1933. Göring to Hitler's right. Dr. Schultze, who treated Hitler's injury in 1923, second row left. DR. SCHULTZE

Above, ceremony for those who died in the Putsch. Memorial designed by Troost. In row behind Hitler, extreme left, Göring and Keitel; extreme right, Dr. Schultze. DR. SCHULTZE

Left, Brownshirt Chief Ernst Röhm. SCHULZE-WILDE

Above, Party Day, Nuremberg, 1934. Dramatized by Leni Riefenstahl's documentary film, *Triumph of the Will.* NATIONAL ARCHIVES

Right, Leni Riefenstahl. LENI RIEFENSTAHL

"Heil Hitler!" Berlin. BIBLIO. FÜR ZEIT.

The Berghof. Hitler's official residence at Berchtesgaden. The famed picture window could be lowered into the floor. Erich Kempka, Hitler's chauffeur, took this and the following three candid photographs of a typical pilgrimage to the Obersalzberg in the first years of Hitler's regime. KEMPKA

Hitler greets admirer gallantly. The two colorfully dressed youths are apprentice carpenters from Hamburg. KEMPKA

Above, in center, Bormann, face partially covered, appears in most unofficial pictures and yet was almost unknown to the German public. KEMPKA

Right, "Mein Führer!" KEMPKA

The Führer laughs at his critics. His first foreign press secretary, Ernst Hanfstaengl (Harvard graduate and acquaintance of Roosevelt), was allowed to publish two books of anti-Hitler cartoons under the title *Facts vs. Ink*. Hanfstaengl, against Goebbels' violent protests, persuaded Hitler that this kind of propaganda would impress Westerners, particularly Americans. HANFSTAENGL

Right, Professor Gerdy Troost, widow of Hitler's favorite architect, objects to the exclusion of the best modern works at the first art exhibition in Munich's Haus der Kunst. One of the few who dared speak frankly to the Führer, she resigned moments later as judge. This is one of seventeen photographs in this book, most of them published for the first time, taken by Hitler's movie cameraman, Walter Frentz. He formerly worked for Leni Riefenstahl. FRENTZ

Below, March 1938. Hitler receives Reichstag ovation after announcing *Anschluss* of Austria. IMPERIAL WAR MUSEUM

these reassurances. If the Reichstag refused this "opportunity for friendly co-operation," the new regime was prepared to fight for its principles. "It is for you, gentlemen of the Reichstag, to decide between war and peace."

During the recess the foes of the measure mobilized and when the session was resumed the leader of the Social Democrats made a courageous if poorly delivered protest despite chanting in the corridors from the Brownshirts: "We want the bill—or fire and murder!" Hitler himself responded, even though Papen tried to restrain him, in a style reminiscent of the early beer-hall days in Munich, by attacking the Social Democrats with sarcasm and invective. "I do not want your votes. Germany will be free, but not through you. Do not mistake us for the bourgeoisie. The star of Germany is in the ascendant, yours is about to disappear, your death knell has sounded."

Hitler's assault not only crushed the futile revolt of the Social Democrats but intimidated the Center Party. The vote was taken and when Göring announced the results—far beyond the required two-thirds majority with 441 for the bill, 94 against—the National Socialists leaped to their feet cheering as if their team had scored a winning goal in the final seconds of play.

Democracy was expunged from the German parliament with scarcely a protest. Only the Social Democrats voted against the bill. The other parties handed over to Hitler powers that he privately vowed never to relinquish. And powers surrendered to a man who has use for them are seldom relinquished.

The victory in the Reichstag also brought into the open a number of industrialists who had secretly supported Hitler. The steel magnate Krupp openly heiled acquaintances on the street. He wrote Hitler a letter of congratulations stating that he and his colleagues were convinced that Germany at last had "the basis for a stable government." He was rewarded by being chosen as czar of German industry, thus sanctifying the marriage between big business and National Socialism. It was also no accident that Hitler chose Hjalmar Schacht as president of the Reichsbank. This brilliant financier had helped bring Hitler into industrial circles and shared his detestation of democracy and parliamentarianism.

4

A revolution was going on but since it was almost bloodless on the surface many Germans did not—or chose not to—realize it. This preliminary stage of the Brown Revolution was given an innocuous name, *Gleichschaltung* (co-ordination). It appeared to be an efficient process of unifying the nation and was received with little alarm. What it did was bring the political, economical and social life of the nation under the control of the NSDAP and plant the seeds of a faceless dictatorship. There was little resistance primarily because Hitler kept within the law. Consequently his opponents believed he wanted a government similar to the Weimar Republic. A set of instructions issued to Social Democratic locals on the day of the enabling law enactment illustrates that party's obtuseness. It was filled with advice on filling out questionnaires and other mundane matters and but one paragraph mentioned the Nazi revolution in progress. While their leaders were being searched at night for weapons, while thousands of Communists and suspected Communists were being jailed, the Social Democratic Party, which should have been the bulwark of democracy, was exhorting its followers to stop making bookkeeping errors.

"The whole city lay under an epidemic of discreet, infectious fear," Christopher Isherwood wrote of Berlin that spring. "I could feel it, like influenza, in my bones." The city was "full of whispers. They told of illegal midnight arrests, of prisoners tortured in the S.A. barracks, made to spit on Lenin's picture, swallow castor-oil, eat old socks. They were drowned by the loud, angry voice of the Government, contradicting through its thousand mouths."

A month after Hitler had failed to persuade a majority of the electorate to vote for him, he had won the temporary confidence of most Germans by his gradual process of co-ordination. Isherwood watched these solid citizens smile approvingly at the young storm troopers "in their big, swaggering boots who were going to upset the Treaty of Versailles. They were pleased because it would soon be summer, because Hitler had promised to protect the small tradesmen, because their newspapers told them that the good times were coming . . . And they thrilled with a furtive sensual pleasure, like schoolboys, because the Jews, their business rivals, and the Marxists, a vaguely defined minority of people who didn't concern them, had been satisfactorily found guilty of the defeat and the inflation, and were going to catch it."

Jews and Marxists had been systematically persecuted since the takeover. Albert Einstein's bank deposits were seized when a bread knife—categorically a lethal weapon—was found in his house. In Germany such stories were branded as foreign propaganda while in the United States Secretary of State Cordell Hull was assuring leaders of American Jewry that the physical mistreatment of German Jews had "virtually terminated." Even so the outcry of liberals from abroad increased to Hitler's annoyance and he announced that Jewish business in Germany would suffer until the Jews in England and America ceased their atrocity propaganda.

They did not and on April 1 Hitler instituted a boycott with these words: "I believe that I act today in unison with the Almighty Creator's intention: by fighting the Jews I do battle for the Lord." It was only a tentative step, almost as if Hitler were testing to see how far his countrymen would let him go.

Brownshirts were posted before the doors of most Jewish stores and offices. There was little violence and the young SA men were, for the most part, polite when reminding shoppers that they were about to patronize a Jewish business. "Little knots of passers-by collected to watch the performance—interested, amused or merely apathetic." In fact a good number went into the department store Isherwood was watching. He too entered, bought the first thing he saw, a nutmeg grater, and walked out twirling his parcel. This act of defiance was greeted by a wink from one of the young SA monitors. Although the boycotters got support from organizations which called upon farmers to support them, it was ineffective against the large department stores and banks and ended after three days.

Hindenburg himself protested further anti-Semitic measures and wrote the Chancellor a strong letter condemning discrimination against Jewish war veterans. "If they were worthy of fighting and bleeding for Germany, they must be considered worthy of continuing to serve the Fatherland in their profession." But the Old Gentleman was no match for a man whose secret goal in life was Jewish extinction. Hitler replied that the Jews, who monopolized up to eighty per cent of the professions of law and medicine, were now pushing their way into government posts. "One of the major reasons why the old Prussian state was such a clean one was that the Jews were granted only a very limited access to the civil service. The officer corps kept itself almost entirely pure." It was an argument that could not fail to impress the field marshal. This, coupled with a vague promise to give some consideration to Jewish veterans, was enough to permit enactment of decrees on April 7 removing all Jews from civil service posts and restricting the freedom of the legal profession. That same day Hitler told the Doctors' Union that he was aware of their present distress, especially among the young members, and in so doing subtly revealed his two-pronged Weltanschauung. "It is precisely for these young Germans that a Lebensraum and possibilities for the exercise of their profession must be created by a vigorous repression of an alien race. . . . This work of cleansing through racial hygiene now being undertaken will perhaps take centuries. The important thing is to lay a firm foundation today for future political development."

Many Jews did leave the country but others did not feel the anti-Semitic program was directed against them personally. For centuries the Jews had survived similar decrees by swimming with the current. What could happen to them in a nation that had produced Goethe and Beethoven? Besides, Hitler's real target was the Eastern Jew.

With all its outward appearance of success, the NSDAP was neither unified nor organized. It had come to power with a weak cadre structure and too many inept "old fighters" in key positions. The party grew rapidly and there were already more than a million and a half members with another million applications awaiting approval. But Hitler was not pleased to see the party become so unwieldy and ordered Schwarz to halt applications on the first of May.

This also marked the beginning of his attack on labor unions. He declared a Day of National Labor and treated it as a celebration of unity between workers and government. The main rally was held that evening at Tempelhof airfield where several hundred thousand workers and their leaders gathered to hear the Führer expound on the dignity of labor and the need for national unity. All lights were extinguished except those beating on the orator and the vast crowd listened in awed silence. He spoke in generalities but with such passion that when he finished the workers cheered as if he had promised them the world, and before they could emerge from the magic of his words they were singing the national hymn and the "Horst Wessel Lied." And as the last strains died down the sky exploded with fireworks.

The next morning the SA and SS, with the help of police, seized union offices throughout the nation. Labor leaders who had yesterday pledged allegiance to the government were arrested in their homes; union files and bank accounts were confiscated and labor newspapers shut down. Before nightfall organized labor in Germany was obliterated. But Hitler promised the workers they would be better off than ever in the new German Labor Front and their rights would be fully protected. There was no uprising, no organized protests, and by the end of the month the vast army of workers was marching obediently behind the swastika. They had changed from red to brown without breaking step.

5

In every German village and town the red and black swastika waved side by side with the black-white-red flags of the old Reich. Hitler's concept of revolution by absorption was working in a nation that wanted its uprisings orderly and legal. The Führer's storm troopers were now accepted almost as an arm of government; and nearly every important post was held by Nazis or someone controlled by the party. In the classroom and the church, the Brown Revolution was receiving commendation and blessing.

Hitler wanted no bloody uprising, no sweeping reforms to repel the average citizen or industrialist, and he laid down guidelines to his own Gauleiters. "To gain political power we had to conquer rapidly with a single blow; in the economic sphere other principles of development must determine our action. Here progress must be made step by step without any radical breaking up of the existing conditions which would endanger the foundations of our life." Such words deliberately courted physical defiance from his strongest supporters, the Brownshirts, who had waited long years to enjoy the fruits of the spoils system. But he carried off the extraordinary feat of dampening the revolution from below by the sheer force of his personality.

He proclaimed the end of the economic revolution and replaced the party's economic specialist with a representative of big business. Hitler's socialism was his own and subordinate to his secret aims. His concept of organized economy was close to genuine socialism but he would be a socialist only so long as it served the greater goal. He had the bohemian's rather than the revolutionary's disdain for private property and wanted only enough capital to rebuild the army and restore the economy so that he could lead Germany to its proper destiny. He was a Caesar rather than a Lenin, using socialism to get the masses moving. If he had believed they could have been propelled by capitalism it is likely he would have carried that banner. To Hitler, saving Germany justified any means.

It appeared as though he was creating a society of workers. To them he was the soldier-laborer, and they helped propagate this image. Thus millions of Germans humiliated by defeat in war and brought to the edge of economic disaster in peace readily identified with the warrior-worker hero. In ever increasing numbers Communists, whose leaders were in concentration camps, found a home in National Socialism. It was not at all difficult to accept Hitler's definition of the difference between socialism and Marxism: "German socialism is directed by Germans; international socialism is an instrument of the Jews."

By mid-1933 the majority of Germans supported Hitler. The bourgeoisie and the workers, the military and the civil service, the racists and some of the best brains in the country swelled the Nazi ranks. It has long been a political principle that power corrupts. It can also sanctify. Hitler the street ruffian a year earlier had been made respectable by the power of his office. Some Germans were seduced by expediency but more by a wave of idealism. Reform seemed to be sweeping the Reich. Moreover, the economy had taken a turn for the better, and the streets of the large cities were no longer filled with beggars.

An increasing number of intellectuals and artists paid homage, if in varying degrees, to the Führer. Spengler spent an hour and a half with him that July; they agreed about German policy toward France and shared the same disdain for the mediocre leadership in the Evangelical Church. On parting, Hitler assured the author that he "considered it of great importance for people outside the party to be won over to a German policy." Spengler agreed and left with a feeling that the Führer, while insignificant, was a "very decent fellow." Richard Strauss, scarcely Hitler's favorite composer, was even more forthcoming and announced that he was quite satisfied with the change in Germany and, when the Führer attended a new performance of *Der Rosenkavalier* in Berlin, was happy to be received in his box during the intermission.

The princes of the Church were more eager to curry his favor. "Hitler knows how to guide the ship," announced Monsignor Ludwig Kaas, leader of the recently outlawed Catholic Party after an audience with the Pope. "Even before he became Chancellor I met him frequently and was greatly impressed by his clear thinking, by his way of facing realities while upholding his ideals, which are noble. . . . It matters little who rules so long as order is maintained." Pius XI subscribed to the same principles, as was proved on July 20 when a concordat between the Vatican and Hitler was signed. The Church agreed to keep priests and religion out of politics while Hitler, among other things, granted complete freedom to confessional schools throughout the country, a notable victory for German Catholics.

The Vatican was so appreciative of being recognized as a full partner that it asked God to bless the Reich. On a more practical level, it ordered German bishops to swear allegiance to the National Socialist regime. The new oath concluded with these significant words: "In the performance of my spiritual office and in my solicitude for the welfare and the interest of the German Reich, I will endeavor to avoid all detrimental acts which might endanger it."

Late in July 1933 Hitler took time off to make another pilgrimage to Bayreuth. He laid wreaths on the graves of Richard and Cosima Wagner and their son Siegfried. He also attended the annual festival. It was the first time he had seen the Wagner family since becoming Chancellor and he wandered around the library at Wahnfried with undisguised satisfaction. "It was right here that you received me ten years ago," he told Winifred Wagner and then became dejected. "If the Putsch hadn't failed everything would have been different; I would have been the right age. Now I am too old. I have lost too much time and must work with double speed." The moment of depression passed as quickly as it had come and he predicted he would stay in power for twenty-two years. "Then I'll be able to retire, but first I must get more power into my hands so I won't have to bother with the cabinet. Just now they think they have a perfect right to meddle in things that are none of their business." During a vegetarian lunch he confided that once he had full power he would dissolve the monasteries and confiscate their property.

That summer Hitler spent much of his time at his mountain villa on the Obersalzberg. He invited the Hanfstaengls for a holiday at Haus Wachenfeld. Hanfstaengl was busy but sent Helene and Egon, who was twelve. Hitler offered them a ride from Munich and sat in the front seat with the chauffeur. At a lonely stretch of road near Rosenheim their car spluttered and came to a stop. In moments seven bodyguards, automatics in hand, surrounded the car. Kempka examined the motor as Hitler held a flashlight. "It's the old trouble again, my Führer," explained the chauffeur. "Some Reds must have dumped sugar lumps in the gas tank." Hitler warned the bodyguards to keep a sharp lookout, then watched with interest as Kempka unscrewed part of the mechanism, sucked and blew through it, spitting gas and sugar on the road.

Like any other proud householder, Hitler showed Helene and Egon through Haus Wachenfeld. His room on the first floor, which faced directly toward Salzburg, was modest, in keeping with the rest of the villa. "He had a small writing table, and a number of simple bookshelves," recalled Egon. "I especially looked to see what kind of literature the Führer had chosen for relaxation." Surprisingly, the majority of the books were the Wild West novels of Karl May, more suitable for Egon himself than a Chancellor.

The Hanfstaengls were the only house guests but other party members who were staying at nearby boardinghouses and inns would visit. "Göring was constantly around. He and Hitler used to walk on the narrow tile paths in the garden, talking confidentially. Round and round the same plot of grass. If you sat on the veranda in front of the house you could catch bits of conversation as they went by. Göring did most of the talking: 'I have just signed twenty death warrants. . . .' That's about the only utterance I remember for sure. Mother heard it too and both of us were surprised at this grim glimpse behind the scenes of glorious statecraft."

They all had meals together in the pleasant but modest dining room downstairs. Egon couldn't stand the Austrian cooking that was prepared by Angela Raubal, particularly string beans served in a sauce made of milk, flour and quantities of sugar, but he was fascinated by the free and easy table conversation. "They talked about music, and politics, and Chinese art—in fact, about anything. Hitler was rather gracious, for his standards. I mean he didn't make you remember all the time that he was the Führer. As a rule, Hitler never converses, he either listens, or—more commonly—preaches, making his utterances as though they were endowed with the authority of revealed religion. But here, in his '*Landhaus*' he frequently appeared wholly in the becoming guise of an ordinary host, an average man. He talked a lot about motorcars, engines, the size and performance of different ships, and technical things of that sort."

By this time it had become known that the Führer was at Haus Wachenfeld and tourists from all over Germany began congregating on the Obersalzberg. He stayed indoors to avoid being seen and one day the crowd called Egon over and asked whether Hitler was likely to appear. The twelve-year-old went to the Führer and said in stilted German: "Herr Hitler, a devoted multitude is eagerly awaiting your appearance at the gateway."

Hitler burst into laughter and followed Egon outside to greet his admirers. "They nearly swooned. After he went back in, they thanked me profusely, and one hysterical woman picked up some pebbles on which Hitler had stepped and put them in a little vial which she crushed ecstatically against her breast." Later, after another crowd had gathered, Egon collected a stack of postcards, photos and pieces of paper from the group, then wordlessly placed the stack in front of Hitler along with a pen. "My God, boy," he exclaimed with a smile, "you don't give up either, do you!"

By the time Hitler came down from his mountain and returned to Berlin he had decided to present a similarly affable face to the world. That August he allowed Egon's father to publish a book of anti-Hitler caricatures from German and foreign magazines and newspapers. Entitled *Fact vs. Ink*, the jacket showed a good-natured Führer laughing indulgently at his critics. Hanfstaengl cannily picked excellent cartoons, some satirical, some savage, covering the past ten years. In his foreword, prefaced by a quotation from Hitler's hero, Frederick the Great ("Pamphlets are to be hung lower"), Hanfstaengl explained that the book was an attempt to differentiate between the real and the fictional Adolf Hitler. This kind of propaganda appalled Goebbels but Hitler was swayed by Hanfstaengl's reasoning that British and Americans would be impressed. There was already a feeling among many foreign observers that Hitler was an object more of fun than fear.

With this good will Hitler set about revising his nation's foreign policy. It was dominated by his dual doctrines of race and space and, though he occasionally made a detour, he always returned to Germany's Lebensraum in the East. Hitler's hope was to inveigle England to join him as a silent partner in the crusade against Communism. To do that he must convince the English that the Reich had renounced world trade and global naval ambitions. Briefly, Germany would control the continent of Europe and be a bulwark against Communism while England ruled the seas. To further strengthen himself before launching his drive to the East, Hitler sought support from Italy, which was sympathetic to Nazi principles and shared a common hostility toward France because of Mussolini's ambitions in the Mediterranean.

The diplomats Hitler had inherited from the Weimar Republic came from a different class and abhorred his methods, but the majority agreed with most of his basic aims—for entirely different reasons—and persuaded themselves that they could use him and his brand of socialism for their own purposes. Hitler was as astute in his manipulation of the diplomatic service as he was with the industrialists and militarists. He allowed all the leading officials to remain at their posts, including one Jew and one married to a Jew. He also declared that the Reich desired to establish friendly relations with the Soviets so long as they did not intervene in German internal affairs. His campaign against home-grown Reds did not represent any hostility to Russia and to show his good faith he secretly allowed the Soviet Union to postpone payments on a long-term credit agreement negotiated before his takeover.

By the fall of 1933 Hitler felt the cautious international game had been played to the end. He decided to walk out on the League of Nations, which, among other things, had a confused policy toward rearmament. "We must make a break," he told Papen in a state approaching exaltation. "All other considerations are completely irrelevant." When Hindenburg questioned the wisdom of leaving the League, Hitler argued that it had to be done to affirm Germany's full equality. Against his better judgment, the Old Gentleman gave grudging consent.

On October 14 Hitler formally announced to the world by radio that Germany was withdrawing from the conference and the League. "To be written down as a member of such an institution possessing no such equality of rights is, for an honor-loving nation of sixty-five million folk and for a government which loves honor, an intolerable humiliation."

There was justification in this charge and, in a sense, his withdrawal from a body that discriminated against the losers was more of a symbolic rejection of the Treaty of Versailles than a challenge to the West. He went out of his way to reassure the French of his peaceful intents by including a hope for German-French reconciliation.

Hitler's shock tactic was a gamble—and yet, with its protestations of peace, a fairly safe one. The British predictably felt more sympathy than condemnation. Lord Allen of Hurtwood told the House of Lords: ". . . we are compelled to admit that we and other nations during the last fifteen years have not handed out to Germany that full measure of wise and fair play which the country merited when it threw out from its own land the regime which made the war."

Hitler characteristically faced the problem of gaining wide approval at home by announcing that he was submitting his decision to a plebiscite to take place by month's end. He campaigned as if for an election, utilizing the resources of the party to convince the people to back his withdrawal from the League of Nations. He appealed to all classes as if they were a unified group. "You cannot afford internal conflict in the fight to regain your position among nations," he told the workers at the Siemens plant. "If Germany does not wish to remain as an outcast, it must insist on equal rights, and that can only be accomplished if all Germans hold together as one man. Accept me as your Führer. I have shown that I can lead, and I do not belong to any class or group, only to you."

On election eve Hindenburg identified himself with Hitler, from whom he had accepted such liberal gratuities. "Tomorrow show your national honor and identify yourself with the Reich government," he advised the nation in a broadcast. "Speak up with me and the Chancellor for the principle of equality and for peace with honor and show to the world that we have restored German unity and with God's help shall preserve it."

It was an invocation that few patriots could resist. When the votes were counted the next day 95.1 per cent approved

Hitler's foreign policy; and in the Reichstag election 92.2 per cent voted National Socialist, the only party on the ticket. Adolf Hitler had won his gamble on foreign policy while solidifying his position at home. His mandate was so overwhelming that he was able, within weeks, to pass a law unifying party and state. It stated that the NSDAP was to be "the representative of the German state idea and indissolubly linked to the state."

With the entire population of Germany incorporated into the new regime, Hitler's policy of Gleichschaltung was officially completed. While the Führer had gained considerable power by consent (and threat), he was not yet a true dictator since resistance was still possible from the military and even from the failing Hindenburg. Hitler had led Germany onto the road to dictatorship. They needed no whip to follow a Siegfried who was bringing them out of economic depression and wiping out the dishonor of Versailles.

This could not have been accomplished, of course, without repression. The concentration camp (a term borrowed from the British of Boer War days) had become an accepted part of the national scene and was as much a threat to those on the outside as punishment for those inside. Nor was there any serious protest in the press after confiscation of Marxist and Social Democratic newspapers and publishing houses. Editors and publishers were brought under control and the last vestiges of independence were obliterated with establishment of the Reich Press Chamber. Along with freedom of the press also went that of literature, radio, theater, music, films and fine arts.

By December of 1933 Germany stood on the threshold of totalitarianism, brought there more by the needs of the time and the wish to conform than by terror. Nor was the spirit of conventionality a matter of class. It existed among scientists as well as workers. "We wish thus to conform to the spirit of the total state and to co-operate loyally and honestly," the president of the German Mathematical Association told his colleagues. "Unconditionally and joyfully we place ourselves—as is a matter of course for every German—at the service of the National Socialist movement and behind its leader, our Chancellor Adolf Hitler."

And so came totalitarianism and conformity to every profession on every level of society. Although other nations and races were congratulating themselves that such compliance was peculiarly Germanic and the repressiveness of this regime was typically Teutonic, both were a result of the intolerable demands of economics, geography and the times. These Germans marching to the tune of National Socialism were not unique in their love of order and militarism, or in their cruelty and arrogance.

6

Hitler's promise to hold in check the SS and SA reassured France to a certain extent but their leaders could not be persuaded that Hitler's rearmament program was designed for defense alone. "The British were eager to get it all over with," recalled Ambassador François-Poncet. "They sent us note upon note urging us to state what guarantees seemed to us to strengthen security sufficiently to gain our consent to a relative rearmament of the Reich." The British themselves were privately concerned, particularly by the rapid growth of the German air force, but there was still considerable public sympathy for the plight of the new Reich, with many ridiculing the notion that Hitler was driving toward war. The French decision was to check German ambitions by setting up an anti-Nazi bloc in the East: Poland, the U.S.S.R. and Czechoslovakia would be the links in this security chain under the aegis of Mother France.

When France and the Soviet Union approached agreement that spring, Hitler understandably feared that this was the beginning of an encirclement of the Reich. To counter the proposed bloc, Hitler needed a strong ally. The best prospect was Italy, whose leader had shown little desire for such a union since 1924 when he refused to lend the Nazis a few million lire. It grated on Hitler to be a supplicant but pride gave way to necessity and he made another effort. Controlling his resentment, he wrote Mussolini, ". . . admiration for the historic efforts of Your Excellency is linked with the desire for cooperation in a spirit of true friendship for our two ideologically related nations which can contribute immeasurably to the tranquilization of Europe through suitable attention to identical interests."

Several weeks later Hitler's foreign press secretary and unofficial court jester, Hanfstaengl, also visited Mussolini and suggested that he meet the Führer. "You are both admirers of Wagner and that will give a common starting point," Hanfstaengl remembered saying. "Think what it would mean if you invited him to the Palazzo Vendramin in Venice where Richard Wagner died. He would gain the benefit of your long experience and obtain much-needed insight into the problems of Europe as seen from outside Germany." Mussolini was not averse to the idea and in his good time sent an invitation which, after a show of reluctance, was accepted.

The historic meeting was doomed from the start. According to Filippo Bojano, Italian press representative in Berlin, Mussolini was motivated primarily by curiosity to see the politician all Europe was talking about. "Hitler is simply a muddleheaded fool," he confided to Bojano. "His head is stuffed with philosophical and political tags that are utterly incoherent. I can't make out why he waited so long to take over power, and why he played the buffoon, with his ridiculous electoral contests, in order to take legal possession of the reins of power. Either he is a revolutionary or he is not. Fascist Italy would never have come into being without a march on Rome. We are dynamic, and Signor Hitler is just a prater."

This contemptuous attitude was so publicized that the Italian press turned out en masse, directors and all, "to see this strange freak, Hitler." When he stepped out of his Junkers at Lido airfield on June 14 he looked like a struggling saleman in his worn trench coat over a blue serge suit. He was met by a Duce wearing black shirt, jack boots and glittering gold braid, backed up by Italian troops in full dress. Mussolini flung his arm out in Roman salute so vigorously that correspondent H. R. Knickerbocker thought "he might lose his hand."

Hitler sidled forward uncertainly, his hand almost apologetically responding with a feeble Nazi salute. He was obviously embarrassed by the show Mussolini had staged and, after blinking in the sunlight, awkwardly descended the steps to shake hands with his *beau idéal*. "They were not over three yards from me," wrote Knickerbocker, "and I was fascinated to watch the expressions on their faces. Beneath the obligatory cordiality I found I could see an expression of amusement in Mussolini's eyes and of resentment in Hitler's." Nor did the Führer's embarrassment ease when his host led him down the line of troops. He acted like a schoolboy at his first formal party. He didn't know what to do with his new fedora. First he took it off to salute the Italian flag, then started to put it back on but stopped himself and clutched it in his right hand. Then as he walked alongside Mussolini, who was chatting away in his voluble but eccentric German, he kept shifting the hat from hand to hand as if it were a hot potato.

There was another bit of comedy when the flustered Hitler tried to get Mussolini to precede him in boarding the launch which was to carry them to Venice. But Mussolini, the perfect host, maneuvered himself behind the Führer and waved him down the gangplank as if he were shooing a chicken into a coop. At the hotel landing, Hitler leaped out and jogged forward with bent head. "Mussolini stepped forth superbly. He was aware of being the cynosure of all eyes. His glances flashed, his figure was upright; he was—histrionically—the Duce."

Once inside his suite, Hitler began loudly abusing his advisers for allowing him to arrive in civilian clothes when Mussolini was so effectively attired. He was so upset that the first conversation with his host, despite a glowing official report, was another disaster. Il Duce dominated the talk, which centered on Austria, speaking in a bravura German which was sometimes incomprehensible to Hitler, while Mussolini in turn misunderstood much of Hitler's Austrian German.

The next morning the two men reviewed a parade of Fascist troops in the Piazza San Marco. At one point two columns had an argument about right of way directly in front of the rostrum. Neither unit would give in and when both plunged straight ahead the musicians began caterwauling. Later Hitler asked his new personal adjutant, Lieutenant Fritz Wiedemann, what he thought of the military value of such troops. Wiedemann, adjutant of Hitler's regiment during the war, replied that fighting ability had nothing to do with parading. "This remark, however, made no impression at all on Hitler, especially since, at the very moment, he glanced out the window at an Italian warship and saw to his amazement an array of sailors' shirts and underwear flying from the masts instead of the usual fleet flags."

Only a fool or a master of comedy would have staged the concluding and most important meeting of the dictators at the Lido golf course. "I noticed," recalled Bojano, "that Hitler was speaking all the time in a very excited way, while Mussolini listened, silent and with a scowl on his face." During the two-hour talk Bojano rarely saw Il Duce open his mouth. "He was so bored by Hitler's drivel that that very evening, in the middle of the official reception, he decamped in a hurry, and left the lagoon, stating that he did not want to see anybody."

Hitler left Venice stung by the realization that he had been not only snubbed by Mussolini but outmaneuvered diplomatically. The Führer had agreed to the full recognition of the independence of Austria which he felt belonged within the Reich, while receiving in turn no definite promise of support on the disarmament question.

THE SECOND REVOLUTION— "ALL REVOLUTIONS DEVOUR THEIR OWN CHILDREN"

FEBRUARY–AUGUST 1934

1

Hitler's promise to reduce the number of storm troopers was sincere. For years the SA had shown an independence that troubled him and for months its commander, Captain Röhm, had been demanding a military role for his men. The army, naturally, opposed it.

Hitler knew that his best chance for survival was to back the military leaders since he could never achieve his ultimate aims without their full support, and so had announced: "The Reichswehr is the sole bearer of arms of the nation; the SA is responsible for the political education of the people." These words stirred up old resentments among the four million Brownshirts, who recalled the long struggle between the northern and southern factions of the party. While remaining loyal to Hitler as their spiritual leader, many felt he had betrayed the Brown Revolution and was selling out to the right. They regarded themselves as the symbol of party radicalism and were not at all satisfied with the reforms of the first year of power. For months Röhm had been calling for a Second Revolution that would bring them the social and material benefits they had fought for.

Hitler sympathized with the radicals but his head told him

that further revolution was not feasible until Germany had recovered from economic disaster and rebuilt her armed forces; and this could not be done without the full support of industry and the military. At the same time, in his continuing role as conciliator, he made Röhm minister without portfolio in his cabinet, promised to appoint him Minister of Defense and sent him a rare commendation on the first day of 1934, remarkable for its use throughout of the familiar second person singular. Hitler meant to praise Röhm while subtly warning him to leave the defense of the country to the military, but Röhm missed the point. Emboldened, he dispatched a memorandum to the Defense Ministry claiming that national security was a prerogative of the SA.

This brought the conflict to a head and General von Blomberg asked Hitler to make a definite ruling. It was thus with regret that the Führer invited SA and Reichswehr leaders to a conference in the marble-pillared lecture hall of the ministry on the last day of February 1934. In a "moving, gripping" speech Hitler urged both sides to compromise. The party, he said, had solved unemployment but within eight years an economic recession would ensue and the only remedy was creation of living space for the surplus population. This might necessitate short, decisive military action in the West and then in the East. But a civilian militia, as suggested by Röhm, would not be the "least bit suitable for national defense." The solution was a people's army, rigorously trained and equipped with the most modern weapons. The SA must confine itself to internal political matters.

At this point Hitler forced Blomberg and Röhm to sign an agreement in his presence. The SA was granted two paramilitary functions: certain units were to operate as a police force along the nation's borders; the premilitary training of youths age eighteen to twenty-one was to be undertaken by the SA while those from twenty-one to twenty-six not serving in the armed forces were to be trained in "SA sport," a code name for organized military training.

It was a blow to Röhm but afterward he invited everyone to a luncheon of reconciliation in his home, formerly a millionaire's mansion. "Hitler did not take part," recalled General von Weichs. "The food was good—the atmosphere frosty. At any rate it seemed as if peace was restored. One certainly believed that the authority of Hitler in the party was so great that his decision would remain binding on the SA."

Once the army men left, Röhm's true feelings, liberated perhaps by drink, exploded. "What that ridiculous corporal says means nothing to us," he told his followers. "I have not the slightest intention of keeping this agreement. Hitler is a traitor and at the very least must go on leave. . . . If we can't get there with him, we'll get there without him."

Secretly enemies of Röhm in the SS were already deeply involved in a plot to destroy him. At first it seemed curious that the prime mover was Reinhard Heydrich, head of the SD (*Sicherheitsdienst*, Security Service), and not the SS chief himself. For some time Himmler was reluctant to support the intrigue, perhaps out of fear that an open conflict with the SA would cause a fatal breach within the party. But he was tempted to forget this upon learning that Göring had also joined the conspirators. Göring was not only one of the Führer's closest associates but could give Himmler a post he coveted, chief of the Prussian Secret State Police Office *(Geheimes Staatspolizeiamt)*.* No sooner had Himmler allied himself with the cabal than he was made head of the Gestapo and he reciprocated by dropping hints to all the SS units that an open struggle with the Brownshirts was on the horizon. This seemed a certainty when Heydrich reported he had collected evidence that Röhm was plotting treason. The truth was that Röhm had not the slightest intention of launching a Putsch. He wanted only to force Hitler to give the SA its proper position in the Reich, by setting the Führer "in a golden cage" as it were, to isolate him from evil advisers. He was waging a war of nerves, not treason, but his threatening words were cause for alarm. On June 4 Hitler summoned Röhm to the chancellery and, according to the former's account, their conversation lasted almost five hours. It is probable that Röhm left at midnight with the impression that the Führer was sympathetic but under pressure from the military to curtail SA activities. It was also likely that Hitler himself imagined he had just made a genuine truce with Röhm since the SD was almost immediately informed that the Führer had come to agreement with the SA chief on several points.

*Some post office officials made up an abbreviated stamp for the new organization—Gestapa. Colloquial usage soon turned this into Gestapo, a name that would soon be a synonym for terrorism.

2

Discontent from an entirely different quarter descended on Hitler hours after his return from the humiliating visit with Mussolini in Venice. On June 17, a pleasant Sunday, Franz von Papen was preparing to make an address at the University of Marburg. There was considerable interest in what the Vice-Chancellor would say since he had delivered a controversial speech six months earlier at the Bremen Club warning of the growing unrest in Germany over the new regime's assaults on the principles of law and the restrictions placed on the Church. As Papen entered the great auditorium, which was packed with students, professors and a scattering of uniformed party members, there was an air of expectancy. He began with a direct attack on the controlled press in general and Goebbels in particular.

The audience was stunned by such words coming from the official who held the second highest position in the government but this was only the beginning. After criticizing Nazi bigots and doctrinaires along with the single-party system, he urged Hitler to break with those calling for Röhm's Second Revolution. "Have we gone through the anti-Marxist revolution in order to carry out the Marxist program? . . . No people can afford to indulge in a permanent revolt from below if it would endure in history. At some time the movement must come to a stop and a solid social structure arise."

The few shouts of protest from party members were drowned out in tumultuous applause. Only the *Frankfurter Zeitung* managed to print a few extracts from the speech in its afternoon edition. Goebbels ordered all copies of this paper impounded and forbade a scheduled replaying of the speech over the radio.

For the first few days Hitler made no public comment. It was Papen who forced the issue by threatening to resign unless Goebbels' ban on his speech was lifted. Hitler tried to calm his Vice-Chancellor. He admitted Goebbels had blundered, then berated the insubordination of the SA as if he approved that part of the speech. He promised to lift the ban and requested Papen to withhold his resignation until the two of them went to Neudeck to see Hindenburg.

Papen agreed to wait but Hitler broke his word. The next day, June 21, he hastily set out for Neudeck alone and without removing the ban on the speech. His announced purpose was to report to the President on the recent meeting with Mussolini, but it is more likely he wished to see the Old Gentleman without the inhibiting presence of Papen. He may also have wanted to check on Hindenburg's health and find out how much time he had left to make arrangements to be his successor. To accomplish this he would need the support of the military and it was significant that the first person he met on the steps of the Hindenburg estate was Defense Minister von Blomberg in full uniform despite the sweltering heat.

The President had his own reasons for seeing the Führer. He wanted to be enlightened on the turmoil caused by Papen's speech, but he left most of the talking to Blomberg, acting stiff and Prussian, who made it clear that internal peace was the first priority. If Hitler could not remove the present intolerable tension, he said, the President would declare martial law and turn over the job to the army. No mention was made of Röhm and the Second Revolution, nor was any necessary. The Old Gentleman, who had left Berlin in a wheel chair—purchased over his protest that it was too expensive—rallied himself and in a somewhat shaky voice reaffirmed Blomberg's words.

Sometime that night Hitler made up his mind to take action against Röhm. In the morning he phoned SA Obergruppenführer Viktor Lutze, who months earlier had warned him against Röhm, and instructed him to report to the chancellery at once. "He led me into his study," wrote Lutze in his diary, "and, taking me by the hand, swore me to secrecy until the whole matter was settled." The Führer revealed with some emotion that Röhm had to be removed because of a determination to arm the SA and set it against the army. "The Führer said that he had always known I would be no party to such matters. Henceforth I was to accept no orders from Munich and take instructions only from him."

In the meantime Heydrich and Himmler were doing their utmost to entrap Röhm and that same day the latter summoned one of his SS commanders, Freiherr von Eberstein, and told him that Röhm was plotting a Putsch. Eberstein was to pass the word on to the military district commanders and put his own troops on "unobtrusive alert," confining them to barracks for emergency action.

By now Hitler had become so convinced that Röhm was plotting an uprising that he told Defense Minister von Blomberg he was summoning all SA commanders to Bad Wiessee, a spa on the Tegernsee where Röhm was taking his rest cure. When they had assembled, continued Hitler, he would personally arrest them and "square accounts." The army was prepared for action.

Hitler traveled to Essen to attend the wedding of a local Gauleiter. No sooner had he arrived with Göring at the wedding breakfast than he was interrupted by a call from Himmler in Berlin, who read off a series of alarming reports. Göring nodded his head in confirmation as he learned of supposed SA machinations and Hitler became so wrought up that he returned at once to his local quarters. "Here in the hotel room," according to Lutze, who was one those hastily summoned, "the telephone was going almost uninterruptedly. The Führer was deep in thought but it was apparently clear that he would now have to take action."

He phoned Röhm in Bad Wiessee and complained about the alleged molesting of foreigners. This could not be tolerated, he said with some heat, and told Röhm he wanted to speak to the top SA leaders gathering at the Tegernsee two days later at 11 A.M.

The conversation either did not perturb Röhm or he pretended it didn't, for when he returned to the dinner table he seemed "very well pleased." He informed his guests, one of whom was General Franz Ritter von Epp, whose Free Corps unit helped overthrow Munich's soviet government in 1919, that Hitler was going to attend the congress of SA leaders on June 30, adding with relish that this would give him the opportunity to "tear the mask from Goebbels." He knew that he could count on his SA and the army. Such an unrealistic comment meant Röhm either was fantasizing or was unaware of the extent of the intrigues swirling around him.

A flood of new evidence—consisting of rumors, fake reports and doctored documents—was already being directed into army channels to convince the doubting Thomases that after the Putsch Röhm would execute or dismiss all senior army officers. Fictitious death lists were passed around from so many sources that they began to seem real.

Adolf Wagner, the Gauleiter of Bavaria, telephoned the Führer to report that rowdy Brownshirts were already in the streets of Munich shouting, "The Reichswehr is against us!" (Certain units had been alerted by a pamphlet of mysterious origin: "SA, take to the streets, the Führer is no longer for us!") Hitler's rage turned to panic. Here was proof positive that Röhm was mutinying. "It was at last clear to me," he later said, "that only one man could oppose and must oppose the Chief of Staff [Röhm]. It was to me that he had pledged his loyalty and broken that pledge, and for that I alone must call him to account."

He made a sudden decision, which caught his comrades by surprise: he was going to Bad Wiessee and personally face the "nest of traitors." He ordered his private plane to be prepared for take-off, then paced between terraces and hall pouring out his feelings. How could Röhm have done such a thing? How could he have betrayed his Führer?

3

It was a shaken Hitler who climbed into the three-motored Junkers 52, a replacement for the regular plane, which had engine trouble. It was about 2 A.M. He slumped into his seat, stared fixedly ahead into the darkness.

In the gray light preceding dawn Baur landed the plane on the drenched runway at Oberwiesenfeld, the military exercise field where Hitler had had his first humiliating confrontation with police and army twelve years earlier. The airport director was distressed. He had been instructed by Chief of Staff Röhm to alert the entire SA leadership as soon as the Führer's plane, D-2600, approached. But with the last-minute change in aircraft there was only a small group—party personages and several army officers—on hand to greet Hitler. "This is the blackest day in my life," he told them. "But I shall go to Bad Wiessee and pass severe judgment."

Hitler was driven to the Bavarian Ministry of the Interior where he leaped out of the car, followed by a rattled Gauleiter Wagner, who was also Minister of Interior. The Führer strode into the building, the skirt of his leather coat flying, and up the stairs toward Wagner's office. As he burst into the anteroom the head of the Upper Bavarian SA started to salute but Hitler rushed at him, shouting, "Lock him up!" He began cursing all traitors in general and the SA leaders whose men had been lured to the streets of Munich by pamphlets in particular. "You," he yelled, "are under arrest and will be shot!"

It was 6 A.M. when the Führer, still in "a terrifying state of excitement," emerged from the building. A second plane with armed reinforcements had not yet landed but he was too impatient to wait. He got into Kempka's car, taking his usual place beside the chauffeur, and instructed him to head for Bad Wiessee. They started off, followed by another car driven by Schreck. In the entire party there were only eight or nine men and the Führer's secretary, Fräulein Schröder. From the back seat Goebbels talked incessantly of the Brownshirt plot but Hitler only stared ahead. The sun was just breaking through clouds on the horizon. It was going to be "Hitler weather."

In less than an hour they reached the Tegernsee, nestling at the gateway to the Alps, its pure waters steaming with early morning mist. "We are now going to the Pension Hanselbauer," Hitler told Kempka. There was "some dirty work afoot" and they had to surprise the Hanselbauer's occupants. It was almost seven and church bells were calling the faithful to early morning mass when Kempka slowly, cautiously pulled up at the pension. Kempka noticed that some of the windows were closed, others open, there was no guard at the door. Hitler was first to enter. The ground floor appeared to be deserted; there was no one in the dining room, which was set for the midday banquet. Then the landlady appeared, understandably shocked to find herself face to face with the Führer. She started to express the honor she felt but he brusquely asked to be taken up to Röhm.

While the others in the party took positions in front of other rooms, a plainclothes detective knocked on Röhm's door. Then Hitler, revolver in hand, went in. Kempka, peering from behind his Führer, glimpsed a sleep-drugged Röhm blinking with genuine amazement and shock. He was in bed alone.

"Ernst," said Hitler, and then used the familiar *Du*, "you are under arrest." There was none of the fury Hitler had shown at the Ministry of Interior. He was "somewhat tense but not visibly excited." Briefly and curtly he accused Röhm of being a traitor and told him to get dressed. Protesting vigorously, the SA chief began pulling on civilian clothes but Hitler had already gone and Röhm's words were wasted on the detectives left behind.

The Führer was banging at the opposite door. It opened and an Obergruppenführer named Heines stared out drowsily. Behind him stood his bed partner—an attractive young man who doubled as his chauffeur. "A disgusting scene, which made me feel like vomiting," wrote Goebbels.

While Hitler was discussing what should be done next, Kempka was sent to a nearby pension to apprehend Max Vogel, Röhm's cousin, who also served as his chauffeur. Vogel was in bed with a girl—the only such case that morning. Kempka, a good friend of his fellow chauffeur, apologetically announced he was under arrest. As they went to the garage for the Röhm car, Vogel made a curious last request: could he drive it just once more? Kempka understood and let him make a few slow turns in the driveway as he himself stood on the running board.

Just as Kempka and his prisoner got back to the Hanselbauer a truck filled with about forty armed Brownshirts of Röhm's "Headquarters Guard" arrived from Munich. Their commander had been locked up in the laundry and they were unhappy about it. One of Hitler's adjutants, Wilhelm Brückner, shouted an order to return to Munich at once. They did nothing except stare back sullenly, and a pitched battle seemed likely.

Then Hitler strode forward. "Didn't you hear what Brückner said?" In a tone of command that managed to be charming, he ordered the guardsmen to return to Munich. "On the way you will meet SS troops and they will disarm you." His manner more than his words took all the fight out of them and the truck drove off.

The prisoners were loaded into two commandeered buses and the caravan started off. Hitler's Mercedes led the way and SA men bound for the lunch banquet at the Hanselbauer would be stopped and interrogated by Hitler. Those whose names appeared on a list hastily drawn up by Goebbels were disarmed and instructed to sandwich their own cars in the cavalcade.

It was about 9:30 A.M. by the time the growing procession reached the Brown House. It had been cordoned off by army troops and Hitler took time to thank them for coming to his aid and give assurances that he had never intended using them against the SA. Once inside party headquarters, Hitler told Goebbels to telephone the code word to Göring. The purge was on. "I gave the order to shoot those who were the ringleaders in this treason and I further gave the order to *burn out down to the raw flesh the ulcers of this poisoning of the wells* in our domestic life and of the poisoning of the outside." The use of words dredging up memories of his mother's cancer and Dr. Bloch revealed the depth of his emotional upheaval.

The cells of Stadelheim were already filled with SA leaders put there by the SS. Those still in the Brown House, such as Röhm, demanded to see the Führer and when he refused asked for Goebbels. He was too occupied with the phone conversation with Göring and, before he finished, the last prisoners were on their way to Stadelheim in an armored car. Their leader was put in a solitary cell, not far from the one he had occupied after the Beer Hall Putsch.

At 11:30 A.M., a conference of SA leaders began in the spacious council chamber. Hitler had not yet regained his composure and his address to his apprehensive audience was a series of disconnected complaints about the SA. Throughout the hour-long tirade Hitler's listeners stood in discomfort. One was fascinated by the foam that kept spewing from his mouth. "In a voice frequently choked with emotion," he accused Röhm of planning to kill him in order to hand Germany over to her enemies. Röhm and his conspirators, he promised, would be shot.

The killings had not yet started since Hitler was waiting for Sepp Dietrich, commander of the elite Leibstandarte, to do the job. He appeared shortly and explained to the exasperated Führer what had kept him so long: his trucks, for one reason, could not travel fast over wet roads on worn tires. For all his show of annoyance at the delay, Hitler had no orders to give. He told Dietrich to wait while he and his advisers argued the fate of the accused. Three hours passed without a decision.

While the Führer vacillated, his associates in Berlin were already carrying out executions. Hitler had given Göring power to deal with the insurgents in the capital. Papen protested on the grounds that he was the Chancellor's deputy and in his absence such authority could be granted only to him. He insisted that Hindenburg declare a state of emergency and bring in the Reichswehr to restore law and order. Göring refused. He and Himmler's SS had complete control of the situation. He cut short Papen's protests and ordered the Vice-Chancellor to return home immediately for his own safety. Before Papen got there police cars were careening through the streets of Berlin rounding up enemies of the regime. One unit surrounded Papen's office, shot to death his press officer and arrested other members of his staff. The Vice-Chancellor might as well have been incarcerated; for as soon as he entered his own house it became a prison. Papen found his telephone wire cut and a police captain in the reception room who informed him that he was to have no contact with the outside world.

In Munich, Hitler still hesitated about passing final judgment on Röhm and his colleagues. The discussion in the meeting room grew so loud that Sepp Dietrich, waiting in the outer office, could hear voices through the double doors of the meeting room. At last this portal opened about 5 P.M. and Martin Bormann, Hess's assistant, emerged. He escorted Dietrich back to Hitler. "Return to the barracks," instructed the Führer, and gave an order that Dietrich felt was wrung out of him: "Select an officer and six men and have the SA leaders shot for treason."

Dietrich examined a list handed over by Bormann. It contained the names of all those taken to Stadelheim but Hitler had checked off only a dozen. They included Heines and the chief of the Upper Bavarian SA—but not Ernst Röhm. Hitler could still not bring himself to make that decision.

When Hans Frank, the Bavarian Minister of Justice, learned that many SA leaders were jailed at Stadelheim he decided to go there in person and take charge. Upon arrival, he ordered the SA prisoners placed in the custody of a detachment of state police, then had himself admitted to Röhm's little cell.

"What does it all mean?" asked Röhm. "What is going on?"

Frank could give little information or assurance. He hoped that everything would proceed legally. Röhm replied that he was prepared for the worst. "I am not concerned about my own life but please take care of my relatives, they are women totally dependent on me." As Frank opened the cell door Röhm pressed his hand. "All revolutions," he said, "devour their own children."

No sooner had Frank returned to his own office than Sepp Dietrich entered with a colleague to announce that he had orders to shoot a number of SA leaders. He produced a list checked personally by Hitler. Stunned, Frank said the executions could not take place under any circumstances. Dietrich insisted that the Führer himself had ordered it but was persuaded to telephone the Brown House. First he talked to Hess. After a pause Dietrich extended the receiver to Frank. "Hitler wants to speak with you."

Hitler began shouting: "You refuse to carry out an order from me? Are you in sympathy with that criminal scum? I'm going to destroy those boys, roots and all!"

Frank protested that there was no written authorization, just a list of six names. "I marked that list myself," said Hitler in more controlled language. "These gentlemen are criminals against the Reich. I am the Reich Chancellor. It is a matter of the Reich, which is never under your jurisdiction."

* * *

At Stadelheim the first six victims were led out into the courtyard, each guarded by two policemen. "The Führer and Reich Chancellor has condemned you to death," an SS officer droned out. "The sentence will be carried out forthwith." When the head of the Upper Bavarian Brownshirts, August Schneidhuber, realized the chief executioner was Dietrich, he cried out: "Sepp, my friend, what on earth's happening? We are completely innocent!" With set face Dietrich clicked his heels. "You have been condemned to death by the Führer," he said. "Heil Hitler!"

The first man was placed before the firing squad. He refused to have his eyes covered. Shots reverberated in the courtyard walls. The next victim and the next also disdained blindfolds. Dietrich witnessed the first few shootings but before it was Schneidhuber's turn he had to walk off. "I had had enough."

For the average Berliner there was little on the surface to indicate that the nation was undergoing an upheaval. True, sinister rumors were beginning to circulate and there were traffic tie-ups on the Charlottenburger Chaussee, what with police barriers and the stream of army trucks. It was also known that house arrests were taking place but the violence was under cover. Few citizens knew that General von Schleicher and his wife had been murdered or that Gregor Strasser had been seized at his lunch table and put into Cell 16 of the Gestapo prison. There he was peppered with shots by unseen assailants from the cell window while he dodged around like a rat in a cage until wounded. Then one of the gunmen entered to finish the job. Thus the enemy of Goebbels and Göring perished, still faithful in his own fashion to the Führer.

The ringmaster of the purge in Berlin was Göring, who briefed foreign correspondents in the Ministry of Propaganda late that afternoon. "Göring arrived in one of his full-dress uniforms," wrote a Gestapo official. "Once again he did not walk; he strutted up to the platform with slow, mincing steps. He began the session with a long, impressive pause, leaning forward slightly, his chin propped in his hand, and rolling his eyes as if he feared his own revelations." When he mentioned Schleicher in connection with the Röhm-Strasser plot, someone asked what had happened to the former Chancellor. "He was foolish enough to resist," said Göring with what one chronicler described as a wolfish smile. "He is dead."

By evening the death toll was appalling. General von Bredow, a friend of Schleicher, was gunned down at his front door. The acting police president of Breslau was disemboweled by a shotgun and an SS cavalry leader murdered in his own smoking room. The ghost writer of the recent controversial Papen speech lay lifeless in an underground cell of the Gestapo prison in the Prinz Albrechtstrasse. Other executions were taking place, under the supervision of the SS, at the Lichterfeld Barracks. Here died an official of the Ministry of Transport, the president of Catholic Action as well as Karl Ernst, head of the Berlin storm troopers, who had been brought back from his honeymoon. His last words were: "Heil Hitler!"

The Brownshirts were in a state of confusion. Some units were alerted, issued revolvers and ordered to catch traitors—only to be rounded up themselves by SS troops and carted off for detention. Others were beaten up in the streets by roving Himmler men and some shot out of hand. Still others were marked for arrest or death but spared by friends in the SS. For thousands, who felt they had sacrificed everything for the party, it was a night of terror and disillusionment.

4

President von Hindenburg took the executions calmly. His first reaction was a cranky "I told you so" to Meissner. "For months I have been telling the Chancellor to lock up this immoral and dangerous Röhm; unfortunately he did not listen to me; now see how much blood has been spilled!"

The next morning, the first of July, those who were privileged to see the Führer knew that he was going through one of the most traumatic crises of his turbulent career. It reached a climax that afternoon when he finally was forced to approve the execution of Röhm. Even Hitler's sentence of death was marked by affection. He instructed Brigadeführer Theodor Eicke to give Röhm the chance to commit suicide.

It was still light by the time Eicke and two subordinates arrived at Stadelheim with Hitler's verbal order. At first the prison governor refused to hand over the prisoner without something in writing but he wilted under Eicke's shouts and ordered a warder to escort the three SS men to Cell 474 in the new prison block. There slumped Röhm on an iron cot, bare to the waist and sweating heavily in the sweltering heat.

"You have forfeited your life," said Eicke. "The Führer

gives you one more chance to draw the right conclusions." He placed a pistol loaded with a single bullet on a table, then left the cell. Eicke waited in the passage for almost fifteen minutes, then he and his deputies drew their own revolvers and pushed back into the cell. "Chief of Staff, prepare yourself!" shouted Eicke. And, when he saw his deputy's gun quivering, said, "Aim slowly and calmly." Two shots reverberated deafeningly in the little cell. Röhm collapsed. "My Führer!" he gasped. "My Führer!"

Throughout the Reich that hot Monday the average German was congratulating himself with grim satisfaction that the roughneck Brownshirts were at last under control. "No one loved Röhm and his parvenu officers," recalled correspondent Delmer, "the ex-waiters, ex-hotel porters and ex-plumbers, who had been bossing the common people more arrogantly than any Prussian Guards Officers in the days of the Kaiser. They and their brand-new, elegant motorcars, roaring ruthlessly about the streets, were feared and hated by the German little man." By eliminating these ruffians Hitler had become his hero.

Hindenburg was having second thoughts. The brutal murder of General von Schleicher and his wife upset him deeply enough to demand an investigation. He simply could not accept the official version that the couple had been shot resisting arrest. At the same time he was incapable of putting his indignation into effect and he dutifully signed a congratulatory telegram to Hitler drafted by the Nazis. It read:

> FROM THE REPORTS PLACED BEFORE ME, I LEARN THAT YOU BY YOUR DETERMINED ACTION AND GALLANT PERSONAL INTERVENTION, HAVE NIPPED TREASON IN THE BUD. YOU HAVE SAVED THE GERMAN NATION FROM SERIOUS DANGER. FOR THIS I EXPRESS TO YOU MY MOST PROFOUND THANKS AND SINCERE APPRECIATION.

With this certificate of support, Hitler now had the uneasy sanction of almost the entire nation.

5

Approval of the purge did not extend beyond Germany's borders and scathing articles and editorials flourished abroad. Much as he flinched from foreign attack, Hitler's primary concern was a faint but growing suspicion among his own people that they might have been deceived.

Tiny as was this seed of doubt, it aggravated Hitler's own distressed state of mind. Genuinely shaken by the liquidation of old friends and comrades, he hid from the public. Privately he commissioned Hess, now his closest friend and associate, to embark on a number of missions of mercy (occasioned by remorse) to widows and relatives of the victims.

Hitler also attempted to make amends to Papen, inviting him to attend an emergency session of the cabinet on July 3 just as if he had never been held in custody. All affability, Hitler invited the Vice-Chancellor to take his usual place at the table. Nettled, Papen said that was out of the question and demanded to see Hitler alone. The two moved into the next room where Papen told about his own house arrest and the murder of his press officer. He requested an immediate judicial inquiry into the matter, then insisted that his resignation be announced immediately. Hitler's polite refusal sent Papen directly to the Bendlerstrasse to see his old friend General von Fritsch. The army commander-in-chief stared as if facing a ghost. "As you can see, I am alive," said Papen. "But this *Schweinerei* has got to be stopped." Why, he asked, hadn't Fritsch prevented the purge in the first place? The army chief sheepishly explained that it had been impossible to act "without explicit orders from Blomberg or Hindenburg." The former had "rigidly opposed any intervention" and the latter could not be reached.

Not a single member of the cabinet protested (including the Minister of Justice, a number of whose right-wing friends had perished), and this group then proceeded to do what it had been brought together to do: promulgate a law legalizing the "measures taken on June 30 and on July 1 and 2" as an "emergency defense of the state."

Papen was not the only official who wanted to resign. Bavarian Minister of Justice Frank also offered to step down. "Does one desert a ship in the middle of the ocean?" said Hitler caustically. "I have quarrels with many but I must hold everything together. We are a troop in battle." Justice and revolution, he argued, were incompatible. "Don't forget that every revolution has its victims!" Hitler could understand Frank's feelings of revulsion at the purge but nothing could be done about that now. "I have too many deadly enemies. Everything now hinges on my authority." When Frank protested that the police were assuming too much power and that too many party members were taking the law into their own hands, Hitler replied: "Justice and jurists serve the community best when they leave all political necessities to other organs."

He even had an answer for the growing number of concentration camps. "If I had a spacious Siberia at my disposal as Moscow has, then I wouldn't need any concentration camps. . . . Who in the world talks about the millions of victims of Bolshevism? The Jewish press of the world pursues me because I am an anti-Semite. Herr Stalin is their darling." Frank tore up his resignation.

Papen was not so easy to bring around. He insisted on getting the remains of his press officer—ashes in an urn—and arranging a proper burial at Schönberg cemetery despite warnings from Himmler against provoking any public demonstration. Papen not only delivered a moving oration at the funeral but kept bombarding the Führer with letters protesting against the continued imprisonment of four of his subordinates and pressing for a public inquiry into his press officer's death. A model of patience himself for a change, Hitler urged Papen to be patient. A special meeting of the Reichstag to explain the purge fully was to be held in forty-eight hours. At the time he, as Führer, would take full responsibility for everything that had happened, including those unfortunate events committed "in an excess of zeal."

At 8 P.M. on July 13 at the Kroll Opera House a grim-faced Führer stepped to the podium clutching the lectern as if for balance. Extending an arm in stiff salute, he began speaking in a voice harsher than usual, as if giving assurance that he was once more in control of events. He gave a lengthy, emotional account of the purge which, he explained, was necessitated by the treasonous actions of various groups which he described as "destructive elements" and "pathological enemies of the state." He could have been describing himself in earlier days—as well as his present role in world politics. With the skill of a born storyteller he gave his version of the events leading up to the dramatic decision to put down the rebellion in person. Except for the foreign observers, almost everyone in the opera house was spellbound by his performance, and throughout Germany enthralled crowds clustered around radios.

The hand-picked audience rose as one to applaud enthusiastically. Almost as an anticlimax, the main purpose of the meeting was promptly accomplished: the Reichstag unanimously approved the bill legalizing the executions as "emergency defense measures of the state." Hitler had been given, ex post facto, a license to murder. There was not a single word of protest. The legislators had enshrined the Führer as the sole source of law.

6

A month earlier, during his frustrating excursion to Italy, the Führer had promised Mussolini to respect Austrian independence. It was a considerable concession since *Anschluss*, incorporation of his homeland into a Greater Germany, had been one of Hitler's first goals. Despite this promise his own SS did not cease sending considerable financial and moral support to Austrian Nazis, who carried on a campaign of terrorism, blowing up railways and power stations with German dynamite and murdering supporters of Chancellor Engelbert Dollfuss with German weapons. Ironically the diminutive Dollfuss was a nationalistic, authoritarian reactionary who was countering the threats of both Nazism and socialism with suspension of parliamentary government.

Perhaps the Austrian Nazis were inspired by the hubbub following the Röhm affair to take direct action. More likely, though there is no proof, Hitler approved it. At any rate, on July 25 they suddenly launched their own Putsch, under the code name Operation Summer Festival. At noon a secret striking force of 150 local Nazis in the uniforms of the Austrian army broke into the chancellery on the Ballhausplatz to seize Dollfuss and his advisers. The plot had already been discovered and all but two of the cabinet had fled, but the plucky Dollfuss had remained. He was shot in the throat from a range of six inches. As he lay on the floor, ignored and bleeding profusely, other rebels were broadcasting the lie that the Chancellor had resigned.

In Berlin the news of the uprising was welcomed in official circles and DNB prepared a statement to the effect that the people had revolted in righteousness. "The inevitable has happened. The German people in Austria have risen against their oppressors, jailers, and torturers." Hitler—in Bayreuth attending the Wagner festival—pretended indifference at first but as the afternoon wore on he became concerned over the possible repercussions of the revolt. Would Mussolini assume he had broken his word and bring his own superior military force into play?

The shock of the purge, followed so quickly by that of the Dollfuss murder, had a perceptible effect on Hindenburg. He declined rapidly and was confined to his bed. It was a spartan iron bed but he refused to get a more comfortable one on the grounds that he had always slept on a field cot. Nor would he buy a robe despite his chills. Soldiers don't have robes, he grumbled. He had no money for such things and besides he was about to die.

The Führer was still at Bayreuth when he learned that the Old Gentleman was sinking fast. He rushed to Neudeck on the first day of August with a small party including two public relations experts. The group was coolly received. Oskar von Hindenburg led the Führer into the President's bedroom. "Father," he said, "the Reich Chancellor is here." Hindenburg, lying with eyes closed, did not react and Oskar repeated the words. Without opening his eyes, the marshal said, "Why did you not come earlier?"

"What does the President mean?" Hitler whispered to the son.

"The Reich Chancellor could not get here until now," Oskar told his father, who only muttered. "Oh, I see." After a silence Oskar said, "Father, Reich Chancellor Hitler has one or two matters to discuss."

This time the Old Gentleman opened his eyes with a start, stared at Hitler, then shut them again and clamped his mouth shut. Perhaps the President had expected to see *his* Reich Chancellor, his Franzchen—Papen.

The next morning, even while Hindenburg was expiring, Hitler's cabinet passed a law combining the offices of President and Chancellor. The vote was unanimous, with the absent Papen's signature affixed by proxy. The measure was to be effective with the death of Hindenburg and this occurred within minutes. The Old Gentleman died with the words: "My Kaiser . . . my Fatherland" on his lips. He was laid out on the iron cot with a Bible in his hands.

Thanks to a legal coup, Hitler now carried the title of Führer and Reich Chancellor. This meant he was also supreme commander of the armed forces and his first act was to summon

General von Blomberg and the three commanders-in-chief of the three armed forces. "We were in his study," Admiral Erich Raeder later testified, "and Hitler asked us to come to his desk without ceremony or staging. There we took the oath which he, as Chief of State and Supreme Commander of the Armed Forces, read to us."

The four men repeated this oath: "I swear before God to give my unconditional obedience to Adolf Hitler, Führer of the Reich and its people, Supreme Commander of the Armed Forces, and I pledge my word as a brave soldier to observe this oath always even at the risk of my life."

It was uprecedented. The previous oath had demanded loyalty and obedience to the constitution and the President. This one to a specific individual established a personal link between Führer and every soldier, sailor and airman. Yet not one officer made the slightest protest or even questioned the unique wording, and before the end of the day every serviceman in the land had taken the same oath of personal fealty.

Chapter Thirteen

TRIUMPH OF THE WILL

1934–1935

1

After victory in the plebiscite Hitler retreated to Berchtesgaden for a late summer holiday. He spent hours strolling around his beloved Obersalzberg, engaging in one of his favorite pastimes, conversation. But he was also making preparations for the impending Party Day Congress in Nuremberg, which could be blighted by bitter memories of the Röhm purge. He was determined to prevent this through his usually reliable combination of threat, promise and conciliation. The nation was still in a state of unrest and a number of intellectuals like Spengler, who had given grudging approval of National Socialism, were now enemies.

He was also concerned by foreign journalists eager for material that would damn or ridicule his regime. Dorothy Thompson had found such a story for an article in *Harper's Bazaar*. "This is not a revolution," an American visitor at the Passion play in Oberammergau (which blamed the Jews for the death of Jesus*) reportedly told her. "It's a revival. They think Hitler is God. Believe it or not, a German woman sat next to me at

*Only in 1975 was the text revised to place the blame instead on Lucifer, the fallen angel of evil.

the Passion play, and when they hoisted Jesus on the cross, she said, 'There he is. That is our Führer, our Hitler!' And when they paid out the thirty pieces of silver to Judas, she said: 'That is Röhm, who betrayed the leader.'"

Hitler chose young Alfred Speer as stage manager of the pageant at Nuremberg that was to consolidate his gains and bring back unity to the party. Speer erected a stone structure 1300 feet long and 80 feet high. Crowning the stadium was a giant eagle with a 100-foot wingspread and on all sides were hung thousands of swastika banners. Positioned around the field at 40-foot intervals were 130 anti-aircraft searchlights with a range of 25,000 feet. Göring had resisted loaning these since they were the greater part of his strategic reserve but Hitler backed Speer. "If we use them in such large numbers for a thing like this," he reasoned, "other countries will think we're swimming in searchlights."

His imagination went beyond propaganda of the moment. Envisaging a permanent record that could be exported, he asked Leni Riefenstahl, the noted actress and director, to produce a commemorative film. She took over the difficult task herself and, to bring additional interest to the six-day program, devised shots from planes, cranes, roller skates and a tiny elevator platform attached to the tallest flagpole. She arrived in Nuremberg a week before the opening day, with a crew of 120, including sixteen cameramen. The city's fire-fighting equipment as well as public utilities were turned over to her.

The participants were already flooding into Nuremberg. Carefully selected months in advance, each had a number, a designated truck, a designated seat in the truck, and a designated cot in the vast tent city near Nuremberg. By the time the ceremonies began on September 4 the thousands of party members had been rehearsed to perfection. That evening the Führer made a short welcoming speech at the old Rathaus, followed by Hanfstaengl's long one urging the foreign press to "report on affairs in Germany without attempting to interpret them."

The next morning Hitler appeared at the Luitpold arena, more as an object of reverence than as an orator. He entered dramatically, followed by Göring, Goebbels, Hess, Himmler and several aides, to the strains of the "Badenweiler March." After a stirring rendition of the *Egmont* Overture, Hess came forward and slowly read the names of those who had died in the 1923 Putsch. To the audience of 30,000, if not to the foreign correspondents, it was a moving experience. The most important words were spoken by Gauleiter Wagner, who read a proclamation of Hitler's in a voice so similar to the Führer's that some correspondents listening on the radio thought it was he. "The German form of life is definitely determined for the next thousand years," read out Wagner. "For us, the unsettled nineteenth century has finally ended. There will be no revolution in Germany for the next thousand years."

Intoxicated as he was by the almost constant ovation from admirers, Hitler was nevertheless nagged by anxiety. Many Brownshirts had brought their resentment and disillusionment to the festivities, and the possibility of an embarrassing or even dangerous episode made him so tense that occasionally his own resentment flared up. During one meal at the restaurant frequented by party officials he suddenly turned on Hans Frank. "You certainly annoyed me by delaying things on the thirtieth of June in Munich!" he exclaimed and, when Frank again offered to resign, cut him off impatiently. "In a few weeks this whole joke of state justice will end."

In the rising excitement of the rally Hitler regained his mood of exultation. This was particularly evident on the evening of the seventh when 200,000 party faithful with more than 20,000 unfurled flags crowded into Zeppelin Field and lined up with military precision. The effect of Speer's 130 giant searchlights was more breath-taking than imagined. "The floodlit stadium gave the impression of a giant hall ringed by titanic gleaming white pillars," Speer recalled, "with an occasional cloud floating surrealistically through the majestic wall of light, like a translucent anemone drifting through the sea." In the awesome silence, Hitler's voice came across the field from loudspeakers with eerie effect. "We are strong and will get stronger!" he said, and made it as much a threat as a promise.

Leni Riefenstahl and her cameramen were filming the scene from a dozen angles, despite interference from officious Brownshirts who, at Goebbels' instigation and unbeknown to the Führer, kept harassing her cameramen, pushing them from the best vantage points and even dismantling several of their camera stations.

September 10 was designated as Army Day and mobile units with the most modern equipment maneuvered flawlessly on the great meadow. It was the first public display of military might in Germany since the war and the audience of 300,000 was raised to a state of almost uncontrollable excitement at the sight of a realistic sham battle. Militarism, wrote American correspondent William L. Shirer in his diary, was not just a product of the Hohenzollerns. "It is rather something deeply ingrained in all Germans. They acted today like children playing with tin soldiers."

Hitler's high spirits were in evidence at the reception in his honor at the presidential palace. All those diplomats who had been avoiding him were forced to be on hand to pay formal respects to the new president. Never had U.S. Ambassador Dodd seen him "quite so happy-looking as while he went down the line greeting the representatives of all foreign countries." Despite some annoyances and a few anxious moments, he had succeeded in accomplishing at Nuremberg what he had set out to do. The party was reunited, and the people and the armed forces were with him.

2

There was gossip that Leni Riefenstahl was Hitler's mistress. This charge was as unfounded as those that he was sleeping with other famous actresses such as Olga Tschechowa, Lil Dagover and Pola Negri. It was not sex that Hitler sought from such charming women but the stimulation that his suppressed bohemian nature craved.

Unity Mitford, daughter of Lord Redesdale, had just come out in England. She was in Munich attending art classes and was caught in the excitement of the new Germany. From the moment Hitler kissed her hand she became a dedicated advocate of National Socialism. Hitler had never met anyone like this gay, irrepressible, golden-haired girl who would make the bluntest and most surprising remarks. Her freedom of expression, original outlook on life and lively humor, which she shared with her five sisters, were a new and refreshing experience to Hitler and his delight in her company soon generated a rumor—as unfounded as the others—that she was his mistress.

With Hitler's rise to power, he found an increasing number of women eager for his company. Perhaps it was his widening range of interest which soured his long-standing relationship with Helene Bechstein. She began to criticize him openly and upbraid him for some of his reforms. According to Friedelind Wagner, she would usually begin by asking the Führer if he were crazy and then shower him with such a deluge of abuse that he was unable to defend himself. "During these violent scoldings, Hitler would stand there like an abashed schoolboy who had committed a misdemeanor."

Eva Braun was even more distressed at Hitler's broadening horizon. A few days after he came to power he had given her a matching ring, earrings and bracelet of tourmalines for her twenty-first birthday. But this was no indication that he planned to marry his mistress. She saw less of him than before. Occasionally he would phone her from Berlin—usually from a public booth. To prevent her parents from finding out how intimate were her relations with the Führer, she had persuaded them to let her have a private phone in her bedroom. Whenever he came to Munich he would invite Eva to his apartment but in Berchtesgaden she stayed at some hotel for appearance's sake.

By the autumn of 1934 Eva was stricken with long spells of melancholy. She had no hope that Hitler would marry her. As head of the Third Reich, he told her, he must devote himself to the nation with no family distractions. He was, in fact, like the Pope. His excuse to Captain Wiedemann was more blunt. Yes, he confided one evening, he did miss family life but if he got married he would lose many female votes. "So," he concluded, "I have a girl at my disposal in Munich." Hitler was even more revealing to his secretary, Christa Schröder. "Eva is very nice," he said, "but, in my life, only Geli could have inspired in me genuine passion. I can never think of marrying Eva. The only woman I could have tied myself to for life would have been Geli."

In the meantime Hitler was devoting much of his time to foreign policy. Since success in this field almost always depends on power, Hitler was doing his best to rearm the Reich overnight. Behind the smoke screen of the disarmament negotiations at Geneva he was hastily building up Germany's armed forces on every level. Heartened by public reaction to the impressive military display at Nuremberg, Hitler issued a secret order three weeks later trebling the size of the 100,000-man army. That same day 70,000 recruits were enrolled. The defense budget rose to 654 million marks.

The sudden activation of nine corps headquarters, fourteen infantry divisions and seven motorized combat battalions even under tight security generated alarming rumors of infringements of the Versailles Treaty. These, combined with a deterioration in Anglo-German relations, were a real concern to Hitler. It was becoming obvious, moreover, that Britain and France were moving closer to military unity in view of German expansion. On the other hand, there were indications that England was not ready to take any great risks.

The French answer to Germany's new show of power was a meaningless appeal to the League of Nations and on the morning of March 25 the official British delegation met Hitler in an atmosphere of amiability. Paul Schmidt, acting as the Führer's interpreter for the first time, noticed his smile was "especially friendly" when he greeted Sir John Simon, Anthony Eden and Ambassador Sir Eric Phipps. They grouped themselves around a low table at the Reich chancellery together with Baron Konstantin von Neurath, the Foreign Minister, and Ribbentrop.

Simon announced that both the government and people of Britain wanted peace above all and earnestly wished Germany could co-operate with other European nations toward that objective. The British public, the decisive factor in England, he said, "was very disturbed" by such events as German "withdrawal from the League of Nations, Austria and certain unilateral announcements." England as a whole "was not at all anti-German, but she was strongly opposed to anything which was liable to disturb the peace."

"Hitler's reply," recalled Eden, who understood enough German to realize that Schmidt was interpreting ably, "was a skillful piece of special pleading which was none the less threatening in its undertones." In his second encounter, Eden was "most unfavorably impressed," by the Führer's personality. He seemed "negative to me, certainly not compelling," and was, moreover, "rather shifty." At the same time Eden admired the way Hitler conducted the meeting, "without hesitation and without notes, as befitted the man who knew where he wanted to go."

3

In Berlin, preoccupation with the international scene was briefly overshadowed by preparation for the wedding of Hermann Göring and Emmy Sonnemann, an actress. (His first wife, Carin, had died after a long illness in 1931.) They were inundated with presents donated by organizations and individuals seeking favor. Museums sent paintings on permanent loan, the most valuable being two priceless oils by Cranach. In addition to oriental rugs, tapestries, silver candelabra and jewels were pepper cake from Saxony, Kirsch from the Black Forest, cheese and cattle. The smaller items were on display in the Berlin residence, the bulkier transported by truck to Karinhall, the country estate near the capital named after his first wife but misspelled.

The wedding on April 10 could have been produced in Hollywood, and a play-by-play account was given by radio to the nation. The pomposity of the ceremony—performed by a bishop and witnessed by the Führer himself—was relieved when two storks were observed circling around the Evangelical Cathedral. An irreverent flying comrade had swooped down and released them over the *Dom*. As the bride and groom left the church a military band thundered out the march from *Lohengrin*. Passing under a long arch of extended swords, they were greeted outside by ecstatic cheers and a mass Roman salute.

On April 11 the British, French and Italians opened their conference at Stresa. Contrary to Hitler's expectations that French suggestions would not win the support of the other two powers, the meeting led to the issuance of a joint communiqué condemning Germany's illegal rearmament. The presence of Laval, MacDonald and Mussolini gave force to the announcement. Hitler, hoping to isolate the French, found himself in danger of being isolated himself. This was emphasized several weeks later by a Franco-Soviet pact of mutual assistance, which was so unsettling to the Führer's basic strategy that he made new efforts to reassure his friend Lord Rothermere that England had no reason at all to fear the Reich. From the earliest days of the party, Hitler wrote on May 3, he had envisaged cooperation with Great Britain. "Such an agreement between England and Germany would represent the weighty influence for peace and common sense of 120,000,000 of the most valuable people in the world. The historically unique colonial aptitude and the naval power of Britain would be combined with that of one of the first military nations of the world."

While Rothermere needed no convincing and continued to present a picture of a benign Germany in his papers, the general reaction in England was one of apprehension. When the MacDonald government leaders learned that Hitler would make a major political announcement after mid-May, they became concerned enough to schedule a Commons debate on rearmament to follow it.

The dreaded speech was delivered on May 21 and once more Hitler surprised the world. Earlier in the day he had promulgated a secret defense law which placed Schacht in charge of war economy and reorganized the armed forces: The Reichswehr officially became the Wehrmacht (Armed Forces) and Hitler was named its supreme commander; Blomberg's title was changed from Minister of Defense to Minister of War and he was given the title of commander-in-chief of the armed forces; and General Ludwig Beck's unrevealing title of *Chef des Truppenamtes* was changed to Chief of the General Staff. In private at least, a spade was being called a spade but when Hitler faced the microphone that evening, relaxed and confident, he was the model of moderation. His chief aim was peace nor had he any dream of conquest. All war ever did, he proclaimed, was destroy the flower of the nation.

After reiterating that "Germany needs peace and desires peace," he offered to make bilateral non-aggression pacts with all his neighbors and promised to observe the Locarno Treaty. All he wanted was a fleet 35 per cent the size of Britain's navy. That, he promised, would be the end of his demands. "For Germany," he vowed, "this demand is final and abiding."

In many influential quarters abroad his words were taken at face value, the London *Times* calling his address "reasonable, straightforward and comprehensive." In a stroke Hitler had reversed the trend of isolation and prepared the way for a sympathetic reception of German demands at the forthcoming naval conference. It opened exactly two weeks later at the British Foreign Office with Joachim von Ribbentrop as head of the German delegation. He seated himself at the conference table armed with good advice from the Japanese naval attaché in London. Captain Arata Oka informed his German counterpart that the Japanese had come to the Washington Conference in 1921 under the false impression that one could make "a deal" with the English. "Consequently we were unprepared when the English quickly drove a wedge between our diplomats and our naval experts, separating them into almost hostile groups." He recommended that the Germans concentrate on one clear demand—such as the 35 per cent ratio—and hold to it tenaciously even if it threatened to wreck the conference. Once the English realized the Germans were firm they would slowly give in—and have greater respect for their antagonists.

Following Oka's advice, Ribbentrop refused to discuss anything but Germany's demand for a 35 per cent ratio. "If the British government does not immediately accept this condition," he said, "there is no point at all in continuing these negotiations. We must insist upon an immediate decision." Once the British accepted this ratio, he promised, the technical details regarding the program of naval construction could be settled promptly.

Schmidt was interpreting, though Ribbentrop spoke good English, and was startled that his principal had immediately brought up—and so undiplomatically!—the most difficult question on the agenda. Schmidt wondered if it was Ribbentrop's lack of experience or blind obedience to instructions. What Ribbentrop was doing, besides following Oka's shrewd advice, was to implement the disconcerting tactic that Hitler had been using so successfully for years. The speech a fortnight ago was the carrot, this was the club.

As Schmidt translated Ribbentrop's words, he could see Simon flush. It was not usual, he replied stiffly, to make such conditions at the beginning of negotiations and he could, of course, make no statement on the subject. So saying, he bowed frigidly and left the room. After a moment's embarrassment Sir Robert Craigie took Simon's place and firmly presented Britain's objections. But the dogged Ribbentrop could not be moved.

The next day the redoubtable Craigie opened the proceedings with the announcement that the British were prepared to meet Herr von Ribbentrop's demands. Full agreement was reached so amicably that Ribbentrop, dropping his "rather awkward manner," became outright sociable. The British not only allowed Germany to fix her naval tonnage at 35 per cent of their own fleet but conceded a 45 per cent ratio for submarines. Ribbentrop returned to Germany as a conquering hero. The attainment of all of Germany's secret naval aims by negotiation had transformed Hitler from a man of force to a statesman. France, stunned at such unilateral action (made incidentally on the anniversary of Waterloo) by a so-called ally, sent an angry note to London but British public opinion was almost universally favorable and (except for Winston Churchill, who damned the agreement as damaging British security) even those politicians generally hostile to Hitler supported the agreement.

The Soviet Union reacted almost as violently to the London pact as the French. It confirmed suspicions that elements of

Britain's ruling class, including the heir to the throne, were helping Germany strengthen its navy in the Baltic Sea for an attack on the U.S.S.R. while supporting Japanese ambitions in the Far East. Despite such apprehensions the Soviets signed a new trade treaty with Hitler, who advanced their credit to 200 million marks and was preparing to boost that figure to 500 million over a ten-year period. This was no abandonment of his dream of Lebensraum but another devious move in the international game of diplomacy. For, while he talked peace with the West and did business with the East, rearmament in Germany continued as secretly as possible at a rate exceeding the estimates of most foreign observers.

4

As the political life of Adolf Hitler expanded so did his personal life. Two inner circles had formed around him—one composed of top associates like Goebbels, Göring, Hess (and their wives) and another on a more personal level: the chauffeurs, secretaries, servants and other intimates. This innermost circle, which included such disparate members as an architect, Speer, and a pilot, Baur, was also taking in some of the younger military adjutants, like Navy Lieutenant von Puttkamer and the representative of the Luftwaffe, Nikolaus von Below. A few belonged to both circles. The most notable was Martin Bormann, who had been working for Hess since the early days and now, as his representative in Berlin, was given the opportunity of assiduously devoting himself to the daily needs of the Führer. Although unknown to most Germans, the indefatigable Bormann had become Hitler's shadow, remaining at his shoulder most of the day ready to jot down on cuff or notebook his slightest whim.

Hitler himself moved easily between the two circles as well as among a constellation of top military and civilian circles. What he could not do was conduct the affairs of high office in a businesslike manner. A night person, he usually arrived at his desk shortly before noon. He would glance through the press dispatches that Otto Dietrich had selected for him and then rush off to lunch. Upon returning, he would postpone matters that bored him to retire in privacy and consider those that did not. For hours he would discuss the rebuilding of

Berlin, Munich and Linz with architects Speer and Giesler, while State Secretary Hans Lammers and Otto Meissner, whom the Führer had inherited from Hindenburg, impatiently waited for decisions that only the head of state could make.

His working methods were a constant concern to Captain Wiedemann. Rarely could his personal adjutant get him to read a file before making an important decision. "He was of the opinion," wrote Wiedemann, "that many matters took care of themselves as long as one didn't stir them up. And he was not often wrong about this. The question was merely how such matters took care of themselves." He was similarly bohemian in his selection of visitors. Some officials would wait for days in the anteroom but if an acquaintance of the old days showed up he was as likely as not to be invited at once to lunch where he could voice problems which were often solved on the spot.

Preoccupation with the international scene disrupted Hitler's already erratic schedule and consequently he found almost no time for his mistress. The love of Adolf Hitler had become Eva Braun's whole life, even though he had made it plain that they could never marry while he was Führer of the Reich. "For me marriage would have been a disaster," he explained to his inner circle seven years later. "There's a point at which misunderstanding is bound to arise between man and wife; it's when the husband cannot give his wife all the time she feels entitled to demand." A woman lived only for her husband's sake and expected him to live for hers. Whereas the man, a slave to his thoughts, was ruled by duty. "I'd have had nothing of marriage but the sullen face of a neglected wife, or else I'd have skimped my duties. . . . The bad side of marriage is that it creates rights. In that case, it's far better to have a mistress. The burden is lightened, and everything is placed on the level of a gift."

Eva had sunk into a deep depression that was momentarily relieved by one of her lover's rare visits. "Yesterday he came quite unexpectedly," she wrote in her diary on February 18, "and it was a delightful evening. . . . I am so endlessly happy that he loves me so much, and pray that it will always be so." Within two weeks she wrote: "I am again deathly unhappy. Since I cannot write him, this diary has to be the depository of all my tales of woe." He came on Saturday but after spending "a few wonderful hours" with her he left and sent no word when he would return. "I am sitting on hot coals thinking every moment he might come."

A week later she wrote disjointedly as if in great haste or under emotional stress:

> I wish that I were very sick since I have not heard from him for 8 days. Why doesn't something happen to me, why do I have to go through all this. I wish I had never seen him. I am desperate. Now I am buying sleeping pills, at least I will be half dazed and don't think about it so much any more. . . . Why does he torment me like this and not just put an end to the whole thing.

What Eva Braun did not know was that at the time Hitler was undergoing an operation. For some months he had been troubled by a sore throat. His voice, abused by numerous speeches of interminable length delivered in all kinds of weather, had become hoarse and discovery of a growth on his larynx revived an old fear; for months, according to Speer, he had been talking of Emperor Frederick III, who died of throat cancer. The throat irritationn was accompanied by stomach pains—perhaps similar to those he suffered as a youth in Vienna—for which he took Neo-Balestol. Apparently he took excessive amounts of the drug, which contained fusel oil, and at least once he was so stricken with a form of intoxication that he summoned Dr. Grawitz to complain of headache, vertigo, buzzing in the ears and seeing double. Professor Karl van Eicken, head of Berlin University's otolaryngology department, removed a one-centimeter polyp from the Führer's vocal cord. It was an easy operation which took place in Hitler's chancellery apartment, requiring only a small amount of morphine as a sedative. Even so Hitler slept deeply for fourteen hours. "I was quite concerned," Eicken later revealed. After the operation Eicken warned him to speak softly for a few days, and in the future not to let his emotions "lead him to shout and scream loudly. . . . He admitted he had been told that before, but forgot himself during a speech.

Feeling hopeless and abandoned, Eva swallowed twenty tablets of Vanoform, a narcotic, in the early hours of May 29. She was found in a coma by her sister Ilse. After administering first-aid treatment, learned while working as a receptionist for a surgeon, she phoned her employer, Dr. Martin Marx, whose discretion she trusted. While he was treating Eva she found the notebook containing the diary. Determined to keep the second suicide attempt a secret, she ripped out the incriminating pages so as not to involve Dr. Marx, a Jew. Ilse also feared her father might react violently and the Führer might question the mental stability of his mistress; she suggested the suicide was part theater. After all, Eva had only taken twenty pills of a type milder than Veronal—aware that one of her sisters would say good night to her after returning home.

Dr. Marx obligingly recorded the case as excessive fatigue resulting in an overdose of narcotics. Hitler accepted this explanation (although Ilse Braun remains convinced that he had guessed the truth). In any case the "accident" accomplished what words of entreaty had not. That summer he found Eva a place of her own. On August 9, 1935, she and her younger sister, Gretl, moved into a three-room apartment in the quiet residential Bogenhausen section—a short walk from the Führer's Munich apartment. He paid the rent indirectly through Hoffmann and furnished the place with furniture bought on sale. The master of the establishment was seldom there, and when he did come it was after the neighbors were asleep. Even then his trysts with Eva were scarcely private since secret police kept watch on the stairs and outside the building.

Hitler's first major speech at Nuremberg came on September 11. It turned from a plea for cultural development into another attack on Jews. He charged that they had never produced an art that was characteristically their own and never would. It was such a mild rebuke that foreign observers wondered if it was true that his anti-Semitic program was being muted as reassurance to the other Great Powers. On the contrary, the growing agitation in the West for a boycott of German goods had convinced him that the time had come to enact some of those legal measures against Jews which had been suggested in his first recorded anti-Semitic declaration almost exactly sixteen years earlier. On September 13 he ordered that a decree be drafted within forty-eight hours under the title "The Law for the Protection of German Blood and Honor."

No sooner had those assigned this task completed a draft prohibiting marriages and extramarital intercourse between Jews and citizens of "German or related blood" than a messenger arrived with new orders from Hitler. They were also to write up a Reich citizenship law. The harried authors soon ran out of paper and were reduced to using old menu cards. It was 2:30 A.M., September 15, by the time it was agreed that only those of "German or related blood" could be citizens.

The other provisions were acceptable and at 9 P.M. Hitler addressed an extraordinary session of the Reichstag in Nuremberg. Passage of these laws, he said, was actually to the advantage of the Jews. It might possibly "create a level ground on which the German people may find a tolerable relation towards the Jewish people." These moderate words were immediately followed by threatening ones: "Should this hope not be fulfilled and the Jewish agitation both within Germany and abroad continue, then the position must be examined afresh."

5

Fortunately for Hitler, the attention of the world was suddenly turned from this new assault on the rights of Jews as well as his illegal expansion of the Wehrmacht by a foolish act of Benito Mussolini, his one-time model. On the third of October Italy invaded Ethiopia. Moral indignation was almost universal. How could a civilized nation attack a weak foe forced to battle planes and tanks with tribesmen on horseback? Britain and America, with conveniently short memories of their own pacification programs, were particularly abusive, and the former led the campaign in the League of Nations to invoke limited economic sanctions against Italy. Despite numerous anti-Italian and pro-Ethiopian sympathizers in Germany, Hitler publicly refused to help Emperor Haile Selassie, while secretly sending him some military aid. At the same time Hitler gave Mussolini raw materials so as to embroil Italy (and, hopefully, England) in a debilitating campaign that would leave Germany more freedom of action. His public support of Il Duce was also a test case to see how Britain would react to German defiance of the League of Nations. It was soon evident that the English would do nothing in reprisal and this must have strengthened his conviction that they were going to come to an agreement with him.

Hitler went into seclusion to regain control of the situation and himself. He was not seen in public during the last four weeks of autumn; Rosenberg assumed that the Führer was ill but it was just as likely that he was suffering one of his pre-Christmas moods of despondency. What is more, he was faced with another crucial, and unpleasant, decision that involved the future of the NSDAP and the course of National Socialism itself. Hitler had reached his Rubicon. While he and the party had gained control over all aspects of public life in Germany, the Brown Revolution remained at a standstill. He had let everything in the domestic scene slide at the expense of foreign policy and was reacting rather than initiating. Public interest in the party as a consequence was at a low level. There were fewer applications for membership and the members themselves were showing less devotion to party activities.

On the third day of January 1936 Hitler summoned his Gauleiters and Reichsleiters to a conference in hopes this group could reconcile the issues that had arisen. He opened his talk with the full revelation of the plans to rearm the nation, hinted at the grand future he envisioned for Germany and then, with an air of desperation reminiscent of the black days of late 1932 when the party seemed about to split apart, begged his listeners to realize that all this could not be achieved unless the party leadership "formed a single community, loyal to him." This plea was followed by an emotional demand for absolute devotion, which was succeeded—as in 1932—by a threat to kill himself. The audience was stunned and Chairman Hess promptly assured Hitler that everyone in the room would follow him wherever he went with unquestioning loyalty.

The Führer's spirits were abruptly revitalized and by mid-January he was prepared to take his next step forward—seizure of the demilitarized Rhineland zone which encompassed all German territory west of the Rhine as well as a thirty-mile strip east of the river that included Cologne, Düsseldorf and Bonn. He was heartened in this ambition by the death of a monarch. On the evening of January 20 King George V died and was succeeded by Edward VIII, a man of individuality and independence who had made no secret of his sympathies with many of Germany's aspirations. In his first broadcast as King he made it clear that he would not change.

On February 12 Hitler summoned his chargé d'affaires in Paris for a conference regarding possible French reactions to remilitarization of the Rhineland. That same afternoon he spoke to General von Fritsch about military action. The army chief of staff was not at all enthusiastic. Why not negotiate? Hitler argued that a conference would take weeks and explained that he was only thinking of a symbolic operation. How long would it take to put nine battalions of infantry and some artillery into the Rhineland? Two days, said Fritsch, but warned that it should not be undertaken if there was the slightest risk of war.

On Friday, March 6, it was announced that the Reichstag

would meet the following noon and the diplomatic community in Berlin guessed something momentous was afoot. That evening reporters and photographers of the leading German newspapers were invited to a conference in the Ministry of Propaganda. The mystified journalists were informed by Goebbels that they were to be taken on a journey next morning so secret that they were being held in custody until then.

Early on Saturday morning the special press group was driven to Tempelhof where a Junkers transport was waiting. When the plane took off the reporters still had no idea where they were going. The pilot himself did not know his destination; at a specified time he was to open a sealed envelope that would direct him to the Rhineland.

At 10 A.M. the German ambassador called on Eden. After some discussion regarding another Anglo-German naval agreement, Hoesch abruptly said: "I have a communication of very great importance to make. I am afraid that the first part of it will not be to your taste, but the later portions contain an offer of greater importance than has been made at any time in recent history." He began to read a memorandum charging that the Franco-Soviet pact violated the Treaty of Locarno. Consequently Germany was taking back the demilitarized zone of the Rhineland. Hoesch hurriedly read on that Hitler offered to sign separate non-aggression pacts with Eastern countries as well as those in the West. He also was willing to re-enter the League of Nations.

Eden expressed deep regret over the Rhineland move but said he would give careful consideration to the German proposals. Her attitude toward the League, he added, was most important. At this point Hoesch said he must make it clear that there were no conditions attached to his country's return to the League, then added casually that as for the Rhineland only a few small German detachments would move into that zone. Once Hoesch left, Eden summoned the French ambassador to express his deep regret at Germany's action. The denunciation of Locarno was "deplorable," said Eden, but it would require consideration by the British cabinet. This could not be done until Monday since most of its members were at their country homes.

After short interviews with the Italian and Belgian representatives, Eden telephoned Prime Minister Baldwin and then set off at once for Chequers to brief him. "Though personally friendly to France," recalled Eden, "he was clear in his mind that there would be no support in Britain for any military action by the French. I could only agree. I told him of the earnestness with which Hitler had spoken to me of Locarno. I could not believe him anymore." Neither did Baldwin but he agreed all they could do was await the French reaction.

At about 11:30 A.M. the Junkers carrying the German press landed at Cologne and half an hour later the reporters were standing with thousands of other patriotic Germans at the Hohenzollern Bridge which stretched across the Rhine. Here eighteen years earlier dejected German soldiers had retreated from France, leaving their guns behind. Suddenly the crowd could hear the tramp of feet, the rumble of iron-clad wheels and the clop of horses' hoofs. There was fervent cheering as the first soldiers moved onto the bridge. Other units were crossing at least five other bridges as a handful of fighter planes flew cover overhead. Only three of the nineteen infantry battalions in Operation Winter Exercise crossed the Rhine but the fervor (for Germans) and fear (for French) inspired by this handful of troops was momentous.

PART 5

WAR IN MASQUERADE

"Such subtle covenants shall be made
Till peace itself is war in masquerade."

DRYDEN

Chapter Fourteen

"WITH THE ASSURANCE OF A SLEEPWALKER"

MARCH 1936–JANUARY 1937

1

London never seriously considered taking action when German soldiers marched into the Rhineland on that Saturday morning, March 7, 1936. From Berlin François-Poncet urged "energetic reaction." Perhaps this sparked a spirit of resistance in the French government, which called on its General Staff to act. Like most such groups, it was conservative to the point of timidity. General Gamelin warned that "a war operation, however limited, entailed unpredictable risks and could not be undertaken without decreeing a general mobilization." He did agree to rush thirteen divisions to the Maginot Line.

A pusillanimous gesture, it panicked Gamelin's opposite number in Berlin. On Sunday morning General von Blomberg begged Hitler to at least withdraw troops from Aachen, Trier and Saarbrücken. If the French attacked, he said, the Germans would have to pull back without a battle, thus suffering a moral and military defeat of the first order. Hitler remained resolute despite misgivings. He told Blomberg to wait. If necessary they could retreat tomorrow. Nor did he waver when the French Premier broadcast a message of stern defiance: Never would France negotiate while Strasbourg was threatened by German guns.

By Monday more than 25,000 German troops, greeted by censer-swinging priests conferring blessings on them, were established in the Rhine zone. While there were still only words from the French, Hitler was consumed by anxiety. He couldn't, he later confessed, endure another such strain for ten years. "The forty-eight hours after the march into the Rhineland," he told his interpreter, "were the most nerve-racking in my life." If the French had retaliated "we would have had to withdraw with our tails between our legs, for the military resources at our disposal would have been wholly inadequate for even a moderate resistance." He made a triumphal tour of the reoccupied area without incident and on the trip back home in his special train relaxed. "Good Lord, am I relieved how smoothly everything went!" he said and then turned boastful from relief. "Yes, the world belongs to the courageous. God helps him." He asked that a record of Wagner's *Parsifal* be played and, as he listened, remarked that he had built his religion out of that opera. "You can serve God only as a hero," he said.

In Paris the Locarno powers convened with results so inconclusive that French Foreign Minister Flandin flew to London for help. The attitude there was typified by Lord Lothian's remark: "The Germans, after all, are only going into their own back garden." Neville Chamberlain, being groomed to succeed Baldwin as Prime Minister, emphasized to Flandin that public opinion was against enforcing any sanctions and then wrote in his diary, "His view is that, if a firm front is maintained by France and England, Germany will yield without war. We cannot accept this as a reliable estimate of a mad dictator's reaction."

Surprisingly, this general feeling of helplessness was overridden the very next day, March 12, when the Council of the League of Nations met in London and unanimously passed a resolution condemning Germany as a treaty-breaker. This occasioned an alarmist telegram to Berlin from the three Wehrmacht attachés. Blomberg rushed with it to the Führer, who jammed the message into his pocket without reading it. He refused to consider Blomberg's pleas to make concessions and gruffly told him to refrain in the future from attempting to influence political matters. Policy, he said, was made in the Reich chancellery and not in the War Ministry. His Foreign Minister was far more bellicose than the generals.

Holding the weakest hand in the game, Hitler had bluffed

England and France, proof that words of condemnation from international bodies were futile without force behind them. At the same time he had learned that his own political instincts were sounder than those of his generals. It was a victory of far-reaching import, reinforcing faith in his own destiny. He had discovered how far a resolute man, unafraid of using force, could go against adversaries terrified by the thought of another world war.

He was also shrewd enough to capitalize on the Rhineland to further solidify his power at home. He dissolved the Reichstag and submitted this policy to plebiscite. Rather than an election campaign, it was a triumphal parade from city to city with the majestic new dirigible, *Hindenburg*, painted all over with swastikas, flying escort overhead. "I have not usurped this office," he told the people of Karlsruhe. "What I have done, I did according to my conscience, and to the best of my knowledge, filled with concern for my people, realizing the necessity of protecting its honor, in order to lead it again to a position of honor in this world. And should unnecessary sorrow or suffering ever come to my people because of my actions, then I beseech the Almighty God to punish me."

On March 29, without benefit of guns, 98.8 per cent of the electorate voted for Hitler.

It was a particularly trying time for Hitler. His chauffeur Schreck had recently been killed in a crash and he himself was having trouble sleeping. He complained to Dr. Brandt of a high, metallic buzz in the left ear. Brandt advised him to stroll before retiring, then have a hot and cold foot bath and several mild sleeping pills. The Führer did take the pills, and he settled into a more regimented schedule at the new Reich chancellery which had been rebuilt according to his own design. At night he would invariably lock himself in his spartan bedroom. The only decoration was an oil portrait of his mother copied from an old photograph. On the right of the bed was a night table; Karl Krause, one of his valets, had strict instructions to have a similar table in the same position whenever he slept. In the morning the Führer insisted on shaving himself and getting dressed without help. Only when he was putting on his jacket would he emerge from his room, greet Krause and proceed to the library for a breakfast of two cups of milk, up to ten pieces of zwieback and several pieces of semi-sweet chocolate. He would eat erect while examining reports from DNB. Breakfast was over in five minutes and, without pause, he set off for the office.

About his only recreation in these busy days was an almost nightly movie in the enormous drawing room. Krause would give him a list of five or six films and he would select several. If one bored him, he would exclaim, "Trash!" and call for another. "His favorite actress was Greta Garbo," according to Sir Ivone Kirkpatrick, "and one of his favorite films *Lives of a Bengal Lancer*, which he saw three times. He liked this film because it depicted a handful of Britons holding a continent in thrall. That was how a superior race must behave and the film was compulsory viewing for the SS." He preferred French productions since, he said, they recorded the life of the petite bourgeoisie so faithfully. "I'm sorry they can't be shown to the public," he told Friedelind Wagner, although it was he who had taken over the responsibility of censoring films not cleared by the Goebbels office.

When Hitler's health showed no improvement, Dr. Brandt advised him to go on vacation, preferably to Berchtesgaden, where he always slept better. He took this advice and spent as much time as possible the next few months at Haus Wachenfeld. That summer he again attended the Wagner festival. Since Unity Mitford and her sister Diana were also on hand, Frau Wagner suggested inviting them to luncheon. Hitler was delighted. "You know Unity lives on little more than a mark a month," he said, according to Friedelind Wagner. "Her parents have cut off her allowance to force her back to England. She has returned once or twice but always runs away again."

The idyl at Bayreuth was disturbed on the night of July 22 when he was visited by two Germans residing in Morocco who belonged to the foreign organization of the NSDAP. They brought a letter from a Spanish general named Franco, leader of a military revolt against the republican government. He desperately needed planes to ferry troops from Africa for action against the "Reds." Hitler immediately summoned Göring, who happened to be at the festival. He urged Hitler to support Franco for two reasons: to prevent the further spread of Communism and "to test my young Luftwaffe." Hitler approved sending part of the transport fleet along with a number of experimental fighter units, bombers and anti-aircraft guns—but no more. It was to Germany's advantage to prolong the Civil War in Spain and keep Mussolini, who was already giving extensive aid to

Franco, from establishing better relations with France and England. An isolated Mussolini would have to turn to Germany.

Ribbentrop advised Hitler to keep out of the Spanish affair. No laurels were to be won there and he feared "fresh complications with Britain, which would undoubtedly dislike German intervention." But Hitler argued that it was his duty as a National Socialist to support Franco. If Spain went Communist, France (already governed by a leftist regime) would also be Bolshevized. "Wedged between the powerful Soviet bloc in the east and a strong Franco-Spanish bloc in the west, we could do hardly anything if Moscow chose to attack us."

2

That summer the Olympics were staged in Berlin despite efforts by liberals in Great Britain, the United States and France to boycott them, largely because of Germany's anti-Semitic policies. In his eagerness to turn the Olympics into a showcase for Nazi achievements, Hitler made a number of concessions. Token Jews—notably Helene Mayer, the fencer, and Rudi Ball, the hockey star—were allowed to represent the Reich, and Captain Wolfgang Fürstner, another Jew, was charged with erecting and organizing the Olympic Village. More important, anti-Semitic posters along the highways as well as notices barring Jews from resorts were removed. In Berlin, Streicher's *Der Stürmer* disappeared from the newsstands. The entire anti-Semitic campaign, in fact, was muted. These marks of conciliation were given such international publicity that foreigners thronged to Berlin, where they were greeted enthusiastically.

The opening ceremonies on August 1 were blessed by a clear blue sky. That afternoon Hitler led the parade to the stadium down the Via Triumphalis. His car, followed by a long caravan, proceeded slowly down the ten-mile boulevard, protected from the crowds by 40,000 Brownshirts and other guards. When the procession reached the stadium Hitler, in the simplest uniform, and the two Olympic officials strode forward, followed by the King of Bulgaria, crown princes from Sweden, Greece and Italy, and Mussolini's sons. They marched through the tunnel into the world's largest stadium to be greeted by a brassy voluntary from thirty trumpets. The orchestra, led by Richard Strauss and assisted by a chorus of 3000, broke into

"Deutschland über Alles" followed by the "Horst Wessel Lied" and the "Olympic Hymn," composed by Strauss for the occasion. The crowd of 110,000 cheered as Hitler took his place in the official stand. Some of the delegations used the Olympic salutation, a stiff right arm extended to the side but, to the delight of the audience, Austrians modified this to the Nazi salute. The Bulgarians outdid them by adding a smart goose step. The greatest applause came for the 250-member French team, whose salute was more Roman than Olympian. They were followed by the British in straw hats who, by merely executing an "eyes right," offended numerous onlookers. The Americans got the least applause, and some derogatory stamping of feet, as they passed the Tribune of Honor, eyes right, without even dipping their flag.

The next day Hitler was present to congratulate Hans Wölke, a German, for breaking the Olympic record for the shot-put. He also congratulated the three Finns who swept the 10,000-meter run as well as the German women who placed first and second in the javelin throw. By the time the German entrants in the high jump were eliminated it was dark and so he was not there to shake hands with the three American winners, two of whom were black.

This led the President of the International Olympic Committee to inform the Führer that, as guest of honor, he should henceforth congratulate all victors or none. Hitler chose the latter course and so did not meet Jesse Owens, who won four gold medals. That the Führer publicly turned his back on the great black athlete was denied by Owens himself, who further claimed that Hitler did pay him a tribute. "When I passed the Chancellor he arose, waved his hand at me, and I waved back at him. I think the writers showed bad taste in criticizing the man of the hour in Germany."

To the surprise of his entourage, the Führer attended almost every track and field event. Face contorted, he would watch the Germans perform with the passionate interest of a boy. (During the hockey game at the Winter Olympics in Garmisch-Partenkirchen he had been too nervous to stay till the end and had to have someone give him a brief account later.) The games ended on August 16 with Hitler on hand for the final ceremonies. As the orchestra played "The Games Are Ended," the crowd joined in the emotional farewell of the athletes, who rocked in time to the music. There were isolated shouts of "Sieg Heil!" for Hitler, who had been given no role at all in the final exercises. Others took up the cry and soon the stadium reverberated with the chant, "Sieg Heil! Unser Führer, Adolf Hitler, Sieg Heil!"

The games had been an almost unqualified Nazi triumph. Germans had won the most gold medals (33), as well as the most silver and bronze; and, surprisingly, defeated the second-place Americans by 57 points. More important, many of the visitors left Germany pleased by their hosts' cordiality and impressed by what they had seen of Hitler's Reich. The success of the games was further enhanced by a two-part documentary filmed by Leni Riefenstahl that won world-wide acclaim, despite Goebbels' attempted sabotage. He even tried to keep her from setting foot in the stadium.

In the paeans of self-congratulation that followed there was a tragic note. Captain Fürstner, replaced at the last moment as commandant of the Olympic Village because he was Jewish, attended the banquet honoring his successor, then shot himself.

3

Hitler did not break stride in his drive for German supremacy. In the summer of 1936 he composed a long memorandum on war economy written in foreboding language and typed in triplicate with one copy each for Göring and Blomberg and a third for his personal file. In it he stated that military strength must be raised to the limits of Germany's potential. Nor did the urgency of the task permit any "gentle scruples." Germany not only lacked raw material but was overpopulated and could not feed itself from its own soil. "To keep on saying these things is absolutely pointless. We must now put measures into effect which can bring the future a final solution, and for the interim a temporary relaxation. The final solution lies in expanding the living space or the raw material and food resources of our people." It was the problem of the government, he continued, to eventually resolve the shortages of raw materials. "It is better to consider and solve these problems in peace than to wait until the next war before attempting to carry out these economic investigations and experiments in the midst of other demands." Autarchy (a self-sufficient economy) must be established as rapidly as possible with the following aims: "I. The German army must be ready for war in four years' time. II. The German economy must be ready for war in four years."

At the same time he was attempting to solidify connections with the British. They, in turn, were demonstrating persistent ineptitude in coping with a leader of such determination and cunning. They were convinced that Hitler could be brought into line with understanding and concessions; and he had kept this misinterpretation alive the past year with conciliatory talk and vague offers of treaties.

Hitler also sought an understanding with Italy. He sent Hans Frank to Rome with an invitation to Mussolini to visit Germany not only as dictator of Italy but as leader of the original Fascist revolution. Now Il Duce showed genuine interest in liaison with Germany, and on October 21 his Foreign Minister and son-in-law, Count Galeazzo Ciano, arrived in Berlin to make preliminary arrangements. First Ciano talked to his opposite number, Neurath, who (so reported the Italian) ridiculed Ribbentrop's illusions of a meaningful Anglo-German friendship. Ciano was equally skeptical of a new Locarno and suggested Italy remain in the League of Nations to perform "a work of sabotage useful for our common ends." Three days later Ciano met Hitler at the Berghof. In a mood to captivate, Hitler began by saying, "Mussolini is the first statesman of the world with whom no one else has the right even remotely to compare himself." The Germans and Latins, he continued, complemented each other. Together they could unite in an invincible coalition against Bolshevism and the Western democracies.

Having charged his son-in-law with the task of driving a wedge between England and Germany, Il Duce had given him a document fallen into Italian hands: a telegram from the British ambassador in Berlin to London referring to the Hitler government as one of dangerous adventurers. Upon reading this, the Führer angrily exclaimed, "According to the English there are two countries in the world today which are led by adventurers: Germany and Italy. But England too was led by adventurers when she built her Empire. Today she is governed merely by incompetents." He assured Ciano that there was no need to be concerned about England since rearmament was proceeding at a far more rapid rate in both Germany and Italy. By 1939 Germany would be ready for war, in four or five years much more than ready.

Their new relationship, providing for co-operation over a wide range, was sealed in a secret agreement and signed in Berlin by Ciano and Neurath. A few days later Mussolini referred to it in a speech delivered in the Piazza del Duomo in Milan, using a term that would come to have an ominous ring in Western ears: ". . . this Berlin-Rome line is not a diaphragm but rather an *axis*, around which can revolve all those European states with a will to collaboration and peace."

For the remainder of the autumn of 1936 one of Hitler's concerns was Spain. Small but significant quantities of German supplies and personnel had already been delivered to Franco, and the Führer considered giving more substantial aid. A special air unit capable of providing vital tactical air support for the insurgents was operational by November, and on the eighteenth Hitler, in concert with Mussolini, finally recognized the Franco regime as the legal government of Spain.

While the Foreign Ministry urged Hitler to proceed with caution, Göring, now in charge of the Four-Year Plan, regarded the Spanish conflict as a prelude to a genuine conflict. "We are already in a state of war," he told a conference of air officials on December 2—though not an official shot had yet been fired. Even so, beginning with the new year, "all factories for aircraft production shall run as if mobilization had been ordered." A few days later he was as frank with a group of industrialists and high officials in Berlin. He revealed that war was in sight and Germany was on the threshold of mobilization. "The battle we are now approaching," he said, "demands a colossal measure of production capacity. No limit on rearmament can be visualized. The only alternatives are victory or destruction."

Diplomatically 1936 was a successful year for Hitler and at minimal cost. England had been charmed and Italy brought to the threshold of an unequal partnership. He also had persuaded Japan to sign an Anti-Comintern Pact with Germany which contained secret agreements (vague to be sure) that each should help the other against the Soviet Union. Admittedly spineless, the agreement was important as a propaganda ploy to justify German rearmament.

The only setback of the season was the constitutional crisis in England caused by the King's determination to marry Mrs. Wallis Warfield Simpson. He told Prime Minister Baldwin, "If I can marry her as King well and good," but if the government opposed the marriage, as Baldwin had given Edward to believe it would, "*then I was prepared to go*." A large segment of the public sympathized with Edward VIII but the Church and the Prime Minister remained adamant.

On the evening of December 9 Edward signed the Instrument

of Abdication to become the first monarch in British history to give up the throne voluntarily. That evening he told his subjects and the world in a moving broadcast that he was unable to "carry the heavy burden of responsibility and to discharge my duties as King, as I wish to do, without the help and support of the woman I love."

Hitler could not understand how any man could give up rule for romance. He telephoned Ribbentrop and dejectedly informed his ambassador he might as well pack his trunks and give up the game for lost. "Now that the King has been dethroned, there is certainly no other person in England who is ready to play with us. Report to me on what you've been able to do. I shan't blame you if it amounts to nothing."

4

This disappointment notwithstanding, 1936 had brought Hitler such success that the Yuletide season was his first happy one "in long years," so he told Frau Göring. "It was, I believe, my most beautiful Christmas." This despite severe stomach cramps, insomnia and eczema. On December 25 he selected a personal physician recommended by Hoffmann, the photographer. Dr. Theo Morell was a skin specialist with a lucrative practice in Berlin's Kurfürstendamm, his patients including the leading film and stage personalities. He was fat, swarthy, with a full round face and peered nearsightedly through thick glasses. His hands were large, hairy, his nails often dirty. In practice too he was occasionally careless. He was known to have wrapped a patient's arm with a bandage he had just used to wipe a table; and to inject the same needle without sterilization into two patients.

For some reason, perhaps out of the friendship that had sprung up between Frau Morell and Eva Braun, Hitler chose him from among all the doctors in Germany. And for the first time since his army days Hitler removed all of his clothes for a complete physical examination. Morell diagnosed the pains and cramps in the epigastric region as gastroduodenitis, for which he prescribed Mutaflor and Gallestol. Hitler also suffered from meteorism, uncontrollable farting, a condition aggravated by his vegetarianism for which Morell prescribed Dr. Köster's Antigas pills. These contained nux vomica but Morell, unaware that this was a seed containing strychnine, instructed his patient to take two to four at every meal. In addition, Morell supplemented Hitler's vegetarian diet with large doses of vitamins, often administering them intravenously together with glucose for energy.

The most prestigious specialists in the country—including Dr. Grawitz, head of the German Red Cross, and Professor Dr. Bergmann of the Berlin Charity Hospital—had failed to cure Hitler's stomach cramps or clear up eczema so painful he couldn't wear boots. The skin specialist from the Kurfürstendamm promised to do both within a year. It took him little more than a month and Hitler jubilantly announced that the miracle doctor had saved his life. "Both Grawitz and Bergmann let me go hungry. I was only allowed tea and zwieback. . . . I was so weak I could hardly work at my desk. Then came Morell and made me well." The Führer insisted all his new-found health came from Morell, claiming that improved gum conditions had come through Mutaflor injections, not the conscientious massaging and brushing prescribed by his dentist, Dr. Hugo Blaschke.

By the time Hitler addressed the Reichstag on January 30, 1937, to commemorate his first four years in office, he was in good spirits and looking younger than his age. He reasserted his divine mission. "Today I must humbly thank Providence whose grace has enabled me, once an unknown soldier in the war, to bring to a successful issue the struggle for our honor and rights as a nation." It was a speech of promise rather than of threat and made an impact because its boasts had a basis in reality. Hitler's achievements in the first four years had truly been considerable and impressive. Like Roosevelt, he had paved the way to social security and old-age benefits. And, like Roosevelt, he had intuitively divined that the professional economists, whose thinking was hobbled by accepted theory, had little understanding of the depression. Both leaders, consequently, had defied tradition to expand production and curb unemployment.* Hitler also was changing the face of the land

*"Hitler also anticipated modern economic policy," commented economist J. Kenneth Galbraith in 1973, ". . . by recognizing that a rapid approach to full employment was only possible if it was combined with wage and price controls. That a nation oppressed by economic fear would respond to Hitler as Americans did to F.D.R. is not surprising." Perhaps he understood economics too little to know what he was doing. "But in economics it is a great thing not to understand what causes you to insist on the right course."

with a network of *Autobahnen* that would help unite the nation in peace and mobilize it in war. To put the population on wheels, he was developing a "People's Car" so compact and inexpensive that the average German could afford it. He asked Ferdinand Porsche to design a vehicle that would get some forty miles per gallon, accommodate four passengers and have an air-cooled engine that would not freeze up in winter. He envisaged other innovations for the future. In large cities there would be automated underground parking, traffic-free centers, numerous parks and green areas, and strict pollution control. In line with his personal obsession with cleanliness (perhaps in connection with his recurring poison-cancer phobia), the problem of pollution so concerned him that he encouraged industry to work toward the complete elimination of noxious gases. Anti-pollution contrivances were already installed in some factories in the Ruhr basin, and new plants were required to construct preventive devices to avoid pollution of the waters.

The welfare and training of the youth of the nation were also given priority. Drastic changes had already been made in the educational system, with high schools specializing in natural science and non-classical curriculum placed on the same level as the humanistic Gymnasia. With five hours a day for physical training, compulsory courses in racial biology and emphasis on German history and literature, subjects such as ancient languages and science suffered. "The goal of our education is formation of character," wrote one Nazi pedagogue. "We don't intend to educate our children into becoming miniature scholars. . . . Therefore, I say: Let us have, rather, ten pounds less knowledge and ten calories more character."

The character-building process was accompanied by semideification of Hitler. Before lunch the children of Cologne were required to recite this invocation:

Führer, my Führer, bequeathed to me by the Lord,
Protect and preserve me as long as I live!
Thou hast rescued Germany from deepest distress,
I thank thee today for my daily bread.
Abide thou long with me, forsake me not,
Führer, my Führer, my faith and my light!
Heil, my Führer!

British Ambassador Phipps reported back to London: ". . . the German schoolboy is being methodically educated, mentally and physically to defend his country . . . but I fear that, if this or a later German government ever requires it of him, he will be found to be equally well-fitted and ready to march or die on foreign soil." This ominous development began in the training of the *Jungvolk*, the organization preparing boys of ten to fourteen to become Hitler Youth. "The Young Folk is the newly won element of eternity in inexorable truth," wrote the author of a booklet on the subject. "For us an order and an imperative are the most sacred duties. For every order comes from the responsible personage, and that personage we trust—the Führer. . . . So we stand before you, German Father, German Mother, we, the young leaders of the German Youth, we train and educate your son, and mould him into a man of action, a man of victory. He has been taken into a hard school, so that his fists may be steeled, his courage strengthened, and that he may be given a faith, a faith in Germany."

Upon graduation into the Hitler Youth each boy was given a dagger on which was engraved "Blood and Honor" and informed that now he could not only wear the brown shirt but defend it by force of arms. "We took this to mean that we were not to put up with anything from anybody," commented one member of the Hitler Jugend, recently escaped to England, "that we were superior to all civilians and could beat them up if they gave themselves airs."

Before 1933 the aim of Hitler Youth was to bring together young people from all walks of life, to break their ties with Communist organizations by persuasion and propaganda, and to indoctrinate them in the Fight for Power. Afterward, the mission was to build them physically, educate them politically and train them to work for Führer and nation.

While preparing the nation mentally and physically for the future, Hitler had managed in four years to raise the standards of health to such a degree that many foreigners were impressed. "Infant mortality has been greatly reduced and is considerably inferior to that in Great Britain," wrote Sir Arnold Wilson, M.P., a seven-time visitor since the take-over. "Tuberculosis and other diseases have noticeably diminished. The criminal courts have never had so little to do and the prisons have never had so few occupants. It is a pleasure to observe the physical aptitude of the German youth. Even the poorest persons are better clothed than was formerly the case, and their cheerful faces testify to the psychological improvement that has been wrought within them."

Working conditions were improved with more windows, less crowding and better washrooms. Under the slogan "Beautification in Every Place," all offices and workrooms were kept clean and neat; there were abundant flowers so that those who labored could also enjoy their surroundings. Such gains were not illusory. Never before had the worker enjoyed such privileges. The *Kraft durch Freude* (Strength through Joy) program initiated by Robert Ley's Labor Front provided subsidized concerts, theater performances, exhibitions, dances, films and adult education courses for the workers. The most revolutionary project was subsidized tourism. The humblest laborer and his family could now travel aboard luxury liners for undreamed-of holidays.

Hitler strove to unite people of all social levels—except, of course, the Jews—and his brand of socialism excluded neither the wealthy nor the middle class. "The bourgeois must no longer feel himself a kind of pensioner of either tradition or capital, separated from the worker by the Marxist idea of property," he told one interviewer, "but must aim to accommodate himself as a worker to the welfare of the community." In practice, this concept glorified the worker while underlining Hitler's theory of social equality. He himself was publicized as construction worker, artist and student; as a man of the people who sat next to his chauffeur and ate simple meals. He refused to accept any honorary doctorates and would address workers in plants with the intimate plural form *Ihr*, boasting that he too was without estates or stocks—but neglecting to note that *Mein Kampf* had made him a millionaire.

The spirit of equality was even felt in the armed forces. There was far more camaraderie than formerly between officers and enlisted men in the regular service and the elite SS units were models of democracy. Here there was no differentiation between ranks but a brotherly spirit of all for one and one for all that would have been frowned upon by most British and American officers. Nowhere was egalitarianism more evident than in the Youth Labor Service where young men and women of all classes between the ages of seventeen and twenty-five were obliged to work for a period as farm hands and laborers for *Volk und Vaterland*. This service had been instituted to alleviate unemployment but went far beyond Roosevelt's Civilian Conservation Corps, which had a similar aim, to become the manifestation of socialism. The walls of the labor camp barracks were hung with flags, pictures of the Führer and other leaders and inspirational slogans such as: "Germany needs you, as you need Germany," "Thy people is everything; thou art nothing," and "Labor service is honor service of the German youth." An American visitor, G. S. Cox, found a pair of remarkable slogans in one camp, a quotation from Hitler: "The Jew is not a German but merely a trader; not a citizen but an exterminator," side by side with another from Kant, "Have the courage to use your reason." Cox found the trainees a cheerful lot. "They were in splendid health, with plenty to eat—a luxury some of them had not experienced for years—and they were kept too busy to have time to criticize."

Of all of the achievements of Hitler's first four years, perhaps the most consequential was his unification of the nation. Hitler had not set the clock back, American diplomat George Kennan warned a superior. "Germany had simply been unified and thoroughly so. What Bonaparte and Napoleon III left undone in this direction, Versailles completed, and Hitler is now stamping out the last vestiges of particularism and class differences. That he is doing this by reducing everything to the lowest and most ugly common denominator is neither here nor there. German unity is a fact. Hitler may go but the unity will remain, and with it, barring outside interference, will remain—must remain—the jealousy, the uncertainty, the feeling of inferiority, the consequent lust to dominate Europe which are all that most Germans really have in common."

No objective observer of the German scene could deny Hitler's considerable exploits and, while labor had lost its unions, so had management lost its right to organize politically. Every individual, in fact, had lost his rights, his liberty, while the nation was gaining in equality and prosperity. But loss of civil liberties was not the only price paid for Hitler's program: although he had lifted the country out of depression and ended unemployment by original means, his insistence on speeding up rearmament at all costs was forcing the nation into a potentially disastrous economic crisis. The brilliant Schacht had done his best to oppose the efforts of Hitler and the military to make Germany economically independent, first, by vetoing plans of the War Ministry and I. G. Farben to produce artificial rubber, and then by refusing Blomberg's request for expansion of fuel oil production for fear it would upset the peacetime balance of the economy. But by early 1936 Schacht's influence had waned and the economy had been thrown off balance by Hitler's order to increase the army to thirty-six divisions. There were two primary reasons: import prices had risen 9 per cent while export prices were falling 9 per cent; and with two successive bad harvests, German agriculture was unable to supply the needs of the nation. Existing raw material stocks were shrinking. There was already a disturbing shortage of food and fuel. This latter crisis was precipitated by a Russian embargo on German exports combined with a Romanian demand for higher prices. Heating, light, lubricating and diesel oil supplies were at a dangerously low level and could not be replaced by home production.

Hitler demanded an economic mobilization "comparable to the military and political mobilization." Nor did he care how it was achieved so long as the Wehrmacht was operational in four years. This was the Four-Year Plan he had announced at the 1936 Nuremberg rally. The following month he chose Göring to administer it and, significantly, his choice of collaborators included but one old party member, the top posts going to co-operative civil servants, representatives of industry and General Staff officers. This meant that the NSDAP, except for Göring, whose loyalty was to himself and Hitler, had been virtually excluded from the decision-making process in the nation's economic life.

In a speech calling for national mobilization, Göring declared that workers and peasants must apply their full strength, inventors must place themselves at the disposal of the state, and business must "think not of profit, but of a strong, independent national German economy."

Two months later Hitler himself made a pressing appeal to an important group of industrialists to trust Göring as executor of this urgent mission: "He is the best man for this job, a man of iron will and determination. Therefore march in serried ranks behind him." At the same meeting Göring told the industrialists it was no longer a question of producing economically but of producing. He was not at all concerned how foreign exchange was brought in. Only those who broke the law *without success* would be prosecuted.

"It was incumbent on me to denounce this economic nonsense," wrote Schacht, "and to oppose this irresponsible and wanton flouting of the law, as openly as possible." He did so in a speech to the Chamber of Commerce on his sixtieth birthday, and his audience was almost the same as Göring's. He also decried Göring's claim that the only important thing was to produce. "If I sow a hundred-weight of grain on a certain area of land and harvest only three-quarters of a hundred-weight, then that is the most utter economic nonsense imaginable." It was a declaration of war by an official already out of favor and within a few months Schacht was forced to resign as Minister of Economics. This left Göring free to carry out his Führer's plan to transform the German economy into a barefaced instrument for rearmament—and war.

If Hitler had died in 1937 on the fourth anniversary of his coming to power—the great economic crisis notwithstanding—he would undoubtedly have gone down as one of the greatest figures in German history.

The accomplishments of Hitler in his first four years of power had done much to encourage others of a like mind. The appeal of Fascism was not only to the disgruntled and disenfranchised but to responsible men of good will. It drew unto itself youthful elements as well as intellectuals who found it a refreshing alternative to bourgeois liberalism. And while each country had its own particular brand of Fascism, all its adherents (including Hitler and Mussolini) believed that, come what may, the spiritual unity of their nation would solve all problems. This end, they believed, justified the means.

Chapter Fifteen

THE RETURN OF THE NATIVE

FEBRUARY–APRIL 1938

On the brink of total dictatorship, Hitler told the Wehrmacht that the aim of German policy was to make secure, to preserve, and to enlarge the racial community. To do so Germany must take the offensive while the rest of the world was still preparing its defense. The first objective was to secure Germany's eastern and southern flanks by seizing Czechoslovakia and Austria. But the two top army officers, Field Marshal von Blomberg and General von Fritsch, opposed the Führer's blueprint for conquest so forcefully that Hitler decided to eliminate them. Fritsch was framed on a charge of committing criminal homosexual acts with two Hitler Youths. But Blomberg brought about his own downfall by unwittingly marrying a prostitute, his young secretary. Blomberg was replaced by General Wilhelm Keitel; Fritsch was replaced by General Walther von Brauchitsch, long an ardent admirer of the Führer.

On February 4, 1938, the leading officers of the Wehrmacht were assembled and informed by Hitler why Fritsch and Blomberg had to be dismissed. The astounded officers meekly accepted Hitler's announcement of the reorganization of the Wehrmacht, and that evening Hitler legalized his takeover of the armed forces at a cabinet meeting. After presenting Keitel and Brauchitsch, he announced that he himself was now in command of the armed forces. It was the last time the cabinet would ever meet and it was fitting that its members merely sat and approved.

Just before midnight the people of Germany were informed by radio of the Führer's momentous decree. They also learned that Blomberg and Fritsch had resigned, that sixteen high-ranking generals had been dismissed, and that forty-four more had been transferred to other posts. Finally, Hermann Göring was granted the baton of a Luftwaffe field marshal as a consolation for not being named Minister of War. The house cleaning extended to the diplomatic service. Foreign Minister von Neurath was replaced by Ribbentrop, who believed that every hour not spent in preparing for war against England was an hour lost to Germany. There was no longer any possibility of an agreement with the British, he had recently told Hitler, since they would not tolerate a powerful Germany.

It was a day to remember in German history. The most powerful dissidents in the Wehrmacht had been eliminated or curbed and the two leading military men in the land, Keitel and Brauchitsch, were both in Hitler's debt and little more than uneasy deputies.

At last Hitler was the supreme dictator of the German Reich. He was ready to embark on his final course.

2

The repercussions of Hitler's bloodless purge were felt almost immediately in Vienna. At the German Legation Franz von Papen—once Chancellor and now merely a minister to a small country—was called on the telephone. It was Lammers, secretary of the chancellery. "The Führer wished to inform you," he said, "that your mission in Vienna has ended. I wanted to tell you before you read about it in the newspapers." Papen was almost speechless. He had been persuaded by Hitler to take the minor post to restore the dangerous situation created by the Dollfuss murder. "I had served my purpose, it seemed, and could now go," he recalled with some bitterness. To "obtain some picture of what was going on" he decided to go at once to Berchtesgaden where he found Hitler exhausted and disturbed. "His eyes seemed unable to focus on anything and his thoughts seemed elsewhere. He sought to explain my dismissal with empty excuses." The distracted Führer paid little attention to the conversation until Papen remarked that only a face-to-face meeting between Hitler and Austrian Chancellor Kurt von Schuschnigg could solve the numerous problems dividing the two countries.

"That is an excellent idea," said Hitler and told Papen to return to Vienna and arrange a meeting for the near future. "I should be very pleased to invite Herr Schuschnigg here and talk everything over with him."

Schuschnigg accepted Papen's invitation with some uneasiness, then confessed to his Foreign Minister, Guido Schmidt, that he did so "to forestall a coup and to gain time until the international situation should improve in Austria's favor." He added ironically that he only wished his place opposite Hitler at the conference table could be filled by a psychiatrist. Schuschnigg was, indeed, ill suited to face such a ruthless opponent. A devout Catholic, an intellectual, a decent man with little vanity or driving ambition, he would enter the contest at a disadvantage.

On the evening of February 11, accompanied by Guido Schmidt, he boarded the night express for Salzburg. Once the train reached the birthplace of Mozart the sleeping car was detached. The next morning the two men drove through the ancient city, past the airport and across the Salzach River to the German border. Papen was waiting with a Hitler salute. The German customs officials also smartly raised their arms, as did their Austrian counterparts in violation of the law. It was an alarming omen and moments later came another. Papen trusted the guests wouldn't mind that three generals had "quite accidentally" arrived at the Berghof. If he had been a Dollfuss, Schuschnigg might have protested, but he disliked scenes and had no desire to provoke Hitler. "No," he said, "I don't mind but it's strange."

On the outskirts of Berchtesgaden they turned sharply to the left, at the foot of the Obersalzberg where half-tracks were waiting to take them up the steep, icy road to the Berghof. They passed neat snowbound farmhouses and an old church, then came upon SS barracks, some still under construction. All at once there was a sharp turn and the tracked vehicle stopped below the large terrace of the Berghof.

Hitler advanced with outstretched hand, the genial host. After introducing the three generals behind him, he led the Austrian Chancellor into his study on the second floor. Here the Führer abruptly shed his affability, bluntly accusing Austria of following anything but neighborly policy. Was it friendly to stay complacently in the League of Nations after Germany withdrew? In fact, Austria had never done anything to help Germany. The whole history of Austria was one uninterrupted act of high treason. "And I can tell you right now, Herr Schuschnigg, that I am absolutely determined to make an end of all this. The German Reich is one of the Great Powers and nobody will raise his voice if it settles its border problems."

Determined not to lose his temper, Schuschnigg retorted that Austria's entire history had been an essential and inseparable part of German history. "Austria's contribution in this respect is considerable."

"Absolutely zero, I'm telling you, absolutely zero!" exclaimed Hitler, sounding like anything but a man born and raised in Austria himself, and, when Schuschnigg brought up Beethoven, reminded him that the composer came from the Lower Rhineland. "I am telling you once more that things cannot go on this way. I have a historic mission; and this mission I will fulfill because Providence has destined me to do so. I thoroughly believe in this mission; it is my life. . . . Look around you in Germany today, Herr Schuschnigg, and you will find that there is but one will."

He accused Austria of fortifying the German border and making ridiculous efforts to mine the bridges and roads leading to the Reich. "You don't seriously believe you can stop me or even delay me for half an hour, do you? Perhaps you will wake up one morning in Vienna to find us there—just like a spring storm. And then you'll see something! I would very much like to save Austria from such a fate, because such an action would mean blood."

When Schuschnigg replied that Austria was not alone in the world and an invasion of his country would probably mean war, Hitler scoffed. Nobody would move a finger for Austria—not Italy, nor England, nor France. "Think it over, Herr Schuschnigg," he said, lowering his voice. "Think it over well. I can only wait until this afternoon. If I tell you that, you will do well to take my words literally. I don't believe in bluffing. All my past is proof of that."

His tactics were getting on Schuschnigg's nerves. He longed

for a cigarette but he had been warned not to light up in the Führer's presence. He asked Hitler exactly what he wanted. "That," replied Hitler, ending the session with dramatic abruptness, "we can discuss this afternoon."

At 4 P.M. Ribbentrop handed Schuschnigg a two-page typewritten draft of an agreement that was essentially an ultimatum: Germany would renew its full support of Austria's sovereignty if all imprisoned Austrian National Socialists, including the assassins of Dollfuss, were set free within three days and all dismissed National Socialist officials and officers were reinstated in their former positions. In addition, Artur Seyss-Inquart, the leader of the moderate Pan-German faction, was to be appointed Minister of Interior with full, unlimited control of the nation's police forces; a "moderate" Austrian Nazi was to be Minister of Defense, and the incumbent propaganda chiefs were to be removed as part of "the smooth execution of a press truce."

To Schuschnigg these concessions amounted to the end of Austrian independence and, suppressing indignation, he began to contest the various points like a dispassionate lawyer. He had just managed to squeeze a few minor concessions from Ribbentrop when word came that the Führer was ready to see him upstairs.

Hitler was excitedly pacing up and down the study. "Herr Schuschnigg, I have decided to make one last attempt." He pushed another copy of the draft agreements at the Austrian. "There is nothing to be discussed about it. I will not change one single iota. You will either sign it as it stands or else our meeting has been useless. In that case I shall decide during the night what will be done next."

Schuschnigg refused to sign. Even if he did, he said, it would be valueless since by constitution President Miklas alone could appoint cabinet members and grant amnesty. Nor could he in any way guarantee that the time limits stipulated in the document would be observed.

"You must guarantee that!"

"I could not possibly, Herr Reichskanzler."

Schuschnigg's studied, courtroom rejoinders infuriated Hitler. He rushed to the door and shouted, "General Keitel!" He turned back to Schuschnigg. "I shall have you called later." The bellow was heard in the winter garden and Keitel trotted upstairs like an obedient dog, entering the study just as Schuschnigg was about to leave. Out of breath, Keitel asked what commands the Führer had. "None at all! Just sit down." Puzzled, the head of OKW perched in the corner dutifully and from now on fellow officers would nickname him *Lakeitel*, for *Lakai* (lackey).

Unaware that Hitler was bluffing, Schuschnigg was badly shaken by the time he reached the winter garden. He related what had happened to Foreign Minister Schmidt, who said he would not be surprised if they were arrested "within the next five minutes."

Upstairs, another Austrian, a moderate Nazi, an art critic, was assuring the Führer that Schuschnigg was a scrupulous man who would honor his promises. Impressed, Hitler made one of his lightning tactical shifts and the next time Schuschnigg walked into the study he found a magnanimous Führer. "I have decided," he said, "to change my mind—for the first time in my entire life. But I warn you—this is your very last chance. I have given you three more days before the agreement goes into effect."

After the shock of the first two conversations, the minor concessions wrung out of Hitler seemed more important than they were and Schuschnigg agreed to sign the compact. Once the revised document was sent out to be retyped, Hitler again became the genial host—one who has just sold the guest an objet d'art for an exorbitant price and is assuring him it is a bargain. "Believe me, Herr Bundeskanzler, it is for the best. Now we can abide by this agreement for the next five years."

3

Schuschnigg had three days to get their agreement approved by his colleagues and President Miklas. It was Sunday when the Chancellor arrived back in Vienna and time would run out on Tuesday the fifteenth. He conferred at once with Miklas, who was willing to grant amnesty to those Austrian Nazis still in prison while vigorously objecting to the appointment of Seyss-Inquart. "I would give him any other post," he said, "but I refuse to give him the police and the army."

News of the secret meeting in Berchtesgaden soon spread to the coffeehouses, the unofficial parliament of Austria, and an uneasy spirit pervaded the nation. Bitter arguments sprang up among the cabinet members with one group complaining that Schuschnigg should publicly proclaim Hitler's brutal tactics at the Berghof and the other commending the Chancellor's policy of caution. Twenty-four hours before Hitler's ultimatum was to run out so much disagreement remained that an emergency conference was held in the office of the President. Present, besides the two principals, were the mayor of Vienna, the president of the National Bank and a former Chancellor. After reviewing the situation Schuschnigg presented three possible courses: select a new Chancellor who would be under no obligation to the commitments at the Berghof; carry out the agreements under a new Chancellor; or carry them out under Schuschnigg. At last Miklas bowed to pressure, reluctantly agreeing to the Chancellor's third proposal: to leave Schuschnigg in office and accept the Berchtesgaden pact. That evening a new cabinet was sworn in.

In Vienna there was a rising demand that Schuschnigg reveal exactly what had happened in Berchtesgaden but, having promised to keep silent until after Hitler addressed the Reichstag on Sunday, he kept his word as a man of honor.

The German Legation phoned Berlin that there was "considerable agitation in Vienna because of the political and economic consequences" of the agreement, that the city "resembled an anthill," and that "quite a few Jews were preparing to emigrate." Secret SD reports confirmed this, one agent informing Heydrich on February 18 that the Chancellor was under heavy attack from both Jews and Catholics. "The Jews were attacking mainly through the stock exchange, to exert pressure on the currency. Since February 17, 1938, there has been an extraordinarily heavy flight of capital, which led to a substantial drop in Austrian securities in Switzerland and London, as well as in other foreign countries. Schilling notes are being taken over the border illegally in large quantities, so that they have not been quoted since last night."

On February 20 Hitler made his eagerly awaited speech to the Reichstag, which was also broadcast throughout Austria. After announcing that he and Schuschnigg had "made a contribution to the cause of European peace," he accused Austria of mistreating its "German minority." It was, he added, "intolerable for a self-conscious world power to know that at its side are co-racials who are subjected to continuous suffering because of their sympathy and unity with the whole German race and its ideology."

Schuschnigg's reply to Hitler came four days later at the opening session of the Federal Diet in a speech broadcast throughout both countries. The stage of the parliament was decorated with a mass of tulips in the Austrian colors of red-white-red. Near the rostrum was a bust of the martyred Dollfuss. Although the Chancellor walked erectly to the podium his restrained manner was that of a Jesuit scholar. He was greeted with shouts of "Schuschnigg! Schuschnigg!" for the word had gone out that he was going to make a fighting speech. "The one and only point on the order of the day," he said in a tired voice, "is: Austria." This brought renewed shouts. Inspired, he began to speak movingly of those who had fought for Austrian independence from the Empress Maria Theresa to Dollfuss. Never before had his delivery been so effective, so fervent. Gone were the restraints of the self-effacing intellectual who had allowed himself to be bullied at the Berghof. His tone hardened when he finally mentioned the Berchtesgaden agreements. "We have gone to the very limit of concessions, where we must call a halt and say, 'Thus far and no further.'" He went on to declare that "neither Nationalism nor Socialism is the watchword of Austria, but patriotism!" The nation would remain free and for this Austrians would have to fight to the end.

4

French indignation at Hitler's threat to Austria took the form of a proposal to London that the two big powers send a joint note of protest to Berlin. It arrived at an inauspicious time. Anthony Eden had just resigned and the Foreign Ministry was momentarily without leadership. The English public had not yet been aroused by the events in Austria and their new Prime Minister Neville Chamberlain remained devoted to the policy of appeasing Germany. Furthermore, Chamberlain was supported by the London *Times*, which consistently played down the importance of the events in Austria. "Fundamentally," it editorialized, "a close understanding between the two German states is the most natural thing possible." Goebbels could not have put it more convincingly. "Austria can never be anti-Germanic."

By the beginning of March Great Britain was irrevocably bound to appeasement. On the third of the month the Ambassador to Germany, Sir Nevile Henderson, called at the chancellery to inform Hitler that His Majesty's Government was ready, in principle, to discuss all outstanding questions.

It took Henderson ten minutes to state the object of his visit: a genuine desire to improve mutual relations between their two countries. Britain, he said, was prepared to make certain concessions to settle the grave problems of limitation of armaments and restrictions of bombing as well as a peaceful solution to the Czech and Austrian problems. What contribution to general security and peace in Europe was Hitler ready to make?

During this lengthy exposition the Führer crouched in his armchair scowling and when Henderson finally stopped he angrily replied that only a small percentage of Austrians supported Schuschnigg. Why did England persist in opposing a just settlement and interfering in "German family matters"? He abruptly went on the offensive, charging that the Franco-Soviet and Czecho-Soviet pacts were definite threats to Germany. That was why Germany had to be so heavily armed. In consequence any limitation of arms depended on the Russians. And this was a problem complicated "by the fact that one could place as much confidence in the faith in treaties of a barbarous creature like the Soviet Union as in the comprehension of mathematical formulae by a savage. Any agreement with the U.S.S.R. was quite worthless and Russia should never be allowed into Europe."

The following day Hitler sent his chief economic adviser, Wilhelm Keppler, to Austria. Presenting himself to Schuschnigg as a personal representative of the Führer, he came bearing fresh demands which included everything deleted at Berchtesgaden. But Keppler's main interest was economic and, since he regarded Anschluss (incorporation of Austria into Germany) as a financial imperative for both countries, he acted more like a benefactor than a predator. "The Führer's wish at the time," recalled Schuschnigg, "was for an evolutionary development; in other words he wished to roll up Austria from within, if possible without any apparent German involvement." The time, concluded the amiable Keppler, had come to accelerate this process.

Schuschnigg reacted sharply to Keppler's new demands, such as the immediate appointment of a Nazi as Minister of

Economics, cancellation of the ban on the *Völkischer Beobachter* and formal legalization of National Socialism. How, asked the incredulous Schuschnigg, could Hitler come along three weeks later with this fresh set of impositions? His government would co-operate with Austrian Nazis only on the basis of long-term recognition of Austrian independence. Schuschnigg recalled that the interview "ended inconclusively" but Keppler reported that it "began tempestuously but concluded in an entirely conciliatory manner," and that he "had the impression that Schuschnigg will by no means submit to force but that, if treated sensibly, he will come along to a great extent, if this is made possible for him without loss of prestige. We can rely on his loyalty as regards the Berchtesgaden agreements." He further reported that the Austrian party was making excellent progress, particularly in Graz where some 80 per cent of the people professed National Socialism. "At present we are inclined to apply the brakes to the movement, in order to wring more and more concessions from Schuschnigg."

Schuschnigg's concessions to the Nazis only incited new disturbances, placing Austria in a quasi state of undeclared civil war. In Vienna storm troopers and Nazi sympathizers would cross the Danube Canal to the Jewish quarter in Leopoldstadt shouting, "Sieg Heil! Sieg Heil!" one night and "Heil Hitler!" the next. They would be confronted by opponents shouting "Heil Schuschnigg!" and "Red-White-Red to the Death!" There were frequent clashes, usually brought to an end by truncheon-wielding police. Generally it was the patriots who got beat up, for the loyalty of the police extended more to Minister of the Interior Seyss-Inquart than to the Chancellor.

In desperation Schuschnigg dispatched an appeal to Mussolini on March 7 warning that he might have to hold a plebiscite to save the situation. Il Duce sent back words of reassurance. Professing to believe the pledge of Göring that Germany would not use force, he urged Schuschnigg not to hold a plebiscite. The message was cold comfort to a Chancellor threatened with invasion from abroad while under attack at home by workers for being too lenient and by Nazis for being too restrictive. He decided to ignore Mussolini's advice.

On March 9 he announced the plebiscite in a Tyrolean city, Innsbruck. He stepped onto the podium in the town square clad in the traditional Austrian gray jacket and green waistcoat and announced emotionally that the nation would go to the polls in four days to answer one question: "Are you in favor of a free and German, independent and social, a Christian and united Austria?" For the second time he spoke as orator rather than scholar. "Tyrolians and Austrians, say 'Yes' to Tyrol. Say 'Yes' to Austria!"

As he feared, the announcement did force the Führer's hand. A vote for a free and united Austria—and this was the likely outcome—meant the delay, if not the end, of Anschluss. And since the union with Austria was a necessary preliminary to eastward expansion, the plebiscite threatened to wreck Hitler's entire program of Lebensraum. He could not tolerate such a challenge and on the morning of March 10 told General Keitel that the Austrian problem was so "acute" that he should make appropriate preparations. Keitel remembered that a General Staff plan, Operation Otto, had been drawn up in case Otto von Habsburg attempted to regain the throne of Austria. "Prepare it," ordered the Führer.

Keitel rushed to OKW headquarters in the Bendlerstrasse where he found to his dismay that Operation Otto was simply a theoretical study. Regretting his haste to please the Führer, he turned over to General Beck the task of submitting a report on the possible invasion of Austria. "We have prepared nothing," complained Beck, "nothing has been done, nothing at all." When Beck reported to Hitler and suggested using two corps and the 2nd Panzer Division for the military occupation of Austria, he was appalled to learn that these troops should be prepared to march across the border by Saturday the twelfth. The thought of preparing such an operation within forty-eight hours was inconceivable to a professional. Beck protested that it meant orders would have to go out to the various formations at 6 P.M. that same evening. Then do it, said Hitler the amateur strategist.

More concerned with Italian reaction to an invasion than with logistics, the Führer hastily dictated a letter to Mussolini. Austria, he wrote, was approaching a state of anarchy and he could not stand idly by. "In my responsibility as Führer and Chancellor of the German Reich and likewise as a son of this soil . . . I am now determined to restore law and order in my homeland and enable the people to decide their own fate according to their judgment in an unmistakable, clear and open manner." He reminded Il Duce of Germany's help in Italy's critical hour, the Abyssinian war, and promised to repay Italian support by recognizing the boundary between Italy and the Reich as the Brenner Pass.

Throughout Austria posters were being plastered on billboards announcing the plebiscite. Sound trucks circulated through towns and cities urging all Austrians to vote "*Ja*" on Sunday. In Vienna patriots were at last making more noise than the Nazis as groups ranged the streets shouting "Heil Schuschnigg!" "Heil Liberty!" and "Sunday is polling day; we vote *Ja*!"

Heartened by public enthusiasm, Schuschnigg continued to act resolute. "I am neither able nor prepared to play the role of puppet," he wrote Seyss-Inquart in reply to the Minister of the Interior's charge that the plebiscite was contrary to the Berchtesgaden agreements. "I cannot be expected to look on with folded hands while the country is ruined economically and politically." He concluded with an urgent request to Seyss-Inquart, as the minister responsible for security, to take measures to bring terrorism to an end. Otherwise he would not be able to hold the opposing forces in check.

Although Seyss-Inquart was generally regarded as Hitler's cat's-paw, he too was concerned for his country's independence, and while he sympathized with some of the policies of the Austrian Nazis, they did not regard him as one of their number. He was much closer in ideology and nature to Schuschnigg. Both considered themselves patriots; both were devout Catholics; both were intellectuals, shy men of culture with a deep love of music. Seyss-Inquart proved he was more patriot than Nazi by promising to appeal to his followers over the radio to vote affirmative on Sunday.

Schuschnigg went to bed that evening "fully satisfied" that the Nazi threat to the plebiscite had been scotched—unaware that Seyss-Inquart by now had little influence in his own party. The hard-core Austrian Nazis were already on the streets marching in columns of four toward the center of disorder, the official German Tourist Bureau which boasted a hastily painted larger-than-life oil portrait of Hitler. Their shouts of "*Ein Volk, ein Reich, ein Führer*!" were greeted at first with amusement by the patriots, who outnumbered them three to one. Then windows were smashed and the police, who had been standing by, formed cordons to prevent further damage. Making no move to subdue the howling mob of Nazis, they concentrated on the patriots to such an extent that eventually the outnumbered wearers of the swastika dominated the streets.

5

At 2 A.M. on March 11 the improvised invasion plan, still bearing the code name Operation Otto, was issued. In it, Hitler took personal control. "If other measures prove unsuccessful," it read, "I intend to invade Austria with armed forces in order to establish constitutional conditions and to prevent further outrages against the pro-German population." The units involved were to be prepared by noon of March 12. "I reserve the right to decide the actual moment of invasion. The behavior of the troops must give the impression that we do not want to wage war against our Austrian brothers."

At 5:30 A.M. Schuschnigg's bedside phone rang. It was his chief of police reporting that the German border at Salzburg had just been closed and all railroad traffic stopped. He hurried to the chancellery on Ballhausplatz where he learned that German divisions in the Munich area had been mobilized, destination presumably Austria.

At about 10 A.M. Glaise-Horstenau, Schuschnigg's minister without portfolio, a Nazi, arrived at the Ballhausplatz with written instructions from Hitler and Göring. He was accompanied by Seyss-Inquart, who had met him at the Aspern airport. Badly shaken, Seyss-Inquart reported the demands from Berlin: Schuschnigg must resign and the plebiscite was to be postponed for two weeks so that a "legal poll," similar to the Saar plebiscite, could be set up. If Göring did not get a telephone answer by noon he would assume that Seyss-Inquart was prevented from making the call and would "act accordingly." It was already eleven-thirty and Seyss-Inquart, a reasonable man, extended the deadline until 2 P.M. in the Führer's name.

Schuschnigg used this time to assess possibilities of resistance. He telephoned the chief of police, who informed him that Vienna remained quiet. He had thrown a cordon—"in as far as that is possible"—around the inner city but so many Nazi policemen had been restored to their jobs that the government could no longer count on its police force. In this extremity Schuschnigg summoned the "inner cabinet," his closest advisers, to discuss the emergency. He presented three alternatives: rejection of the ultimatum followed by an appeal to world opinion; acceptance followed by his own resignation;

and a compromise, accepting Hitler's demands for technical changes in the plebiscite but resisting all other demands. They decided upon compromise.

It was almost 2 P.M. and moments later the two reluctant messengers of doom, Seyss-Inquart and Glaise-Horstenau, were back. They could not accept the proffered compromise and Schuschnigg was faced with the unpleasant choice between complete submission or defiance. He hurriedly conferred with President Miklas and it was decided to call off the plebiscite. Returning to his office, he informed the inner cabinet members of the decision.

Moments later the Chancellor was telling Seyss-Inquart and Glaise-Horstenau that Berlin's demands for postponement of the plebiscite had been granted. At the same time extensive security measures, such as an 8 P.M. curfew, would have to be taken. Concerned, the two men excused themselves to transmit this information to Göring by telephone.*

"These measures of Chancellor Schuschnigg are in no way satisfactory," replied Göring, who then hung up to think things over. He should have conferred with Hitler who, according to Papen, was currently "in a state bordering on hysteria," but instead acted on his own. A few minutes past 3 P.M. he was back on the phone with Seyss-Inquart. "Berlin cannot agree in any way to the decision taken by Chancellor Schuschnigg," he said, ruthless beneath a veneer of joviality. He demanded that Schuschnigg and his cabinet resign. He also repeated the demand to send Berlin a telegram asking for German help.

The two ministers solemnly marched back to the large room where their cabinet colleagues were assembled. Seyss-Inquart, "white in the face and agitated," read from his notebook Göring's ultimatum, and then quailed under a bombardment of questions. "Don't ask me," he replied bitterly, "I'm nothing more than an historic telephone girl." If he himself were not appointed Chancellor within two hours, he added, the German armies would move on Austria.

Life in Vienna was continuing as if nothing had happened. Planes circled overhead dropping clouds of leaflets urging the citizens to vote "Ja" on Sunday. On the streets truck columns of the "Fatherland Front" were greeted with patriotic shouts and waving handkerchiefs; strangers would welcome each other

*This and other telephone conversations between Berlin and various capitals during the next few days are from official transcripts found by Allied authorities in the Reich chancellery.

with: "*Österreich*!" For once the nation appeared to be united. All at once the gay waltzes and patriotic marches that had been coming from every radio station were abruptly changed by an announcement ordering all unmarried reservists of the 1915 class to report immediately for duty. Before long a stream of army trucks loaded with steel-helmeted troops headed for the German border.

In desperation Schuschnigg sought help from London. He told how he had given way to Hitler's demands rather than risk bloodshed and asked "for immediate advice of His Majesty's Government as to what he should do." This telegram ironically reached Prime Minister Chamberlain during a lunch at 10 Downing Street in honor of the Ribbentrops. Chamberlain frostily invited Ribbentrop into his study "for a private word" with himself and Lord Halifax, the new Foreign Secretary. "The discussion," as Ribbentrop reported it to Hitler, "took place in a tense atmosphere and the usually calm Lord Halifax was more excited than Chamberlain, who outwardly at least appeared calm and cool-headed." After the Prime Minister read out the telegram from Vienna, Ribbentrop "professed to be ignorant of the whole situation" and, in fact, expressed doubts about the truth of the reports. If it were true, he added, it might be the best way of achieving a "peaceful solution."

These words were enough to placate a man already determined to keep on good terms with Hitler; Chamberlain agreed with Ribbentrop that there was no proof of violent German action even when his own Foreign Secretary angrily charged that Schuschnigg had been "threatened with invasion." Then Chamberlain asked Lord Halifax to send off a reply to the Austrian government that must have made him wince: "His Majesty's Government cannot take responsibility of advising the Chancellor to take any course of action which might expose his country to dangers against which His Majesty's Government are unable to guarantee protection."

Nazis were already taking over the streets of Vienna in response to orders from Berlin. One mob sweeping toward the inner city shouted, "Heil Hitler! Sieg Heil! Hang Schuschnigg!" In the chancellery Schuschnigg heard the shouts and the tramp of feet. Convinced that this was a prelude to invasion, he went to the President's office to make a final appeal but Miklas remained adamant, stubbornly refusing to appoint a Nazi as Chancellor, and when Schuschnigg insisted, said, "You will desert me now, all of you." Still Schuschnigg saw no other possibility than Seyss-Inquart, a practicing Catholic with a reputation as an honest man, and suggested that he himself speak immediately on the radio to the Austrian people.

Shortly Schuschnigg entered the Corner Room on the first floor of the chancellery adjoining the grand staircase. Here in the middle of the room stood a microphone, barely five paces from the place Dollfuss had been murdered by the Nazis. There was a hush as Schuschnigg stepped to the microphone at 7:50 P.M. and told of the German ultimatum. Throughout Austria people were engrossed by a broadcast which William Shirer described as the most moving he had ever heard. "President Miklas asks me to tell the people of Austria that we have yielded to force. Because under no circumstances, not even in this supreme hour, do we intend that German blood shall be spilt, we have instructed our army to retreat without offering any resistance in the event of an invasion and to await further decisions." Shirer thought Schuschnigg's voice would break into sobs but he controlled himself. "Thus," he concluded, "I take leave of the Austrian nation with a German farewell which also expresses my heartfelt wish: God save Austria!"

Seyss-Inquart must have run from the Corner Room to a telephone because it was only 7:57 P.M. by the time he had Göring on the line. "The government has just put itself out of office," he reported. Austrian troops were being withdrawn from the German border. "The gentlemen here have decided to sit and wait for the invasion."

When Göring learned that Seyss-Inquart had not been nominated as Chancellor he lost his temper. "All right then. I am going to give marching orders now to the troops. And it is up to you to see that you will be in charge. Inform all leading personalities of what I tell you now: everybody who resists our troops or organizes resistance will be summarily dealt with by our tribunals." Seyss-Inquart's halfhearted protests were shouted down. "All right, now. You have got your official orders."

The crowd outside the Austrian chancellery, swollen to an estimated 100,000, was getting rowdy as Nazi supporters of both sexes chanted the name of the Führer and cavorted in the glow of smoking torches. Even more unruly groups ranged through the inner city singing Nazi songs and shouting, "Down with the Jews! Heil Hitler! Sieg Heil! Kill the Jews! Hang Schuschnigg! Heil Seyss-Inquart!"

Between delivering ultimatums to Vienna in an effort to force the situation, Göring had been urging Hitler to invade Austria come what may. The Führer hesitated until about 8:15 P.M. Then as he was reflectively strolling with Göring a police official saw him abruptly slap his thigh. "Now, get moving!" he cried. Half an hour later Hitler signed Instruction Order Number Two for Operation Otto which declared that German troops would march into Austria at dawn the next morning "to prevent further bloodshed in Austrian towns."

Three minutes after Hitler signed the order Göring was at a phone in the winter garden giving further orders to Keppler, the economic expert. Seyss-Inquart was to send a telegram in the name of the provisional Austrian government, urgently requesting that Germany help them restore law and order by dispatching troops to Austria. Seyss-Inquart was to take care of the matter at once. "He does not really have to send the telegram. He only has to say that he did. You get me?"

Hitler was pleased by the arrival of the telegram from the provisional government of Austria requesting the immediate aid of German troops in the exact words dictated by Göring, another case of legality after the fact. It gave Hitler the opportunity to masquerade his troops as liberators and, in high spirits, he ordered them to march in with bands playing and regimental colors flying. One thing was lacking, reassurance from Mussolini. And this arrived at 10:25 P.M. in the form of a long-distance call from Prince Philip von Hessen. "I have just returned from the Palazzo Venezia," he told Hitler, whose heart must have been pounding. "Il Duce took the news very well indeed. He sends his very best regards to you." The Austrian question no longer interested him.

6

Early that Saturday morning Hitler flew to Munich with Keitel to take part in the triumphal entry into his homeland. Before leaving, he signed a proclamation describing his version of the events that led to the crisis. "Since early this morning soldiers of the German armed forces have been marching across the Austro-German frontiers. Mechanized troops and infantry, German airplanes in the blue sky, summoned by the new National Socialist government in Vienna, are the guarantors the Austrian nation shall at an early date be given the opportunity to decide their own future by a genuine plebiscite." This was followed by a personal note, "I, myself, as Führer and Chancellor will be happy to walk on the soil of the country which is my home as a free German citizen."

At 8 A.M. his troops had begun streaming into Austria and at some points frontier barriers were dismantled by the inhabitants themselves. It was more like an improvised maneuver than an invasion. The 2nd Panzer Division, for instance, was advancing with the help of a Baedeker's guide and refueling at local gas stations. As the troops marched in they were bombarded with flowers by ecstatic women and children. Nazi tanks flew flags of both nations and were gaily decorated with greenery. "The populace saw that we came as friends," recalled General Heinz Guderian, "and we were everywhere joyfully received." Almost every village and town, houses decorated with swastika flags, greeted the Germans with jubilation.

In London the cabinet was meeting in emergency session. Chamberlain's glum judgment was that the Anschluss had been inevitable, ". . . unless the Powers had been able to say: 'If you make war on Austria, you will have to deal with us.'" And that had never been a possibility. "At any rate," he concluded, "that question is now out of the way." He dismissed the fait accompli as a matter of little consequence.

It was dark when the first stage of Hitler's sentimental journey ended at Linz, whose streets he had wandered in solitude so many evenings. The crowd of 100,000 waiting in the market square engulfed the caravan in a display of joyous hysteria which amazed Hitler's aides and adjutants. When the Führer appeared on the balcony of the City Hall with the new Chancellor of Austria the people were in a frenzy.

7

Sigmund Freud had promised his family to leave Austria once the Nazis took over. Now he told an English colleague, Dr. Ernest Jones, "This is my post and I can never leave it." This reminded Jones of the officer on the *Titanic* who, when asked why he abandoned ship, replied: "I never left the ship, she left me." Freud got the point. He admitted Austria no longer existed and agreed to depart for England, "the land of his early dreams." He escaped none too soon. The restructuring of Austria in line with the NSDAP's notion of relationship between party and state was already in process under the personal supervision of Rudolf Hess. More sinister was Himmler's administration of the purge of the police and the neutralization of political opposition. Gestapo Chief Heydrich was installed on the Morzinplatz where his agents were examining statute books and records seized from the chief of the Austrian Secret Service. At least one political murder had already been perpetrated, that of Papen's closest adviser, the German Embassy councilor.

Local storm troopers began the persecution of Jews, dragging them from their homes and offices and forcing them to scrub Schuschnigg's propaganda slogans from walls and pavements with acid. Others were rounded up to wash toilets in the SS barracks and sweep the streets. Such bullying was distasteful to many of the Wehrmacht officers, and journalist G .E. R. Gedye watched two of them "kick over the bucket of two very old Jews who were scrubbing the pavements and tell them they could go, cursing the Nazi stormtroopers who were supervising."

Such scenes did not dampen the fervor of most Viennese, intoxicated as they were by the events of the past forty-eight hours. "It is impossible to deny enthusiasm with which both the new regime and last night's announcement of incorporation in the Reich have been received here," telegraphed the British ambassador to Viscount Halifax on Monday. "Herr Hitler is certainly justified in claiming that his action has been welcome by the Austrian population." There was good reason. Anschluss would probably end unemployment. There were 600,000 Austrians out of work, and particularly hard hit were professional men; some doctors were seen begging from door to door.

Later that morning Hitler set out for Vienna. He could average only twenty miles an hour, impeded partly by the crowds, partly by the stalled trucks and tanks. It was almost 5 P.M. by the time his cavalcade reached the outskirts of the capital. Every building, including churches, flew the Austrian and German flags. Masses lined the streets, shouting themselves hoarse at the sight of Hitler in his open car, erect with arm outstretched. The ovation was frantic, spontaneous. His car stopped before the Hotel Imperial and, upon entering, it was another dream come true. As a youth he had always longed to go inside. Now it was bedecked in long red banners, bearing his mark, the swastika.

Chapter Sixteen

"ON THE RAZOR'S EDGE"

MAY–OCTOBER 1938

1

Even before Hitler marched into Austria he had suggested that he would no longer suffer the "severe persecution" of the German minority in Czechoslovakia. While this was in line with a vow to return lost people and land to the Reich, his main concern was Czechoslovakia's threatening geographical and political position. Here, he reasoned, was an artificial country created by the Allies after the war, a peninsula thrust into what remained of the Reich as a perpetual threat from the east.

Hitler was not alone in regarding it as a dagger aimed at the heart of Germany. The specter of simultaneous drives from east and west into the waist of the Reich inspired a counter German military plan known as Case Green: a surprise attack on Czechoslovakia. For about two years, however, Case Green was little more than a staff study; the easy seizure of Austria changed all that. Overnight Hitler had been given the opportunity to upset the balance of power in Europe; a thrust into Czechoslovakia, neutralizing her formidable defense system, would position his army for a drive against Poland or the U.S.S.R. All he needed was an excuse to invade and he had a ready-made one: three and a half million Sudeten Germans, inspired by the absorption of Austria, were now demanding a similar Anschluss, on the debatable grounds that they were a cruelly repressed minority. Their grievances, along with a traditional hostility to all things Czech, had plagued the tiny republic since its foundation. For the past three years Hitler had been covertly subsidizing the Nazi Sudeten Party led by Konrad rad Henlein and it now controlled the entire German minority movement. In late March 1938 German support took a more ominous character when the Führer named Henlein as his personal representative with instructions to make demands that could not possibly be accepted by the Czech government. This strategy, he hoped, would create a constant state of unrest that would finally "necessitate" German armed intervention to prevent civil war and protect the lives of its nationals in the Sudeten.

With an excuse at hand, Hitler was still restrained by apprehension that France, England and perhaps Russia would resist any effort to seize Czechoslovakia. Before facing such odds he needed the blessing of his sole ally. And so on May 2, 1938, he set out for Rome to get it, accompanied by a retinue of five hundred, consisting of diplomats, generals, security agents, party leaders and journalists, all wearing uniforms of one type or another.

It was with mixed feelings that Hitler left Berlin. Elation over the bloodless conquests of the Rhineland and Austria was tempered by recurrence of the gastrointestinal pains "miraculously" cured by Dr. Morell's Mutaflor. Concern over his health spurred him to spend several hours on the train bound for Rome writing out a will; from *Mein Kampf* alone he had amassed a fortune.

The five trains of the Führer's party were met at the Brenner Pass by flowers, banners and formations of Italian soldiers and Fascist troops. A band played the national anthems of both countries as the Duke of Pistoia welcomed the Germans in the name of the King. The German railway cavalcade proceeded into Italy past guards of honor posted on both sides of the tracks. Houses were decorated with placards and banners acclaiming the Führer and Italian-German friendship. As the delegation neared Rome, Hitler summoned an adjutant and—within hearing of his valet, Heinz Linge—ordered him to go through the train informing everyone that a very little man would greet them in Rome but they were to behave themselves and not laugh. "That is an order. The little man is the King of Italy."

It was dark when they arrived at the beflagged San Paolo station specially constructed for the occasion. It annoyed Hitler that he was met by King Victor Emmanuel, not Mussolini, and he annoyed His Majesty by seating himself first in the state carriage. Drawn by four horses, it proceeded past illuminated fountains along the old Roman triumphal way. A profusion of searchlights and torches turned night into day; the gaudily lit Colosseum seemed on fire. Cheering crowds lined the route and at one point African cavalry charged down the avenue at the guest of honor like something out of *The Desert Song*. But Hitler felt demeaned by riding in such an ancient vehicle. Hadn't the House of Savoy ever heard of the automobile? Nor did he find his accommodations in the Quirinal at all to his taste. The palace was uncomfortable as well as gloomy and reminded him of a museum.

From the very beginning he and Victor Emmanuel were on bad terms. Hitler resented the sovereign's open coolness and kept complaining that Mussolini himself should have served as host. The reception banquet at the Quirinal did nothing to ease the situation. Hitler, eyes moving nervously, slowly led the Queen, a majestic figure taller than himself, on his arm. Behind came the diminutive King leading the governor's tall wife. The foursome made a comical sight and Hitler knew it. As the Queen entered the great reception hall the Italians either bent very low or kneeled down. Several kissed the hem of her gown.

During the meal he and the Queen did not exchange a word. Hitler was particularly annoyed by the huge crucifix the Queen wore around her neck. She had done it deliberately, he thought, to annoy him. The royal family was going beyond the bounds of being ungracious. The King was spreading malicious stories about his guest, including one that the Führer demanded a woman on his first night at the Quirinal. "Boundless amazement," wrote Ciano in his diary. "The explanation: it seems he cannot go to sleep unless a woman turns down the bed before his eyes. It was difficult to find one, but the problem was solved by recruiting a chambermaid from a hotel. If this were really true it would be weird and interesting, but is it? Isn't it just a piece of spite on the part of the King, who also alleges that Hitler has himself injected with stimulants and narcotics?" Part of the last charge was only too true and there was reason to believe the bed-turning routine was also accurate.

On May 7, Hitler made an effective speech that, according to Count Ciano, "was extremely successful in melting the ice around him." In effect, he offered the South Tyrol as a present to his host, a most generous gift since it would infuriate his own countrymen, particularly those from Bavaria. This speech was the first event of political significance since Hitler's arrival. Satisfied to stay in the background and let the King play host, Il Duce had cleverly evaded any serious discussion by submitting his guests to a program that kept them busy day and night. Ribbentrop did eventually manage to present to Ciano a draft treaty of an alliance which he scanned without comment. Mussolini's son-in-law, in fact, had already written in his diary: "The Duce intends to make the pact. We shall make it, because he has a thousand and one reasons for not trusting the Western democracies."

More important, Hitler eventually succeeded in broaching the question that most concerned him—Czechoslovakia. Almost offhandedly, Mussolini gave the impression that this little country was not at all important to him and he would look the other way. This assurance was worth all the real and imagined insults Hitler had been subjected to and he now felt free to take the next step in his program.

President Beneš and other Czech leaders were under the illusion that Hitler would never risk an attack on their country for fear of setting off a general war. And if he did, wouldn't France, England and Russia somehow manage to restrain him? But these three were in no mood to act as protectors. "You only have to look at the map," Chamberlain had recently written his sister, "to see that nothing that France or we could do, could possibly save Czechoslovakia from being overrun by the Germans if they wanted to do it. . . . Therefore, we would not help Czechoslovakia—she would simply be a pretext for going to war with Germany. That we could not do, unless we had a reasonable prospect of being able to beat her to her knees in a reasonable time and of that I see no sign. I have therefore abandoned any idea of giving guarantees to Czechoslovakia or the French in connection with her obligations to that country." The Prime Minister's continuing lack of resolve disturbed the French leaders and, though they continued to make bold statements, perceptive observers were convinced that France, whose foreign policy had been in tow of the British since the Rhineland seizure, would not spring to the Czechs' defense. The third potential defender was publicly taking every opportunity to urge England and France to stand up to the Germans, while privately doing nothing. Stalin wanted Hitler controlled by the West, not himself, and on May 6 the Soviet chargé d'affaires in Prague admitted to the American ambassador that his country definitely would not supply Czechoslovakia any military aid unless France did so. Besides, how could they get the troops there? Poland and Romania stood between them and both these countries had understandably refused to allow passage of the Red Army. At the same time Stalin was assuring Beneš in private that the Soviet Union was ready to assist him militarily "even if France does not do so and even if Poland and Romania refuse to permit Soviet troops to pass in transit to Czechoslovakia."

This was all part of the attempt to convince liberals of the world that the Soviets were the true defenders of a brave little beleaguered nation when, in fact, they were no more willing to fly to its aid than England or France. Hitler had guessed as much and now that he had Mussolini's tacit approval of a march into Czechoslovakia he ordered Goebbels to intensify the press campaign against that hapless country. Activity among the Sudetenland Germans increased with assurance that *Der Tag* was at hand. This rumor was given credence by alarming reports on May 19 and 20 that Hitler's troops were mobilizing on the Czech borders: eleven infantry and four armored divisions were already converging on the Bohemian frontier while German and Austrian troops were poised for attack in southern Silesia and northern Austria.

On the afternoon of Friday, the twentieth, Beneš called an emergency meeting of the cabinet and the Supreme Defense Council. Shortly after 9 P.M.—without consulting their French allies—a "partial mobilization" was ordered. By dawn of Saturday, Czech troops occupied the border fortifications and the Sudeten territories—and Europe was swept by a crisis fever not experienced since 1914. A small power had taken the initiative against a powerful one, making known that she would not be a pawn in the game of European power politics. In so doing, Czechoslovakia was also forcing her reluctant sponsors, France and England, to back her up.

As a consequence, French Premier Daladier summoned the German ambassador and showed him a mobilization order lying on his desk. "It depends upon you, Excellency," he said, "whether I sign this document or not." And in Berlin British Ambassador Henderson warned Foreign Minister von Ribbentrop that "France had definite obligations to Czechoslovakia and that, if these had to be fulfilled, His Majesty's Government would not guarantee that they would not be forced by events to become themselves involved." Convinced that England was the prime enemy, Ribbentrop decelerated from outright rage to righteous indignation, stoutly denying that German troops threatened the Czech borders. If France and Britain were "crazy enough" to use armed force against Germany, "then once again we should have to fight to the death."

Ribbentrop left Berlin by special plane that evening to meet Hitler in Berchtesgaden. He was as incensed as his Foreign Minister, for not a single major military movement or concentration aimed at Czechoslovakia had taken place. Who then had started the rumor? It could have been the Communists, the Czechs or the anti-Hitler group which included such disparate elements as Schacht, the self-styled financial wizard, and Admiral Canaris, chief of the German intelligence service. More likely, panic itself was the villain.

The Western press spread the story that the Führer had been forced by foreign pressure to call off his invasion and by so doing made the mistake of humiliating him. "Hitler had embarked on no military enterprise," wrote State Secretary Ernst von Weizsäcker, of the Foreign Office, "and could not therefore withdraw from one. But unfortunate provocation by the foreign press now really set Hitler going. From then on he was emphatically in favor of settling the Czech question by force of arms."

Before the week was out Hitler acted with dramatic suddenness. On May 28 he summoned his top military leaders, officials of the Foreign Office and other important functionaries to a special conference. As this unusually large group was gathering outside the chancellery winter garden, the general assumption was that Hitler was about to call for new military measures. An agitated Göring drew Captain Wiedemann aside. "Doesn't the Führer realize what he is doing? This will mean war with France!" The army was not combat-ready, he said, and promised to tell this to the Chief.

Hitler began speaking calmly but his words were explosive: "It is my unshakable will to wipe Czechoslovakia off the map. . . . We shall have to use methods which, perhaps, will not find the immediate approval of you old officers." This attack, he explained, was but part of a much broader strategy to acquire living space. When Germany made its inevitable drive to the east for Lebensraum, Czechoslovakia would be a threat to the rear. Consequently, she had to be eliminated and this was the propitious moment since neither Britain nor France wanted war, Russia would not intervene and Italy was uninterested.

When Hitler finished, Göring pushed forward, eyes agleam, and grasped his hand. "Mein Führer," exclaimed the man who had vowed to stop him an hour earlier, "let me congratulate you wholeheartedly on your unique concept!"

2

Although Hitler had put Case Green in motion, his intent was primarily to use it for bargaining. The question was how close to the precipice of war he would go, and early that summer he himself probably did not know. Relying on intuition as he had in the Rhineland and Austrian crises, he allowed his personal adjutant, Wiedemann, to go to London in July for an informal talk with Lord Halifax. It was an extraordinary mission of exploration privately arranged by Wiedemann's close friend, Princess Hohenlohe, half Jewish by birth, which completely circumvented Ribbentrop. Wiedemann's official commission was to explore the possibilities of a state visit to England by Göring, but Hitler had also personally instructed him to inform Halifax that the crucial question of the moment was the mistreatment of the Sudeten Germans. "If there is no satisfactory solution in the near future, I will simply have to solve it by force. Tell this to Lord Halifax!"

Wiedemann repeated his warning in mid-July and Halifax replied cordially that much could be settled before that deadline. He also agreed in principle to a visit by Göring and extended a vague invitation to the Führer himself as a guest of the King. Wiedemann flew back to Germany in high spirits.

Several weeks later Fritz Hesse, the covert representative of the Wilhelmstrasse, was recalled from London and chastised by Ribbentrop for sending a report indicating that Chamberlain was prepared to consider the cession of the Sudeten territories to Germany. "What's the good of sending me this kind of stuff?" said the Foreign Minister according to Hesse's account. The Führer, it seemed, was convinced the English planned to smash Germany to pieces once they had completed their own rearmament and had recently told Ribbentrop: "There is no international morality left, everybody snatches whatever booty he can. I shall take this as a lesson." Before he allowed the English to encircle him, he would strike first.

Hesse explained that Chamberlain's personal adviser had

asked him to inform Hitler unofficially that a London *Times* editorial suggesting Britain was prepared to accept a solution favorable to Germany had been planted by the Prime Minister himself. With this in mind, wasn't it likely that Hitler could obtain autonomy for the Sudeten Germans without even a threat of military action? "Autonomy!" exclaimed Ribbentrop. "There can be no question of autonomy any longer." Before the lying reports of German troop movements, he said, Hitler might have been satisfied with autonomy. But now that was not enough.

While Hitler's position hardened, his generals continued to resist his policy of expansion. Beck began openly to circulate gloomy predictions: the question of guilt in a new war would be a greater factor than it had been in the World War; and the aftermath of defeat would be far more disastrous than in 1918. That July he composed a third long memorandum for Brauchitsch declaring that he was positive an attack on Czechoslovakia would bring about another great conflict. "The outcome of such a war would be a general castastrophe for Germany, not only a military defeat." The people, he went on, did not want this war, nor was the Wehrmacht prepared for it.

In early August Brauchitsch was persuaded to convene the senior army commanders. It was he, in fact, who read a memorandum prophesying that a Czech invasion would lead to a general war that Germany was doomed to lose. Was the Sudetenland worth risking the existence of the nation? The consensus was that citizens and soldiers alike were against war. The generals also agreed that the training and equipment of their troops might be up to defeating the Czechs but certainly not the combined powers of Europe. There were only two objections and these rather mild ones. General Busch repeated the cliché that soldiers should not interfere with politicians and Reichenau, the first general to go Nazi, warned his colleagues to confront Hitler singly rather than en masse. Brauchitsch decided to take his advice and faced the Führer alone. It is doubtful if he stated the case as forcefully as he had done to his peers, but even in milder form it brought a verbal explosion that promptly brought him back in line.

Discouraged by the commanders' negative attitude, Hitler invited their chiefs of staff to dinner at the Berghof on August 10. He regaled them for three hours with his political theories, but they too were not impressed. Universal opposition only made the Führer more determined and five days later, after witnessing artillery exercises near Jüterbog, he gathered his senior officers in a mess hall to announce that he had decided to solve the Czech problem by force that fall. He assured his listeners that so long as Chamberlain and Daladier were in power there would be no widespread war, and concluded with a reminder of his own prophetic powers.

Two days later Soviet Ambassador Maisky told Halifax that German policy was "at least 50 per cent bluff," and that the irresolute stance of the French and British "constituted a real danger for peace," since it gave an exaggerated impression of Germany's strength both at home and abroad.

At home Hitler was surrounded by disapproval. The generals were still unconvinced by his arguments. The prime mover, Beck, once more offered his resignation and, when Brauchitsch continued to decline it, refused to serve any longer. Hitler solved the problem by accepting the resignation and ordering Beck to keep it secret from the public "for reasons of foreign policy." As a loyal German, Beck agreed but continued to support the anti-Hitler group which was secretly plotting to arrest the Führer once he gave the final order for execution of Case Green. Rarely in history had so many leading military and civilian leaders plotted to overthrow a government by force.

The Party Congress at Nuremberg that year served as a dramatic prelude to the developing political crisis by its impressive display of Nazi power and discipline. The title of the 1938 festivities was appropriate: "First Party Rally of Greater Germany," as were the trappings. Hitler had brought from Vienna, after a hundred and forty years, the insignia of the First Reich—the Imperial crown, the Orb of Empire, the Scepter and the Imperial Sword. At the presentation of these symbols of imperialism he solemnly vowed that they would remain in Nuremberg forever. But he made no mention of war during his opening address or the following afternoon when he received the entire diplomatic corps.

Hitler's refusal to discuss international politics at Nuremberg inspired conjectures and rumors, including one directed to Henderson, that Hitler had become "quite mad" and was bent on war at all costs. In the next twenty-four hours Henderson spoke to a number of Hitler's close advisers, urging Anglo-German co-operation in a Sudeten settlement. Göring said he planned to go hunting the end of the month and "hoped to goodness the Czechs wouldn't upset his shooting plans by starting trouble in the middle of them," and Goebbels expressed the pious hope that the Führer would refer to co-operation with the English in his final speech. "He appeared to me anxious," reported a suspicious Henderson, "and I begin to doubt whether he is egging Hitler on to extremes."

In the midst of these interviews, Henderson received instructions to deliver a personal warning to Hitler that England "could not stand aside" in the event of a general conflict. Henderson protested: the Führer was on the borderline of madness and a second crisis could push him over the edge. The matter consequently was dropped.

Since Hitler was already convinced England had no intention of risking war over Czechoslovakia, he was going ahead with his invasion plans come what might. It was a decision combining shrewd calculation, intuition and an irresistible impulse. "You know I am like a wanderer who must cross an abyss on the razor's edge," Hitler told Frank. "But I must, I simply must cross."

It was not Hitler but Göring who made the first public announcement on Czechoslovakia the following day. "A trifling piece of Europe," he said, "is making life unbearable for mankind. The Czechs, the vile race of dwarfs without any culture—nobody even knows where they came from—are oppressing a civilized race; and behind them, together with Moscow, there can be seen the everlasting face of the Jewish fiend!"

If such words had been uttered by Hitler, Europe would have trembled but even President Beneš ignored Göring's diatribe. "I firmly believe that nothing other than moral force, good will, and mutual trust will be needed," he broadcast in both Czech and German. Afterward William Shirer encountered the President in the hall of Broadcasting House. The American correspondent wanted to warn Beneš he was dealing with gangsters but didn't have the nerve. He observed that Beneš's face was "grave, not nearly so optimistic as his words, and I doubt not he knows the terrible position he is in."

The final ceremony of the Nuremberg Rally came on September 12. It was the last chance for Hitler to deliver the speech the world dreaded he might make. He arrived at the huge outdoor stadium just before 7 P.M. to the concerted roar of "Sieg Heil!" and slowly walked toward the rostrum in the glare of a spotlight, looking to neither side, right hand raised in salute. He spoke at first only of the party's struggles and at such length that some foreign observers began to hope he was not going to bring up the question of the day. Suddenly he began to condemn the Czechs. "I am in no way willing that here in the heart of Germany a second Palestine should be permitted to arise. The poor Arabs are defenseless and deserted. The Germans in Czechoslovakia are neither defenseless nor are they deserted, and people should take notice of that fact."

The audience roared, "Sieg Heil! Sieg Heil!" This was the moment the world had been waiting for all week, but instead of following such stridency with an ultimatum, he merely demanded justice for the Sudeten Germans, then concluded with bluster rather than threat: "We should be sorry if this were to disturb or damage our relations with other European states, but the blame does not lie with us!"

The French, English and Czechs had feared so much that such words were reassuring; it was generally believed that the sound and fury were for the benefit of German extremists and that Hitler was ready to work for a peaceful solution. Mussolini shared this belief, for he observed as he turned away from his radio, "I had expected a more threatening speech. . . . Nothing is lost."

3

This sense of well-being was brief. Hitler's oratorical condemnation of injustice inspired scenes of protest among the Sudeten Germans. Within twenty-four hours bloody disorders spread through the Sudetenland and the death toll rose to twenty-one. Aroused by Henlein's call for freedom, the Sudeten Germans went on strike and refused to pay taxes. Prague declared a state of siege. Martial law was proclaimed in the border districts and more Sudeten Germans were shot down. Throughout Europe there were renewed rumors of an ultimatum by Hitler—or an outright invasion. Paris and London panicked. That evening Daladier sent an urgent message to Chamberlain. An invasion of Czechoslovakia, he said, had to be avoided at all costs or France would be forced to fulfill the obligations of her treaty. He proposed that they immediately invite Hitler to meet with them and work out a reasonable settlement.

The cryptic reply he got from Chamberlain kept Daladier perplexed for hours: "Some time ago I came to a resolution. I believe it to be useful. . . . I cannot tell you anything yet, but I will let you know about it a little later." That same evening

Chamberlain telegraphed Hitler suggesting a man-to-man conference. Hitler was delightfully taken by surprise and described his feeling with a colorful idiom that would have perplexed Milton: "I fell from Heaven!" That afternoon he sent a reply placing himself at Chamberlain's proposal and suggesting that they meet the next noon at Berchtesgaden.

In England the first reaction of relief was followed by enthusiasm that their Prime Minister was making such an original move to keep peace. In Prague newsboys shouted out: "Extra! Read how the mighty head of the British Empire goes begging to Hitler!" The Czech citizens spontaneously massed in the streets to demonstrate that they stood behind their President's efforts to resist.

Early September 15, Chamberlain left 10 Downing Street to the cheers of an extraordinarily large crowd for that hour. Before boarding his plane at Croydon, in the presence of Halifax and other dignitaries, he paused to speak into the BBC microphones. "My policy has always been to ensure peace. The prompt acceptance of my suggestion encourages me to hope that my visit today will not be without results."

At about 8 A.M. the Lockheed Electra took off. It was the first long flight for the sixty-nine-year-old Prime Minister and he was as excited as a boy. But it would be wrong to assume he was an aging innocent proceeding to the slaughter. Chamberlain was a hard bargainer. "My method is to try and make up my own mind first on the proper course, and then try and put others through the same course of reasoning." Like his father, a successful businessman who became an outstanding statesman, he was a devout Unitarian, the very embodiment of Victorian virtues. His spare, ascetic figure, his chilling manner and his sardonic smile reminded many of a headmaster. Only his intimates knew that this austere exterior emanated from painful shyness and that beneath the armor lay warmth and sensibility.

The question was whether such an individual, convinced as he was that the Führer was half mad and needed to be handled cautiously, could cope with the situation. As he flew over London Chamberlain himself experienced "some slight sinkings," yet was buoyed by the thought that he too held strong cards and that, as long as he could keep negotiating with the Führer, Czechoslovakia would be safe.

He sat through the flight to Munich, according to one fellow passenger, "as always, aloof, reserved, imperturbable, unshakeably self-reliant." Henderson greeted him as he descended from the plane at 12:30 P.M. and was surprised how remarkably fresh he looked for a man of his age. "I'm tough and wiry," explained Chamberlain.

Despite the drizzle, enthusiastic crowds were waiting all along the route to the Munich railroad station shouting "Heil!" and lifting arms in salute. It was after four o'clock by the time the Chamberlain party started up the steep, winding road to the Berghof. The sky was dark and clouds hid the mountains as rain began to pelt down. Hitler, the polite host, waited at the head of the long flight of steps to the terrace. After exchanging stilted pleasantries over tea, Hitler abruptly asked what procedure his guest proposed for the meeting. Chamberlain said he preferred a tête-à-tête. Hitler led the Prime Minister and interpreter Schmidt upstairs to his study, leaving behind a patently annoyed Ribbentrop.

In this simple, wood-paneled room, almost bare of ornament, Hitler began quietly listing complaints against his neighbors as he presented a history of events leading up to the present crisis. Chamberlain listened attentively, answered questions with a friendly smile, then looked the Führer full in the face and said he was prepared to discuss the possibility of righting any German grievances so long as force was not used.

"Force!" said Hitler, excited for the first time. "Who speaks of force?" Wasn't it Beneš who was applying force against the Germans in the Sudetenland? As the mountain wind howled, rain slashed against the window, and he himself poured out such a torrent of words that Chamberlain asked him to stop so he might have a chance to understand what he was talking about. "I shall not put up with this any longer," exclaimed Hitler. "I shall settle the question in one way or another." It was the first time the alarmed Schmidt had heard him use such a phrase with a foreign statesman. "I shall take matters into my own hands."

Chamberlain was startled but answered resolutely, "If I have understood you right, you are determined to proceed against Czechoslovakia. If that is so, why did you let me come to Berchtesgaden?" This trip was a waste of time, and under the circumstances, he said, it was best to return to England at once. "Anything else seems pointless."

Hitler hesitated before this unexpected counterattack. Now, thought Schmidt, was the moment if he really wants to come to war. The interpreter stared at the Führer in agonized suspense: the question of peace was poised on the razor's edge. To Schmidt's astonishment, Hitler backed down. "If, in considering the Sudeten question," he said calmly, "you are prepared to recognize the principle of the right of peoples to self-determination, then we can continue the discussion in order to see how the principle can be applied in practice."

Then came a second surprise. Chamberlain did not immediately assent, objecting that a plebiscite in the Sudetenland held immense practical difficulties. Amazingly, Hitler did not flare up at this rebuff. Perhaps, thought Schmidt, the Führer had been frightened by Chamberlain's threat to go home. The Prime Minister said that he could not give Hitler an answer on the question of self-determination without first consulting his colleagues. "I therefore suggest that we break off our conversation at this point, and that I return to England immediately for consultation, and then meet you again."

Hitler looked uneasy as Schmidt translated the first words but, once he realized that Chamberlain would see him again, could not hide his relief. He expressed immediate agreement and, when Chamberlain asked "how the situation was to be held in the meantime," unhesitatingly promised that he would not give the order to march unless some "particularly atrocious incident occurred."

This ended the three-hour talk. They chatted cordially on the way downstairs, Hitler hoping that his guest would see some of the scenic beauties before he left. But Chamberlain could not spare the time "since lives were being lost." He left the Berghof pleased with the talk. "I had established a certain confidence, which was my aim," he wrote his sister, "and on my side, in spite of the hardness and ruthlessness I thought I saw in his face, I got the impression that here was a man who could be relied upon when he had given his word."

In Washington, Roosevelt was concerned. Fearing that such talks would only postpone the inevitable conflict, he lamented at a cabinet meeting that the Prime Minister was for "peace at any price," and bitterly observed to Harold Ickes that apparently England and France were going to leave the Czechs in the lurch, then "wash the blood from their Judas Iscariot hands." Before the weekend was over, further opposition to Chamberlain began to appear within his own cabinet but he stood firm. American Ambassador Joseph Kennedy had sent the Prime Minister an ominous report by the noted aviator, Charles Lindbergh, of overwhelming German air power based on a recent inspection of the Luftwaffe. Chamberlain had been as impressed as Kennedy and so England, which was poorly prepared for war, remained committed to appeasement.

On September 18 Chamberlain told the French delegation headed by Daladier which had come to England to discuss the problem: "There must be some cession of territorial area to the Reich. But it would be very difficult for us to carve up Czechoslovakia, unless the Czechoslovakian Government themselves were prepared to admit the necessity for frontier rectifications." Daladier agreed that a little "friendly pressure" might persuade the Czechs to cede "some portions of Sudeten territory." At the same time, they had to be assured "of some sort of international guarantee of what remained." And Germany must participate in such a guarantee. Chamberlain hesitated but after a break in the proceedings agreed.

At the same time there remained the unpleasant job of telling the Czechs that they must give up the Sudetenland, and when Beneš was informed the next day after lunch by the British minister, he was so agitated he refused to discuss the matter at first. The embarrassed Sir Basil Newton stressed that a quick ratification must be forthcoming since Chamberlain hoped to resume talks with Hitler within forty-eight hours. Beneš bitterly charged that his country had been abandoned. The guarantees he already possessed, he said, had proven valueless. He feared the proposed solution would not be final, only a stage in the eventual domination of his country by Hitler.

While Chamberlain anxiously waited all that Monday for an answer, Beneš was desperately searching for help from another quarter. On Tuesday he summoned the Soviet minister and asked two questions: Would the U.S.S.R. fulfill her treaty obligations if France did likewise? In the event of a Hitler attack would the Soviets support Czechoslovakia in an appeal to the League of Nations even if France refused to do so? Affirmative answers finally arrived from Moscow at 7 P.M. and forty-five minutes later Czech Foreign Minister Krofta was telling Newton that his government must reject the British-French proposal.

A little later, however, Newton's French counterpart, Victor de Lacroix, was hastily summoned to see Czech Prime Minister Hodža. He begged Lacroix to get a telegram from Paris stating that France would back out of the treaty if it came to fighting.

"It was the only way of saving the peace," he said and assured Lacroix that he was acting with the consent of Beneš—which was a lie.

Lacroix transmitted this information to Paris while Newton was doing the same to London. In his message, Newton concluded with the suggestion that Halifax send Beneš an ultimatum to accept the proposal "without reserve and without further delay failing which his Majesty's Government will take no further interest in the fate of the country."

Despite the late hour, Halifax rushed to 10 Downing Street. He returned to the Foreign Office after midnight and instructed Newton to urge the Czechs to reconsider, otherwise Chamberlain would be forced to postpone or cancel his second meeting with Hitler.

It was two o'clock in the morning by the time Newton, accompanied by his French colleague, arrived at Hradschin Castle to see the President. Wakened from a fitful sleep, Beneš collapsed at Lacroix's first words "as if he had hit him with a club," and burst into tears. Shaken, the betrayed Beneš promised to give a final reply by midday.

The first word of acceptance came from the devious Hodža, who informed Newton that the Czech reply was affirmative and an official answer to that effect would be delivered as soon as possible. But the argument continued until late afternoon when Newton and Lacroix were summoned to the Ministry of Foreign Affairs. Each minister was handed a note stating that the Czechoslovakian government "sadly" accepted the Franco-British proposal.

That evening the Beneš government publicly announced its surrender in a communiqué that brought shame to many Westerners.

> We relied upon the help that our friends might have given us; but when the question of reducing us by force arose, it became evident that the European crisis was taking on too serious a character. Our friends therefore advised us to buy freedom and peace by our sacrifice, and this in proportion to their own inability to help us . . . The President of the Republic and our government had no other choice, for we found ourselves alone.

Hitler had won a victory by proxy.

4

The next morning, September 21, just before boarding a plane for his second flight, Chamberlain told newsmen: "A perfect solution of the Czechoslovakian problem is an essential preliminary to a better understanding between the British and German peoples; and that, in turn, is the indisputable foundation of European peace. European peace is what I am aiming at, and I hope this journey may open the way to it."

This time the two leaders would meet at Bad Godesberg on the Rhine in the Dreesen Hotel. Chamberlain began with a recital of the concessions he and the French had wrung out of the Czechs. After outlining the comprehensive and complicated plan to carry out the turnover of territory, he mentioned the guarantee the British and French had given the Czechs, then leaned back with an expression of satisfaction as if to say, thought Schmidt: "Haven't I worked splendidly during these five days."

To the interpreter's surprise, Hitler quietly, almost regretfully replied, "I am exceedingly sorry, Mr. Chamberlain, but I can no longer discuss these matters. This solution, after the developments of the last few days, is no longer practicable."

The Prime Minister bolted upright. Schmidt noticed that his kindly eyes gleamed angrily under bushy brows. Chamberlain indignantly exclaimed he could not understand. This solution answered the very demands the Führer had made at Berchtesgaden. After hedging on the grounds that it was impossible to make a non-aggression pact with the Czechs before the claims of Poland and Hungary were satisfied, Hitler retaliated by criticizing the British-French proposal point by point, then peremptorily demanded that the Sudetenland be occupied by the Germans "forthwith."

Chamberlain replied that he was both disappointed and puzzled at such an attitude. This was a brand-new demand, going far beyond what Hitler had proposed at Berchtesgaden. He had returned to Germany with a plan that gave the Führer everything he wanted, doing so at the risk of his political career. At this point Sir Ivone Kirkpatrick handed the Prime Minister a note that German troop formations had just crossed the frontier at

Eger. Chamberlain seized on this. There were bound to be such incidents, on both sides, he said and urged the Führer to join him in an effort to do "all that was humanly possible to settle matters in an orderly, peaceful way, and not allow the work for peace to be disturbed by shootings and incidents." What proposal, he asked, could Hitler make so they could reach agreement in principle?

The answer chilled Chamberlain: immediate occupation of the Sudetenland by German troops with the frontier to be determined later by a plebiscite. Since this amounted to almost complete capitulation by the Czechs, an acrimonious, tedious debate followed which was spiced by the arrival of another message from Eger, this one to Hitler that twelve German hostages had been shot. The result, of course, was a dissertation by the Führer on the iniquity of the Czechs, followed by an avowal that, "if Prague fell under Bolshevik influence, or if hostages continued to be shot, he would intervene militarily at once."

After three hours the first conversation ended in complete discord but with the understanding that they would meet again on the morrow.

Despite a calm visage, the Prime Minister was still angry and indignant as he recrossed the Rhine and was driven up the mountain to his own hotel. Only then did he wonder if he had made a mistake by not breaking off the talks and going home. Was Hitler actually on the edge of madness, or a sort of Dr. Jekyll and Mr. Hyde? If so, it was Chamberlain's responsibility to break through the deadlock. The question was how to do it.

He was not the only one at the conference who doubted Hitler's sanity. At the Dreesen several newsmen were circulating a story that the Führer was so distraught over the Czech crisis that he would fling himself to the floor and chew the edge of the carpet. This report had been inspired by a remark of one Hitler aide that the Chief had become so furious that he was "eating the carpet." This slang expression was taken literally by some American correspondents, who should have translated it into "climbing the walls."

Some intimates believed the Führer displayed anger for effect. If so, his outbursts that afternoon had surely placed his opponent on the defensive. Chamberlain was already writing him a conciliatory letter. In it he suggested that he himself ask the Czechs whether they thought there could be an arrangement by which the Sudeten Germans themselves could maintain law and order.

After breakfast on the twenty-third this letter was sent across the river. In no mood for reconciliation, Hitler took it as a flat rejection of his ideas and, after long and "feverish" discussions with Ribbentrop and other advisers, composed an unfriendly reply which was a repetition of what he had said at the conference table. It was too long for a written translation and Hitler instructed Schmidt to deliver it in person and translate it verbally.

Upon the interpreter's return, Hitler's first words were anxious ones: "What did he say? How did he take my letter?" But he visibly relaxed upon learning that Chamberlain had shown no excitement or anger. Within the hour the ferry brought two emissaries from Chamberlain who solemnly delivered the Prime Minister's answer. It was a model of diplomacy, being simultaneously conciliatory and ominous. First Chamberlain promised to put Hitler's proposals before the Czechs and therefore requested a memorandum detailing Hitler's demands. Upon receipt of this document, he proposed returning to England.

The threat of departure must have spurred a second meeting. It was agreed that Chamberlain should return to the Dreesen that evening not only to pick up the memorandum but to listen to Hitler's explanation of it. Their conversation started about 10 P.M. and, since more participants were on hand, took place in a small dining room. Henderson, Kirkpatrick, Ribbentrop and Weizsäcker sat informally in a semicircle around Hitler and Chamberlain while Schmidt translated the memorandum. Hitler demanded withdrawal of all Czech armed forces from an area shown on an accompanying map. Evacuation would start on September 26 and the territory would be formally ceded to Germany on the twenty-eighth.

"But that's an ultimatum!" exclaimed Chamberlain, lifting his hands in protest.

"*Ein Diktat!*" chorused Henderson, who liked to display his German. Chamberlain refused to transmit such a document to the Czechs. Its tone, not to mention its content, would cause indignation among neutrals, he said, and began to scold Hitler as if he were a recalcitrant member of his own cabinet. It was one of the rare occasions when Hitler was placed on the defensive, and was followed by a concerted attack by the three British statesmen on the timetable of the proposal, which allowed the Czechs an impossibly short period to evacuate and turn over the Sudetenland. Impracticable and dangerous, it could lead to a European war.

During the ensuing deadlock an adjutant entered with a message for the Führer. After glancing at it he handed it to Schmidt, who translated it out loud in English: "Beneš has just announced over the wireless general mobilization of the Czechoslovak forces."

It was Hitler who finally broke the silence. "Despite this unheard-of provocation," he said in a barely audible voice, "I shall of course keep my promise not to proceed against Czechoslovakia during the course of negotiations—at any rate, Mr. Chamberlain, so long as you remain on German soil." This remark, misleading by being softly spoken, was followed by a statement that could not be misinterpreted. The Czech mobilization, he said tersely, settled the whole affair. Chamberlain hastily pointed out that mobilization was a precaution, not necessarily an offensive measure, but the Führer replied that so far as he was concerned mobilization was a clear indication that the Czechs did not intend to cede any territory. Again Chamberlain dissented. The Czechs, he argued, had agreed to the principle of self-determination in the Sudetenland and would not go back on their word.

Then why mobilize? persisted Hitler.

Germany mobilized first, said the Prime Minister.

You call that mobilization? retorted the Führer sarcastically and made another threat: the crisis could not drag on very much longer. He quoted an old German proverb: "An end, even with terror, is better than terror without end." The memorandum, he said, represented his last word.

In that event, said Chamberlain, there was no purpose in further negotiations. "He would go home with a heavy heart, since he saw the final wreck of all his hopes for the peace of Europe. But his conscience was clear; he had done everything possible for peace. Unfortunately, he had not found an echo in Herr Hitler."

A walkout was the last thing Hitler wanted and he hastily reassured the British that he would not invade Czechoslovakia during the negotiations. It was as if a thunderstorm had cleared the atmosphere. "To please you, Mr. Chamberlain," he said after a short recess, "I will make a concession over the matter of the timetable. You are one of the few men for whom I have ever done such a thing. I will agree to October 1 as the date for evacuation."

After negotiating a number of other minor alterations, Chamberlain agreed to transmit the memorandum to the Czechs. It was one-thirty in the morning and the meeting adjourned. The Führer thanked the Prime Minister for his work on behalf of peace, assuring him that the "Czech problem was the last territorial demand which he had to make in Europe."

Chamberlain left with a hearty "Auf Wiedersehen!" and those who watched him stride out of the hotel could not discern the slightest strain of displeasure on his face.

5

After a few hours of needed sleep, Chamberlain flew back to England and the following day met with the full cabinet. It was necessary, he explained, to appreciate people's motives and see how their minds worked if one would understand their actions. Herr Hitler "would not deliberately deceive a man whom he respected and with whom he had been in negotiations." Consequently it would be a great tragedy if they "lost this opportunity of reaching an understanding with Germany on all points of difference between the two countries."

Never had there been such opposition from the cabinet. First Lord of the Admiralty Duff Cooper could place no confidence in the Führer's promises and proposed an immediate general mobilization. Chamberlain urged his colleagues to postpone any such decision and it was agreed to first consult the French, who had already ordered a partial mobilization.

When the cabinet met again Sunday morning there was opposition from a new source. "I cannot rid my mind of the fact," confessed Foreign Secretary Halifax, "that Herr Hitler has given us nothing and that he is dictating terms, just as though he had won a war but without having had to fight." So long as Nazism lasted, peace was uncertain.

No sooner had this meeting ended in discord than Chamberlain was subjected to another harrowing experience. Jan Masaryk, the Czech ambassador, arrived with a bitter protest. His government, he said, was "amazed" at the contents of Hitler's memorandum. It was a de facto ultimatum which deprived Czechoslovakia of every safeguard for its national existence. "Against these new and cruel demands my government feels bound to make their utmost resistance and we shall do so, God helping."

That evening the French delegation was back in London to discuss the situation. Its leader, Daladier, declared that France could not recognize Hitler's right to seize the Sudetenland but would give only a vague response to Chamberlain's question: would France declare war if Hitler simply imposed on Czechoslovakia a frontier based on strategic considerations? When Chamberlain pressed for a more specific answer Daladier replied that France might "try a land offensive, after a period of concentration."

This meeting was adjourned for half an hour so that Chamberlain could consult with his cabinet. "I am unwilling to leave unexplored any possible chance of avoiding war," he told his colleagues. "Therefore I suggest that, basing myself on the personal conversations I have had with Herr Hitler, I should write a personal letter." It would be delivered to the Führer by Chamberlain's closest adviser, Sir Horace Wilson, and would contain a last appeal suggesting a joint commission to determine how to put into effect the proposals already accepted by the Czechs. "If the letter fails to secure any response from Herr Hitler, Sir Horace Wilson should be authorized to give a personal message from me to the effect that if this appeal was refused, France would go to war and if that happened, it seemed certain that we should be drawn in."

The following morning, September 26, Wilson, who shared some of Hitler's apprehension about Jews, set off for Berlin with the letter. The Führer listened quietly but with growing restlessness until he heard how shocked the British public had been by the terms of his Godesberg memorandum, then he burst out, "It is no use talking any more!" Hitler shouted that Germans were being treated like niggers. One wouldn't even treat Turks like that. "On 1 October I shall have Czechoslovakia where I want her!" he exclaimed, and if France and England decided to strike, let them. He didn't care a pfennig. Finally calm was restored and Hitler agreed to negotiate with the Czechs. He insisted, however, that they agree to accept the Godesberg memorandum within forty-eight hours. Come what may, he added, German troops would occupy the Sudetenland on the first of October.

The speech brought despair to those hoping for peace. In

London workmen dug trenches near Buckingham Palace; air raid posters were pasted up. From Paris, Ambassador Bullitt, a personal friend of Roosevelt's, phoned Washington: "I believe the chances are about ninety-five in a hundred of war beginning midnight Friday." The President, who had also been getting words of appeasement from his ambassador in London, Joseph Kennedy, cabled Hitler an appeal (his second in two days) to continue the negotiations.

Chamberlain too issued another appeal to the Führer in the form of a statement to the press. The British, he said, would guarantee that the Czechs kept their promise to evacuate the Sudetenland so long as the Germans abstained from force. His envoy, Wilson, was back in the Reich chancellery late the next morning with this new proposal, but Hitler refused to discuss it. There were only two possibilities open to the Czechs: accept or refuse the German proposal. "And if they choose to refuse I shall smash Czechoslovakia!" He threatened to march into the Sudetenland if Beneš did not capitulate by 2 P.M. the next day.

Sir Horace suddenly rose and read out a short message which Schmidt translated as slowly and emphatically as possible so that Hitler could mark its purport: "If France, in fulfillment of her treaty obligations, should become actively involved in hostilities against Germany, the United Kingdom would deem itself obliged to support France."

Hitler was furious. "If France and England strike, let them do so. It's a matter of complete indifference to me. I am prepared for every eventuality. It is Tuesday today and by next Monday we shall all be at war."

On Wednesday, September 28, Chamberlain offered to come to Berlin at once for a conference. Il Duce seconded the idea. He suggested that they all meet in Munich. Hitler agreed and invitations were hastily dispatched to Daladier and Chamberlain. The one to the latter arrived while he was addressing the House of Commons and Queen Mary, who was in the gallery with Halifax, Baldwin and other notables. Chamberlain had just announced Hitler's acceptance of Mussolini's suggestion to delay mobilization and during the resultant mutter of approval the Chancellor of the Exchequer passed him a slip of paper. The Prime Minister's face was transformed. In a broken voice he continued: "That is not all. I have something further to say to the House yet. I have now been informed by Herr

Hitler that he invites me to meet him at Munich tomorrow morning. He has also invited Signor Mussolini and M. Daladier." Some unidentified member shouted: "Thank God for the Prime Minister!" thereby touching off an unprecedented demonstration of hysterical shouting. Queen Mary, a symbol of self-control, wept without restraint as did the Duchess of Kent and Mrs. Chamberlain. One of the few members of Commons not overcome by the moment was Winston Churchill. "And what about Czechoslovakia?" he was heard to mutter bitterly. "Does no one think of asking their opinion?"

With few exceptions the people of the democracies shared the relief. In the streets of Paris, London and New York jubilant crowds read the extras proclaiming the end of the crisis. From Paris, Ambassador Bullitt wrote his friend Roosevelt, "I am so relieved this evening that I feel like embracing everyone and wish I were in the White House to give you a large kiss on your bald spot." And from Washington the President dispatched a two-word cable to Chamberlain: GOOD MAN.

From another President, Beneš, the Prime Minister received a longer message, this a plea: "I ask Mr. Chamberlain very earnestly for help because it is our real desire to contribute to peace. I beg therefore that nothing may be done in Munich without Czechoslovakia being heard."

6

Early the following morning, September 29, the Führer met Mussolini between Munich and the border. Beyond being a mark of courtesy to an ally, it gave Hitler an opportunity to bring Il Duce up to date on the latest developments. As the two dictators headed for the Bavarian capital in the Führer's train, Hitler revealed that, with the Westwall completed, he feared no attack from that quarter. If England and France were foolish enough to make an assault, the war would be over before the enemy could complete mobilization. "I have no need to mobilize. The German army stands ready and asks only to be allowed to realize my aims."

The other two conferees were Munich-bound by air. Chamberlain left Heston in a slight rain after telling journalists, "When I was a little boy, I used to repeat, 'If at first you don't succeed, try, try again!' This is what I am doing. When I come back I hope I may be able to say, as Hotspur says in *Henry IV*, 'out of this nettle, danger, we pluck this flower, safety.'"

Chamberlain and his two colleagues, all in black suits, arrived first. Next came Mussolini, advancing with lively step, his chest thrown out, completely at ease, and patronizing, as if he were the host. The last to arrive was the Führer. The hard, strange look in his eyes impressed Daladier. The conferees and their aides congregated around a buffet set up in a salon, shaking hands courteously but coldly as they surveyed each other. Hitler did his best to be affable but his brows were furrowed with concern since most of his guests spoke no German and he was unable to communicate with them freely. At last the stilted buffet was over and Hitler led the way into a large rectangular room overlooking the Königsplatz. It was an impressive room with leather-covered walls, a profusion of green plants and paintings and a huge marble fireplace over which hung the imposing portrait of Bismarck by Lenbach.

Hastily prepared and poorly organized, the conference began in confusion and became increasingly muddled. With no chairman, no agenda or agreed procedure, it splintered into a series of involved individual discussions. At one point Hitler became so restive at Chamberlain's nagging concern over the matter of compensating the Czechs for property in the Sudetenland that he shouted, "Our time is too valuable to be wasted on such trivialities!"

Mussolini brought some degree of order into the proceedings by submitting a written proposal for the solution of the Sudeten question which he presented as his own even though the Germans had drafted it. By then it was 3 P.M. and there was a recess for lunch. The proceedings were even more chaotic after the bolted meal. Often three or four would talk at once, making Schmidt's task almost impossible. He would have to insist that the preceding translation be heard first and, to friends watching in amusement through glassed doors, he looked like a schoolmaster trying to keep an unruly class in order. To complicate matters, outsiders began to invade the room. One by one Göring, François-Poncet, Henderson, Italian Ambassador Bernardo Attolico and Weizsäcker wandered in with legal clerks, secretaries and adjutants. They all crowded around the principals, who were grouped in a semicircle before the huge fireplace, until it looked like a high-stake game of chance.

After extensive redrafting and tedious delays that continued until past midnight, agreement was finally reached. "Actually the whole thing was a cut-and-dried affair," Göring later told an American psychologist. "Neither Chamberlain nor Daladier was the least bit interested in sacrificing or risking anything to save Czechoslovakia. That was clear as day to me. The fate of Czechoslovakia was essentially sealed in three hours. Then they argued for hours more about the word 'guarantee.' Chamberlain kept hedging. Daladier hardly paid any attention at all. He just sat there like this." (Göring slumped down and assumed a bored expression.) "All he did was nod approval from time to time. Not the slightest objection to anything. I was simply amazed at how easily the thing was managed by Hitler."

At 1:30 A.M. an acceptable document was ceremoniously placed on a mahogany table next to a huge, elaborate inkwell. The pact provided for a four-stage evacuation of the Sudetenland to begin on October 1. An international commission would determine which districts were to hold plebiscites and make final determination of the borders.

Hitler appeared satisfied. The first to sign, he found the pretentious inkwell empty and a substitute had to be hastily provided. The last to arrive, the Führer was the first to leave and William Shirer was struck by "the light of victory in Hitler's eyes as he strutted down the broad steps" of the Führerbau.

It was some time before Chamberlain and Daladier left and it was their painful duty to inform the two Czech representatives, anxiously waiting off stage throughout the long day, of the fate of their country. They were brought to Chamberlain's room at the Regina about 2:15 A.M. The atmosphere was oppressive as the Czechs waited for sentence to be passed. Chamberlain made a long introductory speech, then, as Daladier was handing over a copy of the agreement, he began yawning. One of the Czechs was in tears. "Believe me," François-Poncet consoled him, "all this is not final. It is but one moment in a story which has just begun and which will soon bring up the issue again."

When Chamberlain returned to London, he was given a hero's welcome, rare in the history of England. The streets, as he described in a private letter, "were lined from one end to the other with people of every class, shouting themselves hoarse, leaping on the running board, banging on the windows, and thrusting their hands into the car to be shaken." It seemed that all England wanted to congratulate and thank him. "No conqueror returning from a victory on the battlefield," commented the London *Times*, "had come adorned with nobler laurels."

He was engulfed in front of 10 Downing Street and when the screaming throng refused to disperse he came to an open window. The cheering intensified, finally turning into a raucous rendition of "For he's a jolly good fellow!" Chamberlain stood beaming at the window, the same one at which Disraeli had announced "peace with honour" on returning from the Berlin Congress of 1878. "This is the second time in our history," he said, "that there has come back from Germany to Downing Street peace with honour. I believe it is peace for our time."

The weeks of crisis were at last over and the English, with few exceptions, were unrestrained in their joy but there was no celebration in Prague when the new premier, General Jan Syrovy, announced over the radio that his government had been forced to accept the Munich Diktat since they had been deserted and stood alone. It was a choice, he said, "between a reduction of our territory and the death of the nation."

nounced the London *Times*, come crowned with nobler laurel.

He was smuggled into No. 10 Downing Street and when the cheering throngs refused to disperse he came to an upper window. The cheering intensified, finally turning into a raucous rendition of "For He's a Jolly Good Fellow." Chamberlain stood beaming at the window, the same one at which Disraeli had announced peace with honor on returning from the Berlin Congress of 1878. "This is the second time in our history," he said, "that there has come back from Germany to Downing Street peace with honour. I believe it is peace for our time."

The [illegible] French and the English, with few exceptions, were unrestrained in their joy but there was no celebration in Prague when the new premier, General Jan Syrovy, announced over the radio that his government had been forced to accept the Munich Diktat since they had been deserted and stood alone. It was a choice, he said, "between a reduction of our territory and the death of the nation."

PART 6

"TO THE VERY BRINK OF BOLDNESS"

Chapter Seventeen

CRYSTAL NIGHT

NOVEMBER 1938–MARCH 1939

1

The path of anti-Semitism in Hitler's Germany was tortuous. The first Jewish restrictions in 1933 were so inclusive that it seemed as if the Führer were deliberately compromising his principles. Could this be an attempt to solve the Jewish question by rational means acceptable to those Germans who wanted Jews controlled but not persecuted? There followed a period of struggle between the racial radicals in the party and moderates in the government and civil service which came to a climax during the summer of 1935. At this time the latter took the offensive, objecting openly to the continuing mistreatment of Jews on the grounds that it was bad for business. The "unlawful" activity against Jews must end, Reichsbank President Schacht told a small, influential group including Interior Minister Frick, Finance Minister Schwerin von Krosigk, Justice Minister Gürtner and Education Minister Rust. Otherwise, he warned, he could not complete his task of economic rearmament. For example, the Jewish agent of Alliance Insurance in Egypt had been so harried that he resigned, leaving the market to the English. Many Jewish importers were canceling large orders and it was ridiculous to imagine that it was possible for a nation to succeed economically without Jewish business. Schacht had no objection to the public display of signs such as "Jews not wanted," since these could even be found in the United States, but he bitterly opposed those put up by Streicher proclaiming, "Whoever buys from a Jew is a traitor to the people." It was unanimously agreed by the group that "wild single actions" must cease so that the Jewish question could be solved legally.

The first steps in the direction of legalization were taken a few weeks later at Nuremberg by the Führer himself, when he proclaimed the Law for the Protection of German Blood and Honor, legalizing a number of repressive measures which were promptly justified by the official Catholic *Klervsblatt* as "indisputable safeguards for the qualitative make-up of the German people." Even Streicher seemed to be satisfied now that the matter was being solved "piece by piece" in the best German legal tradition. "We don't smash any windows and we don't smash Jews," he boasted. "Whoever engages in a single action of that kind is an enemy of the State, a provocateur, or even a Jew."

Were the Nuremberg laws an attempt by Hitler to solve the Jewish question by less harsh "acceptable" methods? Or was he merely biding his time before effecting his dream of extermination? In either case solution of the problem, for the time being at least, had been taken from the party and turned over to the law. This resulted in growing resentment among the more radical Nazi racists. Held in restraint during Hitler's ensuing expansion program, they finally broke out three years later, in 1938, with the destruction of synagogues in Munich, Nuremberg and Dortmund. A wave of Jew-baiting swept the nation. "The entire Kurfürstendamn," wrote Bella Fromm, a diplomatic correspondent from Berlin, "was plastered with scrawls and cartoons. 'Jew' was smeared all over the doors, windows, and walls in waterproof colors. It grew worse as we came to the part of town where poor little Jewish retail shops were to be found. The SA had created havoc. Everywhere were revolting and bloodthirsty pictures of Jews beheaded, hanged, tortured, and maimed, accompanied by obscene inscriptions. Windows were smashed, and loot from the miserable little shops was strewn over the pavement and floating in the gutter."

The tide of anti-Semitism was given impetus on November 7, 1938, when a young Jew, Herschel Grynszpan, shot a minor German Foreign Office official in Paris. Grynszpan, whose parents had been deported from Germany to Poland, had gone to the embassy to assassinate the ambassador only to be sidetracked by Counselor Ernst vom Rath. Himself an enemy of anti-Semitism, Rath was being investigated by the Gestapo but it was he who took the bullets intended for his superior.

"Being a Jew is not a crime," sobbed Grynszpan to the police. "I am not a dog. I have a right to live and the Jewish people have a right to exist on this earth. Wherever I have been I have been chased like an animal."

On the afternoon of November 9 Rath died. The news reached Hitler at the Munich town hall where he was attending a meeting of party leaders. He left the room with his escort, conferred briefly with Goebbels before boarding his special train. Goebbels returned to the meeting to announce that Rath's murder had inspired anti-Jewish riots in the districts of Kurhessen and Magdeburg-Anhalt. The Führer, he said, had decided that if the riots spread spontaneously throughout Germany they were not to be discouraged.

Soon after midnight Heydrich sent urgent teletypes to all headquarters and stations of the SD and police, enjoining them to co-operate with the party and SS leaders in "organizing the demonstrations." Finally, as many Jews, particularly rich ones, were to be arrested "as can be accommodated in existing prisons. For the time being, only healthy men, not too old, are to be arrested. Upon their arrest, the appropriate concentration camps should be contacted immediately in order to confine them in these camps as fast as possible."

It was a night of despair for the Jews in Germany, with the police standing by as witnesses of the destruction and beatings. One policeman was found by the deputy police chief of Berlin weeping in front of a looted shoe shop. It had been his duty to enforce order and yet, in violation of all his ideals, he had done nothing. By official count 814 shops, 171 homes were destroyed, and 191 synagogues put to the torch; 36 Jews were killed and another 36 seriously injured. But the figures, Heydrich himself admitted, "must have been exceeded considerably."

The reaction from abroad was immediate and the acts of brutality were given an unforgettable name—inspired by the multitude of smashed windows—Crystal Night. On all sides Germany was assailed as a barbarous nation. Many Germans agreed and other party officials beside Himmler joined in the condemnation of Goebbels.

Göring complained directly to the Führer that such events made it impossible for him to carry out his mission. "I was making every effort, in connection with the Four-Year Plan," he later testified, "to concentrate the entire economic field to the utmost. I had, in the course of speeches to the nation, been asking for every old toothpaste tube, every rusty nail, every bit of scrap material to be collected and utilized. It would not be tolerated that a man who was not responsible for these things should upset my difficult economic tasks by destroying so many things of economic value on the one hand and by causing so much disturbance in economic life on the other hand." Then Hitler, according to Göring's account, "made some apologies for Goebbels, but on the whole he agreed that such events were not to take place and must not be allowed to take place."

Hitler was already giving the impression that he knew nothing of Crystal Night and added his own complaints. "It is terrible," he told Gerdy Troost, widow of the architect Professor Paul Ludwig Troost, whom Hitler admired above all. "They have destroyed everything for me like elephants in a china shop . . . and much worse. I had the great hope that I was about to come to an understanding with France. And now that!" But Fritz Hesse, summoned to Munich from London for a special press conference, claimed he overheard otherwise from Hitler's own lips the very night Crystal Night was set into motion. At dinner the Führer was boasting how he had bluffed the English and French at Munich when an adjutant whispered something to Goebbels. He turned and muttered to Hitler. At first Hesse couldn't hear what was said, but when the others at the table lapsed into silence it became clear that the Propaganda Minister was explaining a mass attack which he and the SA were going to launch against the Jewish shops and synagogues in a few hours. There was no doubting the Führer's approval, recalled Hesse. "Hitler squealed with delight and slapped his thigh in his enthusiasm."

Despite Hitler's protestations to moderates, the pogrom continued and by November 12 an estimated 20,000 Jews had been shipped to concentration camps. That day Göring, who had objected to the destruction of property on economic grounds, called a meeting of the Council of Ministers to determine who would have to pay for it. He began by announcing that this conference was of decisive importance and his next words had a significance his listeners could not fathom at the time. "I have received a letter from Bormann sent me by order of the Führer, asking that the Jewish question be now, once and for all, treated in its entirety and settled in some way. Yesterday the Führer telephoned me to point out again that decisive measures must be undertaken in a coordinated manner." Inspired by this directive, the conferees agreed that the Jews themselves would have to pay for the damage in the form of a billion-mark fine.

"I certainly would not like to be a Jew in Germany!" remarked Göring and brought the four-hour meeting to a close with a grim forecast: "If in the near future the German Reich should come into conflict with foreign powers, it goes without saying that we in Germany should first come to a showdown with the Jews." Furthermore, the Führer was about to suggest to those foreign powers so concerned over the plight of German Jews that they be deported to the island of Madagascar. "He explained it to me November 9," concluded Göring. "He wants to say to the other countries: 'Why are you always talking about the Jews? Take them!'"

While this plan for the complete elimination of Jews from the Reich economy was getting under way, other Germans, including many party leaders, were privately expressing deep concern at the excesses of Crystal Night. The bureaucrats and party leaders, aware that such violent actions always get out of hand, protested that a pogrom was too costly and accomplished almost nothing in the battle against Jews. Others were repelled by the inhumanity of such actions but did little more than grumble cautiously.

Almost every newspaper and radio commentator in the United States responded to Crystal Night with outrage. At a news conference on November 15 Roosevelt read a prepared statement to the reporters. The news from Germany, he said, had deeply shocked American public opinion. "I myself could scarcely believe that such things could occur in twentieth century civilization. With a view to gaining a firsthand picture of the situation in Germany I have asked the Secretary of State to order our Ambassador in Berlin to return at once for report and consultation." But official condemnation did not extend beyond the verbal and the United States continued its trade relations with the Third Reich.

Perhaps the protests from abroad had some effect on Hitler. A week after Crystal Night he supported the civil service, which sought to protect in the part-Jew "that part which is German," rather than the party which looked on the part-Jew as a carrier of the "Jewish influence." His support came in the form of the First Regulation to the Reich Citizenship Law which separated so-called non-Aryans into definite categories. A Jew was defined as anyone descended from at least three Jewish grandparents, or an individual with two Jewish grandparents who also belonged to the Jewish religious community or was married to a Jew.

Then came a curious category: The *Mischlinge* (half-breeds), those descended from only one Jewish grandparent, or those with two Jewish grandparents who neither practiced the Jewish religion nor were married to a Jew. In practice this split non-Aryans into two distinct groups with the Mischlinge no longer subject to repressive measures. With one bureaucratic stroke Hitler made it possible for a substantial portion of the hated enemy to escape his wrath. Was his resolve to exterminate Jews truly weakening or, again, was he merely waiting for a more suitable time to act decisively? Or was this a conscious or even unconscious attempt to save himself, since there was still the possibility that one of his own grandfathers was Jewish? The Mischlinge regulation also saved Jesus, who by Hitler's argument, being the son of God, had but two Jewish grandparents; neither did he practice the Jewish religion, nor was he married to a Jew.

2

Early in 1939 German bankers revolted against Hitler's vast rearmament program. "The reckless expenditures of the Reich," read a memorandum composed by Hjalmar Schacht, president of the Reichsbank, and signed by every governor of the bank, "represents a most serious threat to the currency. The tremendous increase in such expenditures foils every attempt to draw up a regular budget; it is driving the finances of the country to the brink of ruin despite a great tightening of the tax screw, and by the same token it undermines the Reichsbank and the currency." The stability of the currency, warned Schacht, could not be stabilized in the face of such an inflationary expenditure policy and the "time has come now to call a halt."

Days passed but nothing happened. Finally at midnight of January 19, 1939, Schacht's phone rang. He was ordered to report to the Führer the following morning at nine. It was an unusual hour for an interview since Hitler rarely went to bed before three in the morning. According to Schacht, the Führer said, without preamble, "I have called you in order to hand you your dismissal as president of the Reichsbank." Schacht took the piece of paper extended to him. "You don't fit into the National Socialist picture," continued Hitler, then waited for some comment. Schacht remained silent until Hitler reprimanded him for condemning Crystal Night at a Christmas party of bank office boys. "If I had known that you approved of those happenings," Schacht finally said, "I might have kept silent."

This reply seemed to take Hitler's breath away. "In any case," he said indignantly, "I'm too much upset to talk to you any more now." Both men agreed that Schacht should take a long trip abroad and he left for India soon thereafter. Hitler was relieved to be rid of him. "When it is a question of a bit of sharp practice," Hitler later told his inner circle, "Schacht is a pearl beyond all price." But whenever he was called upon to show strength of character, he always failed.

Soon after Schacht's dismissal Captain Wiedemann was summoned to the winter garden. For the past months Hitler had been treating him with increasing coolness and Wiedemann guessed he too was going to be fired. Ever since Crystal Night the Führer had seemed to inhabit an imaginary world which had nothing in common with reality and whenever Wiedemann attempted to discuss any defect in the system Hitler ignored him.

"I have no use for people in high places and in my closest circle who do not agree with my politics," Hitler curtly told Wiedemann. "I hereby discharge you as my personal adjutant and appoint you consul general in San Francisco. You can accept or refuse this new position." Without hesitation Wiedemann accepted, adding that he hoped he wouldn't have to take a cut in salary. At this, Hitler's tone became milder. "I will always keep an open ear for your financial welfare." Thus, after four years' close association, the two war comrades parted without bitterness.

The exit of Schacht and Wiedemann signaled the return to grace of Josef Goebbels, who had fallen from favor due to his sexual adventures. "Every woman inflames my very blood," he wrote in his twenties. "I pace back and forth like a wolf." Nor had marriage to Magda restrained him. At the same time he kept his numerous affairs under control, never compromising himself publicly. That is, until he fell in love with Czech actress Lida Baarova in the summer of the Olympics. Magda imagined it was one of his usual flirtations but finally lost her patience in 1938 and demanded a divorce. Hitler had shown remarkable tolerance to homosexuality but was distressed by the party leaders who abandoned mates who had helped in the rise to power. He demanded that Goebbels give up the actress. At first he refused, offering to resign from his ministry and become an ambassador to Japan or some such distant country. Finally he succumbed to pressure and renounced his great love. No sooner had Baarova returned to Czechoslovakia under "advice" from the police than Hitler summoned the entire Goebbels family to the Berghof. Pictures of the couple and three of their children at the entrance to the Kehlstein tea house were published as public proof that all was well with the household.

This stage reconciliation took place only a few weeks before Crystal Night and the anguish of losing Lida Baarova—along with a desire to rehabilitate himself with people like Himmler and Rosenberg who felt that the scandal had dealt "the severest kind of blow to the moral status of the party"—might have caused him to act so recklessly that November night.

Just as the false accusations of troop movements on the Czech borders early in 1938 had roused Hitler to premature action, so the storm of protests from abroad over Crystal Night may have hardened his resentment toward Jews and prompted him to look for new ways of dealing with them. An indication of this complete loss of objectivity came on January 21, 1939, when he told Czech Foreign Minister Chvalkovsky that no German guarantee would be given to a state which did not eliminate its Jews. "Our own kindness was nothing but weakness and we regret it," he said. "This vermin must be destroyed. The Jews are our sworn enemies and at the end of this year there will not be a Jew left in Germany." They were not going to get away with what they had done in November 1918. "The day of reckoning has come."

A few days later a Foreign Ministry circular on the Jewish question as a factor in foreign policy was dispatched to all diplomatic missions and consulates. "The ultimate aim of Germany's Jewish policy," it said, "is the emigration of all Jews living on German territories." Since the advent of National Socialism only slightly more than 100,000 Jews had legally or illegally left Germany to find homes in new host countries. Even this modest influx of Jews from Germany had already aroused the resistance of the native populations of America, France, Holland and Norway. Despite the moral denunciation of Germany, the Western nations were hermetically sealing their own boundaries against Hitler's Jews. This ground swell of anti-Semitism confirmed the validity of shipping out Jews en masse, and the goal of the new German policy, concluded the circular, "will be an international solution of the Jewish question in the future, not dictated by false sympathy for the 'Jewish religious minority which has been expelled,' but by the mature realization by all peoples of the danger which the Jews represent for the racial preservation of the nations."

On January 29 Hitler proclaimed his abrupt change in tactics even more explicitly. In a speech to the Reichstag on the sixth anniversary of the Nazi rise to power he declared war on world Jewry. Significantly, hours earlier he had ordered the navy to begin building a mighty submarine fleet to be completed within five years. England, America and France, he charged, were "continually being stirred up to hatred of Germany and the German people by Jewish and non-Jewish agitators," when all he wanted was peace and quiet. These lying attempts to bring about a war could not in the slightest influence Germany's manner of settling her Jewish problem, he said, and for the first time since his rise to power he publicly lifted the veil on his ultimate plan: "In the course of my life I have often been a prophet, and have usually been ridiculed for it. . . . I will once more be a prophet: If the international Jewish financiers in and outside Europe should succeed in plunging the nations once more into a world war, then the result will not be the Bolshevization of the earth, and thus the victory of Jewry, but the annihilation of the Jewish race in Europe!" He was crying out to the Jews the paranoiac warning: "Stop, before you force me to kill you!"

3

In the past year Hitler had destroyed one sovereign state, reduced and paralyzed another and, in the process, humbled the West. Nineteen thirty-nine promised even greater political conquests. On January 1 Mussolini finally made up his mind to accept the German offer of the past autumn and transform the Anti-Comintern Pact from a propaganda front to a full-fledged military alliance. "During this month," wrote Ciano in his diary, "he plans to prepare the acceptance of his views by public opinion, about which he doesn't give a damn." The reason: Mussolini feared war with the West was now inevitable.

In his New Year's message Hitler announced that the German government had but one wish: ". . . that in the coming year, too, we may succeed in contributing to the German pacification of the world." The next step in his "peaceful" program of pacification was the complete control of Czechoslovakia. For some time he had regretted the Munich Pact since it had become apparent he could have annexed the entire country without reprisals. Now he would have to find some acceptable excuse to march in and liquidate what was left.

In February he ordered Goebbels to launch a massive propaganda campaign against the Czech government: it was still terrorizing its ethnic German citizens, concentrating troops along the Sudeten borders, conspiring with the Soviets and grossly mistreating its Slovak population. The last accusation proved to be the most fruitful, for radical Slovak nationalists eagerly rose to the bait and began increasing their demands for complete independence. It was an explosive situation that needed but a single misstep from some inexperienced Czech in high places to set off another crisis—and gave Hitler the excuse he needed.

On March 9 the President of Czechoslovakia, Emil Hacha—who once admitted he understood very little about politics—finally committed the blunder Hitler was waiting for: he dismissed the Slovak government from office and ordered troops to prepare to move into the Slovakian district. The next day, Friday, Hacha declared martial law.

Hitler reacted with rapidity. He canceled his trip to Vienna to take part in the celebration of the Anschluss so that he could prepare for his next invasion. The slight but nagging fear that the Soviets might rush to Prague's aid was relieved almost immediately. Even as Hacha was resorting to martial law, Stalin told the Eighteenth Party Congress that they must be cautious and not allow the West to use the U.S.S.R. to pull its own chestnuts out of the fire. It was in line with Soviet policy to proclaim publicly that they were Czechoslovakia's only faithful ally while risking nothing. The excuse for inaction was that their pact with the Czechs required them to provide aid only *after* France had acted.

On Saturday, his favorite day for a coup, Hitler went into action, improvising with customary agility. First he instructed General Keitel to draft an ultimatum demanding that the Czechs submit to the military occupation of Moravia and Bohemia without resistance, then issued disruptive orders to agents in Czech and Slovak territory.

That evening Hitler's two puppet leaders in Austria, accompanied by five German generals, drove across the Danube to break into a meeting of the new Slovak cabinet at their seat of government, Bratislava. The members were told to proclaim the independence of Slovakia but the new Prime Minister stalled for time by announcing that he would first have to discuss the situation with the Prague government. His predecessor, Josef Tiso—a Roman Catholic priest who was a Friar Tuck in the flesh—had been placed in a monastery under house arrest, but he now dramatically re-entered the scene. The corpulent Monsignor Tiso ("When I get worked up I eat half a pound of ham, and that soothes my nerves") escaped from his prison and demanded that a meeting of the new Slovak cabinet be held early Sunday morning, March 12.

At this secret convocation Tiso revealed that he had received an "invitation" to see Hitler in Berlin. He had accepted, he said, under threat of occupation by German and Hungarian troops. At exactly 7:40 P.M., March 13, Tiso was ushered into Hitler's office by Ribbentrop. The Führer, looking stern and implacable, was flanked by his two top military men, Brauchitsch and Keitel; orders had already been issued to the army and air force to stand by for a possible invasion of Czechoslovakia at six o'clock on the morning of the fifteenth.

"Czechoslovakia," said Hitler accusingly, "owes it only to Germany that she has not been mutilated further." Nor did the Czechs appreciate the great self-control exhibited by the Germans. He raised his voice, either in anger or a show of it, and asked what kind of a game they were playing. He assumed the Slovaks wanted independence and that was why he had prevented Hungary from seizing their territory. He wanted one question cleared up "*in a very short time*." He accented each of these words, then put the question directly to Tiso: did Slovakia want to lead an independent existence or not? "Tomorrow at midday," he said, "I shall begin military action against the Czechs, which will be carried out by General von Brauchitsch." He pointed to his commander-in-chief. "Germany does not intend to take Slovakia into her Lebensraum, and that is why you must either immediately proclaim the independence of Slovakia or I will disinterest myself in her fate. To make your choice I give you until tomorrow midday, when the Czechs will be crushed by the German steamroller."

Tiso hesitated briefly, then telephoned the Slovak cabinet in Bratislava and said in German that he was speaking from the Führer's office. He requested them to convene the Slovak parliament for the following morning. Once he was sure his stupefied listeners understood the message, Tiso rang off. He arrived in Bratislava in time to read to the assembled deputies a Slovak declaration of independence drafted by Ribbentrop. Opposition to the proclamation collapsed and a new Slovakia, independent in name only, was born.

That afternoon in London, Chamberlain stoutly parried angry questions in the House of Commons over the government's failure to stand up to Hitler. What about Britain's guarantee to Czechoslovakia? asked one critic. That guarantee, he retorted, referred only to provoked attack. "No such aggression," he said, "has taken place."

While Chamberlain was making excuses in Parliament, Hitler acted and, as usual, made it appear as if he were only reacting. His tool in the final step of the drama was President Hacha of Czechoslovakia. Harried and confused by the events of the past few days, Hacha now urgently requested an interview with the Führer—a case of the fly seeking an invitation to the spider's net.

After keeping Hacha in suspense for hours, Hitler finally agreed to see him. Already psychologically crushed, the President of Czechoslovakia, accompanied by his daughter and his Foreign Minister, boarded a train for Berlin. He could not fly because of a weak heart.

In Berlin Hitler and his guests were assembling in the drawing room of the chancellery to see a movie, *A Hopeless Case*. Next to the Führer sat General Keitel, on hand to issue, if necessary, executive orders to begin the invasion. At 10:40 P.M. the train from Prague pulled into Anhalt Station but it was not until an hour after midnight that Hacha was summoned by the Führer. He had waited that long, so he told Keitel, to give the old gentleman a chance to rest and recover from the tiring trip but the delay only increased Hacha's anxiety and by the time he and Foreign Minister Chvalkovsky passed by an SS guard of honor and entered Hitler's study his face was "flushed with agitation."

Hacha made a personal appeal by assuring the Führer that he had never mixed in politics. In a sad exhibition of abasement, he threw himself on Hitler's mercy. "He was convinced that the destiny of Czechoslovakia lay in the Führer's hands," read the official German minutes of the meeting, "and he believed it was in safekeeping in such hands."

Even this servility could not stem the vitriol stored up in Hitler. After repeating the alleged wrongs perpetrated by Masaryk and Beneš, he charged that "under the surface the Beneš spirit lived in the new Czechoslovakia." Frail little Hacha was a pitiable figure as he cringed under this attack. Abruptly Hitler—either from compassion or a need to change tactics—hastened to add that he did not mean to imply any distrust of Hacha, and he had "come to the conclusion that this journey by the President, despite his advanced years, might be of great benefit to this country because it was only a matter of hours now before Germany intervened."

Both Hacha and his Foreign Minister sat as if turned to stone until Hitler again gave them a glimmer of hope by insisting that he harbored no enmity against any nation and remained convinced of Hacha's loyalty. But this was extinguished by a declaration that the Beneš tendencies still flourished. The die had been cast on Sunday, said Hitler. The order for the invasion by the German troops and for the incorporation of Czechoslovakia into the German Reich had already been given.

The two Czechs sat stupefied. Hitler announced that his army would enter their country from all sides at 6 A.M. while the Luftwaffe occupied all Czech airfields.

Threat was again followed by promise. Hacha could serve Czechoslovakia by a simple decision. He would have to act quickly—or at six o'clock German troops and planes would go into action. "I would have irremediably lost face if I'd had to put this threat into execution," Hitler recalled several years later, "for at the hour mentioned fog was so thick over our airfields that none of our aircraft could have made its sortie."

He suggested that Hacha and his Foreign Minister withdraw to discuss privately what should be done, but to Hitler's relief Hacha said, "The position is quite clear." He admitted that resistance would be folly yet how could he possibly restrain the nation in less than four hours? Hitler replied that it had to be done somehow, then added hopefully that he saw dawning "the possibility of a long period of peace between the two peoples." If the decision was to resist, he concluded sharply, he saw "the annihilation of Czechoslovakia."

With these ominous words, Hitler ended the interview. As the two dejected Czechs were escorted to an adjoining room, Ribbentrop attempted to place a telephone call to Prague. The line was out of order and Schmidt was asked to try again. As the interpreter was dialing he heard Göring exclaim from the adjoining room that Hacha had fainted. A call went out for Dr. Morell, who had been kept on duty in case the ailing Czech President needed him. If anything happens to Hacha, thought Schmidt, the whole world will say tomorrow that he was murdered in the chancellery. Just then the line to Prague was opened. Schmidt went for Hacha and to his surprise found him recovered, thanks to Dr. Morell's vitamin injection. Hacha came to the phone and, after informing his cabinet what had happened, advised capitulation.

In the meantime Schmidt was making a fair copy of a brief official communiqué which had been composed beforehand. It stated that the President of Czechoslovakia confidently laid the fate of the Czech people and country in the hands of the Führer of the German Reich. It was, in reality, a document of surrender, and Hacha asked for another of Morell's injections. This revived him so much that he refused to sign it despite urgings of Ribbentrop and Göring. These two, according to the official French report, then proceeded to hound the two Czechs pitilessly.

At last Hacha gave in and, face still flushed, signed the document at 3:55 A.M. with trembling hand. He turned to Dr. Morell and thanked him for his ministrations. The moment the pen dropped from Hacha's nerveless fingers the Führer rushed from the conference room to his office where his two middle-aged secretaries were waiting. His face was transfigured, recalled Christa Schröder, as he exclaimed, "Children, quickly, give me a kiss. Quickly!" Schröder and Wolf bussed him on both cheeks. "Hacha has just signed," he said in exultation. "It is the greatest triumph of my life! I shall go down in history as the great German!"

Chapter Eighteen

THE FOX AND THE BEAR

JANUARY–AUGUST 24, 1939

1

On the day Hitler announced the protectorate of Bohemia and Moravia from Hradschin Castle, the British Foreign Office was warned by the Romanian ambassador that secret sources indicated Hitler would take over Romania and Hungary within the next few months. Those hastily reconstructing foreign policy in London were led further astray by an alarming note from their own ambassador in Paris. It was filled with errors since Sir Eric Phipps typed it himself for the sake of secrecy. "Hitler's personal wish," he wrote, "backed by Goering, Himmler, Ribbentrop, Goebbels and Reichenau, is to make war on Great Britain before June or July." The information had probably been planted by the German anti-Hitler faction in their continuing effort to start a shooting conflict. The Führer, in fact, had no desire to fight England, and the proposed domination of both Romania and Hungary was still only in the economic sphere. His sights were set on a solution of Germany's festering differences with Poland, which had been created after the World War by the Allies primarily to contain German aggression. Not only had the Reich lost most of the provinces of West Prussia and Posen but a corridor was cut to the Baltic along the Vistula River to give landlocked Poland an outlet to the sea. Danzig, at the end of this corridor, was made a free city so it could serve Poland as a seaport. Nothing aroused patriotic Germans more than this so-called Polish Corridor which isolated their province of East Prussia from the rest of the Fatherland. And the focal point of resentment lay in Danzig, which was populated almost exclusively by Germans.

Surprisingly, the most nationalistic of Germans devoted little space to the Polish question in *Mein Kampf* and his early speeches. It was not that Hitler entertained friendly feelings for the Poles—a non-Aryan inferior people according to his standards—but that he was obsessed by the Soviet Union, the only country large enough to meet Germany's needs for living space. From the beginning of his regime Hitler had minimized the Polish question and in 1934 signed a ten-year non-aggression pact with Warsaw. Publicly he made a show of German-Polish friendship and at Munich graciously invited the Poles to join in the dismemberment of Czechoslovakia. This they did with relish, not realizing that the guests at such banquets usually pay the bill in the end. It was presented a month after Munich when Ambassador Josef Lipski was invited to have lunch with Ribbentrop at the Grand Hotel in Berchtesgaden. At last the time had come, said Ribbentrop, to settle their differences. He proposed—and his manner was friendly—that Poland return Danzig and allow Germany to construct its own corridor linking East Prussia with the rest of the Reich. In return Germany would let Poland use Danzig as a free port, guarantee her existing borders and extend their pact. Ribbentrop further suggested that the two countries co-operate on the emigration of Jews from Poland and establish "a joint policy towards Russia on the basis of the Anti-Comintern Pact."

Since many influential Poles shared Hitler's fear of Red Russia and hatred of Jews, the prospects of a peaceful settlement seemed hopeful. But the Polish Foreign Minister, Colonel Josef Beck, kept avoiding Hitler's invitations to Germany while doing his best to strengthen links with Russia. Late in 1938 a joint statement of Russo-Polish friendship was issued and trade talks were initiated.

This double game could not be played indefinitely with a man such as Hitler and at last Beck was forced to accept his hospitality. Early in January 1939 he came to the Berghof. If he feared being browbeaten like Schuschnigg, Tiso and Hacha, he was pleasantly surprised. There were no threats, only inducements as Hitler hinted of possible liquidation of Czechoslovakia with further benefits to Poland. This approach failed.

As diplomatically as possible Beck refused even to consider the return of Danzig.

Several weeks later Ribbentrop journeyed to Warsaw so he could repeat the German offer. He was treated to a round of dancing, theater and hunting along with an endless supply of caviar and green vodka but at the conference table he got nothing but more Polish charm. It was rumored at the Wilhelmstrasse that Hitler, offended at Beck's continued refusal to accept what he considered a most generous offer, shouted that the only way to deal with the Poles was by threat. This tactic, used so successfully against Austria and Czechoslovakia, was implemented that March. Ribbentrop warned Warsaw that Polish outrages against the German minority were becoming intolerable. This pronouncement was followed by a press campaign with Göring's newspaper, *Die Zeitung*, charging that German women and children were being molested in Polish streets while German houses and shops were smeared with tar. Far from intimidated, Beck summoned the German ambassador and made his own threat: any attempt to change the status quo of Danzig would be regarded as an act of aggression against Poland.

"You want to negotiate at the point of a bayonet!" exclaimed the German ambassador.

"That is your own method," said Beck.

This and other indications of Polish pluck were rewarded by a startling offer of military assistance from London in case of Nazi aggression. Beck accepted "without hesitation" and on the last day of March Chamberlain, "looking gaunt and ill," walked into the House of Commons and dropped wearily into his chair. A few minutes later he rose and began reading a statement slowly and quietly, head lowered as if he could barely make out the words. "In the event of any action, which clearly threatens Polish independence," he said, "and which the Polish Government accordingly considers it vital to resist with their national forces, His Majesty's Government would feel themselves bound at once to lend the Polish Government all support in their power." The Poles, he added, had been assured to this effect, and the French had authorized him to announce that they joined Britain in these assurances. As he sat down there was spontaneous cheering, the first genuine display of approval since his return from Munich. The unconditional offer was the first material proof that Chamberlain had indeed abandoned appeasement. At last England was united and committed.

* * *

The following day, April 1, the Führer responded to this unanimity with a satirical speech. What right, he asked, had the English to interfere with Germany's right to live? "If today a British statesman demands that every problem in the realm of vital German rights must first be discussed in England, then I could demand just as well that every British problem must first be discussed with us."

He turned from sarcasm to threat. "The German Reich," he said, "is in no sense prepared to tolerate intimidation permanently, or even a policy of encirclement." This was relatively mild and it must have taken will power to control his feelings so well. Privately he seethed, and, upon receiving confirmation of the British guarantee to the Poles that afternoon from Admiral Canaris, he flared up. Features distorted by rage, he stormed about the room, hammering his fists on the marble table and spewing curses. "I'll cook them a stew they'll choke on!" Could he have been thinking of a pact with Stalin?

And so, as a result of his failure to realize that Britain had jettisoned appeasement in fact as well as in words, Hitler issued a war directive on April 3 marked "Most Secret" and delivered by hand to senior commanders only. "Since the situation on Germany's eastern frontier has become intolerable, and all political possibilities of peaceful settlement have been exhausted," it began, "I have decided upon a solution by force." The attack on Poland, Operation White, would begin on the first of September.

The responsibility for opening hostilities on the western front would be left to England and France. If these nations attacked Germany in retaliation, the Wehrmacht was to conserve its strength in this quarter as much as possible. "The right to order offensive operations is reserved absolutely in me." So was decision regarding any air attack on London.

This indicated that he did not take seriously the Anglo-French pledge to support Poland. The Allies might, at worst, declare war but it would only be to save face and if the Germans restrained themselves from responding offensively a deal could be worked out. On such miscalculations are the fates of nations decided. This directive was countersigned by Keitel who, together with all the commanders he consulted, opposed any conflict with Poland. All agreed that Germany was not yet ready for war.

Most nations operate their foreign policy on the pragmatic proposition that at least two irons in the fire are better than one. The Soviet Union, no exception, was negotiating simultaneously with England and Germany. This urgent need for allies stemmed in part from the dangerous weakening of the Red Army brought about two years earlier by Stalin's bloody purge (inspired, incidentally, by Hitler's elimination of the Röhm circle) of Marshal Tukhachevsky and other top military leaders. Although it was not generally known, Germany had been secretly strengthening the Red Army for almost two decades. Both Germany and the Soviet Union had been excluded from the negotiations leading to the Versailles Treaty and, since outcast nations are often drawn together by shared grievances, they covertly began an extensive military collaboration.

This mutually profitable secret arrangement developed into a political rapprochement which was formalized on Easter Sunday, 1922, by the Treaty of Rapallo. It was an effective alliance against the Versailles powers, giving assurance to the Soviets that Germany would not join in any international consortium to exploit their economy while freeing the Germans from threat of complete encirclement. But the rise of Hitler marked a turning point in Soviet-German relations which, by 1938, were practically at an end. The tide again changed dramatically when the Munich Pact was signed by France and England without consulting the Soviets.

Ignored by the West, the Soviet Union once more looked to Germany. Early in 1939 it accepted a Hitler overture to discuss a new trade treaty by inviting one of Ribbentrop's aides to Moscow; and a few days later Stalin gave credence to a sensational story in the London *News Chronicle* that he was signing a non-aggression pact with the Nazis. In a speech to the eighteenth congress of the Communist Party he declared that the Soviet Union was not going to be drawn by the West into any war with Germany. "We are in favor of peace and consolidation of our business relations with all countries." German newspapers seized upon the *all* as a further overture to the Reich, and Soviet newspapers responded by congratulating them for their discernment.

April 20, was Hitler's fiftieth birthday and perhaps his recent show of anger was an indication of impatience. Time was fleeting and he believed he had only a few more years of good health to accomplish his mission. The 1939 birthday was celebrated as usual by a major military parade. This magnificent spectacle—with all three branches of the Wehrmacht as well as the *Waffen* (armed) SS represented—was designed as a warning to enemies. At Hitler's express request the latest medium artillery, heavy tank guns, anti-aircraft guns and air force searchlight units were displayed. Overhead roared a menacing cloud of fighter and bomber squadrons. The attending foreign diplomats were suitably impressed by this greatest military display in German history, nor did they miss the significance of the guest of honor at Hitler's side, President Hacha of Czechoslovakia.

Although numerous Germans were appalled by the demonstration, the majority felt a surge of pride to see such armed might. The fiftieth birthday was also an excuse to subject the public to another flood of propaganda in praise of Hitler.

For a multitude of worshipers he was Germany's savior: "The Führer is the only man in our century who has possessed the strength to take into his hand the thunderbolt of God and fashion it anew for mankind." For others he was more than Messiah—God himself: "My children look upon the Führer as He who gives orders for everything, arranges everything. To them the Führer is the Creator of the world."

When Soviet newspapers reported that Maxim Litvinov had been succeeded by V.M. Molotov, it was sensational news and nowhere was it more appreciated than in the German Embassy. The German chargé telegraphed the Wilhelmstrasse that the Foreign Commissariat was giving no explanations but the dismissal appeared to be the result of differences of opinion between Stalin and Litvinov, whose wife, Ivy, was English. He himself symbolized collective security against the Axis, and his exit meant that Stalin was abandoning this line. The replacement of the Jewish Litvinov by a gentile further indicated that Stalin, already distrustful of Britain's tentative overtures, was opening the door wider to his fellow anti-Semite in Berlin. The embarrassing fact that Molotov had a Jewish wife was kept from Hitler, not only by the Russians but by his own diplomats.

The news of Litvinov's replacement by Molotov struck the Führer "like a cannon ball." Beyond their common violent hatred and fear of Jews, he had long grudgingly admired Stalin's ruthless methods. Even so Hitler was not yet convinced that collaboration with the Soviets was wise. On May 10 he summoned an expert on Russian affairs to Berchtesgaden to determine whether Stalin was prepared for a genuine understanding with Germany. Gustav Hilger, economic attaché at the German Embassy in Moscow, with two decades' experience in Russia, was somewhat taken aback by such a query. He was "tempted to give Hitler a résumé of German-Soviet relations since 1933, and to remind him how often the Soviet government, during the first years of his rule, had expressed the desire of maintaining the old friendly relationship" but restrained himself, merely reminding Hitler of Stalin's declaration to the party congress exactly two months ago that there was no reason for war with Germany.

On his part, Stalin ordered Georgi Astakhov, his chargé d'affaires in Berlin, to resume trade talks with the Germans. On May 20 Molotov inserted himself into the negotiations by inviting Ambassador von der Schulenburg to the Kremlin. The usually dour Molotov was a genial host but beneath the veneer of amiability lay a flintlike obduracy and once serious discussion got under way he complained that Hitler's apparent reluctance to conclude a new economic agreement gave the Soviets the impression that the Germans were not in earnest and were only playing at negotiating for political reasons.

For the present, at least, the Führer was more concerned with strengthening his ties with Mussolini. Upset as he was by Il Duce's surprise invasion of Albania (Hitler had wanted a diversion, not the real thing), he had been negotiating ever since then for a more binding Axis treaty. This was signed with considerable ceremony in Berlin on May 22. Dubbed the Pact of Steel, it bound Italy's destiny inextricably to Germany's. To Hitler the agreement was a diplomatic triumph, pledging as it did each party to support the other in case of war "with all its military forces on land, on sea, and in the air." Incredibly Mussolini had been so anxious to please Hitler that he had not had his cabinet or his political and legal experts check the text, which did not even include a clause specifying that it was in effect only in case of attack by an enemy. Il Duce had carelessly placed the fate of Italy in his partner's hands.

It was almost as if Hitler had received a license to risk war and the next day a confident Führer gathered the senior Wehrmacht officers in his study at the chancellery. The solution of Germany's economic problems, he explained, had somehow become inextricably tied to her differences with Poland. "Danzig is not the subject of the dispute at all. It is a question of expanding our Lebensraum in the East and of securing our food supplies, of the settlement of the Baltic problems."

Therefore Poland (which would always side with Germany's enemies despite treaties of friendship) must be destroyed. "We cannot expect a repetition of the Czech affair," he warned. "There will be war. Our task is to isolate Poland." He reserved to himself the right to give the final order to attack since battle with Poland would be successful only if the West stayed on the sidelines. "If this is impossible, then it will be better to attack in the West and settle Poland at the same time."

The contradiction puzzled his listeners and, while most were staggered by Hitler's words, faithful Keitel convinced himself that the Führer was only trying to show his commanders that their misgivings were unfounded and that war would not really break out. This despite Hitler's next words: a bald prediction of a "life and death" war against England and France.

This was not the irrational ranting of a man possessed by the will to conquer but an admission that Germany could not continue as a great nation without war. Only the limitless resources of the East could save the Reich; and the alternative, accommodation with the West, entailed unacceptable risks. If he exposed to the world that he had been bluffing and shirked the test of war, German prestige and power would deflate like a leaky balloon.

With the possible exception of Keitel and Raeder, the other listeners filed out of the winter garden in shock. As for the Führer, he set out for his refuge on the Obersalzberg in high spirits, stopping off at Augsburg to see a local production of *Lohengrin*. Even as he relaxed at the Berghof, Hitler kept exploring the possibilities of a deal in the East. Although he had ordered Schulenburg to "sit tight" he began fretting about the English negotiations in Moscow. What if they concluded a treaty with the Bolsheviks before he did? If so, what would Stalin do if Germany invaded Poland? He had to know and on May 26 Ribbentrop dictated instructions for Schulenburg to inform Molotov that Germany's former policy of hostility to the Comintern was to be abandoned if Hitler could be assured that the Soviets had, in fact, renounced their aggressive struggle against Germany as indicated by Stalin's recent speech. If so, then the time had come "to envisage the tranquilization and normalization of German-Russian foreign political relations."

Hitler was willing to postpone the dream of Lebensraum.

He instructed Schulenburg to convince Molotov that the Germans had no intention at all of expanding into the Ukraine. The Russian also should not fear the recent Pact of Steel, which was aimed exclusively at the Anglo-French combination. Schulenburg was further enjoined to assure Molotov that, should Hitler find it necessary to use military force against Poland, the Soviet Union would not suffer.

This offer was made so spontaneously that the Wilhelmstrasse was thrown into a mild panic. First Ribbentrop hastily informed the Japanese ambassador of Hitler's proposal, then urged him to wire Tokyo for concurrence. While General Oshima's critics at home looked upon him as Hitler's toady, he could, if the occasion demanded, be extremely intransigent. He refused even to send such a telegram, arguing that any Axis accord with the Soviet Union (whose troops and tanks were battling the Japanese on the Manchurian-Outer Mongolian border in a bitter if undeclared war) would destroy all chances of bringing Japan into the three-power pact with Germany and Italy that Hitler desired and the Japanese had kept side-stepping.

Concluding that he had approached the Russians on too high a level, Hitler ordered Weizsäcker to sound out Astakhov. He did so on the last day of May and the tone and content of their talk were so reassuring that the Führer authorized a message to Schulenburg later that same day instructing him to "undertake definite negotiations with the Soviet Union." On the heels of this message came another suggesting that economic talks with the Russians also be resumed. But Stalin's suspicions exceeded Hitler's and when nothing substantive had been achieved by the end of June the latter reluctantly ordered suspension of negotiations. The honeymoon that each side seemed so eager to consummate was off.

2

Stalin's Western suitors were no nearer to a treaty than Hitler. In London Lord Halifax was reaching the end of his patience with the Kremlin's reluctance to get down to business. Saying no to everything, he complained to Ambassador Maisky, was not his idea of negotiation since it had "a striking resemblance to Nazi methods of dealing with international questions." The Soviet answer was a tart article in *Pravda* on June 29 with this headline: BRITISH AND FRENCH GOVERNMENTS DO NOT WANT A

TREATY ON THE BASIS OF EQUALITY FOR THE USSR. What actually lay behind Soviet hesitation was a lively suspicion that the British aimed to get Russia embroiled in a war with Hitler while reducing their own military contribution to a minimum. The Japanese ambassador in London, equally skeptical, reported to Tokyo his impression that the English were playing their usual double game: using the Soviet treaty negotiations as a threat against Hitler while utilizing a German-oriented peace plan against Stalin.

In the meantime Hitler remained at the Berghof much of the summer, removing himself from the diplomatic scene and making no important announcements. Perhaps this silence was born of his own uncertainty, perhaps it was in line with his conviction that most problems solved themselves if left alone. In any case, he could have done nothing more calculated to confuse his opponents.

Hitler attended Bayreuth enjoying the year's Wagner festival which, besides *The Ring*, included stirring performances of *Tristan* and *Parsifal*. He had invited his old school friend Kubizek to attend every performance but did not see him until August 3, the day after the final performance of *Götterdämmerung*. That afternoon an SS officer escorted Kubizek to Haus Wahnfried. Hitler grasped his old friend's right hand in both of his, and Kubizek could hardly speak.

Kubizek hesitatingly brought out a large bundle of postcards with the Führer's picture and wondered if they could be autographed for friends back in Austria. Hitler put on his reading glasses—he was careful to remove them for photographers—and obligingly began signing cards as Kubizek methodically blotted each signature. Afterward Hitler led him into the garden to Wagner's tomb. "I am happy," he said, "that we have met once more on this spot which always was the most venerable spot for us both."

This episode was one of the rare evidences of Hitler's private life, which had become overshadowed by his responsibilities as Führer. He had little time for Eva Braun, and it was not until the beginning of 1939 that she was moved into quarters in the chancellery. She slept in Hindenburg's former bedroom, whose main decoration was a large picture of Bismarck, and there were standing orders from the Führer never to open the window curtains. This bleak room, along with an adjoining boudoir, led directly to Hitler's library, but she was required to enter his suite through the servants' entrance.

Although they lived as husband and wife, the two went through an elaborate charade to persuade the staff that they were merely good friends. In the morning she would address him as "Mein Führer," and this form of address became such a habit that she used it, so she confessed to her best friend, even in private.

When important guests arrived at either the chancellery or at Berchtesgaden, where Eva's pleasant apartment adjoined the Führer's, she was confined to quarters and this was hard to endure. She longed to meet Admiral Horthy, President Hoover, King Carol of Romania, the Aga Khan and other notables and yet was forced to stay in her room like a child. She was particularly disturbed, she confided to friends, when Hitler refused her pleas to meet the Duchess of Windsor since the two women, she thought, had so much in common. She did console herself with the thrill of knowing that the great of the world were coming from all over the world to honor her lover. This knowledge made her "Back Street" existence endurable. Moreover, anything was better than the earlier days of loneliness and doubt which had led to two attempted suicides.

By August Hitler had become even more impatient about talks with the Soviets. His campaign deadline against Poland was less than a month off and he needed assurance from Stalin that the Red Army would not intervene. At this point he either forced the issue or was blessed by luck. A crisis in Poland arose. Danzig Nazis informed the Polish customs officials that they could no longer carry out their normal duties. Poland responded with an irate demand to withdraw the order, whereupon the president of the Senate of the Free City of Danzig indignantly denied that any such order had been issued and charged that Poland was only looking for a pretext to threaten Danzig.

If it was indeed a case of the tail wagging the dog, the latter quickly took command on August 9. Berlin warned Warsaw that any repetition of the ultimatum to Danzig "would lead to greater tension in the relationship between Germany and Poland." The tempest in the teapot grew into a serious crisis with Poland's retort that she would consider any possible German intervention an aggression.

From his mountain retreat Hitler became personally involved by sending his private plane to Danzig for Carl Burckhardt, the League of Nations' high commissioner for the Free City.

Burckhardt arrived at the Obersalzberg on August 11 and was driven up to the tea house on the Kehlstein.

Hitler was occupied by a different matter. "Perhaps something enormously important will happen soon," he remarked to Speer as they rode up in the elevator to the main room. Almost as though speaking to himself, he mentioned something about sending Göring on a mission. "But if need be I would even go myself. I am staking everything on this card." He was referring to a treaty with Stalin but by the time Burckhardt walked in he had worked himself into an excess of rage over Poland. "If the slightest thing happens without warning," he exclaimed, "I will pounce on the Poles like lightning with all the power of mechanized forces which they don't even dream of!" He shouted at the top of his voice, "Do you understand me?"

"Very well, Monsieur Chancellor, I quite realize that means a general war."

A look of pain and fury came over Hitler's face. "Very well," he said, "if I am forced into this conflict, I prefer to do it today rather than tomorrow. I will not conduct it like Wilhelm II, who always had scruples of conscience before waging total warfare. I will fight relentlessly to the bitter end."

He calmed down as if he had let off sufficient steam and quietly assured his guest that he had no desire to fight Britain and France. "I have no romantic aspiration," he said pleasantly, "no appetite for domination. Above all I seek nothing in the West. Neither today nor tomorrow." But he had to have a free hand in the East. "I must obtain a sufficient quantity of wheat for my country." He also needed a colony outside of Europe for timber. That was as far as his ambitions extended. "Once and for all," he said somberly, "it is necessary that you realize that I am ready to negotiate and discuss all these matters."

He reaffirmed that, given freedom in the East, he would happily conclude a pact with the British and guarantee all their possessions. This promise was obviously meant to be transmitted to London, as was the threat that followed. "Everything that I have in mind is directed against Russia; if the West is too stupid and blind to understand this then I will be forced to come to terms with the Russians, to crush the West and then after its defeat, turn with all my forces against the Soviet Union. I need the Ukraine so they can't starve us out as in the last war."

3

What Burckhardt did not know was that the British had recently made a secret offer to Hitler through one of Chamberlain's top advisers. In a private conversation at his house in West Kensington, Sir Horace Wilson assured Fritz Hesse, Ribbentrop's undercover representative, that the Prime Minister would be prepared to offer the Führer a defensive alliance for twenty-five years that could include economic advantages for the Reich and the return of German colonies by stages "in due course." In return Hitler must promise to take no more aggressive action in Europe.

When Hitler first heard the proposals, so an eyewitness informed Hesse, he was transported with joy. "It's the greatest news I've had for a long time!" he exclaimed and began romancing like a child. The dream of his life, an alliance with mighty England, was coming true! But almost immediately he had misgivings.

That week Ribbentrop asked Hesse if he was "completely convinced" that England would go to war over Danzig. All of his sources, he answered, indicated that Chamberlain could not act otherwise. Any invasion of Polish territory would result in war. "The Führer doesn't believe this at all!" exclaimed Ribbentrop. "Some donkeys told him that the English would only bluff and a German counterbluff would drive them to their knees." Puzzled by the contradiction between Ribbentrop's personal convictions and his public posture, Hesse asked if he really thought the English were bluffing. The Foreign Minister asserted that he *had* warned the Führer that the English were not soft and degenerate and would fight if they believed the balance of power in Europe depended on it or their empire was seriously threatened.

Ribbentrop promised to speak again to Hitler and marveled at the "surprisingly calm way" the Führer considered Hesse's alternatives. Still, Hitler was consumed by fear that it was merely a maneuver to trick him. What guarantee was there that the English would keep their word? "The Führer," Ribbentrop reported, "would only consider solid guarantees." This hardened attitude was reflected in Ribbentrop's own diplomatic posture upon meeting Mussolini's son-in-law on August 11 in Salzburg. Ciano had come with emphatic instructions from Mussolini to insist upon postponement of any invasion of Poland. The matter must be solved by conference.

Ribbentrop, as well as his Führer, had resented Il Duce's sending an emissary instead of coming himself. Besides both despised Ciano for the drinking bouts and sexual escapades he reportedly indulged in whenever he visited the Reich. Ribbentrop dutifully mouthed his master's thoughts at the meeting with Ciano. Perhaps the Foreign Minister had even come to share them. At any rate, he acted like a carbon copy of Hitler as he peremptorily brushed aside all of Ciano's eloquent pleas for a peaceful solution. Finally Ciano asked what Ribbentrop wanted: the Corridor or Danzig? "Not that any more," was the answer. "We want war."

Surprisingly Ciano, who had allowed himself to be bullied by Ribbentrop, stood up to the Führer the following day at the Berghof. During lunch Ciano poked fun at the floral decorations, which interpreter Dollmann guessed had been arranged by Eva Braun; and once serious discussions began, he countered Hitler's arguments with energy and wit. He warned that a war with Poland could not be confined to that country, since this time the West would surely declare war. In the most explicit terms, Ciano pointed out that Italy was not prepared for a general war, in fact, didn't have sufficient matériel to remain in combat for more than a few months. All affability, Hitler suggested they postpone further talk until morning and drive up to his retreat on Kehlstein mountain while there was still good light.

By morning Ciano was a beaten man. At the second talk with Hitler he said not a word of Italy's inability to take part in the war. His brilliant debating power had suddenly deserted him, and to Schmidt's amazement, "he folded up like a jackknife." Gone was the cool decisiveness and statesmanship of yesterday as he listened apathetically to the Führer's assurance that England and France would never go to war on Poland's account. "You have been proved right so often before when we others held the opposite view," said Ciano, "that I think it very possible that this time, too, you see things more clearly than we do."

The supreme confidence exuded by Hitler to Ciano was largely play-acting. He was deeply concerned at Stalin's reluctance to come to an agreement. This anxiety was aggravated by a report that a British-French delegation had recently arrived in Moscow and was about to conclude successful negotiations with the Soviets. In truth, the Russians were in no mood to negotiate, concerned as they were that the Allies were toying with them.

Not knowing all this, the Führer ordered Ribbentrop to put more pressure on the Kremlin, and a conference between Molotov and Schulenburg was hastily arranged. On the evening of August 15 the Foreign Commissar listened attentively to everything the German ambassador had to say but could give no quick answer. First, he said, an understanding must be reached on several points. Would the Germans, for example, be willing to influence Japan to take a different attitude toward the Soviets? Would the Germans conclude a pact of non-aggression? If so, under what conditions?

Hitler was too impatient for deliberations. He ordered Ribbentrop to reach an understanding at once with Molotov; and thereby let his adversary set the pace of events. Stalin took immediate advantage. Through Molotov he replied that before any political pacts could be signed their economic agreements must be concluded. Ribbentrop responded with a further plea to Schulenburg for haste, pointing out that the first stage of the economic agreements had just been completed.

Stalin realized that every hour of delay was painful to Hitler (perhaps his agents had learned of Hitler's September 1 deadline) and so ordered Molotov to procrastinate as usual at his next meeting with Schulenburg on August 19. The Foreign Commissar consequently argued tediously over every point despite his guest's repeated and emphatic pleas for action. But half an hour after Schulenburg departed the Soviets surprisingly reversed their tactics. Molotov invited the German back to the Kremlin. He arrived late that afternoon and it was immediately apparent that Molotov had good news. After apologizing for inconveniencing Schulenburg, the Foreign Commissar said he had just been authorized to hand over a draft of a non-aggression pact and to receive Herr von Ribbentrop in Moscow. He did not explain, naturally, that the Anglo-French-Soviet military talks in Moscow had reached such an impasse that Stalin had lost all patience with the West. Perhaps he had intended to join with Hitler all along and only used the Anglo-French talks as a maneuver to get better conditions from Hitler.

Even so the Russians proceeded deliberately. Molotov told Schulenburg he could not receive Ribbentrop until a week *after* the signing of their economic agreement. If that took place today, the date would be August 26, if tomorrow, the twenty-seventh. Hitler must have read Schulenburg's report with mixed feelings—delight at the probability of concluding the treaty and exasperation at Stalin's insistence on first signing their economic agreement. It was little better than blackmail but Hitler felt there was no alternative. The trade agreement was rushed through and signed in Berlin two hours after midnight. It granted the Soviet Union a merchandise credit of 200 million Reichsmarks, at the reasonable interest of five per cent, to be used to finance Soviet orders of machine tools and industrial installations. Armaments "in the broader sense," such as optical supplies and armor plate, were to be supplied in proportionately smaller amounts. The credit would be liquidated by Soviet raw materials.

Outmaneuvered by Stalin, just as he had outmaneuvered the Austrians and Czechs, Hitler could not possibly wait the week that Molotov proposed. He composed a personal message to Stalin which was dispatched from Berlin at 4:35 P.M., August 20. In it Hitler sincerely welcomed the signing of the new German-Soviet commercial agreement as a first step in the reordering of German-Soviet relations. He also accepted the Soviet draft of the non-aggression pact although there were a few questions connected with it which should be clarified as soon as possible. Then he got down to the crux of the matter: speed in concluding this pact, he said, was of the utmost importance since tension between Germany and Poland was becoming intolerable. A crisis might arise "any day."

Two hours after Schulenburg delivered the message to the Kremlin, he was summoned back for a personal reply from Stalin himself: "I thank you for the letter," it began. He hoped the pact would mark a decided turn in their political relations. "The people of our countries need peaceful relations with each other." He agreed to see Ribbentrop on August 23.

Throughout the twentieth Hitler had been silently pacing up and down the great hall in the Berghof waiting anxiously for news from Moscow; the expression on his face kept anyone from disturbing him. In expectation he had already sent the pocket battleship *Graf Spee* to a waiting position in the Atlantic; twenty-one U-boats were in offensive positions around the British Isles.

At dinner (according to Speer) Hitler was handed a telegram.

After reading it, his face flushed a deep red and he stared vacantly out the window. All at once he slammed both fists on the table, making the glasses rattle. "I have them!" he exclaimed in a voice choked with emotion. "I have them!" He slumped back and, since no one dared to ask any questions, the meal resumed in silence.

On the face of it, Stalin and Hitler *were* most unlikely allies. What could they possibly have in common? In fact, there were a number of similarities. One admired Peter the Great while the other saw himself as the heir of Frederick the Great. Both were advocates of ruthless force and operated under ideologies that were not essentially different. Communists and Nazis alike were self-righteous and dogmatic; both were totalitarian and both believed that the end justified the means, sanctifying injustice, as it were, in the name of the state and progress.

Hitler had long admired Stalin, regarding him as "one of the extraordinary figures in world history," and once shocked a group of intimates by asserting that he and the Soviet leader had much in common since both had risen from the lower classes, and when one listener protested comparison with a former bank robber, he replied, "If Stalin did commit a bank robbery, it was not to fill his own pockets but to help his party and movement. You cannot consider that bank robbery."

Nor did the Führer look upon Stalin as a true Communist. "In actual fact, he identifies himself with the Russia of the Czars, and he has merely resurrected the tradition of Pan-Slavism. [Perhaps Hitler was unconsciously speaking of himself and Germany.] For him Bolshevism is only a means, a disguise designed to trick the Germanic and Latin peoples."

Both Stalin and Hitler felt sure they could use each other. Both dictators were wrong but in that hectic summer of 1939 there was not a major nation in the world which was not operating under some misconception. Europe was a cauldron of distrusts, deceit and double-dealing. Even as Ribbentrop prepared to leave for Moscow, Stalin had not completely abandoned the hope of an Anglo-French-Soviet military alliance against Hitler. And while the English were doing their halfhearted best to consummate this agreement, they were secretly inviting Göring to England. On all sides nation was dealing behind the back of nation, each mouthing platitudes of sincerity or uttering threats.

4

The apparent winner was Hitler. He wakened on the morning of August 22 full of confidence. After Ribbentrop had left the Berghof with final instructions for his mission to Moscow, the Führer summoned his senior commanders and their chiefs of staff for a special meeting in the spacious reception hall. It was a lecture, not a conference, with Hitler sitting behind a large desk doing all the talking. "I have called you together to give you a picture of the political situation, in order that you may have insight into the various elements on which I have based my decision to act, and in order to strengthen your confidence." The conflict with Poland, he said, was bound to come sooner or later and there were a number of reasons why it was best to act promptly. "First of all two personal factors: my own personality and that of Mussolini. Essentially all depends on me, on my existence, because of my political talents. Probably no one will ever again have the confidence of the German people as I have. There will probably never again be a man with more authority than I have. My life is, therefore, a factor of great value. But I can be eliminated at any time by a criminal or an idiot." The second personal factor was Il Duce. If something happened to him, Italy's loyalty to their alliance would be questionable.

On the other hand there was no outstanding personality in either England or France. "Our enemies have men who are below average. No personalities. No master, no men of action..." Furthermore, the political situation was favorable, with rivalry in the Mediterranean and tension in the Orient. All these fortunate circumstances would no longer prevail in two or three years. "No one knows how long I shall live. Therefore conflict is better now."

Then he became specific. Relations with Poland, he said, had become unbearable. "We are facing the alternative to strike or to be destroyed with certainty sooner or later." What could the West do? Either attack from the Maginot Line or blockade the Reich. The first was improbable and the second would be ineffective since now the Soviets would supply Germany with grain, cattle, coal, lead and zinc. "I am only afraid that in the last minute some *Schweinehund* will produce a plan of mediation!"

The commanders, led by Göring, clapped enthusiastically. "Mein Führer," said the Reichsmarschall, "the Wehrmacht will do its duty!" Despite their applause, Göring and the other military commanders were unanimously against war since all were convinced that Germany was not yet properly prepared to wage one. There was only a six weeks' supply of ammunition, as well as alarming shortages of steel, oil and other important materials.

Hitler was as aware of all this as his generals but envisaged a different type of warfare: the *Blitzkrieg*, a sudden all-out attack of such force and intensity that victory would be assured quickly. The concept was strategic as well as tactical. The dehumanizing years of trench combat in the Great War, not to mention the deprivations of those on the home front, were still searing memories to Hitler. He had vowed that the misery of a long conflict would never again be visited on Germany. That is why he geared the Wehrmacht to armament in breadth rather than in depth. He had purposely organized Germany's economy for a relatively high production of ready armaments but not to wage long-range war with mass-productive powers. His goal was to produce armaments quickly, not to increase Germany's armament-producing plant or to retool her armament-producing machinery.

A series of Blitzkrieg attacks—sustained by short, intensive bursts of production—would permit Hitler to act as if Germany were stronger than she actually was by avoiding the massive production for conventional war that would have meant economic ruin. His was a poor man's philosophy that could only succeed with audacity. Already he had achieved a series of cheap victories by risking a conflict that his more affluent enemies were eager to avoid at almost any cost.

Blitzkrieg not only appealed to his gambling instinct but was perfectly suited to his position of dictator. A democracy could hardly have sustained the necessary bursts of economic effort, the concentration on turning out tanks, for instance, followed by an abrupt concentration on civilian items. What would have brought down a democracy did not apply to the National Socialist state with the peculiar weaknesses and strengths of its economy.

By choosing Blitzkrieg, Hitler confounded some of his own

generals, whose theories were still rooted in the past. They did not realize, as he did, that Germany was far readier for combat than England and France. It was a gamble but he figured he could achieve victory over Poland so rapidly that he would never even have to cross swords with England or France. The odds were that they would then see the futility of retaliation. Somehow he had to neutralize the West—whether by threat or force of arms—so that by 1943 he could achieve his true aim, conquest of Russia. With eyes open, Adolf Hitler was prepared to meet his destiny.

The two German Condors landed at Moscow airport where Ribbentrop was pleased to see the swastika flying side by side with the hammer and sickle. After the Foreign Minister reviewed an honor guard of the Soviet air force, he was driven to his quarters, the former Austrian Embassy. (Was this Tartar irony?) Count von der Schulenburg informed him that he was expected in the Kremlin at 6 P.M. but couldn't say whether it would be Molotov or Stalin who would negotiate with him. "Odd Moscow customs," thought Ribbentrop to himself.

After Schulenburg and Hilger had made their reports, both advised Ribbentrop to allow himself plenty of time and not give the impression of being in a hurry. Interrupting with an impatient movement of the hand, he enjoined the ambassador to inform the Russians that he had to be back in Berlin within twenty-four hours. So saying, he hastily had a snack before heading for the Kremlin.

At 6 P.M. Ribbentrop was facing Stalin. He was affable, good-natured. Molotov was impassive. Ribbentrop spoke first, expressing his nation's desire to establish German-Soviet relations on a new footing. He understood from Stalin's March speech that he felt the same. Stalin turned to Molotov. Did he want to speak first? The Foreign Commissar dutifully replied that it was Stalin's prerogative to reply.

He did in a manner which Ribbentrop had never encountered before. "For years," said Stalin concisely, "we have poured pails of manure at one another. That should not stop us from coming to an understanding. This was the drift of my speech in March, the meaning of which you have understood perfectly." With a notebook opened in front of him for reference, he continued without pause to practical matters: the spheres of influence in the countries between Germany and the U.S.S.R. were defined, with Finland, most of the Baltic States and Bessarabia in the Russian orbit; in the event of war between Germany and Poland they would meet at a definite "line of demarcation."

It was obvious that Stalin had come to the room to do business, not dally, and by the end of three hours he and Ribbentrop had agreed upon everything except two Baltic ports which Stalin insisted on having in his sphere. Ribbentrop said he would have to check with the Führer first and the talks were adjourned so he could do so.

Hitler was as eager to do business as Stalin. Within an hour a phone call from the Wilhelmstrasse brought this laconic reply: "Answer is yes. Agreed." In the meantime Ribbentrop sat down to another quick meal at his quarters, bubbling over with enthusiasm for Stalin and Molotov.

The Foreign Minister was in high spirits as he drove back to the Kremlin with the favorable answer from Hitler, this time with a larger retinue, which included two photographers. Secret police rushed out of the darkness as the German cars slowly moved into the mysterious inner city and proceeded past the largest cannon of its time, so huge that no one had ever dared fire it, past little wooden houses and cathedrals. Finally the procession reached a modern administration building where Stalin was waiting. In short order, final agreement on the nonaggression pact was reached. It was a concise, clear contract. Each party was to desist from any aggressive action against the other and lend no support to any power attacking the other. The treaty was to last for ten years and continue for another five unless renounced by either party a year prior to its expiration.

It was a conventional agreement, but not so its secret protocol, which carved up Eastern Europe. Equally extraordinary was Stalin's willingness to be photographed at the signing of the documents. He entered into the spirit and stage-managed the best-known picture of the signing.

Toast followed toast but the most noteworthy was one from Stalin that was never revealed to the Russian people: "I know how much the German nation loves its Führer," he said. "I should therefore like to drink to his health." One of the most important treaties in world history had been completed and signed without argument in a few hours, proof that both Hitler and Stalin wanted the agreement, that both knew exactly what they would give to get what they wanted, and that both wished the deed done swiftly.

Upon learning the treaty was signed, Hitler jumped up from the dinner table, exclaiming, "We've won!" Although he had waived the opportunity to seize all of Poland, the argument had neutralized Russia. Now he was free to proceed against Poland. Without the Soviet Union on their side, neither England nor France would do more than mouth threats. In addition he was assured of getting from the East all those raw materials he might be deprived of by a possible British blockade.

He was paying Stalin to do exactly what he would undoubtedly have done without a pact. The economy of the Soviet Union as well as its military efficiency was still in such disarray after the purges that Stalin could not even think of fighting the Reich. In fact he had never seriously sought a protective alliance against Hitler. What he and his associates in the Kremlin desired above all was neutrality; the pact with Germany not only gave this but fulfilled their aim of provoking war among the capitalist powers. To Stalin, Nazi Germany was just another capitalist enemy.

Chapter Nineteen

"A CALAMITY WITHOUT PARALLEL IN HISTORY"

AUGUST 24– SEPTEMBER 3, 1939

1

The world awakened Thursday morning, August 24, to headlines proclaiming a treaty that was a traumatic shock not only to ordinary citizens but to diplomats. The Polish people were extremely upset by the German-Soviet pact despite attempts by their newspapers to belittle it as a sign of German weakness. The government itself expressed supreme confidence that British and French assistance would turn the tide in case of war with Hitler. French Communists seemed to be torn between loyalty to their own country and Mother Russia. Confusion was even greater among their American colleagues. At first the *Daily Worker* ignored the treaty as if waiting for instructions from Moscow. Finally Earl Browder, the party leader, announced that it had weakened Hitler. With nary a qualm most extreme left-wing "progressives" obediently accepted a new party line: the agreement with Hitler had been consummated so that Russia could prepare herself for the eventual battle against Fascism. President Roosevelt's response was to send another of his moral telegrams to Hitler urging him "to refrain from any positive act of hostility for a reasonable and stipulated period" but, like its predecessors, it was filed and forgotten.

In Moscow Stalin was congratulating himself. Convinced that the British would compromise in the face of political reality, he imagined that the spheres of influence he had been granted would fall to him bloodlessly, by negotiation. Hitler's other allies were not so sanguine. The Italians, while admitting that Hitler had "struck a master blow," were uneasy and the Japanese feared that the alliance would encourage Stalin to increase pressure on Manchuria.

The German public was generally pleased and relieved: the threat of encirclement, a war on two fronts, had miraculously evaporated thanks to the Führer. Those who found the pact the hardest to swallow were his staunchest followers but most of them quickly convinced themselves that the Chief knew exactly what he was doing.

Hitler flew up to Berlin to greet the returning hero, Ribbentrop, and he spent the evening in the chancellery listening to his Foreign Minister rhapsodize over the masters of the Kremlin, who made him feel "as if he were among old party comrades." Further, a picture of Czar Nicholas in the Winter Palace had convinced Ribbentrop that they could do business with Russia since it indicated that the Communists themselves revered a Czar who worked for the people. While Hitler took all this in with some interest, he was much more enthralled by the pictures Hoffmann had taken. Hitler, it seemed, had requested a close-up of the Soviet leader to see if his earlobes were "ingrown and Jewish, or separate and Aryan." One profile view in particular was most reassuring. His new brother-in-arms, according to the earlobe test, was no Jew.

But Hitler shook his head disapprovingly at the photographs of the final ceremonies. Every one showed Stalin with a cigarette. "The signing of the pact is a solemn act which one does not approach with a cigarette dangling from one's lips," he said and instructed the photographer to paint out the cigarettes before releasing the pictures to the press.

The following day, Friday, August 25, was a crucial and crowded one. It began with a letter to Mussolini, explaining with some embarrassment what had taken place in Moscow. After giving assurances that the treaty only strengthened the Axis, Hitler trusted that Il Duce would understand why he had been forced to take such a drastic step. Hitler's next act was to ask Schmidt to translate the key passages of the speech Chamberlain had made in Commons the previous day. He listened intently to the Prime Minister's admission that the Moscow Pact had come as "a surprise of a very unpleasant character," but that the Germans were laboring under a "dangerous illusion" if they believed that the British and French would no longer fulfill their obligations to Poland.

"These words," recalled Schmidt, "made Hitler pensive, but he said nothing." Perhaps this confirmed a nagging uncertainty. The assault on Poland was scheduled to start early next morning but he was in such doubt that just before noon he instructed the high command to postpone the issuance of the executive order to attack for one hour—until three that afternoon. Then he summoned the British ambassador to the chancellery. Henderson arrived at 1:30 P.M. to find the Führer in a conciliatory mood. He was now prepared "to make a move toward England which should be as decisive as the move towards Russia which had led to the recent agreement." His conscience, Hitler said, compelled him to make this final effort to secure good relations. But this was his last attempt.

To Henderson he appeared to be calm and normal. But he did lose his temper as soon as he began enumerating the charges against the Poles, such as firing on civilian aircraft. These conditions, he shouted, "must cease!" The Danzig problem and the Corridor must be solved without further delay. The only result of Chamberlain's last speech could be "a bloody and unpredictable war between Germany and England." But this time Germany would not have to fight on two fronts. "Russia and Germany will never again take up arms against each other."

When Henderson kept repeating stolidly that England could not go back on her word to Poland, Hitler's threatening posture reverted to one of reasonableness. Once the Polish question was solved, he was prepared and determined to approach Britain again with a large comprehensive offer: he would, for instance, accept the British Empire and pledge himself personally to its continued existence. But if the British rejected his proposal, he concluded ominously, "there will be war." And this was his last offer.

Half an hour later, at exactly 3:02 P.M., he confirmed the order to attack Poland at dawn. On the surface his gamble appeared to have been motivated by mere opportunism. Admittedly a cunning virtuoso of day-to-day politics, his foreign policy did have a basic thrust: a step-by-step play to gain domination over continental Europe that was closely allied to his radical anti-Semitic program.

While Hitler was waiting for a visit from French Ambassador Coulondre, an aide brought in a news report from England which Schmidt glimpsed over his employer's shoulder. England and Poland had just concluded a pact of mutual assistance in London. Visibly concerned, the Führer brooded in silence. For months the signing of this agreement had been delayed for one reason or another. That it should take place on this of all days, a few hours after he had made his "last" offer to England, was no coincidence. This guarantee of military aid (even though it could never be implemented) might give the Poles such a false sense of security that they would refuse to negotiate with Germany.

At 5:30 P.M. Coulondre was finally escorted into the office. After exhibiting rage over Polish provocations, Hitler expressed regret over a possible war between Germany and France. "I had the impression at times," recalled Schmidt, "that he was mechanically repeating what he said to Henderson, and that his thoughts were elsewhere. It was obvious that he was in a hurry to bring the interview to an end." He half rose to his feet in a gesture of dismissal but the elegant Coulondre would not be put off without a retort. He spoke with forcible words that Schmidt would never forget: "In a situation as critical as this, Herr Reichskanzler, misunderstandings are the most dangerous things of all. Therefore, to make the matter quite clear, I give you my word of honor as a French officer that the French army will fight by the side of Poland if that country should be attacked." Then he assured Hitler that his government was prepared to do everything for the maintenance of peace right up to the last.

A minute later, at 6 P.M., Ambassador Attolico entered. He bore with him the text of Mussolini's letter, which had been dictated over the phone by Ciano. The announcement that Italy was not prepared for war, on the heels of the British-Polish pact and Coulondre's crystal-clear declaration of France's intentions, hit the Führer like "a bombshell." To him it was the completely unexpected defection "of an ally." But he controlled himself, dismissing Il Duce's envoy with the curt comment that he would send an immediate reply. As Attolico went out the door Schmidt heard Hitler mutter, "The Italians are behaving just as they did in 1914."

Hitler told General Keitel: "Stop everything at once. Get Brauchitsch immediately. I need time for negotiations." Keitel rushed out into the anteroom. "The order to advance must be delayed again," he excitedly told his aide. The news spread that the threat of war had been averted at the last minute. The

Führer was returning to negotiation! There was general relief except from Hitler's chief adjutant, Rudolf Schmundt, who was glum. "Don't celebrate too soon," he told Warlimont. "This is only a postponement."

Göring was convinced that the English were not merely mouthing words of warning and was surreptitiously negotiating for peace. A man of action, he had already initiated discussions with England without consulting Ribbentrop, whom he distrusted. It was not as daring as it appeared, for he intended keeping his Führer informed of any developments. His desire for peace was hardly altruistic. Being a freebooter with the touch of the gangster, his prime aim in life was to enjoy the fruits of the plunder he was amassing thanks to his privileged position. War could bring an end to his sybaritic existence. On the other hand, Hitler was driven by principle, warped though it was, and could not be bribed. He might compromise but only if it brought him closer to his long-range goal. Realizing all this, Göring carried on his devious policy of peace with caution. As unofficial go-between in this intrigue he selected a wealthy Swedish businessman named Birger Dahlerus. He had a German wife as well as interests in the Reich and so shared Göring's desire to prevent war between Germany and England. Furthermore, he was in a position to do something about it, for he had influential English friends who were willing to work clandestinely on the project.

Earlier that month Dahlerus had arranged a secret meeting between Göring and seven Englishmen in a house conveniently close to the Danish border. Here it was that the Reichsmarschall first expounded his views and hopes for peace to the foreign businessmen. Little was done except talk until the historic military conference at the Berghof two weeks later. This spurred Göring to telephone Dahlerus in Stockholm and urge him to come as soon as possible. The situation, he guardedly revealed, had worsened and the chances of a peaceful solution were rapidly diminishing. Göring persuaded Dahlerus to fly at once to England with an unofficial message to the Chamberlain government, urging that negotiations between Germany and England take place as soon as possible.

And so on that eventful morning of August 25 Dahlerus had flown to London by ordinary passenger plane but it was not until early evening that he was ushered into the office of Lord Halifax. The Foreign Secretary was in an optimistic mood and—since Hitler, it will be recalled, had just called off the invasion—it did not appear that the services of a neutral would be of further use. Dahlerus was not so optimistic and telephoned Göring for his opinion. The Reichsmarschall's reply was alarming. He feared that "war might break out at any moment."

Dahlerus repeated these words to Halifax the next morning and offered to deliver to Göring—the only German in his opinion who could prevent war—a personal message from Halifax confirming England's genuine desire to reach a peaceful settlement. Lord Halifax excused himself so he could discuss the matter with Chamberlain. In half an hour he returned with the Prime Minister's approval. The letter was written and Dahlerus was rushed to Croydon airdrome.

In Berlin Ambassador Attolico was on his way to the chancellery with another message from Mussolini. It contained an imposing list of the material Italy would need if she participated in a war: six million tons of coal; seven million tons of petroleum, two million tons of steel and a million tons of lumber. Since Attolico was opposed to war, he deliberately made Mussolini's terms impossible to fulfill. To Ribbentrop's icy query as to when this vast amount of material was to be delivered, Attolico answered, "Why, at once, before hostilities begin."

It was an unreasonable demand. Surprising, considering the strain he must have been under, was Hitler's calm reply, which was relayed to Mussolini by telephone at 3:08 P.M. He could meet Italy's requirements in most areas, he said, but regretted it was impossible to deliver before the outbreak of war for technical reasons. "In these circumstances, Duce, I understand your position, and would only ask you to try to achieve the pinning down of Anglo-French forces by active propaganda and suitable military demonstrations such as you have already proposed to me." In the light of his pact with Stalin, he concluded, he did not "shrink from solving the Eastern question even at the risk of complications in the West."

At 6:42 P.M. Attolico got another call from Rome. It was Ciano with another urgent message for the Führer. In it Mussolini apologetically explained that Attolico had misunderstood the delivery date. He didn't expect the raw materials for a year. He regretted not being more helpful at such a crucial time and then, unexpectedly, made a plea for peace. A satisfactory political solution, he said, was still possible. When Hitler read these words he concluded that his ally was abandoning him. Somehow he controlled his feelings and sent off another conciliatory reply. "I respect the reasons and motives which led you to take this decision," he said and tried to infuse his partner with his own optimism.

Disappointed and exhausted, the Führer retired earlier than usual, only to be awakened soon after midnight. Göring had to see him at once on urgent business: the Swedish go-between he had mentioned the other day was back with an interesting letter from Lord Halifax. It was about 12:30 A.M. August 27, when Dahlerus was ushered into the Führer's study. Hitler waited solemnly, staring fixedly at the neutral who was striving for peace. Göring stood beside him, looking pleased with himself. After a brief friendly greeting, Hitler launched into a lecture on Germany's desire to reach an understanding with the English, which degenerated into an excited diatribe. After describing his latest proposals to Henderson, he exclaimed, "This is my last magnanimous offer to England." His face stiffened and his gesticulations became "very peculiar" as he boasted of the Reich's superior armed might.

Dahlerus pointed out that England and France also had greatly improved their armed forces and were in good position to blockade Germany. Without answering, Hitler paced up and then suddenly stopped in his tracks, stared and began talking again (Dahlerus recalled), this time as if in a trance. "If there should be a war, then I will build U-boats, build U-boats, build U-boats, build U-boats, U-boats, U-boats." It was like a stuck record. His voice became more and more indistinct. Abruptly he was orating as if to a huge audience, but still repeating himself. "I will build airplanes, build airplanes, airplanes and I will destroy my enemies!" In consternation, Dahlerus turned to see how Göring was reacting. But the Reichsmarschall appeared not at all perturbed. Dahlerus was horrified: so this was the man whose actions could influence the entire world!

"War doesn't frighten me," continued Hitler, "encirclement of Germany is an impossibility, my people admire and follow me faithfully." He would spur them to superhuman efforts. His eyes went glassy. "If there should be no butter, I shall be the first to stop eating butter, eating butter." There was a pause. "If the enemy can hold out for several years," he finally said, "I, with my power over the German people, can hold out one year longer. Thereby I know that I am superior to all the others." All at once he asked why it was that the English continually refused to come to an agreement with him.

Dahlerus hesitated to answer honestly but finally said that the trouble was founded on England's lack of confidence in

Hitler. At this the Führer struck his breast. "Idiots!" he exclaimed. "Have I ever told a lie in my life?" He continued to pace, again stopped. Dahlerus, he said, had heard his side. He must return to England at once and tell it to the Chamberlain government. "I do not think Henderson understood me, and I really want to bring about an understanding."

Dahlerus protested that he was a private citizen and could go only if the British government requested it. First he must have a clear definition of the vital points on which agreement could be reached. For example, what exactly was Hitler's proposed corridor to Danzig? Hitler smiled. "Well," he said, turning to Göring, "Henderson never asked about *that*." The Reichsmarschall tore a page out of an atlas and began outlining with a red pencil the territory Germany wanted.

This led to a clarifying discussion of the main points in Hitler's offer to Henderson: Germany wanted a treaty with Britain that would eliminate all disputes of a political or economic nature; England was to help Germany get Danzig and the Corridor; in return Germany would guarantee Poland's boundaries and let her have a corridor to Gdynia; the German minority in Poland would be protected; and, finally, Germany would give military aid whenever the British Empire came under attack.

Dahlerus ingenuously took Göring at face value and was inclined to think the best of Hitler. Moreover, he had no training in diplomacy. In his favor were a sincere desire for peace, courage and admirable persistence. A soon as he returned to his hotel he put in a long-distance call to an English friend. Before long he had assurance that the British government would welcome him as a messenger. At eight that peaceful Sunday morning he boarded a German plane at Tempelhof. As it headed at low level for London he wondered if he was merely a pawn in a game of intrigue. He was fairly sure that Göring was honestly working for a peaceful settlement. But was Hitler?

A little after noon a German plane landed at Croydon. Birger Dahlerus stepped out. The place seemed dead since civilian air traffic between England and the Continent had come to a standstill. He was driven to the Foreign Office past air raid wardens patrolling streets where shop-windows were pasted over with strips of paper, then taken through back alleys to 10 Downing Street. Chamberlain, Halifax and Sir Alexander Cadogan, the Permanent Under Secretary of State for Foreign Affairs, were waiting. They were grave but "perfectly calm." As Dahlerus told about the long meeting with Hitler he sensed an air of skepticism. His report differed from that of Henderson on several points and Chamberlain asked if he was absolutely certain he'd understood what Hitler said. Dahlerus, whose command of German was superior to Henderson's, replied that any misinterpretation was out of the question.

Throughout this conversation Chamberlain's remarks were colored by distrust of Hitler; he asked what impression the Führer had made on Dahlerus. The answer ("I shouldn't like to have him as a partner in my business") brought the only smile of the day from the Prime Minister. Since the British doubted his interpretation of Hitler's demands, Dahlerus suggested that they allow him to return to Berlin with their reactions. Chamberlain hesitated. Ambassador Henderson, presently in London, was scheduled to fly back to Berlin that day with their answer to Hitler's proposals. Dahlerus suggested that the ambassador wait a day. Then he could let the British know exactly how Hitler felt *before* they made an official reply based only on Henderson's assessment.

He suggested phoning Göring so he could ask point-blank if the German government would agree to Henderson waiting a full day. "Do you intend to phone from the Foreign Office?" asked Chamberlain. Dahlerus did and Chamberlain agreed. In a few minutes the go-between was in Cadogan's room hearing Göring say that he could not possibly give an immediate answer without conferring with the Führer. Half an hour later Dahlerus again phoned. This time Göring announced that Hitler accepted the plan "on the condition that it was genuine."

It was 11 P.M. by the time Dahlerus arrived at Göring's Berlin residence. After assuring the Reichsmarschall of his personal conviction that both the English government and her people truly wanted peace and were acting in good faith, Dahlerus outlined the British response to the Hitler proposals. Göring rubbed his nose. The British reply, he said, was hardly satisfactory and the whole situation was highly precarious. He would have to confer with Hitler alone. Dahlerus nervously paced the floor of his hotel room as he waited for the answer. Finally at 1:30 A.M. Göring telephoned. Hitler, he said in a robust voice, *did* respect England's views and welcomed her desire to reach a peaceful agreement. He also respected England's decision to honor her guarantee of Poland's boundaries as well as her insistence on an international guarantee in this matter of five great powers. Dahlerus was particularly relieved by his last concession since it surely meant that Hitler had shelved any other plans he might have had for Poland.

2

Often amateur diplomats merely confuse matters, but this time Dahlerus had succeeded in breaking a log jam. By 9 P.M. when Henderson's plane landed at the Berlin airport matters had progressed substantially. The ambassador had returned to his post armed with an official version of the offer Dahlerus had delivered unofficially. It also contained a clause stating that Polish Foreign Minister Josef Beck had just agreed to enter at once into direct discussions with Germany.

As Hitler read the German translation of the British note he registered no emotion even though it ended with the mixed expression of promise and threat that had become the Führer's own trademark: a just settlement of the questions between Germany and Poland could open the way to world peace; failure to reach it would bring Germany and Great Britain "into conflict and might well plunge the whole world into war. Such an outcome would be a calamity without parallel in history."

Henderson took the offensive for the first time in memory and did more talking than Hitler. Ordinarily this would have caused an eruption but Hitler sat calmly, occasionally staring out at the dark garden where his famed predecessor, Bismarck, had so often strolled.

In the meantime Henderson was proclaiming that England's word was her bond and she "had never and would never break it." In the old days Germany's word also had the same value and he quoted Field Marshal von Blücher's exhortation to his troops when hurrying to support Wellington at Waterloo: "Forward, my children, forward; I have given my word to my brother Wellington, and you cannot wish me to break it." Things were quite a bit different a hundred and twenty-five years ago, commented Hitler but with no asperity, and then insisted that while *he* was quite ready to settle his differences with Poland on a reasonable basis the Poles were continuing their violence against Germans. Such acts seemed to be a matter of indifference to the British.

* * *

There was pessimism at the chancellery. The Führer, Major Gerhard Engel, Hitler's army adjutant, wrote in his diary, "is exceptionally irritated, bitter and sharp," and he made it clear to his adjutants that he would not take advice from the military on the question of peace or war. "He simply could not understand a German soldier who feared war. Frederick the Great would turn in his grave if he saw today's generals." All he wanted was liquidation of the unjust conditions of the Poles, not war with the Western Allies. "If they were stupid enough to take part that was their fault and they would have to be destroyed."

The air of depression and anxiety in the winter garden heightened as Hitler composed an answer to the British, and this turned to alarm when the noon papers reported in glaring headlines that at least six German nationals had been murdered in Poland. Whether this report was true or not, Hitler himself believed it and was incensed. And so by the time Henderson reappeared early that evening there was a feeling in the waiting rooms and corridors of the chancellery that little less than a miracle could prevent war. Once Henderson entered Hitler's study and was handed a copy of the German reply, however, he sensed an attitude more uncompromising than last night. With the Führer and Ribbentrop eying him closely, he began reading the German note. It started reasonably. Germany readily consented to the proposed mediation by the British; Hitler was pleased to receive a Polish emissary in Berlin with full powers to negotiate. But the next words were completely unacceptable: the German government calculated that "this delegate will arrive on Wednesday, 30 August, 1939."

"It sounds like an ultimatum," protested Henderson. "The Poles are given barely twenty-four hours to make their plans." Supported by Ribbentrop, the Führer heatedly denied the charge. "The time is short," he explained, "because there is the danger that fresh provocation may result in the outbreak of fighting."

Henderson was not impressed. He still could not accept such a time limit. Hitler at last lost his temper. He angrily made a countercharge: neither Henderson nor his government cared a row of pins how many Germans were being slaughtered in Poland. Henderson shouted back that he would not listen to such language from Hitler or anybody else. It seemed the ambassador had also lost his temper, but he explained in his report that this was a trick; the time had come to play Herr Hitler at his own game. Glaring into his opponent's eyes, at the top of his voice he bellowed that if Hitler wanted war he could have it! England was every bit as resolute as Germany and would in fact "hold out a little bit longer than Germany could!"

Later that evening Göring summoned Dahlerus to his residence and revealed a secret: Hitler was working on a *grosszügiges Angebot* (magnanimous offer) to Poland. It was going to be presented the next morning and would include a lasting and just solution of the Corridor by a plebiscite. Once more Göring tore a page out of an atlas and hastily sketched with a green pencil the territory that would be settled by plebiscite; then he outlined in red the area Hitler regarded as pure Polish.

Göring urged Dahlerus to fly immediately to London so he could once more stress Germany's determination to negotiate and "hint confidentially" that Hitler was going to present the Poles with an offer so generous they would be bound to accept.

Chamberlain himself was now so determined to resist Hitler that he never even asked the Poles if they would submit to the time limit and by the time Dahlerus was back at 10 Downing Street negotiation seemed impossible. Chamberlain, Wilson and Cadogan listened to the Swede, but their reaction to Hitler's "magnanimous offer" was that it was all talk and only a trick to gain time. Why not phone Göring and find out if the offer had actually been typed up? suggested Dahlerus. In a few minutes he was talking to the Reichsmarschall, who assured him that the note to Poland was not only finished but its terms were more generous than he had predicted.

Encouraged, Dahlerus did his utmost to allay British distrust, going over the terms of the offer with the help of the map Göring had marked up. While the terms seemed reasonable, the British were still disturbed by Hitler's insistence that a Polish delegate present himself in Berlin on the thirtieth, that very day. Beyond the time limit, Chamberlain and his colleagues opposed the place, Berlin. Look what had happened to Tiso and Hacha!

Dahlerus phoned Göring again, this time with the suggestion that the negotiations with Poland take place out of Berlin, preferably in a neutral territory. "Nonsense," was the annoyed reply, "the negotiations must take place in Berlin where Hitler had his headquarters, and anyhow I can see no reason why the Poles should find it difficult to send emissaries to Berlin." Despite the rebuff, as well as their own continuing distrust, the British decided to at least keep the door to peace open. Dahlerus was urged to fly back to Berlin and reassure Hitler that England remained willing to negotiate. Further, as evidence of good faith, Halifax telegraphed Warsaw cautioning the Poles not to fire on troublemakers from their German minority and to stop inflammatory radio propaganda.

The Polish response was to order a general mobilization. Hitler was indignant, for his Foreign Office had spent the day drafting an offer to Poland so generous that his objective interpreter, Schmidt, could scarcely believe his eyes. Besides suggesting a plebiscite in the Corridor under an international commission, it gave the Poles an international road and railway through territory which would become German. "It was a real League of Nations proposal," recalled Schmidt. "I felt I was back in Geneva." Despite his wrath at the Polish mobilization, Hitler instructed Brauchitsch and Keitel to postpone the invasion of Poland another twenty-four hours. This, he said, was the final postponement. Unless his demands were accepted by Warsaw the attack was to begin at 4:30 A.M. September 1.

It was 10 P.M. Berlin time before Henderson phoned Ribbentrop proposing they meet at midnight. This happened to be the deadline for the Polish representative to arrive in Berlin and Ribbentrop thought it was deliberate. It was done in all innocence—more time was needed to decipher the London message—but it set an unwholesome atmosphere of suspicion for the interview. After Henderson suggested the Germans follow normal procedure by transmitting their proposals through the Polish Embassy in Berlin, Ribbentrop leaped to his feet. "That's out of the question after what has happened!" he shouted, the last vestige of self-control gone. "We demand that a negotiator empowered by his government with full authority should come here to Berlin."

Henderson's face grew red. London had warned him to keep calm this time and his hands trembled as he read the official answer to Hitler's last memorandum. Ribbentrop fumed as if listening under duress. Undoubtedly he knew its contents since most telephone calls at the British Embassy, particularly the overseas line to London, were being monitored by a German intelligence agency known as the Research Office. The note itself, while conciliatory in tone, offered little more than the previous phone messages of the day.

"That's an unheard-of suggestion!" Ribbentrop angrily interrupted at the suggestion that no aggressive military action take place during the negotiations. Crossing his arms belligerently, he glared at Henderson. "Have you anything more to say?" Perhaps he was paying the ambassador back for yesterday's shouting match with the Führer. The Englishman responded to this rudeness by remarking that His Majesty's Government had information the Germans were committing acts of sabotage in Poland.

This time Ribbentrop was truly enraged. "That's a damned lie of the Polish government!" he shouted. "I can only tell you, Herr Henderson, that the position is damned serious."

Henderson half rose in his seat and shouted in return, "You have just said 'damned!'" He wagged an admonitory finger like an outraged schoolmaster. "That's no word for a statesman to use in so grave a situation."

Then Ribbentrop took a paper out of his pocket. It was Hitler's offer to Poland which had so surprised Schmidt. Ribbentrop began reading the sixteen points in German. Henderson had difficulty in understanding them, he later complained, because Ribbentrop "garbled through" the document at top speed and he asked for the text so he could transmit it to his government. It was such normal diplomatic procedure that Schmidt wondered why the ambassador bothered asking at all and he could scarcely believe what he heard next. "No," said Ribbentrop quietly, with an uneasy smile, "I cannot hand you those proposals." He couldn't explain that the Führer had expressly forbidden him to let the document out of his hand.

Henderson, also unable to believe his ears, repeated his request. Once more Ribbentrop refused, this time emotionally slapping the document on the table. "It is out of date, anyhow," he said, "as the Polish envoy has not appeared."

Watching in agitation, Schmidt suddenly realized that Hitler was playing a game: he feared that if the British passed on the proposals to the Poles they might accept them. It was a mortal sin for an interpreter to make a comment but he did stare fixedly and "invitingly" at Henderson, silently willing him to ask for an English translation. Ribbentrop could hardly refuse such a request and Schmidt was determined to translate with such deliberation that the ambassador could copy every word in longhand. But Henderson did not understand the signal and all the interpreter could do was make a thick red mark in his notebook, a personal notation meaning that the die was cast for war.

3

At four forty-five Friday morning, September 1, the German cruiser *Schleswig-Holstein*, in Danzig harbor on a courtesy visit, began shelling the little peninsula where Poland maintained a military depot and eighty-eight soldiers. Simultaneously artillery fire crashed along the Polish-German border, followed by a massive surge eastward of German infantry and tanks. There was no formal declaration of war but within the hour Hitler broadcast a proclamation to his troops. He had no other choice, he said, "than to meet force with force."

In Rome Il Duce was outwardly calm. A few hours earlier, spurred by his own fear and a deluge of cautionary advice, he had come to a wise but embarrassing decision: Italy would remain neutral. He personally telephoned Attolico and urged him to beg the Führer to send him a telegram releasing him from the obligation of their alliance. Hitler quickly composed an answer that hid his anger. "I am convinced that we can carry out the task imposed upon us with the military forces of Germany," he said and thanked Mussolini for everything he could do in the future "for the common cause of Fascism and National Socialism."

The world was shocked by the sudden attack even though it was expected. There was no condemnation from the Vatican, which had been secretly exerting pressure on the Polish government, through Cardinal Hlond, to negotiate with Hitler. President Roosevelt's first action was a plea that both belligerents promise not to bomb civilians or "unfortified cities." It was a vow that Hitler had already publicly made and Roosevelt's statement only annoyed him. His irritation escalated to indignation when his chargé in Washington reported that the deputy of the press chief in the U. S. State Department had told the DNB representative: "We only pity you people, your government already stands convicted; they are condemned from one end of the earth to the other; for this bloodbath, if it now comes to war between Britain, France and Germany, will have been absolutely unnecessary. The whole manner of conducting negotiations was as stupid as it could possibly be." Hitler blamed American hostility on the Jewish-controlled press and the Jews around President "Rosenfeld." He retaliated by prohibiting all German Jews, as enemies of the state, from henceforth going outdoors after 8 P.M. in the winter and 9 P.M. in the summer. Before long all Jewish radios would be confiscated.

Henderson and Coulondre arrived at the Wilhelmstrasse just before 9:30 P.M. to deliver a final warning: unless hostilities ceased, England and France would fulfill their obligations to Poland. But Ribbentrop refused to meet them together. First he saw the British ambassador, receiving him with pointed courtesy. Ribbentrop remarked that it was Poland which had provoked Germany and began arguing, though not raucously. This time they did not stand nose to nose but conducted themselves correctly. No sooner had Henderson left than Coulondre entered with an almost identical note from France. Ribbentrop repeated that it was Poland's fault, not Germany's, but promised to pass on the message to Hitler.

In London Chamberlain was telling the Commons about the note sent to Hitler. England's only quarrel with the German people, he said, was that they allowed themselves to be governed by a Nazi government. "As long as that government exists and pursues the methods it has so persistently followed during the last two years, there will be no peace in Europe. We shall merely pass from one crisis to another, and see one country after another attacked by methods which have now become familiar to us in their sickening technique. We are resolved that these methods must come to an end." There were cheers from all benches.

4

Sunday, September 3, dawned clear and balmy. It was a lovely day and ordinarily Berliners would be streaming out to the nearby woods and lakes to enjoy the holiday. Today they were depressed and confused to find themselves at the threshold of a major war.

Of all mornings, this was the one that Schmidt, in bed only a few hours, overslept. Rushing by taxi to the Foreign Office, he saw Henderson enter the building and himself raced into a side entrance. He was standing, somewhat breathless, in Ribbentrop's office as the hour of nine struck and Henderson was announced. The ambassador shook hands but declined Schmidt's invitation to sit down. "I regret that on the instructions of my government," he said with deep emotion, "I have to hand you an ultimatum for the German government." He read out the statement, which called for war unless Germany gave assurances that all troops would be withdrawn from Poland by eleven o'clock, British Summer Time.

Henderson extended the document. "I am sincerely sorry," he said, "that I must hand such a document to you in particular as you have always been most anxious to help." While Henderson would not be remembered for astuteness, retaining as he did a naïve conception of the Führer to the end, he had succeeded in outshouting him and staring down Ribbentrop on successive evenings, feats worthy of some applause.

In a few minutes Schmidt was at the chancellery. He made his way with some difficulty through the crowd gathered outside of the Führer's office. Hitler was at his desk; Ribbentrop stood by the window. Both turned expectantly as Schmidt entered. He slowly translated the British ultimatum. At last Hitler turned to Ribbentrop and abruptly said, "What now?"

"I assume," said Ribbentrop quietly, "that the French will hand in a similar ultimatum within the hour."

Schmidt was engulfed in the anteroom by eager questions but once he revealed that England was declaring war in two hours there was complete silence. Finally Göring said, "If we lose this war, then God have mercy on us!" Everywhere Schmidt saw grave faces. Even the usually ebullient Goebbels stood in a corner, downcast and self-absorbed.

One man refused to give up hope. Dahlerus located Göring at his private train. Why didn't the Reichsmarschall fly to London and negotiate with the British? Göring was persuaded to telephone Hitler. Surprisingly, he reported, the Führer liked the idea, but first wanted British concurrence. Dahlerus telephoned the counselor at the British Embassy, who replied that the Germans must first answer the ultimatum. Undeterred, Dahlerus phoned the Foreign Office in London. He got the same answer. Still he persisted. He somehow persuaded Göring to ring up Hitler again and suggest sending a conciliatory official reply to the British. Dahlerus waited outside the train, nervously pacing up and down, while Göring talked with the Führer. Finally Göring stepped out of the train, seating himself at a large collapsible table in a stand of beech trees. He muttered that a plane was standing by to take him to England. But Dahlerus concluded from the "disappointed" look on his face that he had been refused by the Führer; but the Swede was not perspicacious and could have been taken in by Göring's play-acting. The extent of Dahlerus' naïveté was revealed in his own recorded reaction to the moment: "My blood boiled as I saw the hopelessness of this powerful man. And I could not understand why, knowing what he did, he did not jump into his car, drive to the chancellery and tell them what he really thought—always supposing he really meant all the things he had been telling me for the past two months." So ended the stout, if amateurish, efforts of Dahlerus to prevent war.

At 11:15 A.M. Ambassador Henderson received a message to call upon Ribbentrop. Within fifteen minutes he was handed Germany's reply to the ultimatum—a flat refusal. Henderson looked up from the statement and remarked that it "would be left to history to judge where the blame really lay." Ribbentrop replied that "nobody had striven harder for peace and good relations with England than Herr Hitler had done," and wished Henderson well personally.

At noon loudspeakers in the streets of Berlin blared out the news of war with England to shocked listeners.

London, where it was 11 A.M., was hot and summery and Chamberlain was steeling himself for his broadcast to the people. Fifteen minutes later he announced that England was at war. The British government, he said, had done everything possible to establish peace and had a clear conscience. "Now may God bless you all and may He defend the right."

Even as he was speaking, Coulondre handed over to Ribbentrop France's ultimatum—and was told that France would therefore be the aggressor. But it was England that bore the brunt of Hitler's resentment. He who so readily perceived British weakness had completely failed to judge British strength. His localized war was turning into a general conflagration because of this miscalculation. It was an impasse born of his first crucial mistake: the decision to seize all of Czechoslovakia. If he had not done so and had waited for that country to fall in his lap, it is doubtful that the English would have reacted so positively to his demands on Poland. What Hitler had refused to accept—even though he may have guessed as much—was that an Englishman will go so far but not one inch farther. Despite information to the contrary by Hesse and intelligence reports, Hitler had been misled by his own distorted picture of British character. It was with unprecedented embarrassment, therefore, that he informed Admiral Raeder of the Western ultimatum.

There was little doubt that the occupants of the Kremlin were surprised by the British declaration. "The news of war," reported the Moscow correspondent of the London *Daily Telegraph*, "astonished the Russians. They expected a compromise." Curiously the Soviets showed so little inclination to join the attack on Poland that Ribbentrop invited them to do so in a telegram dispatched early that evening to Ambassador von der Schulenburg. "In our estimation," explained Ribbentrop, "this would be not only a relief for us, but also be in the sense of the Moscow agreements, and in the Soviet interest as well."

Hitler was already preparing to leave the chancellery with his entourage to board a special train bound for the fighting front. Nine minutes before it left Berlin, the Führer sent off a message to the ally who had failed to support him in his greatest crisis. Unlike the telegram to Moscow, this one to Mussolini was sent in the clear and was replete with dramatic phrases. He was aware, said Hitler, that this was "a struggle of life and death" but he had chosen to wage war with "deliberation," and his faith remained as "firm as a rock." As the Führer's train pulled out of the station at exactly 9 P.M. he did not show the confidence of this letter. One secretary, Gerda Daranowsky, noticed he was very quiet, pale and thoughtful; never before had she seen him like that. And another, Christa Schröder, overheard him say to Hess: "Now, all my work crumbles. I wrote my book for nothing."

But to his valet he seemed the epitome of assurance; there was, he said, nothing to worry about in the West; Britain and France would "break their teeth" on the Westwall. As the train headed east Hitler called Linge to the dining salon and ordered an even more spartan diet from that day on. "You will see to it," he said, "that I have only what the ordinary people of Germany can have. It is my duty to set an example."

PART 7

BY FORCE OF ARMS

Chapter Twenty

VICTORY IN THE WEST

SEPTEMBER 3, 1939–JUNE 25, 1940

1

The invasion of Poland proceeded rapidly. Polish cavalrymen, carrying long lances, were no match for German tanks. In a concentrated land and air attack, the defenders were overwhelmed. Harried from the air by fighter planes, bombers and screeching Stukas, the Polish ground forces were quickly dispersed by a million and a half men supported by heavy self-propelled guns and tanks. It was this incredible mass of Panzers in particular which wreaked havoc. They burst through defenses and ravaged the rear. The Blitzkrieg was almost as terrifying to foreign observers as the victims, for it presaged a frightening turning point in the art of warfare. By morning of September 5 the Polish air force was destroyed, the battle for the Corridor ended. Two days later most of Poland's thirty-five divisions were either routed or surrounded.

Hitler closely followed the action in his special train, designating it as Führer Headquarters even though Jodl's operations staff remained in Berlin. Once he had donned a uniform his way of life changed drastically. Assuming the old role of front-line soldier, he imposed on Führer Headquarters an austere simplicity. His new motto was: "Front-line troops must be assured that their leader shares their privations." Every morning, after dictating orders of the day to Fräulein Schröder, he set out for the battlefield with pistol and oxhide whip. He rode in an open vehicle, weather permitting, so the troops would recognize him while his valet and adjutant tossed out packs of cigarettes. To the wonder of his entourage, he began devoting himself tirelessly to the most minute details of operations. He spent hours, for example, personally inspecting kitchens and mess halls, tyrannically imposing the enlisted man's diet on officers. This aspect of the new regimen soon ended but in all matters of the battlefield he continued to have unflagging interest—that is, with one significant exception. When Schmundt asked him to speak to the first trainload of wounded he could not do so. The sight of their suffering, he confessed, would be intolerable.

As the one-sided campaign drew to a close an unexpected visitor appeared at Führer Headquarters. Fritz Hesse had come to report that the German official delegation in London had been given a friendly farewell not only by their high-ranking British friends but by the population. A crowd outside the embassy had shouted, "See you at Christmas!" Hesse had also come to Poland out of personal concern; he understood he was in disfavor because of his persistence in seeking peace. But Walther Hewel, Ribbentrop's liaison man at the chancellery, who presently enjoyed Hitler's complete confidence, assured him that the Führer had sincerely sought negotiations with the British. What provoked him into invading Poland were the reports of atrocities inflicted on German nationals. Hesse could not believe that the order to invade had come in a moment of rage. "Yes, this was without a doubt the cause," insisted Hewel. "And he soon regretted that he had given way to his temper." That was why he had permitted Hesse to negotiate with Sir Horace Wilson after the invasion. "Yes, Hitler would have just liked to say, 'Everybody about face, march, march!'"

"My God," exclaimed Hesse bitterly, "couldn't anyone make it clear to him that although a dictator can order, 'About face, march, march!' it is impossible in a parliamentary nation to cancel a decison for war made after long and thoughtful preparation? How can he imagine such a thing? I always warned that there was a war party in England and that the collapse of Chamberlain's foreign policy would certainly bring victory to this war party. Didn't anyone read this report?"

After a silence the disconcerted Hewel admitted that the Führer had a rather strange concept of the workings of a democracy. "He snorted at me when I tried to explain to him your report on the statements Chamberlain made in the House of Commons. He simply did not want to believe it. Don't be afraid though. In the meantime he has realized your report was correct. But for heaven's sake don't make use of this. Nothing irritates the Führer more than people who were right when he was wrong."

What concerned Hitler more than England—for there was no action at all on the western front—was the reluctance of the Soviet Union to join in the attack on Poland. Apparently Stalin wanted to wait until the last possible moment so as to minimize Red Army losses. It was not until 2 A.M., September 17, that the German ambassador in Moscow was personally informed by Stalin that the Red Army would cross the Polish frontier in several hours. At 4 A.M. local time the Red Army crossed the long eastern frontier of Poland. At one point men of the Polish Frontier Corps saw a horde of horse-drawn carts filled with soldiers coming through the morning mist. "Don't shoot," shouted the Red Army men, "we've come to help you against the Germans." The defenders were so confused—white flags were attached to the leading Russian vehicles—that the Soviets passed through in many places without receiving a shot. It was the end of eastern Poland.

Ribbentrop was not awakened until 8 A.M. and when he learned that Schmidt had let him sleep three hours he shouted angrily, "The German and Russian armies are rushing toward each other—there may be clashes—and all because you were too slack to waken me!" The interpreter tried to calm him by reminding him that a demarcation line had been set up. But the Foreign Minister, his face lathered, continued to rage as he brandished a razor: "You have meddled with the course of world history! You have not enough experience for that!" What really infuriated Ribbentrop, who was up front with a skeleton staff, was that the delay allowed Goebbels and not his own office to issue the news to foreign journalists in Berlin.

The only contest now was between the victors. Before the first day of Russian participation ended the two allies were wrangling over the text of the joint communiqué which would attempt to justify the conquest of Poland. Stalin objected to the German draft ("It presented the facts all too frankly"), then wrote out in his own hand a new version. No sooner had Hitler bowed to this revision than Stalin presented another far more important one: an out-and-out partition of the spoils which would deprive the Poles of even the semblance of independence. On the face of it the Russian proposal was advantageous to Germany but Hitler's suspicion was such that it was four days before Ribbentrop was empowered to endorse it. Stalin formally offered all Polish territory east of the Vistula, which included most of Poland's populated areas. In return, all he wanted was the third Baltic state, Lithuania.

Shrewd Stalin knew his Hitler. Beyond a need for continuing good relations with the Soviets, the Führer could not resist the opportunity of controlling this breeding ground of Jews. He authorized Ribbentrop to sign the treaty and presented Stalin with the last of the Baltic States. It was a heavy price to pay for keeping his rear in the East free while he dealt with the West.

While Stalin was digesting the three Baltic States and eastern Poland, Hitler was transforming the rest of that nation into a massive killing ground. He had already ordered Jews from the Reich massed in specific Polish cities having good rail connections. Object: "final solution, which will take some time," as Heydrich explained to SS commanders on September 21. He was talking of the extermination of the Jews, already an open secret among many high-ranking party officials.

These grisly preparations were augmented by a "house cleaning " of Polish intelligentsia, clergy and nobility by five murder squads known as *Einsatzgruppen* (Special Action Groups). Hitler's hatred of Poles was of relatively recent origin. He was convinced that during the past few years numerous atrocities had been inflicted on the German minority in Poland. By mid-autumn 3500 intelligentsia (whom Hitler considered "carriers of Polish nationalism") were liquidated. "It is only in this manner," he explained, "that we can acquire the vital territory which we need. After all, who today remembers the extermination of the Armenians!" This terror was accompanied by the ruthless expulsion of 1,200,000 ordinary Poles from their ancestral homes so that Germans from the Baltic and outlying portions of Poland could be properly housed. In the ensuing bitter months more Poles lost their lives in the resettlement than those on the execution list.

2

Even as the SS carried out Hitler's radical program in the East, he turned his attention to the West. With the better part of Poland his, he sought to end the war with France and England, one way or the other. First he launched a peace offensive in press and radio. "Hitler will again reach an understanding with the English," Hewel assured Fritz Hesse, "and wants to make it as easy as possible for them."

Almost certainly Hitler had no intention of accepting a permanent peace with two great powers capable of threatening the Reich's security. A temporary one, however, might enable him to divide France from England and so vanquish them separately. Throughout Germany there was a feeling of widespread relief over the Führer's plea for peace and even premature celebrations of joy, only slightly dampened by Daladier's quick answer that France would never lay down arms until assured of a "real peace and general security." The Führer, however, was preparing for the worst. On October 9 he issued Directive No. 6 for the Conduct of War, which outlined an invasion through Luxembourg, Belgium and Holland.

The next morning at eleven, seven of his military commanders reported to the chancellery. Before presenting the new directive Hitler read out a memorandum of his own composition which indicated that he was a student of military and political history. Germany and the West, he said, had been enemies since the dissolution of the First German Reich in 1648 and this struggle "would have to be fought out one way or the other." But he had no objection "to ending the war immediately," so long as the gains in Poland were accepted. His listeners were not asked for comment nor did they volunteer any. They were called upon only to endorse the German war aim: "the destruction of the power and ability of the Western powers ever again to be able to oppose the state consolidation and further development of the German people in Europe."

He acknowledged the objections to haste in launching the attack. But time was on the enemy's side. Because of the Russian treaty and the great victory in Poland, Germany was at last in position—for the first time in many years—to make war on a single front. With the East secured, the Wehrmacht could throw all its forces against England and France. It was a situation that could terminate abruptly. "By no treaty or pact can a lasting neutrality of Soviet Russia be insured with certainty." The greatest safeguard against any Soviet attack lay "in a prompt demonstration of German strength."

Furthermore, hope of Italian support depended primarily on how long Mussolini remained alive. The situation in Rome could change in a flash. So could the neutrality of Belgium, Holland and the United States. Time was working against Germany in many ways. At present she enjoyed military superiority but England and France were closing the gap since their war industries could call upon the resources of most of the world. A long war presented great dangers. The Reich had limited supplies of food and raw materials, and the fount of war production, the Ruhr, was dangerously vulnerable to air attack and long-range artillery.

He proceeded to purely military matters. They must avoid the trench warfare of 1914–18. The attack, he said, would depend on the new tank and air tactics developed in Poland. Panzers would lead the breakthrough. He urged his commanders to improvise, improvise; and illustrated how they could "prevent fronts from becoming stable by massed drives through identified weakly held positions."

It was a brilliant display but almost every one of his commanders remained convinced that the Wehrmacht was not yet prepared or suitably supplied for war with the West. Yet there was not a single objection, not even after the Führer's announcement that the start of the attack could not begin "too early. It is to take place in all circumstances (if at all possible) this autumn."

After a week's delay, Chamberlain finally answered Hitler. He announced in Commons that the German proposals were hereby rejected as "vague and uncertain." If Hitler wanted peace, "acts, not words alone must be forthcoming"; he must supply "convincing proof" that he truly sought peace. Applause from the House was moderate.

In Berlin a circular from the Press Department of the Foreign Ministry was immediately telegraphed, in the clear, to all foreign stations. It denounced the Prime Minister's reply as an outrageous affront. To Hitler the rejection was disappointing but not unexpected. He summoned Göring and the two men responsible for Luftwaffe production—Field Marshal Erhard Milch and Colonel General Ernst Udet. "My attempts to make peace with the West have failed," he said. "The war continues. Now we can and must manufacture the bombs."

3

As word spread of Hitler's decision to attack the West, various resistance groups inside Germany concocted plans for coups d'état and assassinations. Some wanted to execute the Führer;

others simply to kidnap him and set up either a military junta or a democratic regime. Lists of ministers were drawn up; peace feelers were extended to the United States and other neutrals. The most serious group of conspirators came from the OKW itself and its leading spirit was an impetuous cavalry officer, Colonel Hans Oster. As chief assistant to Admiral Canaris in the *Abwehr*, the Intelligence Service, this impatient, often imprudent man could not have been in a more strategic position. Moreover, he had connections with every faction in the Wehrmacht, private individuals like Schacht, the Foreign Ministry, and even the SS.

Oster found a valuable recruit in a Munich lawyer, Josef Müller, who had detested Hitler for years. Müller—a devout Catholic—made a clandestine trip to Rome early that October with the connivance of Oster, his object to discover if the British were prepared to make peace with an anti-Nazi regime. He met Pius XII and found him willing to act as intermediary. The Pope's secretary sounded out the British minister and was informed that Great Britain was not averse to making a "soft peace" with an anti-Hitler Germany.

Müller was empowered to take this information orally back to Germany but begged for something in writing that would prove to the Abwehr and military commanders that this peace proposal was authorized by the Holy Father himself. Surprisingly, the Vatican agreed and a letter was written by the Pope's private secretary outlining the main bases for peace with England.

The Oster group was cheered. Of all their attempts to make contact with the West, this was the most promising. Perhaps the Pope's promise of participation would at last induce Brauchitsch to take an active part in the conspiracy. But the army commander-in-chief was not impressed. He was convinced that the German people were "all for Hitler." General Halder proved to be almost as timid, but under pressure from Oster and others he finally agreed to help carry out a Putsch. All at once it appeared as if the leading officers were willing to take action. The conspirators were even assured that Brauchitsch himself was prepared to join them if Hitler refused to call off the invasion.

A showdown between army chief and Führer was set for Sunday, November 5—the day the troops were scheduled to move to attack positions on the western front. Brauchitsch appeared as scheduled at the chancellery. After presenting a memorandum, he elaborated on the main arguments against the invasion. It would be impossible, he said, to mount such a massive offensive in the autumn or spring rains. "It rains on the enemy too," replied Hitler curtly. In desperation, Brauchitsch argued that the Polish campaign indicated that the fighting spirit of the German infantryman was far below that of the World War. There were even signs of insubordination similar to those in 1918.

Hitler had been listening politely, if coolly. This remark enraged him. "In what units have there been any cases of lack of discipline?" he demanded. "What happened? Where?" Brauchitsch had deliberately exaggerated "to deter Hitler" and he shrank before such fury.

Brauchitsch was still in a state of shock when he staggered into army headquarters at Zossen, eighteen miles away, and stammered out an incoherent account of what had taken place. Almost simultaneously a telephone call from the chancellery reaffirmed November 12 as the date for invasion. An exact hour was set—7:15 A.M. General Franz Halder, the army chief of staff, requested written confirmation and got it immediately by messenger.

The army conspirators now had the necessary documentary evidence to overthrow Hitler. But there was no call for revolt, no signal for assassination. Instead they furtively burned all incriminating papers. Colonel Oster alone did not panic; through Count Albrecht von Bernstorff, whose father had been ambassador to Washington during the Great War, he warned the Belgian and Netherlands legations to expect an attack at dawn on November 12.

Sunday's storm in the chancellery was followed by anticlimax. The Luftwaffe needed five consecutive days of good weather to destroy the French air force and the meteorological report on Tuesday the seventh was so unpromising that Hitler postponed A-Day.

Although Hitler knew nothing of the military plot, Göring had warned him against Brauchitsch and Halder: "My Führer, get rid of these birds of ill omen." A more definite admonition came from the Swiss astrologer, Karl Ernst Krafft, hired by Himmler's secret intelligence service as an astral adviser. He had recently submitted a paper indicating that Hitler would be in danger of assassination between November 7 and 10; but the document was hastily filed since astrological speculation concerning the Führer was *verboten.*

Hitler went to Munich on the morning of November 8 to attend the annual reunion of the Old Fighters. He spent much of the afternoon on a speech he had just decided to make that evening at the Bürgerbräukeller. It would be another attack on England, designed primarily for German ears. The main room of the vast beer hall was already gaily decorated with banners and flags and by late afternoon the microphones were in place and tested. At dusk a small, pale man with a high forehead and clear bright eyes entered carrying a box. He was a skilled artisan named Georg Elser and he had recently been discharged from Dachau concentration camp where he had been held as a Communist sympathizer. His goal was peace and he had come here to kill Hitler. In the box was a timing device connected to sticks of dynamite. As waiters and party officials made the final preparations for the meeting Elser inconspicuously walked up to the gallery and hid behind the pillar rising from the back of the festooned speakers' platform. Several days earlier he had cut the wooden paneling of the pillar with a special saw—he was a cabinetmaker as well as a mechanic—fixed several hinges and replaced the piece of wood as a little door.

At last the lights of the hall were extinguished, the doors closed. Elser waited another half hour, then placed the bomb in the pillar and set it to detonate at about 11:20 P.M. The Führer would start speaking at 10 P.M. and the explosion would come midway in the speech.

At his apartment on the Prinzregentenplatz, Hitler summoned his young ordnance officer, Max Wünsche. Would it be possible, he asked, to leave Munich earlier than planned? Wünsche assured him it would be no problem; there were always two trains at the Führer's disposal as a security precaution. The young man immediately made arrangements to use the early one.

The Führer was greeted at the Bürgerbräukeller with such wild acclaim that he did not begin speaking until ten minutes past ten. His audience reveled in the insults and jibes he heaped upon the English. It took little, in fact, to draw applause and there were so many interruptions that Wünsche, seated in the front row, feared the Führer would miss the early train.

At 11:07 P.M. Hitler unexpectedly brought his tirade to a hurried conclusion. A few yards away, inside the pillar, Elser's clock was ticking. In thirteen minutes the bomb was supposed to explode. Ordinarily Hitler spent considerable time after a speech chatting with the comrades of the Putsch but tonight, without shaking hands, he rushed out of the building accompanied by Hess and several adjutants and into the car waiting outside. Kempka headed directly for the railroad station. Before they arrived—exactly eight minutes after Hitler left the Bürgerbräukeller—Wünsche heard a distant explosion. He wondered what it was. If Hitler heard the noise he did not think it worth mentioning.

In the hubbub that followed the explosion—the shrieking of sirens from police cars and ambulances—a rumor started that the war was over. It might have been if Hitler had been standing on the platform. He surely would have died. The bomb killed seven and wounded sixty-three, including Eva Braun's father, who had gained admission thanks to a special low-numbered membership card, though he was actually party member No. 5,021,670. His daughter, accompanied by her best friend, Herta Schneider, arrived at the station just as the Führer's train was leaving. Aboard they found an air of carefree gaiety. No one knew of the explosion and almost everyone was drinking. The lone teetotaler, Hitler, was animated but it was Goebbels who enlivened the conversation with his caustic wit.

At Nuremberg the propaganda chief left the train to send several messages and gather the latest news. When he returned to the Führer's compartment he told of the bomb in a trembling voice. Hitler thought it was a joke until he noticed Goebbels' pale face. His own became a grim mask. Finally in a voice hoarse with emotion he exclaimed, "Now I am completely content! The fact that I left the Bürgerbräukeller earlier than usual is a corroboration of Providence's intention to let me reach my goal."

Elser was arrested at the Swiss border and returned to Munich. Under glaring arc lights in an interrogation room at Gestapo headquarters Elser admitted he had planted the bomb. No, he had no accomplices. He had done it to end the war. He described in detail how he had cut the panel and come back to set the clock.

Upon reading the Gestapo report Hitler angrily scrawled on it: "What idiot conducted this interrogation?" It was ridiculous, he thought, to imagine that Elser was a lone wolf. Wasn't it obvious that this was a wide conspiracy involving his worst enemies: the English, the Jews, the Freemasons and Otto Strasser?

The official version of the plot was bizarre: Elser was a

Communist "deviationist" who had been persuaded by the National Socialist "deviationist," Otto Strasser, to become the tool of the British Secret Service. To this main plot propagandists added subplots. One pamphlet claimed that the English agents not only set off the bomb in Munich but were responsible for the political murders and mysterious deaths of such notable figures as Lord Kitchener, Archduke Franz Ferdinand and King Alexander of Yugoslavia.

Besides inciting hatred for England, the attempted assassination was exploited to bolster the Führer's popularity. Messages of congratulation on his narrow escape arrived from Germans on every level of society. The Catholic press throughout the Reich piously declared that it was the miraculous working of Providence which had protected the Führer.

4

On November 30 Stalin invaded Finland, which had repelled a Communist rebellion in 1918 with the help of German troops. It was an embarrassment for Hitler, not only because of the extremely friendly relations between Germans and Finns but also because it weakened the already tenuous bonds with Mussolini. The Italians, from the first opponents of the Russo-German pact, were as indignant over the unprovoked Soviet invasion of Finland as the West. The official organ of the papacy, *Osservatore Romano*, which had followed the Pope's lead in failing to condemn Fascist or Nazi incursions, now joined him in excoriating the Soviet attack as a calculated act of aggression. So much pressure was exerted on Mussolini from church and civilian sources that, "for the first time," wrote Ciano, "he desired German defeat." In fact, on December 26 he authorized his son-in-law to inform the representatives of Belgium and Holland that they were about to be invaded by Hitler.

Neither Hitler nor Mussolini knew that the British were seriously considering declaring war on the U.S.S.R. over the Finnish invasion, thanks in large part to the pressure exerted by church groups and the Cliveden Set, which argued that the real enemy was Red Russia, not Germany. After all, Hitler's demands on Poland were reasonable and only his manner was obnoxious. In the meantime the shooting war against Hitler had diminished to one in name only. On a train trip skirting the French frontier, the crew told William Shirer that not a shot had been fired on this front since the war began.

Hitler's main offensive weapon in these unsettled days was Goebbels, brought back to full favor by the outbreak of war. The force of his propaganda campaign was directed against the French; his purpose was to divide them from the British. Goebbels visited the Westwall in the bitter rain and snow so he could determine first hand what the poilu a few hundred yards away in the Maginot Line was experiencing. He concluded that the average French soldier was so weary, miserable and bored that he would be a ready victim of his concerns and prejudices. The Propaganda Minister, therefore, instructed German soldiers to shout friendly greetings across no man's land and engage the French in brotherly conversation. Propaganda teams blasted information and news over loudspeakers, aimed at proving that France and Germany were really not enemies. The French civilians were approached differently. They were bombarded with broadcasts over secret transmitters illustrating the corruption of their government, the profiteering of Jews and the terrifying might of Hitler's army and air force.

At home Goebbels ordered Germans to harden themselves for the coming battle. Their very existence was at stake since the enemy was "determined to annihilate Germany for good." In mid-December he forbade newspapers to print a word about peace. "In line with this point of view any sentimental note in connection with Christmas must be avoided in the press and on the radio." Only one day would be celebrated, December 24. To unite front and homeland, the theme of 1939's radio Christmas program would be: "Soldiers' Christmas—People's Christmas."

The British soldiers in France were not at all concerned by Goebbels' propaganda. The war, in fact, had turned into a contest of lame jokes. British civilians were as bored as their troops and referred to it as the *Sitzkrieg* or Phony War. More and more members of Parliament dozed as Chamberlain read off his weekly reports.

Hitler was waiting for a stretch of five clear days to turn a joke into grim battle. His own air chief was in a quandary. Göring had to give the impression of being eager while privately praying for a continuation of the bad weather since he feared his Luftwaffe was not yet ready for combat. In desperation Göring hired a rainmaker, Herr Schwefler, for 100,000 marks.

It is not clear whether the field marshal ordered him to bring five clear days or to continue the bad weather but it would not have made any difference since Schwefler's only equipment turned out to be a defunct commercial radio set.

On January 10, 1940, the impatient Führer fixed another specific date for invasion: a week later at exactly fifteen minutes before sunrise. Fate intervened before the day was over. A light Luftwaffe plane strayed across the frontier, crash-landing in Belgium. Of all of the German planes in the sky that day, this was the most important. It carried an unauthorized passenger, Major Helmut Reinberger, who had a briefcase filled with the operation plans for the airborne attack on Belgium. While Reinberger was burning the papers he was seized by Belgian soldiers; but he reported optimistically to Luftwaffe headquarters through the German Embassy in Brussels that he had succeeded in burning the plans to "insignificant fragments, the size of the palm of his hand." Göring, in a state of consternation, experimented by burning a similar packet of papers. The results were so inconclusive that his wife suggested using clairvoyants, not unusual advice to a man who utilized a rainmaker. The team of clairvoyants unanimously agreed that not a scrap of the documents remained.

Their report may have relieved Göring but not Hitler. He canceled the invasion order on the assumption that the plans had been revealed to the enemy. He, not the clairvoyants, was correct. Enough fragments had remained for the Belgians to learn of the invasion. This information was passed on to London where it was received with considerable suspicion. Halifax, for instance, told the cabinet, "I doubt very much whether the documents are genuine." The General Staff agreed; obviously the papers had been planted. They were engrossed in their own offensive, the landing of an expeditionary force in Norway. The very concept of such a *coup de main* appealed to Churchill, the new First Lord of the Admiralty; and, despite his sad experience in a similar venture in the Great War, he pressed the issue until the cabinet was won over.

Hitler was also preparing to seize Norway. He had not even considered such action—after all, these were Nordic peoples who could be counted on to remain neutral as they had in 1914—until his ally, Stalin, upset calculations by invading Finland. This, Hitler feared, might give the Allies an excuse to move into Norway, thus outflanking Germany from the north. He authorized a study of a possible invasion but it was given low priority. Then, late in February, alarming reports of an imminent British landing in Scandinavia turned the Führer into an ardent advocate—out of concern that a British foothold in Norway would close off the Baltic and bottle up all his submarines. Equally foreboding was the economic threat. More than half of Germany's iron ore came from Norway and Sweden; an end to this supply would cripple her war production. On March 1, 1940, therefore, Hitler issued a directive for the simultaneous occupation of Denmark and Norway. It was to have "the character of a *peaceful* occupation, designed to protect by force of arms the neutrality of the northern countries," but resistance would be "broken by all means available."

Hitler became so concerned by the time element that within two days he decided to launch his attack—the "most daring and most important undertaking in the history of warfare"—before invading the West. It would begin on March 15.

In the meantime he had been attempting to shore up deteriorating relations with his two allies. Those with Russia, in particular, had entered a disturbing phase. Negotiations for a trade agreement had started soon after the conquest of Poland. A visit of a thirty-seven-man German economic delegation to Moscow was followed by an even larger Soviet mission to Berlin, which brought a list of industrial and military orders totaling more than one and a half billion Reichsmarks. The Germans were dismayed since most of the orders were for machinery and armaments essential to their own war production. The result was a bitter and lengthy wrangle finally brought to a head by Stalin himself. He querulously declared that if Germany did not give way "the treaty would not be concluded."

Hitler could not permit this, and early in February Ribbentrop was instructed to send a personal letter to Stalin urging him to re-examine the German position. Apparently Stalin, whose hardheaded negotiations had already wrung concessions from the Germans, realized he had pushed his ally to the limit. In one of his lightning changes, Stalin called for an end of bickering. He agreed to accept German deliveries over a period of twenty-seven months while promising delivery of raw materials over a period of eighteen months. With all difficulties removed, the trade pact was signed three days later.

Hitler was pleased as well as relieved. He had become even more fascinated by his counterpart in the Kremlin. Stalin was the only world leader he wanted to know intimately and he interrogated envoys from Russia at length for the most trivial details about his ally. Often, recalled Christa Schröder, he would interrupt to exclaim enthusiastically, "That Stalin is a brute, but really you must admit he's an extraordinary fellow." It was almost as if he were talking about himself.

The solution of this Russian problem was accompanied by the termination of another when the Finns were forced to accept harsh Soviet peace terms that March to end their brief, bloody war. Greatly relieved at being freed from the embarrassment of having to give moral support to such an unpopular cause, Hitler turned to more productive arenas. One of these was Italy.

On March 9, Foreign Minister von Ribbentrop left Berlin with a large retinue: advisers, secretaries, barbers, a doctor, a gymnastics teacher and a masseur. At their first meeting Il Duce gave a guarded answer to Ribbentrop's question: Would Italy participate in the war? He intended, he said, "to intervene in the conflict and to fight a war parallel to that of Germany." *But* he must be free to choose the date. Ribbentrop attempted in vain to tie Mussolini down more definitely but he would merely agree to see Hitler. The following Monday, March 18, the two dictators met at the Brenner Pass in a snowstorm. The session was cordial with Hitler dominating the conversation. But he spoke quietly and made few gestures. He had come, he said, "simply to explain the situation" so Il Duce could make his own decision.

To Schmidt's surprise, Mussolini used his few minutes of talk to reassert emphatically his intention of coming into the war. It was merely a matter of choosing the best moment, he said. The two men departed in an aura of eternal trust and friendship.

5

On Sunday morning, April 7, five German naval groups put to sea destined for six Norwegian cities. At three of these ports—Narvik, Trondheim and Stavanger—waited German merchant ships with combat troops hidden in their holds. British ships were laying mines in Norwegian waters below Narvik in preparation for their own invasion and HMS *Glowworm* sighted two German destroyers. It was assumed in London that these ships were part of a limited force intent on capturing Narvik.

Not until Monday morning did the cabinet learn that enemy warships were also approaching at least three other Norwegian ports. The ministers were aghast but it was too late to thwart Hitler.

Early Tuesday morning the Germans struck. By 8 A.M. Narvik was seized by two battalions of special mountain troops under the command of Brigadier General Eduard Dietl, an intimate of the Führer since the Beer Hall Putsch. Before noon four other important ports fell but the raiders were delayed long enough by defenders in the ancient fortress of Oskarberg to allow the royal family, the government and members of Parliament to escape from Oslo by special train while twenty-three trucks were carting off the gold of the Bank of Norway and the secret papers of the Foreign Office.

In Denmark the Germans met little resistance, their plan working as it had been laid out on paper. For some reason the Danish navy never opened fire and the land troops only managed to inflict twenty casualties on the invaders. It was all over by midmorning. The King capitulated, ordering all resistance to cease. He assured the chief of staff of the German task force that he would do everything possible to keep peace and order in the country. Then he turned complimentary. "You Germans," he said, "have done the incredible again! One must admit that it is magnificent work!"

By the end of the day it appeared as if Hitler had scored a complete triumph in Norway as well—until the British navy unexpectedly appeared. On Wednesday morning five destroyers broke into Narvik harbor to sink two destroyers and all but one cargo ship. Three days later the *Warspite* returned with a flotilla of destroyers and sank the rest of the German vessels.

This news so agitated Hitler that he told Brauchitsch it didn't look as though they could possibly hold Narvik. By April 17 his vexation was apparent. He railed at everyone in sight. While Brauchitsch, Keitel and Halder held their tongues, Chief of Operations Jodl brusquely announced that there was but one thing to do: "Concentrate, hold on and do not give up." To the consternation of the onlookers, he and Hitler began arguing as if they were equals. Finally, in a temper, the chief of operations stormed out of the room, slamming the door. Hitler said not a word. Tight-lipped, he left by another door but that night he signed an order to Dietl: "Hold on as long as possible." The nineteenth brought a new crisis. From his hide-out on the rugged northern coast of Norway, King Haakon VII, the sole monarch of the century elected to the throne by popular vote, steadfastly refused to name a government headed by Vidkun Quisling, the leader of a Norwegian Fascist party and a disciple of Rosenberg.

By this time the British had finally landed two brigades of 13,000 men near Narvik and Trondheim. As their attack gained momentum more British arrived, and by the end of the week the Germans were in desperate straits. But Milch came to the rescue by taking personal command of the Luftwaffe attack. He sent two huge seaplanes loaded with mountain troops to Narvik; then supervised dive-bombing strikes that weakened the British and Norwegian resistance in central Norway. By April 28 the British ordered evacuation of the bulk of their troops. The following day King Haakon and members of his government were transferred by British cruiser to Tromsö, a city far above the Arctic Circle, where a provisional capital was established.

Most of Norway was now under German control except for Narvik where Dietl's 6000 men still gallantly held off 20,000 Allied troops. On the last day of April Jodl informed Hitler that communications had finally been established overland between Oslo and Trondheim. At lunch Hitler, "beside himself with joy," admitted his error and thanked Jodl for his contributions to the victory. The Führer also showed his gratitude to Dietl and Milch with promotions.

With the northern flank secure, Hitler again devoted his energy to the invasion of the West. He had never liked the original plan of attack, an unimaginative version of that used in the World War: an attack through northern France and Belgium to the Channel ports. Its objective was not only to smash the French army but, by occupying the Channel coast, to cut the British off from their ally while establishing submarine and air bases for attacks on the British Isles.

Hitler envisioned a daring thrust farther south through the Ardennes with a sudden armored breakthrough at Sedan and a sweep to the Channel. The main force would then swing to the north, in a reversal of the Schlieffen plan, for a drive into the rear of the retreating Anglo-French army. Night after night his adjutants would see him poring over a specially constructed relief map to make sure that Sedan was, after all, the correct place to penetrate.

Independently, perhaps the most brilliant strategist of the Wehrmacht, Colonel General Fritz Erich von Manstein, had devised a similar offensive. He presented it to Brauchitsch, who rejected it on the grounds that it was too risky. But the Führer heard talk of Manstein's "risky" proposal and asked him for the details. To Manstein's surprise, Hitler was delighted with what he heard. It not only reinforced his own convictions but contained a number of improvements to his own plan. The supreme command liked Hitler's revised version no more than they had Manstein's. To a man they opposed it but the Führer overrode all objections, deriding opponents as "Schlieffen worshipers," embalmed in a "petrified" strategy.

He was determined to strike by Friday, May 10th, without waiting for the five-day favorable weather prerequisite which had already cost three months. He was gambling on the tool that had proved so valuable in the past—his "intuition," that is, a suspension of logic born of impatience. On Thursday morning a corps commander near Aachen reported heavy fog in his area. This was followed by a prediction that the fog would lift and the tenth would be a good day. Hitler ordered his special train prepared for departure from a small station outside of Berlin and went through elaborate measures to keep his own inner circle in the dark as to its destination and purpose. Outwardly calm during the tedious train trip, he was gnawed with worry that evening as the deadline for confirmation of the attack order approached. The train stopped near Hannover for a final weather report. This time Chief Meteorologist Diesing (who later got a gold watch as a reward) predicted good weather for the tenth. Hitler confirmed the order to attack at dawn, then retired earlier than usual. But he could not get to sleep. Despite the report he kept worrying about the weather.

A greater peril to success came from his own intelligence service. Of the few Hitler had entrusted with the final details of the invasion, one was Admiral Canaris and whatever he knew was passed on to his impetuous deputy, Colonel Oster. Earlier that evening Oster had reported to his old friend the Dutch military attaché, over the dinner table, that Hitler had issued the final attack order. After the meal Oster stopped off at OKW headquarters in the Bendlerstrasse and got information that there would be no last-minute postponement. "The swine has gone to the western front," he told the Dutch attaché, who first informed a Belgian colleague, then phoned The Hague in code: "Tomorrow, at dawn. Hold tight!"

At 4:25 A.M. on the tenth the Führer's train reached its destination, Euskirchen, a town near the Holland-Belgian borders. Under a canopy of stars, the party was driven to the Führer's new headquarters, *Felsennest* (Rocky Nest). Dawn was breaking as they settled into the bunker installation which had been blasted out of a wooded mountaintop. Checking his watch, Hitler got an unwelcome surprise ("I was filled with rage"). Dawn had come fifteen minutes earlier than he had been told it would.

Twenty-five miles to the west his troops were charging across the Belgian, Holland and Luxembourg borders. The air was darkened with his Luftwaffe. Twenty-five hundred aircraft had been gathered for the attack, far outnumbering those the Allies could send up. Wave after wave of German planes swept westward to devastate more than seventy enemy airfields. Airborne troops captured key points in Holland while glider forces swooped down prepared to capture Belgian fortresses by surprise. The Führer was particularly interested in the attack on Fort Eben Emael. He had personally briefed the commanders and non-coms involved in this glider operation, using a scale model for the purpose, and he awaited reports "feverishly." By noon of the eleventh, this supposedly impregnable fortress, along with a bridge over the Meuse, was in German hands. On hearing this Hitler literally hugged himself with joy. Later came even more meaningful information: the enemy was striking back! "When the news came that the enemy was advancing along the whole front," Hitler recalled, "I could have wept for joy; they'd fallen into the trap! It had been a clever piece of work to attack Liège. We had to make them believe we were remaining faithful to the old Schlieffen plan."

6

On May 10 England and France were caught by surprise, their General Staffs not heeding the warnings from Brussels and The Hague or their own intelligence experts. Pale and somber, Chamberlain wanted to stay on as Prime Minister but he was persuaded to step down. King George VI accepted his resignation regretfully and suggested that Halifax succeed him. But it was obvious that Winston Churchill alone had the confidence of the nation and at 6 P.M. His Majesty summoned him to the palace. Churchill had once paid a grudging compliment to the Führer in a letter to the *Times*: "I have always said that I hoped if Great Britain were beaten in a war we should find a Hitler who would lead us back to our rightful place among nations." These words had not mollified the Führer, who continued to look upon Churchill as his worst enemy, the tool of those English Jews who had scotched an Anglo-German alliance. It was a profound hatred contrasting strangely with his admiration for Stalin, and Churchill's elevation to Prime Minister was galling news.

The drive into western Belgium gained the most impressive victories. This, of course, was part of Hitler's plan to divert attention from the main attack through the hills of the Ardennes. By May 13 these troops had crossed the Meuse at several points to approach Sedan where Hitler hoped to break through the weak link in the Maginot Line.

Despite the steady advance in the north, Hitler was disturbed by the stubborn defense put up by the outnumbered Dutch troops and, on the morning of the fourteenth, issued a directive to break this resistance "speedily." Detachments of the Luftwaffe were sent from the Belgian area "to facilitate the rapid conquest of Fortress Holland." Within hours the Luftwaffe dropped ninety-eight tons of high explosives on Rotterdam. The intent was to eliminate Dutch resistance at the bridges over the Nieuwe Maas but the bombs slammed into the center of the city, killing 814 civilians. The facts were grossly misrepresented by the democratic press, which listed the death toll as between 25,000 and 30,000. Nor did Western newspapers reveal that the tacit agreement between the two sides to limit bombing to military targets had been first violated by the British. Three days earlier, over strenuous French objections, thirty-five Royal Air Force bombers had attacked an industrial city in the Rhineland, killing four civilians, including an Englishwoman. Despite Hitler's frightful retaliation in Holland, he resisted proposals to bomb London itself. He was not willing to go that far—as yet. The tragedy of Rotterdam ended Dutch resistance, the commander-in-chief of the Dutch forces ordering his men to lay down arms a few hours later. That same day German tanks burst through the French Ninth and Second Armies at Sedan. Supported by screaming Stuka dive bombers, three long columns of Panzers rattled and rumbled toward the English Channel.

Churchill was wakened the next morning by a telephone call from Paris. "We have been defeated!" exclaimed Premier Reynaud. "We are beaten!" Churchill could not believe it, nor could his generals, who had misread the armored conquest of Poland as a simple maneuver against an inept, primitive defense.

The terror that seized France was aggravated by Goebbels. "The task of the secret transmitter, from now on," he told his staff on May 17, "is to use every means to create a mood of panic in France. . . . It must further utter an urgent warning against the dangers of a 'Fifth Column' which undoubtedly includes all German refugees. It should point out that, in the present situation, even the Jews from Germany are nothing but German agents."

By the morning of May 19 several armored divisions were within fifty miles of the Channel and one, the 2nd, rolled into Abbeville at the mouth of the Somme the following evening. The trap was sprung and inside the giant net were the Belgians, the entire British Expeditionary Force and three French armies. Hitler was so surprised when Brauchitsch telephoned him of the capture of Abbeville that his voice choked with emotion.

Things were turning out exactly as he had dreamed. Within three days the tanks of Army Group A had wheeled north, closing on the Channel ports of Calais and Dunkirk, whose capture would cut off the British from a sea retreat to England. Göring slammed his big hand on a table when he heard the report. "This is a special job for the Luftwaffe!" he exclaimed. "I must speak to the Führer at once. Get a line through by phone!" In moments he was assuring Hitler unconditionally that the Luftwaffe by itself could annihilate the trapped remnants of the enemy. All he asked was withdrawal of German tanks and ground troops so that they wouldn't be hit by friendly bombs. Having resumed his feud with both the Wehrmacht and army high commands, Hitler might have seen this as an opportunity to strengthen his hold on the military. He gave Göring consent to finish off the enemy from the air.

Overhearing this, Jodl sarcastically remarked to an adjutant, "There goes Göring shooting off his big mouth again!" then dutifully began making the necessary arrangements over the phone with Göring's chief of staff. "We have done it!" Göring exulted to Milch on his return to air force headquarters. "The Luftwaffe is to wipe out the British on the beaches. I have managed to talk the Führer round to halting the army." Milch did not share his enthusiasm and objected that their bombs would sink too deeply into the sand before exploding. Besides, the Luftwaffe was not strong enough for such an operation. "Leave it to me, it's not your business," said Göring and returned to his boasting. "The army always wants to act like gentlemen. They round up the British as prisoners with as little harm to them as possible. But the Führer wants to teach them a lesson they won't easily forget."

The following morning, May 24, Hitler visited General Gerd von Rundstedt and his staff at Army Group A's forward headquarters. In high spirits, the Führer predicted that the war would be over in six weeks. Then the way would be free for an agreement with the English. All he wanted from them was their acknowledgment of Germany's position on the Continent. When they got down to tactics, General von Rundstedt did not oppose the use of planes to reduce the entrapped enemy at Dunkirk. He proposed that tanks be halted at the canal below the besieged city. Hitler agreed with his observation that this armor should be saved for operations against the French. At 12:45 P.M. the halt order was issued to the Fourth Army in the Führer's name.

That evening four Panzer divisions were stopped at the Aa Canal. The tank crews were astounded. No fire was coming from the opposite shore. Beyond they could make out the peaceful spires of Dunkirk. Had Operations gone crazy? The division commanders were even more amazed. They knew they could take Dunkirk with little trouble since the British were still heavily engaged near Lille. Why weren't they allowed to seize the last escape port to England?

The ground commanders reiterated their request to move into Dunkirk with tanks and infantry, but Hitler would not listen. It was only on May 26, after reports of heavy shipping in the Channel (was it possible the British were preparing to evacuate their forces?), that he grudgingly authorized an advance on Dunkirk from the west. But that same day Göring assured him that the Luftwaffe had destroyed Dunkirk harbor. "Only fish bait will reach the other side. I hope the Tommies are good swimmers."

As the English and Allied troops fell back into the cul-de-sac, a crazy-quilt fleet of almost 900 vessels began leaving dozens of English ports. There were warships and sailboats, launches and strange-looking Dutch craft—manned by career officers, fishermen, tugboat operators, expert amateur seamen and Sunday sailors who had never before ventured beyond the three-mile limit. This was Operation Dynamo, a mission to evacuate 45,000 men in two days. But this modest estimate had not taken into consideration Hitler's low opinion of democracy in action. He was completely surprised by a sporting operation carried out gallantly and effectively by a pickup group of amateurs and professionals. By the thirtieth of May, 126,606 men were back in England—and more were coming every hour.

In the meantime the Stukas of the Eighth Air Corps were doing surprisingly little damage to the flotilla of small vessels; and those bombs dropped on the beaches dug so deeply before exploding that casualties were low. Equally surprising was the performance of a new British fighter plane, the Spitfire, which ravaged Göring's fighter squadrons; and once the weather cleared enough for bombers to get into the air, they too were picked off by the deadly little Spitfires.

The thin perimeter of the Dunkirk defense line held until June 4 but by then 338,226 British and Allied troops had been ferried to England to fight another day. Now speculation arose on both sides of the Channel regarding Hitler's strange behavior. Why had he given Göring the license to bomb the encircled army "to teach them a lesson," then apparently assisted in their escape by not acting forcefully? His own words only confused matters. He told his naval adjutant that he had expected the BEF would fight to the last man as they had done in *his* war, and hoped to contain them until they ran out of ammunition, thus gaining for himself a mass of prisoners for use in peace negotiations. Yet when this strategy failed—if it had been his strategy—and almost no British were captured, he showed no sign of rage or even petulance.

7

Hitler left Felsennest on the eve of the fall of Dunkirk with instructions to preserve the entire area as a "national monument." Every room in the complex was to be kept intact, every name-plate to remain on its door. Führer Headquarters was moved to the small Belgian village of Brûly-de-Pesche, near the border of France. By the time Hitler arrived the place was deserted, every inhabitant evacuated. A special garden had been laid out along with gravel paths but the cement of the Führer bunker was still wet. He gave this peaceful scene a warlike name, *Wolfsschlucht* (Wolf's Gorge), after his own nickname of early party days.

By this time King Leopold had not only surrendered Belgium but refused to go into exile. "I have decided to stay," he told his Prime Minister. "The cause of the Allies is lost." This seemed certain on June 5 when 143 German divisions turned on the remnants of the French army—65 divisions. The defenders had few tanks and almost no air cover and the Wehrmacht swept forward on a 400-mile front. In Paris Reynaud made a desperate impossible plea to Roosevelt for "clouds of planes," then packed his bags.

It was an auspicious moment to enter the war on Hitler's side and Mussolini expressed his desire to join the lists. But his ally urged him to wait until the Luftwaffe wiped out the French air force. Il Duce could only restrain himself until June 10 before declaring war, and the supremely confident tone of his explanatory letter to Hitler brought this burst of sarcasm: "I have quite often in the past wondered about his naïveté," the Führer told his military staff. "The whole letter is proof that in the future I must be much more careful with the Italians in political matters. Evidently Mussolini thinks of this as a walk in *Passo romano*." The Italians would get a rude surprise. "First they were too cowardly to take part, now they are in a hurry so that they can share in the spoils."

At dawn thirty-two Italian divisions attacked six French divisions in the south, but with such a lack of drive that any advance had to be measured in feet. By this time both ends of the French line in the north had crumbled and on the morning of the fourteenth German troops began entering Paris. On the seventeenth the French asked for an armistice.

Although the British were stricken by the French capitulation, Churchill revived their courage with talk of England's "finest hour." And from the British Broadcasting Corporation came another voice of resistance, this beamed to France. "The flame of French resistance cannot go out," proclaimed General Charles de Gaulle from Studio B-2. "It will not go out." France, he said, had lost only a battle. "She has not lost the war."

On the first day of summer, Hitler motored to the same woods near Compiègne where the Kaiser's representative had surrendered. It was a vindictive as well as historic choice. There stood the famous wooden railroad dining car used on that occasion, hoisted from its museum through a torn-out wall to the original site. At exactly 3:15 P.M. the Führer motorcade arrived. Hitler walked toward the car with springy step, face grave, manner solemn. He stopped at a granite block which read:

HERE ON THE ELEVENTH OF NOVEMBER 1918 SUCCUMBED
THE CRIMINAL PRIDE OF THE GERMAN EMPIRE—VANQUISHED
BY THE FREE PEOPLE WHICH IT TRIED TO ENSLAVE

William Shirer was watching through binoculars to catch Hitler's expression. "I have seen that face many times at the great moments of his life. But today! It is afire with scorn, anger, hate, revenge, triumph."

A long plain table had been set up in the old railroad car with half a dozen chairs on each side for the two delegations. At the head stood Schmidt where he would be able to hear both groups. After the Führer seated himself next to his interpreter, Göring, Raeder, Brauchitsch, Ribbentrop and Hess took their places. Several minutes later General Charles Huntziger led in the French delegation—an admiral, an air force general, and a former ambassador, their faces still showing the shock of learning at the last moment where the negotiations would take place.

Hitler and his associates rose. Not a word was spoken. Both delegations bowed and sat down. First Keitel read out the preamble to the armistice conditions, which had been composed by Hitler. The French and the Germans stared at each other, thought Schmidt, like wax figures as Keitel spoke the Führer's words: Germany did not intend that the conditions should cast any aspersion on so courageous an enemy. "The aim of the German demands is to prevent a resumption of hostilities, to give Germany security for the further conduct of the war against England which she has no choice but to continue, and also to create the conditions for a new peace which will repair the injustice inflicted by force on the German Reich." It seemed as though Hitler addressed England rather than France, offering them an honorable peace too if they chose.

Once Schmidt finished reading the French text, Hitler got to his feet. So did the others. After more polite bows, the Führer left with most of his followers. Keitel and Schmidt stayed behind and were joined directly by Jodl and several other German officers. After the French had re-examined the terms, they insisted upon transmitting them to their government at Bordeaux. "Absolutely impossible!" said Keitel. "You must sign at once."

But the French stubbornly demanded the same courtesy extended to the German delegation in 1918 and in a few minutes Huntziger was talking to General Weygand, the French commander-in-chief. "I am telephoning from the coach"—he paused—"from the coach you know." He reported that the conditions were hard but not dishonorable. Even so, Huntziger felt they were "merciless," far worse than the conditions France had forced on Germany in the previous war, and the negotiations continued without resolution until dusk. They resumed the following morning, June 22, dragging on into late afternoon. By 6 P.M. Keitel lost all patience and sent Schmidt to the French with an ultimatum: "If we cannot reach an agreement within an hour, the negotiations will be broken off, and the delegation will be conducted back to the French lines."

There was no alternative. At 6:50 P.M., after more telephone conversations with Bordeaux, General Huntziger signed the armistice treaty. After the ceremony Keitel asked him to stay a moment. When they were alone the two generals looked at each other silently and Schmidt noticed both had tears in their eyes. Controlling his emotion, Keitel congratulated the Frenchman for having represented his country's interests with such dignity, then held out his hand. Huntziger shook it.

Back at Wolf's Gorge Hitler was planning a sightseeing tour of Paris. He had summoned a sculptor and his two favorite architects—Speer and Giesler—to go along as guides. Hitler admitted that it had long been one of his most ardent wishes to visit the City of Light. It was a metropolis of art and that was why he insisted on seeing it first with his artists. He was sure they would find inspiration for the rebuilding of important German cities. "I am interested in actually seeing the buildings with which I am theoretically familiar."

It was pitch-dark when the party—which included Keitel and Bormann and several adjutants—arrived at a meadow outside Brûly-de-Pesche and climbed into a plane piloted by Baur, but by the time they reached Le Bourget the sun was up. June 23 was going to be a bright, hot day. Hitler climbed into the first open car of a motor column, seating himself as usual beside the driver. Behind him sat the rest of the party. As they headed for the first stop, the Opéra, the streets of the city were deserted except for an occasional gendarme who would dutifully greet the Führer with a smart salute. Arno Breker, whose heroic-classical works were admired by Hitler, had spent his most decisive years in Paris and was shocked to see the almost complete absence of life.

Hitler's features slowly relaxed as he took in the architectural wonders of the Opéra, which he had admired since his early days in Vienna. He was as familiar with the building as with his own chancellery and his eyes shone with excitement.

After a stop at the Eiffel Tower they visited Napoleon's tomb. Here Hitler placed cap over heart, bowed and gazed for some time down into the deep round crypt. He was very moved. Finally he turned to Giesler and said quietly, "You will build my tomb."

The three-hour tour ended on the heights of Montmartre, the mecca of art students. Perhaps it reminded Hitler of his own student days. Lost in thought for some moments, he finally turned to Giesler, Breker and Speer. "Now your work begins," he said. The rebuilding of cities and monuments was entrusted to them. "Bormann," he said, "help me with this. Take care of my artists." Hitler again surveyed the city which stretched below. "I thank Fate to have seen this city whose magic atmosphere has always fascinated me," he said. That was why he had ordered his troops to by-pass Paris and to avoid combat in its vicinity. "So that picture below us would be preserved for the future." But the few Parisians who saw him that morning were reduced to panic. As his cavalcade came upon a group of boisterous market women the fattest pointed in terror at Hitler. Her shriek of "It's him! It's him!" spread pandemonium.

Chapter Twenty-one

"EV'N VICTORS BY VICTORY ARE UNDONE" (DRYDEN)

JUNE–OCTOBER 28, 1940

1

That summer Hitler made it evident he was more interested in negotiating than in fighting. In France his weapons were persuasion and the projection of himself as the magnanimous victor who offered the French a share in the fruits of a united and prosperous Fascist Europe, a hegemony designed not only for moral regeneration but as a bulwark against Godless Bolshevism. One of the first acts in this campaign was a demand that his troops act like liberators, not conquerors. "I do not wish my soldiers to behave in France the way the French behaved in the Rhineland after the first war!" He told Hoffmann that anyone found looting would be shot on the spot. "I want to come to a real understanding with France."

Consequently troops who entered Paris did not swagger around the city demanding homage and free food. They conscientiously paid for every purchase and enjoyed the late June sun outside the cafés of the Champs-Élysées side by side with Frenchmen. It was an embarrassed, often silent and indifferent companionship but fear was leaving Parisians who had expected their women to be raped and their shops and banks to be sacked. By now it was common knowledge that the Wehrmacht was actually assisting those refugees trekking back to the capital, and there was some acceptance of the placard plastered all over the city showing a child in the arms of a friendly German with the admonition: "Frenchmen! Trust the German soldier!"

Hitler would have been proud of his troops. They were neat, quiet and ingratiating; courteous to women but not too gallant, and respectful to their mates. They stood bareheaded at the tomb of the Unknown Soldier, armed only with cameras. They acted more like a horde of tourists brought in at special holiday rates than the fearsome creatures who had just humiliated the French armies. It was astute public relations, part of a program designed to turn France into a working and productive vassal.

Hitler still had no definite plan for the invasion of the British Isles. Victory in the West, in fact, had come so quickly that there was not a single landing craft or barge ready for launching across the Channel. He seemed to be waiting instead for England to sue for peace. But when Brauchitsch and Halder flew to the Berghof on July 13 he readily approved their plan to invade England, yet moments later protested that he had no desire to fight his English brothers. He had no desire to dismantle the Empire; bloodshed would only draw the jackals eager to share in the spoils. Why was England still so unwilling to make peace? he asked and answered, so Halder wrote in his diary, "that England still has some hopes of action on the part of Russia."

Three days after, he issued a specific invasion directive designed to eliminate the English homeland as a base for the prosecution of the war against Germany and, if necessary, to occupy it completely. The operation was given an imaginative code name: Sea Lion. No sooner had Hitler approved it than he decided to make a peace proposal of his own. When it came on July 19, it began with a derisive attack on Churchill, continued with a threat that any battle between their two countries would surely end in the annihilation of England, and concluded with a vague proposal: "I can see no reason why this war should continue."

The first English reply to Hitler's bleak offer came from someone who knew him well. Sefton Delmer, now working for BBC, was on the air within the hour. "Herr Hitler," he said in his most deferential German,"you have on occasion in the past consulted me as to the mood of the British public. So permit me to render Your Excellency this little service once again tonight. Let me tell you what we here in Britain think of this appeal of yours to what you are pleased to call our reason and common sense. *Herr Führer* and *Reichskanzler*, we hurl it right back to you, right in your evil-smelling teeth."

President Roosevelt too was unimpressed by Hitler's offer. Later that evening, in a radio address from the White House accepting the nomination for the presidency, he declared there was only one way to deal with a totalitarian country—by resistance, not appeasement.

Still no official rejection came from London and when Hitler summoned his commanders to Berlin for a conference on Sunday, July 21, he seemed more puzzled than bellicose. "England's situation is hopeless," he said. "The war has been won by us. A reversal of the prospects of success is impossible." He speculated on the chances of a new cabinet under Lloyd George before lapsing into grim conjecture.

Suddenly the musing ended. He called for "a speedy ending of the war" and suggested that Sea Lion was the most effective way to do so. But his assurance—or show of it—almost immediately began to dissipate. He warned that invasion across the Channel commanded by the enemy was no one-way trip as in Norway. There could be no element of surprise. How could they solve the problem of logistic supply? He went on and on, pointing out grave problems that Admiral Raeder (who was taking diligent notes) silently seconded. Complete air superiority was essential and first-wave landings must be completed by mid-September before worsening weather prevented the Luftwaffe from full participation.

With some embarrassment Raeder replied that he hoped to have an answer on technical details in a few days but how could he commence practical preparations until air superiority was a fact? Brauchitsch responded to his pessimism with a positive expression of faith. He liked Sea Lion. Göring's deputy said the Luftwaffe was only waiting for the word to start a massive air offensive; without comment, Hitler instructed Raeder to submit his report as soon as possible. "If preparations cannot be completed with certainty by the beginning of September, it is necessary to consider other plans." The burden of Sea Lion was on the navy.

Although Hitler had achieved an astounding military victory in the West it had not brought him the political stability he needed to begin his holy war against Russia. His blows against England had merely made this stubborn nation more stubborn and his attempts to placate the Vichy French into joining his crusade were being thwarted by a reluctant compliance that stopped short of active assistance.

These failures notwithstanding, he was still confident he could prevent the conflict from becoming a world war, still so sure England was on the verge of surrender that he ordered an immediate intensification of the propaganda war against England.

That summer Hitler decided that the time had come for Lebensraum and to destroy Bolshevism. He instructed the military to make preparations in this direction and on July 29, 1940, Jodl journeyed to the Bad Reichenhall railroad station to discuss the matter with Colonel Warlimont, chief of OKW's planning section, in his special train. Warlimont and his three senior officers thought the unusual visit might mean promotion or some award. To their mystification, Jodl checked to see that all doors and windows of the dining car were closed and then abruptly announced in a quiet, dry voice that Hitler had decided to rid the world "once and for all" of the danger of Bolshevism. A surprise attack was to be launched on the Soviet Union as soon as possible—May 1941. "The effect of Jodl's words was electric," recalled Warlimont, who at the time grasped his chair because he could not believe his own ears.

A chorus of protests erupted. This was the two-front war which had defeated Germany in the First World War. And why this sudden change after the Moscow Pact? Hadn't Stalin kept his promise to deliver raw materials and food punctually and fully? Jodl tersely answered every objection: a collision with Bolshevism was inevitable; it was better to attack now at the peak of German armed strength.

On the last day of July the Führer summoned his commanders to the Berghof for a conference that purported to concern Sea Lion but would lead in the opposite direction. Admiral Raeder spoke first. Preparations were in full swing: matériel had been brought up according to plan and the conversion of barges would be finished by the end of August. On the other hand, the merchant shipping situation was unfavorable due to losses sustained in Norway and from mines; and while minesweeping had commenced it was hampered by Allied air superiority. Therefore, he concluded, it would be better to postpone the invasion until the following May.

Hitler protested. Waiting that long, he said, would enable England to improve her army and stockpile considerable supplies from America—and perhaps even Russia. "How can we bridge the gap until May?" he asked and set the operation for

September 15. No sooner had he made this categorical decision than he diluted it. That is, he added, if a concentrated weeklong bombing attack on southern England could damage the RAF, the Royal Navy and key harbors. "Otherwise it is postponed until May 1941."

2

Within twenty-four hours the man of decision was again vacillating. He issued two directives, one calling for quick conquest of Britain and the other expressing doubt of its execution. The first began in confidence: "In order to establish the conditions necessary for the final subjugation of England, I intend to intensify the air and naval war against the English homeland." The Luftwaffe was to overpower the RAF as quickly as possible, then stand by in force for Operation Sea Lion. "I reserve for myself," he pointed out, "the decision on terror attacks as a means of reprisal."

The second order, signed by Keitel in the name of the Führer, directed preparations for Sea Lion to be completed by mid-September, then stated: "Eight to fourteen days after the launching of the air offensive against Britain, scheduled to begin about August 5, the Führer will decide whether the invasion will take place this year or not; his decision will depend largely on the outcome of the air offensive."

In 1938 MI-6, the British secret intelligence service, had bought the secret of a German cipher machine (called "Enigma") from a Polish mathematician for £10,000, a British passport and a resident's permit in France for himself and his wife. He had memorized diagrams of the main parts of the machine and created a replica in an apartment on the Left Bank in Paris. A working model of Enigma was successfully completed and installed in Bletchley Park, a Victorian mansion forty miles north of London. By the time England declared war in 1939 the machine, code-named Ultra, was operational; and its first major contribution was to warn the British General Staff of Hitler's plan to invade the West.

It did not occur to Hitler that the substance of his two directives on that August 1 had been decoded by Ultra. The messages assured Churchill that he truly possessed the German code and his faith was confirmed beyond doubt when Ultra shortly decoded a signal from Göring designating August 13 as the beginning of Operation Eagle, the all-out air assault on England.

The offensive began on schedule, but because of worsening weather only the Third Air Force took part. There were almost five hundred bombing sorties, but, thanks primarily to radar and secondarily to the Ultra warning, damage was slight and German losses were serious: 45 Luftwaffe aircraft against 13 RAF fighters. The next day was equally disappointing to Göring. On the fifteenth he launched all three of his air fleets. This time Ultra disclosed exactly what forces Göring would use and approximately where each would strike and with this knowledge the RAF was able to assemble its few fighter squadrons at the right place and altitude, parceling them so economically that each German wave met fierce resistance. In the greatest air battle to date, the RAF shot down 75 planes while losing 34. Operation Eagle was turning sour: on the seventeenth the score was 70 to 27. That was the day the slow Stuka dive bomber, which had wreaked such havoc in France, was taken out of the campaign by Göring. It was simply no match for the Spitfires.

Bad weather began on the nineteenth and kept the Luftwaffe grounded four days. During the respite Göring summoned his commanders. The daylight attacks on aircraft factories and other such targets, he said, would have to be replaced by night raids. Göring also took the opportunity to bitterly reproach the single- and double-engine fighter pilots for their performances. "Neither type of fighter is allowed to break off its escort mission because of weather," he ordered. Any pilot who did so would be court-martialed.

When the weather lifted on August 23 the Luftwaffe came over the Channel that night en masse. One flight of a dozen bombers strayed off course and, instead of hitting aircraft factories and oil tanks outside of London, dropped their loads directly on the city. Nine civilians were killed and the RAF, assuming it had been done on purpose, retaliated the next night by bombing Berlin. Little damage was suffered but the Berliners were stunned.

The success of invasion or British capitulation depended on the air assault and Hitler sanctioned mass raids on London. Wave after wave of planes took off for England. The first group of 320 bombers, heavily protected by fighters, passed over the head of Göring, who was watching from the cliffs of Cape Blanc Nez. The tightly massed planes swarmed over the Channel, then flew up the Thames to blast Woolwich Arsenal, power stations and docks. As soon as Göring got the report that the last target was "a sea of flames," he hurried to a microphone and began broadcasting that London was being destroyed. His planes, he boasted, were striking "right into the enemy's heart." The devastating attack continued until dawn and was resumed the following dusk. Eight hundred and forty-two Londoners died in those two days of terror. Making good his threat to "raze their cities to the ground," Hitler authorized another massive raid for September 15. This would be the grand finale, designed not only to punish London but to destroy the RAF.

Again Ultra warned Churchill and, four days before the raid, he broadcast an exhortation to the nation. "There is no doubt that Herr Hitler is using up his fighter force at a very high rate, and that if he goes on for many more weeks he will wear down and ruin the vital part of his air force." At the same time he warned that "no one should blind himself to the fact that a heavy full-scale invasion of this island is being prepared with all the usual German thoroughness and method, and that it may be launched now—upon England, upon Scotland, or upon Ireland, or upon all three." It could come in the next few days. "Therefore, we must regard the next week or so as a very important period in our history. It ranks with the days when the Spanish Armada was approaching the Channel, and Drake was finishing his game of bowls; or when Nelson stood between us and Napoleon's Grand Army at Boulogne." His words lifted spirits in the fortress island, inspiring civilians to feel that they too were involved in the battle.

In the meantime the Battle of Britain intensified, with increasingly heavy German losses. On the fifteenth, for instance, 60 planes were destroyed while the British were losing 26. Consequently Hitler was forced at last to face reality on Tuesday, the seventeenth. He admitted to himself that bombing would probably never bring the English to their knees, then curtly announced his decision: due to inability to achieve air superiority, Operation Sea Lion was hereby postponed until further notice. Postponement meant cancellation; from that moment on the invasion of England existed only on paper. Ultra and a small band of British pilots, typifying the united spirit of the people, had dealt Adolf Hitler his first military defeat.

"This blessed plot, this earth, this realm, this England," was saved.

3

Hitler devoted October to diplomacy. On the fourth he met Mussolini at the Brenner Pass. "The war is won! The rest is only a question of time," he said. While admitting that the Luftwaffe had not yet achieved air supremacy, he claimed that British planes were being knocked out of the air at a ratio of three to one. For some reason, however, England continued to hold out even though her military situation was hopeless. Her people were under inhuman strain. Why does she keep on? he complained and answered his own question: hope of American and Russian aid.

That, he said, was an illusion. The Tripartite Pact was already having a "dampening effect" on the cowardly American leaders and forty German divisions on the eastern front discouraged any Russian intervention. Therefore the time was ripe to strike a new blow at the very roots of the British Empire: to seize Gibraltar. This digressed into a diatribe against the Spaniards, who demanded 400,000 tons of grain and considerable gasoline as their price for entry into the war. And, complained Hitler, when he had brought up the matter of eventual repayment, Franco had the gall to reply that this "was a matter of confusing idealism with materialism." Almost beside himself with resentment, Hitler exclaimed that he had been practically represented "as if I were a little Jew who was haggling about the most sacred possessions of mankind!"

After the two dictators parted in a spirit of warmth and trust, the Führer made for Berchtesgaden "to think over quietly the new political scheme." He paced the rooms of the Berghof and took long walks by himself on the slopes of the Obersalzberg. He spoke out some thoughts over the dinner table, some at conferences. The result of these monologues was a decision to sound out the French during his trip to see Franco. Then, and only then, would he speak to the Russians.

The Führer planned to extend his program reducing France to complete vassalage. He hoped to do it with the willing help of the victims but was ready to use force and ruthless reprisals if necessary. Beyond subjecting France, as he had other conquered nations, to what Göring blandly called plunder economy (which included the outright theft of everything of value from raw materials and slave labor to national art treasures), he hoped to gain Vichy France as an active ally against England. From Deputy Premier Pierre Laval's attitude, Hitler was assured that this could be done and he was in a confident mood as his train continued its journey through the night for the crucial meeting with Franco.

They were to meet next day at a little French border town more suitable for a holiday than a conference of world importance. Hendaye lay just below Biarritz in the resort area of southwest France, with beaches and palm trees worthy of a travel poster. The rendezvous was at the edge of town where the French narrow-gauge and Spanish wide-gauge rails met. The Führer train arrived in good time for the two o'clock meeting but there was no Spanish train on the adjoining platform. It was a sparkling, clear October day, so pleasant that the punctual Germans were not annoyed. After all, what could you expect from those lazy Spaniards with their interminable siestas?

Hitler was convinced that once he met Franco face to face he would bring him around just as he had Chamberlain, Laval and the others. Where would the Generalissimo be without the help of Germany? It was not, as devout Spaniards believed, the intervention of the Mother of God which had won the Civil War but the bombs German squadrons had "rained from the heavens that decided the issue."

While they waited, Hitler and Ribbentrop chatted on the platform. "We cannot at the moment," Schmidt overheard the Führer say, "give the Spaniards any written promises about transfers of territory from the French colonial possessions. If they get hold of anything in writing on this ticklish question with these talkative Latins, the French are sure to hear something about it sooner or later." Tomorrow he wanted to induce Marshal Henri Philippe Pétain, the Vichy Premier, to start active hostilities against England and so could not give away French territory today. "Quite apart from that," he continued, "if such an agreement with the Spaniards became known, the French colonial empire would probably go over bodily to De Gaulle."

At last, an hour late, the Spanish train appeared on the International Bridge over the Bidassoa River. The tardiness had been deliberate, not due to any siesta. "This is the most important meeting of my life," Franco told one of his officers.

"I'll have to use every trick I can—and this is one of them. If I make Hitler wait, he will be at a psychological disadvantage from the start." The *Caudillo* (Leader) was short and plump with dark, piercing eyes.

Although a peasant at heart, Franco was not even a man of the people. He also was too close to the Church and the monarchists and, while giving lip service to the Falangists (a Fascist-type party), it was obvious he was not one of them. As his train drew alongside of Hitler's, Franco knew the fate of his country rested on his ability to keep it out of the European conflict. The Civil War had left Spain's economy in a shambles and with the failure of last year's harvest his people faced starvation. But would Hitler let him remain neutral? If he gave the Führer a flat refusal, what could stop a German invasion? The solution was to give the impression of joining the Axis, yet find some slight point that needed further clarification.

Franco began with a set speech laden with compliments and vocal promises. Spain had always been "spiritually united with the German people without any reservation and in complete loyalty," and, in fact, "at every moment felt herself united with the Axis." Historically there were only forces of unity between their two nations and, in the present war, "Spain would gladly fight at Germany's side." The difficulties of doing so, he added, were well known to the Führer: in particular the food shortage and the difficulties anti-Axis elements were making for his poor country in America and Europe. "Therefore, Spain must mark time and often look kindly toward things of which she thoroughly disapproves." He said this with a tone of regret but quickly noted that despite all these problems Spain—mindful of her spiritual alliance with the Axis—was assuming "the same attitude toward the war as had Italy in the past autumn." This artful dodge was followed by a promise from Hitler. In return for Spanish cooperation in the war, he said, Germany would let Franco have Gibraltar—it would be seized on the tenth of January—as well as some colonial territories in Africa.

Franco sat huddled silently in his chair, face expressionless. Finally he began to talk, slowly and deliberately, offering up excuses while insisting on more concessions. His country, he said, needed several hundred thousand tons of wheat immediately. Fixing Hitler with "a slyly watchful expression," he asked if Germany was prepared to deliver it. And what about the large number of heavy guns Spain needed to defend the coast from attacks by the Royal Navy, not to mention anti-aircraft guns? He shifted in seemingly haphazard manner from one subject to another, from recompense for the certain loss of the Canary Islands to the impossibility of accepting Gibraltar as a present from foreign soldiers. That fortress must be taken by Spaniards! Abruptly he pragmatically assessed Hitler's chances of clearing the British out of Africa: to the edge of the desert, perhaps, but no farther. "As an old African campaigner I am quite clear about that." Similarly, he cast doubt on the Führer's ability to conquer Britain itself. At best England might fall but Churchill's government would flee to Canada and continue the war with America's aid.

That evening the Germans entertained the Spaniards at a state dinner in the dining car of the Führer's train. Franco was warm and friendly, his brother-in-law Foreign Minister Suñer, charming. Perhaps their ingratiating manner throughout the meal encouraged Hitler to draw Franco aside as the guests were rising to depart. For almost two hours the two men talked in private with the Führer becoming increasingly agitated at his inability to manipulate the imperturbable Caudillo, who stood firm on every important point. He believed, for instance, that the eastern gate of the Mediterranean, the Suez Canal, should be closed before the western gate, Gibraltar; nor was he moved by Hitler's protests. Even when his firmness drove Hitler from insistence to an outburst of temper, Franco remained impassive, insisting that if Spain did not get the ten million quintals of wheat, history (he was referring to the rising against Napoleon) might repeat itself. The Führer left the banquet car in a fume.

In the meantime Ribbentrop was in his train trying to work out an agreement with Suñer, but he had become as frustrated as the Führer with the Spaniard's polite but insistent objections. Losing all patience, he dismissed Serrano Suñer and his aides as if they were schoolboys, instructing them to bring in the completed text by eight in the morning.

Serrano Suñer failed to appear in person on the twenty-fourth, entrusting the text instead to his subordinate, a former ambassador to Berlin who spoke German with a Viennese accent. Ribbentrop was so infuriated at the substitution that his rude shouts could be heard outside the train. "Unsatisfactory!" exclaimed Ribbentrop in his role as schoolmaster after reading Serrano Suñer's draft, which described the French Zone of Morocco as a territory later to belong to Spain. He demanded that the Spaniards submit a new draft, then drove off with Schmidt to the nearest airport so they could reach Montoire in time for the Hitler-Pétain meeting. Spluttering with rage all the way, the Foreign Minister cursed Suñer as a "Jesuit" and Franco as an "ungrateful coward." Secretly the interpreter was delighted by the tactics of the Spaniards. For the first time Hitler had been outwitted before he could play his own tricks.

Hitler had already arrived in Montoire and was waiting in his train to meet Marshal Pétain, who had recently elevated himself from French Premier to Head of State, a new title disassociating him from the old republican regime. It would have made the Führer even unhappier with Franco to know that he had already warned Pétain not to assume the burden of leading France out of chaos. "Make your age your excuse," he had said. "Let those who lost the war sign the peace. . . . You are the hero of Verdun. Don't let your name be mingled with the others who have been defeated."

The aged marshal, smartly uniformed, was greeted at the entrance of the railway station by Keitel. Pétain returned his salute and walked erectly past the German honor guard, eyes front, with Ribbentrop and Laval at his heels. They silently filed through the station to the Führer's train. As Pétain emerged from the ticket hall, Hitler came forward, hand outstretched. The marshal allowed himself to be led into the private coach but sat very straight facing Hitler, listening to Schmidt translate.

After listing French sins in a moderate tone, the Führer repeated what he had said to Franco: "We have already won the war. England is beaten and will sooner or later have to admit it." And, he added meaningfully, it was obvious someone would have to pay for the lost war. "That will be either France or England. If England bears the cost, then France can take the place in Europe which is due her, and can fully retain her position as a colonial power." To do this, of course, France would have to protect her colonial empire from attack as well as reconquer the central African colonies, which had gone over to De Gaulle. At this point he indirectly suggested that France join the war against Britain.

Pétain replied that his country was in no position to wage another war. He countered with a request for a final peace treaty "so that France may be clear about her fate, and the two million French prisoners of war may return to their families as soon as possible." Hitler glided over this problem and the two Frenchmen, in turn, made no response to another hint that France should enter the war. The two sides were at cross-purposes and although Pétain expressed his personal admiration for the Führer and seemed to agree with many of his opinions, he expressed himself so curtly that Schmidt took it as an overt rebuff. "The great stake for which Hitler had played," recalled the interpreter, "had been lost as a result of the prudent reticence shown by Pétain and Laval." In his opinion France was not shamed by the actions of their two representatives at Montoire.

It was with honor, Pétain told his countrymen a few days later over the radio, that he accepted collaboration with Germany. He did so to maintain French unity. It would also lighten the weight of France's sufferings and better the lot of her prisoners. "This collaboration," he warned, "must be sincere. It must exclude all idea of aggression. It must carry with it a patient and confident effort." France had numerous obligations to the victor. Hadn't Hitler let France keep her sovereignty? "So far," continued Pétain, "I have spoken to you as a father. Today I am addressing you as a leader. Follow me. Trust in eternal France."

The mood aboard the Führer train was glum. Hitler had failed to get what he wanted at both Hendaye and Montoire. The third disappointment came with delivery of a letter from Mussolini dated six days earlier. In it he venomously attacked the French. In their hearts, he wrote, they hated the Axis and, despite the sweet words coming from Vichy, "one cannot think of their collaboration." Anxious lest Il Duce's vengeful attitude toward France endanger his own plan to draw Vichy into the anti-democratic crusade, Hitler instructed Ribbentrop to move up his meeting with Mussolini in Florence to October 28.

Rather than return to Berlin as planned Hitler ordered his train to Munich so he could rest and prepare for the hastily updated trip to Italy. On October 27, just before heading south late that afternoon, word came from the German military attaché in Rome that it was now "practically certain" that Mussolini would attack Greece early the next morning. According to Schmidt, the Führer "was beside himself" at this news and that evening at supper Ribbentrop reflected his master's ire. "The Italians will never get anywhere against the Greeks in the autumn rains and winter snows," he said. "Besides the consequences of war in the Balkans are quite unpredictable. The Führer intends at all costs to hold up this crazy scheme of the Duce's, so we are to go to Italy at once, to talk to Mussolini personally."

The next morning at 10 A.M. Hitler learned that the Italians had just marched into Greece. His first outburst of swearing and cursing, recalled Engel, was directed not at Mussolini but at the German liaison staffs and attachés who had "spoiled many a recipe for him." Only then did Hitler begin berating the Italians for their duplicity. "This is the revenge for Norway and France!" he exclaimed, then complained that "every second Italian is either a traitor or a spy." His emotions released, he turned to a more sober analysis of the situation. Il Duce, he guessed, had gone into Greece to counter Germany's growing economic influence in the Balkans. "I am greatly disturbed," he said. The Italian invasion, he feared, would have "grave consequences and give the British a welcome opportunity to set up an air base in the Balkans."

An hour later his train pulled into the gaily decorated station of Florence. An exuberant Duce rushed forward to embrace his ally. "Führer," he exclaimed, "we are on the march!" Hitler controlled himself. The damage had been done and it would be useless to complain. His greeting was aloof, a far cry from the usual warm reception he gave Mussolini, but even this coolness was momentary. In moments both dictators, being politicians, were put in good spirits by the ecstatic cries of "Führer, Heil Führer! Duce! Duce!" from the crowd outside the Palazzo Pitti where the talks would take place. Several times the two dictators had to appear at the balcony to appease the crowd. "It was a greeting such as the Romans gave their Caesars," Hitler later told his valet. "But they did not deceive me. They are trying to soften me now because of the way they have messed up my plans."

During the talk Hitler controlled himself well to Schmidt's surprise, with not "the slightest sign of his mental gnashing of teeth." Mussolini was in exceptional good humor. Any guilt he may have felt for doing what Hitler had only given reluctant consent to had been dispelled by his own resentment over Hitler's recent dispatch of troops to Romania days after they both had promised at the Brenner Pass to preserve peace in the Balkans. "Hitler always faces me with a fait accompli," he had complained to Ciano. "This time I am going to pay him back in his own coin. He will find out from the papers that I have occupied Greece. In this way the equilibrium will be re-established."

Apparently he had succeeded, for the Führer never uttered a syllable of complaint about Greece. Instead he devoted most of his time to the problem that had brought him to Florence. He told Mussolini of the meeting with Pétain and Laval in which he had been much impressed by the dignity of the former—and had not been at all deceived by the servility of the latter. He described his talks with Franco as an ordeal and rather than go through another he would "prefer to have three or four teeth out." The Caudillo, he complained, had been "very vague" about entering the war; he must have become leader of Spain by an accident.

The long meeting ended in brotherliness with Hitler repeating the promise made at the Brenner Pass that he would "on no account conclude peace with France if the claims of Italy were not completely satisfied." On his part, Mussolini observed that their two countries were, as always, completely in accord.

The return trip through the snow-covered Alps was a morose one for the Führer. In little more than six months he had conquered more land than even the most optimistic German could have imagined. Norway, Denmark, Luxembourg, Belgium, Holland and France were his. He had outstripped Alexander and Napoleon. Yet nothing, it seems, fails like success; this incredible string of victories had been followed by frustration at Hendaye, Montoire and Florence. The mediocre leader of a second-rate country and the chief of a defeated nation were avoiding being led into the crusade against England and his own dependable ally was stupidly endangering the Axis position in the Mediterranean out of need for personal glory on the battlefield. As if that were not enough, the air campaign designed to bring England to the green table was now an admitted failure—at a frightful cost in planes.

Chapter Twenty-two

"THE WORLD WILL HOLD ITS BREATH"

NOVEMBER 12, 1940–JUNE 22, 1941

1

Although Hitler had given only reluctant support to the Tripartite Pact with Japan and Italy, he was persuaded by its father, Ribbentrop, to invite the Soviets to make it a four-power agreement. And so, on November 12, 1940, Foreign Commissar Molotov arrived in Berlin to talk of coalition. The meeting began without Hitler at Ribbentrop's new office in the former presidential palace and the host did his utmost to make the Soviet delegation feel at home, bestowing smiles on all sides. "Only at long intervals," recalled Schmidt, "did Molotov reciprocate, when a frosty smile glided over his intelligent, chess player's face." He listened impassively to Ribbentrop voice loud assurance that the Tripartite Pact was not aimed against the Soviet Union. In fact, Ribbentrop observed, Japan had already turned her face to the south and would be occupied for centuries in consolidating her territorial gains in Southeast Asia. "For her Lebensraum Germany, too, will seek expansion in a southerly direction, that is in central Africa, in the territories of the former German colonies." Everyone, he said reassuringly, was going south, as if talking of the latest fad. He suggested in his heavy-handed manner that the Soviets also head south and named the Persian Gulf and other areas in which Germany was disinterested. It was an obvious reference to India but Molotov just peered without expression through his old-fashioned pince-nez.

That afternoon Molotov listened impassively to the Führer, but when Hitler finally stopped talking complained politely that his statements had been of too general a nature. He wanted details; and began posing a succession of embarrassing questions: "Does the German-Soviet agreement of 1939 still apply to Finland? What does the New Order in Europe and Asia amount to, and what part is the U.S.S.R. to play in it? What is the position with regard to Bulgaria, Romania and Turkey; and how do matters stand with regard to the safeguarding of Russian interests in the Balkans and on the Black Sea?"

Molotov was skeptical. "If we are to be treated as equal partners and not mere dummies," he said, "we could, in principle, join the Tripartite Pact. But first the aim and object of the pact must be closely defined, and I must be more precisely informed about the boundaries of the Greater Asia area." Obviously disconcerted at being put on the defensive, Hitler abruptly ended the interrogation with the announcement that they would have to break off their discussion. "Otherwise we shall be caught by the air-raid warning."

Later Ribbentrop escorted Molotov to his own air shelter in the Wilhelmstrasse and while there took the opportunity to show Molotov a draft of the four-power treaty he so devoutly sought. It called for Germany, Russia, Japan and Italy to respect each other's natural spheres of influence and settle any dispute "in an amicable way." It defined the Soviet's "territorial aspirations" as south "in the direction of the Indian Ocean."

Molotov was not impressed. Russia, he said, was more interested in Europe and the Dardanelles than the Indian Ocean. "Consequently," he said, "paper agreements will not suffice for the Soviet Union; she would have to insist on effective guarantees of her security." He made an exhaustive list of other Soviet interests: Swedish neutrality, access to the Baltic Sea; and the fate of Romania, Hungary, Bulgaria, Yugoslavia and Greece.

Ribbentrop was so taken aback that, according to the minutes of that meeting, he could "only repeat again and again that the decisive question was whether the Soviet Union was prepared and in a position to cooperate with us in the liquidation of the British Empire." Molotov replied with sarcasm: if Germany was waging a life-and-death struggle against England as Hitler had remarked that afternoon, he could only assume this meant that Germany was fighting "for life" and England "for death." And when Ribbentrop persisted that England was beaten but didn't know it, the Russian replied, "If that is so, why are we sitting in this air-raid shelter? And whose bombs are those that are falling so close that their explosions are heard even here?"

Molotov won the argument but lost the case. When Hitler read the report of the air-shelter discussion he was galled. Convinced that the Russians were not serious about a four-power pact, he gave up the last scant hope of entente and resolved to do what he had vowed to do since 1928. At last he irrevocably decided to attack Russia.

2

On the surface relations between the two unnatural allies prospered. Within days after setting into action the invasion of Russia, code-named Barbarossa (red Beard) after Frederick I, the Holy Roman Emperor who marched east in 1190 with his legions to take the Holy Land—on January 10, 1941—Hitler authorized promulgation of two agreements with the Soviets: an economic treaty specifying reciprocal deliveries of commodities; and a secret protocol in which Germany renounced its previous claim to a strip of Lithuanian territory for 7,500,000 gold dollars.

Behind the façade of amity, however, dissension increased between the trade delegations. The flow of raw materials from the Soviet Union was steady and on schedule, while German deliveries were painfully slow and erratic.

Stalin became involved in the argument over German deliveries but he always restrained his own negotiators. He was determined to maintain good relations with his obstreperous ally for as long as possible. While he was striving for peace—at least until the Red Army was brought up to fighting strength—Hitler continued to prepare his people for war and the New Order. He did so in an ominously oblique manner in his annual January 30 address at the Sportpalast. After a rousing introductory speech by Goebbels, he strode rigidly to the platform, raising an arm diffidently in the party salute, amidst wild cheers. He stood silent for a moment and then began speaking. "His voice," recalled Shirer's replacement at CBS, "was first a slow, low rumble." Then, with sudden vehemence, his arms began sweeping in wide gestures.

He could have been thinking of Barbarossa and the racial cleansing that would follow when he said, "I am convinced that 1941 will be the crucial year of the great New Order in Europe," but the enemy he attacked was Britain, leader of the "pluto-democracies," which, he charged, were under the control of an international Jewish clique and supported by dissident émigrés. These words provided cover for his attack on the Soviet Union while preparing his own people for the final assault on Jewry and, upon hearing Halder's report four days later that German troop strength would be equal to Russia's and far superior in quality, Hitler exclaimed, "When Barbarossa commences the world will hold its breath and make no comment!" His vision of conquest, in fact, soared beyond the limits of his own continent; on February 17 he ordered preparation of a drive to the heart of Britain's empire, India. This would be accompanied by seizure of the Near East in a pincer movement: on the left from Russia across Iran and on the right from North Africa toward the Suez Canal. While these grandiose plans were primarily designed to force Britain onto the side of Germany, they indicated the extent of Hitler's vaulting aspirations. Russia was as good as won and his restless mind was already seeking new worlds to conquer, new enemies, America and Roosevelt in particular, to bring to heel.

For a dreamer Hitler could, quite often, be practical. No sooner had he envisaged vast fields of conquest than he began devoting himself to a relatively modest one. The defeat of Italian troops in Albania and Greece had, in his own words, indirectly "struck a blow at the belief of our invincibility, that was held by friend and foe alike." Greece, therefore, had to be occupied and order re-established throughout the area before Barbarossa could safely be launched. This was not his sole motivation. Hitler also looked upon Italian failure in the Balkans as a golden opportunity to gain more territory and economic assets.

The occupation of Greece, no simple matter, was particularly complicated by geography. Four countries lay between Hitler and his target—Hungary, Romania, Bulgaria and Yugoslavia. The first two, virtual German satellites, had been invested by his troops for some months; and the third, under considerable pressure, had joined the Tripartite Pact on the first of March. While this gave German troops a clear road to Greece, strategic Yugoslavia remained a military as well as political concern. Its leaders wanted neither German nor Russian intervention in the Balkans and, after veiled threats and vague promises failed to bring them into the Axis, Hitler invited Prince Paul, the Yugoslav Regent, to the Berghof so that he could exert his personal influence.

Tempted as he was by Hitler's promise to guarantee Yugoslavia territorial integrity, Prince Paul protested that the decision was most difficult for personal reasons: his wife's Greek ancestry, her personal sympathies for England and his own antagonism toward Mussolini. The Prince left without giving an answer but three days later—an interminable wait for Hitler—he replied that he was willing to sign the Tripartite Pact, provided Yugoslavia was not required to lend any military assistance or allow passage of German troops through its territory. This was unsatisfactory but Hitler, controlling his feelings, sent back word that Germany accepted these conditions. This conciliatory offer unexpectedly brought a rebuff. The Yugoslavs could do nothing that might involve them in a war, "possibly with America or even Russia."

By mid-March it was evident that the Yugoslav government would not yield and the strain on the Führer was visible as he spoke on the sixteenth at the Memorial Day ceremony in the Berlin War Museum. "His face was drawn and haggard," recalled the American journalist Louis Lochner, "his skin was ashy gray, his eyes devoid of their usual luster. Care and worry was stamped on him. But that was not the most striking thing. What amazed me was the matter of fact, uninterested, detached way in which he rattled off his usual platitudes appropriate to such an occasion." He read the brief speech as though it bored him, making no attempt to rouse the millions listening to him over the radio.

The next day the situation in Yugoslavia changed with dramatic suddenness. The Crown Council agreed to sign the Tripartite Pact. This brought a public outcry of indignation and, after three ministers resigned in protest, high-ranking air force officers led a revolt. By dawn of March 27 the rebels had overthrown the government and the youthful heir to the throne, Peter, was King.

In Berlin that morning, Hitler was congratulating himself on the happy conclusion of the Yugoslav problem; he had just received a message that the local population had been "universally most impressed" by Yugoslavia's acceptance of the new pact and that the government was "entirely master of the situation." Five minutes before noon, a telegram arrived from

Belgrade. When Hitler read that the former members of the Yugoslav government were reportedly under arrest, he first thought it was a joke. Then he was seized with indignation. To be robbed of victory at the last moment was insupportable. This time his rage was genuine. He felt he'd been "personally insulted." He shouted an order for military commanders to report at once to the chancellery, then burst into the conference room where Jodl and Keitel were waiting for the daily briefing. Brandishing the telegram, Hitler exclaimed that he was now going to smash Yugoslavia once and for all!

Like a lover spurned moments after being accepted, the more he talked the angrier and more excited he became. He vowed he would issue orders for immediate, simultaneous attacks from north and east. Keitel protested that such an ambitious operation was impossible. The Barbarossa deadline could not be postponed since troop movements were already proceeding according to their planned maximum railway-capacity program. Furthermore, Field Marshal Sigmund List's army in Bulgaria was too weak to pit against Yugoslavia and only a fool would rely on help from the Hungarians.

"That is the very reason why I have called in Brauchitsch and Halder," said Hitler. They would have to find some solution. "Now I intend to make a clean sweep of the Balkans—it is time people got to know me better."

By ones and twos, Brauchitsch, Halder, Göring, Ribbentrop and their adjutants joined the meeting. All listened in awe as Hitler declared in a harsh and vengeful tone that he was determined "to smash Yugoslavia militarily and as a state."

3

Athough Hitler blamed the delay of Barbarossa on the Yugoslav campaign, the general shortage of equipment for the Wehrmacht—his responsibility—could have been a more determining factor. In any event, he did not regard the postponement as a calamity despite a gnawing dread: "I was haunted by the obsession that the Russians might take the offensive." He did not seem perturbed when he summoned his field commanders to the chancellery to announce a definite date of attack and, more important, deliver a doctrinal lecture on the coming "struggle of two opposing ideologies." By 11 A.M. March 30 the senior commanders for Barbarossa, along with their leading staff officers, were gathered in the small cabinet chamber where a speaker's lectern had been set up. More than two hundred were seated in long rows according to rank and seniority by the time Hitler entered from the rear. With a shuffling of chairs the assemblage smartly rose, then sat down once Hitler stepped to the rostrum. His mood was grave as he spoke of the military and political situation. The United States could not reach the peak of production and military power for four years. Consequently this was the time to clean up Europe. War with Russia was inevitable, he said, and merely to sit back and wait would be disastrous. The attack would begin on June 22.

It could not be postponed, he said, since no successor would ever again exercise sufficient authority to accept responsibility for unleashing it. He and he alone could stop the Bolshevik steamroller before all Europe succumbed to it. He called for the destruction of the Bolshevik state and the annihilation of the Red Army, adding an assurance that victory would be quick and overwhelming. The only problem, he added ominously, was how to deal with the conquered Russians, how to treat prisoners of war and non-combatants.

The military sat stiff in their chairs, wondering if they would be called upon to take part in this program. As military professionals most of them had been repelled by Hitler's ruthless measures, after the conquest of Poland, against Polish Jews, intelligentsia, clergy and nobility. Their fears were quickened by Hitler's next loud threat: "The war against Russia will be such that it cannot be fought in a knightly fashion! This struggle is one of ideologies and racial differences and will have to be conducted with unprecedented, merciless and unrelenting harshness." There was no utterance of protest, any more than there had been in Poland, not even an involuntary gesture of protest.

That morning Hitler had put his military leaders to the final humiliating test with his demand that they compromise their honor as warriors. Now they, like so many in Germany who shared his fear and hatred of Jews and Slavs, were reluctant partners in his crusade. Today Lebensraum, which they considered just recompense for the Russian territories won in battle but lost at Versailles, had been relegated to the background and Hitler's real grounds for invasion lay exposed: annihilation of Bolshevism—that is, annihilation of the Jews.

In the meantime preparations for the Yugoslav-Greek invasions were brought to a conclusion. In Belgrade there were daily patriotic demonstrations, some instigated by local Communists carrying out Soviet Balkan policy. Russia, in fact, was so eager to bolster the Yugoslavs against German incursion that she signed a pact with the new government on April 5. This did not daunt Hitler. The following dawn German troops crossed the Yugoslav border in overwhelming force. Bombers began systematically destroying Belgrade in an operation to which Hitler had given a significant code name, Punishment. The Soviet leaders, their signature hardly dry on the treaty with Yugoslavia, reacted with striking indifference, relegating the attack on Yugoslavia and Greece to the back pages of *Pravda*. Mere passing mention was made of the devastating air raids on Belgrade which were continuing around the clock.

Hitler warned Goebbels that the entire campaign would take at least two months and this information was passed on to the people. It was based on a gross overestimation of enemy strength. Within a single week German and Hungarian troops marched into a shattered Belgrade which was little more than rubble. In the process of Punishment, 17,000 civilians had died. On the seventeenth the remnants of the Yugoslav army surrendered. Ten days later the Grecian campaign was virtually concluded when German tanks rumbled into Athens. Twenty-nine German divisions had been transported into the battle zones over primitive roads and rail systems at an extravagant cost of energy, fuel and time. Of this huge force, only ten divisions saw action for more than six days. A sledge hammer had been used to kill mosquitoes. It was this shocking failure of German intelligence which was more responsible for the delay of Barbarossa than Mussolini.

Hitler's dismay at the cost of the Balkan invasion was more than mitigated by a startling development in North Africa. With only three divisions at his disposal, General Erwin Rommel burst across Cyrenaica to within a few miles of Egypt. This triumph, which surprised Hitler as much as the enemy, compromised Britain's hold on the entire eastern Mediterranean. It also damaged British prestige and persuaded Stalin to maintain good relations with the Germans despite provocations. Besides shutting his eyes to their aggressions in the Balkans, the Soviet leader persistently ignored the growing rumors that Hitler was planning to invade his own country.

For months the Soviet intelligence service itself had been predicting the attack. But Stalin did not trust his own informants and his paranoia increased with the volume of reports. Convinced that Hitler would not be stupid enough to attack Russia without first neutralizing England, he imagined these were rumors manufactured by the capitalist West, which hoped to come between him and Hitler. He wrote in red ink on one alarming report from a Czech agent: "This information is a British provocation. Find out where it comes from and punish the culprit."

Stalin was spurred to action by the emergency landing of a German plane almost a hundred miles inside the Soviet Union; aboard were found a camera, unexposed rolls of film and a torn topographical map of the districts of the U.S.S.R. The Soviets lodged a formal complaint with Berlin, adding that eighty other violations of Soviet air space had occurred since the end of March. Still it was a mild protest and Stalin persisted in ignoring a new flood of warnings, the latest from British Ambassador Sir Stafford Cripps, who predicted Hitler would attack on June 22.

While everyone in the German Foreign Office suspected an attack on Russia might be imminent, it was not until now that Hitler told Ribbentrop of Barbarossa. The unhappy Foreign Minister "wanted to try one more diplomatic approach to Moscow but Hitler refused to allow any further démarche." He forbade Ribbentrop to discuss the matter with anyone, and then assured Ambassador von der Schulenburg in Moscow: "I do not intend a war against Russia." Two days later Hitler again confirmed the attack date, the one Cripps had mentioned, June 22.

There was no doubt that Germany was entering this contest with the most powerful armed force in the world. Yet she had no valid ally. Japan was on the other side of the world; Italy was a liability; Spain was intransigent; and Vichy France was unreliable. Hitler's alliances had been diminished by victory. His easy conquests had made all his friends—including little ones like Yugoslavia, Hungary and Romania—uneasy. His only strength was the Wehrmacht and reliance on force was fatal for any conqueror. Wars are won by politics, not by arms. Napoleon had learned this hard lesson from the British, who had a tradition of losing battles and winning wars. They had lost the battle against Hitler on the Continent but had already won the battle for their dominions and the battle for American aid.

Hitler's only chance for victory in the East was an alliance with those millions in the Soviet Union who hated Stalin but, unless he followed the advice to treat them liberally, he would not only lose his last chance for a genuine Grand Alliance but turn potential allies into relentless enemies.

4

Although Hitler's military leaders had first been appalled by the thought of invading Russia, they now almost universally shared his conviction that victory would come quickly. The consensus was that the campaign would be successfully completed within three months and Field Marshal von Brauchitsch had just drastically reduced this estimate. After "up to four weeks" of major battle, he predicted, the war would degenerate into a mopping-up operation against "minor resistance." The hard-headed Jodl concurred and curtly silenced Warlimont who questioned the categorical statement that "the Russian colossus will be proved to be a pig's bladder; prick it and it will burst."

The Führer, according to General Guderian, "had succeeded in infecting his immediate military entourage with his own baseless optimism. The OKW and OKH were so serenely confident of victory before winter set in that winter clothing had only been prepared for every fifth man in the army." There were, of course, a few dissidents in high places. From the beginning Ribbentrop and Admiral Raeder openly opposed Barbarossa. Keitel, too, had serious reservations but he had learned to keep any objections to himself. There was also opposition within Hitler's inner circle. Rudolf Hess—second in line after Göring to succeed the Führer—heartily approved the theory of Lebensraum but opposed attacking Russia so long as the war with England continued. The Bolsheviks alone, he confided to Schwerin von Krosigk, were profiting by this unfortunate conflict. Determined to resolve the question of how to neutralize Britain, he had met with Professor Karl Haushofer, the geopolitician, in the Grunewald Forest the previous summer. Until two in the morning they discussed the best means of negotiating a peace. Haushofer suggested a secret rendezvous with some prominent Englishman in a neutral city. From this modest beginning sprang an adventure that would intrigue the world.

Excited by the prospect of a secret mission, Hess took the plan to Hitler, hoping perhaps that this would restore his own waning influence. Despite Hess's lofty rank, Hitler had not taken him seriously for over a year. "I hope he never becomes my successor," he reportedly told Hanfstaengl. "I wouldn't know whom to be more sorry for, Hess or the party." But his affection for "*mein Hesserl*," his second Kubizek, had not diminished and he gave the Deputy Führer grudging approval to make inquiries through Albrecht Haushofer, the professor's elder son, who worked in the Foreign Office.

Young Haushofer, a member of the Resistance for several years, diffidently suggested to Hess that the best possibility would be a meeting with his own closest English friend, the Duke of Hamilton, since he had ready access to Churchill and the King. Hess left the meeting with enthusiasm but Albrecht wrote his father that "the whole thing is a fool's errand." At the same time he decided to do what he could, as a patriotic German, to make peace with England. He wrote the Duke of Hamilton proposing a meeting with Hess in Lisbon. He signed the message "A" and sent it, via Hess's brother, to a Mrs. V. Roberts in Lisbon. She transmitted it to England but the letter was intercepted by the British censor. He turned it over to the Secret Service, which eventually instructed RAF intelligence to take appropriate action. So much time had passed by then that Hess decided to act on his own without the knowledge of the Haushofers or Hitler. His plan was to embark on the mission himself, doing so in a dramatic manner that would strike the English as a sporting gesture. He would fly over the estate of the Duke of Hamilton, land by parachute and secretly conduct negotiations under a false name. He was an expert flier, a flight officer in the First World War, the winner in 1934 of the hazardous air race around the Zugspitze, Germany's highest peak, near Garmisch. A solo flight over enemy lines to a remote area of Scotland would surely appeal to young Hamilton, the first to fly over Mount Everest. "I was confronted by a very hard decision," Hess later told interrogators. "I do not think I could have arrived at my final choice unless I had continually kept before my eyes the vision of an endless line of children's coffins with weeping mothers behind them, both English and German; and another line of coffins of mothers with mourning children."

Hess's woolly scheme was organized and prepared with exquisite efficiency. He persuaded Willy Messerschmitt, the aeronautical engineer, to let him borrow an ME-110 two-man plane for practice flights, then criticized its limited range. It should, he said, have two auxiliary tanks of 700 liters fitted on each wing. After reluctantly making this change, Messerschmitt was talked into adding special radio equipment. Then came training under the excuse of recreation, and after twenty flights Hess felt he had mastered the modified plane. Hess rose early on the morning of May 10, a Saturday, and, upon learning that the weather forecast was good, he made arrangements for the flight. Never had he been more gallant to his wife. After tea he kissed her hand and then stood gravely at the door of the nursery "with an air of one deep in thought and almost hesitating." She asked him when he was returning and, told it would be Monday at the latest, she bluntly said, "I cannot believe it. You will not come back as soon as that!" She guessed he was bound for a meeting with someone like Pétain but he feared that she had guessed the truth. He "turned hot and cold in turns" and, before she could say anything more, he dashed into the nursery to take a last look at their slumbering son.

At 6 P.M., after giving his adjutant a letter for Hitler, Hess took off from the Augsburg airport and headed for the North Sea. Abruptly, contrary to the weather report, the cloud cover vanished and for a moment he thought of turning back. But he kept going and found England covered by a veil of mist. Seeking shelter, he dived down with full throttle, at first unaware that a Spitfire was on his tail. Outdistancing the pursuer, he hedgehopped over the dark countryside at more than 450 miles an hour, narrowly skimming trees and houses. Baur had always claimed Hess was the type of pilot who liked to fly through open hangar doors and it was in this barnstormer's spirit that he aimed at the mountain looming ahead. It was his guidepost and he literally climbed up the steep slope and slid down the other side, always keeping within a few yards of the ground. Just before 11 P.M. he turned east and picked out a railway and small lake which he remembered were just south of the duke's residence. He climbed to 6000 feet, a safe height from which to parachute, and switched off the motor. He opened the hatch—then suddenly realized he had overlooked one step in his elaborate training: "I had never asked how to jump; I thought it was too simple!" As the ME-110 plummeted, he recalled a friend mentioning that a plane should be on its back. After a half roll, he found himself upside down, held inside by centrifugal force. He began to see stars; just before passing out, he thought: "Soon the crash must come!" Regaining consciousness, he saw the speed gauge indicate zero. He flung himself out of the plane, pulled at the parachute ring. Fortunately, while unconscious, he had automatically brought the plane out of its semi-looping curve to finish almost perpendicular on its tail. And so, to his amazement, he found himself safely in mid-air.

He hit the ground, stumbled forward and blacked out a second time. He was found by a farmer, marched off to the Home Guard and brought to a barracks in Glasgow. Insisting that he was one Oberleutnant Alfred Horn, he asked to see the Duke of Hamilton.

It was not until Sunday morning that his letter was delivered to Hitler at the Berghof. Hitler put on his glasses and began to read indifferently but as soon as he saw the words "My Fuhrer, when you receive this letter I shall be in England" he dropped into a chair and shouted so loudly he could be heard downstairs: "Oh, my God, my God! He has flown to England!" He hastily read of the technical difficulties of the flight and that Hess's goal was to further the Führer's own aim of alliance with England but he had kept the flight secret since he knew the Führer would have forbidden it.

> And if, my Führer, this project—which I admit has but very little chance of success—ends in failure and the fates decide against me, this can have no detrimental results either for you or for Germany; it will always be possible for you to deny all responsibility. Simply say I am crazy.

Chalk white, the Führer ordered Engel to get the Reichsmarschall on the phone. As soon as he was located near Nuremberg, Hitler shouted, "Göring, come here immediately!" He yelled at Albert Bormann to fetch his brother and Ribbentrop, placed Hess's hapless adjutant under arrest, and began pacing the room angrily. When Martin Bormann arrived out of breath, Hitler demanded to know if Hess could possibly reach England in an ME-110. The question was answered by the famous ace of the Great War, Luftwaffe General Udet. Never, he said, not with its limited range. And the Führer muttered, "I hope he falls into the sea!"

No announcement came from England even though Hess, admitting his true identity to the Duke of Hamilton, told about his mission of peace and how he and Albrecht Haushofer had tried to arrange a meeting in Lisbon. Hamilton rushed off to see Churchill, who said, "Well, Hess or no Hess, I am going to see the Marx brothers." Only after the film ended did the Prime Minister interrogate Hamilton thoroughly.

A few hours after the Germans announced that Hess was missing, the British finally revealed that he had arrived in England. No details were released. Goebbels flew to Berchtesgaden to attend an emergency convocation of Gauleiters and Reichsleiters. After Bormann had read aloud the Hess letter, the Führer appeared. Hans Frank had not seen him for some time and was shocked at his "disturbed appearance." At first he spoke about Hess "very softly, hesitatingly and with a deep sense of melancholy," but soon his tone changed to one of anger. The flight, he said, was sheer insanity. "Hess is first of all a deserter and if I ever catch him, he will pay for this as any ordinary traitor. Furthermore, it seems to me that this step was strongly influenced by astrological cliques which Hess kept around him. It is time, therefore, to put an end to all these stargazers. Because of this insanity our position is made much more difficult though not shaken, particularly my belief that the victory in this Jewish war against National Socialism belongs to our unblemished flag." His listeners had already heard stories of Hess's pet lion, as well as his interest in homeopathic medicine and astrology, and were prepared to believe he was mentally disturbed. Yet they wondered, as ordinary citizens did, why then had Hitler retained him in high office?

In England the government had decided not to make public the interrogations of Hess; it would be best to keep the Nazis guessing. Hess was transported secretly to the Tower of London during the night of May 16 to become the world's most famous prisoner of war.

Stalin was far more perturbed by the Hess flight than Mussolini who, according to his son-in-law, was "glad of it because this will have the effect of bringing down German stock, even with the Italians." Those in the Kremlin, particularly in light of the invasion rumors, suspected the British were really intriguing with Hitler. New regulations were imposed. Travel outside of Moscow by foreigners was forbidden except in rare cases.

Irate as he was, Hitler confided to several intimates that he respected Hess for his willingness to sacrifice himself on such a dangerous mission. On reflection he realized that his deputy had made the hazardous flight for him. Hitler did not believe that Hess was mad, only foolish not to have seen what a disastrous political mistake he was making.

As for Hess, it was enough that he had done his utmost. He was glad, he wrote his wife from the Tower of London, that he had been impelled to fly to England, an urge which he described as "the obstinate dragon" that would not let him go. "True, I achieved nothing. I was not able to stop the madness of the war and could not prevent what I saw coming. I could not save the people but it makes me happy to think that I tried to do it."*

5

The day after learning about Hess, Hitler issued two repressive decrees. One declared that Russian civilians taking arms against the Wehrmacht in the coming invasion should be considered outlaws and shot without trial. The other empowered Himmler to carry out "special tasks which result from the struggle which has to be carried out between two opposing political systems." He was to act independently of the Wehrmacht "under his own responsibility." There would be no interference from any source and "the highest personalities of the government and party" were to be forbidden entrance into the occupied Russian areas which would be "cleansed" of Jews and other troublemakers by special SS units of assassins known as *Einsatzgruppen* (Special Action Groups).

Both directives troubled Alfred Rosenberg, who had recently been appointed Commissioner for the Central Control of Questions Connected with the East European Region. A Balt himself, he believed the Soviet people should be treated as anti-Stalinists rather than as enemies of the Reich. He assured Hitler that they would welcome the Germans as liberators from Bolshevik-Stalinist tyranny and could be trusted with a certain amount of self-rule. Each state would have to be treated differently. The Ukraine, for instance, would be "an independent state in alliance with Germany" but Caucasia must be ruled by a German "plenipotentiary."

*As a reward Hess has already served almost forty years of solitary confinement. He remains the last Allied prisoner at Spandau prison. In all those years he has been separated from visitors by a wide table. Never has he been allowed to embrace or kiss a loved one.

Convinced that a heavy-handed policy in the East would destroy the spirit of Lebensraum, Rosenberg submitted a memorandum to Hitler objecting to the two directives. How could one possibly build a civil administration in the occupied areas without using the Soviet civil commissars and officials now administering them? He recommended that "only senior and very senior officials" should be "liquidated." Hitler gave no definite answer. Characteristically, he was content to take no active part in the power struggle between Himmler and Rosenberg that would surely begin once the Wehrmacht advanced into the Soviet Union. Bormann, the rising star in the National Socialist hierarchy, would be a decisive factor in this contest. He had already joined forces with Himmler.

In the meantime, final preparations for Barbarossa continued. Admiral Raeder informed Hitler on May 22 that he would cease delivering important materials to Russia. Comparatively few shipments had, in fact, been sent to the Soviet Union, while many had come from the East. In addition to almost 1,500,000 tons of grain, the Soviets had delivered 100,000 tons of cotton, 2,000,000 tons of petroleum products, 1,500,000 tons of timber, 140,000 tons of manganese and 25,000 tons of chromium. Despite suspicions over the Hess flight, Stalin was still so eager to appease Hitler that he authorized further shipments by express trains from the Far East of other important raw materials, such as copper.

Barbarossa was in motion and nothing short of catastrophe could postpone it. Hitler's greatest concern was security. Haunted by the mishap in Belgium a year earlier, he still had not informed Mussolini of the invasion. When he met his senior ally at the Brenner Pass on June 2, he talked at length of his determination to force British capitulation (this time by U-boats), of Hess, and of the situation in the Balkans. Not a word did he utter about Barbarossa, not only for the sake of secrecy but because Il Duce had already cautioned him in explicit terms not to attack Russia, which had become "a running sore" to Germany.

The roads and rail lines leading east were dense with traffic as the final phase of preparations for Barbarossa began. On June 6 Hitler summoned Japanese Ambassador Oshima to Berchtesgaden and revealed that large numbers of troops were being sent east because of Soviet border violations. "Under such circumstances," he concluded with a confidence that impressed his listener, "war might be unavoidable between us." To Oshima this was tantamount to a declaration of war and he immediately warned Tokyo that an invasion of Russia was imminent.

It was a significant day for the Führer. He legalized his threat to wage ruthless ideological warfare by instructing Field Marshal von Brauchitsch to issue a directive to liquidate captured Soviet commissars as bearers of an ideology diametrically opposed to National Socialism. His commander-in-chief objected violently until Hitler curtly said, "I cannot demand that my generals should understand my orders, but I do demand that they follow them." The terms of this directive could not be misinterpreted. "These commissars are the originators of barbarous, Asiatic methods of warfare, and they must therefore be treated with all possible severity and dispatch. . . . Whether captured during battle or while offering resistance, they must be shot at once." This ideologically motivated order was to be executed by the Wehrmacht together with Himmler's Einsatzgruppen and its issuance by OKW was more than another victory for Hitler over the military. It bound them to his political program and made them unwilling accomplices, along with the SS, in his grand plan of the future.

To achieve this goal he must first conquer the Red Army and to do this he needed the help of those states bordering the Soviet Union that could be trusted—and that, sharing his own fear and hatred of Bolshevism, had accounts of their own to settle with Stalin. The Finns, forced to accept harsh terms to end their brief, bloody war with Russia, needed little urging to join the crusade; and on June 8 the first elements of a German infantry division landed in Finland. Two days later Field Marshal Mannerheim ordered a partial mobilization. Hitler also trusted Romania and on June 11 he intimated to General Ion Antonescu that he had decided to attack Russia. He was by no means asking Antonescu for assistance in such a war, he said, and "merely expected of Romania that in her own interest she do everything to facilitate a successful conclusion of this conflict." Stirred by visions of spoils and military glory, the Romanian dictator hastily declared that he wanted to be in on the fight from the first day.

6

On June 14 Soviet secret agent Sorge dispatched a definite warning from Tokyo: "War begins June 22." But Stalin still chose not to credit this or similar alarums. He had reassured himself, despite qualms, that the war could not possibly start until 1942 and that very day ordered publication of a Tass communiqué ridiculing the numerous rumors of war: "All this is nothing but clumsy propaganda by forces hostile to the U.S.S.R. and Germany and interested in an extension of the war." This statement was so reassuring that there was an easing of tension in the forward positions of the Red Army.

In Berlin selected combat officers were arriving at the chancellery for a special briefing and luncheon. By now each one had digested his own orders and become reconciled (if grudgingly) to the inhumane methods Hitler had imposed on the enemy. At 2 P.M. there was a break for lunch and this, unlike so many other meals at the chancellery, was mellow and relaxed. Nor was the atmosphere of camaraderie dispelled when Hitler ascended to the podium and began a persuasive lecture on the need to launch Barbarossa. The collapse of Russia, he said, would lead to England's surrender.

A final signal went out on June 17 confirming 3 A.M., Sunday, June 22, as zero hour. That day a German sergeant, who had struck an officer and feared execution, crossed into Soviet lines to surrender. He revealed that the German attack would begin before dawn on the twenty-second. Front-line officers who learned of the report were disturbed but their commanding general's reaction was: "No use beating an alarm."

As zero hour approached, Hitler appeared calm and confident. On Friday the twentieth he sent for Frank—formerly his personal lawyer and now governor general of German-occupied Poland. "We are facing a war with the Soviet Union," he said and, when the other reacted with consternation, added, "Calm yourself." He promised that the German attack units would soon pass through Frank's area and then waved off his attempt to make another objection. "I understand your problem very well. But I must insist that you come to an understanding with Himmler." He was referring to their conflicting concepts of treating the occupied areas. "I can tolerate no more differences;

you two must come to an understanding." That evening Hitler's proclamation to the troops was secretly distributed and, under cover of darkness, assault units began moving forward. By dawn of the twenty-first more than three million men were in attack position.

In Moscow Molotov had just summoned German Ambassador von der Schulenburg. "There are a number of indications," he told Schulenburg, "that the German government is dissatisfied with the Soviet government. Rumors are even current that a war is impending between Germany and the Soviet Union." It was an embarrassing situation and all Schulenburg could do was promise to transmit the question to Berlin. He returned to his office as ignorant as Molotov that an attack was coming in a few hours.

One of the eastern front commanders was reading out Hitler's exhortation to the troops. "Weighed down for many months by grave anxieties, compelled to keep silent, I can at last speak openly to you, my soldiers." He told of the Russian build-up on the German frontier, of the numerous border violations. That was why they had been brought up to the "greatest front in world history" along with allies from Finland and Romania. "German soldiers! You are about to join battle, a hard and crucial battle. The destiny of Europe, and future of the German Reich, the existence of our nation now lie in your hands alone."

All along the tortuous 930-mile front, from the Baltic to the Black Sea, three million men listened and believed. With fear and expectation they huddled in their positions. It was the shortest night of the year, the summer solstice, but it seemed endless to those waiting in the pale light for the command to attack. Just before midnight the Moscow-Berlin express rumbled over the frontier bridge into German territory. It was followed by a long freight train filled with grain, the last delivery Stalin would make to his ally, Adolf Hitler.

At 3 A.M., June 22—exactly a year after the surrender of France at Compiègne—German infantrymen moved forward. Fifteen minutes later flame and smoke burst out all along the eastern front. The pale night sky was turned to day by the flash of guns. Barbarossa, long a dream, was reality. But its creator was already nagged by concern. The five-week delay caused by the Yugoslav venture loomed more ominously. Being of historic bent, perhaps Hitler recalled that on that same day in June a hundred and twenty-nine years before Napoleon had crossed the Niemen River on his way to Moscow.

* * *

In Moscow Schulenburg was en route to the Kremlin with an accusation that the Soviet Union was about to "fall on Germany's back." Consequently the Führer had ordered the Wehrmacht "to oppose this threat with all the means at its disposal." Molotov listened silently to a solemn reading of the statement, then said bitterly, "It is war. Your aircraft have just bombarded some ten open villages. Do you believe that we deserved that?"

At the Wilhelmstrasse Ribbentrop finally sent word that he would see the Russian ambassador at 4 A.M. Never before had Schmidt seen his chief so excited. Pacing up and down the room like a caged animal, Ribbentrop kept repeating, "The Führer is absolutely right to attack Russia now." It seemed, thought Schmidt, as if he were trying to reassure himself. "The Russians would certainly themselves attack us, if we did not do so now."

At exactly 4 A.M. Soviet Ambassador Dekanozov entered, right hand innocently extended. Ribbentrop interrupted his attempt to relay the Soviet grievances. "That is not the question now," he said and announced that the Soviet government's hostility had compelled the Reich to take military countermeasures. "I regret that I can say nothing further," he said, "especially as I myself have come to the conclusion that, in spite of serious endeavors, I have not succeeded in establishing reasonable relations between our two countries."

Correspondents all over Berlin were being wakened for a 6 A.M. press conference at the Foreign Office. Several heard the news en route to the Wilhelmstrasse from outdoor loudspeakers as a message from the Führer was broadcast: "People of Germany! National Socialists! The hour has come. Oppressed by grave cares, doomed to months of silence, I can at last speak frankly." He told of the machinations of Russia and England to crush the Axis with the aid of American supplies. "I therefore decided today to lay the fate and future of the German Reich in the hands of our soldiers. May God help us above all in this fight!"

Chapter Twenty-three

"A DOOR INTO A DARK, UNSEEN ROOM"

JUNE 22–DECEMBER 19, 1941

1

The Soviet Union was in disarray. Within hours the Red Air Force had admittedly lost 1200 aircraft, and infantry resistance was unco-ordinated. Refusing to believe in the gravity of first reports, Stalin ordered the Red Army to keep out of German territory and the Red Air Force to restrict raids to within ninety miles of the frontier. He was so convinced that the Nazi invasion was a mistake and he could halt the war by diplomatic means that he kept open radio communications with the Wilhelmstrasse while requesting Japan to mediate any political and economic differences between Germany and the Soviet Union.

Within twenty-four hours German public interest began to slacken. After the first rush for the newspapers, which contained only general reports from the front, the citizens returned to their normal life as if it were only another of Hitler's exploits. At 12:30 P.M. on June 23 he and his entourage left the capital in the Führer train: destination *Wolfsschanze* (Wolf's Lair), the new headquarters in a forest several miles from Rastenburg, East Prussia. Confidence in a quick victory ran high among the staff as they settled into the wooden huts and concrete bunkers but the Führer had mixed feelings. "We have only to kick in the door and the whole rotten structure will come crashing down," he told Jodl, yet shortly remarked to an aide, "At the beginning of each campaign one pushes a door into a dark, unseen room. One can never know what is hiding inside."

The early victories seemed to justify the highest hopes. Within two days hordes of prisoners were taken and bridges seized intact. There seemed to be no organized enemy resistance as German tanks burst through Soviet lines and roamed at will. There were such piercing advances, such mass surrenders—almost half a million to date—that Halder wrote in his diary on July 3, "It is no exaggeration to say that the campaign against Russia has been won in fourteen days." The Führer also told his entourage that "to all intents and purposes the Russians have lost the war." How fortunate it was, he exulted, "that we smashed the Russian armor and air force right at the beginning!" Never, he said, could the Russians replace them. Many Western military experts shared this estimate and talk in the Pentagon was that the Red Army would fold up in a month or so.

Following in the wake of the advancing troops were four SS Einsatzgruppen of 3000 men each, whose mission was to insure the security of the operational zone; that is, prevent resistance by civilians. These were police of a very special nature, given an additional task by their chief, Reinhard Heydrich. They were to round up and liquidate not only Bolshevik leaders but all Jews, as well as gypsies, "Asiatic inferiors" and "useless eaters," such as the deranged and incurably sick.

To supervise this mass killing, Heydrich and Himmler had been inspired to select officers who, for the most part, were professional men. They included a Protestant pastor, a physician, a professional opera singer and numerous lawyers. The majority were intellectuals in their early thirties and it might be supposed such men were unsuited for this work. On the contrary, they brought to the brutal task their considerable skills and training and became, despite qualms, efficient executioners.

The majority of the victims were Jews. They had no idea of Hitler's "racial cleansing" program since few German anti-Semitic atrocities were reported in the Soviet press. Consequently, many Jews welcomed the Germans as liberators and were easily trapped by the Special Units. "Contrary to the opinion of the National Socialists that the Jews were a highly organized group," testified Obergruppenführer von dem Bach-Zelewski, the senior SS and police commander for Central

Russia, the appalling fact was that they were taken completely by surprise. It gave the lie to the old anti-Semitic myth that the Jews were conspiring to dominate the world and were thus highly organized. "Never before has a people gone as unsuspectingly to its disaster. Nothing was prepared. Absolutely nothing."

The exterminations proceeded with cool calculation. It was a tidy, businesslike operation; and the reports were couched in the arid language of bureaucracy as if the executioners were dealing with cabbages, not human beings. The methodical work of the killing units was rarely marred by resistance. "Strange is the calmness with which the delinquents allow themselves to be shot," reported one commander, "and that goes for non-Jews as well as Jews. Their fear of death appears to have been blunted by a kind of indifference which has been created in the course of twenty years of Soviet rule."

Heydrich's most awkward problem was coping with the psychological effects of the exterminators. Some enlisted men had nervous breakdowns or took to drinking, and a number of the officers suffered from serious stomach and intestinal ailments. Others took to their task with excess enthusiasm and sadistically beat the prisoners in violation of Himmler's orders to exterminate as humanely as possible.

Rumors of these atrocities distressed Rosenberg, ordered by Hitler to draw up a blueprint for occupation of the conquered Eastern territories. He had envisaged a far different program with a degree of self-rule. Since the Führer had earlier agreed to establish "weak socialist states" in the conquered lands of Russia, Rosenberg optimistically assumed that Hitler approved his own plan in principle and that it would be accepted at a special conference on the subject to be held at the Wolfsschanze on July 16. "It is essential," said Hitler (according to Bormann's notes of the meeting), "that we do not proclaim our views before the whole world. There is no need for that but the main thing is that we ourselves know what we want." If this did not reveal to Rosenberg that Hitler had changed his mind about establishing "weak socialist states," what followed surely did. "This need not prevent our taking all necessary measures—shooting, resettlement, etc.—and we shall take them. . . . In principle we must now face the task of cutting up the giant cake according to our needs in order to be able: first, to dominate it; second, to administer it; third, to exploit it. The Russians have now given an order for partisan warfare behind our front. This guerrilla activity again has some advantage for us; it enables us to exterminate everyone who opposes us."

Although Rosenberg left the meeting with the title of Reich Minister of the East, it was a hollow one, for he realized his own dream of the East now had little chance to materialize. What a tragedy, he thought, that Hitler still maintained the false conception of Slavs, born during his youthful days in Vienna out of inflammatory pamphlets which described the Slavs as lazy primitives, a hopelessly second-class race. Equally disastrous was Hitler's complete misunderstanding of the structure of the Soviet Union. The Ukrainians and other tribes under the yoke of the Great Russians were potential allies of the Third Reich and could be a bulwark of defense against Bolshevism if treated properly and given a measure of self-rule. But the Führer had been persuaded by Bormann and Göring that they were enemies to be controlled by the whip. The struggle to turn Hitler from this path seemed hopeless but Rosenberg resolved to keep trying. It was a diluted resolve, for no one knew better than he that, once the Führer looked into his eyes, he would, as usual, be too frightened to speak out.

2

During these early summer days of 1941 Hitler became sick. To begin with there were recurrent stomach pains which may have been of hysterical nature. His system was already undermined by an overdose of drugs—120 to 150 anti-gas pills a week as well as ten injections of Ultraseptyl, a strong sulfonamide. Then he was struck down by dysentery—a common malady in the swampy surroundings of the Wolfsschanze. A victim of diarrhea, nausea and aching limbs, he would shiver one moment, sweat the next. A more serious threat to his health came to light during a hot argument with Ribbentrop late in July. The Foreign Minister, opposed to Barbarossa from the beginning, lost his temper and began to shout his disapproval. Hitler paled at the extraordinary attack. He tried to defend himself but halted in mid-sentence, clutched his heart and sank into a chair. There was a frightening moment of silence. "I thought I was going to have a heart attack," Hitler finally said. "You must never again oppose me in this manner!"

Dr. Morell was so perturbed he sent an electrocardiogram

of the Führer's heart to Professor Dr. Karl Weber, director of the Heart Institute at Bad Nauheim and a leading authority on heart disease. He had no idea that the patient was Hitler, only that he was "a very busy diplomat." His diagnosis was: a rapidly progressive coronary sclerosis, a virtually incurable heart disease. Morell probably did not pass this information on to Hitler; at least once announcing in his presence that the Führer's heart was in good shape. Morell did add a number of other medicines to his patient's growing list of prescriptions: a heart tonic, Cardiazol (a quite harmless solution for circulatory weakness, fainting and exhaustion) and Sympathol 3, one per cent as efficacious as adrenalin.

Hitler's illness came at the height of a bitter conflict with his commanders on the conduct of the campaign in the East. He had already ordered the direct attack on Moscow halted; he stripped Army Group Center of its most powerful armored units, one being sent north to facilitate the capture of Leningrad, the other south to bolster the drive into the Ukraine. Both these areas, in Hitler's opinion, superseded Moscow in importance; the first because it was a key industrial center (and was named after Lenin), and the second because of its economic importance. Not only was the Ukraine vital for its industry and grain but the Crimea itself was a potential Soviet aircraft carrier for the bombing of the Ploesti oilfields in Romania. Further, once the Crimea was occupied, the Wehrmacht would have easy access to the Caucasus.

Hitler's sick spell gave Brauchitsch and Halder the chance to sabotage the Führer's strategy. Quietly they began trying to put their own plan into operation, with Halder exerting his personal influence on Jodl to gain his support. It was not until Hitler was on the road to recovery in mid-August that he fully realized what had been going on behind his back: neither his own strategy nor that of Halder had been put into effect but a compromise of both. To clarify the situation, Hitler composed an order on August 21 that could not possibly be misunderstood: "The most important objective to be reached by winter is not Moscow, but the Crimea." The attack on Moscow could not begin until Leningrad had been isolated and the Russian Fifth Army in the south destroyed. This order was followed a few hours later by a lengthy memorandum, dictated in anger and read with indignation. Little better than a stern lecture on how to wage a campaign, it charged that unnamed commanders were driven by "selfish desires" and "despotic dispositions," then characterized the army high command as a gathering of minds "fossilized in out-of-date theories."

3

This minor crisis was soon overshadowed by the highly publicized visit of Mussolini to the front. He was coming to persuade Hitler to enlarge the Italian Expeditionary Force on the Russian front and so share some of the glory of crushing Communism. But as his special train approached Wolfsschanze Il Duce was in poor condition to match wits with his ally; he was still pale and grieving over the recent loss of his son Bruno in an air crash.

Hitler met Mussolini at the little railroad station near the Wolfsschanze and for the rest of the day scarcely gave him a chance to open his mouth. The Führer talked incessantly of the forthcoming victory in the East, the stupidity of France and the civil machinations of the Jewish clique that surrounded Roosevelt. When his guest finally managed to make his offer of more troops Hitler changed the subject.

On the long rail trip back home Mussolini was dejected. He had not only failed to get approval for a large Italian contingent but had gained the uneasy feeling that the war in the East would be a lengthy and bloody one.

At the Wolfsschanze Hitler changed his mind and decided it was now time to launch the attack on Moscow. During tea in the casino with his secretaries and aides, he stared fixedly at a large map on the wall. "In several weeks we will be in Moscow," he said in a deep, rough voice. "There is no doubt of it. I will raze that damned city and I will construct in its place an artificial lake with central lighting. The name of Moscow will disappear forever." And so on the afternoon of September 5 he told Halder, "Get started on the central front within eight to ten days." His mood at supper that night was light, almost frolicsome. His comments were noted down by Werner Koeppen, Rosenberg's liaison man at Führer Headquarters. Since early July that year, at Rosenberg's behest, he had been circumspectly recording the Führer's table conversations. Koeppen assumed Hitler knew what he was doing and would furtively jot down notes on his paper napkin, then immediately after the meal write out only those parts of the conversation he could distinctly remember. An original and one copy of his records were forwarded to Berlin by courier.

Unbeknown to Koeppen, there was a second Boswell at the main table. Shortly after their arrival at Wolfsschanze, Bormann had suggested almost offhandedly to Heinrich Heim, his adjutant, that he surreptitiously note down what the Chief said. So Hitler wouldn't know he was being put on record, Bormann instructed his adjutant to rely on his memory. But Heim wanted more accurate results and on his own initiative he began making copious notes on index cards which he hid on his lap. Bormann was taken aback but he gave Heim tacit approval to continue taking notes.*

The records of Heim and Koeppen gave rare insight into the momentous events unfolding each day on the eastern front. On September 17, for instance, Hitler expounded on the spirit of decision, which consisted, he said, "in not hesitating when an inner conviction commands you to act. Last year I needed great spiritual strength to take the decision to attack Bolshevism. I had to foresee that Stalin might pass over to the attack in 1941. It was therefore necessary to get started without delay, in order not to be forestalled—and that wasn't possible before June. Even to make war, one must have luck on one's side. When I think of it, what luck we did have!" The tremendous military operation presently in progress, he said, had been widely criticized as impracticable. "I had to throw all my authority into the scales to force it through. I note in passing that a great part of our successes have originated in 'mistakes' we've had the audacity to commit."

He assured his fascinated listeners that the hegemony of the world would be decided by the seizure of Russian space. "Thus

*Some of these notes were later published in various editions in England, France and Germany, the last under the title *Hitler's Tischgespräche*, by Henry Picker, who deputized for Heim as court reporter from March through July 1942. Heim was never consulted by any of the publishers or given the opportunity of commenting on the notes and correcting misconceptions on their history. While the published portion of his notes sounds quite accurate, he misses many important passages. Only about one sixth of his original notes, for instance, appear in the Picker edition. Heim is positive that Hitler never knew his table talk was being recorded. After the war he was assured of this by Hitler's personal adjutant, Schaub. Heim presently lives in Munich within blocks of Koeppen but was unaware until recently that the other was also making notes. Their two accounts complement each other. Heim purposely omitted all military matters for security; Koeppen did not. The latter's notes, moreover, are valuable as corroboration of Heim's far more detailed and personalized minutes.

Europe will be an impregnable fortress, safe from all threat of blockade. All this opens up economic vistas which, one might think, will incline the most liberal of the Western democrats toward the New Order. The essential thing, for the moment, is to conquer. After that everything will be simply a question of organization." The Slavs, he said, were born slaves who felt the need of a master and Germany's role in Russia would be analogous to that of England in India. "Like the English, we shall rule this empire with a handful of men."

He talked at length of his plans to make the Ukraine the granary for all Europe and to keep its conquered people happy with scarves and glass beads, then ended in a confession: while everyone else was dreaming of a world peace conference, he preferred to wage war for another ten years rather than be cheated of the spoils of victory.

The capture of Kiev, three days later, caused elation at Wolfsschanze. It meant, predicted Hitler, the early conquest of the entire Ukraine and justified his insistence on giving priority to the southern offensive. At dinner on September 21 Hitler glowed with satisfaction as he told of the capture of 145,000 prisoners in the valley near Kiev. This battle of encirclement, he claimed, was the most confused in the entire history of warfare. The Soviet Union was on the verge of collapse.

At the noon meal on September 25 he revealed his fear of the subhuman farther east: Europe would be endangered until these Asians had been driven back behind the Urals. "They are brutes, and neither Bolshevism nor Czarism makes any difference—they are brutes in a state of nature." Late that evening he extolled the virtues of battle by comparing a soldier's first battle to a woman's first sexual encounter, as if he regarded each as an act of aggression. "In a few days a youth becomes a man. If I weren't myself hardened by this experience, I would have been incapable of undertaking this Cyclopean task which the building of an empire means for a single man." It was with feelings of pure idealism that he had set out for the front in 1914. "Then I saw men falling around me in thousands. Thus I learned that life is a struggle and has no other object but the preservation of the species."

The table talk was almost exclusively of the battle in the East, since there was little action on the only other active war front, North Africa. The British effort to throw back Rommel had failed miserably; and by the beginning of autumn there was a standoff in the desert with neither side prepared to mount another offensive. Hitler's energy and the might of the Wehrmacht were being concentrated for an all-out assault on Moscow but Field Marshal von Bock warned that it was too late in the season. Why not spend the winter in fortified positions? Hitler replied with an allegory of sorts: "Before I became Chancellor, I used to think the General Staff was like a mastiff which had to be held tight by the collar to keep it from attacking anyone in sight." But it had turned out to be anything but ferocious. It had opposed rearmament, the occupation of the Rhineland, the invasion of Austria and Czechoslovakia, and even the war in Poland. "It is I who have always had to goad on this mastiff."

He insisted upon attacking the capital in force and the operation, code-named Typhoon, was launched on the last day of September by Bock. His mission was to destroy the central Soviet forces with a fearsome aggregation of sixty-nine divisions before advancing on the capital; his basic strategy was a drive aimed at Moscow with a double tank envelopment, the pincers meeting eighty miles behind the Red Army.

The Soviet high command, unable to conceive of a major offensive started so late in the year, was caught so completely by surprise that Guderian's 2nd Panzer Group raced fifty miles in the first twenty-four hours through the Red Army ranks. German infantrymen rushed into the vacuum to mop up disintegrating pockets of resistance.

By October 2 Hitler was confident enough of victory to set off for Berlin in his special train. He had not spoken to the people for months and the next afternoon he strode into the Sportpalast purportedly to make an appeal in support of the Wartime Winter Assistance Program. But he had come to issue a major proclamation. "On the morning of June 22," he said, his words booming over loudspeakers throughout the Reich, "the greatest battle in the history of the world began." Everything had gone according to plan, he said, and then announced that the enemy was "already beaten and would never rise again!" The audience broke into wild acclaim.

He began listing the statistics of victory: 2,500,000 prisoners, 22,000 destroyed or captured artillery pieces, 18,000 destroyed or captured tanks, more than 14,500 destroyed planes. The figures rolled on: German soldiers had advanced up to 1000 kilometers ("This is as the crow flies!"), over 25,000 kilometers of Russian railway were again in operation with most of this already converted to the German narrow gauge.

For a man who had just professed that Russia was beaten and would never rise again, he entertained deep concerns. The war in the East, he admitted, was one of ideologies, therefore all the best elements in Germany must now be welded into one indissoluble community. "Only when the entire German people becomes a single community of sacrifice can we hope and expect that Providence will stand by us in the future. Almighty God never helped a lazy man. Nor does He help a coward."

Hitler's declaration that the Soviets were defeated and total victory assured was not merely propaganda to raise morale at home. He believed what he said. But he had not quite convinced his pragmatic propaganda chief. Josef Goebbels started the briefing to his subordinates on the fourteenth with optimism: "Militarily this war has already been decided. All that remains to be done is of predominantly political character both at home and abroad." Then he contradicted himself by warning that the German people must reconcile themselves to continued fighting in the East for another ten years. Therefore it was the task of the German press to help strengthen the people's "staying power" and when that was done "the rest will follow of its own accord, so that, within a very short space of time, no one will notice that no peace has been concluded at all."

If Hitler had similar reservations they were dispelled upon learning that the Soviet diplomatic corps had fled Moscow on October 15 for Kuibyshev, six hundred miles to the east. Panic was truly sweeping the city and at the Kremlin Stalin reputedly had lost his nerve. A report that two German tanks had reached a suburb caused stampedes at railway stations. High-ranking party officials and secret police joined the pell-mell flight in cars, causing the first traffic jam in Soviet history. Pedestrians stormed the stalled cars, robbing and blackmailing the occupants, particularly those thought to be Jews.

Other bands of deserters and workers were plundering stores since no police were on hand to stop them. One rumor circulated that Lenin's body had been removed from Red Square for safekeeping, another that Stalin himself had taken to his heels. A grim minority was building barricades and preparing to die rather than let a single Nazi pass, but most Moscovites were demoralized, awaiting the Germans with a strange mixture of expectancy and apathy. Many of them bought German-Russian dictionaries so they could greet the conquerors in their own language.

On the nineteenth Stalin asked the chairman of the Moscow

Soviet, "Should we defend Moscow?" and without waiting for an answer proclaimed a state of siege. Breaches of law and order were to be dealt with promptly; all spies, diversionists and agents provocateurs were to be shot without trial. With firm direction from the top, morale throughout the city began to lift.

Before Moscow, the Soviet troops stiffened and the German spearheads which had driven to within forty miles of the capital were slowed. Then came a break in the weather. The fall rains began and while the powerful German Mark IVs became mired in the muddy roads, the more maneuverable Soviet T-34 tanks rolled free. Hitler's victories of the past two years had come through the superior mobility and firepower brought about by massed Panzer attacks closely supported by tactical air forces. But the seas of mud below foundered the armor and the low visibility above grounded the Luftwaffe, which had already gained air supremacy. With mobility went firepower—and Blitzkrieg, upon which Hitler based his hopes.

To say that Typhoon was stemmed by the mud and freezing rain and the Red Army was only partially true. The principal reason for failure, so asserted most of his commanders, was Hitler's refusal to launch it a month earlier. If he had followed their advice Moscow would have been a mass of rubble and the Soviet government and its forces defeated.

In late October the sleet turned into snow and the mud froze. Conditions for the troops were almost unbearable. There were few advances along the entire line and these were modest ones. By the end of the month the situation was so desperate that Giesler, the architect, was ordered to stop work on the reconstruction of German cities. All workers, engineers, building materials and machinery were to be transported at once to the East to construct highways, repair railroad tracks and construct stations and locomotive sheds.

At meals Hitler appeared as confident as ever. On the eve of his departure for the annual celebration of the Munich Putsch he enlivened supper with jokes and reminiscences. In Moscow his admired enemy was making a speech at the annual Eve-of-Revolution Day meeting in the huge hall of the Mayakovsky subway station. It was an odd mixture of dejection and confidence. First Stalin admitted that the building of socialism had been greatly impeded by the war and that casualties on the battlefield already were almost 1,700,000. But the Nazi claim that the Soviet regime was collapsing had no basis in fact.

"Instead," he said, "the Soviet rear is today more solid than ever. It is probable that any other country, having lost as much territory as we have, would have collapsed." Admittedly Russia faced a tremendous task since the Germans were fighting with numerous allies—Finns, Romanians, Italians and Hungarians—while not a single English or American soldier was yet in position to help the Soviet Union.

He made an impassioned appeal to Russian national pride in the name of Plekhanov and Lenin, Belinsky and Chernyshevsky, Pushkin and Tolstoy, Gorki and Chekhov, Glinka and Tschaikovsky, Sechenov and Pavlov, Suvorov and Kutuzov. "The German invaders want a war of extermination against the peoples of the Soviet Union. Very well then! If they want a war of extermination, they shall have it."

Stalin was back in command and the next morning, November 7, he spoke with equal force to troops gathered in Red Square. In the distance guns boomed and overhead came the snarl of patrolling Soviet fighter planes as he compared their position with that of twenty-three years ago. How could anyone doubt that they could and must defeat the German invaders? Again he shrewdly used names of the past—the conquerors of the Teutonic Knights, the Tartars, the Poles and Napoleon—as a rallying cry. "May you be inspired by the heroic figures of our great ancestors, Alexander Nevsky, Dimitri Donskoi, Minin and Pozharsky, Alexander Suvorov, Michael Kutuzov!"

Hitler arrived in Munich the following afternoon. He made an impassioned appeal to a convocation of Reichsleiters and Gauleiters and later delivered a speech at the Löwenbräukeller which included a warning to President Roosevelt that if an American ship shot at a German vessel "it will do so at its own risk." His threatening words did not have Stalin's forceful ring. In fact, he was depressed by the stalemate on the eastern front and the next day reminded his staff what had befallen Napoleon's army in Russia. "The recognition that neither force is capable of annihilating the other," he predicted, "will lead to a compromise peace."

But Marshal von Bock argued against such pessimism. He urged that their offensive be continued. So did Brauchitsch and Halder. On November 12 the latter was the picture of optimism as he announced that in his opinion the Russians were on the verge of collapse. Hitler was impressed and three days later the push for Moscow resumed.

At first the weather was good but soon ice, mud and snow

began taking control of the battlefield. The cold intensified, provoking bitter denunciation of Hitler's earlier edict prohibiting the preparation of winter clothing. On November 21 Guderian phoned Halder to say that his troops had reached the end of their endurance. He was going to visit Bock and request that the orders he had just received be changed since he could "see no way of carrying them out." But the marshal, under direct pressure from the Führer, would not listen to Guderian's pleas and ordered the attack on Moscow resumed. After short, spasmodic advances the drive once more faltered. Taking over personal direction from an advanced command post, Bock called for another assault on November 24 despite a brewing storm. The attack was halted by snow, ice and fanatic Soviet resistance.

Frustration in the center was compounded five days later by a crisis in the south. Field Marshal von Rundstedt was forced to evacuate Rostov, the gate to the Caucasus, captured only a week previously. Angered by this thirty-mile retreat, Hitler telegraphed Rundstedt to remain where he was. The marshal immediately wired back:

> IT IS MADNESS TO ATTEMPT TO HOLD. FIRST THE TROOPS CANNOT DO IT AND SECOND IF THEY DO NOT RETREAT THEY WILL BE DESTROYED. I REPEAT THAT THIS ORDER MUST BE RESCINDED OR THAT YOU FIND SOMEONE ELSE.

The message was drafted by a subordinate, except for the last sentence, which Rundstedt added in his own hand. It was these final words that infuriated Hitler and, without consulting the commander-in-chief of the army, he replied that same night:

> I AM ACCEDING TO YOUR REQUEST. PLEASE GIVE UP YOUR COMMAND.

After replacing Rundstedt with Field Marshal von Reichenau, one of the few who dared speak openly to him, the Führer flew to Mariupol for firsthand information. He sought out an old comrade, Sepp Dietrich, commander of the SS Leibstandarte, but to his chagrin learned that the officers of this elite division agreed with Rundstedt that they would have been wiped out if they had not fallen back.

After giving Reichenau orders to do what he had fired his predecessor for doing, Hitler summoned Rundstedt. He was packing to go home and thought the Führer might make some sort of apology. But their personal discussion turned into a threat; Hitler said that in the future he would not tolerate any more applications to resign. "I myself, for instance, am not in a position to go to my superior, God Almighty, and say to Him, 'I am not going on with it, because I don't want to take the responsibility.'"

Announcement of the fall of Rostov caused gloom in Berlin in both the Propaganda Ministry and the Foreign Office. But this defeat soon paled before a looming disaster on the central front. The all-out offensive against Moscow was foundering. Although an infantry reconnaissance reached the edge of Moscow early in December and sighted the Kremlin's spires, it was dispersed by several Red Army tanks and an emergency force of factory workers. Field Marshal von Bock, suffering from severe stomach cramps, admitted to Brauchitsch on the phone that the entire attack had no depth and the troops were physically exhausted. On December 3 Bock phoned Halder. This call was even more pessimistic and when Bock suggested going over to the defensive the chief of the General Staff tried to inspirit him with the kind of admonition that comes from those far from the front line; he said that "the best defense was to stick to the attack."

The following day Guderian reported that the thermometer was down to 31 degrees below zero. It took fires under the tank engines to get them started and the cold made telescopic sights useless. Worse, there were still no winter overcoats and long woolen stockings and the men suffered intensely. On the fifth it was five degrees colder. Guderian not only broke off his attack but began to withdraw his foremost units into defensive positions.

That same night the new Soviet commander of the central front, General Georgi Zhukov, launched a massive counteroffensive—one hundred divisions—on a two-hundred-mile front. This combined infantry-tank-air assault caught the Germans off guard and Hitler had not only lost Moscow but seemed destined to suffer Napoleon's fate in the winter snows of Russia. Despair and consternation swept the German Supreme Command. Commander-in-Chief of the Army von Brauchitsch, sick and discouraged, wanted to resign.

Hitler himself was confused. In the Great War the Russian infantrymen had fought poorly; now they were tigers. Why? Despondent, he admitted on December 6 to Jodl that "victory could no longer be achieved."

4

For the past two years Hitler had been sedulously avoiding confrontation with the United States. Convinced that the entire nation was in the clutches of the "Jewish clique," which not only dominated Washington but controlled the press, radio and cinema, he exercised the utmost restraint in the face of Roosevelt's increasing aid to Britain. Although he despised Americans as fighters, he did acknowledge their industrial strength and was set upon keeping them neutral—until he was prepared to deal with them properly.

Despite the steady flow of war matériel to the British Isles, Hitler was so eager to avoid incidents that he had forbidden attacks on United States naval or merchant ships. "Weapons," he ordered, "are to be used only if U.S. *ships fire the first shot.*" But Roosevelt's quick reaction to Barbarossa threatened to end Hitler's patience. On the day after the attack the President authorized Acting Secretary of State Sumner Welles to release a statement that Hitler must be stopped even if it meant giving aid to another totalitarian country. Although Roosevelt was vague as to how this was to be done, he soon made it clear, first by releasing some forty million dollars in frozen Soviet assets, and then by announcing that the provisions of the Neutrality Act did not apply to the Soviet Union, thus leaving the port of Vladivostok open to American shipping.

Two weeks later, July 7, German claims that Roosevelt was intervening in the European war were reinforced; it was revealed that American forces had arrived in Iceland to eventually replace British forces then occupying that strategic island. The German chargé d'affaires in Washington, Hans Thomsen, cabled the Wilhelmstrasse that this was a further attempt on FDR's part to provoke Hitler into attacking America through some naval incident so she could declare war on Germany.

Disturbed by these reports, Hitler made a proposition to Japanese Ambassador Oshima in mid-July that was a reversal of his former determination to limit Japan to the task of holding off England and keeping America neutral. "The United States and England will always be our enemies," he said. "This realization must be the basis of our foreign policy." It was a sacred conviction reached after lengthy deliberations. "America and England will always turn against whomever, in their eyes, is isolated. Today there are only two states whose interests cannot conflict with one another, and these are Germany and Japan."

The proposition was received in Tokyo with polite reserve. The Japanese had already decided not to attack Russia from the east but instead move south to Indochina. They did so and its peaceful seizure brought a quick response from Roosevelt on the night of July 26. Taking the advice of those like Harold Ickes, who had long been urging him to act forcefully against all aggressors, the President ordered Japanese assets in America frozen, an act which deprived Japan of her major source of oil. To the New York *Times* it was "the most drastic blow short of war." To Japan's leaders it was the last step in the encirclement of the Empire by the ABCD (American, British, Chinese, Dutch) powers, denying Nippon her rightful place as leader of Asia, a challenge to her existence. In any case, it was a giant step toward war in the Far East and, to some observers, Roosevelt's backdoor entrance to war against Hitler.

A month later the President went further when he met Churchill at sea off Newfoundland and signed the Atlantic Charter, a joint declaration of British and American war aims. Its terms not only left no doubt that Roosevelt was Hitler's implacable enemy but, ironically, disillusioned the Führer's enemies inside Germany, for no difference was made between a Nazi and an anti-Nazi. Those in the Resistance regarded the charter as Roosevelt's unofficial declaration of war against all Germans. They particularly resented Point 8, which stipulated that Germans must be disarmed after the war; a demand which, Ulrich von Hassell, former Ambassador to Italy, wrote in his journal, "destroys every reasonable chance for peace."

Roosevelt's determination to smash Hitler was opposed to the sentiments of millions of Americans. In addition to the right-wing America Firsters of Charles Lindbergh and the German-American Bund, there was the traditional isolationist Midwest which, though sympathetic to Britain and China, wanted no part of a shooting war. Other Americans hated Communism so intensely that they resented any aid going to the Soviet Union. Roosevelt was undeterred by violent press and radio attacks. "From now on," he announced in a radio broadcast on September 11, "if German or Italian vessels of war enter these waters [i.e., Iceland and similar areas under United States protection] they do so at their peril."

Candid shot of Hitler on the veranda of the Berghof in 1938. WÜNSCHE

Hitler standing in limousine outside the Rheinhotel Dreesen in Bad Godesberg, where he was to meet with British Prime Minister Neville Chamberlain. September 1938. IMPERIAL WAR MUSEUM

Hitler, Chamberlain and Ribbentrop talk peace in Munich one week later. NATIONAL ARCHIVES

Left, General von Fritsch, shortly before his death in Poland. IMPERIAL WAR MUSEUM. Right, General Halder, wearing rimless glasses, and Field Marshal von Brauchitsch pose over map. July 3, 1939. IMPERIAL WAR MUSEUM

Left, two months after invading Poland in 1939 Hitler narrowly escapes death at Burgerbraukeller in Munich. A bomb hidden in a column behind Hitler exploded a few minutes after he unexpectedly ended his speech and rushed to the railroad station. That afternoon, Frau Troost had warned him of possible assassination and he decided to take an earlier train. The ordnance officer in charge of scheduling, Max Wünsche, stares intently at his chief from the front row. BIBLIO. FÜR ZEIT. Right, Polish Jews humiliated by Nazis. IMPERIAL WAR MUSEUM

Rare pictures of Hitler planning invasion of the West in early 1940 in the old Reich Chancellery. Left, Göring and Captain von Puttkamer, the Führer's naval adjutant, watch Hitler explain how to skirt the Maginot Line. Almost all his commanders opposed the unorthodox plan—which worked. PUTTKAMER. Right, Keitel, Jodl, Hitler, Schmundt (chief adjutant) and Puttkamer. PUTTKAMER

Hitler's military inner circle, May 1940. Front row, l. to r., Brückner (personal adjutant), Otto Dietrich (press chief), Keitel, Hitler, Jodl, Bormann, Below (Hitler's Luftwaffe adjutant), Hoffmann the photographer. Middle row, Bodenschatz (Göring's chief of staff), Schmundt, Wolf, Dr. Morell (Hitler's chief physician), Hansgeorg Schulze (Hitler's ordnance officer, killed in battle and replaced by his brother Richard). Back row, Engel (Hitler's army adjutant), Dr. Brandt (Hitler's surgeon), Puttkamer, Lorenz (DNB), Walther Hewel (Foreign Office), unknown, Schaub (Hitler's personal adjutant), Wünsche. BIBLIO. FÜR ZEIT.

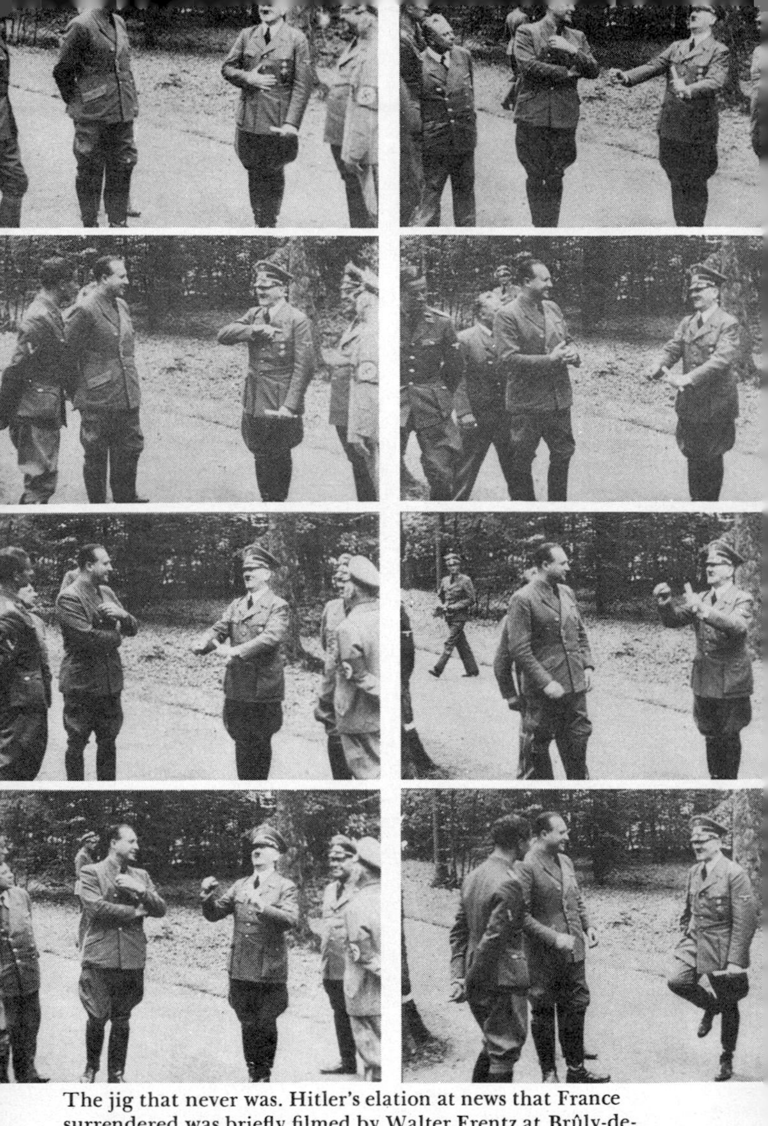

The jig that never was. Hitler's elation at news that France surrendered was briefly filmed by Walter Frentz at Brûly-de-Pesche, not as generally believed, in Compiègne. The above frames (and there were no others, Frentz revealed to the author) were cleverly "looped" (repeated) by a Canadian film expert, making it appear that Hitler was executing a dance. The same technique was later used in cat food commericals. TRANSIT FILM, MUNICH

SENTIMENTAL JOURNEY, JUNE 1940.
HITLER REVISITS HIS BATTLEFIELDS OF 1914-18.

Hitler tells a joke. Extreme right, Below. FRENTZ

"Never again trench warfare," he assures entourage. PUTTKAMER

Bormann, Himmler, Keitel, Hitler and Puttkamer. PUTTKAMER

Fun on the auto tour. Arno Breker, the sculptor, threatened with a dagger by his wife if he ever should be disloyal. Left, Gerda Daranowsky Christian, Hitler's secretary and former employee of Elizabeth Arden. FRENTZ

Hitler in Paris with Speer and Breker. U.S. ARMY

Hitler in Paris, l. to r., Architect Giesler, Breker, Keitel, Hitler, Bodenschatz, Engel, Bormann, Schaub and Speer. FRENTZ

Two faces of Adolf Hitler. PUTTKAMER

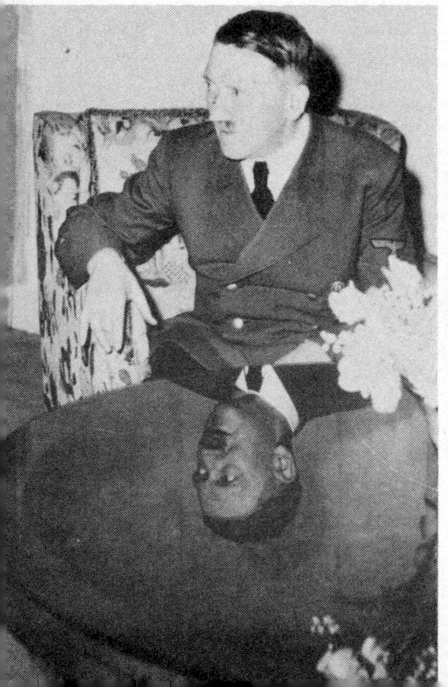

Generalissimo Franco leans forward from train car to speak with Hitler and the German interpreter. October 1940. Part Jewish, Franco refused Hitler's offer to join the Axis. U.S. ARMY

Hitler talks peace with Soviet Foreign Minister Molotov, November 1940. The man in the center is Stalin's interpreter. After this meeting Hitler decides definitely to invade Russia. IMPERIAL WAR MUSEUM

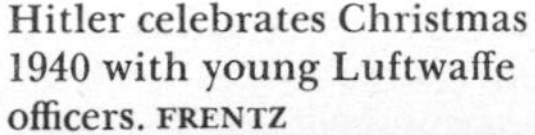

Hitler celebrates Christmas 1940 with young Luftwaffe officers. FRENTZ

Hitler and Papen on the Berghof veranda. FRENTZ

The same day. Engel is promoted to major. Puttkamer affixes the new insignia. FRENTZ

RARE PICTURES OF THE HESS FAMILY

Bormann at wheel with Frau Hess. Hess in jump seat; in back Professor Haushofer, the geopolitician, and Hildegard Fath, Hess's secretary. FATH

Hess with his wife on a skiing holiday in the mid-thirties. He usually kept a stiff upper lip—to cover his buck teeth. FATH

Athlete Hess takes off. FATH

Just before his flight to England in May 1941, Hess and his son. The girl is Bormann's daughter. FATH

THE FÜHRER TRAIN

Hitler with Keitel and Engel aboard the special Führer train. FRENTZ

Hitler reads latest radio dispatch. FRENTZ

Hitler and his dog Blondi inspect Flak crew. To his left, Albert Bormann (brother of Martin), valet Linge and Richard Schulze (Hitler's ordnance officer). FRENTZ

Engel, Puttkamer and Jodl outside train. PUTTKAMER

Göring's favorite trains, in his basement at Karinhall. FRENTZ

Left, on February 15, 1942, after the military reverses in Russia of November–December 1941, Hitler exhorts recent SS officer graduates to stem the Red tide and save civilization. Behind: Schaub and Schulze. The latter, recently made the Führer's personal adjutant, was so moved he wanted to join the fight. The young lieutenants, Schulze recalled, jumped onto their seats and cheered in a spontaneous demonstration. SCHULZE

Below, a few days later Hitler loses his Minister of Armaments, the famed engineer Fritz Todt, in a mysterious plane crash on the eastern front. Todt was replaced by architect Speer. PUTTKAMER

Mussolini flies over the Russian lines in 1941. Moments after this unusual picture was taken, he insisted on taking the controls from pilot Baur. Hitler consented, to his regret. Il Duce maneuvered the plane with boyish élan. PUTTKAMER

Mussolini's son-in-law, Count Ciano, visits Hitler at Wolf's Lair, his headquarters in Poland. Behind: Schmundt, Ribbentrop and Schulze. BIBLIO. FÜR ZEIT.

Hitler and Speer at Wolf's Lair. Behind is Otto Günsche, Hitler's SS adjutant. GÜNSCHE

In July 1942 Hitler moves east to Werwolf, the new headquarters in the Ukraine, so he can personally direct the attack on Stalingrad. Birthday celebration that August for Bormann's secretary Fräulein Wahlmann. L. to r., Schaub, Hewel, Fräulein Wahlmann, Bormann, Engel, Fräulein Fugger (another Bormann secretary) and Heinrich Heim, instructed by Bormann to note down surreptitiously Hitler's table conversations. PUTTKAMER

A month later the inner circle celebrates Below's birthday. L. to r., Schulze, Johanna Wolf (Hitler's secretary), Below, Christa Schröder (Hitler's secretary), Dr. Brandt, Hewel, Albert Bormann, Schaub, Puttkamer, Engel. PUTTKAMER

Christmas card from Uncle Adolf to his favorite nephew, son of Alois Hitler, Jr., Heinz Hitler, who was later captured at Stalingrad. HANS HITLER

22/Dez. 1938

Die besten Weihnachtsgrüsse

lieber Heinzi,
sendet Dir und Papa und
Mama
Dein Onkel Adolf.

Eva Braun, right, and sister Ilse. FR. SCHNEIDER

The wedding of Eva's friend Marion Schönemann to Herr Theissen, at the Berghof, August 1937. Kneeling near groom, Gretl Braun, Eva's sister. Standing, l. to r., Heinrich Hoffmann, Frau Hanni Morell, Erna Hoffmann, Eva Braun, Frau Dreesen (her husband owned the Hotel Dreesen), Dr. Morell, Herta Schneider (Eva's best friend), two unidentified men and Hitler. U.S. ARMY

Eva at nineteen. Hitler's favorite photograph. FR. SCHNEIDER

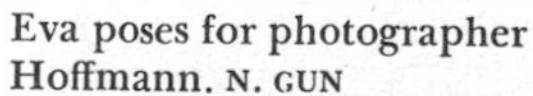

Eva poses for photographer Hoffmann. N. GUN

EVA IN THE WAR YEARS

FR. SCHNEIDER

NATIONAL ARCHIVES

NATIONAL ARCHIVES

Eva's bedroom at the Berghof. NATIONAL ARCHIVES

The passageway leading to Eva's bedroom.
NATIONAL ARCHIVES

Hitler's study at the Berghof.
NATIONAL ARCHIVES

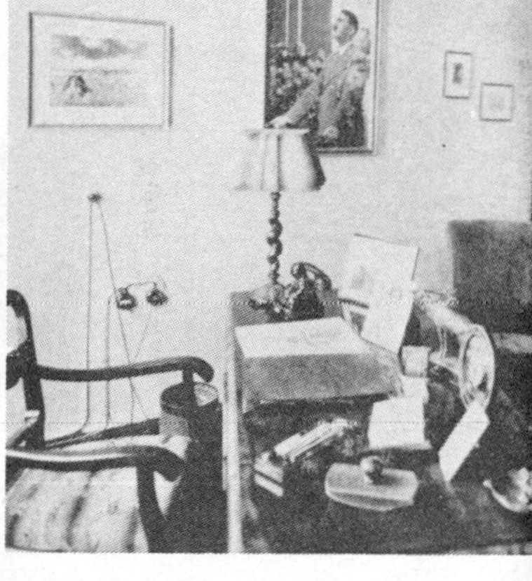

Adolf dozes after dinner with Eva at the tea house. NATIONAL ARCHIVES

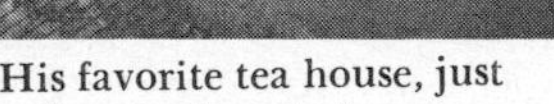

His favorite tea house, just below the Berghof. FRENTZ

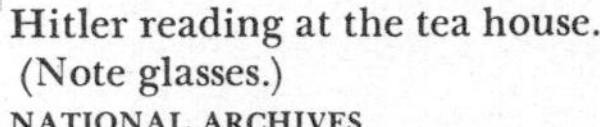

Hitler reading at the tea house. (Note glasses.) NATIONAL ARCHIVES

Above, omnipresent Bormann in the Führer's car. FRENTZ

Left, Frau Gerda Bormann with one of their nine children. FATH

Above, Frau Gertraud "Traudl" Junge (Hitler's youngest secretary) and her husband, Hans Junge (Hitler's valet), dine on the Führer's train with the oldest secretary, Fraülein Wolf. (Note reflection.)
FRENTZ

Left, the two other Hitler secretaries waiting for the train. Gerda Daranowsky Christian, left, and Christa Schröder.
FRENTZ

Hitler leaves the eastern front for relaxation on the Obersalzberg.
FRENTZ

Left, Hitler and SS adjutant Günsche on the Obersalzberg. GÜNSCHE

Below, Hitler and ordnance officer Wünsche visit a girls' school in Berchtesgaden. WÜNSCHE

Recently rescued by the famous commando Otto Skorzeny (September 1943), Mussolini is about to face Hitler. From rare movie film. TIEFENTHALER

Hitler's trousers after the blast. BUNDESARCHIV

Hitler marveling at his miraculous escape from death earlier that day. L. to r., Mussolini (who had just arrived for a visit), Bormann, Admiral Dönitz, Hitler, Göring, SS General Fegelein (husband of Eva's sister Gretl), General Lörzer. BIBLIO. FÜR ZEIT.

Shortly after the explosion, Hitler has changed his uniform and had a bandage put on his left hand, which is supporting his injured right arm. L. to r., Keitel, Göring (Günsche, Jodl and Below in background), Hitler, Bormann. To the right, Himmler jabs finger at General Lörzer. BIBLIO. FÜR ZEIT.

Major Otto Remer, promoted to colonel by Hitler for his part in squashing the army bomb plot, is congratulated by Goebbels. On the left, Hans Hagen, an author in uniform, who helped Remer. REMER

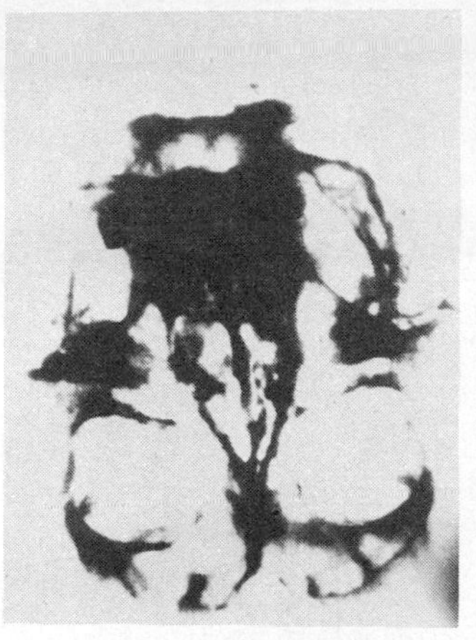

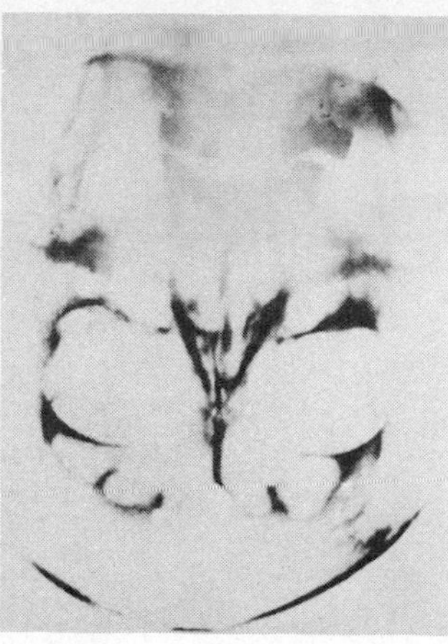

After the bombing, Dr. Erwin Giesing persuaded Hitler to allow X rays of his skull taken. NATIONAL ARCHIVES

Field Marshal Rommel was forced to take poison for participating in the plot. Here, two years earlier, he is being honored for his victories in the desert. Behind, l. to r., Engel, Keitel and Schulze. U.S. ARMY

Right, Field Marshal Walther Model, Hitler's personal choice to command his last gamble, the Battle of the Bulge, December 1944. Left, Bodenschatz; center, Luftwaffe General von Richthofen. U.S. ARMY

General Hasso von Manteuffel, German pentathlon champion, whose tanks almost reached the Meuse River. MANTEUFFEL

Left, the Reich Chancellery, March 1945. FRENTZ
Right, Hitler driven underground by Allied bombs. The waiting room of the Führer bunker. Extreme left, Dr. Morell. Center, Hitler's former valet Krause and Admiral von Puttkamer. PUTTKAMER

Nuremberg, home of the Nazi Party Day. AMERICAN COMMISSION FOR THE PROTECTION AND SALVAGE OF HISTORICAL MONUMENTS

Cologne. AMERICAN COMMISSION FOR THE PROTECTION AND SALVAGE OF HISTORICAL MONUMENTS

In the midst of destruction, Hitler dreams of a new Munich, above, and a new Linz, below. Both cities were designed by Professor Hermann Giesler with Hitler's help. Behind, as usual, is Bormann. FRENTZ

One of the last pictures of Hitler. He visits Oder front, March 1945. BIBLIO. FÜR ZEIT.

On October 10, 1943, Hitler congratulates Himmler, who has privately revealed progress in implementing the Final Solution.

Millions more Jews and non-Jews died in concentration camps in the spring of 1945. Belsen. U.S. OFFICE OF WAR INFORMATION

Nachdem nunmehr beide Verlobte die Erklärung abgegeben haben die Ehe einzugehen, erkläre ich die Ehe vor dem Gesetz rechtmäßig für geschlossen.

Berlin, am [illegible] April 1945

Vorgelesen und unterschrieben:

1.) Ehemann:

2.) Ehefrau:

3.) Zeuge zu 1:

4.) Zeuge zu 2:

5.)

als Standesbeamter

The wedding certificate of Eva and Adolf Hitler, dated April 29, 1945. Note blurred date—it was originally April 28 and then mistakenly altered—and Eva's writing mistake. EISENHOWER LIBRARY

The End. After twelve years of imprisonment in the East, SS adjutant Günsche views the ruins of the Berghof. Left, personal adjutant Schulze. MONIKA SCHULZE-KOSSENS

Hitler's hardening attitude toward America was reflected by Ribbentrop. On the evening of November 28 he summoned General Oshima and urged Japan to declare war against both the United States and Britain. Oshima was surprised. "Is Your Excellency indicating that a state of actual war is to be established between Germany and the United States?" Ribbentrop had not meant to go that far. "Roosevelt is a fanatic," he explained, "so it is impossible to tell what he would do." He promised that if Japan should fight the United States, Germany would join her ally. "There is absolutely no possibility of Germany's entering into a separate peace with the United States under such circumstances. The Führer is determined on this point."

This information was a great relief to the Japanese high command. A carrier task force was already en route to Pearl Harbor. On the last day of November Oshima was ordered to inform Hitler and Ribbentrop immediately that the English and Americans were planning to move military forces into East Asia and this must be countered:

> ...SAY VERY SECRETLY TO THEM THAT THERE IS EXTREME DANGER THAT WAR MAY SUDDENLY BREAK OUT BETWEEN JAPAN AND THE ANGLO-SAXON NATIONS THROUGH SOME CLASH OF ARMS AND ADD THAT THE TIME OF THE BREAKING OUT OF THAT WAR MAY COME QUICKER THAN ANYONE DREAMS.

These instructions were quickly followed by orders to obtain specific pledges from the Germans, yet when Oshima approached Ribbentrop late on the evening of December 1 the Foreign Minister was surprisingly evasive. He excused himself on the grounds that he would first have to consult with the Führer, who was still at the Wolfsschanze. Both men knew that Hitler had little time to devote to the drama brewing on the other side of the world and so Oshima was not surprised that he did not receive a draft treaty until 3 A.M. on the fifth. In it Germany promised to join Japan in any war against the United States and not to conclude a separate peace.

The first to learn of Pearl Harbor at the Wolfsschanze was Otto Dietrich. Late in the afternoon of December 7 he hurried to Hitler's bunker with word that he was bearing an extremely important message. Hitler had just received depressing reports from the Russian front and feared Dietrich was bringing more bad news, but as his press chief hastily read the message his look of surprise was unmistakable. He brightened. Extremely excited, he asked, "Is this report correct?"

Dietrich said that he had received a telephone confirmation from his office. Hitler snatched the paper and, without putting on coat or hat, strode to the military bunker. Keitel and Jodl were amazed to see him, telegram in hand, a "stunned" look on his face. It seemed to Keitel as if the war between Japan and America had suddenly relieved Hitler of "a nightmare burden." With Hewel, the Führer could barely conceal the elation in his voice. "We cannot lose the war!" he exclaimed. "Now we have a partner who has not been defeated in three thousand years."

5

The desperate reports streaming in from the Russian front on Pearl Harbor day forced Hitler to draft a new directive which he issued twenty-four hours later. "The severe winter weather," it began, "which has come surprisingly early in the East, and the consequent difficulties in bringing up supplies, compel us to abandon immediately all major offensive operations and to go over to the defensive." He set down the general principles for defense while turning over to Halder the task of issuing subsequent instructions. Then he set off for Berlin to take personal charge of the crisis raised by Pearl Harbor. By this time his initial relief at the Japanese attack had been replaced by concern. In one stroke, Pearl Harbor had freed Stalin from worry over attack from the east; he could now transfer almost all his strength in Asia against Germany. "This war against America is a tragedy," Hitler later admitted to Bormann.

One of Hitler's first visitors in Berlin on the morning of the ninth was Ribbentrop with the unwelcome information that General Oshima was requesting an immediate declaration of war against America. But the Foreign Minister didn't think Germany was obligated to do so since, according to the Tripartite Pact, she was bound to assist her ally only in case of a direct attack upon Japan.

Hitler could not accept this loophole. "If we don't stand on the side of Japan, the pact is politically dead," he said. "But that is not the main reason. The chief reason is that the United States already is shooting at our ships. They have been a forceful factor in this war and through their actions have already created a situation of war."

His decision to declare war on America was not lightly taken, nor was its motivation simple. Beyond upholding the spirit of the Tripartite Pact there were far weightier arguments: the assistance received from Japan would considerably offset the disadvantages caused by America's entry into the war; from a propaganda point of view the acquisition of a new, powerful ally would have a tremendously heartening effect after the recent setbacks in Russia. Further, an outright declaration of war was in line with his ideological world view. Why not make 1941 the year in which he declared total war upon the two major enemies of human survival—international Marxism (Russia) and international finance capitalism (America), both the creatures of international Jewry?

His Foreign Office regarded the decision as a colossal mistake. In addition to the obvious reasons it neatly solved another of Roosevelt's domestic problems. The President would not have to declare war on Germany and risk opposition from a substantial segment of the citizenry. American national unity, so unexpectedly won by the surprise attack on Pearl Harbor, would remain intact.

On December 11 Hitler convoked the Reichstag. After equating international Jewry with Bolshevik Russia and Roosevelt's regime, Hitler made his declaration of hostilities. "I have therefore arranged for passports to be handed to the American chargé d'affaires today and the following . . ." His words were drowned in a bedlam of cheers, and it was some time before he could announce that Germany was "at war with the United States, as from today."

Anxiety over America was soon overriden by new reverses in the East. The German retreat on the central front threatened to degenerate into panic flight. The area west of Moscow and the Tula area was a snow-covered graveyard of abandoned guns, trucks and tanks. German despondency was accompanied by rising Russian confidence. On December 13 the Soviets publicly announced the failure of Hitler's attempt to surround Moscow and two days later the Politburo ordered the principal organs of government to return to the capital.

The exhausted Brauchitsch wanted to continue the withdrawal but Hitler overruled him and sent out a general order that spread despair among the military hierarchy: "Stand fast, not one step back!" Marshal von Bock, commander of the central front, already suffering from a stomach ailment, reported himself physically unfit for duty. He was replaced by Field Marshal Günther von Kluge. The next day, the nineteenth, Brauchitsch—just recovering from a heart attack—summoned up nerve enough to face Hitler. For two hours they argued in private. Brauchitsch left the Führer, ashen and shaken. "I am going home," he told Keitel. "He has sacked me. I can't go on any longer."

"What is going to happen now, then?" asked Keitel.

"I don't know; ask him yourself."

A few hours later Keitel was summoned. The Führer read out a brief Order of the Day he had composed. He was assuming personal command of the army, inextricably binding the fate of Germany with his own. The news was to be kept secret for the moment but he felt Halder should be informed at once. Hitler did so, minimizing the difficulties of the post. "This little affair of operational command is something anybody can do," he said. "The commander-in-chief's job is to train the army in the National Socialist idea and I know of no general who could do that as I want it done. For that reason I have taken over command of the army myself."

Previously he had been de facto commander of the army, keeping himself in the background and allowing the military to take blame for all setbacks. Now he was the official commander-in-chief and would have to accept praise or blame for whatever happened.

PART 8

THE FOURTH HORSEMAN

And I looked, and behold a pale horse: and his name that sat on him was Death, and Hell followed with him. And power was given unto them over the fourth part of the earth, to kill with sword, and with hunger, and with death, and with the beasts of the earth.

REVELATION 6:8

Chapter Twenty-four

"AND HELL FOLLOWED WITH HIM"

1941–1943

1

Two days after the invasion of the Soviet Union the man responsible for the deportation of Jews, Reinhard Heydrich, complained in writing that this was no answer to the Jewish problem. Deporting these misfits to the French island of Madagascar, for instance, would have to be dropped in favor of a more practical solution. It was fitting, therefore, that on the last day of July Heydrich received a cryptic order (signed by Göring upon instructions from the Führer) instructing him "to make all necessary preparations regarding organizations and financial matters to bring about a complete solution of the Jewish question in the German sphere of influence in Europe."

Behind the innocuous bureaucratic language lay sweeping authority for the SS to organize the extermination of European Jewry. As a preliminary step, Himmler asked the chief physician of the SS what was the best method of mass extermination. The answer was: gas chambers. The next step was to summon Rudolf Höss, the commandant of the largest concentration camp in Poland, and give him secret oral instructions. "He told me," testified Höss, "something to the effect—I do not remember the exact words—that the Führer had given the order for a final solution of the Jewish question. We, the SS, must carry out that order. If it is not carried out now the Jews will later on destroy the German people." Himmler said he had chosen Höss's camp since Auschwitz, strategically located near the border of Germany, afforded space for measures requiring isolation. Höss was warned that this operation was to be treated as a secret Reich matter. He was forbidden to discuss the matter with his immediate superior. And so Höss returned to Poland and, behind the back of the inspector of concentration camps, quietly began to expand his grounds with intent to turn them into the greatest killing center in man's history. He did not even tell his wife what he was doing.

Hitler's concept of concentration camps as well as the practicality of genocide owed much, so he claimed, to his studies of English and United States history. He admired the camps for Boer prisoners in South Africa and for the Indians in the wild West; and often praised to his inner circle the efficiency of America's extermination—by starvation and uneven combat—of the red savages who could not be tamed by captivity.

Until now he had scrupulously integrated his own general policy with that of Germany, since both led in the same general direction. The resurgence of German honor and military might, the seizure of lost Germanic territories, and even Lebensraum in the East were approved heartily by most of his countrymen. But at last had come the crossroads where Hitler must take his personal detour and solve, once and for all, the Jewish question. While many Germans were willing to join this racist crusade, the great majority merely wanted a continuation of the limited Jewish persecution which had already received the tacit approval of millions of Westerners.

It was Hitler's intent to start eliminating the Jews secretly before leaking out the truth a little at a time to his own people. Eventually the time would be ripe for revelations that would tie all Germans to his own fate; his destiny would become Germany's. Complicity in his crusade to cleanse Europe of Jewry would make it a national mission and rouse the people to greater efforts and sacrifices. It would also burn all bridges behind the hesitant and weak-hearted.

Until now all this was kept secret from Hitler's innermost circle—the secretaries, adjutants, servants and personal staff. But in the autumn of 1941 the Führer began making overt remarks during his table conversations, perhaps as an experiment in revelation. In mid-October, after lecturing on the necessity of bringing decency into civil life, he said, "But the first thing, above all, is to get rid of the Jews. Without that, it will be useless to clean the Augean stables." Two days later he was more explicit. "From the rostrum of the Reichstag, I prophesied to Jewry that, in the event of war's proving inevitable, the Jew would disappear from Europe. That race of criminals has on its conscience the two million dead of the First World War, and now already hundreds and thousands more. Let nobody tell me that all the same we can't park them in the marshy parts of Russia! Who's worrying about our troops? It's not a bad idea, by the way, that public rumor attributes to us a plan to exterminate the Jews. Terror is a salutary thing." He predicted that the attempt to create a Jewish state would be a failure.

The Führer made it known to those entrusted with the Final Solution that the killings should be done as humanely as possible. This was in line with his conviction that he was observing God's injunction to cleanse the world of vermin. Still a member in good standing of the Church of Rome despite detestation of its hierarchy ("I am now as before a Catholic and will always remain so"), he carried within him its teaching that the Jew was the killer of God. The extermination, therefore, could be done without a twinge of conscience since he was merely acting as the avenging hand of God—so long as it was done impersonally, without cruelty. Himmler was pleased to murder with mercy. He ordered technical experts to devise gas chambers which would eliminate masses of Jews efficiently and "humanely," then crowded the victims into boxcars and sent them east to stay in ghettos until the killing centers in Poland were completed.

The time had come to establish the bureaucracy of liquidation and the man in charge, Heydrich, sent out invitations to a number of state secretaries and chiefs of the SS main offices for a "Final Solution" Conference, to take place on December 10, 1941. The recipients of his invitation, aware only that Jews were being deported to the East, had little idea of the meaning of "final solution" and awaited the conference with expectation and keen interest.

Their curiosity was whetted by a six-week postponement. Frank, head of the *Generalgouvernement* (German-occupied Poland), became so impatient that he sent Philipp Bouhler, his deputy, to Heydrich for more details, then convened a conference of his own at Cracow in mid-December. "I want to say to you quite openly," said Hitler's former lawyer, "that we shall have to finish the Jews, one way or another." He told about the important conference soon to take place in Berlin which Bouhler would attend for the Generalgouvernement. "Certainly the major migration is about to start. But what is to happen to the Jews? Do you think they will actually be settled in Eastern villages? We were told in Berlin, 'Why all this fuss? We can't use them in the *Ostland* either; let the dead bury their dead!'" He urged his listeners to arm themselves against all feelings of sympathy. "We have to annihilate the Jews wherever we find them and wherever it is at all possible." It was a gigantic task and could not be carried out by legal methods. Judges and courts could not take the heavy responsibility for such an extreme policy.

When Bouhler arrived in Berlin on January 20, 1942, for the Heydrich conference he was far better prepared than most of the conferees to understand the generalities uttered. At about 11 A.M. fifteen men gathered in a room at the Reich Security Main Office at number 56–58 Grossen Wannsee. There were representatives from Rosenberg's East Ministry, Göring's Four-Year Plan agency, the Interior Ministry, the Justice Ministry, the Foreign Office and the party chancellery. Once they had seated themselves informally at tables, Chairman Heydrich began to speak. He had been given, he said, "the responsibility for working out the final solution of the Jewish problem regardless of geographical boundaries." This euphemism was followed by a veiled and puzzling remark which involved Hitler himself. "Instead of emigration," he said, "there is now a further possible solution to which the Führer has already signified his consent—namely deportation to the East."

At this point Heydrich exhibited a chart indicating which Jewish communities were to be evacuated, and gave a hint as to their fate. Those fit to work would be formed into labor gangs but even those who survived the rigors would not be allowed to go free and so "form a new germ cell from which the Jewish race would again arise. History teaches us that."

Thirty copies of the conference record were distributed to the ministries and SS main offices and the term "Final Solution" became known throughout the Reich bureaucracy yet the true meaning of what Heydrich had said was fathomed only by those privy to the killing operations, and many of this select group, curiously, were convinced that Adolf Hitler himself was not totally aware that mass murder was being plotted. SS Lieutenant Colonel Adolf Eichmann, in charge of the Gestapo's Jewish Evacuation Office, for one knew this was a myth. After the Wannsee conference he sat "cozily around a fireplace" with Gestapo Chief Müller and Heydrich, drinking and singing songs. "After a while we climbed onto the chairs and drank a toast; then onto the table and traipsed round and round—on the chairs and on the table again." Eichmann joined in this celebration with no qualms. "At that moment," he later testified, "I sensed a kind of Pontius Pilate feeling, for I was free of all guilt. . . . Who was I to judge? Who was I to have my own thoughts in this matter?" He, Müller and Heydrich were only carrying out the laws of the land as prescribed by the Führer himself.

A few days later Hitler confirmed in spite of himself, that he was indeed the architect of the Final Solution. "One must act radically," he said at lunch on January 23, in the presence of Himmler. "When one pulls out a tooth, one does it with a single tug, and the pain quickly goes away. The Jew must clear out of Europe. It's the Jew who prevents everything. When I think about it, I realize that I'm extraordinarily humane. At the time of the rules of the Popes the Jews were mistreated in Rome. Until 1830, eight Jews mounted on donkeys were led once a year through the streets of Rome. For my part, I restrict myself to telling them they must go away. If they break their pipes on the journey, I can't do anything about it. But if they refuse to go voluntarily I see no other solution but extermination." Never before had he talked so openly to his inner circle and he was so absorbed by the subject that on the twenty-seventh he again demanded the disappearance of all Jews from Europe.

His obsession with Jews was publicly expressed a few days later in a speech at the Sportpalast on the ninth anniversary of National Socialism's rise to power. "I do not even want to speak of the Jews," he said, and proceeded to do so at length. "They are simply our old enemies, their plans have suffered shipwreck through us, and they rightly hate us, just as we hate them. We realize that this war can only end either in the wiping out of the Germanic nations, or by the disappearance of Jewry from Europe."

2

To the Führer the extermination of Jews and Slavs was as important as Lebensraum. He had turned the invasion into ideological warfare and his military decisions, therefore, could only be understood in this context. What appeared irrational to his generals was no sudden mental lapse but the fruit of decisions made in 1928. Ironically, never had he shown more military acumen than after the shocking defeats at the gates of Moscow. Surrounded by demoralized military leaders pleading for general retreat, Hitler did not lose his nerve. He refused to grant any requests to withdraw. He was not swayed by the most successful tank commander, Guderian, who argued that taking up positional warfare in such unsuitable terrain would lead to the useless sacrifice of the best part of the army. He accused Guderian of being too deeply impressed by the suffering of the soldiers. "You feel too much pity for them. You should stand back more. Believe me, things appear clearer when examined at longer range."

Enforcing his order ruthlessly, Hitler managed to rally the army and stem the Russian advance. The cost was great but a number of his generals, including Jodl, were forced to agree that he had personally saved his troops from the fate of Napoleon's army.

All was well on the other war fronts. In France the Resistance, still hopelessly splintered, was of little concern; and in the Mediterranean, U-boats, Italian "human torpedoes" and mines had recently sunk or crippled a carrier, three battleships and two cruisers, thus eliminating Great Britain's Eastern battle fleet as a fighting force. Moreover, Rommel was almost ready to launch another major offensive in North Africa and Germany's Japanese allies were continuing their unbroken series of victories in the Pacific. At the same time Hitler knew the crisis in the East was by no means over and so ordered a general mobilization of the industry and economy of the Reich. The present effort, he said, was insufficient and the Blitzkrieg strategy must be abandoned. Although he couched this call for a long war in hopeful terms, he privately retained the nagging fear, so recently confided to Jodl, that victory could no longer be achieved.

In the meantime preparations for the Final Solution were maturing and Himmler's Einsatzgruppen had begun another deadly sweep. While this second roundup of Jews, commissars and partisans was carried out in a co-ordinated manner in the military areas, progress in civilian territories proceeded less smoothly. Even so the death toll was massive and Rosenberg's staff begged him once more to urge Hitler to treat the peoples of the occupied areas as allies, not enemies. Rosenberg's aides warmly supported his relatively liberal concept of setting up separate states with varying degrees of self-government, but his turn toward liberalism had not been accompanied by a strengthening of character and he still trembled at the thought of antagonizing his Führer. A stronger man might have proved as ineffective; to approach the Führer it was necessary to go through Bormann, who had solidly aligned himself with Himmler and Heydrich.

While it was true that Hitler had little time for internal matters, it was more likely that Bormann always followed his personal instructions; and there was no doubt that Hitler always took time to oversee the Final Solution. In this matter he neither needed nor took advice. He made this clear in his message on the anniversary of the promulgation of the party program in late February. "My prophecy," he said, "shall be fulfilled that this war will not destroy Aryan humanity but it will exterminate the Jew. Whatever the battle may bring in its course or however long it may last, that will be its final course." The elimination of Jewry overrode victory itself.

Despite such open hints, few had yet been initiated into the secret. Goebbels himself still did not realize the enormity of the measures being prepared. One of his employees, Hans Fritzsche, did learn about the Einsatzgruppen killings from a letter sent by an SS man in the Ukraine. The writer complained that he had suffered a nervous breakdown after receiving an order to kill Jews and Ukrainian intelligentsia. He could not protest through official channels and asked for help. Fritzsche immediately went to Heydrich and asked point-blank, "Is the SS there for the purpose of committing mass murders?" Heydrich indignantly denied the charge, promising to start an investigation at once. He reported back the next day that the culprit was Gauleiter Koch, who had acted without the Führer's knowledge, then vowed that the killings would cease. "Believe me, Herr Fritzsche," said Heydrich, "anyone who has the reputation of being cruel does not have to be cruel; he can act humanely."

Only that March did Goebbels himself learn the exact meaning of Final Solution. Then Hitler told him flatly that Europe must be cleansed of all Jews, "if necessary by applying the most brutal methods." The Führer was so explicit that Goebbels could now write in his diary:

> . . . A judgment is being visited upon the Jews that, while barbaric, is fully deserved. . . . One must not be sentimental in these matters. If we did not fight the Jew, they would destroy us. It's a life-and-death struggle between the Aryan race and the Jewish bacillus. No other government and no other regime would have the strength for such a global solution of this question.

By spring six killing centers had been set up in Poland. There were four in Frank's Generalgouvernement: Treblinka, Sobibor, Belzec and Lublin; two in the incorporated territories: Kulmhof and Auschwitz. The first four gassed the Jews by engine-exhaust fumes but Rudolf Höss, commandant of the huge complex near Auschwitz, thought this too "inefficient" and introduced to his camp a more lethal gas, hydrogen cyanide, marketed commercially under the name of Zyklon B.

3

Within the SD it was no secret that Himmler distrusted Heydrich, who had monumental files on everyone in the party, including the Führer, and was despised in return. But Hitler had great plans for Heydrich. He was even considering him as a successor now that Göring had fallen from favor after the disappointing performance of his Luftwaffe, and made him Acting Protector of Moravia and Bohemia in addition to his other high offices. After initiating a wave of terror in Czechoslovakia that quickly crushed the resistance movement, Heydrich adopted the guise of benefactor, particularly to workers and peasants. He raised the fat ration for industrial laborers, improved the social security system and requisitioned luxury hotels for the working class. "He plays cat and mouse with the Czechs," observed his fellow intellectual, Goebbels, "and they swallow everything he places before them. He has carried out a number of extremely popular measures, particularly the almost complete conquest of the black market."

The Reich Protector's achievements in Czechoslovakia roused the Czech government-in-exile to action. Since it appeared that the population might passively accept domination by the Third Reich under such a benevolent despot, they decided to assassinate Heydrich. Two non-coms, Jan Kubis and Josef Gabcik, trained at a school for sabotage in Scotland, were parachuted into the protectorate from a British plane.

On the morning of May 27 the assassins, accompanied by two compatriots, hid at a curve on the road between Heydrich's country villa and Hradschin Castle in Prague. As the Protector's green open Mercedes was approaching, Gabcik jumped to the road and pressed the trigger of his Sten. Nothing happened. He cocked the gun. Again it jammed. Behind him, Kubis lobbed a grenade at the car, which was slowing to a halt. Heydrich shouted, "Step on it, man!" but the driver, a last-minute substitute, kept slamming on the brakes. The grenade exploded, wrecking the rear of the car. Apparently unwounded, Heydrich leaped to the road, revolver in hand, shooting and yelling as if he were "the central figure in a scene out of any Western." Kubis escaped on a bicycle; Gabcik, still unhurt, stood momentarily immobilized when his weapon jammed, then escaped. Suddenly Heydrich dropped his revolver, grasped his right hip and staggered. Fragments of leather and steel springs from the Mercedes' upholstery had penetrated his ribs and stomach. He was taken to a nearby hospital but his wound did not seem serious and he refused to be attended by any but a German doctor. One was finally found who announced that an operation was necessary since grenade fragments were lodged in the membrane between the ribs and lungs as well as the spleen.

Himmler, at temporary headquarters near Wolfsschanze, wept upon learning that his right-hand man was dying, but some SS men were convinced these were crocodile tears since he resented Heydrich's rise to favor with Hitler. As Heydrich lay dying in Prague he whispered a warning to his subordinate Syrup to beware of Himmler.

The two assassins, along with five other members of the Czech Resistance, were finally trapped in a Budapest church by the SS and executed. But this was only the beginning of the reprisal. A reign of terror which made Heydrich's actions seem benevolent descended on Bohemia and Moravia. More than 1300 Czechs were executed out of hand, including all the male inhabitants of Lidice on the fake charge that these villagers had harbored the assassins. Lidice itself was burned, the ruins dynamited and the ground leveled. The eradication of this obscure village not only aroused the disgust and indignation of the Western world but rekindled the spirit of resistance within Czechoslovakia.

It was the Jews who suffered most by the assassination. On the day Heydrich died 152 were executed in Berlin. Three thousand others were removed from the concentration camp of Theresienstadt and shipped to Poland where the killing centers were already receiving a steady flow of victims.

Perhaps the most diabolical innovation of the Final Solution was the establishment of Jewish Councils to administer their own deportation and destruction. This organization, comprising those leaders of the community who believed that co-operation with the Germans was the best policy, discouraged resistance. "I will not be afraid to sacrifice 50,000 of our community," reasoned a typical leader, Moses Merin, "in order to save the other 50,000."

By early summer the mass exterminations began under the authority of a written order from Himmler. Eichmann showed this authorization to one of his assistants, Dieter Wisliceny, with the explanation that Final Solution meant the biological extermination of the Jewish race. "May God forbid," exclaimed the appalled Wisliceny, "that our enemies should ever do anything similar to the German people!"

What Kurt Gerstein learned, as head of the Technical Disinfection Service of the Waffen SS, had already driven him to despair. "He was so appalled by the satanic practices of the Nazis," recalled a friend, "that their eventual victory did not seem to him impossible." During a tour that summer of the four extermination camps in the Generalgouvernement, Gerstein saw with his own eyes what he had read about. At the first camp he and two companions—Eichmann's deputy and a professor of hygiene named Pfannenstiel—were informed that Hitler and Himmler had just ordered "all action speeded up." At Belzec, two days later, Gerstein saw these words translated into reality.

"There are not ten people alive," he was told by the man in charge, Kriminalkommissar Christian Wirth, "who have seen or will see as much as you." Gerstein witnessed the entire procedure from the arrival of 6000 Jews in boxcars, 1450 of whom were already dead. As the survivors were driven out of the cars with whips, they were ordered over a loudspeaker to remove all clothing, artificial limbs, and spectacles and turn in all valuables and money. Women and young girls were to have their hair cut off. "That's to make something special for U-boat crews," explained an SS man, "nice slippers."

Revolted, Gerstein watched the march to the death chambers. Men, women, children—all stark naked—filed past in ghastly parade as a burly SS man promised in a loud, priestlike voice that nothing terrible was going to happen to them." All you have to do is breathe in deeply. That strengthens the lungs. Inhaling is a means of preventing infectious diseases. It's a good method of disinfection." To those who timorously asked what their fate would be, the SS man gave more reassurance: the men would build roads and houses; the women would do housework or help in the kitchen. But the odor from the death chambers was telltale and those at the head of the column had to be shoved by those behind. Most were silent, but one woman, eyes flashing, cursed her murderers. She was spurred on by whiplashes from Wirth, a former chief of criminal police in Stuttgart. Some prayed, others asked, "Who will give us water to wash the dead?" Gerstein prayed with them.

By now the chambers were jammed with humanity. But the driver of the diesel truck, whose exhaust gases would exterminate the Jews, could not start the engine. Incensed at the delay, Wirth began lashing at the driver with his whip. Two hours and forty-nine minutes later the engine started. After another interminable twenty-five minutes Gerstein peered into one chamber. Most of the occupants were already dead. At the end of thirty-two minutes all were lifeless. They were standing erect, recalled Gerstein, "like pillars of basalt, since there had not been an inch of space for them to fall in or even lean. Families could still be seen holding hands, even in death." The horror continued as one group of workers began tearing open the mouths of the dead with iron hooks, while others searched anuses and genital organs for jewelry. Wirth was in his element. "See for yourself," he said, pointing to a large can filled with teeth. "Just look at the amount of gold there is! And we have collected as much only yesterday and the day before. You can't imagine what we find every day—dollars, diamonds, gold! You'll see!"

Gerstein forced himself to watch the final process. The bodies were flung into trenches, each some hundred yards long, conveniently located near the gas chambers. He was told that the bodies would swell from gas after a few days, raising the mound as much as six to ten feet. Once the swelling subsided, the bodies would be piled on railway ties covered with diesel oil and burned to cinders.

The following day the Gerstein party was driven to Treblinka near Warsaw where they saw almost identical installations but on a larger scale: "eight gas chambers and veritable mountains of clothing and underwear, 115 to 130 feet high." In honor of their visit, a banquet was held for employees. "When one sees the bodies of these Jews," Professor Pfannenstiel told them, "one understands the greatness of the work you are doing!" After dinner the guests were offered butter, meat and alcohol as going-away presents. Gerstein lied that he was adequately supplied from his own farm and so Pfannenstiel took the former's share as well as his own.

Upon arrival in Warsaw, Gerstein set off immediately for Berlin, resolved to tell those who would listen of the ghastly sights he had witnessed. A modern Ancient Mariner, he began spreading the truth to incredulous colleagues. As a rock thrown into a pond creates ever widening ripples, so did the tale of Kurt Gerstein.

4

Hitler's conviction that he was surrounded by traitors was confirmed by the discovery late in August of a spy ring, the *Rote Kapelle* (Red Orchestra), which was comprised of prominent Germans. This group had succeeded in informing Moscow about the attack on Maikop, the fuel situation in Germany, the location of chemical warfare materials in the Reich, and Hitler's insistence on taking Stalingrad. After wholesale arrests, forty-six members of the ring, including Mildred Harnack, an American citizen, were executed. But secret information continued to flow to Moscow from another German spy, Rudolf Rössler, a publisher of leftist Catholic books in Lucerne. Rössler, whose code name was Lucy, had informants inside Germany, including General Fritz Thiele, the number two man in the OKW signal organizations; and his reports consequently were far more important than those of the Rote Kapelle; he could provide the Red Army with the German daily order of battle.

Hitler suspected there was a spy at Führer Headquarters since all his moves seemed to be anticipated. Suspicion bred irritability and his military leaders took the brunt of it.

The briefing conferences now took place in his hut deep in the Ukraine near Vinnitsa where Hitler had moved his headquarters. He pointedly refused to shake hands with any staff officer. The atmosphere of the meetings was glacial, with stenographers recording every word of the Führer's instructions. He was determined that never again would his orders be disputed. It was also the end of the camaraderie at mealtimes that he cherished. From now on the Führer ate alone in his room, attended only by Blondi, the Alsatian bitch which Bormann had recently given him to take his mind off escalating problems.

At conferences Hitler continued to display dogged confidence. When General von Weichs of Army Group B and General Friedrich Paulus, the field commander whose task it was to take Stalingrad, warned of the extremely long and lightly held Don front on the northern flank, the Führer made light of their concern. He assured them that the Russians were at the end of their resources and the resistance at Stalingrad was "a purely local affair." Since the Russians were no longer capable of launching a major counteroffensive, there was no real danger on the Don flank. The vital thing, he said, was "to concentrate every available man and capture as quickly as possible the whole of Stalingrad itself and the banks of the Volga." That was why he proposed to reinforce Paulus' Sixth Army with three more divisions.

This time there were some grounds for Hitler's optimism. Disorder was rampant among Soviet troops in the Stalingrad area. Numerous units between the Don and the Volga had already disintegrated as officers and troops deserted or fled to the rear. Columns of refugees, taking cattle and farm equipment with them, cluttered all roads to the east. One recently assigned commander found that his armor had vanished without orders and that leading artillery, anti-tank and engineer commanders, some holding the rank of general, had decamped. By September 14 disaster seemed imminent. Luftwaffe planes were already mining the Volga behind Stalingrad as German infantrymen ranged through the center of the city, seizing the main railroad station and driving as far as the waterfront.

Abruptly the Soviet defense stiffened. Reinforcements, ferried across the river, began challenging the Germans. On the fifteenth the main railroad station changed hands several times and Paulus felt obliged to narrow his attack.

Hitler decided to rid himself of Halder, who had annoyed

him above all others as a prophet of doom, but whom he tolerated for his competence. The end came on September 24. "You and I have been suffering from nerves," said Hitler. "Half of my exhaustion is due to you. It is not worth while going on. We need National Socialist ardor now, not professional ability. I cannot expect this of an officer of the old school such as you." Tears welled in Halder's eyes, a sign of weakness to Hitler, further grounds for dismissal. Halder said not a word in his own behalf. He rose when Hitler finished his tirade. "I am leaving," he said simply, and walked out of the room with dignity. He was convinced that Hitler was dominated by feminine characteristics. "The intuition which mastered him instead of pure logic," he later wrote, "was only one of the many proofs of this fact."

As a replacement, Hitler wanted the antithesis of Halder, and chose Kurt Zeitzler. A newly appointed major general, he had none of the advantages of seniority and authority enjoyed by Halder and it seemed doubtful he could have much influence with OKW and the army group commanders. But Zeitzler's relative youth and inexperience made him all the more attractive to the Führer. He promoted Zeitzler two grades to colonel general.

Those expecting a new spirit of defiance at Führer Headquarters were quickly disillusioned. In his inaugural address to the officers of OKH, Zeitzler said, "I require the following from every staff officer: he must believe in the Führer and in his method of command. He must on every occasion radiate this confidence to his subordinate and those around him. I have no use for anybody on the General Staff who cannot meet these requirements."

Reassured that he had at last found the right army chief of staff, Hitler set out for Berlin to make another speech. It came on the last day of September at the Sportpalast rally for Winter Relief. Eagerly awaited by a hand-picked audience which had no idea what their Führer would say, it was a short, uninspired speech delivered without the usual sparkle. It struck many foreign listeners as pure bombast of no import, but they missed the implications of the anti-Semitic remarks that accompanied Hitler's pledge to take Stalingrad. Perhaps it was because his words about the Jews had been so oft repeated. For the third time that year he reiterated his prediction that if the Jews instigated "an international war to exterminate the Aryan peoples it would not be the Aryan peoples that would be annihilated but Jewry itself." The motivation for this repetition was obscure except to those privy to the secret of the Final Solution. Each mention was a public acknowledgment of his program of extermination; each gave reassurance and authority to the elite charged with the task of mass murder.

5

November proved to be a month of disaster for Germany with the enemy scoring victories in both East and West. Since conquest of Egypt was low among Hitler's priorities, he had made defeat in North Africa inevitable by failing to send Rommel sufficient supplies and reinforcements. With the pyramids practically in sight, the Desert Fox was forced into defensive warfare. When his southern section (held by Italians) was pierced by British General Montgomery, Rommel radioed for permission to retreat. On the evening of November 2 the Führer sent his reply: Do not fall back "one inch." The troops must "triumph or die."

Just before receiving this message Rommel radioed that he had been forced to withdraw; in fact a retreat had been under way for five hours. This information reached OKW at 3 A.M. and since the Operations Staff duty officer knew nothing of Hitler's original message, he did not think it important enough to pass on to the Führer. Hitler, of course, was angry that he had not been awakened.

Rommel's retreat, an augury of total defeat in the desert, was closely followed on November 7 by a disturbing report: a huge armada of Allied ships had entered the Mediterranean and was approaching the north coast of Africa. Although these ships had been sighted outside Gibraltar for several days Hitler and OKW had assumed they were bound for Sardinia or Sicily. The main reason for German surprise, explained Jodl, "probably was that we did not expect such a political false play after the upright, one can properly say, noble treatment which France had received [from Germany] since the collapse in the Forest of Compiègne. For this landing was only possible in agreement with the French and not against the will of France."

Hitler neither bothered to make excuses nor reflected the alarm of his military commanders. He cut short the midday briefing conference and, accompanied by most of the high-ranking population of Wolfsschanze, boarded his special train. Their destination was Munich; the occasion, the nineteenth anniversary of the Putsch. While the Führer slept, the first American and British troops landed on the beaches of Morocco and Algeria. Early reports indicated the French were repelling the landings and Hitler chided his advisers for their initial panic. To their dismay he ordered reinforcements sent to Crete at the other end of the Mediterranean.

By evening the reports from Africa were too grim for Hitler to ignore. He ordered Ribbentrop to summon Mussolini for an immediate conference. But Il Duce refused to make the trip to Bavaria. Already ill, he did not relish facing the Führer under the shadow of defeat. By the time his substitute, Ciano, arrived in Munich, Hitler had accepted the significance of the Africa landings. It was clear to him that "the God of war had now turned from Germany and gone over to the other camp."

There were increasing rumors in Berlin that Hitler had gone mad. At one large gathering the wife of Reichsminister Funk reportedly told the wife of Reichsminister Frick, "The Führer is leading us headlong into disaster." "Yes," replied Frau Frick, "the man is insane." This opinion was echoed by Dr. Ferdinand Sauerbruch, the noted surgeon. He told friends that during a recent visit to the Führer he had heard an old and broken Hitler muttering such disjointed phrases as, "I must go to India," or "For one German who is killed ten of the enemy must die."

6

Hitler faced another defeat at Stalingrad. For weeks the Sixth Army of Paulus had made little progress. Advances were measured in yards and the cost of each yard was exorbitant. Both Paulus and Lieutenant Colonel Reinhard Gehlen, chief of intelligence in the East, warned of dangerous enemy concentrations to the north. "While it is not possible to make any over-all assessments of the enemy situation with the picture as uncertain as it is at present," reported Gehlen on November 12, "we must expect an early attack on the Romanian Third Army, with the interruption of our railroad to Stalingrad as its objective so as to endanger all German forces further to the east and to compel our forces in Stalingrad to withdraw."

At dawn November 19 forty Soviet divisions attacked the

Romanians. The defenders fought ably and with gallantry but were crushed by overwhelming numbers. The Army Group B commander reacted quickly. First he ordered Paulus to cease attacking Stalingrad and prepare units to meet the threat to his left flank; then once it became obvious that the Romanians would collapse, he suggested immediate withdrawal of the Sixth Army.

Hitler peremptorily vetoed this. Convinced by earlier reports that the Soviets had been bled to the point of death and this counteroffensive was only a last gasp, he ordered the men at Stalingrad to stand firm. Help was on the way. The reassuring words did not reflect the state of disarray within Hitler's headquarters itself. Major Engel recorded in his diary that there was complete confusion. "Führer himself completely unsure what is to be done." During these trying hours he incessantly paced the great hall of the Berghof, inveighing against his commanders for repeating the same old mistakes.

The tanks he had sent so reluctantly into the battle had already been thrown back and by November 21 the Romanians, half of whose tanks had been disabled by mice which had gnawed through wires, were cut off. Only that day did Paulus and his chief of staff, Major General Arthur Schmidt, realize their own peril. The appearance of Soviet tanks a few miles from their battle headquarters confirmed that vital links in Sixth Army lines of communication had been captured. After hastily transferring his own headquarters, Paulus asked permission to withdraw. His superior approved the proposal and passed it on to OKW. At the evening's conference in the Berghof, Jodl proposed a general evacuation of the Sixth Army but again the Führer said no. "No matter what happens we must hold the area around Stalingrad."

The next morning, the twenty-second, the two arms of a tremendous Soviet pincer movement met, encircling the entire Sixth Army. More than 200,000 of Germany's finest troops along with 100 tanks, 1800 big guns and more than 10,000 vehicles were caught in a giant *Kessel* (cauldron). At a Sixth Army conference that morning someone suggested they break out to the southwest. "We can't," said Chief of Staff Schmidt, "because we haven't got the necessary fuel. And if we tried we should end up with a catastrophe like that of Napoleon." Sixth Army, he added, would have to go into a "hedgehog" defense. By afternoon the situation had worsened so much that Schmidt began to question his own argument. At this point

Paulus received fresh orders: Stand fast and await further orders. "Well," said Paulus, turning to his chief of staff, "now we'll have time to think over what we ought to do. This we'll do separately. Meet me, please, in an hour's time and we'll compare the conclusions we have reached." They were identical: break out to the southwest.

Hitler could not contemplate retreat. That evening he sent a personal message to Paulus. "Sixth Army must know," he said, "that I am doing everything to help and to relieve it. I shall issue my orders in good time." Paulus accepted the decision but one of his corps commanders began a withdrawal on his own initiative in order to force Paulus into ordering a general retreat. Paulus had authority to remove or arrest him but did neither, since the situation was so critical. Ironically, once Hitler learned a retreat was under way, he put the blame on the innocent Paulus and rewarded the guilty man, in whom he had great faith, by giving him an independent command.

His suspicion of Paulus was one reason Hitler ignored a personal plea from the Sixth Army commander, late on the night of November 23, to break out of the trap. Instead he chose to accept Göring's assurance that the Luftwaffe could keep the encircled Sixth Army supplied by air despite the Reichsmarschall's poor performance record, and he dispatched a radio signal next morning ordering Paulus to hold "at all costs" since supplies were coming by air. In a display of wishful thinking, Hitler eagerly seized upon Göring's rash promise and declared Stalingrad a fortress, thus sealing the fate of the almost 250,000 German and allied troops.

Having lost faith in Paulus' superior, Hitler turned over most of that commander's responsibility to Field Marshal von Manstein, whose ingenious invasion plan of the West had coincided so closely with his own. Manstein was to command a new force, Army Group Don, his task to halt the Soviet advance westward so as to take all pressure off the defenders of Stalingrad. Manstein sent a reassuring message to Paulus that noon: "We will do all we can to get you out of this mess." Paulus' present task, he added, was to "maintain the Volga and north front according to the Führer's order and prepare strong forces to break out to the rear." Taking this to mean that Sixth Army was to stand firm while Manstein opened up a corridor, Paulus and Schmidt abandoned their own plan to break out without Hitler's permission.

Twenty-two of the planes flying supplies to Stalingrad were

shot down before the end of the day. On the twenty-fifth another nine were destroyed, and a mere seventy-five tons of food and armaments reached Paulus.

Paulus sent a handwritten letter to Manstein, thanking him for the recent promise to help Sixth Army. He told of his request to Hitler asking for freedom of action if it should become necessary. "I wanted to have this authority," he explained, "in order to guard against issuing the only possible order in that situation too late. I have no means of proving that I should only issue such an order in an extreme emergency and I can merely ask you to accept my word for this."

Paulus got his answer from the Führer at five minutes before midnight. In a personal message to the men of Sixth Army, Hitler ordered them to stand fast with the assurance that he would do all in his power to send them relief.

The relief operation, Winter Storm, was relatively stingy, consisting of a single thrust by two armored divisions. Scheduled to begin in early December, there were so many delays in assembling this minimal force that it was not mounted until the morning of December 12. As 230 tanks rolled northeast toward Stalingrad, some sixty miles distant, there was very little resistance. In some places there were no Russians at all and the Germans were puzzled. Even so only twelve miles were made; the frozen ground began to melt under the sun's rays and slopes were turned into slippery traps.

For six days the men of Sixth Army anxiously waited for sight of friendly tanks but all they could see were streams of Russians plodding west to stem Winter Storm. Manstein was equally depressed and requested permission on the eighteenth for Paulus to break out so that most of his men could be saved.

The following afternoon Manstein once more radioed Hitler for permission to break out Sixth Army. At first Hitler refused but he showed signs of relenting under Zeitzler's continued urgings. His indecision encouraged some staff officers to hope against hope that Paulus, on his own responsibility, would attempt the breakout. Paulus would have done so if he could. He was prepared to disobey the Führer's original order, but by now had less than a hundred tanks with fuel enough, at best, for twenty miles. Moreover, there was hardly enough ammunition for defense, let alone an offensive. He and Schmidt rested their hopes on the columns driving to their relief.

But the tanks coming to their aid would get no farther east.

On December 23 Manstein was forced to call off the relief attack since one Panzer division of this force had to be diverted to plug up the hole left by the fleeing Italians. At 5:40 P.M. he got in touch with Paulus by teleprinter and asked, "if worst came to worst," could he break out? Did this mean, asked Paulus, that he was now authorized to initiate the move? "Once it is launched," he said, "there'll be no turning back."

"I can't give you full authority today," replied Manstein. "But I hope to get a decision tomorrow."

Early in January the main Soviet assault began and Sixth Army's western front was slowly pushed back. Food and ammunition supplies rapidly dwindled; the daily ration of most big guns was a single round and each man got a slice of bread and a little horse meat. The amount of supplies coming into the pocket remained far below that promised by Göring and by now Hitler was disillusioned to the point of biting sarcasm, referring to him as "this fellow Göring, this fat, well-fed pig!" Perhaps the greatest insult was selecting a subordinate to reorganize the airlift and save Sixth Army. The Führer had already twice praised Field Marshal Milch as one who did not know the word "impossible." In mid-January he was instructed by Hitler to get three hundred tons of supplies daily into the cauldron. To do so he was given special powers, including authority to issue orders to any military command. Milch's energetic reforms raised the daily level of supply from sixty to eighty tons and there was a glimmer of hope inside the pocket. But it soon became obvious that even Milch could do little better and finally he himself realized his mission was impossible.

By January 20 the pocket, already reduced to half its size, showed unmistakable signs of disintegration, particularly in those areas where the fighting was fiercest. Moved by the suffering he saw with his own eyes, Paulus felt duty-bound to appeal once more to higher authority. That day he summoned Schmidt and two staff members for their opinion. Only one of the three, an operations officer, favored continuing the fight and Paulus dispatched identical messages to Manstein and Führer Headquarters requesting permission, once operations were no longer possible, "to avoid complete annihilation."

Both Manstein and Zeitzler urged Hitler to reply favorably but he continued to demand that Sixth Army "fight to the last man." In a last desperate measure to bring him around, a major named Zitzewitz was flown out of Stalingrad to make a first-hand report of the hopeless situation. Hitler gripped both Zitzewitz's hands when he was presented on January 22. "You have come from a deplorable situation," he said, then talked of another relief drive through enemy lines by a battalion of new Panther tanks.

Zitzewitz was flabbergasted. How could a battalion succeed where an entire Panzer army had failed? During a pause in Hitler's dissertation the major read off figures from a slip of paper he had prepared. He spoke movingly of the trapped men's hunger and frostbite, the dwindling supplies, the feeling that they had been written off. "My Führer," he concluded, "permit me to state that the troops at Stalingrad can no longer be ordered to fight to their last round because they are no longer physically capable of fighting and because they no longer have a last round."

Hitler turned to him in surprise, and, Zitzewitz felt, stared straight through him. "Man recovers very quickly," Hitler said. He dismissed the major and ordered this message sent to Paulus: "Surrender out of the question. Troops will resist to the end."

Isolated groups of Germans were already surrendering in considerable numbers but Paulus himself stood firm. He told two divisional commanders who brought up the subject of capitulation that the general situation did not permit such action. They must obey the Führer's injunction to hold out to the last possible moment. His own decision weighed heavily on his conscience since he knew the torments his men were suffering. Until recently their fighting spirit had been remarkable. With faith in their leaders, they had taken it for granted that relief was coming. Today, the tenth anniversary of the National Socialist take-over, an air of hopelessness pervaded the air. There was no place to put the newly wounded since every cellar in Stalingrad was crowded almost to suffocation. The supply of drugs, medicines and bandages was fast disappearing. It was no longer possible to bury the dead in the frozen ground.

In a final letter Paulus wrote his wife, a Romanian of noble birth, "I stand and fight—these are my orders!" On the evening of January 30 he armed himself with a rifle for his last battle. Then came word from Wolfsschanze that the Führer had promoted him to the rank of field marshal. It was an honor that every officer dreamed of, yet at this moment it seemed of little consequence. The promotion was followed, after midnight, by a message from Zeitzler, which was its price tag: "The Führer asks me to point out that each day the fortress of Stalingrad can continue to hold out is of importance."

Just before dawn of the thirty-first, Chief of Staff Schmidt peered out a window and in the glare of innumerable fires saw an incredible sight. In the market place a large group of German and Russian soldiers were standing together, smoking cigarettes, talking animatedly. Schmidt told Paulus that the end had come. Further local resistance was senseless unless they were willing to fire at their own troops. Paulus agreed that surrender was the only alternative. Within the hour the two men were in a Soviet car bound for the headquarters of General M. S. Shumilov's Sixty-fourth Army.

Early the following morning, February 1, Moscow announced the surrender of Paulus and Schmidt. At the midday conference Zeitzler could not believe this was true but Hitler had no doubts. "They have surrendered there formally and absolutely," he insisted. "Otherwise they would have closed ranks, formed a hedgehog, and shot themselves with their last bullets." Zeitzler continued to express doubt that Paulus had capitulated. Perhaps he was lying somewhere badly wounded. "No, it is true," said Hitler. "They'll be brought straight to Moscow and put into the hands of the GPU and they'll blurt out orders for the northern pocket to surrender too." He rambled on, commending those military men who, unlike Paulus, ended their problems with a shot in the head. "How easy it is to do that! A revolver—makes it easy. What cowardice to be afraid of that. Ha! Better be buried alive! And in a situation like this where he knows well enough that his death would set the example for behavior in the pocket next door. If he sets an example like this, one can hardly expect people to go on fighting."

The next day the northern pocket surrendered. The Soviets claimed the capture of 91,000 prisoners including 24 generals and 2500 officers. Thanks in large part to Hitler's own brutal treatment of Soviet prisoners, these men were treated inhumanely. Reportedly more than 400,000 German, Italian and Romanian prisoners of war died between February and April 1942. Starvation was the chief cause of death and cannibalism became a common practice. The strong alone survived and these lived on excrement from which undigested corn and mullet was picked and washed. Only a few thousand of those captured at Stalingrad would ever return to Germany. One was

Paulus, who pleased the Soviets by publicly condemning Hitler and Nazism.

After visiting the wreckage of Stalingrad, General Charles de Gaulle remarked to a correspondent, "Ah, Stalingrad, a remarkable people, a very great people." The correspondent assumed he was talking of the Russians. "*Mais non*, I'm not speaking of the Russians but of the Germans. To have come so far!"

Chapter Twenty-five

THE FAMILY CIRCLE

1943

1

As the Battle of Stalingrad approached its climax the Führer returned to Wolfsschanze and slowly emerged from solitary confinement. Occasionally he would invite an adjutant or visitor from Berlin to share his meager repast. As the group enlarged to include the secretaries and other select members of the family circle, the meals were transferred back to the communal dining hall. The military leaders were still excluded and he still refused to shake hands with them at briefings. For their part, they felt constrained in his presence, most considering him a tyrant and more than a little mad.

Even in the depth of his depression the Führer had treated his adjutants with polite consideration and his interest in the younger ones, like Richard Schulze, a former Ribbentrop aide, was avuncular. This was the side of Hitler that the Halders never knew. They did not see the man who could be gracious to servants and at ease with chauffeurs and secretaries. Isolation from the military drove him even closer to this family circle and so his new secretary, Gertraud Humps, had a special opportunity to get to know her Führer.

Traudl Humps, the granddaughter of a general, was twenty-two, naïve and impressionable. She was so nervous the first time she took dictation that Hitler soothed her as if she were a child. "You don't have to get excited," he said, "I myself will make far more mistakes during the dictation than you will." She was summoned again on January 3, 1943. This time Hitler asked if she would like the job of permanent private secretary. It was an exciting and flattering offer and, without hesitation, she accepted it. She soon became accustomed to this new, strange world. With no full office routine or fixed duty time, she had leisure to spend much of the day wandering in the snow-covered forest. She particularly enjoyed watching her new employer play with Blondi in the morning. The big dog would jump through hoops, leap over a six-foot wooden wall, climb up a ladder, then beg at the top. Whenever Hitler noticed Traudl, he would come over, shake hands and ask how she was doing.

This affable Hitler was not in evidence at the military briefings. After the fall of Stalingrad his irascibility was such that attendance at situation conferences was kept to a minimum. Guderian, who hadn't seen the Führer since the failure to take Moscow, noticed that, while he hadn't aged greatly, he "easily lost his temper and raged, and was then unpredictable in what he said and decided."

At mealtimes he managed to control his temper with the family circle but his conversation deteriorated in quality. "After Stalingrad," recalled Fräulein Schröder, "Hitler would not listen to music any more, and every evening we had to listen to his monologues instead. But his table talk was by now as overplayed as his gramophone records. It was always the same: his early days in Vienna, the *Kampfzeit*, the history of man, the microcosm and the macrocosm. On every subject we all knew in advance what he would say. In the course of time these monologues bored us. But world affairs and events at the front were never mentioned: everything to do with the war was taboo."

In Berlin, Goebbels proclaimed a three-day mourning in honor of Stalingrad's dead. During that period all places of entertainment, including theaters and cinemas, were closed. He also began preparing the nation for hard times ahead. Everywhere—on trains, walls, shopwindows and billboards—was splattered the slogan: "The Wheels Must Turn Only for Victory." On February 15 he issued a decree addressed to Reichsleiters, Gauleiters and all army headquarters demanding complete mobilization for victory.

That same day in a speech at Düsseldorf, entitled, "Do You Want Total War?" he all but announced Hitler's Final Solution. Two thousand years of Western civilization, he said, were in danger from a Russian victory, one forged by international Jewry. There were cries from the audience of "Hang them!" and Goebbels promised that Germany *would* retaliate "with the total and radical extermination and elimination of Jewry!" This brought wild shouts and manic laughter.

The gravity of the military situation was underlined, next day, in a letter from Bormann to his wife, whom he addressed as his dearest Mummy-Girl. "Should the war take a turn for the worse, either now or at some later stage, it would be better for you to move to the West, because you simply must do everything in your power to keep your—our—children out of any danger. In due course they will have to carry on the work of the future."

2

Correspondent Louis Lochner had already made several attempts to inform Roosevelt of the resistance movement inside the Reich. In hopes of convincing Roosevelt that not all Germans were Nazis, Lochner was prepared to give him the radio code of two separate groups opposed to Hitler so that Roosevelt could inform them directly what political administration in Germany would be acceptable to the Allies. After failing to reach the President through his appointments secretary, Lochner wrote a personal note revealing the existence of these codes and emphasizing that they could be handed over to Roosevelt alone. There was no reply but several days later Lochner was informed that his insistence was viewed by official sources as "most embarrassing." Would he please desist? What Lochner did not know was that the President's refusal to see him was official American policy in line with unconditional surrender, designed not only to withhold encouragement to German resisters but to avoid any important contact. Recognition of the existence of any anti-Hitler movement within Germany was forbidden.

The Resistance was discouraged but continued to plot the overthrow of Hitler. It was agreed that seizure of power alone was not sufficient. The Führer himself must first be assassinated and General Oster and his group selected General Henning von Tresckow, Field Marshal von Kluge's chief of staff, as executioner. He decided to lure Hitler up front, then plant a bomb in his plane that would explode on the return flight. On the evening of March 13, 1943, one of Tresckow's junior officers, Fabian von Schlabrendorff, arrived at the airport with a parcel supposedly containing two bottles of brandy. It was a bomb made from British plastic explosives. Using a key, Schlabrendorff pressed down hard on the fuse, triggering the bomb. Moments later he delivered the parcel to a colonel in Hitler's party who had promised to deliver it to a friend at Wolfsschanze.

The Führer boarded the plane and it took off. The bomb was expected to explode above Minsk but two hours passed without news of any accident. Then came word that the plane had landed safely in Rastenburg. The conspirators were confounded. Now they had to retrieve the erratic bomb before it exploded or was discovered. Schlabrendorff did so and discovered that its firing pin had been released but the detonator was a dud.

A few days later the conspirators tried again. Near midnight, March 20, in a room at a Berlin hotel, the Eden, Schlabrendorff turned over plastic explosives to Colonel Rudolf Christoph Freiherr von Gerstdorff, Kluge's chief of intelligence. His mission was suicidal. He was to approach the Führer at tomorrow's celebration of Heroes' Memorial Day at the Zeughaus in Berlin and blow himself and Hitler to bits.

The next day Gerstdorff appeared at the Zeughaus, a bomb in each overcoat pocket. At 1 P.M. Hitler arrived, and after listening to a passage from Bruckner by the Berlin Symphony he gave a short speech in the inner court. As he headed for the exhibition hall where captured Russian trophies were on display, Gerstdorff reached into his left pocket and broke the acid capsule of the British fuse, which needed at least ten minutes to detonate. Hitler was accompanied by Himmler, Keitel, Göring and a dozen others but the would-be assassin had no difficulty getting to his left side.

Schmundt had assured Gerstdorff that the Führer would spend half an hour at the exhibit but he showed little interest and, to Gerstdorff's consternation, was out of the building in five minutes. There was no possibility of following and Gerstdorff knew he had only another five minutes to dispose of the fuse without being observed. He elbowed his way to the corridor. Finally he found a men's room. Fortunately it was empty. He hastily removed the fuse from his pocket and—seconds before it was due to explode—flushed it down the toilet and left the building with the bombs.

Although the Gestapo had no suspicion of these two attempts against the Führer's life, they suspected that traitors infested the Abwehr. Fifteen days later they arrested Hans von Dohnanyi at Abwehr headquarters. Oster managed to destroy most of the papers incriminating himself but before long he too was placed under arrest. The conspirators had lost not only an able leader but their best means of communicating with each other and any friends in the West.

3

Early that April Hitler and his entourage boarded the train for Berchtesgaden, which would be a welcome respite from the gloomy surroundings at the Wolfsschanze. It was a clear, mild winter night and as they left the snow-covered forest of Rastenburg, Traudl Humps was a bit saddened to leave, yet exhilarated by the promise of new experiences. There was every comfort on the train including a special car equipped with showers and bathtubs; the food was excellent and the seats could be converted into comfortable beds. As the train rolled quietly toward its destination the next morning, she thought of other trains in the Reich, without light or heat, their passengers uncomfortable and hungry. Her thoughts were interrupted by an invitation to join the Führer for lunch. The following morning she breakfasted in less exalted company. The gossip among the servants and secretaries was about Eva Braun, who was to board the train at Munich. To them she was "the lady at the Berghof," and as such was silently accepted by all guests. That is, except by the wives of Ribbentrop, Göring and Goebbels. The first ignored her regally; the other two snubbed her openly, despite Hitler's request that she be treated with respect.

Traudl was given a tour of the Berghof by one of the older secretaries. They started on the second floor where the Führer lived. The walls of the hallway were decorated with paintings by the old masters, beautiful pieces of sculpture and exotic vases. Everything, thought Traudl, was wonderful but strange and impersonal. There was deadly silence since the Führer still slept. In front of one door were two black Scotch terriers—Eva's dogs, Stasi and Negus. Next came Hitler's bedroom. The two rooms, it seemed, were connected by a large bathroom and it was apparent they lived discreetly as man and wife. Traudl was taken downstairs to the large living room which was separated from the famous picture-window room by a heavy velvet curtain. The furnishings were luxurious but despite the beautiful Gobelins and thick carpets she got the impression of coldness. The accommodations were far superior to those at Wolfsschanze but here she felt ill at ease. While she was treated as a guest, she was not there of her own free will but as an employee.

The daily schedule at the Berghof was something of a strain even though it never varied. Hitler's noon briefing rarely ended before midafternoon and it was usually 4 P.M. before the last officer left and the Führer entered the living room where his hungry guests were gathered. As if by signal, Eva would then make her appearance, accompanied by her two scampering dogs. Hitler would kiss her hand, before greeting each guest with a handshake. The transformation of man of state burdened by the tragedies of battle to jovial host eager to please guests and helpmate was unexpected and somewhat ludicrous. His private life in fact was not much different from that of a very successful businessman.

The men addressed Eva with a slight bow and a polite "Gnädiges Fräulein"; the women called her Fräulein Braun. Several seemed very intimate, particularly Herta Schneider, a school friend. The women began an animated discussion on children, fashion and personal experiences. Finally Hitler interrupted, ridiculing Eva's dogs as "hand-sweepers." She blithely retorted that Hitler's dog, Blondi, was a calf.

The banal pleasantries, enlivened by not so much as an aperitif, were ended when Hitler escorted one of the ladies to the table. They were followed by Bormann and Eva, who heartily disliked him, primarily for his flagrant philandering.

The guests enjoyed sauerbraten but Hitler kept to the vegetarian meals cooked under the supervision of Dr. Werner Zabel in his Berchtesgaden clinic and warmed over at the Berghof kitchen. Nothing would induce Eva to so much as taste Hitler's thick gruel, oatmeal soup or baked potato liberally soaked in raw linseed oil. The Führer teased her about her own meager diet. "When I first met you," he said, "you were pleasingly plump and now you are quite thin." Women underwent these sacrifices, he added sardonically, "only to make their girl friends envious."

The conversation was gay and superficial until Hitler abruptly began propagandizing for vegetarianism by describing in detail the horrors of a slaughterhouse he had recently visited in the Ukraine. The guests blanched as he described work girls in rubber boots, standing in fresh blood up to their ankles. One, Otto Dietrich, laid down knife and fork with the comment that he was no longer hungry.

After lunch Hitler set out on the daily twenty-minute walk to his tea house. It was a round stone building located below the Berghof, reminding some of the guests of a silo or power plant. Tea was served in a large round room whose six large windows provided a wide vista. From one end there was a magnificent view of the Ach River roaring down the mountainside between houses that looked like matchboxes. Beyond lay the baroque towers of Salzburg.

Hitler drank apple-peel tea while Eva talked of plays and movies. His only comment was that he could not watch a film while the people were making so many sacrifices. "Besides, I must save my eyes for studying maps and reading front-line reports." The conversation that day palled on Hitler. He closed his eyes and shortly was asleep. His guests continued to chat but in lowered voices, and when the Führer wakened he joined in as if he had just closed his eyes momentarily to think.

At 7 P.M. a parade of vehicles arrived at the Berghof, and the business of government resumed. Two hours later Hitler left the conference and led the way to the dining room where he ate mashed potatoes and a tomato salad while his guests dined on cold meat. He charmed everyone with tales of his youth, until he noticed the lipstick on Eva's napkin. Did she know what it consisted of? Eva protested that she only used French lipstick made of the finest materials. With a pitying smile Hitler said, "If you women knew that lipstick, particularly from Paris, is manufactured from the grease of waste water, you certainly wouldn't color your lips any more." Everyone laughed. He had won another argument—if no adherents.

An adjutant quietly informed Hitler that everyone had arrived for the evening military conference. Not wanting his guests, particularly the women, to come in contact with the military, he told them to remain seated. "It won't take too long," he said and left, head lowered but with a strong step. The secretaries went to an office to type air raid reports, while

Eva and most of the guests descended to the basement to see a movie. Before it concluded a telephone rang: a servant reported that the conference was over and the Führer expected everyone in the main hall. Eva hurried to her room to refresh her make-up; her sister Gretl smoked a last cigarette, then chewed peppermint candy to camouflage her breath; and the rest dutifully repaired to the great hall. It was almost midnight by the time Hitler came down the stairs and seated himself at the fireplace next to Eva and her two little terriers. Since they did not get along with Blondi, the latter was excluded except on the rare occasions when Hitler asked Eva to banish her two darlings so his dog could have a moment in the limelight.

Liquor was served but Hitler took tea and apple cake. The group sat silently around the fire in the semidarkness waiting for him to begin the general conversation. Finally he raised his voice for another lecture on the evils of tobacco. His dentist declared that smoking disinfected the mouth. In moderation, it was not at all dangerous. Hitler dissented. "I wouldn't offer a cigar or cigarette to anyone I admired or loved since I would be doing them a bad service. It is universally agreed that nonsmokers live longer than smokers and during sickness have more resistance." He never tired of this crusade against pollution of the body, and had a standing offer of a gold watch for anyone within the circle who renounced tobacco. To Eva, however, he gave an ultimatum: "Either give up smoking or me."

The argument turned to liquor, which he thought less dangerous, and on to painting. Dr. Morell, after a single glass of port, was fighting to stay awake. He lolled back, fat hands folded over his paunch, and his eyes suddenly closed from bottom to top. Magnified by his thick glasses, it was a frightening sight. Colonel von Below nudged Morell, who wakened with a start and broke into a big smile, assuming that the Führer had told a joke.

"Are you tired, Morell?" asked Hitler.

"No, mein Führer, I was just daydreaming," he said and, to show how wide awake he was, began an oft-told anecdote about his experiences in Africa. The Führer began softly whistling a popular song. No, said Eva, and demonstrated how the tune should go. They argued amiably. She wanted to bet but Hitler complained that if he won he always had to forgive the bet in a spirit of generosity, but if she won he had to pay. Refusing to be put off, she suggested they play the music to see who was right. Albert Bormann dutifully rose and put on the record. Eva was triumphant. "The composer made the mistake," said Hitler, who had written an opera in his youth. "If he were really talented he would have written my melody." Everyone laughed as Hitler made this joke. At last at 4 A.M. Hitler summoned a servant to ask if the air raid reports had arrived; he could not go to bed until he was assured no enemy plane was over Germany.

4

On May 7 Hitler made a sad pilgrimage to the capital to attend the funeral of another old comrade. Viktor Lutze, the successor to Röhm, had died in an auto accident. At least that was the official story; some survivors of the Röhm Putsch suspected foul play. After the funeral Reichleiters and Gauleiters attended a luncheon at the chancellery. This was followed by a detailed survey of the general situation which began with the Führer's statement that in 1939 Germany—a revolutionary state—had faced only bourgeois states. It was easy, he explained, to knock out such nations since they were quite inferior in upbringing and attitude. A country with an ideology always had the edge over a bourgeois state since it rested upon a firm spiritual foundation. This superiority, however, had ended with Barbarossa. There the Germans had met an opponent which also sponsored an ideology, if a wrong one. He praised Stalin for purging the Red Army of defeatists and installing political commissars with the fighting forces. Stalin enjoyed the further advantage of having rid himself of "high society" by other liquidations so that Bolshevism could devote all its energy to fighting the enemy.

Another reason for failure in the East was the poor performance of Germany's allies, particularly the Hungarians. Lasting resistance to the Soviets, he concluded, could be offered in Europe only by the Germans since victory in battle was linked with ideology. Consequently the anti-Semitism which formerly animated party members must once more become the focal point of their spiritual struggle. It should also be a rallying cry for the troops; if they did not stand firm as a wall, the hordes of the East would sweep into Europe. A constant, untiring effort must therefore focus on taking the necessary measures for the security of European culture. "If it be true today that the Bolshevism of the East is mainly under Jewish leadership and that the Jews are also the dominant influence in the Western plutocracies, then our anti-Semitic propaganda must begin at this point." That was why there was practically no possibility of any compromise with the Soviets. "They must be knocked out, exactly as we formerly had to knock out our own Communists to attain power. At that time we never thought of a compromise either."

Despite the vigorous tenor of his talk, it was apparent that Hitler's health was failing. Dr. Morell doubled the hormone injections as well as adding still another drug, Prostakrin, but there was little improvement. Another electrocardiogram indicated a worsening of his heart condition. Fearing that the diet regime of Dr. Zabel was aggravating matters, Morell recommended that the Führer hire a special cook. They settled on a woman from Vienna, a Frau von Exner, who would surely know how to please an Austrian palate. Neither was aware there was Jewish blood in her mother's family.

On May 12 Hitler returned to Wolfsschanze satisfied that his leadership had ended the withdrawals after the fall of Stalingrad. His complacency ended the next day upon learning that two German-Italian armies in Tunisia, some 300,000 men, had been bagged by the Allies. It was another Stalingrad. A week later there was worse news. Mussolini's regime was close to collapse. Italians in high places were using phrases such as "you never know what's going to happen" and "when the war is over." On the streets German soldiers were openly cursed as enemies.

Despite the reverses in North Africa, Hitler was still considering the all-out attack on Kursk so vigorously opposed by Milch. Armored expert Guderian came to Berlin and added his objections: first on the grounds that the new Panther tank had a limited supply of spare parts; and second—in answer to the Führer's argument that the attack was necessary for political reasons—that few people even knew where Kursk (on the southern wing of the central front) was. Hitler confessed that the mere thought of this offensive churned his stomach, but in the ensuing days he was persuaded by both Zeitzler and Kluge to launch it while there was still time. The operation was entitled Citadel and, on the first of July, Hitler addressed his senior commanders. Germany, he said, must either tenaciously hold on to all conquered territory or fall. The German soldier had to realize he must stand and fight to the end. He admitted Citadel was a gamble yet felt sure it would succeed. Hadn't he been right, against all military advice, about Austria, Czechoslovakia, Poland and the Soviet Union? His inclusion of the last country struck a chill in the audience.

Manstein's attack force in the north consisted of eighteen divisions but less than 1000 tanks and 150 assault guns were fit for combat. In the south General Model had fifteen divisions and only 900 tanks. The assault began at an unusual hour, 3 P.M. on the fourth of July. It was hot and sultry. Thunder rumbled threateningly in the distance. At first it seemed as if the Soviets had been caught by surprise, for Red Army artillery did not respond until long after dark. But visions of a quick victory vanished once heavy rains began to fall. By dawn roads and trails were veritable quagmires. Later that morning a cloudburst transformed streams into roaring cascades, and it took sappers twelve hours to bridge them for tanks.

By July 9 the leading German tanks were still fifty-five miles from Kursk. The disappointment was followed next day by news that an Anglo-American force had landed on Sicily and were meeting a spiritless defense. This came as no surprise to Hitler and on July 13 he stopped the offensive he had so reluctantly supported so he could send reinforcements, including the SS Panzer Corps, to western Europe. Manstein argued that failure to continue the Kursk operation would endanger a long salient stretching all the way to the Black Sea. A gambler, Hitler accepted the loss of Kursk in return for more probable success in another quarter. But Citadel turned out to be more than a lost campaign. Thereafter the initiative in the East would belong to the Soviets.

5

Turning his back on the East, Hitler journeyed to northern Italy for another meeting with Il Duce, their thirteenth, on July 19. The conference, held at the imposing Villa Gaggia near Feltre, began promptly at 11 A.M. with the two men facing each other from large armchairs. Circling them was an elite group of military and diplomatic dignitaries. There were a few moments of embarrassed silence as both Mussolini and Hitler waited for the other to begin. It was a strange prelude, more like the stiff meeting of two families arranging a dowry. At last the Führer began speaking quietly of the general military and political situation. Il Duce sat cross-legged, hands clasped on knees, on the edge of a chair that was too large and too deep, listening with impassive patience. Then he began to fidget and he nervously passed a hand over the lower part of his face as Hitler abruptly assailed the Italians for their defeatism.

Occasionally Mussolini would press a spot behind his back that apparently pained him; occasionally he would heave a deep sigh as if resigned but wearied by a monologue which grew increasingly strident. Struggling to hide his distress, he mopped his brow with a handkerchief. Hitler showed no mercy, and even after an adjutant whispered something into his ear at five minutes to one, he did not pause in his reiterated assurance to the wilting Duce that the crisis could be overridden if Italy emulated Germany's fanatic determination to fight.

Five days later Il Duce was forced to listen to another diatribe, this from his own Fascist Grand Council, which was convening for the first time since 1939. After a long exhausting debate on his conduct of the war, a resolution was proposed demanding restoration of a constitutional monarchy with the King in command of the armed forces. The vote was taken and the motion passed 19 to 8. The next day, July 25, a sultry Sunday, Mussolini called on Victor Emmanuel III. He tried to control himself, but the notes in his hand rattled. The King stopped his arguments; it was useless to go on; Italy was defeated and the soldiers would no longer fight for Fascism. He requested Mussolini's resignation, then revealed he had already appointed Marshal Pietro Badoglio as head of government. "I am sorry, I am sorry," he was heard to say through the door. "But the solution could not have been otherwise." The little King accompanied Il Duce to the front door where he shook his hand warmly. As Mussolini stepped out of the villa he was approached by a Carabinieri officer who said His Majesty had charged him with the protection of Il Duce's person. Mussolini, protesting that it was not necessary, was led into an ambulance. He was under arrest.

At nine-thirty that night Hitler shocked his military advisers by announcing, "The Duce has resigned." The government had been taken over by Badoglio, their bitterest enemy. He quelled the rising panic and when Jodl suggested they do nothing until receiving a complete report from Rome Hitler curtly replied:

"Certainly, but we have to plan ahead. Undoubtedly, in their treachery, they will proclaim that they will remain loyal to us; but this is treachery. Of course, they won't remain loyal. . . . Anyway what's-his-name [Badoglio] said straightaway that the war would be continued but that doesn't mean a thing. They have to say that. But we can play the same game; we'll get ready to grab the whole mess, all that rabble."

The catastrophe in Italy was almost immediately followed by the carpet bombing of Hamburg. By the morning of August 3 the city was a blazing mass of ruins. More than 6000 acres of homes, factories and office buildings were gutted. Seventy thousand people were dead. Hitler was enraged, convinced as he was that such terror raids were a product of the Jews; he accused the leading British air commanders, including Portal and Harris, of being Jews or part Jewish. Psychologically Hamburg's destruction was as devastating as Stalingrad, not only to ordinary citizens but to Hitler's paladins.

6

Hitler's categorical refusal to negotiate with Stalin came at a curious time. Forty-eight hours earlier, on September 8, shortly after Allied troops breached the narrow channel between Sicily and the toe of Italy, it had been announced that the new Italian regime under Marshal Badoglio had signed an armistice with the West. Hitler was badly shaken even though he himself had predicted Badoglio would betray Germany. But he hadn't thought it possible (so he told the hastily summoned Goebbels) that this treachery would be committed so dishonorably.

Hitler's concern over the fate of 54,000 German troops in Sardinia and Corsica was succeeded by fear that the Allies might take the opportunity to launch their second front; the recent heavy English bombings were certainly suspicious. He was similarly haunted by another critical situation on the eastern front: the Wehrmacht, under heavy Soviet pressure, was withdrawing to the Dnieper.

At this point Goebbels wondered whether anything might be done with Stalin. "Not for a moment," said Hitler. It would be easier to make a deal with the English. At a given moment they would come to their senses. Goebbels disagreed. Stalin was more approachable, being a practical politician. Churchill was a romantic adventurer with whom one could not even talk sensibly. "Sooner or later," predicted Goebbels, "we shall have to face the question of inclining toward one enemy side or the other. Germany has never yet had luck with a two-front war; it won't be able to stand this one in the long run either." Concessions would have to be made, he said, pointing out how they had not come to power in 1933 by making unqualified demands. "We did present absolute demands on August 13, 1932, but failed because of them." The first thing to do was admit that Italy was lost, and he urged Hitler to address the nation on this subject without delay. The people were entitled to frankness, as well as a word of encouragement and solace from the Führer.

With reluctance Hitler agreed and on the night of September 10, from his bunker at Wolf's Lair, delivered a twenty-page speech which was taped in Berlin and broadcast to the nation. "My right to believe unconditionally in success," he said, "is founded not only on my own life but also on the destiny of our people." Neither time nor force of arms would ever bring the German people down.

Hitler, too, realized that words alone could not bolster his people's morale and decided to act drastically, dramatically. He would rescue Mussolini, now held prisoner in a hotel near the top of Gran Sasso, the loftiest peak in the Apennines range of mountains a hundred miles from Rome. An attack up the steep, rocky slope would not only cost many casualties but give guards time to kill Mussolini. Parachuting into such terrain was about as risky and so it was decided to use gliders. To carry off this piece of derring-do, Hitler chose a fellow Austrian. SS Captain Otto Skorzeny, a Viennese who stood six foot four, was, apart from his size, an imposing figure. He bore deep scars on his face from the fourteen duels he had fought as a student and carried himself with the air of a fourteenth-century condottiere. Skorzeny was not only a bold man of action but a canny one who believed commando operations should be carried out with a minimum force and as few casualties to both sides as possible. At 1 P.M. on Sunday, September 12, he and 107 men boarded gliders which, once airborne, began jerking erratically on their tow lines. The plan was to land on what appeared in photographs to be flat grassy meadow near Il Duce's hotel.

Mussolini, who had been threatening to commit suicide,

was sitting by an open window with arms folded when a glider suddenly loomed and a parachute, acting as a brake, blossomed behind just before it crashed with a shattering noise a hundred yards away. Four or five men in khaki piled out and began assembling a machine gun. Mussolini had no idea who they were, only that they were not English. An alarm rang and Carabinieri guards and police excitedly rushed from their barracks, as other gliders began landing. One skidded to rest less than twenty yards from the hotel. It was Skorzeny's. Looking up, he saw Il Duce staring out at him. "Away from the window!" he shouted and lunged into the lobby.

Skorzeny and his band literally bowled over the detachment of soldiers trying to stop them; then he bolted up a staircase, three steps at a time, to the next floor and flung open a door. Mussolini stood in the middle of the room. "Duce," he said, "the Führer has sent me. You are free!" Mussolini embraced him. "I knew my friend Adolf Hitler would not abandon me," he said and profusely thanked his rescuer. Skorzeny was surprised at Il Duce's appearance. He looked sick and unkempt in ill-fitting civilian clothes. He was unshaven; his usually smooth head was covered with short, stubbly hair.

By 3 P.M. they were in a small Fieseler-Storch which had managed to land safely on the sloping meadow. While happy to be free, Mussolini was apprehensive. Being a pilot, he knew how risky the take-off from this unlikely strip would be. As the plane gathered speed it bumped erratically over rocks toward a yawning gully. The Storch finally lifted but its left wheel almost immediately struck the ground. The little plane bounced into space, then plunged straight into the gully. Skorzeny closed his eyes and held his breath, awaiting the inevitable crash. Somehow the pilot managed to pull the plane out of its dive and, to the shouts and waves of Germans and Italians on the meadow, guided it safely down into the valley.

Nobody uttered a word. Only now, in "most unsoldierly fashion," did Skorzeny lay a reassuring hand on Il Duce's shoulder. Within the hour they landed in Rome, transferred to a trimotor Heinkel and were bound for Vienna. They arrived late at night and were driven to the Hotel Imperial. When Skorzeny brought Il Duce a pair of pajamas he rejected them. "I never wear anything at night," he said, "and I would advise you to do the same, Captain Skorzeny." He grinned roguishly. "Especially if you sleep with a woman."

As midnight struck Skorzeny's telephone rang. It was Hitler, who until he received word of the rescue had been "like a caged lion, pacing to and fro, listening for every ring of the telephone." His voice was husky with emotion. "You have performed a military feat which will become part of history," he said. "You have given me back my friend Mussolini."

After a stopover in Munich, where Mussolini was reunited with his family, he and Skorzeny set off for East Prussia early on the morning of September 14. The Führer was waiting at the Wolfsschanze airstrip. He warmly embraced his ally and for some time the two stood hand in hand. Finally Hitler turned to Skorzeny, who had discreetly waited before disembarking, and thanked him effusively. This one daring feat had forever endeared him to Hitler. It had also captured the imagination and admiration of foes as well as friends. More important, the spirits of Germans were uplifted not only by the rescue of Mussolini but by the manner in which it was done.

The Führer expected Mussolini to wreak vengeance on Badoglio and the regime in power. But Il Duce's only ambition was retirement to the Romagna. Privately he knew that his political life was over. His only future was as Hitler's pawn and the latter reacted with sarcasm and resentment. "What is this sort of Fascism which melts like snow before the sun!" he said. "For years I have explained to my generals that Fascism was the soundest alliance for the German people. I have never concealed my distrust of the Italian monarchy; at your insistence, however, I did nothing to obstruct the work which you carried out to the advantage of your King. But I must confess to you that we Germans have never understood your attitude in this respect." These words of intimidation were followed by a promise—even more ominous—to treat Italy well despite Badoglio's treachery *if* Il Duce would assume his role in a new republic. "The war must be won and once it is won Italy will be restored to her rights. The fundamental condition is that Fascism be reborn and that the traitors be brought to justice." Otherwise Hitler would be forced to treat Italy as an enemy. The country would be occupied and governed by Germans.

Mussolini wilted. If Hitler did not have his way the Italian people would undoubtedly suffer. Renouncing his plans to retire, he issued an official communiqué announcing that he had today assumed the supreme direction of Fascism in Italy. This was accompanied by four orders of the day which reinstated those authorities dismissed by Badoglio, reconstituted the Fascist militia, instructed the party to support the Wehrmacht and investigate the conduct of members relative to the July 25 coup d'état. By sheer force of will, Hitler had turned things around in Italy. But he no longer had any illusions about his partner. "I admit that I was deceived," he told his family circle. "It has turned out that Mussolini is only a little man."

Chapter Twenty-six

"AND WITH THE BEASTS OF THE EARTH"

APRIL 1943–APRIL 1944

1

To most Germans, Hitler's treatment of the Jews was a matter of minor importance. They had been indifferent to the lot of Jewish neighbors forced to wear the Star of David—after all, didn't they deserve it? And even after the same neighbors began to disappear it was assumed they had been deported. It was only wisc to discount unspeakable rumors in a land where listening to a foreign broadcast was punishable by death.

Not many knew about the killing centers. These were all in Poland and each was surrounded by a barren stretch several miles wide posted with notices that trespassers would be shot on sight. To ensure secrecy, the process from deportation to murder was not only executed speedily but done so under a smoke screen of euphemism: the over-all operation was referred to as "special treatment"; collectively the centers were described as the "East"; individual installations were called labor, concentration, transit or PW camps; and gas chambers and crematorium units were "bathhouses" and "corpse cellers."

Rumors of atrocities were answered by lies. When an important Nazi official, Hans Lammers, brought Himmler several reports that Jews were being executed in large numbers, the Reichsführer was vehement in denial. He explained that the so-called Final Solution order, received from the Führer through

Heydrich, merely entailed evacuation of Jews from the homeland. During these movements there had unfortunately been some deaths from sickness and attacks by enemy aircraft—and a number of Jews, he admitted, had to be killed during revolts as examples. Himmler assured Lammers that the majority of Jews were being "accommodated" in camps in the East and brought out photo albums to show how they were working for the war effort as shoemakers, tailors and such. "This is the order of the Führer," emphasized Himmler. "If you believe you have to take action, then tell the Führer and tell me the names of the people who made these reports to you." Lammers refused to divulge any information and sought more information from Hitler himself. He gave almost identical information. "I shall later on decide where these Jews will be taken," he said, then added reassuringly—"and in the meantime they are being cared for there."

While some of those closest to Hitler truly did not know what was going on in the East, many others, victims of self-deception, guessed if they did not know the terrifying facts. "Don't let anyone tell you he had no idea," Hans Frank later wrote, including himself in the accusation. "Everyone sensed that there was something horribly wrong with this system, even if we didn't know all the details. We didn't *want* to know! It was too comfortable to live on the system, to support our families in royal style, and to believe that it was all right."

This was the man who had recently told his subordinates that they were all accomplices in the elimination of the Jews which, disagreeable as it might be, "was necessary in the interests of Europe." In his role as head of the Generalgouvernement in Poland, Frank knew the order had come directly from the Führer. But the average German still was convinced that Hitler had no part in any brutality. "People are now clinging to the hope that the Führer doesn't know about such things, can't know, otherwise he would take some steps," wrote an ardent Nazi woman to a friend in reference to the Euthanasia Program, the overture to the Final Solution. "Anyway, they think he can't know how this is being done or on what scale. I feel, however, that this can't go on much longer without even this hope being lost."

Those in Hitler's family circle could not imagine Uncle Adi authorizing the murder of Jews. It was unthinkable. Hadn't both Schmundt and Engel successfully persuaded the Führer to let a number of part Jewish Wehrmacht officers keep their commissions? The villain had to be either Bormann or Himmler, acting behind his back. But these two were only Hitler's faithful agents. He alone conceived the Final Solution and he alone could have ordered its execution. Without him there would have been no Final Solution, and he was confident he could get away with it if it were presented to the world as a fait accompli.

In a secret conversation on June 19, 1943, the Führer instructed Himmler to proceed with the deportation of Jews to the East "regardless of any unrest it might cause during the next three or four months." It must be carried out, he added, "in an all-embracing way." While these words would certainly not have convinced the family circle that Hitler was a mass murderer, those he uttered some time later to Bormann would have. "For us," he said after proudly admitting that he had purged the German world of the Jewish poison, "this has been an essential process of disinfection, which we have prosecuted to its ultimate limit and without which we should ourselves have been asphyxiated and destroyed." Hadn't he always been absolutely fair in his dealings with the Jews? "On the eve of the war, I gave them one final warning. I told them that, if they precipitated another war, they would not be spared and that I would exterminate the vermin throughout Europe, and this time once and for all. To this warning they retorted with a declaration of war and affirmed that wherever in the world there was a Jew, there, too, was an implacable enemy of National Socialist Germany. Well, we have lanced the Jewish abscess; and the world of the future will be eternally grateful to us."

One particularly horrifying aspect of Hitler's Final Solution had recently come to an apocalyptical ending. Of the 380,000 Jews crowded into the Warsaw ghetto, all but 70,000 had been deported to the killing centers in an operation devoid of resistance. By this time, however, those left behind had come to the realization that deportation meant death. With this in mind, Jewish political parties within the ghetto finally resolved their differences and banded together to resist further shipments with force. They did so to Himmler's amazement and he thereupon ordered the total dissolution of the Warsaw ghetto. At three in the morning of April 9, 1943, more than 2000 Waffen SS infantrymen—accompanied by tanks, flame throwers and dynamite squads—invaded the ghetto, expecting an easy conquest, only to be met by determined fire from 1500 fighters armed with weapons smuggled into the ghetto over a long period: several light machine guns, hand grenades, a hundred or so rifles and carbines, several hundred pistols and revolvers, and Molotov cocktails. Himmler had expected the action to take three days but by nightfall his forces had to withdraw. The one-sided battle continued day after day to the bewilderment of the SS commander, General Jürgen Stroop, who could not understand why "this trash and subhumanity" refused to abandon a hopeless cause. He reported that, although his men had initially captured "considerable numbers of Jews, who are cowards by nature," it was becoming more and more difficult. "Over and over again new battle groups consisting of twenty to thirty Jewish men, accompanied by a corresponding number of women, kindled new resistance." The women, he noted, had the disconcerting habit of suddenly hurling grenades they had hidden in their bloomers.

The defenders fought two, three weeks with reckless heroism, taking refuge, as a last resort, in the sewers. Finally, on May 15, firing from the few remaining Jewish nests of resistance became sporadic and the following day General Stroop blew up the Tlomacki Synagogue, in the "Aryan" section of Warsaw, to celebrate the end of the battle. For exactly four weeks the little Jewish army had held off superior, well-armed forces until almost the last men was killed or wounded. Of the 56,065 who were rounded up, 7000 were shot out of hand; 22,000 were sent to Treblinka and Lublin; the remainder to labor camps. The German losses were 16 dead and 85 wounded. Of far more significance was the blow dealt to Hitler's concept of Jewish cowardice.

2

Early that June Pius XII secretly addressed the Sacred College of Cardinals on the extermination of the Jews. "Every word We address to the competent authority on this subject, and all Our public utterances," he said in explanation of his reluctance to express more open condemnation, "have to be carefully weighed and measured by Us in the interests of the victims themselves, lest, contrary to Our intentions, We make their situation worse and harder to bear." He did not add that another reason for proceeding cautiously was that he regarded

Bolshevism as a far greater danger than Nazism.

The position of the Holy See was deplorable but it was an offense of omission rather than commission. The Church, under the Pope's guidance, had already saved the lives of more Jews than all other churches, religious institutions and rescue organizations combined, and was presently hiding thousands of Jews in monasteries, convents and Vatican City itself. The record of the Allies was far more shameful. The British and Americans, despite lofty pronouncements, had not only avoided taking any meaningful action but gave sanctuary to few persecuted Jews. The Moscow Declaration of that year—signed by Roosevelt, Churchill and Stalin—methodically listed Hitler's victims as Polish, Italian, French, Dutch, Belgian, Norwegian, Soviet and Cretan. The curious omission of Jews (a policy emulated by the U.S. Office of War Information) was protested vehemently but uselessly by the World Jewish Congress. By the simple expedient of converting the Jews of Poland into Poles, and so on, the Final Solution was lost in the Big Three's general classification of Nazi terrorism.

Contrasting with their reluctance to face the issue of systematic Jewish extermination was the forthrightness and courage of the Danes, who defied German occupation by transporting to Sweden almost every one of their 6500 Jews; of the Finns, allies of Hitler, who saved all but four of their 4000 Jews; and of the Japanese, another ally, who provided refuge in Manchuria for some 5000 wandering European Jews in recognition of financial aid given by the Jewish firm of Kuhn, Loeb & Company during the Russo-Japanese War of 1904–5.

But the man who did most to hinder the atrocities in the East was a thirty-four-year-old German lawyer who worked for Himmler. Konrad Morgen, son of a railroad conductor, had become imbued with the ethics of law from his student days and even as an assistant SS judge was outspoken in his disapproval of illegality whoever committed it. His judgments, based strictly on the evidence, so exasperated his superiors that Morgen was posted to a front-line SS division as punishment. Because of his outstanding reputation he was transferred in 1943 to the SD's Financial Crimes Office with the understanding that he was not to deal with political cases. Early that summer he was given a routine investigative mission to clear up a long-standing corruption case at Buchenwald concentration camp. The commandant, Karl Koch, had been suspected of hiring out camp laborers to civilian employers, racketeering in food supplies and, in general, running the camp for his own personal profit. The initial investigation had failed to bring conviction when a parade of witnesses categorically supported Koch's plea of innocence.

Morgen journeyed in July to Weimar where he installed himself in Hitler's favorite local hostelry, the Elephant Hotel, and quietly began his research. To his surprise he found the concentration camp, located on a hill above Weimar, a prospect pleasing to the eye. The installations were clean and freshly painted; the grounds covered with grass and flowers. The prisoners appeared to be healthy, sun-tanned, normally fed. They enjoyed regular mail service and a large camp library which boasted books in foreign languages. There were variety shows, movies, sporting contests and even a brothel. As Morgen began to dig deeper he learned that the corruption at Buchenwald had started with the influx of Jews after Crystal Night. Unfortunately, the closer he got to the truth about Koch, the further he was from proof. Too often for coincidence he found that prisoners said to have information of corruption were now dead. From their files he discovered that the dates of death were years apart and in each case a different cause was given. Suspecting murder, he ordered an investigation but his own special agent could not find a single clue and refused to continue his search.

An ordinary man would have abandoned the investigation, but Morgen was so convinced that crime had been committed that he turned detective himself. He went to local banks where he briefly displayed official-looking papers and pretended that he had been authorized by Himmler to examine Koch's accounts. His persistence was rewarded. At one bank he found undeniable evidence that Koch had embezzled 100,000 marks. Finally proof of murder came when Morgen burrowed deep into the prison records to discover that witnesses were taken to a secret cell and eliminated.

Armed with a bulging briefcase of records and affidavits, Morgen set out for Berlin. His superior, the chief of criminal police, blanched at the evidence. He had not expected Morgen to take his assignment so seriously and hurriedly passed him on to Kaltenbrunner. Heydrich's successor was equally aghast —or pretended to be—and said, "That's not my business. Take it to your own boss in Munich." Morgen dutifully took the evidence to the head of the SS Legal Department, who was just as unwilling to take any responsibility. "You'll have to tell all that to Himmler," he said. Morgen proceeded to the Reichsführer's field headquarters where he was refused an interview. With the help of a sympathetic member of Himmler's personal staff, Morgen proceeded to draft a cautiously worded telegram outlining the case. The problem was to get it delivered personally. Somehow it was slipped through the bureaucratic barrier and came to Himmler's attention. To the amazement of almost everyone, he gave Morgen complete authority to proceed against Koch, his wife and anyone else connected with the sordid case. Some thought it was because of Himmler's mistrust of Oswald Pohl, the administrator of all concentration camps; others believed that he did not realize the case was a potential Pandora's box; but those who knew Himmler most intimately felt it was another instance of his peculiar sense of honor.

3

"Cruelty has a human heart."

WILLIAM BLAKE

There was no more paradoxical figure in the higher reaches of National Socialism than Heinrich Himmler. He impressed many by his charm and politeness, his modesty at meetings, his reasonableness. Diplomats described him as a man of sober judgment and the resistance movement regarded him as the sole leading Nazi who could be utilized in ending Hitler's rule. To General Friedrich Hossbach, Hitler's chief adjutant, he was the Führer's evil spirit, cold and calculating, the "most unscrupulous figure in the Third Reich." To Max Amann he was "a kind of Robespierre or witch-burning Jesuit." What made him sinister to Carl Burckhardt, the former League of Nations High Commissioner of Danzig, was "his capacity to concentrate upon little things, his pettifogging conscientiousness and his inhuman methodology; he had a touch of the robot." To his young daughter Gudrun he was a loving father. "Whatever is said about my *Papi*," she recently said, "what has been written or shall be written in the future about him—he was my father, the best father I could have and I loved him and still love him."

Most of his subordinates regarded Himmler as a warm, thoughtful employer with a deep sense of democracy. He played skat with secretaries and soccer with aides and adjutants. Once he invited a dozen young charwomen to his birthday dinner and ordered his reluctant officers to choose them as table companions, then himself led off the head charwoman.

The key to this enigmatic character did not lie in his youth. He came from a well-to-do Bavarian middle-class family. Young Himmler was neither more nor less anti-Semitic than the average young Bavarian of his class and the remarks about Jews in his diary were those of a bigot trying to be fair rather than of a racist. He had rigid convictions concerning sex and these were not unusual for his day. In short, he seemed to be the predictable product of Bavarian education and training—a promising young bureaucrat, meticulous and regulated.

It was not strange that a young man of such bent should be attracted by the theories of National Socialism and its charismatic leader; a bureaucrat by training and loyal by nature, he was a perfect Nazi career man. As he rose in the party he became the victim of a battle raging within himself. He was a Bavarian, yet fervently admired Prussian kings like Frederick the Great and constantly praised Prussian austerity and hardness. Himself dark, of average size and somewhat oriental features, he believed fanatically that the ideal German was Nordic and, like his master, preferred to surround himself with tall, blond, blue-eyed subordinates. He admired physical perfection as well as athletic skill, yet was constantly suffering from stomach cramps. He presented a ridiculous figure on skis or in the water and once collapsed trying to win a lowly bronze medal in the mile run.

With more personal power than anyone in the Reich except Hitler, he remained unpretentious and conscientious. Born and bred a Catholic, he now relentlessly attacked the Church and yet, according to a close associate, conscientiously rebuilt his SS on Jesuit principles by assiduously copying "the service statutes and spiritual exercises presented by Ignatius Loyola."

Dreaded by millions, he trembled before the Führer who, he confessed to a subordinate, made him feel like a schoolboy who hadn't done his homework. Like his Führer, Himmler was indifferent to things material and, unlike Göring and others, never profited from his position. He lived in frugal simplicity, eating moderately, drinking sparingly and restricting himself to two cigars a day. He maintained one household on the Tegernsee for his wife and daughter, another near the Königsee for his personal secretary, Hedwig Potthast, who bore him a son and a daughter. And as a man of responsibility, he provided for each family in a style which left him very little for his personal use.

Some of his tenets were so eccentric that even his faithful followers found them difficult to accept: glacial cosmogony, magnetism, homeopathy, mesmerism, natural eugenics, clairvoyance, faith healing and sorcery. He sponsored experiments in obtaining gasoline by having water run over coal and in producing gold out of base metals.

While his power had all come from Hitler, the Führer wanted nothing to do with him personally. "I need such policemen," he told his personal adjutant, Julius Schaub, who had been entreated by Himmler to get him an invitation to the Berghof, "but I don't like them."

At the same time, he put Himmler in full charge of the operation closest to his heart, the Final Solution. In some respects it was an appropriate appointment. From the beginning Himmler had been under Hitler's spell and he remained totally Hitler's man, his disciple and subject. Furthermore, Himmler was the epitome of National Socialism, for it was as a diligent professional party worker that Himmler had overcome his own problems of identity. He was the Führer's faithful right hand who, despite squeamishness in the face of blood or beatings, had become a mass killer by remote control, an efficient businessman murderer.

If approached diplomatically he found it difficult to resist a reasonable plea for mercy. In one case he freed a deserter; in another, forgave an official for writing a biting critique of SS treatment of the Poles. But his sense of honor forbade him to show mercy to his own flesh and blood. When a nephew, an SS officer, was brought up on charges of homosexuality he immediately signed the order sending him to a punishment camp. During imprisonment, the young man committed other homosexual acts and the uncle ordered his execution. Rolf Wehser, an SS judge, urged leniency but Himmler refused. "I do not want anyone to say that I was more lenient because it was my own nephew." It was Hitler himself who had to revoke the judgment of death.

Under Himmler's supervision the work of the killing centers reached the peak of efficiency by the fall of 1943. At Auschwitz those selected for death marched to the gas chambers, unaware of their fate, past an inmate symphony orchestra conducted by the Jewish violinist Alma Rose. At Treblinka, however, the

Jews almost always knew they were about to die and would cry and laugh from shock. Annoyed guards lashed away at them; babies, who hindered attendants while shaving their mothers' hair, would be smashed against a wall. If there was any resistance, guards and *Kapos* (trusties) would use whips to drive the naked victims into trucks bound for the gas chamber.

The thought of refusing the order to murder never entered the heads of the executioners. "I could only say *Jawohl*," Höss, the commandant of Auschwitz, later confessed. "It didn't occur to me at all that I would be held responsible. You see, in Germany it was understood that if something went wrong, then the man who gave the orders was responsible." Nor did these executioners ever question whether the Jews deserved their fate. "Don't you see, we SS men were not supposed to think about these things; it never even occurred to us. . . . We were all so trained to obey orders, without even thinking, that the thought of disobeying an order would simply never have occurred to anybody, and somebody else would have done it just as well if I hadn't."

Some of the executioners thoroughly enjoyed their work but these were sadistic at the peril of punishment from their chief. Years earlier Himmler had forbidden independent action against the Jews by any member of his organization. "The SS commander must be hard but not hardened," he instructed one Sturmbannführer. "If, during your work, you come across cases in which some commander exceeds his duty or shows signs that his restraint is becoming blurred, intervene at once."

Training his men to become hard but not hardened was a difficult task for Himmler and he attempted to do so by transforming the SS into an order of knights with the motto: "Loyalty is my honor." He imbued the SS, therefore, not only with a sense of racial superiority but with the hard virtues of loyalty, comradeship, duty, truth, diligence, honesty and knighthood. His SS, as the elite of the party, was the elite of the German Volk, and therefore the elite of the entire world.

Himmler summoned his SS generals to Posen on October 4, 1943. His primary purpose was to enlarge the circle of those privy to the extermination of the Jews. The recent revelations by Morgen, combined with persistent rumors of terrors in the concentration camps, were causing apprehension and some revulsion among the most loyal adherents of the Führer. Now that the truth was leaking out, he had decided to involve the party and the military in his Final Solution. By making them, in effect, co-conspirators, he would force them to fight on to the end. The war was probably lost, but this would give him time to fulfill his main ambition. If worse came to worst he would take millions of Jews to death with him.

4

While Hitler envisaged grandiose plans of conquest that encompassed five continents, his armies in the East were being steadily driven back toward the homeland. Inspired by success in repelling Operation Citadel, the Soviet high command had gone over to the attack with confidence and daring. In the last six months of 1943 the Red Army had advanced in some places as much as two hundred and fifty miles, throwing the Germans in the south and center back across the Dnieper River.

This only spurred Hitler to accelerate the Final Solution and early in 1944 he allowed the secret to be revealed to a large non-party, non-SS group. On January 26, 1944, Himmler made his third address, this to some 260 high-ranking army and navy officers in a theater at Posen. In his cool, antiseptic manner he told how Hitler had given him the mission of extermination. "I can assure you that the Jewish question has been solved. Six million have been killed." A wave of applause swept the auditorium. One Wehrmacht officer near Colonel von Gerstdorff (who had tried in vain to bomb Hitler and himself to bits) stood up on a chair in his enthusiasm. From the rear of the hall an aghast general checked to see how many of his colleagues were *not* applauding. He could count but five.

Himmler continued this campaign of enlightenment in the next weeks. He admitted to a group of navy leaders that he had ordered women and children killed. "I would be a weakling, a criminal to our descendants if I allowed hate-filled sons to grow to manhood in this battle of humans against subhumans . . . but we must recognize more and more that we are engaged in a primitive, original, natural racial battle." He told much the same story to another group of generals at Sonthofen. "The Jewish question in Germany and in general throughout the occupied territories is solved," he said. And when he added that it had been done "without compromise," there was applause. In all, Himmler made some fifteen speeches on the Final Solution, covering a wide range of audiences but, significantly, never one of Foreign Office personnel.

The last days of 1943 were oppressive ones for Hitler. Not only did his troops face new setbacks at Leningrad and throughout the Ukraine, but his extermination program was threatened when SS Judge Morgen finally uncovered the network of corruption at Buchenwald. An accomplice of Camp Commandant Koch's, named Köhler, lost his nerve and agreed to testify. He was jailed as a material witness but within days was found dead in his cell. In the light of such damning evidence, Koch wilted under Morgen's relentless interrogation. He confessed that, besides enriching himself at the expense of the inmates, he had executed a number of them to cover up his secret.

The successful prosecution of Koch by no means satisfied Morgen's sense of justice. He pursued the trail of corruption to Poland. In Lublin Morgen was warmly greeted by the camp's commandant, Kriminalkommissar Wirth, who had acted as Gerstein's guide in Belzec. He revealed with pride that it was he who had not only built the four extermination camps in the Lublin area but organized the system of extermination. Each establishment, he said, had been built up like a Potemkin village. As trains pulled into a dummy railroad station, the occupants imagined they were entering a city or town. With relish, Wirth described how he or one of his representatives would greet the newcomers with a set speech: "Jews, you were brought here to be resettled but before we organize the future Jewish state, you must of course learn how to work. You must learn a new trade." After these calming words the victims would innocently start off on their march to death.

Wirth's description of the entire process seemed "completely fantastic" to Morgen but not after he toured the buildings which housed the loot. From the massive piles—including one incredible heap of watches—he realized that "something frightful was going on here." Never had he seen so much money at one time, particularly foreign currency. There were coins from all over the world. He gaped in wonder at the gold-smelting furnace and its prodigious stack of gold bars.

Morgen inspected all four camps built by Wirth—Maidanek, Treblinka, Sobibor and Belzec. In each one he saw evidence of execution—the gas chambers, the ovens, the mass graves. Here was crime on a ghastly scale, yet he was helpless to act since the order had come directly from the Führer's chancellery. Morgen's only recourse was to prosecute the "arbitrary killings" of prisoners; these could be brought before the SS judicial system. He set out to get evidence and persevered, despite continued hindrances, until he found sufficient proof to bring charges of murder against the two top officials at Maidanek.

The guiding spirit of all four camps, the helpful Christian Wirth, continued to talk freely to Morgen. One day he remarked casually that a man named Höss ran another large extermination complex near Auschwitz. This sounded like fertile ground for Morgen, but his authority was limited and he had to find some good reason to go so far afield. He soon found his excuse: an unsolved case of gold smuggling involving several men on Höss's staff. And so by early 1944 the doughty Morgen was investigating the death camps near Auschwitz. He had no trouble locating numerous sheds loaded with loot, gas chambers and crematories. But investigations of "illegal" killings and corruption were blocked every time one of his men got too close to the truth and Morgen decided to return to Germany so he could attend to a more important matter—the mass official killing themselves. Morgen decided to approach Himmler personally and make it clear that the extermination system was leading Germany "straight into the abyss." To reach the Reichsführer he again had to go through channels. First on the list was his immediate superior, the chief of the criminal police. Nebe listened in shocked silence ("I could see his hair stand on end when I made my report") and when he found tongue he told Morgen to report the matter immediately to Kaltenbrunner. He too was appalled and promised to take his protest to both Himmler and Hitler. Next came Chief Justice of the SS Court Breithaupt. He was so incensed that he promised to arrange a meeting between Himmler and Morgen. But this time the machinery of bureaucracy prevented Morgen from getting beyond the Reichsführer's anteroom. This convinced Morgen that he would have to take a more practical route to justice: "that is, by removing from this system of destruction the leaders and important elements through the means offered by the system itself. I could not do this with regard to the killings ordered by the head of the state, but I could do it for killings outside of this order, or against this order, or for other serious charges."

He returned to his task with spirit, determined to institute proceedings against as many leaders as possible in hopes of undermining the entire system of mass murder. He expanded the scope of investigation to concentration camps despite threats and attempted reprisals. At Oranienburg one of his informers—a prisoner named Rothe—was saved at the last moment from a public execution designed to warn other inmates not to collaborate with Morgen. Even so he won the nickname, "The Bloodhound Judge," bringing some 800 cases of corruption and murder to trial, 200 of which resulted in sentences. Karl Koch of Buchenwald was shot. The commandant of Maidanek was also executed, his chief assistant condemned to death. The commandant of Hertogenbosch was posted to a penal unit for maltreatment of prisoners and the head of Flossenburg was fired for drunkenness and debauchery.

These trials caused such reverberations in the hierarchy by the early spring of 1944 that Himmler, undoubtedly at Hitler's order, instructed Morgen to cease further investigations. "The Bloodhound Judge" was going too far, too successfully and was about to launch a full-scale inquiry into Rudolf Höss and the Auschwitz constellation of camps. The shock wave of Morgen's one-man house cleaning had already compromised the Lublin killing complex. Kriminalkommissar Wirth was instructed to destroy three of the four camps he had built—Treblinka, Sobibor and Belzec—without leaving a trace. That task completed, Wirth was dispatched to Italy to defend roads against partisans. Here the man who had escaped Morgen's justice was soon brought down by a ruder one—a partisan bullet in the back. In the meantime, despite the Himmler-Hitler order, Konrad Morgen was surreptitiously continuing his lonesome attempt to end the Final Solution.* He was particularly interested in a rather low-ranking SD officer named Eichmann.

*Morgen also did his best to convict Ilse Koch, the wife of the Buchenwald commandant. He was convinced that she was guilty of sadistic crimes, but the charges against her could not be proven. After the war Morgen was asked by an American official to testify that Frau Koch made lampshades from the skin of inmates. Morgen replied that, while she undoubtedly was guilty of many crimes, she was truly innocent of this charge. After personally investigating the matter, he had thrown it out of his own case. Even so, the American insisted that Morgen sign an affidavit that Frau Koch had made the lampshades. Anyone undaunted by Nazi threats was not likely to submit to those of a representative of the democracies. His refusal to lie was followed by a threat to turn him over to the Russians, who would surely beat him to death. Morgen's second and third refusals were followed by severe beatings. Though he detested Frau Koch, nothing could induce him to bear false witness. Fortunately, Morgen survived and is presently practicing law in West Germany.

PART 9

INTO THE ABYSS

Chapter Twenty-seven

THE ARMY BOMB PLOT

NOVEMBER 1943–JULY 21, 1944

1

On the eve of the twentieth anniversary of the Beer Hall Putsch Germany's strategic position was frankly revealed to a hundred or so Reichsleiters and Gauleiters by General Jodl. In a top secret lecture at Munich he told of the bitter defeats in Russia, of the failure to draw Spain into the war and thus seize Gibraltar (because of that "Jesuit Foreign Minister Serrano Suñer"), and of the "most monstrous of all betrayals in history"—that of the Italians. Jodl spoke extemporaneously of the future, alarming his listeners with the admission that the Western Allies enjoyed such tremendous air superiority that a mass landing could not possibly be contained by the present defense forces. There was, he concluded, only one solution: to mobilize every German able to bear arms. It would not be possible to drain troops and supplies from the East, he said, since things were indeed "getting warm" there. New ways had to be found to solve the dilemma of manpower shortage in the West. "In my opinion, the time has come to take steps with remorseless vigor and resolution in Denmark, Holland, France and Belgium, to compel thousands of idle ones to carry out the fortification work, which is more important than any other work. The necessary orders for this have already been given."

The glum picture of the present ended with the acknowledgment that the terror air raids by the West "weighed most heavily on the home front" and that U-boat reprisals were declining drastically because of enemy air superiority over the Atlantic. At the same time, he said, there were considerable grounds for confidence in final victory. They were blessed with a leader who was "the soul not only of the political but also of the military conduct of the war," and it was his will power alone that was animating "the whole of the German armed forces, with respect to strategy, organization, and munitions of war. Similarly the unity of political and military command, which is so important, is personified by him in a way such as has never been known since the days of Frederick the Great."

The politicians cheered. Jodl's talk was a tour-de-force mixture of candor and hope that was followed two days later by a purely inspirational performance on the part of Hitler. In a speech from the Löwenbräu cellar, he spoke with such confidence and fire that many of those listening on the radio were as uplifted as those present.

These attempts to inspire the party and the people were undermined within weeks by deterioration in both the political and the military situations. Hungarians were eying Italy's desertion with envy and Romanians were bitter at the destruction of eighteen divisions on the Don and Volga. The Wehrmacht itself had suffered 1,686,000 casualties in the past twelve months and it was so difficult to find replacements that the conscription law exempting the youngest or only son of a family was suspended, and fifty-year-old men, veterans of the First World War, were deemed eligible for service.

That spring enemy planes ravaged Bavaria. Almost every day the warning sirens screeched and Hitler would climb down the sixty-five steps to the deep bunker under the Berghof. But no bombs dropped on the Obersalzberg; the raiders were bound for Vienna, Hungary or other populated targets.

The air raid alerts became so common that some of the guests at the Berghof began to ignore them. One early morning Traudl rushed from her bed to safety but found no one in the bunker. When she came up to see why, there was Hitler standing at the entrance like Cerberus, scanning the skies anxiously. He wagged an admonishing finger at her. "Don't be so careless, young lady. Get back to the bunker; the alarm is not yet over." She didn't tell him that the other guests were still in their beds but obediently descended the long flight of steps. During lunch Hitler delivered a lecture on the stupidity of not taking shelter.

"My co-workers, some of whom are irreplaceable, simply have an obligation to go to the bunker," he scolded. "It is idiotic to prove your courage by placing yourself in danger of being struck by a bomb."

He was placing his own body in jeopardy by steadfastly refusing to exercise, rest or undergo massage, while depending more and more on medication. In addition to the other pills and injections, he allowed himself to be dosed with a heart and liver extract and four to six multivitamin tablets a day. It was almost as though his health was no longer important and he was only keeping himself alive until he had accomplished his mission in life. He did succeed in lifting himself out of depression and resumed preaching his message of hope. One fine day, he assured the family circle, something would change the entire situation. The Anglo-Saxons would eventually realize their best interests lay with his anti-Bolshevist crusade. *It had to happen.*

The Allies responded with a new strategic bombing campaign of coordinated and concentrated raids. By early May attacks by American daylight bombers on fuel plants in central and eastern Germany seriously endangered Hitler's entire armament program. The daily output of 5850 metric tons abruptly fell to 4820 tons. "The enemy has struck us at one of our weakest points," Albert Speer reported to Hitler. "If they persist this time, we will soon no longer have any fuel production worth mentioning. Our one hope is that the other side has an air force General Staff as scatterbrained as ours!"

2

The war of mobility which the Germans had so successfully employed in the early stages of the war was now turned against them. In the First World War the protracted stalemate had enabled German propaganda to argue plausibly almost to the end that the war could still be won. No such assertions were possible amid the military realities of World War II. There could no longer be any question of another German summer offensive. Notwithstanding the staggering losses of manpower in the past three years, Russia still had some 300 divisions of over 5,000,000 men in the field, opposing 20 undermanned German divisions totaling 2,000,000 men. The most painful surprise to the Germans was not the astounding reserve strength of the Red Army but its tenacious fighting spirit. During the siege of Stalingrad Hitler had captiously explained the inability of Paulus to take the city with the fact that the Russians fought like "swamp animals." Whatever the designation, the vigor and valor of these *Untermenschen* of the East had proved more than a match for the Teutonic race. So much for the underlying premise of Hitler's *Ostpolitik*. He had no thought of even a token victory in 1944. His concern, in fact, was invasion from the West. "It will decide the issue not only of the year but of the whole war," he told his military advisers one day in early June as he gazed absently out the window. "If we succeed in throwing back the invasion, such an attempt cannot and will not be repeated within a short time. It will mean that our reserves will be set free to use in Italy and the East." Then the latter front could at least be stabilized. But if they could not throw back the Western invaders it meant final defeat.

Hitler had turned over the task of repelling the West to Rommel, who had already presided over one catastrophe, the loss of North Africa, through no fault of his own. Rommel was convinced that the invasion could best be stopped at the beaches where the enemy was at his weakest. "The troops are unsure and possibly even seasick," he argued. "They are unfamiliar with the terrain. Heavy weapons are not yet available in sufficient quantity. That is the moment to strike and defeat them." His elderly superior, Gerd von Rundstedt, Commander-in-Chief West, held the opposite view. The decisive battle should be fought far behind the coast. All armor and tactical reserves, therefore, should be well inside France so they could encircle and destroy the oncoming enemy. Hitler settled the dispute by a compromise that pleased neither. He took all armored units from Rommel but placed them much closer to the coast than Rundstedt wanted.

On the morning of June 4 Rommel set out for Germany by car, ostensibly to visit his wife, whose birthday fell on the sixth, but his main purpose was to drive on to Berchtesgaden and persuade Hitler to transfer two additional armored divisions and one mortar brigade to Normandy. "The most urgent problem," he wrote in his diary, "is to win the Führer over by personal conversation." It was an appropriate time for a brief holiday. The Luftwaffe meteorologist in Paris had just reported that no Allied invasion could be expected for two weeks because of stormy conditions.

* * *

Across the Channel General Dwight Eisenhower, the Allied commander-in-chief, was faced with his own dilemma. The invasion, Operation Overlord, was scheduled to start the next day but the unfavorable weather reports induced him to postpone the great venture for at least another twenty-four hours. He spent most of the day alone in his cramped house trailer in a woods near Portsmouth, mulling over the pros and cons of risking an attack under bad conditions or waiting until July. More than 200,000 men had already been briefed on the operation and it seemed inevitable that the secret would leak out by that time. That evening a new weather front was reported: there would be relatively good conditions until the morning of June 6, when the weather would deteriorate. Eisenhower polled his commanders. Air Chief Marshal Sir Arthur Tedder feared the cloud cover would hinder his planes but Montgomery's reply was, "I would say go." Eisenhower made the decision: On June 6 the Allies would hit the beaches of Normandy.

June 6 was barely fifteen minutes old, British Double Summer Time, when an eighteen-year-old paratrooper named Murphy dropped into the garden of a schoolmistress in Ste. Mère Église. It was the beginning of D-Day. Within an hour vague and contradictory reports began flooding German Seventh Army command posts. It was 3 A.M., German time, before Rundstedt informed Supreme Headquarters, presently located on the Obersalzberg, that major paratroop and glider landings had been made in Normandy. Three hours later Rundstedt's chief of staff informed Warlimont that this, in all probability, was the invasion. He urged that the four motorized-armored divisions of OKW reserves be sent nearer the landing area.

But Jodl was positive it was merely a diversionary attack. He had been tricked by a secret Allied operation known as Bodyguard: a fake war plan was cleverly leaked to Führer Headquarters indicating the main landings would be farther north near Calais where the Channel was narrowest. In consequence, Jodl refused to wake up Hitler for consultation.

This caused consternation at Rundstedt's headquarters. The elderly field marshal, according to his chief of operations, "was fuming with rage, red in the face, and his anger made his speech unintelligible." Another commander might have telephoned Hitler directly but the aristocratic Rundstedt, who openly referred to his Führer as "that Bohemian corporal," would not stoop to petition. He left the entreaties to his subordinates, who kept pestering OKW with phone calls in an effort to change Jodl's mind.

It was not until 9 A.M. that the Führer was finally wakened. This, in fact, was earlier than usual but he was scheduled to receive Horthy, Tiso and Antonescu—the dictators of Hungary, Slovakia and Romania—at Klessheim Castle. Emerging from his bedroom in dressing gown, Hitler listened placidly to the latest reports before sending for Keitel and Jodl. He was not so calm by the time they arrived. "Well, is it or isn't it the invasion?" he shouted, then spun on his heel and left. But before long his mood abruptly changed. He clapped people on the back with unaccustomed familiarity as if revitalized by at last coming to grips with the West. "Now, we can give them a nice little packet!" he exclaimed with a slap on his own thigh. He was jubilant throughout the hourlong scenic auto trip to Klessheim. "I can hold the Russians as long as I like," he told his companions and then boasted how he would destroy the Anglo-Saxon powers in front of the Atlantic Wall.

Events in the West dominated the midday situation conference, which was held just before the meeting with the three dictators. As Hitler entered the conference room his military advisers, anxiously clustered around maps and charts, turned with some excitement and apprehension. To their amazement he strode in confidently, face beaming. In exceptionally broad Austrian he said, "So, we're off!" and began chuckling in a carefree manner. What he had wanted all the time had finally come true, he told them. "I am face to face with my real enemies!"

At 4 P.M. Hitler was back at the Berghof in time for a late lunch with Eva and a number of party dignitaries and their wives. The highlight of the meal was his comment on vegetarianism: "The elephant is the strongest animal; he also cannot stand meat." The party adjourned as usual to the tea house where the Führer treated himself to lime-blossom tea. This was followed by an hour's nap and another military conference at 11 P.M. He doubted, he said, that this was the real invasion. It was only a feint to trick him into deploying his forces to the wrong place. The main invasion would surely come at Calais since it was the shortest route across the Channel. He could not be shaken from the lie so assiduously planted by Bodyguard—perhaps because that was the route in reverse he had selected when he was planning to invade England.

By midnight the Allies had broken into Hitler's western

Festung on a front of thirty miles. The Germans had been completely taken by surprise, their air force and navy rendered powerless and their coast defenses shattered. The enemy had achieved a great victory at the cost of fewer than 2500 lives but there was still time to throw them back into the Channel—if the right decisions were made without delay.

3

Hitler was still so convinced that the Normandy landing was a trick that he had not yet taken resolute action against this bridgehead, and by refusing to give his field commanders a free hand he had deprived them of their last chance to seize the initiative. The battle was already lost. By now it was obvious that the Allies had won complete air supremacy over France, and Hitler turned to Göring, whom he had praised a few days earlier. He sarcastically asked whether it was true that his vaunted Luftwaffe had taken out a "knock-for-knock" insurance policy with the West.

In desperation the Führer inaugurated the V-1 rocket campaign against London on June 12, two days ahead of schedule. The harassed catapult crews could launch only ten flying bombs. Four crashed immediately, two disappeared, and the others destroyed a single railway bridge. After this fiasco Göring hastily reminded Hitler that this was Milch's program, not his, but when the second launching of 244 rockets two days later set disastrous fires in London the Reichsmarschall was quick to claim the credit.

All this had no effect on the situation in Normandy. Within ten days the Allies had managed to land almost a million men and 500,000 tons of matériel. The situation was so desperate that on June 17 Hitler motored west to a village north of Soissons. Here, for the first time since D-Day, he met Rundstedt and Rommel. "He looked pale and sleepless," recalled General Hans Speidel, "playing nervously with his glasses and an array of colored pencils which he held between his fingers . . . then in a loud voice he spoke bitterly of his displeasure at the success of the Allied landings, for which he tried to hold the field commanders responsible."

It was Rommel, not Rundstedt, who carried the burden of rebuttal. He pointed out, "with merciless frankness," that the struggle was hopeless against the Allies' overwhelming superiority in the air, at sea and on land. There was but one chance: to abandon the suicidal policy of holding onto every meter of ground and abruptly withdraw German forces so that all armored forces could be reorganized for a decisive battle to be fought outside the range of the withering enemy naval fire. Hitler answered by assuring his commanders that his new rocket bombs "would make the British willing to make peace." This was a sore subject to Rundstedt and Rommel, whose request to use these bombs against English south coast ports supplying the invasion had been declined by Hitler on the grounds that all rockets must be concentrated on a political target. The two field marshals confined themselves to criticism of the Luftwaffe: how could one win on the ground without a minimum of help from the air? Hitler's answer was that "masses of jet fighters" would soon sweep the skies clear of American and British planes. He neglected to explain that, against the vigorous opposition of Milch, the jet plane in production was a hybrid fighter-bomber which was efficient at neither task.

The distant drone of approaching enemy planes forced adjournment to an elaborate underground concrete bunker. The change of venue encouraged Rommel to become even more forceful. The West, he said, would inevitably smash through the Normandy front and break into the homeland. Hitler listened with compressed lips as Rommel further predicted that the eastern front would also collapse and the Reich would become politically isolated. He urgently requested, therefore, that the war be brought to an end. "Don't you worry about the future course of the war," Hitler interrupted sharply. "Look to your own invasion front."

Hitler stubbornly refused to hear out his field commanders in Normandy and as a result the situation there was beyond repair. On June 26 Cherbourg fell to American troops. Largely because of Hitler's abiding fear of a main invasion at Calais and Ultra intercepts, which were often read in London within minutes of their origin, Germany had no hope of regaining the initiative. With her armies now dedicated to a dreary, enervating period of purely passive resistance, the Third Reich faced catastrophe.

4

The men who had already tried in vain to destroy Hitler's plane with brandy bottles filled with explosives or to blow him up with bombs concealed in an overcoat were not at all deterred by failure. They made four more unsuccessful attempts between September 1943 and February 11, 1944. The last failure was followed by a crippling blow to the Resistance. Hitler ordered Himmler to amalgamate the Abwehr and the SD. This meant the virtual destruction of the heart of the conspiracy. General Oster had already been dismissed on suspicion. Although he was at liberty he was too closely watched to be of use. It seemed as though fate indeed was protecting Hitler and a sense of hopelessness permeated the ranks of the conspirators. This might have been the end of their secret war against Hitler but for the inspiration of a new leader, Count Claus Schenk von Stauffenberg, a staff officer with the rank of lieutenant colonel. Like so many other German officers, he applauded Hitler's introduction of conscription, approved the Anschluss with Austria as well as the occupation of Czechoslovakia, and was caught up in the glory of victory in Holland and France. It was Barbarossa that destroyed his illusions. He heartily approved Rosenberg's attempt to free the non-Russian peoples of the Soviet Union and, after this policy was superseded by oppression and murder, he told a fellow officer that the only solution for Germany now was to kill the Führer. By chance he met resistance leaders who had no trouble enlisting him in their cause. His role, however, seemed short-lived; his car ran over a mine and he lost an eye, his right hand and two fingers of the other hand. Almost any other man would have retired, but Stauffenberg was convinced that he alone could assassinate Hitler and was back on duty late in 1943.

His new position as chief of staff to the commander of the General Army Office in Berlin made it possible for him to rebuild the weakened ranks of the conspiracy. He seized the reins from the tired, older leaders and, by the dynamism of his personality, got definite commitments from a powerful group in the Wehrmacht: his own chief, the first quartermaster general of the army, the chief of signals at OKW, the general whose troops would take over Berlin after the assassination, and other key officers of middle rank.

As yet, however, not a single field marshal wholeheartedly supported the plot. Kluge was a dubious factor and Manstein refused to commit himself prematurely since he felt "any such coup d'état would collapse the eastern front." The most promising candidate was Rommel but even he had reservations. "I believe it is my duty to come to the rescue of Germany," he said—but opposed assassination. It would only make Hitler a martyr. The Führer should be arrested by the army and brought before a German court to answer for his crimes.

Rommel was brought deeper into the plot during the spring of 1944 by his new chief of staff, Lieutenant General Dr. Hans Speidel, a soldier-philosopher who had received his doctorate in philosophy summa cum laude from the University of Tübingen. Speidel persuaded Rommel to meet secretly with General Karl Stülpnagel, military governor of France, in a country home near Paris. Here the two men, with the help of their energetic chiefs of staff, worked out a plan to end war in the West by an armistice. All German troops would retire into Germany and the Allies would cease bombing the homeland. Hitler would be arrested, with the resistance forces temporarily taking over the country. In the meantime the war in the East would continue, the assumption being that American and British troops would join the crusade against Bolshevism. Rommel was now so enthusiastic, he tried to involve Rundstedt in the plot but, while approving it, he refused to be personally involved. "You are young," Rundstedt said. "You know and love the people. *You* do it."

Stauffenberg and his group were not too pleased with the entrance of Rommel into the conspiracy, for they considered him a Nazi who was only deserting Hitler because the war was lost. They also disapproved of the plan to continue fighting Russia, and felt it was unrealistic to expect the West would make a separate peace. Further, the Stauffenberg circle was dedicated to assassination rather than arrest and by the first of June 1944 they felt it had to be done before the Allied invasion. Once enemy forces overran the homeland there would be no possibility for any decent kind of peace. By now they had a definite scenario for a coup d'état based, ironically, on a measure approved by the Führer himself. The official operation was entitled Walküre and was Hitler's plan to put down any unrest among the millions of war and foreign slave workers employed in Germany. It called for a proclamation of a state of emergency and instant mobilization of adequate forces to quell any uprising. Stauffenberg's scheme was to use the Walküre alert as the signal to start their own coup throughout the Reich and on every battle front. Hitler had specified that the orders to issue the Walküre alert be issued by the commander of the Reserve Army, General Friedrich Fromm—who was flirting halfheartedly with the idea of joining the Resistance.

D-Day caused consternation among the conspirators. The older ones argued that even a successful coup would not save Germany from enemy occupation. It was best to rely on the West to treat Germany decently and prevent Russia from ravaging the homeland. But Stauffenberg was resolved to make one final assassination attempt and chance almost immediately took a hand. He was promoted to full colonel and made Fromm's chief of staff. Now the coup did not depend on such a dubious factor. Stauffenberg himself could issue orders directly to the Reserve Army and thus seize Berlin. The new post also gave him frequent access to the Führer. He made plans to act early in July: he would report to the Führer at the daily conference, plant a time bomb which would blow up Göring and Himmler as well as the Führer, then fly back to Berlin and personally direct the military take-over of the capital.

Stauffenberg's chance came at last on July 11 when Hitler summoned him to report on replacements. He arrived at the Berghof with a briefcase carrying official papers and an English bomb but, to his dismay, Himmler was not in the conference room. He excused himself to phone the huge General Staff building on the Bendlerstrasse near Berlin's Tiergarten. "Shouldn't we do it anyhow?" he asked the chief of the General Army Office, General Olbricht. The bomb could still kill both Hitler and Göring. Olbricht advised him to wait until he could kill all three at once.

The opportunity came in four days; Stauffenberg was again ordered to see Hitler, who had moved his headquarters to Wolfsschanze. He arrived with bomb in briefcase and this time the conspirators were so sure of success that General Olbricht issued the orders for Operation Walküre at 11 A.M., two hours before the scheduled conference. This would give the troops of the Reserve Army and the tanks from the nearby Panzer school time to move into the capital by early afternoon.

At exactly 1:10 P.M. the conference began. Stauffenberg

briefly reported to the Führer, then left the room to telephone the Bendlerstrasse that Hitler was in the room and he was going back to plant the bomb. But on his return he discovered that Hitler had left for some reason and would not be back. It took Stauffenberg another quarter of an hour to excuse himself again and warn Berlin. By this time it was 1:30 P.M. and troops were already converging on Berlin. Olbricht hurriedly canceled the Walküre alarm and the units on march were returned to their barracks as inconspicuously as possible.

Some of the conspirators were discouraged and shaken by this latest fiasco but not Stauffenberg. He met with younger colleagues at his home in Wannsee and they heard an encouraging report from a cousin of Stauffenberg, who was their liaison with the Rommel-Speidel group in France. An imminent Allied breakthrough was expected, he said, and Rommel was determined to support the conspiracy no matter what Rundstedt's replacement, Marshal von Kluge, did. But again fate intervened on behalf of Hitler. The very next day Rommel was badly injured when his car was strafed by Allied planes.

5

On the afternoon of July 18 Stauffenberg received a summons from Wolfsschanze to report in two days. He was to brief Hitler on replacements that might be thrown into the battle in the East, where the central front was in peril of imminent collapse following recent defeats on both flanks. Stauffenberg spent the nineteenth at the Bendlerstrasse making last-minute preparations and that afternoon presided over a final conference of conspirators. The signals for the following day were hastily arranged; it was agreed that most of the messages would be passed orally in a prearranged sequence. Code words would be used on telephone and teleprinter and would be reserved for important matters since the entire system of communications was tapped by the Gestapo.

The conspirators knew this since their number included several Gestapo officials, including the SS general who had taken over the Gestapo main office in Berlin. There was, in fact, considerable anti-Hitler feeling throughout the SS. General Felix Steiner, for instance, had already evolved a vague plan of his own to kidnap the Führer, then "declare him mentally deranged," and with other Waffen SS commanders had recently assured Rommel of support in any revolt against Hitler. The hierarchy of the SD itself was infected with rebellion.

At the Bendlerstrasse late on the afternoon of the nineteenth Stauffenberg completed arrangements for the next day's operation. He instructed his driver, who knew nothing at all about the plot, to collect a briefcase from a certain colonel in Potsdam. It contained, Stauffenberg explained, two very important and confidential packages and was not to be left out of sight. As instructed, the chauffeur kept the case next to his bed that night. It held two bombs.

During evening tea at Wolfsschanze, Hitler was so nervous and uneasy that Fräulein Schröder asked why he was so preoccupied. "I hope nothing is going to happen to me," he replied cryptically. After an awkward silence, he said, "It would be too much if something troublesome happened now. I cannot allow myself to fall ill, since there is no one who can replace me in the difficult situation Germany finds herself in."

July 20, 1944

Shortly after 6 A.M. Stauffenberg was driven from his home to the city. Here he was joined by his adjutant, a lieutenant. At Rangsdorf airfield they met General Helmuth Stieff, who in September 1943 failed in an attempt to plant a time bomb at the Wolfsschanze, and all boarded a plane provided by the quartermaster general. It touched down at the air base near Rastenburg at 10:15 A.M. The pilot was instructed to stand by until noon to take the passengers back to Berlin.

After half an hour's drive through woods, the three conspirators were passed through the first gate of Führer Headquarters. They proceeded through minefields and a ring of fortifications for almost two miles to a second gate. This opened into a large compound surrounded by electrified barbed wire. After another mile they reached the officers' checkpoint. As usual their passes were examined but not their briefcases. In two hundred yards they arrived at a third enclosure. This was Security Ring A, where Hitler and his staff lived and worked. This innermost compound, surrounded by a barbed-wire fence, was constantly patrolled by SS guards and Secret Service personnel. To enter, a field marshal himself needed a special pass issued by Himmler's chief of security, but again the shiny briefcase containing the bombs was not inspected.

While his adjutant took charge of this case, Stauffenberg

carried another containing official papers. He proceeded nonchalantly to a mess hall where he had a leisurely breakfast with the camp commander's adjutant. Outwardly unperturbed and casual in bearing, he later sought out General Fellgiebel, OKW chief of signals, the key to success once the bomb exploded. It was his task to inform the Berlin conspirators that it was time to act, then to isolate Wolfsschanze by cutting all telephone, telegraph and radio communications.

Assured that Fellgiebel was ready to do his part, Stauffenberg chatted briefly with another OKW officer and at noon strolled over to the office of Keitel. The field marshal greeted him with slightly disconcerting news: since Mussolini was due to arrive that afternoon, the midday situation conference would start half an hour earlier—in just thirty minutes. Keitel urged Stauffenberg to keep his report brief since the Führer wanted to leave as soon as possible. Keitel kept glancing impatiently at the clock and, just before 12:30 P.M., said it was time to walk over to the conference barracks. In the hallway Stauffenberg approached Keitel's adjutant, Ernst John von Freyend, and asked where he could clean up. He was directed to a nearby lavatory. His own adjutant was waiting here with the brown briefcase. It was not a suitable place to arm the bombs so they returned to the hall and asked Freyend where the colonel could change his shirt. Freyend took them to his own bedroom and left them alone. Stauffenberg grasped a pair of tongs in the three fingers of his only hand and began shoving in the fuse of one bomb. This crushed a glass capsule containing acid which would eat eat through a thin wire within fifteen minutes and set off the bomb. His adjutant was entrusted with the second "back-up" bomb.

No sooner was the armed bomb carefully packed in the brown briefcase than a sergeant entered to hurry them up and from the hall Freyend shouted, "Come on, Stauffenberg! The Chief is waiting"

Keitel was waiting impatiently at the doorway. The conference was already under way. He led the way down the central corridor of the building past the telephone room and into the conference room through a double-winged door. There were ten or so windows and all were open against the sultry midday heat. The conferees gathered around a long, narrow oak map table, notable for its thick top and two massive supports. Only Hitler was sitting, his back to the door, at the middle of the table. A pair of spectacles rested on the map. He toyed with a magnifying glass as General Adolf Heusinger, standing to his immediate right, read out a glum report on the eastern front. Hitler looked at the newcomers, acknowledged their salutes. Stauffenberg moved to the other side of Heusinger, then casually shoved the brown briefcase under the table as close to Hitler as possible. The case leaned against the inside of the heavy oaken support only six feet from the Führer. It was twelve thirty-seven and in five minutes the bomb would explode. The others were so engrossed by Heusinger's tale of doom that Stauffenberg managed to sidle out of the room without being noticed. He hurried down the long corridor and out of the building.

Heusinger was also on the periphery of the anti-Hitler conspiracy but knew none of the details of the plot. When he saw Stauffenberg enter it hadn't occurred to him that anything was awry since the conspirators had promised to warn him when the next assassination attempt would take place. But he happened to glance down just as Stauffenberg shoved the brown briefcase under the table and thought fleetingly: "Something might happen!" But under Hitler's absorbed attention, Heusinger's suspicion evaporated almost as soon as it was aroused. His aide leaned over the conference table to get a better look at the map but was impeded by the brown briefcase. He couldn't budge it with his foot so leaned down and transferred it to the *outside* of the heavy table support. It was a trivial move which would alter the course of history.

Admiral von Puttkamer had moved to a window to get some air and was perched on the sill debating whether he should quietly leave and change to his best trousers for the Mussolini visit. It was twelve forty-one. The Führer was intently leaning far over the table to check the map. Heusinger was saying, "Unless at long last the army group is withdrawn from Peipus, a catastrophe . . ."

At exactly 12:42 P.M. his words were obliterated by a deafening roar. Flames shot up and a hail of glass splinters, timber and plaster rained down. Smoke erupted in the room. Puttkamer had felt a strange jerk a split second before the explosion. Falling down, he saw the heater under the window and thought, "My God, it exploded!" then realized this was nonsense; it was summer. Maybe it was a plot by the foreign laborers who were working on the construction. Dazed as he was, he realized the best thing was to remain on the floor. Then he heard someone shout, "Fire!" and scrambled for the door. It was lying flat on the floor and he leaped over it. Suddenly he wondered where everyone else was and turned to locate the Führer. Just then Hitler, trousers in tatters, face blackened by soot, came toward him with Keitel. Both men were covered with dust and wood fiber. They passed him as if sleepwalking and he realized he could hardly breathe the acrid air. He followed Hitler and Keitel down the long corridor. Outside a knee gave way and he collapsed on the ground. He gulped air greedily and saw Hitler and Keitel heading toward the Führer bunker, followed by some third person.

SS Adjutant Günsche didn't even hear the explosion. His eardrums had burst. His forehead bled, his eyebrows were burned off. The room was black with smoke; the floor had buckled up at least three feet. "Where is the Führer?" he wondered. With the instinct of a soldier, he scrambled out a shattered window and hurried to the other side of the building just as Keitel and Hitler were emerging. The Führer's trousers were in tatters, his hair tousled, but there was no blood in sight. *"Was ist los?"* asked Hitler as Günsche helped guide him down the path. A bomb from a Russian plane?

Upon leaving the conference room, Stauffenberg had hurried to the OKW Signals Office in Bunker 88. He and General Fellgiebel stood outside waiting for the bomb to explode. They were talking as unconcernedly as possible when the headquarters signal officer reported that Stauffenberg's car was ready, then reminded him that the headquarters commandant was expecting him for lunch. Stauffenberg confirmed the invitation but said he would first have to return to the conference. Just then came an explosion.

"What's happening?" exclaimed Fellgiebel and the signals officer nonchalantly explained that some animal must have set off another land mine. Stauffenberg now contradicted himself. He said he was *not* going back to the conference but would drive directly to the commandant's for lunch. He bade Fellgiebel a knowing farewell and set off with his adjutant in the car. Moments later their driver, wondering why Stauffenberg wore neither hat nor belt, pulled to a stop at the first checkpoint. The guard there had closed the gates upon hearing the explosion and refused to open them. Without a word, Stauffenberg hurried to the guard room and asked for the lieutenant on duty, an acquaintance, for use of the telephone. He dialed, said a few quiet words, replaced the receiver and said calmly, "Lieutenant,

I am allowed to pass." The barrier was opened without question and at 12:44 P.M. the Stauffenberg party was through the gate.

Ninety seconds later an alarm was sounded and Stauffenberg could not talk his way through the next barrier. A sergeant major of the guard battalion refused flatly to let any car pass. Once more Stauffenberg used the phone, this time calling the camp commandant's aide. "Colonel Count von Stauffenberg speaking," he said, "from outer Checkpoint South. Captain, you'll remember we had breakfast together this morning. Because of the explosion the guard refused to let me pass. I'm in a hurry." Then he told a lie. "Colonel General Fromm is waiting for me at the airfield." He hastily hung up. "You heard, Sergeant Major, I'm allowed through." But the sergeant major could not be bluffed. He telephoned for confirmation and, to Stauffenberg's relief, got it.

It was almost 1 P.M. by the time Stauffenberg and his adjutant drove up to their Heinkel 111. Moments later they were in the air. Ahead lay a three-hour flight. There was nothing to do but worry since the plane's radio did not have the range to hear any announcements from Berlin. Had Fellgiebel gotten the word through to the conspirators in the Bendlerstrasse? If so, would they have the resolve to seize the capital and send out the prepared messages to the military commanders on the western front?

Hitler would probably have been killed had not the brown briefcase been shifted to the outer side of the table support. It was also fortunate for the Führer that the door behind him led to a long narrow hallway through which the main force of the explosion escaped. Again, luck, incredible luck, had saved Adolf Hitler.

Doctors and rescue workers were in action minutes after the explosion. Ambulances took the seriously wounded to the field hospital at Rastenburg. Dr. Hanskarl von Hasselbach, the Führer's personal physician, was the first to treat him. He bandaged Hitler's wounds, then put his right arm—the elbow was rather badly sprained—in a sling. "Now I have those fellows!" he exclaimed with more glee than anger. "Now I can take steps!"

Dr. Morell arrived, examined Hitler's heart and administered an injection. The patient was in a state of ecstasy, repeating over and over, "Think of it. Nothing has happened to me. Just think of it." To Morell's amazement his pulse was normal. The three secretaries rushed in to see with their own eyes that the Führer still lived. Traudl Junge (who had been married a year ago to Hans Junge, Hitler's valet) almost burst into laughter at the sight of his hair, which stood on end like a porcupine's. He greeted them with his left hand. "Well, my ladies," he said with a smile, "once again everything turned out well for me. More proof that Fate has selected me for my mission. Otherwise I wouldn't be alive." He was talkative, blaming the plot on a "coward," undoubtedly one of the construction workers. "I don't believe *in any other possibility*," he emphasized, turning to Bormann for confirmation. As usual Bormann nodded.

The next to arrive with congratulations was Himmler. He too thought laborers had built the bomb into the barracks. It took an amateur to set the trail straight. Valet Linge went to the conference barracks and learned from the sergeant in charge of the telephone room that Stauffenberg had been expecting an urgent call from Berlin. Then someone recalled that the colonel had left a briefcase under the table. A telephone call to the airstrip revealed that Stauffenberg had left hastily for Berlin a little after 1 P.M. Hitler now had no doubts that Stauffenberg alone was responsible. He ordered his arrest.

This order never was transmitted to Berlin because of a curious set of circumstances. Moments after the explosion one of Hitler's adjutants ordered the headquarters signals officer, Colonel Sander, to cut all telephone and teleprinter communications. He did so, then told Chief Signals Officer Fellgiebel what he had done. Fellgiebel, whose assignment as a conspirator was to isolate Führer Headquarters, solemnly agreed that proper action had been taken by Sander but upon discovering, moments later, that Hitler was not dead, the general called his own office. "Something frightful has happened," he told his chief of staff. "The Führer is *alive*. Block *everything*!" The chief of staff understood the odd message, for he too was a conspirator. Within minutes the major switch centers at *both* Führer and army headquarters went dead.

This communication blackout gave the conspirators in Berlin time to seize the capital, but they failed to act since confusion was the order of the day at the Bendlerstrasse. The plotters, uncertain whether Hitler had been killed or not, were reluctant to activate Operation Walküre. The information from Wolfsschanze was too vague to risk a repetition of the false alarm of July 15.

At 3:42 P.M. Stauffenberg finally landed at an airport outside

Berlin. To his surprise, no one was waiting, friend or foe. His aide telephoned the Bendlerstrasse, got General Olbricht and gave the code word signifying that the assassination attempt had succeeded. Olbricht's vague reply made it clear that Walküre had not even been activated. Stauffenberg seized the phone, demanded they do so without waiting for his arrival. He commandeered a Luftwaffe car to take him to Berlin.

Only at 3:50 P.M. did Olbricht act. The Wehrmacht commandant of Berlin, General Kortzfleisch, was ordered to alert all units of the guard battalion, the Spandau garrison and two army weapons training schools. Kortzfleisch, who was not in the plot, did so.

To speed matters, General Olbricht personally alerted General von Hase, the Berlin garrison commander, another conspirator. By 4:10 P.M. his troops were ready to march. So were those outside Berlin. At the Bendlerstrasse itself the guards were alerted and their commander orally instructed by Olbricht to use force if any SS units tried to enter. Within minutes transit traffic was stopped, all exits blocked.

Olbricht was now doing what he should have been doing three hours earlier. He burst in on General Fromm, who was neither all the way in nor all the way out of the conspiracy, and explained that Hitler was really dead. He urged Fromm, as commander of the Replacement Army, to issue the Walküre alert to the military district commanders. Fromm, an ambitious man with a grand manner, hesitated as he had been doing for months. He insisted on telephoning Keitel for assurance that Hitler was dead.

"Everything is as usual here," said Keitel from the tea house, and when Fromm said that he had just received a report that the Führer had been assassinated, he exploded. "That's all nonsense." The Führer was alive and only slightly injured. "Where, by the way, is your chief of staff, Colonel von Stauffenberg?" The agitated Fromm replied that the colonel had not yet reported to him—and silently resigned from the conspiracy.

A few minutes later most of the conspirators were congregated in Olbricht's large office waiting anxiously for Stauffenberg. Someone announced excitedly that he had just driven into the courtyard! In moments the colonel bounded energetically into the room, bringing with him a spirit of enthusiasm and confidence. Stauffenberg told what he had seen—a great explosion, flames and smoke. "As far as one can judge," he said, "Hitler is dead." They must act decisively without wasting another moment! Even if Hitler was alive they should do their utmost to overthrow the regime. Beck agreed.

Stauffenberg did his utmost to bring General Fromm back into the conspiracy. He assured him that Hitler was truly dead, but Fromm repeated what Keitel had said. "Field Marshal Keitel is lying as usual," said Stauffenberg and proceeded to lie. "I myself saw Hitler being carried out dead."

"In view of this," cut in Olbricht, "we have sent out the code signal for internal unrest to the military district commanders." Fromm leaped from his chair, a startling act for such a huge, ponderous man. He banged the table and shouted in his best parade ground manner. "This is rank insubordination. What do you mean by 'we'?" He ordered the Walküre alert canceled.

Stauffenberg made another attempt to convince Fromm that Hitler was dead. "No one in that room can still be alive," he argued but Fromm was not impressed. "Count von Stauffenberg," he said, "the attempt has failed. You must shoot yourself at once." Stauffenberg refused and Olbricht added his plea to strike now. Otherwise the Fatherland would be ruined forever. Fromm turned on him. "Olbricht, does this mean that you, too, are taking part in the coup d'état?" "Yes, sir. But I am only on the fringe of the circle."

Fromm glared down from his height at Olbricht. "Then I formally put you under arrest." Olbricht was not cowed. He returned the glare. "You can't arrest us. You don't realize who's in power. It's we who are arresting you." The two generals went from words to blows. Stauffenberg intervened and in the scuffle was struck in the face. Big Fromm was subdued only under threat of a drawn pistol. He was placed under arrest and locked in the next room. By 5 P.M. guards were posted at all entrances to the huge building, as well as the bombed area in the rear. Everyone entering now needed an orange pass signed by Stauffenberg; no one could leave without a similar pass or signed orders.

6

Although the Bendlerstrasse was at last under the complete control of the conspirators, their comrade, General von Hase, was in deep trouble at his office on Unter den Linden. An hour earlier, as commandant of the Berlin Garrison, he had ordered the guard battalion to seal off the government quarter; not a general or minister was to cross the barrier. Major Otto Remer, commander of the battalion, was a former Hitler Youth Leader and he first wanted assurance that his Führer was really dead. Hase gave it, adding that he had been murdered by the SS. Who was his successor? asked Remer, who felt "something was fishy." Hase told him to stop asking stupid questions and get his battalion on the move.

Remer's companion, Lieutenant Hans Hagen (in Berlin to lecture the guard battalion on National Socialism), was equally suspicious and once they were alone he convinced Remer that this looked like a military Putsch. He asked for permission to clarify the matter with Goebbels, his prewar employer. Remer put a motorcycle at his disposal with instructions to report back immediately. As the major set out to supervise the blockade of the inner city, Hagen (an author in civilian life) was bouncing in the sidecar of a motorcycle bound for the official residence of the Minister of Propaganda. He was heard to shout out periodically, like a Teutonic Paul Revere: "Military Putsch!"

The Goebbels establishment was already a center of confusion. The burgomeister of Berlin was there, along with a city councilor, and both were bewildered by the conflicting rumors. So was Speer, who had just noticed a group of Remer's men trotting toward Brandenburg Gate with machine guns; others stood guard outside the ministry. Sweating profusely, Goebbels was on the telephone querying party officials and regional military commanders. Troops from Potsdam and provincial garrisons, it seemed, were already marching toward the city. The situation was desperate but Goebbels saw a ray of hope in the fact that the rebels hadn't yet broadcast their success over the radio. He now busied himself making arrangements for his own broadcast, a tricky matter since a simple account of the facts might cause panic.

Just then Hagen, rumpled from his motorcycle ride, pushed his way into Goebbels' presence. After listening impatiently to the soldier-author's breathless account, Goebbels demanded to know if Remer could be trusted. Absolutely! Hadn't he been wounded eight times in action! Still somewhat suspicious, Goebbels instructed Hagen to fetch Remer. If the two were not back within half an hour, Goebbels would assume the major was either a traitor or held by force—and he would order SS troops to seize the headquarters of the Berlin Garrison at Unter den Linden.

Moments later, at 5:30 P.M., Goebbels was again called to the telephone. It was Hitler, who urged an immediate broadcast to let the people know that his life had been spared. Goebbels promptly phoned the text of a broadcast to the Rundfunkhaus. It was already occupied by rebellious troops of the infantry school but their commanding officer was so confused—or terrified—by Goebbels' voice that he readily agreed not to interfere with transmission of the announcement.

In the meantime Hitler, swayed by agitated advisers, had come to suspect his Propaganda Minister was a traitor. He again phoned Goebbels, this time bitterly reproaching him for delaying the newscast so long. Goebbels gave vehement assurance that he was not to blame; it was someone in the Radio Division, Hitler believed him—at least he said he did—and hung up.

In Berlin, Major Remer had just finished sealing off the government area. He was glum, for he had not yet heard that the Führer was alive. Remer had carried out his mission with misgivings, reinforced when he reported back to Hase only to be given vague answers to every question. Dissatisfied, Remer was in a rebellious mood by the time Hagen accosted him outside with the news that Minister Goebbels demanded his immediate presence! This was civil war, Remer thought, and brought Hagen upstairs to repeat Goebbels' message to Hase. The general pretended to be alarmed and, when Remer said he must report at once to the Propaganda Minister, ordered him to remain in the anteroom. But another conspirator, also a major, intervened, with a knowing wink at Hase; he suggested that it *was* Remer's duty to see Goebbels—and place him under arrest. Remer left the building in a state of confusion. "Well, I've got to gamble for my life," he finally told his adjutant and set off for the Propaganda Ministry with twenty men.

Goebbels was checking the time. He had been unsuccessful in attempts to reach Remer by phone and it was only two minutes before the deadline—7 P.M. Then Remer marched in. He did not tell Goebbels he had orders to arrest him nor did he believe the Minister's claim that he had just spoken to the Führer. He would believe Hitler was alive only, he said, if he heard it from his own mouth.

"As you wish, Major," said Goebbels and put in a call to Rastenburg. In less than a minute he was telling Hitler, "Here is Major Remer, commander of the guard battalion." Remer took the receiver warily. It could be a recording or someone imitating the Führer. "Are you on the line, Major Remer?" he heard. "What are you doing now?" The voice certainly sounded like the Führer's and Remer told what he had done to date. But he must have sounded doubtful. "Do you believe that I am alive?" The answer was Jawohl even though Remer was not entirely convinced.

Hitler said that he was giving Remer complete authorization to insure the security of the government. "Do whatever you think necessary. Every officer, regardless of rank, is now under your command." He ordered Remer to restore full order immediately. "If necessary by *brachial* (brutal) armed force." The "*brachial*" completely convinced Remer this really was Hitler. He snapped to attention. "You are responsible only to me," repeated Hitler and promoted him to the rank of colonel.

Remer turned the ministry into a command post. First he telephoned General von Hase and said he had just spoken to the Führer, who had put him in complete command. He ordered Hase to report to him at once. Hase refused indignantly. "Since when does a general come trotting to a little major?"

"General, if you don't want to come, I will have you arrested," said Remer and sent troops to occupy Hase's headquarters. He then informed all military units in the Berlin area that they were now under his personal command, and was not surprised that their commanders, regardless of rank, accepted his authority without protest. As a finishing touch, Colonel Remer assembled his own battalion in the ministry garden so they could hear about the *Attentat* (assassination attempt) from the lips of Goebbels himself.

By this time a subdued General von Hase had arrived. He was no longer angry and, in fact, seemed at the point of embracing Remer. He was so full of compliments and questions that Remer had to politely put him off so he could get on with the job of restoring order. Goebbels was somewhat condescending to Hase, who began to stammer slightly under his curt questioning. Would the Minister mind if he telephoned his wife and had something to eat? "There go our revolutionaries," jibed Goebbels after the general left to enjoy his snack. "All they think about is eating, drinking and calling up Mamma."

The switchboard at the Bendlerstrasse was jammed with calls from officers seeking fuller details on the newscast. The recipients of the Walküre alert were also asking for direct confirmation from Fromm of the earlier report of Hitler's death. They were answered by Stauffenberg, who insisted that Hitler *was* dead and, if they were conspirators, he gave assurance that the plot was still operative. He told them the newscast was a trick. The army was in control and all was well.

At Wolfsschanze Keitel had just succeeded in dispatching an order putting Himmler in command of the Replacement Army. Keitel added that "only orders from him and myself are to be obeyed." This teleprint went out at 8:20 P.M. Ten minutes later Party Chancellor Bormann dispatched an urgent message informing all his Gauleiters of the "murderous attempt on the Führer's life by certain generals." He ordered his people to honor only orders from the Führer himself.

At 9 P.M. the people were informed by radio that the Führer would soon speak to them in person. There would be a long delay, however, since there were no facilities at Wolfsschanze to broadcast directly. The nearest recording van was in Königsberg, the capital of East Prussia, and it would take several hours to fetch it.

By chance Hitler's favorite commando, Otto Skorzeny, was in Berlin, but once he heard that the Führer was alive he saw no reason to delay a trip to Vienna to inspect his school of frogmen saboteurs. As he was boardinq the train at Anhalt Station at dusk an officer raced down the platform shouting that there was a military revolt in the city and Skorzeny had been commanded to establish order.

He hurried to SD headquarters where he was told that some traitorous military leaders were seizing control of the capital. "The situation is obscure and dangerous," said General Walter Schellenberg, head of the Foreign Intelligence Service. His face was pale; a revolver lay in front of him on the table. He made a dramatic gesture. "I'll defend myself here if they come this way!" It was a ridiculous picture and Skorzeny could not resist laughing. He advised Schellenberg to put his weapon away before he shot himself.

Skorzeny alerted a company from another of his sabotage schools located in the Berlin suburbs before setting out on a personal reconnaissance of the city. Everything was quiet in the government compound. Checking a report that the Waffen SS was in the conspiracy, he hastily inspected their barracks at Lichterfeld. All was serene. He drove to the headquarters of the SS Leibstandarte Division for information but learned very little and continued at top speed to paratroop headquarters near the Wannsee. He found General Student on the terrace of his villa poring over a mass of papers. The general was wearing a long dressing gown; his wife sat beside him, sewing. It was comic, in a way, to see one of Germany's most important commanders presiding over such a placid scene during a revolt. Student refused to take the matter seriously until a phone call from Göring confirmed Skorzeny's alarm: all orders except those issued from Wehrmacht headquarters were to be ignored. While Student began relaying these orders, Skorzeny raced back to Schellenberg's office. No sooner had he arrived than he was called to the phone. "How many men have you?" asked Jodl. Only one company. "Good. Take them to the Bendlerstrasse and support Major Remer and his guard battalion who have just been ordered to surround the building."

There was a feeling of growing desperation at the Bendlerstrasse. The guard battalion units which had been protecting the high command headquarters were withdrawing, on orders from their commander to assemble in the garden behind Goebbels' official residence. This left only about thirty-five soldiers at the main gate. Inside, General Olbricht collected his officers at 10:30 P.M. for the third time that evening and said they would now have to take over the protection of the building since the guards had left. Each of the six exits, he said, would have to be manned by a General Staff officer.

No one objected but one armed group of loyalists was secretly determined to stand by their oath to the Führer. At about 10:50 P.M. these men, eight in all, burst into Olbricht's office, grenades fastened to their belts and armed with submachine guns and pistols. As Olbricht was trying to calm them, Stauffenberg entered. He spun around and escaped in a fusillade through the anteroom. He staggered as if hit, then darted into an adjoining office. But in short order he was captured along with Beck, Olbricht and other conspirators. Soon they were faced by Fromm, who had been released from captivity. "Well, gentlemen," said the big general, brandishing a pistol, "I am now going to treat you as you treated me." He told them to lay down their weapons.

"You wouldn't demand that of me, your former commanding officer," said Beck quietly. "I will draw the consequences from this unhappy situation myself." He reached for a revolver on a suitcase.

Fromm warned him to keep the gun pointed at himself. The

elderly Beck began to reminisce. "At a time like this I think of the old days . . ." "We don't want to hear about that now," interrupted Fromm. "I ask you to stop talking and do something." Beck mumbled something and fired. The bullet grazed his head; he reeled back, slumped in a chair. "Help the old gentleman," Fromm told two junior officers. They approached Beck and tried to take his gun. He resisted so he could try again but dropped back in a daze. Fromm turned to the other conspirators. "Now, you gentlemen, if you have any letters to write you may have a few minutes to do so." He returned in five minutes and informed them that a court-martial "in the name of the Führer" had just pronounced death sentences on Olbricht, Stauffenberg and their two adjutants. Stauffenberg, his left sleeve soaked in blood, stood stiffly as he and his three colleagues were led into the courtyard.

Beck's face was splotched with blood. He asked for and was given a pistol. He was left in the anteroom but those outside heard him say. "If it doesn't work this time, please help me." There was a shot. Fromm looked in and saw that the former chief of the General Staff had failed again. "Help the old gentleman," he told an officer, who refused. A sergeant dragged the unconscious Beck from the room and shot him in the neck.

Outside, the courtyard was dimly lit by the hooded lights of an army vehicle. It was midnight. The four condemned men were lined up in front of a sand pile for use in air raids. Olbricht was calm. At the order to fire, Stauffenberg shouted, "Long live our sacred Germany!" and died.

The huge form of Fromm appeared at the doorway of the building. He marched across the yard to review the firing squad. He talked briefly, ending with a resounding "Heil Hitler!" then somewhat pompously made for the gate. He called for his car and disappeared in the darkness. At the message center in the Bendlerstrasse a teleprint message was being transmitted: "Attempted Putsch by irresponsible generals bloodily crushed. All ringleaders shot. . . ."

Just as Fromm was walking through the gate a white sports car arrived with a screech of brakes. The driver was Speer, his passenger Colonel Remer. "Finally an honest German!" said Fromm as if he himself were innocent. "I've just had some criminals executed." And when Remer said he wouldn't have done that, Fromm blustered. "Do you intend to give me orders?"

Speer chauffeured Fromm back to the Propaganda Ministry

where Goebbels disregarded the latter's demand to speak privately with Hitler. Instead he put him in another room, asked Speer to leave, and telephoned the Führer in private. After some time Goebbels came to the door of his office and ordered a guard posted in front of Fromm's room.

Himmler was among those present at the ministry. He had recently arrived from Rastenburg with express orders and full powers from the Führer to crush the rebellion. "Shoot anyone who resists, no matter who it is," Hitler had told him. Despite such credentials—including a temporary assignment as commander-in-chief of the Reserve Army—he let Goebbels take over the visual command, remaining his usual quiet, contained self. Before coming to Goebbels' he had already unleashed the terror of a counter-Putsch and set up the machinery for a special investigation of the uprising.

At Wolfsschanze General Fellgiebel knew his fate was decided but he did not attempt to kill himself since he wanted to testify to his motives at an official trail. "If you believe in a Beyond," he told his youthful aide in farewell, "we could say *auf Wiedersehen*!"

Hitler was in his tea house impatiently waiting for the recording van from Königsberg so that he could make his speech to the nation. In anticipation of its imminent arrival, he summoned his family circle to hear him read a hastily drafted message. The secretaries and adjutants arrived along with Keitel and the bandaged Jodl, but there was still no van and Hitler used the time to enlarge on the Attentat. "These cowards!" he shouted. "That's exactly what they are! If they had had the courage at least to shoot me I'd have some respect! But they didn't want to risk their lives!"

At last the van arrived and just before 1 A.M., July 21, there was a fanfare of military music over every German radio station. After a brief pause Hitler began telling of the plot, and of the death and injury to colleagues very dear to him. He repeated his mistaken conviction that the circle of conspirators was extremely small and had nothing in common with the spirit of the Wehrmacht or the German people. It was a tiny band of criminal elements which would be promptly and ruthlessly exterminated. "I was spared a fate which held no horror for me, but would have had terrible consequences for the German people. I see in it a sign from Providence that I must, and therefore shall, continue my work."

7

Soon after midnight, July 21, Otto Skorzeny was in complete command of the Bendlerstrasse, and the affairs of the high command were again on course. He also found details of the Putsch in Stauffenberg's safe and placed a number of officers under arrest.

At the Propaganda Ministry, Goebbels and Himmler were interrogating a number of generals including Fromm. They were treated courteously, given wine and cigars, and some, like Kortzfleisch, were allowed to go home when their innocence was established. At 4 A.M. the investigations ended. Goebbels emerged from his office with a radiant smile. "Gentlemen," he announced, "the Putsch is over." He escorted Himmler to his car, taking leave of his old rival with a long handshake, then returned upstairs to regale his closest associates with his own exploits. Utterly pleased, he spryly perched himself on a table next to a bronze bust of the Führer. "This was a purifying thunderstorm," he said. "Who would have dared to hope when the horrible news arrived early this afternoon that all this would end so quickly and so well." It was nothing short of a miracle. If Hitler had died the people would have believed it was God's judgment. "The consequences would have been incalculable. For in history only facts speak as evidence. And they are this time on our side." The press consequently should be instructed to belittle the conspiracy.

At the Wolfsschanze it was apparent that Hitler's head injury was not superficial. He could hear nothing with his right ear and his eyes constantly flickered to the right. That evening while strolling outside he twice wandered off the path. Dr. Karl Brandt urged him to rest in bed for several days, but the Führer would not listen. "That's impossible." He had too much work to do. Besides it would certainly look ridiculous to foreign guests to see such a healthy man lying in bed.

Although Hitler was convinced he would never hear with his right ear, he remained in relatively good spirits. He took the time to peck out a letter on a typewriter to "My dear Tschapperl," the Viennese diminutive which he often used affectionately for Eva Braun. Illustrated by a sketch of the bombed barracks, it assured her that he was fine, just somewhat tired.

"I hope to come back soon and so be able to rest, putting myself in your hands. I greatly need tranquillity."

She replied at once on her blue monogrammed stationery that she was deeply unhappy. "I am half dead now that I know that you are in danger." She asserted she could not go on living if anything happened to him. "From the time of our first meetings, I promised myself to follow you everywhere even in death. You know that my whole life is in loving you."

On July 23 Gestapo investigators by accident found incriminating diaries in the ruins of a bombed house which implicated Canaris and other important officials in the coup. The admiral was arrested, as was former Minister of Economics Schacht. At first Hitler could not believe that such high-ranking people—and so many of them!—were involved. It was a blow to his convictions that only a small clique of traitors existed and he was hurt. "My life is so full of sorrow, so heavily leaden," he told Traudl Junge, "that death itself would be salvation." And another secretary heard him chide his dog for disobeying him: "Look me in the eyes, Blondi. Are you also a traitor like the generals of my staff?"

8

The day after the bombing Hitler replaced his ailing chief of staff, Zeitzler, with a man he had previously banished from a front-line command for differing with him. By the time Heinz Guderian, perhaps the most respected Panzer expert in the Wehrmacht, arrived in Rastenburg to take charge, he found the offices of OKH practically deserted. Zeitzler had already departed in semi-disgrace. Heusinger was gone and many department heads had been removed by the Gestapo.

One of Guderian's first tasks was to issue a loyalty order of the day, pledging to Hitler "the unity of the generals, of the officer corps and of the men of the army." By the end of the week Guderian went further; he ordered every General Staff officer to be a National Socialist officer-leader "by actively cooperating in the political indoctrination of younger commanders in accordance with the tenets of the Führer." Any officer who could not conform was ordered to apply at once for transfer.

None did and the subjugation of this elite band, begun in 1933, came to a degrading finale.

By now the western front was collapsing in the face of a savage American attack on the western flank of the Normandy beachhead. At dusk of July 30 a fierce tank battle raged for the Avranches defile, the last barrier to an American break-through into the open spaces of France. Warlimont and others pressed for an immediate withdrawal from France while there was still time but Jodl contented himself with presenting to the Führer a draft of an order "for possible withdrawal from the coastal sector."

By the next evening American tanks were storming into Avranches. Hitler wanted to rush west and take personal charge, but both Dr. Erwin Giesing and Professor Karl van Eicken, the eminent eye-ear-nose-throat specialist, who had been summoned from Berlin to examine Hitler, forbade him to fly. Restricted to Wolfsschanze, he was forced to do nothing while six of George Patton's divisions poured through the gap at Avranches and sealed the fate of France. This was but one of many concerns. On August 1, 35,000 ill-armed Poles of all ages assaulted the German garrison in Warsaw and the next day Turkey broke off diplomatic relations with the Reich.

Himmler had recently assured that he would ruthlessly bring to justice not only the criminals in the conspiracy but their families. "The Stauffenberg family," he said, "will be exterminated root and branch! That will be a warning example, once and for all." He pressed the investigation in this spirit. Next of kin and other relatives of the chief conspirators were arrested, including at least a dozen women over seventy. Scores of detectives covered every angle of the conspiracy—with such dispatch and thoroughness that the first trial got under way on August 7. Eight officers were brought before a People's Court presided over by Roland Friesler, an expert on Soviet law and methods of punishment. Characterized by Hitler as "our Vishinsky," he had been instructed by the Führer to proceed harshly and "with lightning speed."

The defendants entered the great courtroom of the Kammergericht in Berlin wearing old clothes. They looked haggard and unkempt, as movie cameras recorded the event so the German people could see what happened to traitors. Field Marshal von Witzleben, deprived of his false teeth, looked like a tramp in a comedy as he kept hitching up his oversized beltless pants. Friesler, dramatically clothed in red, began shouting like one of the Soviet judges he so admired: "You dirty old man, why do you keep fiddling with your trousers?"

This was the tone and level of the show trial. "Never before in the history of German justice," recalled one shorthand secretary, "have defendants been treated with such brutality, such fanatic ruthlessness as at these proceedings." The judgment was foreordained and, in a trumpet voice, Friesler pronounced all eight men guilty of treason against the Führer (which, in fact, they were) and against German history (which they were not). In line with Hitler's specific instructions, the eight men were trucked to Plötenzee prison, then into a small room where eight meathooks dangled from the ceiling. Here the condemned were stripped to the waist and hung by nooses of piano wire. Their agonized jerking was recorded by a movie camera, and that same evening was reproduced on a screen at the Wolfsschanze. According to Speer, "Hitler loved the film and had it shown over and over again," but Adjutant von Below and others in the family circle still assert he never saw it.

There were further investigations and other trials but only the execution of the first eight victims was publicized. Almost 5000 other men and women, most of them not even directly involved in the uprising of July 20, were also executed.

9

The military situation was desperate. From the Baltic to the Ukraine, Red Army offensives had routed or surrounded the Wehrmacht along the entire eastern front. In the south Soviet troops were seizing the oilfields of Romania; in the north they had just surrounded fifty German divisions; and in the center they were closing in on Warsaw. On Hitler's personal orders, preparations were made to remove the coffin of President von Hindenburg from the tomb at Tannenberg, scene of his great victory in the First World War.

In the emergency, Goebbels proclaimed a new Draconian policy on August 24: all theaters, music halls, drama schools and cabarets were to be closed within a week. Soon, he warned, all orchestras, music schools and conservatories (except a few leading ones) would be shut down and the artists put either in uniform or in armaments factories. There would be an end to publication of fiction or belles-lettres and of all but two illustrated papers.

On the following day Paris was liberated after four years of occupation; both Romania and Finland sued for an armistice. Twenty-four hours later the Romanians, who had thrown out Marshal Antonescu by a coup, declared war on Germany. With defeat imminent on all fronts, Hitler did not waver. His answer to signs of disintegration within the Wehrmacht was a threat to arrest the kin of any deserter.

He told Keitel and two other generals on the last day of August that the time was not yet ripe for a political decision. "Such moments come only when you are victorious." There was still hope of success, he said. The tension between the Allies would soon become so great that a major break would occur. "The only thing is to wait, no matter how hard it is, for the right moment." He mused glumly on the problems facing him in both East and West, then began feeling sorry for himself. "I think it's pretty obvious that this war is no fun for me. I've been cut off from the world for five years. I haven't been to the theater, I haven't heard a concert, and I haven't seen a film." His voice rose in wrath. "I accuse the General Staff of failing to give the impression of iron determination and so of affecting the morale of combat officers—and when General Staff officers go up front I accuse them of spreading pessimism!" He would fight until Germany got a peace which secured the life of the nation for the next hundred years "and which, above all, does not besmirch our honor a second time, as happened in 1918." His thoughts reverted momentarily to the bomb plot. Death, he said, "would only have been a release from sorry, sleepless nights and great nervous suffering. It is only a fraction of a second and then a man is freed from everything and has quiet and eternal peace."

This mood of fatalism might have been the result of deteriorating health. Although he joked with his secretaries about his right hand, which trembled so much he could no longer shave himself, he was seriously affected by a head cold which was aggravated in turn by an incessant earache. His condition was complicated a few days later by a slight feeling of pressure in his head, particularly in the brow area. His voice grew hoarse. He began complaining of stomach pains but disregarded Dr. Giesing's warning that this might be the result of the numerous pills prescribed by Dr. Morell. By the beginning of September, however, Hitler had come to accept Dr. Giesing's prescription of a ten per cent cocaine solution to relieve the sinus pain and would faithfully crouch for hours each morning and evening over an inhalator.

Giesing's visits indeed became so pleasurable that Hitler began to show the same gratitude he had bestowed on Morell. Gratitude ripened into trust and before long the new doctor enjoyed a rare personal relationship with the Führer. The treatments were invariably followed by long discussions on a variety of subjects, ranging from the future of the Reich to the evils of smoking. During all these conversations Giesing continued to take detailed notes. He also undertook something even more dangerous: secret psychological tests. This was done so subtly and over such a long period that Hitler never guessed he had been the object of, in Giesing's terms, "rather primitive psychological tests," and had been diagnosed as "a neurotic with Caesar-mania."

Touchy as he was in these days of pain and depression, Hitler never lost his temper with his youngest secretary, Traudl Junge, or failed to show keen interest in her personal welfare. But at one noonday meal she noticed he acted strangely. He said not a word to her and when their eyes met his were serious and probing. She wondered if anyone had spread gossip about her. Later in the day SS General Otto Hermann Fegelein phoned and asked if she could come to his barracks. Putting an arm around her in a fatherly manner, he revealed that her husband had been killed in action. The Chief, he explained, had known about it since yesterday but was unable to tell her the bad news. Later she was summoned to the Führer's study. He took both her hands and said softly, "Oh, child, I am so sorry. Your husband was such a fine fellow." He asked her to remain on the job and promised to "always help" her.

In early September Professor van Eicken returned for another examination and, upon learning of Morell's injections and pills, became as concerned as Giesing and Hitler's two surgeons, Brandt and Hasselbach. The four doctors met secretly but Eicken doubted that their patient would heed his warnings any more than those of his three colleagues since Morell enjoyed Hitler's complete confidence.

A week later Hitler reported that he was getting almost no sleep. He would lie awake all night long from the agony of stomach spasms. Nor was there any relief from the sinus inflammation; the left side of his head continued to ache constantly. This was aggravated by the rattle and grind of pneumatic drills used around the clock by construction workers in an effort to strengthen his bunker from expected Soviet air attacks. A side effect of his bad health was deterioration of his remarkable memory. He had always been able to glance at a long document and repeat it word for word; now he had difficulty remembering names. It was fortunate, he wryly observed, that he only had to deal with a few people these days.

On September 12 Hitler suddenly became dizzy immediately after Giesing had administered the cocaine treatment. He complained that everything was going black and grabbed a table to keep from falling. His pulse was rapid and weak but in ninety seconds the attack—it might have been a mild coronary—passed and the pulse returned to normal. Hitler suffered a similar attack on the fourteenth. This time he broke out into a cold sweat. He summoned Morell, who gave him three injections which gave him temporary relief, but on September 16 there was a third mild attack. This time he agreed to do what Giesing had been urging for a month: undergo head X rays.

Chapter Twenty-eight

THE BATTLE OF THE BULGE

JULY 21, 1944– JANUARY 17, 1945

1

That same day Hitler issued an order demanding "fanatical determination" from every able-bodied combat man in the West. The Americans had just reached the German frontier and at one point, south of Aachen, pierced it. "There can be no large-scale operations on our part. All we can do is to hold our position or die." Hitler seemed to be calling only for a last-ditch defense of the Fatherland but it was a ruse to fool the enemy who, he feared, had a spy at Führer Headquarters privy to all directives. (The spy, of course, was Ultra.) No sooner had the regular Führer conference ended than Hitler invited four men to an inner chamber. Keitel and Jodl were followed into the new conference room by Chief of Staff Guderian and General Kreipe, representing Göring. As they were conjecturing in undertones on what surprise the Führer had in store for them, he entered, stooped, still wan and wary from the third attack. His blue eyes were watery and distant, his mouth slack.

He nodded to Jodl, who succinctly summed up their position: their allies were either finished, switching sides or attempting to do so. While the Wehrmacht listed more than 9,000,000 men under arms, there had been 1,200,000 casualties in the last three months—almost half of them on the western front. There was a respite in the East where the Soviet summer offensive seemed to have run its course. "But in the West we are getting a real test in the Ardennes." This was the last hilly area in Belgium and Luxembourg that had been the highway to German victory in the Great War and again in 1940.

At the word "Ardennes" Hitler abruptly came to life. Raising his hand, he exclaimed: "Stop!" There was a dead pause. Finally Hitler spoke: "I have made a momentous decision. I am taking the offensive. Here—out of the Ardennes!" He smashed his left fist on the unrolled map before him. "Across the Meuse and on to Antwerp!" The others stared in wonder. His shoulders were squared, his eyes luminous, the signs of care and sickness gone. This was the dynamic Hitler of 1940. In the next few days he was a model of his former vigor as he pressed preparations for the ambitious counteroffensive: he issued orders for the establishment of a new Panzer army and envisaged ways of bringing 250,000 men and thousands of machines up to the Ardennes in absolute secrecy.

Only then did he keep his promise to get X rays taken of his head. Late in the afternoon of September 19 he was driven to the field hospital at Rastenburg and escorted to the X-ray room, which had been searched carefully for hidden explosives. Outside Hitler was greeted by loud shouts of "Sieg heil!" from a crowd of civilians from the town and recuperating soldiers. Their excitement at the sight of their Führer—probably for the first time—was understandable but what impressed Giesing most was the ardent enthusiasm in the eyes of the amputees and other badly wounded men.

The following morning Giesing checked the three X rays with Morell and was amazed that his colleague identified the cheekbones as the sinuses. There followed the daily examination of the patient in his bunker and Giesing noticed Hitler's face had an odd reddish tinge in the artificial light. Afterward Hitler was stricken with stomach pains and insisted on taking more than half a dozen of the "little black pills" prescribed by Morell. Concerned by the continuing dosage, Giesing began to make cautious inquiries. Linge showed him the pill container. Its label read: Antigas Pills, Dr. Koster, Berlin, Extract nux vomica 0.04; Extract belladonna 0.04.

Giesing was appalled. Hitler had been heavily dosing himself with two poisons—strychnine and atropine. Perhaps that explained his attacks, his growing debility; his irritability and aversion to light; his hoarse throat and the strange reddish tinge of his skin. Two cardiograms revealed clearly abnormal T waves. It could be hardening of the arteries or high blood pressure, but in any case it was an alarming development in the light of his other disabilities. At their regular session Hitler again complained to Giesing of intestinal discomfort. "The cramps are so severe that sometimes I could scream out loud."

After their next meeting on September 25 Dr. Giesing chanced to see his patient outside the bunker. To his surprise the tinge of Hitler's skin was not red in sunlight but yellow. His eyes were starting to turn yellow. He obviously had jaundice. After a night of agonizing pain, Hitler could not get out of bed the following morning. His secretaries, adjutants and servants were in a state of alarm; no one could remember the Führer staying in bed no matter how sick. He would see no one, wanted no food. In great excitement, Günsche told Traudl Junge that he had never seen the Chief so listless, so indifferent. Even the critical situation on the eastern front failed to interest him.

Morell advised Hitler to remain in bed all day but he insisted on getting up for his regular examination by Giesing. He, in turn, advised discontinuance of the cocaine treatment but Hitler wearily shook his head. "No, dear Doctor," he said. "I think that my physical weakness the past few days is due to the poor functioning of my intestines and cramps." Giesing hesitated, then warned his patient to take care lest he suffer another collapse. On his way out he confiscated a box of Morell's black pills and showed them to Dr. von Hasselbach. He too was horrified to learn they contained strychnine and atropine but warned Giesing to say nothing until they could confer with Dr. Brandt.

For the rest of the month Morell did his utmost to isolate the patient from the other doctors. He insisted that the Führer was *not* suffering from jaundice. It was more likely a temporary gall bladder inflammation. During this time Hitler lost six pounds and lay in bed, racked with pain. He ate nothing and showed little interest in the battle fronts. Occasionally he would see his secretaries but then he would almost immediately dismiss them. "It gave me a feeling of despair," recalled Traudl Junge, "to see the one man who could have stopped this tragedy with a single stroke of a pen lying disinterested in his bed, looking around with tired eyes—while around him all hell had broken out."

Physical pain was not the only cause of Hitler's deep depression. Another cache of incriminating documents was unexpectedly discovered in a safe at army headquarters in Zossen.

They implicated a considerable segment of the army leadership in the assassination plot. The Führer was shattered and some of those in the family circle felt that this, more than the jaundice or the stomach pains, which he had endured for years, had broken his spirit.

Dr. Brandt returned to the Wolfsschanze on the twenty-ninth. Enthusiastic at the chance to finally unmask Morell as a charlatan, he managed to get into Hitler's room that afternoon. At first the patient took Brandt's denunciation seriously; but Morell convinced the Führer that he was absolutely innocent of any wrongdoing.

Then, late in the afternoon on October 1, Linge telephoned Giesing. The Führer was suffering from a bad headache and insisted on seeing Giesing at once. He was lying on his spartan bed in a nightgown. He lifted his head slightly to greet Giesing but immediately dropped back to the pillow. His eyes were empty, expressionless. He complained of pressure in his head. He also could not breathe through his left nostril. As Giesing seated himself next to the bed, Hitler abruptly changed the subject. "Doctor," he asked, "how did you come upon the story of the anti-gas pills?"

Giesing explained. Hitler frowned. "Why didn't you come directly to me? Didn't you know that I have great confidence in you?" The doctor felt chills—not from the excessive air conditioning in the little cell. He explained that he had been prevented from coming. Hitler shrugged this off as well as Giesing's conviction that his intestinal problems were due to strychnine. He had suffered similar attacks frequently, if not as severely. "It is the constant worry and irritation that give me no rest; and I must work and think only of the German people day and night." He was already feeling much better and should be out of bed in a few days. "You gave Morell a great fright," he said. "He looked quite pale and disturbed and reproaches himself. But I have assured him. I myself always have believed they were simple pills to absorb my intestinal gases and I always felt very well after taking them." Giesing explained that the feeling of well-being was an illusion. "What you say is probably right," interrupted Hitler, "but the stuff did me no harm. I'd have had intestinal cramps anyway because of the continuous nervous strain of the last month and, after all, at some time the twentieth of July would have reacted on me. Up to now I'd had the will power to keep all this inside me—but now it has broken out."

Giesing diagnosed his problems as jaundice but Hitler protested. "No, you want to make a gall bladder patient out of me! Go ahead, examine my gall bladder." He folded back the bedclothes so Giesing could make his own examination. It was Giesing's first chance to give his patient a complete physical. He examined Hitler's neurological reflexes, his glands, every part of his body. Giesing satisfied himself, for instance, that the malicious rumor about the Führer's deficient sex organs was a canard; in this respect he was intact and normal.

"You see, Doctor," he said as Linge and Giesing helped him into the nightgown, "aside from this nervous hyperactivity, I have a very healthy nervous system and I hope that soon all will be well again." He was talking himself into a state of euphoria. He thanked Giesing for everything he had done to relieve his discomfort. "And now Fate has sent you again to ferret out this anti-gas story and you have saved me further damage because I would have kept on taking these pills after I recovered." This paradoxical conclusion was followed by a perplexing outburst of gratitude and praise. "My dear Doctor, it was Providence that led you to make this examination and discover what no other doctor would ever have noticed. I am in any event very grateful to you for everything and will remain loyal to you—even if you did attack Morell—and I thank you again for everything." He took both of Giesing's hands, pressed them tightly, then requested another dose of "that cocaine stuff." The Führer instantly luxuriated under the treatment. His head was clearing up, he said, and he would soon be well enough to get up. But his words began to fade and his eyes fluttered. His face turned a deathly white. Giesing grasped Hitler's pulse. It was rapid and weak. "My Führer, are you all right?" he asked but got no answer. Hitler had passed out.

The doctor looked around but Linge had left to answer a knock on the door. It suddenly occurred to Giesing that Hitler was entirely at his mercy. He saw before him a tyrant whose knowledge of people seemed very inadequate. "At that moment," so he claimed in his diary, "I did not want such a man to exist and exercise the power of life and death in his purely subjective manner." Some inner command drove him to plunge a swab stick into the cocaine bottle—a second dose could be lethal—and he rapidly began brushing the interior of Hitler's nose with the substance that had just knocked him out. As Giesing finished the left nostril he was startled by a voice: "How much longer will the treatment take?" It was Linge.

Giesing forced himself to say he was about finished. Just then Hitler's face, paler than before, twitched and he drew up his legs as if in pain. "The Führer is having another one of his intestinal cramps," observed Linge. "Let him rest." Outwardly composed, Giesing bade farewell to Linge and quickly bicycled back to the field hospital, still wondering if he had killed Hitler. In a state of terror, he telephoned Hasselbach, telling what had happened and that he was taking a day off, ostensibly to check on his Berlin office, which had been bombed.

The next day Giesing phoned from the capital to learn that Hitler was alive and no one suspected the double cocaine treatment. It was safe to return to Wolfsschanze. He arrived in an atmosphere of suspicion but not from the Führer, who was as friendly as ever. Still he made it clear that he wanted the whole anti-gas pill episode relegated to the past since he had "total faith" in Morell. He was personally going to clear up the matter and had asked Brandt to see him that afternoon.

Hitler settled the question by dismissing both Brandt and Hasselbach. Early that evening Giesing was summoned to Bormann's quarters. "But, my dear Doctor," Bormann said, upon observing that the doctor had come in full uniform, "why do you come in such official style? I only wanted to discuss something with you." He seemed amused at Giesing's apprehension. "There's no need to take the whole matter so tragically. We have nothing against you. On the contrary, the Führer is full of praise and asked me to give you this letter." It thanked him for his excellent treatment. Enclosed was a check for 10,000 marks. The doctor laid the check on the table. But Bormann forced it upon him with the warning that a refusal would be an insult to Hitler.

After packing, Giesing reported to the Führer bunker. Hitler extended his hand. "You will understand," he said, "that this anti-gas pill business has to be cleared up once and for all. I know that you yourself acted only out of idealism and purely professional motives." He again thanked Giesing for his excellent treatment and promoted him on the spot.

So ended the affair of the little black pills—with the dismissal of three doctors of good reputation. Few in the family circle gave any credence to the growing rumor that Dr. Morell had willfully attempted to poison the Führer. Most of them shared Gerda Christian's opinion that Morell was a good doctor despite his slovenly appearance. (The former Gerda Daranowsky, she had married Hitler's Luftwaffe liaison officer in the winter of 1943.) Even the trio who denounced Morell for incompetence did not believe he was trying to poison Hitler. They remembered the truly shocked look on his face when Brandt pointed out that these pills—though harmless if taken in moderation—contained some strychnine. Morell, it seemed, had never checked the analysis on the label, only the name, nux vomica. And it came as a blow to discover that this was a strychnine-containing seed.

By the time Hitler left his sickbed there was considerable evidence of Rommel's implication in the bomb plot and the Führer assigned two generals the unpleasant task of offering him a deadly proposition. On October 14 they visited Rommel, who was recuperating at his castle near Ulm from the auto accident. When they left an hour later an ashen Rommel told his wife, "In a quarter of an hour I shall be dead." He explained that he had been accused of complicity in the plot and Hitler offered him the choice of taking poison or facing the People's Court.

After bidding his wife and son farewell, he took his aide aside. "Aldinger," he said, "this is it." He repeated Hitler's proposition and plan: he was supposed to drive to Ulm with the two generals and, en route, take poison. Half an hour later his death by accident would be reported. He would be given a state funeral and his family would not be persecuted. Aldinger begged him to resist but Rommel said that was impossible. The village was surrounded by SS men and the lines of communication to his own troops had been cut. "I have therefore decided to do what, obviously, I must do."

At 1:05 P.M., wearing his Afrika Korps leather jacket and carrying his field marshal's baton, Rommel was driven off. In transit to the Ulm Hospital he committed suicide. His death, according to the medical report, was caused by an embolism due to previous skull fractures. The field marshal's face, recalled his relatives, was marked by an "expression of colossal contempt."

2

By the end of September 1944 Hitler had lost three allies: Finland, Romania and Bulgaria. October brought a further defection. Horthy, the Hungarian admiral without a navy, who was nominally ruler of a kingdom without a king, sent envoys to Moscow to beg for an armistice. After all, the fiction of his independence had ended with the Nazi occupation of Hungary earlier that year—and Soviet troops were less than a hundred miles from the capital. Hitler sent his favorite commando, Otto Skorzeny, to Hungary to bring her leaders back in line. He did so with a minimum of bloodshed in probably the most imaginative operation of the war, aptly titled Mickey Mouse. He simply kidnaped Horthy's son Miki, wrapped him in a carpet (Skorzeny got the idea from Shaw's play, *Caesar and Cleopatra*) and delivered him to the airport. He then proceeded to capture the citadel where Admiral Horthy lived and ruled with a single parachute battalion. It took half an hour and cost seven lives.

Six days later he was greeted at Wolfsschanze by Hitler with a warm "Well done!" His description of the kidnaping of young Horthy greatly amused Hitler. As Skorzeny rose to go, Hitler stayed him. "I am now going to give you the most important job of your life." He told of the surprise attack in the Ardennes. Skorzeny, he said, would play a leading role by training men to masquerade as Americans. They would work behind American lines—in American uniforms, with American vehicles. They would seize bridges over the Meuse, spread rumors, issue false orders, breed confusion and panic.

By this time Jodl had presented Hitler with the draft of his plan for the offensive. First it was given the symbolic name of Christrose but that morning the Führer himself changed it to Watch on the Rhine to deceive any spy. It called for the use of three armies with a combined strength of twelve Panzer and eighteen infantry divisions. Watch on the Rhine was based on two premises: complete surprise, and weather that would ground Allied planes. It was designed to break through on a wide front, cross the Meuse on the second day and reach Antwerp on the seventh day. It would not only destroy more than thirty American and British divisions but drive a great wedge—psychological as well as physical—between the Americans and British. The defeat would be so smashing that the West would sue for a separate peace. Then all German troops would be thrown against the Red Army.

To insure absolute secrecy only a select few were told of the offensive; a different code name for the offensive was to be used at every command level and changed every two weeks; nothing of the offensive was to be trusted to telephone or teletype: officers, sworn to silence, would be used as couriers. Only with such precautions, reasoned Hitler, could the spy at his headquarters be foiled.

Field Marshal Model, the Führer's personal choice to command the offensive, read the plan with dismay. "This damned thing hasn't got a leg to stand on!" he complained. Rundstedt shared his concern and offered a counterplan, a more modest attack of twenty divisions on a forty-mile front. "Apparently you don't remember Frederick the Great," Hitler remarked sarcastically. "At Rossbach and Leuten he defeated enemies twice his strength. How? By a bold attack." It was the same old story. His generals lacked imagination for the Big Solution. "Why don't you people study history?"

On November 10 Hitler signed an order to prepare for the Ardennes offensive. He made it clear that this was a do-or-die proposition, a last gamble. The tone of his directiveness incurred the protests of the senior commanders in the West and Hitler decided to leave Wolfsschanze so he could explain his purpose in person despite a sudden relapse in spirit and body.

On November 20 he entrained with his entourage. He must have known it was the last time he would ever see the Wolfsschanze, but he kept up the fiction of returning by allowing the reconstruction work to continue. His train did not leave until dawn since Hitler wanted to arrive in Berlin after dark. He sat in his compartment with all the shades drawn until lunch, then joined the others in the dining car. Traudl had never seen him so downcast and absent-minded. "His voice was only a soft whisper; his eyes were either glued to his plate or staring at a spot on the white tablecloth. It was such a depressing atmosphere that all of us had a strange ominous feeling."

Without preamble Hitler announced that Professor van Eicken would perform another operation on his throat. It was not dangerous, he said, as if assuring himself. "But it is quite possible that I am losing my voice and . . ." He never finished the sentence. He remained in seclusion for the next few days and the family circle knew only that Eicken had removed a polyp the size of a millet seed. Finally he appeared unexpectedly for breakfast; he was obviously looking for company. Everyone extinguished cigarettes; windows were opened to clear the air. He could only whisper. Doctor's orders, he said, and before long everyone was unconsciously imitating him. "My ears are fine and there is no need to spare them," he murmured softly, and everyone laughed, more in relief that he was again in good spirits than at the joke.

By now Otto Skorzeny, wielding more power as lieutenant colonel than some colonel generals, had reached mid-term of his "School for Americans." Though he had never been to the United States, his volunteers were doing well. The course: American slang, habits, folkways, and how to spread panic as pseudo GIs behind enemy lines. On December 11 the build-up was nearly complete. The Reichsbahn, achieving a miracle in railroading, had delivered the first wave to the Zone of the Offensive—without being observed by the enemy. Early that morning Hitler moved into his new headquarters near the medieval castle of Ziegenberg.

Later in the day he met with half of his division commanders; the rest would come tomorrow. Upon arrival the first group of generals and their staffs were stripped of revolvers and brief-cases by the Gestapo. Each man was forced to swear on his life that he would reveal nothing of what he was about to hear. Not one knew why he had been summoned; only that every division had been going in circles for weeks.

The meeting took place in a large underground room. The Führer sat at a narrow table flanked by Keitel and Jodl. Across were Rundstedt, Model and Lieutenant General Hasso von Manteuffel, who would command the most powerful of the three armies in the offensive. A descendant of a famous family of Prussian generals, Baron von Manteuffel was an ex-gentle-man jockey and German pentathlon champion. Standing little more than five feet tall, he was tough-minded, possessed for-midable energy and was one of the few who dared to disagree openly with Hitler.

For over an hour Hitler lectured to the sixty or so officers on Frederick the Great, the history of Germany and National Socialism. His voice was strong, his eyes flashed excitedly as he explained the political motives for deciding upon an all-out offensive. Then Autumn Fog—its final code name—was ex-plained in detail. It would start at 5:30 A.M. on December 15. The divisional commanders listened in awe, impressed not only by the grandiosity of the plan but by the Führer's vigor and good health. But Manteuffel was almost close enough to touch him and saw he was actually "a broken man, with an unhealthy color, a caved-in appearance in his manner, with trembling hands; sitting as if the burden of responsibility seemed to oppress him, and compared to his looks at the last conference in the beginning of December, his body seemed still more decrepit; he was a man grown old."

3

The offensive was set back by a day. The night of December 15 was cold and quiet along the Ardennes front. Twisting eighty-five miles through terrain similar to New England's Berkshires, it was held by six American divisions. Of these, three were new, the other three exhausted and bled white in battle. This was known as the Ghost Front—a cold quiet place where for over two months both sides had rested and watched and avoided irritating each other.

That night no Allied commander seriously feared a German attack. Hours earlier Montgomery had stated flatly that the Germans "cannot stage major offensive operations." In fact things were so dull he asked Eisenhower if there was any objection to his going off to England the next week.

Three German armies—250,000 men and thousands of machines—had been moved secretly to the line of departure, the noise of half-tracks drowned out by low-flying planes. By midnight of the fifteenth the troops were assembled at their assault posts. They stood shivering but listened with genuine enthusiasm as officers read a message from Field Marshal von Rundstedt:

> *We gamble everything!* You carry with you the holy obligation to give all to achieve superhuman objectives for our Fatherland and our Führer!

The excitement of old victories rose in the men. Once more they were on the attack. Deutschland über Alles!

At 5:30 A.M. an eruption of flame and smoke burst all along the Ghost Front. For eighty-five miles mortars coughed, rockets hissed up their launching platforms, 88s roared. The ground shook. Hundreds of tanks rumbled and clanked, and from the rear came the hollow boom of railroad guns hurling their fourteen-inch shells at targets miles behind the American lines.

After an hour the barrage stopped. There was a stunned, momentary silence. Ghostly white-sheeted forms, almost invisible against the new-fallen snow, came out of the haze toward GIs advancing in a slow ominous walk twelve and fourteen abreast. As Hitler's infantrymen filtered into the American forward position, planes of a new design came out of the east with a strange crackling roar, streaking by at unbelievable speed. The Germans looked up at their new jets and many cheered, wild with excitement. Hitler's "miracle weapons" were not talk but fact.

The power, fervor and surprise of their attack were met with a stubborn, if makeshift, defense by the green or worn-out American troops. Cooks and bakers, clerks and musicians, loggers and truck drivers were thrown pell-mell into the line to stem the tide. Some turned in terror and ran; many stood and fought. In some places the Americans held; in others the Germans burst through almost unopposed.

By dusk the northern part of the United States lines was in a shambles but General Omar Bradley, leader of more combat troops than any American field commander in history, had received such fragmentary reports that he assured Eisenhower it was merely a "spoiling attack." Eisenhower disagreed. "This is no local attack, Brad," he said. "It isn't logical for the Germans to launch a local attack at our weakest point." He didn't think they could afford "to sit on their hands" until they found out, and told Bradley to send two armored divisions to the rescue.

Hitler was elated at the reports of breakthrough in the north. Success continued and at noon, December 18, German broadcasters raised the hopes of the people. "Our troops are again on the march," said one announcer. "We shall present the Führer with Antwerp by Christmas." At Eagle's Eyrie Hitler was learning that a Manteuffel column had opened up the road to Bastogne. Major penetrations had been achieved just as predicted and he talked confidently of a victory that would turn the tide. He felt so good he took a short walk in the countryside and was so refreshed he decided to do it every day.

By midnight the Ardennes battlefield was in turmoil, a scene of indescribable confusion to those involved in the hundreds of struggles. No one—German or American, private or general—knew what was really happening. In the next two days a series of disasters struck the defenders. On the snowy heights of the Schnee Eiffel at least 8000 Americans—perhaps 9000 for the battle was too confused for accuracy—were bagged by Hitler's troops. Next to Bataan, it was the greatest mass surrender of Americans in history.

Only seven jeeploads of Skorzeny men in American uniforms managed to break through the lines but these were raising havoc beyond his initial hopes. The leader of one team was directing an American regiment down the wrong road while his men were changing signposts and snipping telephone wires. Another jeepload, stopped by a United States column for information, feigned fear so convincingly that the Americans caught their panic and turned tail. A third group severed the main telephone cables connecting the headquarters of Bradley and his commander in the north, General Courtney Hodges.

But the greatest damage was done by a team that had been captured. When the four confessed their mission to an American intelligence officer the news was immediately broadcast that thousands of Germans in American uniforms were operating as saboteurs behind the lines. At once this information was associated with a verified report of widely dispersed parachutists north of Malmédy—an abortive paradrop which had failed even more dismally than Skorzeny's operation. Out of two fiascos was developing a formidable success.

By December 20 half a million Americans throughout the Ardennes were quizzing each other on lonely roads, in dense pine forests and in deserted villages. Passwords and dog tags no longer proved identity. You were an American only if you knew the capital of Pennsylvania, the identity of "Pruneface" or how many homers Babe Ruth had hit.

In Paris terror of Skorzeny and his men had reached panic peak. According to one hysterical report, Skorzeny men dressed as nuns and priests had just floated to earth. Their destination, according to the confession of a captured Skorzenyite, was the Café de la Paix. There they would join forces and kidnap Eisenhower. American security officers firmly believed this fabrication. SHAEF headquarters was surrounded with barbed wire and the guard quadrupled. Tanks stood at the gates, passes were examined and re-examined. If a door slammed, Eisenhower's office was pestered with calls asking if he was still alive. Skorzeny's twenty-eight men had done their work well.

By the following morning, the twenty-first, the battle had assumed a recognizable shape. It was a giant bulge. In the middle, at Bastogne, completely surrounded, was a collection of Americans under an acting commander of the 101st Airborne Division, Brigadier General Anthony McAuliffe, the division artillery officer. Called upon to surrender by a German *parlementaire*, he offhandedly replied, "Nuts." The one-word message spread throughout the Ardennes and helped raise the flagging spirits of the defenders. The time for running had stopped. The spirit of resistance was followed by an abrupt end of "Hitler weather." A bright sun shone next morning on the Ardennes for the first time and before noon sixteen big C-47s were dropping supplies to the encircled men at Bastogne.

The tide of battle was threatening to turn but Hitler did not yet know it. Manteuffel's tanks were already far beyond the American enclave of Bastogne and approaching the Meuse. But Manteuffel himself was deeply concerned; the German infantry army on his left was far behind. On December 24 he phoned Führer Headquarters from a château near La Roche. "Time is running short," he told Jodl. His left flank was exposed and the time had come for a complete new plan. He could not keep driving toward the Meuse and still take Bastogne. When Jodl protested that the Führer would never abandon the drive to Antwerp, Manteuffel argued that there was still a chance for a great victory *if* they followed his plan. "I'll wheel north on this side of the Meuse. We'll trap the Allies east of the river." The proposal shocked Jodl but he promised to pass it on to the Führer.

But Hitler would not believe that full success could not be achieved. His confidence carried over to Christmas, which he celebrated, to the amazement of his circle, with a glass of wine. It was the first time Fräulein Schröder had ever seen him take wine with any pleasure. Later in the day he refused another request by Manteuffel to abandon the attack on Bastogne even though his most advanced Panzer division had just been cut off by an American armored division and was being smashed to pieces. December 26 was a day of Allied might. The snows that now blanketed the entire Ardennes were red with blood but nowhere was the carnage greater than in the pocket a few miles from the Meuse River where General Ernest "Gravel Voice" Harmon's 2nd Armored Division was savaging Manteuffel's 2nd Panzer Division in a hundred small engagements.

At Eagle's Eyrie an argument over Autumn Fog had continued since morning. Jodl was now saying, "Mein Führer, we must face the facts squarely. We cannot force the Meuse." The 2nd Panzer was close to disaster and Patton had just opened up a narrow corridor from the south to besieged Bastogne. Throughout the Ardennes it was the same story. For the moment it was a static struggle; the great offensive had been temporarily stalled.

Everyone had a plan and Hitler listened to them all. Finally he spoke. "We have had unexpected setbacks—because my plan was not followed to the letter." He frowned. Then his face lightened with a new hope. "But all is not yet lost." He issued new orders: Manteuffel was to turn to the northeast, thus outflanking most of the Americans in the top half of the bulge. "I want three new divisions and at least 25,000 fresh replacements rushed to the Ardennes," he announced to a semicircle of somber faces. Granted the Allies could not be wiped out in a single dramatic blow as planned, Autumn Fog could still be turned into a successful battle of attrition. And this would surely bring Germany a substantial political victory.

These orders were intercepted by the Ultra team and passed on to Eisenhower—and he was assured that Hitler's attack had shot its bolt. What Ultra did not learn was that the Führer and his chosen successor had just engaged in a violent quarrel. At least the violence was on Hitler's side when Göring proposed they seek a truce. "The war is lost," he said. "Now we must get in touch with Count Bernadotte." Folke Bernadotte, whose father was Swedish King Gustavus V's brother, would surely act as mediator for any armistice negotiations.

Hitler, so a pale-faced Göring reported shortly to his wife, had raged and screamed about betrayal and cowardice but he himself had replied in an earnest and composed manner: "Mein Führer, I could never do anything behind your back." He assured Hitler that he would remain faithful in bad times as well as good, then repeated his conviction that an immediate armistice was essential. Hitler, he said, calmed down a bit but then sharply replied: "I forbid you to take any step in this matter. If you go against my orders I will have you shot." Never had Frau Göring seen her husband so shaken as he told her all this. "This is the final break," he said glumly. "There is no sense my attending any more daily briefings. He does not believe me any more. He does not listen to me."

4

To the Germans the classic struggle was known as the Ardennes Offensive but to the Americans it was the Battle of the Bulge. By December 28 its third and final phase was fast approaching. At a special meeting of his top military leaders that day Hitler admitted the situation was desperate, but he had never learned the word "capitulation" and would pursue his aim with fanaticism. During the military conference that same day Rundstedt made the mistake of urging Hitler to abandon Autumn Fog and retreat before an Allied counteroffensive started. Hitler flared up. They would renew the drive to the Meuse, he said, just as soon as North Wind got under way. He jabbed a finger at a point on the large wall map a hundred miles south of the Bulge. "In the meantime," he continued, "Model will consolidate his holdings and reorganize for a new attempt on the Meuse. And he will also make another powerful assault on Bastogne. Above all, we must have Bastogne!" By midnight nine Panzer and Volksgrenadier divisions began to converge on the town Hitler wanted at all costs.

Just before midnight Operation North Wind, designed to take Allied pressure from the Bulge, was launched and eight German divisions rushed from their Westwall position with great élan to assault the Seventh U. S. Army near the boundary of northern Alsace. To the north in the Ardennes, a tremendous artillery barrage erupted at the stroke of midnight. The irrepressible George Patton had ordered every available gun in his command to fire a New Year's salute.

Five minutes later Adolf Hitler's voice, somewhat raspy but confident, was broadcast throughout the Reich. Germany, he said, would rise like a phoenix from its ruined cities and go to ultimate victory. Afterward he entertained the family circle in his private bunker. Everyone was relaxed by champagne but there was a subdued atmosphere. The most enthusiastic was Hitler, who needed no alcohol. The others listened in silence to his prophecies of great success for Germany in 1945. At first Bormann alone seconded them but as Hitler went on for more than an hour the others became infected by his enthusiasm in spite of themselves.

At 4:35 A.M. the Führer left the gathering so he could hear the first reports of North Wind. It started auspiciously but the Ultra team had succeeded in passing on his battle directives to Eisenhower, who quickly reduced the U. S. Seventh Army front and prevented the Germans from cutting off a salient. Thanks to the warning, the Americans were able to hold off the German attack, which came to a standstill after a fifteen-mile advance.

In the Ardennes the Allies went over to the offensive on January 3, 1945, with massive attacks on the center of the Bulge from north and south designed to cut the huge salient in two. The Germans fought tenaciously, yielding every yard of snow at heavy cost to both sides. They were dug in with their usual efficient use of terrain. American troops moved slowly since the dense fog eliminated air support and cut down the use of artillery. Tanks and self-propelled guns slipped and skidded on the iced trails and roads, often crashing into each other.

Churchill flew over from England to observe the counter-offensive, which was being supported by a considerable British assault on the western tip of the Bulge. On January 6 he met with Eisenhower, who was vexed by the slow, arduous progress of the British and American troops. Was it possible, he asked, to get help from the Russians to take pressure from the Ardennes? Churchill knew that Stalin was mounting a new offensive but not when it would start. "You may find many delays on the staff level," he told Eisenhower. "But I expect Stalin would tell me if I asked him. Shall I try?" The answer was a relieved yes, and that same day Churchill cabled a request for a major Russian offensive during January. The response from Moscow was immediate. A large-scale attack, said Stalin, would be launched not later than the second half of January.

Simultaneously Allied drives from north and south, designed to pinch the Bulge in its midriff, began to gain ground on the morning of January 7 and by the following day had drawn so close together that Hitler was forced to authorize a withdrawal of those units in the western half of the salient. Within an hour those Panzers which had almost crossed the Meuse did an about-face and hastened to get east of the Bastogne-Liège highway.

It was the end of Hitler's great dream. Now the question was: would the hundreds of thousands of German tanks and self-propelled guns lumbering eastward cross the highway in time or be caught in a sack? Would the attempted retreat be another Stalingrad?

On the ninth of January Guderian once more journeyed to Eagle's Eyrie and warned Hitler for the third time that the Red Army was about to launch a massive offensive. Today he brought maps and charts made up by Gehlen, his chief of intelligence, showing the relative distributions of strength—and Gehlen's recommendation that East Prussia be evacuated immediately if Berlin itself were to be held.

When Guderian displayed the maps and charts, Hitler angrily labeled them "completely idiotic" and ordered his chief of staff to have the man who had made them shut up in a lunatic asylum. Guderian lost his temper. "The man who made these," he said, "is General Gehlen, one of my best General Staff officers. I should not have shown them to you were I in disagreement with them. If you want Gehlen sent to a lunatic asylum, then you had better have me certified as well!" Hitler's flare-up subsided and he mixed reassurances with praise. "The eastern front," he said, "has never before possessed such a strong reserve as now. That is your doing. I thank you for it."

Three days later Stalin kept his word to Churchill. Almost 3,000.000 Red Army troops—more than a dozen times those landed by the Allies on D-Day—attacked some 750,000 poorly armed Germans on a four-hundred-mile front extending from the Baltic Sea right down the middle of Poland. Supported by massed artillery and led by seemingly inexhaustible streams of "Stalin" and T-34 tanks, hordes of Red infantrymen began storming the pitifully inadequate defense system devised by Guderian. Although weather grounded most of the Red Air Force tactical support, by dusk the first echelon of attackers had pushed forward as much as twelve miles.

Germany was now caught between powerful forces on east and west, for that day also saw substantial victory in the Ardennes. American infantry divisions joined with the 6th Armored Division to trap thousands of first-rate German troops east of Bastogne.

At Eagle's Eyrie Hitler appeared serene to Traudl Junge, who was just returning from Christmas holidays in Munich. At dinner he answered her grim stories of the heavy air raids on Munich with a promise. "This nightmare will abruptly stop in a few weeks," he said. "Our new jets are coming out in quantity now, and then the Allies will be leery of flying over Germany." In mid-January Hitler and his entourage left Eagle's Eyrie for new headquarters in Berlin. Outwardly Hitler did not appear at all depressed, and in fact laughed with the others when someone joked that Berlin was now the only practical place for headquarters since one could travel between the west and east fronts by subway.

A fresh pincer attack had just been launched on the evaporating Bulge from north and south. On January 16 the two forces met a few miles north of Bastogne. In one great bite, half of the Bulge had been eliminated and about 20,000 Germans cut off.

By January 17 there was no consolation at all for Hitler. Manteuffel's army had joined the full retreat. A few picked infantrymen were left behind—the very young, old and useless. These men fought a gallant rearguard battle in lonely hopelessness. Boys of fourteen and fifteen died, rifles frozen to their hands; men in their fifties were found in cellars, feet black with putrefaction. The retreating columns were harassed by planes and big guns. None who survived would ever forget the overpowering American artillery. Winding lines of trucks, tanks and self-propelled guns rumbled toward the Fatherland over icy roads and trails clogged with snowdrifts. Long columns of infantrymen tramped in the snow, tormented as much by the bitter weather as by the retreating enemy.

The Battle of the Bulge was over. Left behind were two tiny ravaged countries, destroyed homes and farms, dead cattle, dead souls, dead minds—and more than 75,000 bodies.

Autumn Fog was creeping back to the Führer like some huge wounded beast. It reminded many of Napoleon's retreat from Moscow. Men shuffled painfully through the snow, feet encased in burlap bags, with shawls wound around their heads like careless turbans. They plodded on frozen feet, bedeviled by biting winds, bombs and shells. The wounded and sick crept back to the homeland with rotting insides, ulcers oozing, pus running from destroyed ears. They staggered east on numb feet with despair in their hearts, stricken by dysentery, which left its bloody trail of filth in the snow.

Their will was broken. Few who survived the retreat believed there was now any chance of German victory. Almost every man brought back a story of doom, of Allied might and of the terrifying weapon forged in the Ardennes: the American fighter. The GI who came out of the battle was the quintessential American, the man Hitler did not believe existed.

Chapter Twenty-nine

"THIS TIME WE MUST NOT SURRENDER FIVE MINUTES BEFORE MIDNIGHT"

JANUARY 17–APRIL 20, 1945

1

By January 17, 1945, the Red Army had overrun or by-passed German troops in the Baltic and crossed the Vistula River from Warsaw to Lower Silesia. The Soviets were so close to Auschwitz that inmates could hear the rumble of their artillery. For the past weeks SS guards had been burning storehousefuls of shoes, clothing and hair to hide traces of mass exterminations. Within two days most German officials in the area were in flight and the over-age *Volkssturm* (People's Militia) had disintegrated. That afternoon guards lined up 58,000 ill-clothed, hungry inmates in a freezing wind and marched them to the west for possible use as hostages. Some 6000 others, too ill to struggle to their feet, were left behind, it was hoped, to be disposed of by bombs and shells in the Soviet advance, but when the Red Army troops finally, on January 27, streamed through the front gate with its slogan Work Brings Freedom, there were still almost 5000 emaciated survivors, so weak they could barely cheer. Efforts to obliterate all traces of the murders at the vast complex had continued until that morning with the final blasting of the gas chambers and five crematoria, but even this could not wipe out the grisly proof of what had gone on in Hitler's death factory. Despite fires and detonations, Red Cross officials found 368,820 men's suits, 836,255 women's coats, 13,964 carpets and seven tons of hair. They came upon mountains of toothbrushes, eyeglasses, shoes, artificial limbs—and the mass graves of hundreds of thousands of human beings.

In Berlin that afternoon General Guderian and his aide climbed the dozen steps up to the main door of the chancellery to attend the Führer military conference. Once inside they took a long detour to Hitler's office; direct passage was closed off by damage from Allied bombs. They passed windows covered by cardboard, through corridors and rooms barren of pictures, carpets and tapestries, finally reaching an anteroom where guards stood poised with machine pistols. An SS officer politely requested them to hand over their side arms and carefully examined their briefcases. This, a regulation since July 20, applied even to the army chief of staff.

At 4:20 P.M. Adolf Hitler shuffled in, shoulders stooped, left arm hanging loose. He greeted a few with a limp shake from his incapacitated right hand, then heavily sank into a chair pushed forward by an aide. The conference opened with Guderian reporting realistically on the growing disaster in the East. Hitler made remarkably few suggestions, almost as if it were beyond his scope, but once the western front came up for discussion he showed lively interest, interspersing criticism with nostalgic reminiscences from his war, then engaging in a lengthy argument with Göring about the reduced rank given officers called out of retirement to active duty. The conference ended at 6:50 P.M. and Guderian started back to Zossen. He was disgusted. They had talked for two and a half hours without reaching a single important decision on the problems of the critical eastern front.

One of those problems was Himmler, who had just been placed in command of an emergency army group designed to stop the main thrust of Marshal G. K. Zhukov. To Guderian his selection was plain idiocy but Hitler had argued that the Reichsführer was the only man capable of forming a major force overnight; his name alone would inspire a fight to the end. Bormann had encouraged this appointment but those close to Himmler were convinced it was a plot to ruin their chief. Sending him to the East would not only keep him away from Führer Headquarters and allow Bormann to strengthen his growing hold on Hitler, but would inevitably give convincing proof of Himmler's military incompetence.

Himmler, an ex-army cadet who secretly longed to lead

troops into battle, took the bait, if a bit reluctantly. While he feared Bormann, it never occurred to him that his rival was preparing his downfall. He started east in his special train determined to halt the Russians at the Vistula River. To do so he had a few staff officers, one outdated map and a name for his unit, Army Group Vistula. Except for several scattered units, his command existed only on paper. As new divisions arrived, Himmler foolishly began forming an east-west defense line running from the Vistula to the Oder, which merely served as protection for Pomerania to the north. In other words, he barricaded the side door while leaving the front gate wide open.

Zhukov, consequently, simply by-passed this lateral line and kept moving due west, impeded only by isolated groups, and, as the Führer conference ended on January 27, his troops were a hundred miles from Berlin. Ahead lay the Oder, the last major geographical obstacle they would have to hurdle before reaching the Reich chancellery.

Three days later Hitler spoke to the people. He raised the specter of international Jewry and Asiatic Bolshevism before calling on every German to do his duty to the last. "However grave the crisis may be at the moment," he concluded, "it will, despite everything, finally be mastered by our unalterable will, by our readiness for sacrifice and by our abilities. We shall overcome this calamity, too, and this fight, too, will not be won by central Asia but by Europe; and at its head will be the nation that has represented Europe against the East for 1500 years and shall represent it for all times: our Greater German Reich, the German nation."

The Führer predicted that the West was bound to realize before long that Bolshevism was their real enemy and then would join Germany in the common crusade. Churchill knew as well as he that if the Red Army conquered Berlin half of Europe would immediately become Communist and in a few years the other half would be digested. "I never did want to fight the West," he said bitterly. "They forced it on me."

On the last day of January Hitler was wakened with alarming news: enemy tanks had just crossed the Oder River! No natural barrier of any consequence lay between them and Berlin. The panic in the capital was heightened three days later when the city was subjected to the heaviest bombing of the war.

Hitler's headquarters was also badly damaged in the raid and the next day Bormann described its woeful state to his wife. There was no communication with the outside, not even any light, power or water. "We have a water cart standing before the Reich chancellery, and that is our only supply for cooking and washing up! And the worst thing of all, so Müller tells me, is the toilets. These Kommando pigs use them constantly, and not one of them ever thinks of taking a bucket of water with him to flush the place." By this time Bormann, who now attended the daily military discussions, had insinuated himself into an impregnable position with the Führer. No longer were Göring, Speer and Himmler rivals for his trust and affection, and Goebbels had come to realize his own influence depended on a continuation of the uneasy alliance with the Reichsleiter.

A final mark of honor came to Bormann early in February. The Führer began dictating to him a political testament. If the Reich *did* fall—and Hitler still entertained the faint hope of some miracle—he wanted to record for history how closely he had come to achieving his magnificent dream. It was typical that he wanted the last word. And so on February 4, with the Bolsheviks at the gates of Berlin, the indefatigable Bormann began jotting down the Führer's final explanation to history of what went wrong. The British, he said, could have put an end to the war at the beginning of 1941. "But the Jews would have none of it. And their lackeys, Churchill and Roosevelt, were there to prevent it." Such a peace would have kept America from meddling in European affairs and, under German guidance, Europe would have speedily become unified. With the Jewish poison eliminated, unification would have been simple. And Germany, her rear secure, could have achieved "the ambition of my life and the raison d'étre of National Socialism—the destruction of Bolshevism." How simple it all would have been if only the English had been logical and reasonable! But they were neither and so he had been forced, as custodian of the fundamental interests of Germany, to wage total war.

Next to Bormann, the man he saw most in these days was his favorite architect, Paul Giesler. They would spend many hours poring over an illuminated wooden model of the new Linz, which would outrank Vienna as the jewel of Austria, or talk until early morning of architecture and Bolshevism, of art and the Western Allies, of his dream of saving Europe and uniting it into one grand unity. It was the large model city that was an unfailing inspiration to him and sometimes Goebbels would be dragged out of bed so Hitler could demonstrate with lights how Linz would look in morning, noon and night. He could have been the young Hitler lecturing to Kubizek on the wonders of their rebuilt city.

2

A month earlier Hitler had complained to Fräulein Schröder, "I am lied to on all sides." He could rely on no one, and if anything happened to him Germany would be without a Führer. His successor, Göring, had lost the sympathy of the people, and Reichsführer Himmler would be rejected by the party. He apologized for talking politics during lunch, then said: "Rack your brains again and tell me who my successor is to be. This is a question that I keep on asking myself, without ever getting an answer."

His spirits were raised a week later by Eva Braun's return to Berlin. She had been ordered out of the capital earlier in the month for the relative safety of Munich but after two weeks announced to her friends that she had to return to her man's side no matter what happened. She told them that death no longer mattered and she had to share the fate of the one she loved. Hitler pretended to be angry at her sudden reappearance and made a show of scolding her, but all that evening he repeated how proud he was of Fräulein Braun's devotion.

Several days later, near the end of February, Hitler convened his Gauleiters for a final meeting. They were alarmed by his appearance. He had to be supported by Schaub. His voice was low, his left hand shook badly. Everyone expected a sensational announcement, but instead he delivered a paradoxical sermon that was both inspiring and depressing. First he assured the Gauleiters that, although no wonder weapon was going to rescue the Reich at the last moment, the war could still be won so long as they inspired a "Teutonic fury" in the German people. If the nation failed to respond it had no moral worth and deserved destruction.

He thanked the Gauleiters for their co-operation and loyalty before doing something totally unexpected: he told them frankly of his failing health. He confessed that the trembling in his leg had traveled to his left arm, and made a joke: hopefully it would not move to his head. His last words were vague but ominous: in the future he would be forced to take harsh measures. He hoped they would not feel betrayed should he take steps they did not understand.

Faced as he was by almost certain disaster, Hitler's dominant mood in the days to follow became one of defiance and ire. He railed at Allied airmen who had already killed half a million civilians, and reviled those Germans who were greeting the advancing Americans almost as though they were liberators. His fury knew no bounds on March 7. The railroad bridge over the Rhine at Remagen was seized intact by Hodges' First Army before the defenders could blow it up. To Hitler this was another betrayal and he was determined to punish those responsible. It also gave him an excuse to get rid of the aging Rundstedt, who seemed only bent on retreat. In the emergency he ordered his most trusted trouble-shooter, Otto Skorzeny, to destroy the bridge. One group of Skorzeny frogmen managed to approach it with packages of "Plastit," a plastic explosive, but were discovered in time by an Allied secret weapon, Canal Defense Lights, a powerful beam whose source was undetectable.

By this time the entire German defense system in the West was in jeopardy. Model's Army Group B had been smashed, its remnants shoved back across the Rhine. To the south SS General Paul Hausser's Army Group G had been backed up against the river's west bank and was about to be surrounded. The situation in the East was no better and during these desperate days of mid-March Hitler decided to visit this front. His generals warned him that the situation was so fluid he might be captured or killed but he would not listen. As a concession he had Kempka drive him forward in a Volkswagen rather than the famous Mercedes. Their destination was a castle near the Oder where he pleaded with the commanders of the Ninth Army to contain the Russian drive on Berlin. Every day, every hour was precious he said, since new secret weapons would be ready momentarily. On the trip back to Berlin, Hitler sat silently beside Kempka, deep in thought. He knew that his talk of secret weapons was visionary and had recently confessed so to his Gauleiters. His atom bomb was many months from completion and his other secret weapons were unrealistic political ones, such as the hope that the West would join in the crusade against Bolshevism. By the time he returned to the city he had seen enough out front. Never again would he venture beyond the chancellery grounds. His only hope was a last-minute political miracle.

Hitler was aware that plots were being woven around him.

He knew, for example, of Ribbentrop's negotiations in Sweden and that Himmler was dickering with the Jews but he continued to allow these men to negotiate as if in his own name, even while declaring that all negotiations were futile. If a negotiation failed, he would deny any knowledge of it; if it succeeded, he could take the credit.

It is doubtful, however, that Hitler knew his trusted Speer was urging commanders such as Manteuffel to disobey orders to destroy bridges, dams and factories rather than leave them to the enemy. On March 18 Speer brought his protest against this "scorched earth" policy directly to the Führer. "At this stage of the war," he wrote in a memorandum, "it makes no sense for us to undertake demolitions which may strike at the very life of the nation." If Hitler had ever wavered in determination to scorch German earth, Speer's words spurred him to action. He summoned his quondam architect moments after reading his memorandum and said icily, "If the war is lost, the people will be lost also. It is not necessary to worry about what the German people will need for elemental survival. On the contrary, it is best for us to destroy even these things. For the nation has proved to be the weaker, and the future belongs to the stronger Eastern nation [the Soviet Union]. In any case only those who are inferior will remain after this struggle for the good have already been killed."

3

The rapid advance east of both Montgomery and Patton in the next few weeks caused consternation at Führer Headquarters. Hitler was particularly aroused by the action of Cardinal Galen, who drove out from Münster to surrender the city to an American unit. "If I ever lay hands on that swine," exclaimed Hitler, "I'll have him hanged!" He had also reached the limit of tolerance for his outspoken and feisty army chief of staff. Guderian knew it and, on the morning of March 28, drove up to Berlin determined to have a showdown. He was particularly upset by the fate of 200,000 German soldiers needlessly trapped hundreds of miles behind Russian lines in Kurland. Once inside the partially destroyed chancellery, Guderian and his aide were escorted by a guard down a flight of stairs to a steel-reinforced door guarded by two SS men. This was the entrance to Hitler's new home: a huge bunker buried far below the chancellery garden.

They descended more stairs to a narrow corridor, which was covered with a foot of water. They balanced their way across duckboards to a door, then went down another short flight of stairs to the upper level of the bunker. Twelve small rooms opened on a central vestibule which also served as the general mess hall. Guderian and his aide traversed this passageway, then proceeded down a curving stairway and a final dozen steps to the lower level. Here, in the Führer bunker, were eighteen cubicles, separated by an entrance hall which was divided into a waiting room and the conference room. Beyond these, in a small vestibule, was the emergency exit to four steep flights of concrete steps leading up to the chancellery garden. On the left of the conference room was a small map room, a rest room for the Führer's bodyguard and the six-room suite of Hitler and Eva Braun. The air was stuffy despite a ventilating system whose shrill, monotonous whine penetrated every room of the bunker. The whole structure was protected by a twelve-foot-thick reinforced ceiling, topped by thirty feet of concrete. This would be Hitler's tomb or his bastion of miraculous victory. Perhaps it reminded him of the terrible but heroic trench life of the Great War.

Hitler shuffled in from his adjoining apartment and the noon conference opened with a report by General Theodor Busse on his unsuccessful attempts to relieve a town on the east bank of the Oder. Hitler's criticism of Busse was interrupted by a spirited defense from Guderian. Stung, Hitler suddenly got to his feet with an agility which amazed the conferees. But Guderian was not intimidated. He boldly brought up the subject he and Hitler had fought over for weeks. "Is the Führer going to evacuate the Kurland army?" he asked. "Never!" exclaimed Hitler with a wave of an arm. Large red blotches appeared on his deathly white face. Guderian stood rooted to the spot, then started toward Hitler. Jodl and his deputy shepherded Guderian away, but he kept talking in a loud voice. Finally his aide inveigled him into the anteroom "to answer a phone call" and by the time Guderian returned to the conference room he had control of himself.

Hitler was back in his chair, face pinched, and though his hands trembled, he too had regained his poise. He quietly asked all to leave the room except Guderian and Keitel, then said, "General Guderian, the state of your health requires that you immediately take six weeks' sick leave." As Guderian started to leave Hitler told him to remain until the end of the conference. It continued as if nothing had happened. After several hours, which seemed interminable to Guderian, the session was over. But he was not yet free to go. "Please take good care of yourself," the Führer said solicitously. "In six weeks the situation will be very critical. Then I shall need you urgently." Guderian said he would pick a place to rest that wouldn't be overrun before the weekend, raised his arm in salute and walked away.

4

Even as fronts everywhere were collapsing, Hitler did his utmost to instill hope of a last-minute miracle. He pointed out that the foundation for the Brave New Europe set up by his enemies at Yalta was already beginning to crack. This was not wishful thinking. The Big Three had drawn up the plan in relative harmony but were indeed already deeply embroiled in its implementation. Their representatives, meeting in Moscow to form a new Polish government, had reached an impasse, with Molotov proclaiming that the Lublin Government truly represented the people of Poland, whereas Averell Harriman and the British ambassador contended that a more representative government must be set up to include émigré Poles.

This conflict was but a preamble to a more disruptive one. For several months General Karl Wolff—formerly Himmler's personal adjutant and presently SS chief in Italy—had been negotiating with the Americans through an agent of Allen Dulles, the OSS representative in Switzerland. Wolff had the Führer's vague approval to explore the matter but on his own initiative proposed surrendering all German troops in Italy, then secretly met with two Allied generals in Ascona, Switzerland, to discuss how this could be done without Hitler's knowledge.

From the beginning the Allies had kept Stalin informed about Operation Sunrise, as this venture was named, and from the beginning he had adamantly demanded that a Soviet officer take active part in the negotiations. The Allies explained, with reason, that Wolff would never come to a meeting under such circumstances but this merely raised Stalin's suspicions. When he learned of the rendezvous at Ascona his reaction was violent.

He accused the Allies of conniving with Germany, "behind the backs of the Soviet Union, which is bearing the brunt of the war against Germany," and labeled the whole affair "not a misunderstanding but something worse."

By the end of March Stalin was charging that, because of the talks at Ascona, the Germans had felt free to send three divisions from Italy to the eastern front. He further complained that the agreement at Yalta to attack Hitler simultaneously from the east, west and south was not being observed in Italy by the Allies. An explanation by Roosevelt resulted in an irate cable from Stalin openly accusing the Allies of playing a deceitful game. This so irritated the President that on April 5 he sent off the most aggressive and indignant message he had ever addressed to an ally: "Frankly I cannot avoid the feeling of bitter resentment toward your informers, whoever they are, for such vile misrepresentations of my actions or those of my trusted subordinates." Stalin hastily replied that he had never doubted Roosevelt's integrity or trustworthiness. But it was an aggressive apology; he added that a Russian should have been invited to the Ascona meeting and described his own point of view as "the only correct one."

Hitler did not know the details of the discord in the enemy camp, only that there was one and he had predicted it. It fanned the faint hope of a miracle and he was in a receptive mood when Goebbels read to him Carlyle's description of the desperate days of the Seven Years' War: Frederick the Great, dejected by apparent defeat in Prussia, declared that if there was no change before February 15 he would take poison. "Brave King," wrote Carlyle, "wait yet a little while, and the days of your suffering will be over. Already the sun of your good fortune stands behind the clouds, and soon will rise upon you." On February 12 the Czarina died and brought about the incredible change in Frederick's fortunes.

"At this touching tale," Goebbels later told Schwerin von Krosigk, "tears stood in the Führer's eyes." It also whetted Hitler's interest in his own horoscope and he sent for two that were kept in Himmler's research departments. Both predicted victories until 1941, and then a series of reversals culminating in disaster during the first half of April 1945. But there would be a temporary success in the second half of that month, followed by a lull until peace in August. Germany would endure hard times until 1948 when she would rise once more to greatness.

Across the Atlantic, in Warm Springs, Georgia, Franklin Roosevelt was murmuring, "I have a terrific headache," before losing consciousness. He died two hours and twenty minutes later. Goebbels received the news upon arrival at his office. "This is the turning point!" he exclaimed and then asked incredulously, "Is it really true?" Some ten people hung over him as he telephoned Hitler. "My Führer," he said, "I congratulate you! Roosevelt is dead. It is written in the stars that the second half of April will be the turning point for us." It was a miracle! He listened to Hitler a moment before mentioning the possibility that Truman would be more moderate than Roosevelt. Anything could happen now. Goebbels hung up, eyes shining, and launched into an impassioned speech. It was as if the war was nearly over.

Ribbentrop did not share his enthusiasm. Next morning, April 13, he returned from a short visit with Hitler in a black mood. "The Führer," he told his staff, "is in seventh heaven!" That scoundrel Goebbels had convinced him that Roosevelt's death was the turn of the tide. "How nonsensical, and how criminal! How could Roosevelt's death change anything to our advantage?"

Hitler called a special meeting and revealed a bizarre strategy to save Berlin: German troops falling back toward the capital would create a hard nucleus of defense which would irresistibly draw Russian troops toward it. This would relieve other German forces from pressure and enable them to attack the Bolsheviks from the outside. The decisive battle would be won in Berlin, he assured a dubious audience; and he himself would remain in the city to inspire the defenders. Several urged him to go to Berchtesgaden but he would not consider it. As commander-in-chief of the Wehrmacht and as leader of the people, it was his obligation to stay in the capital. He drafted an eight-page proclamation—the last he would write to the troops—and sent it to Goebbels. Even the Propaganda Minister thought its bombast too ridiculous. He began revisions with a green pencil but had to give up and threw the statement in the wastebasket. Then he pulled it out and changed a few sentences. Without bothering to clear the final version, Goebbels had copies distributed along the front on the fifteenth. If every soldier on the eastern front did his duty, it said, Asia's last assault would fail. For Fate had removed Roosevelt, the greatest war criminal of all times, from the world, and the war would take a decisive turn.

Incredibly, many of the soldiers were heartened by Hitler's words. Even the majority of citizens still kept faith with him, despite the relentless bombings from the West and the rapidly shrinking borders of the Reich. To the average German the Führer was more than a man, he was a supernatural phenomenon. They held positive belief in his invulnerability, many clinging to the popular myth that a house wall bearing his picture could withstand any bomb. His miraculous escape on the twentieth of July bore witness to his indestructibility, making it that much easier to raise their spirits and hopes with such slogans as "Hitler Is Victory Itself."

In private, the creator of this slogan had lost his own faith. Goebbels disconsolately began preparing for the end, and started by burning his papers and personal mementos. He hesitated before destroying a large autographed photograph of his great love, Lida Baarova. "Now, there's a beautiful woman!" he remarked. After staring at the picture a long moment, he ripped it into pieces then threw them into the fire.

The following day Germany received two great blows: one from the West where all German troops within the Ruhr pocket surrendered; another from the East where Zhukov's all-out attack on Berlin breached the ridge defense lines west of the Oder, thus opening the road to the Führer bunker forty-five miles away. Though he still talked of victory, Hitler prepared for the worst. He entrusted a visiting party official with two assignments: he was to remove the German gold reserves to a salt mine in Thuringia and convey to safety a sealed package that Bormann would give him. The package contained Hitler's dictations to Bormann, his testament to Germany and the world.*

*The document was deposited in the vault of a bank in Bad Gastein by the party official, who was later arrested for war crimes and imprisoned. Fearing the testament would incriminate him further, the official asked a legal friend to destroy it. The lawyer did so, but not before making a photostatic copy. In 1959 these revealing statements, each page authenticated by Bormann's signature, were finally published under the title *The Political Testament of Adolf Hitler, the Hitler-Bormann Documents*.

Chapter Thirty

FIVE MINUTES PAST MIDNIGHT, OR, "THE CAPTAIN ALSO GOES DOWN WITH THIS SHIP"

APRIL 20–30, 1945

1

The Allies celebrated Hitler's birthday with another thousand-bomber raid on the capital. But nothing seemed to dampen Hitler's confidence. Throughout the twentieth of April he told birthday visitors that he still believed the Russians would suffer defeat in Berlin. In the afternoon he met a group of Hitler Youth in the chancellery garden and thanked them for their gallantry in the battle for the capital. Then he climbed down into the bunker and received Grossadmiral Karl Dönitz, who thought he looked like a man carrying an intolerable burden. Afterward he greeted Keitel with warmth. "I will never forget that you saved me at the time of the Attentat and that you got me out of Rastenburg—you made the right decisions and took the right actions."

Keitel blurted out that negotiations for peace should be initiated at once before Berlin became a battlefield. Hitler interrupted. "Keitel, I know what I want. I am going to go down fighting, either in or outside Berlin." After a tête-à-tête with Jodl, he slowly passed down a line of military and civilian leaders—including Bormann, Ribbentrop and Speer—shaking hands and saying a few words to each man. Almost everyone urged Hitler to flee to Berchtesgaden while there was still an open road but he was adamant. From now on, he said, the

Reich would be divided into two separate commands, with Dönitz in charge of the northern sector. Field Marshal Albrecht Kesselring, commander of the western front, was the logical choice for the south, but Hitler was also considering Göring—perhaps for political expediency—and said he would leave it to Providence to decide. He recommended that the various command staffs split in two, and those selected for the south should leave that evening for Berchtesgaden. Göring asked if he should go south or send his chief of staff, Koller. "You go," said the Führer. The two old comrades, once so close, parted with polite coolness. Göring headed for Karinhall where his butler was waiting with fourteen carloads of clothing and art treasures.

Hitler dined alone with Eva and his secretaries. Again he was urged to go south but he said that would be like a Tibetan lama turning an empty prayer wheel. "I must force a decision here in Berlin—or perish!" After midnight he summoned the two older secretaries to his private room and revealed that they were to leave in half an hour or so by car for the Obersalzberg along with Admiral von Puttkamer and eighty others.* The two women were wide-eyed with astonishment. His explanation was that they had been with him the longest. Besides, Fräulein Wolf supported her mother. "I will join you as soon as possible." He spoke in a whisper, vainly trying to hide the trembling of his left hand. A sigh escaped him; one, thought Fräulein Schröder, which seemed to come from a man without hope. A little later he phoned her to say that Berlin was surrounded. She could not leave until first light. A second call followed in minutes. The plane would take off as soon as the air raid all-clear was sounded. She didn't quite understand, since his voice gurgled imperceptibly, and asked him to repeat himself. He said nothing. His last words to her colleague Fräulein Wolf were: "It is all over."

Earlier that evening Himmler, after paying respects to the Führer on his birthday, left the bunker and drove through the beating rain for several hours to meet Norbert Masur, the representative of the World Jewish Congress. Himmler explained

*Among those sent south was Dr. Morell. He was banished in anger for suggesting that Hitler take an injection of caffeine for his fatigue. "You will probably give me morphine!" shouted Hitler and ordered him to remove his uniform as the Führer's private physician. "And act as if you've never seen me." Morell collapsed at Hitler's feet and had to be led away. He died, a broken man, soon after the war.

that he had been empowered to solve the Jewish problem and had first planned a humane solution through emigration. But even those countries which boasted of their friendliness toward the Jews refused to take them. "Through the war," Himmler said, "we came into contact with the masses of the Eastern Jewish proletariat, and this created new problems. We could not have such an enemy in our back." These Jews not only helped the partisans but were infected by typhus and other diseases. "In order to curtail the epidemics," he explained, "we had to build crematoria where we could burn the corpses of the large number of people who died because of these diseases. And now they'll get us just for doing that!"

"Much has happened which cannot be undone," Masur said. "But if we are ever to build a bridge between our peoples for the future, then all Jews who are today alive in the areas dominated by Germany must remain alive." Himmler protested that he had always intended turning over the camps to the Allies without resistance. Hadn't he done so with Bergen-Belsen and Buchenwald? And look what he got in return: faked atrocity pictures were being circulated by the Americans! And when he let 2700 Jews go to Switzerland, the foreign press claimed that he had done so only to get himself an alibi. "I don't need an alibi. I have always done what I felt would fill the needs of my people, and I take full responsibility. It certainly didn't make me a rich man."

At the moment Himmler assured Masur that all evacuations had ceased, the inmates of Sachsenhausen, which lay directly athwart the path of Zhukov's advance on Berlin, were being herded out of the barracks into the rain and lined up for departure; ten miles to the east Zhukov's guns roared ominously. The Red Cross delegate requested the camp commandant to turn over Sachsenhausen to his organization, but he refused, on the grounds that he had standing orders from Himmler to evacuate everything except the hospital at the approach of the Russians. And so almost 40,000 prisoners—starved, sick, poorly clothed—were shoved into two surging columns. The guards harried them through the pummeling rain in a northwesterly direction, and those who couldn't keep up the pace were shot and left in the ditches.

On the eastern front there were rumors that the leaders in Berlin had given up all hope and that OKW was fleeing to

Berchtesgaden. The Russians had broken through the lines of Army Group Vistula at half a dozen points and one Red Army task force was but twenty miles from Berlin and the Führer's bunker. By noon of April 21 it had closed to artillery range, and the explosions of its shells could be heard faintly in the bunker as Jodl reported that a Zhukov column was threatening to encircle Manteuffel's army. To counter this, the last small reserve under SS General Felix Steiner had just been positioned twenty-five miles north of Berlin.

Hitler jerked upright from a slump. Like Skorzeny and Rudel, (Colonel Hans Ulrich Rudel, the Stuka pilot who had sunk a Soviet battleship and knocked out 500 Red tanks), Steiner was a magic name; it was his desperate attack from Pomerania that had slowed Zhukov's advance in February. Hitler began poring over a map. Finally he looked up. His eyes glistened. Counterattack! he said with rising excitement. Steiner was to drive to the southeast and cut straight through the Zhukov spearhead: this would, with one bold blow, save Berlin and prevent Manteuffel from being encircled. He dispatched a personal order to Steiner expressly forbidding any retreat to the west. "Officers who do not comply unconditionally with this order are to be arrested and shot immediately. You, Steiner, are answerable with your head for execution of this order." Of all the impossible orders Steiner had received from the Führer, this was the most fantastic. His Panzer corps was one in name only. He had no intention of sacrificing his troops in such a hopeless cause and would only make a show of compliance—an easy decision for a man who had once considered kidnaping the Führer.

Bormann also knew there was no hope. He telephoned his wife at Berchtesgaden and told her he'd found a "wonderful hiding place" for their children in the Tyrol. She was to pose as a director of bombed-out children seeking refuge. He had kidnaped six youngsters from the party kindergarten in Garmisch to make the group look more plausible.

2

In the bunker, on the morning of April 22, Steiner was the main topic of conversation. Had his attack from the north been launched to relieve Berlin? If so, how far had it gone? With each passing hour Hitler became increasingly upset every time

General Hans Krebs, Guderian's replacement as OKH chief of staff, told him there was nothing definite to report. At the afternoon Führer conference, after learning that Berlin was three-fourths surrounded, Hitler demanded to know once and for all how far Steiner had progressed in his attack. At last Krebs was forced to admit that the Steiner corps was still being organized and there just wasn't anything to report.

Hitler's head jerked and he began breathing heavily. Harshly he ordered everyone out of the room except his generals and Bormann. The rest stumbled over one another in their eagerness to escape. In the waiting room they stood in silent apprehension. Once the door closed Hitler lunged to his feet. As he lurched back and forth, swinging his right arm wildly, he shouted that he was surrounded by traitors and liars. All were too low, too mean to understand his great purpose, he shouted. He was the victim of corruption and cowardice and now everyone had deserted him. His listeners had never before seen him lose control so completely. He flung an accusing finger at the generals and blamed their ilk for the disasters of the war. The only protest came from Bormann. The officers were surprised, but Bormann's words were undoubtedly meant not so much as a defense of the military as to calm the Führer.

Hitler shouted something about Steiner and abruptly flopped into his chair. In anguish he said, "The war is lost!" Then with a trembling voice he added that the Third Reich had ended in failure and all he could do now was die. His face turned white and his body shook spasmodically, as if torn by a violent stroke. Suddenly he was still. His jaw slackened and he sat staring ahead with blank eyes. This alarmed the onlookers more than his fury. Minute after minute passed—afterward no one could remember how many. Finally a patch of color came to the Führer's cheeks and he twitched—perhaps he had suffered a coronary attack or fibrillation. Bormann, Keitel and Burgdorf, chief of army personnel, begged him to have faith. If *he* lost it, then all indeed was lost. They urged him to leave for Berchtesgaden immediately, but he slowly shook his head and in a dead, tired voice said that if they wanted to go they were free to do so, but he was meeting his end in the capital. He asked for Goebbels.

Those in the outer room had heard almost everything. Fegelein grabbed a phone and told Himmler what had happened. The shaken Reichsführer phoned Hitler and begged him not to lose hope. He promised to send SS troops at once. In the meantime Hitler sent for Traudl Junge, Gerda Christian and his new cook, Konstanze Manzialy. They came to his anteroom where he was waiting with Eva Braun. His face was expressionless, his eyes dead. In an impersonal yet imperious manner he told the four women to leave for the south by plane within the hour. "All is lost, hopelessly lost," he said.

The women stood rigid with shock. Eva was the first to move. She went up to Hitler, took both his hands in hers. She smiled softly as if to a sad child. "But you surely know that I shall stay with you. I won't let you send me away." This brought life back to his eyes and he did something no one in the family circle had ever before seen: he kisssed Eva on the lips.

In spite of herself, Traudl found herself saying, "I also am staying." Gerda and the cook joined the chorus. Hitler again ordered them to leave but they stood firm. He seized their hands in turn and said with emotion, "If only my generals were as brave as you are!" As if totally exhausted, he dragged himself to the next room where a group of officers was waiting. "Gentlemen," he said, "this is the end. I shall remain here in Berlin and shoot myself when the time comes. Each of you must make his own decision on when to leave."

3

That evening General Eckard Christian, the Luftwaffe chief of operations, burst into Koller's headquarters just outside Berlin. "The Führer is in a state of collapse!" He gave a frightening account of what had happened. Koller drove to the new OKW headquarters and asked Jodl for confirmation of Christian's incredible story. Jodl calmly replied that it was true. Koller asked if the Führer would carry out his threat to commit suicide. Yes, he was stubborn on that point. Koller was indignant. He said he must leave at once to tell Göring in person that the Führer had said: "If it comes to negotiating, the Reichsmarschall can do it better than I can."

Koller did not reach Göring's comfortable, unostentatious house on the Obersalzberg until noon. Excitedly he told about Hitler's collapse. Göring, asked if Hitler was still alive. Had he appointed Bormann as his successor? Koller replied that the Führer was alive when he left Berlin and that there were still one or two escape routes. The city would probably hold out for a week. "Anyway," he concluded, "it is now up to you to act, Herr Reichsmarschall!"

Göring was hesitant. Might not Hitler have appointed Bormann as his successor? he asked again. Bormann, an old enemy, could have sent the telegram to make him usurp power prematurely. "If I act, he will call me a traitor; if I don't, he will accuse me of having failed at a most critical time!" He sent for Hans Lammers, the legal expert and custodian of the two official documents establishing a successor, drafted by Hitler himself in 1941. In these directives Göring was appointed Hitler's deputy upon his death. He would also be Hitler's successor in case the Führer was prevented—permanently or temporarily—from performing his office.

Göring wanted to know if the military situation in Berlin warranted his taking over, but Lammers could make no decision. Well aware that his influence with the Führer had waned as Bormann's waxed, Göring asked if Hitler had issued any orders since 1941 which might have invalidated his own succession. No, said Lammers, he had made sure from time to time that the documents had not been rescinded. The decree, he declared, had the force of law and didn't even need to be promulgated again.

Someone suggested that a radio message be sent asking the Führer if he still wanted Göring to be his deputy. One was drafted: "My Führer, is it your wish, in view of your decision to stay in Berlin, that I take over complete control of the Reich, in accordance with the decree of June 29, 1941?" Göring read it and added: ". . . with full powers in domestic and foreign affairs," so that he might negotiate a peace with the Allies. Still concerned, he said, "Suppose I don't get any answer? We must give a time limit, a time by which I must receive an answer."

Koller suggested that they make it eight hours and Göring scribbled down a deadline, then added hastily, "You must realize that I feel for you in this most difficult hour of my life and I can find no words to express myself. God bless you and speed you here as soon as possible. Your most loyal, Hermann Göring." Leaning back heavily, he said, "It's frightful." If no answer came by 10 P.M. he had to do something drastic. "I'll stop the war at once."

At the bunker his telegram—the last from Göring to be intercepted in England by Ultra—seemed to outrage Bormann more than anyone else. He demanded Göring's execution. Hitler refused to go that far and sent his Reichsmarschall three conflicting messages. The first offered to disregard the death penalty for high treason if Göring resigned all his offices; the second rescinded the decree establishing Göring as his successor; and the third, perhaps more accurately reflecting Hitler's confused feelings, was couched in such vague terms that Bormann must have feared it was a prelude to forgiveness. On his own he radioed the SS commandant at the Obersalzberg to arrest Göring for treason.

4

With the Russians closing in on the capital, Eva Braun's normal cheerful nature had changed to one of controlled terror. Once she seized Traudl Junge's hands and in a trembling voice confessed how frightened she was. "If only everything would finally be over!" She penned a farewell letter to her best friend, Herta: "These are my last lines, and therefore the last sign of life from me," she began and explained that she was sending her jewelry to be distributed according to her will. She apologized for the letter's incoherence: the Goebbelses' six children were in the next room making an infernal racket. "I can't understand how all this can have happened, it's enough to make one lose one's faith in God!" In a postscript she added that Hitler himself had lost hope. But the next day, Monday, April 23, Eva wrote her sister that there was still a chance. "It goes without saying, however, that we will not let ourselves be captured alive." She asked Gretl to destroy all her business papers but to pack the Führer's letters and her replies in a watertight package and bury them. The message ended with a pitifully hopeful postscript: "I just spoke to the Führer. I think he is also more optimistic about the future than he was yesterday."

At the military conference next morning, April 24, Hitler learned that Manteuffel's army had been completely cut off by a deep Soviet tank thrust. "In view of the broad natural barrier formed by the Oder," he said after a tense silence, "the Russian success against the Third Tank Army can only be attributed to the incompetence of the German military leaders there!" Krebs tried to defend the front-line commander but this only reminded

Hitler of Steiner's abortive attack. He pointed shakily at a map and said that another drive from north of Berlin must be started within twenty-four hours. "The Third Army will make use of all available forces for this assault, ruthlessly depleting those sections of our front line which are not under attack. It is imperative that the link to Berlin from the north be restored by tomorrow evening. Have that passed on at once." A suggestion that Steiner lead the attack incensed him. "Those arrogant, tedious, indecisive SS leaders are no good to me any more!"

Goebbels left the meeting to issue his last proclamation to the citizens of Berlin. He hoped that by telling the truth he could frighten them into continuing the holy crusade against the Reds to the end. "Our hearts must not waver and not tremble. It must be our pride and our ambition to break the Bolshevist mass onslaught which is surging from the East against the heartland of Europe at the walls of the Reich capital." Even as these last words were disseminated, Julius Schaub was burning the last of the Führer's private correspondence. This done, Hitler's personal adjutant enplaned for the south with orders to destroy other private documents in the Munich apartment and at the Berghof.

5

The SS commandant at Berchtesgaden had acted immediately upon receipt of Bormann's telegram by placing Göring and his family under house arrest. The past two days had been the most tempestuous in the Reichsmarschall's dramatic career: his Führer had collapsed; he thought he himself had been called upon to inherit the Third Reich; then came Hitler's three telegrams; and now he feared he was going to be executed. That morning—April 25—several SS officers tried to persuade Göring, in the presence of his wife and his butler, to sign a document stating that he was resigning all positions because of poor health. Göring refused; in spite of the telegrams he could not bring himself to believe Hitler really meant what he said. But once the SS men drew their guns Göring quickly signed. The ceremony was interrupted by the drone of approaching aircraft.

Allied planes had often passed over Berchtesgaden on their way to Salzburg, Linz and other targets, but as yet Hitler's retreat was undamaged. Today, however, 318 Lancaster bombers were bent on wiping it out. At 10 A.M., the first wave swept over the mountain, dumping high explosives on the edge of the Führer area. Half an hour later came a larger wave. For almost an hour plane after plane unloaded blockbusters directly onto the Obersalzberg. After the last bomber had disappeared Air Force General Robert Ritter von Greim, commander of Luftflotte 6 in Munich, drove up to the Berghof. It was a mass of twisted wreckage. Greim looked around in dismay. The Führer's home had been hit directly; one side was demolished and the blasted tin roof hung in mid-air.

By midmorning the Red Army pincers around Berlin were about to close and the conferees at the 10:30 A.M. meeting waited in an atmosphere of gloom for Hitler's arrival. He too was despondent until Heinz Lorenz of the official German news agency reported that he had just monitored an announcement from a neutral country that an argument had broken out between Russians and Americans at the first meeting of their troops on the Mulde River. There were disagreements regarding the sectors to be occupied, with the Russians accusing the Americans of infringing on area agreements made at Yalta.

Hitler sat upright, eyes gleaming. "Gentlemen," he said, "here again is striking evidence of the disunity of our enemies. The German people and history would surely brand me as a criminal if I made peace today while there is still the possibility that tomorrow our enemies might have a falling out!"

By late morning it appeared that General Paul Wenck's Twelfth Army was driving to the rescue of Hitler. Radio reports of his steady progress heartened Berliners. No one waited more eagerly than Hitler. He was counting on Wenck to prolong the battle at least until May 5 so he could die on the same day as Napoleon. It was a vain hope. Only a single corps of Wenck's army, the XX, was attacking toward the capital, and its limited mission was to reach Potsdam and provide a corridor of retreat for the Berlin garrison. The bulk of Wenck's army was driving east—against the Führer's orders—to save comrades of the entrapped Ninth Army.

Early that evening another general, the epitome of loyalty, was risking death to report to his Führer. Ritter von Greim was at the controls of a small observation plane flying at treetop level toward embattled Berlin. Overhead the sky raged with dogfights. Suddenly a gaping hole appeared in the flooring of the cockpit and Greim slumped over. As the plane plunged down out of control his passenger, Hanna Reitsch, the aviator and glider pilot, reached over and seized the stick. Somehow she managed to right the Storch and make a safe landing on the broad avenue running through the Brandenburg Gate. She commandeered a car and helped Greim aboard.

After his injured right foot was treated, Greim was carried on a stretcher down to the Führer bunker. The little party encountered Magda Goebbels, who stared wide-eyed, marveling that any living soul could have found his way there. She had never met Hanna Reitsch but embraced her and began sobbing. In a moment they came upon Hitler in the narrow passageway. His head drooped heavily, his arms twitched continually, his eyes were glassy. But Greim's report gave Hitler new life. He seized both Greim's hands, then turned to Reitsch. "Brave woman! So there is still some loyalty and courage left in the world!"

Hitler told them about the treacherous telegram Göring had sent. "An ultimatum, a blatant ultimatum! Now there's nothing left. Look what I have to go through: no allegiances were kept, no honor lived up to; there are no disappointments or betrayals I have not experienced—and now this above all." He stopped as if unable to go on. Then, looking at Greim with half-closed eyes, he said in a little more than a whisper, "I hereby declare you Göring's successor as Oberbefehlshaber der Luftwaffe. In the name of the German people I give you my hand." Deeply moved, both newcomers asked to be allowed to remain in the bunker to atone for Göring's deceit. Equally moved, Hitler assented. Their decision, he said, would long be remembered in the history of the Luftwaffe.

By dawn April 27 Berlin was completely encircled and the last two airports overrun by the Red Army. Still a flurry of optimism swept through the bunker with arrival of a radiogram from Wenck, announcing that XX Corps had come to within a few miles of Potsdam. Goebbels' office immediately proclaimed over the radio that Wenck had reached Potsdam itself and predicted that he would soon be in the capital. And if Wenck made it, why not others? "The situation has changed decisively in our favor," Berliners were told. "The Americans are marching toward Berlin. The great change of the war is at hand. Berlin must be held till Army Wenck arrives, no matter at what costs!"

The daily army communiqué, also broadcast in the clear,

divulged Wenck's exact position. He was appalled. "We won't be able to move a single step farther tomorrow!" Wenck exclaimed to his chief of staff. The Russians surely had heard the same broadcast and would concentrate everything available at his position. It was, he said, almost a betrayal.

At the afternoon conference, Hitler reverted to reminiscences. He talked of compromises he had been forced to make upon assuming power in 1933 and how this situation had lasted until Hindenburg's death. This led to another pledge to remain in Berlin. He did so, he said, so he could proceed harshly against weakness. "I would otherwise not have this moral right. I cannot constantly threaten others if I run away from the German capital in a critical hour. I must now obey the dictates of Fate. Even if I could save myself, I would not do so. The captain also goes down with this ship."

6

In San Francisco, where the conference to set up a United Nations Organization was in session, a Reuters reporter was told that Himmler had just offered to surrender Germany unconditionally. His telegram got through to Reuters without censorship and a bulletin was dispatched throughout the world. A DNB man on the upper level of the bunker heard a BBC version of this story just before 9 P.M. on the twenty-eighth and brought it to Hitler. He read the message without emotion, as if resigned that the end had come, then summoned Goebbels and Bormann. The three conferred behind locked doors.

The bunker was in a turmoil by the time General Helmuth Weidling, the military commandant of Berlin, arrived for the evening conference. He informed Hitler of the latest Russian advances. All ammunition, food and supply dumps were either in enemy hands or under heavy artillery fire. In two days his troops would be out of ammunition and no longer able to resist. "As a soldier, I suggest therefore that we risk the breakout at once." He immediately launched into the details of his plan before Hitler could comment. Pure hysteria! Goebbels exclaimed. But Krebs said it was feasible from a military viewpoint. "Naturally," he added quickly, "I must leave the decision to the Führer." Hitler was silent. What if the breakout did succeed? he finally asked. "We would merely flee from one frying pan to another. Am I, the Führer, supposed to sleep in an open field or in a farmhouse, and just wait for the end?"

He left the conference to visit the wounded Greim; Hanna Reitsch was already there. He slumped down on the edge of Greim's bed, his face ashen, and told them of Himmler's betrayal. "Our only hope is Wenck," he said, "and to make his entry possible we must call up every available aircraft to cover his approach." He ordered Reitsch to fly Greim to the Rechlin airport so he could muster his aircraft from there. Only with Luftwaffe support could Wenck get through. "That's the first reason you must leave the shelter. The second is that Himmler must be stopped." His lips and hands trembled, his voice quavered. "A traitor must never succeed me as Führer. You must get out to make sure he will not." Painfully Greim began to dress. In tears, Reitsch asked Hitler for permission to stay. Hitler refused. "God protect you."

Frau Goebbels gave Reitsch two letters to her son. She took off a diamond ring and asked her to wear it in her memory. Eva Braun also gave Hanna a letter for her sister, Frau Fegelein. Later Reitsch couldn't resist reading it; she thought it was "so vulgar, so theatrical and in such poor, adolescent taste" that she tore it up.

The dark night was lit up by flaming buildings, and Greim and Reitsch could hear intense small-arms fire as an armored car brought them to an Arado 96 trainer, hidden near the Brandenburg Gate. She taxied the little plane down the east-west axis, taking off in a hail of fire. At rooftop level Russian searchlights picked up the Arado and flak explosions began tossing it about like a feather. With full power she climbed out of the maelstrom—below lay Berlin, a sea of flames. She headed north.

7

"Better to reign in hell than serve in heaven."

Lucifer in MILTON'S *Paradise Lost*

Himmler's betrayal brought an end to Hitler's last hesitation and flickering hope. He sent for Traudl Junge. She wondered what he had to dictate, then noticed a table elaborately decorated for some festivity: a tablecloth with the initials A.H., the silver service, champagne glasses. Was he intending to celebrate his final farewell?

He winked. "Perhaps we can begin now," he said and led the way to the conference room. He stood at his usual place before the map table—today it was barren—and stared at the polished surface. "My last political will," he said. As she took down his words her hand trembled. This was history in the making! She was sure it was going to be a confession, a justification. Who would lie at the brink of death? But the words she jotted down were only recriminations, accusations. Usually he made numerous corrections, rephrasing every sentence. Tonight he spoke almost without pause, his eyes glued on the table. He charged that neither he nor anyone else in Germany wanted war and that it had been "provoked exclusively by those international statesmen who either were of Jewish origin or worked for Jewish interests."

He declared that he would die "with a joyful heart" but had ordered his military commanders "to continue to take part in the nation's continuing struggle." To Traudl's wonder he began to name a new government. As his successor—both as President of the Reich and Supreme Commander of the Armed Forces—Hitler appointed Admiral Dönitz. Goebbels was made Chancellor and Bormann Party Minister. Traudl could not understand, if everything was lost, if Germany was destroyed, and National Socialism dead forever, what would these new officials do?

He was still staring at the table when he finished. For a moment he said nothing; then he began to dictate his personal will. "Since I did not feel that I could accept the responsibility of marriage during the years of struggle, I have decided now, before the end of my earthly career, to take as my wife..." Traudl looked up, startled, at last realizing why the table had been set for a celebration. She recalled Eva's cryptic words an hour earlier to Gerda Christian and herself: "This evening I bet you I shall cry!" But Traudl could find no tears. "...as my wife," continued Hitler, "the girl who, after many years of loyal friendship, came of her own free will to this city, already almost besieged, in order to share my fate. At her own request she goes to her death with me as my wife. Death will compensate us for what we were both deprived of by my labors in the service of my people." He left his possessions to the party, "or if this no longer exists, to the state," and appointed his most faithful party comrade, Martin Bormann, executor of his will. He ended with words that might have been inspired by Wagner and the opera libretto he himself composed as a young man in Vienna: "My wife and I choose to die in order to escape the shame of overthrow or capitulation. It is our wish that our bodies be burned immediately, here where I have performed the greater part of my daily work during the twelve years I served my people."

There were eight guests: Bormann, the Goebbelses, Gerda Christian, Chief Adjutant Burgdorf, Krebs, Arthur Axmann, head of the Hitler Youth, and Fräulein Manzialy, the cook. A minor offical was found in a nearby Volkssturm unit and brought into the bunker to officiate—appropriately, his name was Wagner. Eva wore a long gown of black silk taffeta; Hitler was in uniform. The ceremony was brief and notable only for two slight mishaps and a minor embarrassment. The rings were too big; they had been hastily located in the Gestapo treasury. Then Eva signed the marriage certificate and like many nervous brides, made a mistake. She started to sign it "Eva B . . .," then hastily crossed out the "B" and wrote, Eva Hitler, née Braun. Wagner also was so nervous he signed his name wrong—with a double "a"—then Goebbels and Bormann added their signatures as witnesses. It was just before midnight, April 28.

Arm in arm with his bride, Hitler led the way into the study for the wedding feast. He joked and drank a little Tokay. Eva was radiant. She sent for the phonograph with its single record, "Red Roses," and went out into the corridor to receive congratulations from the staff. The word spread and smaller parties began celebrating the event throughout the bunker. Hitler was jovial but distracted and kept leaving the festivities to find out how Traudl was progressing with the two testaments. Just as she was finishing, Goebbels rushed in, pale and excited. He exclaimed that the Führer had ordered him to quit Berlin so as to take over a leading position in the new government. But how could he leave his side? He stopped abruptly, oblivious of the tears rolling down his cheeks. "The Führer has made so many decisions too late! Why this one, the last one, too early?" He made her leave the typewriter so she could take down *his* last will, one to be attached to Hitler's. "For the first time in my life," he dictated, "I must categorically refuse to obey an order of the Führer. My wife and children join me in this refusal." In the nightmare of treachery surrounding Hitler, he continued, there must be at least one willing to stay unconditionally with him until death.

It was almost 4 A.M. by the time Traudl finished all three documents. By then Bormann, Goebbels and Hitler were hovering over her and one of them ripped the last page from her typewriter. The three returned to the conference room where Hitler scratched his signature at the bottom of his official political testament. Goebbels, Bormann, Burgdorf and Krebs signed as witnesses. It reaffirmed the obsession of his life and career by taking credit for the annihilation of the Jews. They had started the war, he said, and he had made them pay, "even if by more humane means, for their guilt." He had no remorse for what he had done. He was proud that he had never weakened. "Above all," he concluded, "I enjoin the leaders of the nation and those under them to uphold the racial laws to their full extent and to oppose mercilessly the universal poisoner of all peoples, International Jewry." He was proud for having accomplished his mission of extermination and his words reaffirmed that, though he had many accomplices, without him there would have been no Final Solution.

8

By mid-morning of April 29 Russian ground forces were driving toward the bunker in three main attacks: from the east, south and north. The circle around the dying city tightened as advance Soviet units infiltrated the zoo. A mile away in the bunker Martin Bormann was making preparations to send Hitler's testament as well as his personal will to his successor, Admiral Dönitz. To help guarantee their delivery, Bormann decided to dispatch two separate emissaries: his own personal adviser and Heinz Lorenz. Goebbels also wanted his testament to reach the outside world and gave a copy to Lorenz.

A third copy of Hitler's political testament was entrusted to the Führer's army adjutant by General Burgdorf, who ordered it delivered to the newly appointed commander-in-chief of the army, Field Marshal Schörner. The messenger was also given a handwritten covering note, explaining that the will had been written "under the shattering news of Himmler's treason," and was the Führer's "unalterable decision." It was to be published "as soon as the Führer orders it, or as soon as his death is confirmed."

Eva did not get up until midday. She was greeted by an orderly with an embarrassed "Gnädiges Fräulein." With a smile she told him it was all right to call her Frau Hitler. She asked her maid, Liesel, to take her wedding ring and nightgown to her best friend, Herta Schneider, then gave Liesel a ring as a keepsake. A little later she turned over to Traudl Junge another cherished possession, her silver fox coat. "I always like to have well-dressed people around me," she said. "Take it, and I hope it will give you much pleasure." Traudl was too overwhelmed by the gift to foresee how absurd it would be to escape Berlin in such style.

The day dragged on for those in the bunker. There was little to do but gossip and smoke. By now everyonc—even Eva—was smoking openly. The fumes did not seem to bother the Führer. Finally, at 6 P.M., he assembled the family circle in his study, which was screened from the anteroom by a red velvet curtain with gold fringes. After announcing that Wenck was not coming, he said that he and his wife were going to die unless some miracle intervened. He passed out phials containing cyanamide. It was a poor parting gift, he told the two secretaries, and again praised their courage. Goebbels wondered if the phials had lost their deadly effect with time. Hitler was seized with doubts of a different nature: they had been supplied by that traitor Himmler. He sent for his new surgeon, Dr. Ludwig Stumpfegger—who proposed one phial be tested on Blondi. Hitler agreed, then, recalling that Stumpfegger himself belonged to the SS, sent for a doctor in the hospital bunker. This man dutifully forced the liquid down the throat of the dog Hitler adored. It killed her.

Early that evening word arrived that Mussolini and his mistress had been assassinated by Italian partisans, their bodies strung up by the feet in a Milan gas station. "I will not fall into the hands of the enemy dead or alive!" said Hitler. "After I die, my body shall be burned and so remain undiscovered forever!" The news from Italy depressed Hitler and he would have suffered additional anguish had he known that SS General Wolff had just succeeded in secretly surrendering to the Allies all German forces in Italy.

At the final briefing of the day General Weidling told of

the bitter, hopeless battles in the streets. His divisions, he said with heavy heart, were little more than battalions. Morale was poor, ammunition almost exhausted. He brandished an army field newspaper filled with optimistic stories of the imminent relief of Berlin by Wenck, The troops knew better, he charged, and such deceptions only embittered them. Goebbels sharply accused Weidling of defeatism; and another argument erupted. It took Bormann to calm them down so that Weidling could continue. He concluded his report with the devastating prediction that the battle would be over within twenty-four hours.

There was a shocked silence. In a tired voice Hitler asked the commandant of the chancellery area, an SS general, if he had observed the same conditions. He had. Weidling again pleaded for a breakout. Hitler pointed to a map and, in a resigned but sarcastic tone, said he had marked down the positions of the troops according to information from foreign radio announcements, since his own troop staffs were not even bothering to report to him any longer; his orders were not executed any more and so it was useless to expect anything.

As he rose painfully from his chair to say good-by, Weidling once more begged him to change his mind before ammunition ran out. Hitler murmured something to Krebs, then turned to Weidling: "I will permit a breakout of small groups," he said, but added that capitulation was out of the question. Weidling walked down the passageway wondering what Hitler meant. Wasn't the breakout of small groups a capitulation? He radioed all his commanders to congregate at his headquarters in the Bendlerstrasse the next morning.

After midnight Hitler bade farewell to a group of twenty officers and women secretaries in the main dining room. His eyes were covered with a film of moisture and, to Frau Junge, he seemed to be looking far away. He passed down the line shaking hands, then descended the curving staircase to his suite.

Throughout the bunker barriers dropped and high-ranking officers chatted familiarly with their juniors. In the canteen where soldiers and orderlies ate, a dance began spontaneously. It became so boisterous that a messenger from Bormann brought a warning to hold the noise down. He was trying to concentrate on a telegram he was writing to Dönitz. In it Bormann complained that all incoming reports were "controlled, suppressed or distorted" by Keitel, and ordered Dönitz "to proceed at once, and mercilessly, against all traitors."

9

By late morning of April 30 the Tiergarten was overrun by the Soviets and one advance unit was reported in the street next to the bunker. It was difficult to see that the news had any effect on Hitler. During lunch with the two secretaries and the cook, he chatted as if it were merely another family circle gathering. He was self-possessed and, if anything, quieter than usual. To Traudl it seemed to be "a banquet of death under the cheerful mask of resignation and composure."

But it was no ordinary day and no sooner had the three ladies left than Hitler summoned them back, along with Bormann, the Goebbelses and several others. More stooped than ever, he slowly came out of his room with Eva, who was wearing the black dress that was his favorite; her hair was neatly combed. Hitler began shaking hands with everyone. He was pale and there were tears in his eyes. He looked directly at Traudl as he held her hand but did not seem to see her, and mumbled something she could not understand. She stood motionless in a trance, oblivious of everything in the room. The spell was broken somewhat when Eva Hitler, with a sad smile, put an arm around her. "Please, at least try to get out of here," she said. Her voice broke into a sob. "Then please greet Munich for me."

Hitler took Günsche aside and said that he and his wife were going to commit suicide. He wanted their bodies burned. "After my death," he explained, "I don't want to be put on exhibition in a Russian wax museum." Günsche phoned Kempka's quarters at the bunker, asked for something to drink and said he was coming over. Kempka knew something was wrong. In the last days no one had thought of alcohol. He found a bottle of cognac and waited. The phone rang. It was Günsche again. "I need two hundred liters of gasoline immediately," he said huskily. Kempka thought it was some kind of joke and wanted to know why he needed so much fuel.

Günsche could not tell him on the phone. "I want it at the entrance of the Führer bunker without fail." Kempka said the only gasoline left—about 40,000 liters—was buried in the Tiergarten, which was under deadly fire. They would have to wait until five o'clock when the barrage let up.

"I can't wait a single hour. See what you can siphon out of the wrecked cars."

Hitler was bidding his personal pilot for so many years an emotional farewell. As they clasped hands, Baur begged him to escape by plane to Argentina, to Japan, or to one of the Arab countries where his anti-Semitism had made him such staunch friends. But the Führer would not listen. "One must have the courage to face the consequences—I am ending it all here! I know that by tomorrow millions of people will curse me—Fate wanted it that way." He thanked Baur for his long service and offered his cherished portrait of Frederick the Great as a present. "I don't want this picture to get lost. I want it to remain for the future. It has great historical value."

The Hitlers sat together on a couch in their suite. Behind them was the bare space where the portrait of Frederick had hung. Eva was the first to die—by poison. At about 3:30 P.M. Hitler picked up his 7.65-caliber Walther pistol (Geli killed herself with a Walther and Eva had tried to but failed). It had been his companion for years: a defense against the Reds in the early days of the party; the means of gaining attention at the Bürgerbräukeller in 1929. He had threatened to kill himself with it during several fits of depression. This time his intention was genuine. On a console was a picture of his mother as a young woman. He put the pistol barrel to his right temple and pulled the trigger.

On the upper floor, Traudl Junge was telling the Goebbels children a fairy story to keep them from going downstairs, when a shot echoed along the damp concrete. Young Helmut thought it was an enemy bomb and said, "Bull's-eye!" In the conference room Goebbels, Bormann, Axmann and Günsche hesitated momentarily after hearing the shot, then broke into Hitler's anteroom with Goebbels in the lead. Günsche saw the Führer on the couch sprawled face down across a low table. To his left lay Eva, slumped over the armrest, her lips tightly closed in death, her nostrils discolored by cyanamide. Her dress was wet, but not with blood. A jug lying on the table must have been knocked over as the Führer pitched forward. Unnerved, Günsche stumbled back into the conference room where he was accosted by Kempka.

"For God's sake, Otto," the chauffeur said, "what's going

on? You must be crazy to have me send men to almost certain death just for two hundred liters of gasoline." Günsche brushed past him, slamming the door to the cloakroom so that no one else could wander in. Then he closed the door to the Führer's suite and turned, eyes wide. "The Chief is dead!"

The only thing Kempka could think of was that Hitler had had a heart attack. Günsche lost his voice. Though he had seen the bullet hole in Hitler's right temple, he pointed a finger like a pistol and put it in his mouth, his shocked gesture inspiring the widely believed story that Hitler had shot himself in the mouth.

"Where is Eva?"

Günsche indicated Hitler's anteroom and was finally able to say, "She's with him." It took Günsche several minutes to stammer out the whole story.

Linge peered out of Hitler's anteroom and asked for the gasoline. Kempka said he had about a hundred and seventy liters in jerricans at the garden entrance. Linge and Dr. Stumpfegger carried out Hitler's body in a dark brown army blanket. The Führer's face was half covered, his left arm dangled down. Bormann followed, carrying Eva. Her hair was hanging loose. The sight of her in Bormann's arms was too much for Kempka. She had always hated Bormann and the chauffeur thought, "Not one more step." He called to Günsche, "I'll carry Eva," then took her away from Bormann. Halfway up the four flights of stairs to the garden, her body almost slipped from his grasp. Kempka stopped, unable to continue until Günsche moved to his aid, and together they carried Eva into the garden.

Another Russian barrage had begun, with shells smashing into the rubble. Only the jagged walls of the chancellery remained and these trembled with every shattering explosion. Through a cloud of dust Kempka saw Hitler's body not ten feet from the bunker entrance. His trousers were pulled up; his right foot was turned in—the characteristic position he always assumed on a long auto trip.

Kempka and Günsche stretched Eva's body out on Hitler's right. All at once the artillery barrage increased in tempo, forcing them to take cover in the bunker entrance. Kempka waited a few minutes, then seized a jerrican of gasoline and ran back to the bodies. He placed Hitler's left arm closer to his side. It was done only to delay a repellent duty; he could not bring himself to drench the body with gasoline. A gust of wind moved Hitler's hair. Kempka opened the jerrican. A shell exploded, showering him with debris; shrapnel whizzed past his head. Again he scrambled back for refuge.

Günsche, Kempka and Linge waited in the entrance for a lull in the shelling. When it came they returned to the bodies. Shivering with revulsion, Kempka sprinkled them with gasoline. He thought, "I can't do it but I'm doing it." He saw the same reaction in the faces of Linge and Günsche, who were also pouring gasoline. From the entrance Goebbels, Bormann and Dr. Stumpfegger peered out with morbid concern.

The clothing of the corpses became so soaked that even the strongest gust of wind brought no stirring. The bombardment resumed, but the three men emptied can after can until the shallow depression in which the Hitlers lay was filled with gasoline. Günsche suggested igniting it with a hand grenade but Kempka said no. The idea of blowing up the bodies was too repugnant. He saw a large rag lying near a fire hose at the entrance. He pointed it out to Günsche, who doused it with gasoline.

Goebbels handed Kempka a pack of matches. He set fire to the rag and tossed it onto the bodies. A boiling ball of fire mushroomed, followed by dark clouds of smoke. It was a small blaze in a burning city, but horrifying. The men watched, hypnotized, as the fire slowly began to consume Adolf and Eva Hitler. Shaken, Güsche and Kempka stumbled back to the entrance. More jerricans of gasoline were delivered, and for the next three hours they kept pouring the liquid on the smoldering corpses.

That evening the charred remains of Hitler and Eva were swept into a canvas and, so Güsche recalled, "let down into a shell hole outside the exit from the bunker, covered over with earth, and the earth pounded firm with a wooden rammer."

He was buried in the rubble of defeat; not, as he had instructed architect Giesler, in Munich ("Here I was born, here I started this movement, and here is my heart"). There should have been someone present to recite the poem Baldur von Schirach had made from the Führer's own words:

Could be that the columns which halt here,
That these endless brown rows of men,
Are scattered in the wind, split up and dispersed
And will desert me. Could be, could be . . .
I shall remain faithful, even though deserted by all—

I shall carry the flag, staggering and alone.
My smiling lips may stammer mad words,
But the flag will only fall when I fall
And will be a proud shroud covering my corpse.

The flag fell where he fell and when he died so did National Socialism and the Thousand-Year Third Reich. Because of him, his beloved Germany lay in ruins.

The greatest irony of all was that the driving force of his life—his hatred and fear of Jews—was thwarted. He had intended the elimination of six million Jews to be his great gift to the world. It would lead, instead, to the formation of a Jewish state.

Epilogue

1

To the surprise of the world, Hitler's death brought an abrupt, absolute end to National Socialism. Without its only true leader, it burst like a bubble. There were no enclaves of fanatic followers bent on continuing Hitler's crusade; the feared Alpine Redoubt proved to be a chimera. What had appeared to be the most powerful and fearsome political force of the twentieth century vanished overnight. No other leader's death since Napoleon had so completely obliterated a regime.

In death the Führer remained controversial and mysterious. Even as his body smoldered, a rumor spread in the bunker that Axmann, the Youth leader, had put some of Hitler's ashes in a box with instructions to secrete it outside of Berlin. News of his suicide was received with disbelief by some Germans. The parents of Fegelein, for instance, assured an American counterintelligence agent that a courier had brought a message from their son that he and Hitler were "safe and well in Argentina." Stalin also professed doubt. He told Harry Hopkins that Hitler's end struck him as "dubious." Hitler had surely escaped and was in hiding along with Bormann. The version became U.S.S.R. history until 1968 when a Soviet journalist, Lev Bezymenski, published a book revealing that the Russians *had* found the bodies of Adolf and Eva Hitler outside the bunker on May 4, 1945. As evidence, Bezymenski included an autopsy report of the Forensic Medical Commission of the Red Army, which stated that splinters of a poison ampule had been found in the Führer's mouth—and there was no bullet hole in the skull. In other words, the Soviets implied that Hitler had taken a cowardly route to death. Moreover, added the report, he had but one testicle—a conclusion made much of by some psychohistorians despite reports from three doctors who had examined Hitler indicating he was normal. The long-delayed Soviet revelation was received with some suspicion. Although the detailed report was authenticated by five pathologists and experts in forensic medicine, it was supported only by photographic evidence of Hitler's corpse. The remains themselves, Bezymenski admitted, had been "completely burned and their ashes strewn to the wind."

Skeptics wondered why Stalin had spread the story in 1945 that Hitler had escaped when he knew the body had been found. They were not at all convinced by Bezymenski's explanation: "First, it was resolved not to publish the results of the forensic medical report but to 'hold it in reserve' in case someone might try to slip into the role of 'the Führer saved by a miracle.' Secondly, it was resolved to continue the investigations in order to exclude any possibility of error or deliberate deception." Neither reason accounts for the wait of twenty-three years, nor was any explanation given for the destruction of the remains. Pictures of the corpse's dentures had been kept on file and in 1972 Dr. Reidar Soggnaes, a dental forensic expert from U.C.L.A., discovered that these teeth exactly matched those in the X-ray head plates of Hitler taken in 1943. This hard evidence, Dr. Soggnaes told the 6th International Meeting of Forensic Sciences at Edinburgh, proved beyond doubt that Hitler was dead and that the Soviets had autopsied the right body. But where was the proof that Hitler had not shot himself? The skull "proving" that there was no bullet hole had been conveniently destroyed. Moreover, none of the eyewitnesses in the bunker had noticed the telltale discolorations of cyanamide on Hitler's lips; and only one empty poison capsule had been found.

No mystery clouded Goebbels' death. On the first of May, after a futile attempt to negotiate with the Soviets, he told his adjutant, Günther Schwägermann, "Everything is lost." He handed Schwägermann a silver-framed photograph of Hitler and bade him farewell. Frau Goebbels roused their six children from bed. "Children, don't be afraid," she said, "the doctor is going to give you an injection, a kind that is now given to all children and soldiers." After a dentist named Kunz injected morphine to make the children sleepy, Frau Goebbels herself placed a crushed ampule containing potassium cyanide in the mouth of each child.

Others in the bunker were getting last-minute instructions for escape. They were divided into six separate groups. At 9 P.M. the first section would make a run for the nearest subway entrance and walk along the tracks to the Friedrichstrasse station. Here they would emerge, cross the Spree River and head west or northwest until they reached the Western Allies or Dönitz. The other five groups would follow the same course, at intervals. Some were captured but, miraculously, few died.

At 8:45 P.M. Kempka went to the Goebbels suite to say good-by. The children were already dead. Frau Goebbels asked Kempka in a calm voice to send greetings to her son Harald and tell him how she had died. The Goebbelses left their room arm in arm. Utterly calm, he thanked Naumann for his loyalty and understanding; Magda could only hold out her hand. Naumann kissed it. Goebbels wryly remarked that they were going to walk up the steps to the garden so that their friends wouldn't have to carry them. After shaking hands with Naumann, he escorted his silent, pale wife toward the exit. They disappeared up the steep concrete stairway. Then came a shot, followed by a second. Schwägermann and the Goebbelses' chauffeur hurried up the stairs to find the Goebbelses sprawled on the ground. An SS orderly was staring at them—he had shot them. He and the two newcomers poured four jerricans of gasoline on the bodies and set them afire. Without waiting to see the effect of the blaze, they returned to the bunker, which they had been ordered to destroy. They dumped the last can of gas in the conference room and ignited it.

The fate of Martin Bormann was more controversial than his master's. It was generally assumed that he had died while attempting to escape from Berlin but declassified United States and British intelligence documents indicated that he might have escaped to Bolzano, Italy, where his wife had already fled from Berchtesgaden with their nine children. For the next twenty-seven years there were recurring reports of Bormann's reappearance, particularly in Argentina. Then, late in 1972, an American author, Ladislas Farago, claimed he had positive proof Bormann was alive in South America. This sensational announcement was followed a few days later by another. The German authorities declared that they had just found Bormann's body near the Führer bunker. Dr. Soggnaes, who had authenticated the Hitler corpse, asked permission to examine the skull so he could corroborate the dental identification. At first permission was withheld, adding suspicion that the corpse might be a hoax. Finally in the summer of 1973 Dr. Soggnaes was allowed to examine the skeletal remains as well as the maxillary incisor bridge which had been found three months after the skull was unearthed. Dr. Soggnaes returned to U.C.L.A. to prepare a forensic analysis of the data. In September 1974 he presented his material to the World Congress of the Federation of Dentaire Internationale in London. The skull, he concluded, was indeed that of Bormann. And the mystery of Hitler's most faithful servant was finally solved.

2

To the very end, Heinrich Himmler hoped for some arrangement with the Allies while fearing that something would go wrong. After Hitler's death he fled to the north and requested the Führer's successor to appoint him the second man in his new German state. But Admiral Dönitz said, "That is impossible. I have no job for you." In desperation Himmler turned to Schwerin von Krosigk for advice. "Please tell me what is going to become of me?" he asked the new Foreign Minister. "I am not interested in the least what will happen to you or any other man," was the exasperated answer. "Only our mission interests me, not our personal destinies." Krosigk gave Himmler two choices: either commit suicide or disappear with a false beard. "But if I were you I would drive up to Montgomery and say, 'Here I am, Himmler the SS general, and ready to take responsibility for my men.'"

That evening Himmler cryptically told his closest friends that an important new task remained. A few could accompany him. He shaved off his mustache, put a patch over one eye, changed his name and—with some nine followers, including his chief Waffen SS adjutant, Werner Grothmann—went into hiding. When Grothmann discovered his chief had a cyanide capsule and intended to use it if necessary, he accused Himmler of taking an easy way out that was not open to his followers. It was the Reichsführer's duty, he said, not only to assume responsibility for his men's actions but to make clear that the Waffen SS, the SD and the concentration camp guards were from distinctly different organizations. Himmler demurred. "After I take the poison," he said, "then you young officers must tell the world what happened here in Germany—what I did and what I did not do." Within two weeks Himmler was captured by the British. A doctor conducting a routine examination noticed something in his mouth, but when he reached in to pull out the object Himmler bit down on the cyanide capsule and died instantly. There were other suicides but their number were fewer than expected, particularly among the hierarchy, one of whom—Robert Ley—did commit suicide while awaiting trial at Nuremberg.

Göring was by far the most defiant prisoner at Nuremberg. He arrived at the prison with an incredibly large cache of Paradocin pills and was taking forty daily. By the time he testified, however, he was completely free of the drug habit and had cut his weight down more than forty percent to 153 pounds. In the courtroom he, almost alone, defended his Führer. Unlike so many of the other defendants, he never put blame on others or hid behind the figure of Hitler. He took charge of the prisoners' dock, aggressively dictating a concerted strategy of defense. Back in the cell block, he would rub his hands enthusiastically and call himself the captain of the first-string team, boasting that he would give the prosecutors and the audience a run for their money. If any fellow defendant protested or weakened, the revivified Göring would bully and insult him into silence. "It makes me sick to see Germans selling their souls to the enemy!" he said during one lunch, then banged a fist on the table. "Damn it," he added, "I just wish we could all have the courage to confine our defense to three simple words: *Lick my ass!*"

Of the twenty-two major defendants only three (Schacht, Papen and Fritzsche) were acquitted. Eight received long terms of imprisonment; the rest were sentenced to death. At 10:45 P.M. October 15, 1946, Göring cheated the hangman with a cyanide capsule. Two hours later the executions began. The first to climb the thirteen steps of the gallows was Ribbentrop. "God protect Germany," he said loudly. "My last wish is that Germany's unity shall be preserved and that an understanding be reached between East and West." It had taken the incontrovertible evidence at Nuremberg to convince him that masses of Jews had been killed, for Hitler had assured him time and again that the Jewish problem would be solved by deportation. "I never dreamed," he told G. M. Gilbert, an American psychologist, "it would end like this!"

Next came Keitel. Minutes earlier he had sobbed while the chaplain gave him a last benediction. Now his chin was thrust out. "I call on the Almighty God to have mercy on the German people. For Germany—everything. Thank you!" He turned to the chaplain, an American. "I thank you and those who sent you with all my heart." The hangman, Master Sergeant John Woods, had looked forward with relish to these executions. He adjusted the rope around Keitel's neck, then placed a black hood over his head. At the very last moment the field marshal shouted, "Deutschland über Alles!" During the trial Keitel had confided to Gilbert that Hitler had betrayed him. "If he did not deceive us by deliberate lies, then he did it by deliberately keeping us in the dark and letting us fight under a false impression!"

3

A surprising number of Hitler's family circle survived the last cataclysmic days: the four secretaries; his two favorite architects, Speer and Giesler; his pilot, Baur; his chauffeur, Kempka; his valet, Linge; Heim and Koeppen, who copied down his table conversations; the best friend of his wife, Frau Schneider; his two favorite fighters, Skorzeny and Rudel; the three women he particularly admired: Leni Riefenstahl, Gerdy Troost and Helene Hanfstaengl.

A number of his adjutants and ordnance officers not only survived but were willing to talk freely of their experiences: Puttkamer, Engel, Below, Wünsche, Schulze and Günsche. When the last returned to West Germany after twelve years of imprisonment in the Soviet Union and East Germany, he was bewildered by the sight of young men with beards and long hair. "Dear friend," Schulze told him, "we have lost the war and all is now changed. The young people don't live as we did." To shock Günsche back to reality, Schulze took him to the Berghof. The building had been set afire by the SS on May 4, 1945, and its remains had been gradually destroyed by the

Americans. Everything looked different and it was very difficult even to figure out where the long flight of steps leading up to the house had been. As the two men surveyed the scene, Schulze's wife took their picture, capturing in their stunned faces, as no words could, the definitive end of the man they had worshiped. The most extraordinary figure in the history of the twentieth century had vanished—unlamented except by a faithful few.

Notes

ABBREVIATIONS

BA	Bundesarchiv, Koblenz
BFP	*Documents on British Foreign Policy*
BH	Bayerisches Hauptstaatsarchiv, München
CAB	British Cabinet Papers
CIC-PH	CIC interview with Paula Hitler, June 5, 1946. U. S. Army Military History Research Collection, Carlisle Barracks, Pa.
EGD	*The Early Goebbels Diaries*
GFP	*Documents on German Foreign Policy*
HA	Hauptarchiv der NSDAP
HBN	Maser, *Hitlers Briefe und Notizen*
HH	Fritz Hesse, *Hitler and the English*
HSB	OSS *Hitler Source Book*
HSC	*Hitler's Secret Conversations*
IMT	International Military Tribunal, Nuremberg
MK	*Mein Kampf*, Houghton Mifflin edition
MY	Hanfstaengl, *The Missing Years*
NA	National Archives, Washington
ND	Nuremberg Document
NSR	*Nazi-Soviet Relations*, 1939–41
OCMH	Office, Chief of Military History, U.S. Army, Washington, D.C.

PHP	Protokoll des Hitler-Prozesses
TAH	*The Testament of Adolf Hitler*
TMWC	*Trial of the Major War Criminals before the International Military Tribunal*
VB	*Völkischer Beobachter*

Chapter One.
DEEP ARE THE ROOTS

page 4
"laced his tiny knapsack." MK 5.
pages 3–5
Information on Schicklgruber birth register from documents in Ph.D. dissertations, University of Vienna, at Institut für Zeitgeschichte, Vienna.
page 8
"shabby and primitive . . . in exemplary order." Jetzinger 57.
page 8
"It was at this time . . . a little ringleader." MK 5–6.
page 8
"He was imperious . . . over any triviality." Gilbert, *Psychology*, 18.
page 9
"solemn splendor of brilliant church festivals." MK 6.
page 9
"as a small boy it was his most ardent wish . . ." Interview with Helene Hanfstaengl, 1971.
page 10
"who challenged my father to extreme harshness . . ." CIC-PH.
page 10
"Toga boy" incident: Interview with Helene Hanfstaengl, 1971.
page 10
"I then resolved never again to cry . . ." Zoller 55.
page 11
"It was not long before . . ." MK 6.
page 11
"Woods and meadows were the battlefields . . ." Ibid. 9.
page 12
"I thought that once my father saw . . ." Ibid. 10.
page 12
"We all liked him . . ." Heinz 25.

page 12
"You are not German . . ." Interview with Josef Keplinger, 1971.
page 13
"The sharp words that fell . . ." Jetzinger 53.
page 13
"a great artist." Bradley Smith, *Adolf Hitler*, 100.
pages 13–14
Hitler's play with the Schmidt children, including all quotes: Interviews with Maria Schmidt Koppensteiner and Johann Schmidt in Oct. 1938, HA, File 17, Reel 1.
page 14
"complete waste of time." HSC 625.
page 14
"He had definite talent . . . not uncommon amongst immature youths." Jetzinger 68–69.
pages 14–15
"Even today I think back with gentle emotion . . ." MK 14.
page 15
"I often used to practice shooting rats from the window." HSC 201.
page 16
"I've completely forgotten what happened . . ." HSC 202.
page 16
Hitler's health: CIC-PH.
pages 16–17
Kubizek-Hitler quotes: Kubizek 11–13, 26–27.
page 17
Hitler postcards: Kubizek's *Erinnerungen* as quoted in Jetzinger 98–99.
page 18
"sitting for hours at the beautiful Heitzmann grand piano . . ." CIC-PH.
page 18
"a strange almost hostile glance . . . a special mission one day would be entrusted to him." Kubizek 99–100.
page 19
"those dull, monotonous finger exercises . . ." Jetzinger 94.
page 19
"poor people's doctor." Kubizek 119.
pages 19–20
Frau Hitler examination: Dr. Bloch article in *Collier's*, 1941.

page 20
Hitler's romance with Stephanie. Kubizek 59–60.
page 20
"Adolf never took painting seriously . . . was completely carried away by it." Ibid. 84.
page 21
"When it was pointed out that he lacked . . ." HA, File 17, Reel 1, "Adolf Hitler in Urfahr."
page 21
Hitler as baker's apprentice: Interview with Fräulein Johanna Mayrhofer, 1971.
page 21
"showed my unfitness for painting . . ." MK 20.
page 22
"there were already metastases in the pleura." OSS interview with Dr. Bloch. HSB 21.
page 22
"so deeply engrossed." Kubizek 122.
page 22
Many historians believe that Hitler did not arrive until after his mother's death. Franz Jetzinger, for example, bases his conclusions on testimony from people who interviewed Frau Presenmayer, the postmaster's wife, after 1938. According to Jetzinger: "she told them all she could remember: how she and Frau Klara's sister, Johanna, had nursed her together and how—the old woman stressed this particularly—it was only after Frau Klara's death that her son, Adolf, had arrived from Vienna, and how sorry she had been for him that he was too late to see his mother alive." In the article, "Adolf Hitler in Urfahr!" HA, File 17, Reel 1, the same woman testified that it was she who informed Hitler of his mother's condition and that he "interrupted his studies and rushed to the sickbed of his mother." She also corroborated Dr. Bloch's statement about the sketch—"He drew a picture of his mother on her deathbed." Moreover, in 1938 she told a reporter that Hitler had come home before his mother died and nursed her with the solicitude of a loving son. (HA, Folder 17A.) Jetzinger has chosen to discount completely the accounts of both Dr. Bloch and Kubizek. It is true that Dr. Bloch's story in *Collier's* is filled with mistakes, particularly about those events where he was not present. It is also true that Kubizek's account of Hitler, both in his *Memoirs* and *The Young Hitler I Knew*, contains a number of errors, particularly in

dates. Kubizek should be read with care; he has a tendency toward exaggeration, overemphasis and occasional flights of imagination. Most of Jetzinger's criticisms of Kubizek, I believe, are justified, but he himself has a tendency to accent events that make Hitler look bad. (He had been imprisoned in Vienna by the Hitler regime.) His own well-documented book borrows extensively from Kubizek's account, which is admittedly the best firsthand source on Hitler as a young man.

A new piece of evidence, which corroborates the accounts of Dr. Bloch and Kubizek regarding Hitler's ministrations to his mother at the end, is from Paula Hitler's interview with a CIC agent in 1946: "Assisting me, my brother Adolf spoiled my mother during this last time of her life with overflowing tenderness. He was indefatigable in his care for her, wanted to comply with any desire she could possibly have and did all to demonstrate his great love for her." Further corroboration comes from Dr. Rudolph Binion, who recently deciphered Dr. Bloch's casebook for 1907 and thereby reconstructed the case history it contains. The casebook indicates that on October 22, 1907, Dr. Bloch consulted Hitler in Linz.

page 22

Klara's iodoform treatment: Article by Binion, *History of Childhood Quarterly*, 197–201.

pages 22–23

"The pleasure of having her son back . . . meanwhile realized his own faults." Kubizek 124–25.

page 23

"She bore her burden well . . ." Bloch, *Collier's*.

page 23

"Gustl, go on being a good friend to my son . . ." Kubizek 126.

page 23

"In all my career I never saw anyone so prostrate . . ." Bloch, *Collier's*.

Chapter Two. "THE SCHOOL OF MY LIFE"

page 24

"stern and composed." Kubizek 127.

page 25

"I had no idea I had such a clever friend . . . Never mind." Kubizek 149, 152–53, 157–58.

page 26
"For days on end he could live on milk... Isn't this a dog's life!" Kubizek 150–51.
page 27
"developing a taste for symphonic music." Ibid. 204.
page 27
"Swamped for long centuries by the Slavs..." Arthur J. May, *The Hapsburg Monarchy* (Cambridge, Mass., 1951), 308.
page 28
Hitler's lectures on "conscientious planning": Kubizek 166–68.
page 28
"Holy Mountain in the background, before it the mighty sacrificial block..." Kubizek 154.
page 29
"I'm going to work up Wieland..." Jetzinger 121. On writing the opera: Kubizek 193–202.
page 29
"depraved (sexual) customs": Kubizek to Jetzinger, May 6, 1949, Oberösterreichisches Landesarchiv, Folder 64.
page 30
Letter Hitler to Kubizek about Aug. 17, 1908: Jetzinger 127–28; Kubizek 260–62.
page 30
"last attempt to persuade him... and yet each spoiled each other's pleasure of living together." CIC-PH.
page 37
Hitler by no means anti-Semitic in Vienna: Ibid. Honisch 272.
page 38
"the practical application of anthropological research..." Hanser 31.
page 38
Hitler's hatred of Jews a "personal thing": Interview with Helene Hanfstaengl, 1971.
page 39
Hitler's "failure in painting" caused by Jews: CIC-PH.
page 40
An orphan's pension: Jetzinger 1938; interview with Johanna Mayrhofer.
page 41
"I, Anna Csillag, with the very long Lorelei-hair... There is no end of stupid people." Greiner 41–42.

page 42
"in a disdainful way that he was only a dilettante . . ." Statement by Karl Honisch, HA, File 17, Reel 1.
page 42
"I learned to orate less . . ." MK 68.
page 42
"This place is occupied . . . a pity for every word wasted on you, you won't ever understand." Honisch, op. cit.
page 43
"I had set foot in this town . . ." MK 125.

Chapter Three. "OVERCOME WITH RAPTUROUS ENTHUSIASM"

page 44
"The city itself was as familiar . . ." MK 126.
page 44
"for this city more than any other place . . ." Ibid. 126.
page 44
"The young man and I soon came to terms." Heinz 50.
page 45
"achieve the goal I had set myself." MK 126.
page 46
"this doctrine of destruction . . ." MK 154.
pages 46–47
Hitler letter to Linz: Deuerlein, *Der Aufsteig* 76–77; Jetzinger 149–56; Maser, HBN, 40–42.
page 47
"unfit for combatant duties, too weak . . ." Jetzinger 155.
page 47
"a state of imminent threat of war." Fritz Fischer 86.
page 48
"If only the King has already read my application . . ." Julius Hagemann interview with Ignaz Westenkirchner in Schulz-Wilde Collection.
page 48
"looked at it with the delight that a woman . . ." Mend 15.
page 49
"turned tail and ran." Heinz 53.
page 51
"What I noticed first was his unmilitary manner . . ." Wiedemann 13 (translation).

pages 51–52
Letter Hitler to Popp, Jan. 26, 1915: Maser, HBN, 73.
page 52
Letter Hitler to Hepp, Feb. 5, 1915: BA, NSR 26/4.
page 52
"Amen in the prayer." Westenkirchner interview, op. cit.
page 52
"I learned a great deal from him." HSC 662.
page 53
"like a race horse at the starting gate." Mend 124.
page 53
"I was eating my dinner in a trench . . ." Price 40.
page 65
"How many times at Fromelles . . ." HSC 235.
page 54
"It isn't so bad, Lieutenant, right?" Wiedemann 13 (tr.).
page 54
"for the first time in two years . . ." MK 191.
page 55
"Nearly every clerk was a Jew . . ." Ibid. 193.
page 55
One of the most quoted incidents of Hitler's wartime anti-Semitism appears on p. 161 of Mend's book, *Adolf Hitler im Felde*: Hitler refuses to salute a Jewish officer, Hugo Gutmann, and, after Gutmann angrily leaves, says, "I'll only acknowledge this Jew on the battlefield. Here he struts with Jewish arrogance but at the front he'd hide in a mouse hole and wouldn't concern himself with a salute." The veracity of this incident is lessened by later issuance of a "Mend Protocol," in which the author contradicted material in his own book. In the case of Gutmann, Westenkirchner testified that the lieutenant was generally disliked by the men. "Our dislike, however, had nothing to do with anti-Semitism." Once he heard Hitler say, "Gutmann is an ass-crawler and a coward." Westenkirchner interview, op. cit. Lieutenant Gutmann later initiated the award to Hitler of the Iron Cross, First Class.

The 16th Regiment, in fact, was known for its courageous Jewish officers. Two are commended in Wiedemann's book. Reserve Lieutenant Kuh, an assault leader, a painter like Hitler, had a reputation for fearlessness. "The most beautiful thing to me," Kuh told Wiedemann, "is the night before an assault!" One of the battalion physicians, Dr.

Georg Kohn, was decorated with the Bavarian Military Medical Order, the highest decoration awarded doctors for extreme bravery in the performance of their duties. The Great War was the first major opportunity which had been given German Jews to demonstrate their patriotism to a nation which had given them legal if not social equality. Almost unanimously they supported the Fatherland in its hour of peril. The Jewish soldier consequently often did more than his duty as a retort to anti-Semitic propaganda that the Jew was a coward by nature. (Perhaps Hitler's own eager attitude was also to prove that he was a better German than his German-born comrades.)

page 55

Letter Hitler to Wiedemann: Wiedemann 30 (tr.).

page 56

"War forces one to think deeply . . ." Frank 45–46.

page 57

"became furious and shouted . . ." Schmidt interview, op. cit.

pages 57–58

Dr. Rudolph Binion of Brandeis University believes that Hitler's vision at Pasewalk released his unconscious resentment against Dr. Bloch, a Jew. "Hitler was then nearly nineteen, and intellectually and emotionally retarded after having lived idly with his widowed mother for some years past at suffocatingly close quarters. Consciously, he loved Bloch like a kind father; unconsciously, he blamed Bloch for his mother's cancer, for the toxic treatment, for the huge terminal bill paid on Christmas Eve. This blame surfaced after 1918 as a burning rage against the Jewish profiteer, the Jewish poison, the Jewish cancer. On balance, the evidence that he was not an anti-Semite until after World War I, despite his own account in *Mein Kampf*, is compelling. At all odds, his deadly hate for 'the Jew' along with his political vocation itself can be dated quite precisely from his hospitalization of October–November 1918 for a gas poisoning that blinded him temporarily. The gas—mustard gas—was actually a liquid spray that burned through the skin just like iodoform. Hitler associated his gas poisoning with his mother's iodoform poisoning as he felt himself succumbing. By the time he was hospitalized at Pasewalk (north of Berlin) he must have been raving, as he was assigned to psychiatric care. The chief psychiatrist took his blindness to be hysterical—wrongly. But just when he was recovering his vision in the normal course, he relapsed at the news of the Revolution and Armistice. This relapse *was* hysterical. It may have been prompted by the false diagnosis that governed his treatment. . . . In that hallucination Hitler was summoned from on high to undo, and reverse, Germany's defeat. The Germany that he was to restore and avenge was transparently his mother: this is graphic in one of the accounts of the hallucination that Hitler himself gave in the early 1920s and especially in an official party version of it that he must have approved. In his trance he was not expressly called upon to kill the Jews; nonetheless he emerged from his trance resolved on entering politics in order to kill the Jews by way of discharging his mission to undo, and reverse, Germany's defeat." Binion, unpublished article, "Hitler's Concept of *Lebensraum*: The Psychological Basis."

page 59
"no longer complained of anything . . ." Ibid.

page 59
"The medical records at the hospital . . ." Deuerlein, *Hitler*, 68.

page 60
"Their whole activity was so repellent . . ." MK 207.

page 61
"parental religion was largely sham . . . shot through with hypocrisy." Howard Becker, *German Youth: Bond or Free* (London, 1946), 51.

page 63
"to gain a fatherland for myself." Rosenberg, *Memoirs*, 29.

page 63
"Can you use a fighter against Jerusalem?" Alfred Rosenberg, *Dietrich Eckart: Ein Vermächtnis* (Munich, 1927), 45.

page 65
"who bears arms against government troops . . ." *Vorwärts*, Mar. 10, 1919.

page 65
"The Jewish Mafia." David Mitchell 119.

page 67
"This is the New Man, the storm soldier . . ." Ernst Jünger, *Der Kampf als inneres Erlebnis* (Berlin, 1933), 76–77.

page 67
"When I first met him he was like a tired stray dog . . ." Mayr 194.

page 68

"Involuntarily I saw thus my own development..." MK, Eher edition, 296.

page 68

Throughout the whole world others besides Hitler saw Jews as the fountainhead of revolution and Communism. That July, at a meeting of the Anglo-Russian Club in London, Winston Churchill had called for support of White General Denikin against Lenin, Trotsky "and the sinister gang of Jewish anarchists around them," and a few months later told the House of Commons, "No sooner did Lenin arrive than he began beckoning a finger there to obscure persons in sheltered retreats in New York, in Glasgow, in Bern, and other countries, and he gathered together the leading spirits of a most formidable sect, the most formidable sect in the world." (Lacquer 313–14.) Churchill called for a fourteen-nation anti-Bolshevik crusade to support the White forces in Russia battling the Soviets, and declared it was a delusion "to suppose that all this year we have been fighting the battles of the anti-Bolshevik Russians. On the contrary, they have been fighting ours: and this truth will become painfully apparent from the moment they are exterminated and the Bolshevik armies are supreme over the whole vast territories of the Russian empire." D. Mitchell 236–37.

The anti-Bolshevik crusade had also crossed the Atlantic with the U.S. Attorney General, A. Mitchell Palmer, persuading Congress to finance a Red hunt to be directed by J. Edgar Hoover. Throughout the Western world a whispering campaign spread to the effect that it was Jewish money which had started the Russian Revolution: one German primarily responsible for financing Lenin was Max Warburg, whose brother was Paul Warburg, a director of the U.S. Federal Reserve System; and wasn't the father-in-law of brother Felix Warburg the same Jacob Schiff of Kuhn, Loeb and Company who had financed the Bolshevik revolution? This charge was repeated years later on Feb. 3, 1939, in the New York *Journal-American*: "Today it is estimated by Jacob's grandson, John Schiff, that the old man sank about 20,000,000 dollars for the final triumph of Bolshevism in Russia."

page 68

"For me the value of the whole affair..." MK 208.

page 68
"Right after listening to Feder's first lecture . . ." MK 120.
page 69
"and now for the first time . . ." Ibid. 215.
page 69
"The men seemed spellbound by one of their number . . ." Karl Alexander von Müller, *Mars und Venus* (Stuttgart, 1954), 338.
page 69
"I started out with the greatest enthusiasm . . ." MK 215–16.
page 69
"Herr Hitler, if I may put it this way . . ." Remak 25.
page 70
"spoke very well." Heinz Zarnke, in letter to his parents, BA, NS 26/107. "I came to a meeting once by choice," he continued. "23 people were present and just think: Herr Gottfried Feder, whose wife is a Richter, was there too. A Herr Hitler also spoke very well, he is said to be a 'construction worker,' but he is probably a colleague of Herr Feder's, for only an educated man can speak like that. Herr Hitler served through the whole war and was badly wounded. He was even blinded for a short time and took a lively interest in my eye ailment."
page 71
"Our meetings were private . . ." Heinz 106-7.
page 71
"sprang out of the ground . . ." MK 218.
page 72
"left the hall like a wet poodle . . ." Ibid. 219.
page 72
"watching the droll little beasts . . ." Ibid. 219–20.
page 72
"Involuntarily I saw my own development . . ." Ibid. 220.
page 72
"Terrible, terrible! This was club life . . ." MK 222.
page 73
"frozen into an 'organization,' but left the individual . . ." Ibid. 222.
page 73
"to please Ludendorff, whose wishes were . . ." Mayr 195.
page 73
"He burrows into the democracies . . ." Deuerlein, *Der Aufsteig*, 91–93.

Chapter Four.
BIRTH OF A PARTY

page 77
"When we were assembled . . . in our hands as a 'walking stick.'" *Illustrierter Beobachter* 31, Aug. 3, 1929.
page 78
"We were again seven men . . ." MK 354.
page 78
"and what before I had simply felt . . ." MK 355.
page 78
"flew down the stairs with gashed heads." Ibid 358.
page 78
"The misery of Germany . . ." Deuerlein, "Hitlers Eintritt," 207.
page 79
Police repcrt: Deuerlein, *Der Aufsteig*, 99.
page 79
"a funeral vault than an office." MK 390.
page 79
"We cracked our brains over it . . ." Heinz 141.
page 80
"swift as greyhounds, tough as leather . . ." MK 356.
page 80
"The first thing you felt was that there was a man . . ." Frank 39.
page 81
"made things understandable even to the foggiest brain . . ." Ibid. 41.
page 81
"if anyone could master the fate of Germany . . ." Ibid. 52.
page 81
"When I closed the meeting . . ." VB, Feb. 22, 1922.
pages 82–83
"I prefer a vain monkey . . ." Eckart quoted in MK 687.
page 83
"This is the man who will one day . . ." Dietrich, *Hitler*, 163.
page 85
"I would be lying if I said . . ." BA, NSR–177.
page 85
On speech in general: Phelps, "Hitlers Grundlegende"; Franz-Willing 150, 152.

page 86
"The bloody Jew. Butchering of spiritual leadership..." Maser, HBN, 229–353.
page 86
"We are tied and gagged..." Phelps, "Hitler als Parteiredner," 314.
page 86
"For us the enemy sits on the other side of the Rhine..." Maser, HBN, 305.
page 87
"We wanted something red enough..." Heinz 143.
page 88
"With this the cord of my patience..." MK 498.
page 91
"It's all right. We got what we wanted." Konrad Heiden, *A History of National Socialism* (London, 1936), 31. Ballerstedt incident in general: Deuerlein, *Der Aufsteig*, 46.
page 92
"One heard nothing but yells..." Heinz 119.
page 93
"We shall *be* the State..." Lüdecke 74.
page 94
"His eyes grew thoughtful..." Ibid. 81.
page 95
"Seeing that one brawls as well in an English suit..." Ibid. 90.
page 96
"That's typical of your bourgeois world..." Hitler to Jurgen von Ramin.
page 96
Indicative of the wave of approval in western Europe and the United States for the Mussolini coup d'état was a poem which appeared in Jan. 1923 in the *Wall Street Journal*:

On constitutional technique
And precedents he's lame,
On grace and glamor rather weak.
Such lacks don't cramp his game!
Instead they're assets for his job,
Rough, rude, plain word and act,
To mold a nation through a mob,
To make a dream a fact!
Red nonsense had its mischief proved:
His black-shirts curbed and quelled,

Perhaps in ways not graced or grooved,
How the reins be held?
A blacksmith's son to purple Rome.
A brusque command he brought;
Italia, cleansed and rescued home
But more than her he's taught!
Word-froth and demagogues and drones
Banned; sweat and service praised;
Desks manned when A.M. intones,
Languorous Italy dazed!

Chapter Five.
"SUCH A LOGICAL AND FANATICAL MAN"

page 98
"wipe out the disgrace of Versailles . . ." Gilbert, *Psychology*, 93.
pages 98–99
"precisely because it was revolutionary . . ." Ibid.
page 100
Quotes from the Hess essay: Heiden 98–99.
page 100
"restlessly wandered from place to place . . ." Philipp Bouhler, *Kampf um Deutschland* (Munich, 1938), 83.
pages 101–103
Captain Smith's trip to Munich: Truman Smith report.
page 103
"the unmistakable soldier in mufti . . ." MY 33.
page 104
"There was honesty, there was sincerity . . ." HSB 891.
page 104
"His technique resembled the thrusts . . ." MY 35.
page 104
"The muffled restlessness of the masses . . ." Hanfstaengl, *Out of the Strong*, unpublished.
page 104
"Captain Truman Smith asked me . . . we will have to talk about that." HSB 892.
page 105
"I am sure we shall not have to quarrel . . ." HSB 892.
page 105
"My prognostication on the general . . ." NA, U.S. Embassy, Berlin report, State Dept. file.

page 106
"neither during the war nor during the revolution . . ." Karl Alexander von Müller, *Im Wandel einer Welt* (Munich, 1966), 144.
page 107
"And you should have seen the bathroom . . ." MY 43.
pages 107–108
"This music affected him physically . . ." Ibid. 49.
page 108
"Whereas he otherwise kept the different groups . . ." Hanfstaengl, *Out of the Strong*.
page 108
"He was respectful, even diffident . . ." MY 39.
page 108
"He was at the time a slim, shy young man . . . 'Please, Uncle Dolf, spank the naughty chair.'" Helene Hanfstaengl, *Notes*, 281–83. Helene Niemeyer (the former Frau Helene Hanfstaengl) agreed to write a book for Lippincott in 1940. "Got to the end of the Putsch story," explained her son Egon, "and told Lippincott she didn't want to go on. She never showed them what she'd written. . . . Today said that, in 1940, she was sick of the whole Nazi business and it also occurred to her that if she published the story, the Nazis might take it out on her relations." Letter to author, Feb. 16, 1973.
page 109
"Someone who does not understand . . . bite off your head." CIA files: Hanfstaengl, OSS Biography, 31–32.
page 109
"in spite of the many pictures . . ." MY 60.
page 109
"at least it was better than this duelling . . ." Ibid. 61.
pages 109–10
Hitler's speech: Baynes 51–53.
page 110
"It had something of the quality of . . . annihilating his supposed adversary." MY 68-69.
page 110
"When I talk to people . . ." Ibid. 267–68.
page 111
"I'd read the description . . ." HSC 183.
page 111
"At six o'clock gangs of Reds . . ." HSC 270.

page 112
"I have fallen in love with the landscape." HSC 218.
pages 112–13
Eckart story: Hanfstaengl, OSS Biography, op. cit., 35–37.
page 113
"such enthusiasm as had not been seen . . . so overcome were they by emotion." Deuerlein, *Der Aufsteig*, 181–82.
page 113
"In a few weeks the dice will roll . . ." Hanser 321–22.
page 114
"The task of our movement . . ." VB, Sept. 7, 1923.
page 114
Hitler trip to Switzerland: According to Wilhelm Hoegner, who conducted an extensive investigation of the NSDAP's financial sources from 1924 to 1928, Hitler went to Switzerland in 1921 and 1922 to collect money so he could lead the fight against the Catholic Church in Germany. (Hoegner interview, 1971.) Nov. 25, 1924, two Geneva newspapers claimed that the previous September Hitler had stayed at the Hotel St. Gotthard in Zurich where he received donations of 33,000 Swiss francs, some of it from French sources. Other money came from Frau Gertrud von Seidlitz, who owned shares in Finnish paper mills, the Bechsteins, a locomotive manufacturer named Borsig, and a Munich industrialist, Hermann Aust. Reputedly, the largest single contribution, 100,000 gold marks, came from Fritz Thyssen of the United Steelworks. At this time there were approximately 170,000 gold marks in the NSDAP treasury.
page 114
"We must compromise these people . . ." MY 88.
page 114
"Absolutely no one could ever persuade . . ." Helene Hanfstaengl, *Notes*.
page 115
"Hitler now had definite Napoleonic . . ." BH, NA 103476, 1151.

Chapter Six.
THE BEER HALL PUTSCH

For information on the Putsch I am particularly indebted to Prof. Ernst Deuerlein, Richard Hanser, and Dr. Harold J. Gordon, Jr.

page 116
"an old member and fanatic member . . ." Letter from Maria Heiden, Munich, Sept. 30, 1923.
page 116
"A man of action born on April 20 . . ." Ellic Howe, *Urania's*, 90–91.
page 116
"violence with a disastrous outcome . . ." Wulff 39.
page 117
"his voice took on a tone . . ." F. Wagner 9.
page 117
"Don't you feel that he is destined . . ." HSB 933.
page 118
"I can only take action . . ." Stein 97–98.
page 119
"until an adjustment between Bavaria . . . and is Bavaria's duty to right it." NA, U.S. Embassy, Berlin, report, Oct. 22, 1923.
page 120
"The German problem will be solved . . ." E. Röhm, *Die Geschichte eines Hochverräters*, 229.
page 120
"Our people are under such economic . . ." BH, NA 103476, 691.
page 121
"I am ready to support a rightist . . ." Gordon 256.
page 122
Hitler toothache: Egon Hanfstaengl, *Memoirs*, 101.
page 122
"Where is Captain Göring? . . . Tonight we act!" MY 91.
page 123
Hitler-Esser meeting: Interview with Esser, 1971.
page 123
"Hansl, if things don't go right . . ." BH, NA 1042221, Aigner Bericht.
page 125
"Take your hand out." NA, EAP, 10517, I, 97.
page 125
"Komödie spielen . . . but I had no other means." Ibid. 98.
page 125
"There are five rounds . . ." Idem.

page 126

"What followed then was an oratorical . . ." Müller, *Im Wandel*, 162–63.

page 126

"The task of the provisional . . ." Bullock 80.

page 126

"provincial bridegroom . . ." MY 100.

page 126

"such a change of attitude in a few minutes . . . dead by dawn!" Müller, op. cit., 163.

page 126

One listener not converted by Hitler's speech was the man next to Müller, Dr. Max von Gruber, professor of "racial hygiene" at Munich University. Himself an ardent nationalist, he was not impressed by this first close look at Hitler: "Face and head: bad race, mongrel. Low, receding forehead, ugly nose, broad cheekbones, small eyes, dark hair; facial expression, not of a man commanding with full self-control, but betraying insane excitement. Finally, an expression of blissful egotism." Heiden 190.

page 126

"amazed and far from pleased." Goodspeed 239.

page 127

"I am going to fulfill the vow . . ." Bullock 81.

page 127

"the only thing missing is the psychiatrist . . ." Bavarian State Document #72 from Allgemeine Staatsarchiv, Munich.

page 130

Schwander story: Gordon 293–94.

pages 130–31

Message "to all German wireless stations": Hanser 356.

page 131

"March to Berlin! . . ." Frank 61–62.

page 132

"We march!" Ludendorff 65.

page 133

"the most desperately daring decision in my life . . ." Hitler speech, Nov. 11, 1935.

page 134

"If Ludendorff is marching that way . . ." Ludendorff 67.

page 135

Dr. Schultze account: Interviews with Dr. Schultze, 1974–75.

page 136
"Pfui! Jew defenders! . . ." BH, MA 104221, Salbey Bericht.
page 136
Dr. Schultze account: Interviews, 1974–75.
pages 137–39
Helene Hanfstaengl account: *Notes* 322–27.
page 138
"He refused a bite or soup . . ." Heinz 170.

Chapter Seven. IN LANDSBERG PRISON

page 143
Dr. Brinsteiner report, Jan. 8, 1924: Otto Lurker, *Hitler hinter Festungsmauern, ein Bild aus trüben Tagen* (Berlin, 1933), 9–11, 68. Dr. Walter Schultze, who treated Hitler on Nov. 9–11, stated in 1974 that a break such as Dr. Brinsteiner described was impossible; and that Dr. Brinsteiner was either incompetent or a liar. Interview with Dr. Schultze, 1974.
pages 144–45
Ehard account: Interview with Ehard, 1971.
page 145
Angela letter: Hans Hitler Collection.
page 145
Wagner letter: Edward Whalen Collection.
page 146
"Adolf Hitler in Prison." Hoffmann 57.
page 146
Schacht account: *Old Wizard*, 181–83.
page 147
"Hitler was at all times . . ." Brinsteiner report, op. cit.
page 147
"From its failure I learned . . ." Hitler speech, Prange 160.
page 147
"It was the greatest good fortune . . ." Gordon 408–09.
page 148
Frau Ebertin account: Howe, *Urania's*, 92–93.
page 148
Ludendorff quote: Frank 52.
pages 149–50
Quotes from trial: PHP.

page 149
"I can never think without melancholy . . ." Hans von Hülsen, *Zwillings-Seele* (Munich, 1947), I, 207ff.
pages 150–51
Trial quotes: PHP.
page 151
The sentence: BA, NSR 26/114.
page 151
Hemmrich quote: Heinz 171.
page 151
Hitler's diary: Müller-Schönhausen 117.
pages 151–52
Hemmrich quotes: Heinz 182, 174. The prison routine as described in following pages by Heinz was corroborated by Hans Kallenbach, *Mit Adolf Hitler auf Festung Landsberg*.
page 152
Hemmrich quotes: Heinz 183–84.
page 154
"pioneers and forerunners . . ." NA, Microcopy, T-81, Reel 116, Frame 136437.
page 154
"The various groups quarreled . . ." Lüdecke 210.
page 155
Hemmrich account: Heinz 185, 188, 189.
page 156
Hitler quotes: HSC 46.
page 156
Hemmrich account: Heinz 179, 181–82.
page 157
Leybold report, Sept. 22, 1924: BH, State Ministry of Interior file.
page 157
Hemmrich account: Heinz 185, 192.
page 158
Göring-Negrelli correspondence: Ben E. Swearingen Collection.
page 158
Hitler account: HSC 282.
page 159
Hoffmann account: Hoffmann 61.
page 159
Hitler-Müller quotes: HSC 282–83.

pages 159–60
Hitler quote: HSC 284.
page 160
Hitler at the Hanfstaengls': MY 119–22; HSB 893; interviews with Helene and Egon Hanfstaengl, 1971.

Chapter Eight. HITLER'S SECRET BOOK

page 161
Hoffmann account: Hoffmann 145.
page 162
"This wild beast is checked..." Strasser, *Hitler and I*, 71.
page 163
Feb. 27, 1924 meeting: Müller, *Im Wandel*, 301.
page 164
"Fight Marxism and Judaism...reports will be circulated..." BH, Munich police report, Nov. 1929.
page 167
Röhm letter to Hitler: Ernst Röhm, *Die Memoiren des Stabschefs* (Saarbrücken, 1934), 160.
page 167
Hanfstaengl to Hitler: MY 133, 129, 134.
pages 167–68
Mitzi Reiter story: Gun, *Eva Braun*, 61.
page 168
Hitler at Wahnfried: F. Wagner 30, 41.
page 170
"the bridge from left to right..." Richard Hunt, *Joseph Goebbels*, Ph.D. thesis, Harvard Univ., 1960, 101.
pages 170–71
Diary entries: EGD 47, 50. The Goebbels diaries of 1925–26, for all their self-dramatization and exaggeration, present a revealing self-portrait of the author. They were discovered only after the war and turned over to ex-President Hoover. They were much more valuable testimonials than Goebbels' *Struggle for Berlin*, which was probably based on his journals.
pages 172–73
Goebbels quotes: EGD 91, 95, 100–1.
page 174
Freud quotes: Tell 136.
page 174
Hitler quotes: MK 652, 651.

pages 174–75
Haushofer quote: E. A. Walsh, *Total Power* (Garden City, Garden City Publishing Co., 1948).
page 175
Hitler speech, Dec. 18, 1926. BH, Sonderabgabe I, #1762.
page 175
Footnote: Interview with Erich Kempka, 1971.
pages 175-76
"The finances were a mess . . ." Riess 32.
page 176
Goebbels quotes: Bramsted 20.
page 177
"What record must I use . . ." Strasser, *Mein Kampf*, 31.
page 179
"Socialism and nationalism . . ." *Der Angriff*, Apr. 2, 1928.
page 179
"I immediately rang up my sister . . ." HSC 221.
page 179
On Geli: Interviews with Ilse Hess, Ernst and Helene Hanfstaengl, 1971; Hoffmann 48; Schirach 178–79.
pages 179–80
It was Hitler who suggested that Hess and Ilse Pröhl get married. At first Hess had not appreciated the Führer's intervention. But then he was amused. "Hitler took a personal interest in all of us who were with him in the beginning," Frau Hess revealed in a 1971 interview. "We were a very close circle. We were also intimate friends of Geli. As far as my husband and I were concerned, we were too busy to get married; he was always away and I was working. He devoted his time more to political matters, and he didn't have much of a private life."
page 180
Ilse Hess account: Interview, 1971.
page 180
"The compulsion to engage . . ." *Hitler's Secret Book*, 6.
page 181
"It is not my task . . . exactly so with Jewry too." Ibid. 211–12.
page 181
"Never before had Hitler gone quite that far in his equation of the Jews with other peoples. But what, then, was the difference? Was it only the absence of a territorial state? No, the difference was found in the struggle for life." Jäckel

103. The author is indebted to Professor Jäckel for information on this subject.

page 181
"His ultimate goal . . ." *Hitler's Secret Book*, 213.
page 181
Hitler quotes: Ibid. 23, 29, 41, 76, 79.
page 182
Dr. Schwenninger story: Interview with Prof. Ernst Deuerlein, 1971.

Chapter Nine. A DEATH IN THE FAMILY

page 183
Goebbels quote: *Der Angriff*, Nov. 19, 1928.
page 184
Hitler speech: Prange 40–41.
page 185
"he hovered at her elbow . . ." MY 162.
page 185
Hoffmann account of Geli: Hoffmann, 148, 150.
page 186
Henriette Hoffmann account: Schirach 73.
page 186
"She was a terror . . ." Gun, *Eva Braun*, 21.
page 186
First meeting Hitler-Eva Braun: Ibid. 42–43.
page 188
Wessel story: Heiber 68–69.
page 188
"His spirit has risen . . ." *Der Angriff*, Feb. 27, 1930.
page 188
"If anything goes wrong . . ." MY 149.
page 188
Burial of Wessel: Heiber 70.
page 189
August Wilhelm letter: unpublished letter, dated Apr. 7, 1930, from Ben E. Swearingen Collection.
page 191
"Do it jokingly, do it seriously . . ." *Der Angriff*, Sept. 14, 1930.
page 192
"Hitler was not often there . . ." Frank 93–94.

page 193
"I understand your distress . . ." Heiden 409.

page 194
Stennes Putsch: Höhne, *Order of Death's Head*, 67–68; interviews with Hein Ruck, 1971.

page 194
"I found him a very decent fellow . . ." MY 157–58.

page 194
"When a mother has many children . . ." Interview with F. K. Florian, 1970.

page 195
"We were not loved everywhere . . ." Leaders' Conference, June 13–14, SS HQ Report, Berlin Documentary Center, Microfilm 87.

page 195
"I am the SA and SS . . ." *Münchener Post*, Apr. 11/12, 1931.

page 195
"The SA is a collection . . ." Feb. 3, 1931; NA, German Documents, Reel 85.

page 195
Maurice account: Gun, *Eva Braun*, 8.

page 196
Winter account: Ibid. 9.

page 196
Hanfstaengls' quotes: Interviews with Ernst and Helene Hanfstaengl, 1970, 1971.

page 196
Winter quote: Gun, *Eva Braun*, 10.

page 197
Geli to Frau Hoffmann: Hoffmann 151.

page 197
Hoffmann account: Hoffmann 154.

page 198
Frau Reichert account: Interview with Frau Reichert, Schulze-Wilde Collection.

page 198
Eva letter to Hitler: Gun, *Eva Braun*, 13.

page 198
Hoffmann account: Hoffmann 153.

pages 198–99
There are conflicting versions of the discovery of the body. According to Frau Winter, she knocked on the door and when Geli didn't respond she summoned her husband and

together they forced their way in. Frau Hess informed the author that her husband was summoned by Frau Winter and *he* broke down the door.

Eva Braun told her two sisters that Hitler himself had said Geli had wrapped the gun in a face cloth to muffle the explosion, then fired it in her mouth. There was also a report of an unfinished letter from Geli to a professor of music in Vienna stating that she wanted to take lessons from him. A fortuneteller (so Hitler told Friedelind Wagner) had once prophesied that a revolver bullet would end Geli's life, and since then she had a "hysterical fear" of guns. Wagner OSS 938.

page 199
Frank account: Frank 98.

page 200
Frauenfeld account: Interviews with Frauenfeld, 1971; correspondence with Frauenfeld, 1975.

page 200
"So. Now let the struggle begin . . ." Hoffmann 159.

page 201
"It is like eating a corpse!" Gilbert, *Psychology*, 62.

Chapter Ten.
"IT IS ALMOST LIKE A DREAM"

page 205
"The movement is today so united . . ." VB, Oct. 31, 1931.

page 206
"An interesting man with exceptional . . ." Werner Conze, in *Vierteljahreshefte für Zeitgeschichte*, 1 Jahrg. (1953), 261ff.

page 206
"the chess game for power . . ." Goebbels, *Vom Kaiserhof zur Reichskanzlei* (Munich, 1936), 19–20.

pages 206–7
Hitler speech in Düsseldorf: Schweitzer 100, Prange 253.

page 208
"I know that I shall come to power . . ." Frank 101.

page 209
"dream of power was temporarily over . . ." Goebbels, *Vom Kaiserhof*, 55–56, 62.

page 209
"The first election is over . . ." Dietrich 15.

page 210
Frank account of Röhm's homosexuality: Frank 88–89.

page 210
"Hitler is a fool . . ." A. M. Koktanek, *Oswald Spengler in seiner Zeit* (Munich, 1968), 246.
page 211
"When one has a chance . . ." Hamilton 142–43.
page 211
"I very much doubt if I'm the right man." Papen 152.
pages 211–12
"Well, my dear Papen, I hope . . ." Dorpalen 333–34.
page 214
"The President is not prepared . . ." Papen 196.
page 215
Hitler-Hindenburg meeting: Memorandum by Meissner in Walther Hubatsch, *Hindenburg und der Staat* (Göttingen, 1966), 338–39.
page 216
"The decision was right . . ." Dorpalen 356.
page 217
Eva's attempted suicide: Hoffmann 161–62.
page 218
"We must endeavor to put aside . . ." Papen 213.
page 219
"His entire manner of handling . . ." Hegner 16.
page 219
"Not long ago at Tannenberg . . ." HSC 226–27.
pages 219–20
Hitler-Hindenburg meeting: Dorpalen 379–81; Hegner 18–19.
page 221
Hindenburg meeting with Papen and Schleicher: Meissner memo, Dec. 2, 1932, in *Vierteljahreshefte*, VI, 1958, 105–7. Papen 217–18.
page 222
Papen-Hindenburg meeting: Dorpalen 395–406.
page 222
"Along comes Hindenburg, a man of honor . . ." Frank 108.
page 223
Strasser quote: MY 190–91; Heiber 104.
page 224
On Hitler and Christmas decorations: Krause 52.
page 224
Hitler letter to Frau Wagner: Wagner 73.
page 224
Bullitt report: Bullitt 23.

pages 225–26
Oskar Hindenburg-Hitler meeting: Meissner, IMT, XXXII, 152; same, Case No. 11 transcript, 4494; Hans Otto Meissner and Harry Wilde, *Die Machtergreifung* (Stuttgart, 1958), 161–64. Papen's account of the January negotiations in his memoirs is inaccurate. He states, for example, that he "had no contact whatever with Hitler between January 4 and 22," a palpable lie; nor does he mention his abrupt switch to Hitler on the evening of January 22.
page 227
"Whether what I am going to do . . ." Unsigned memorandum on Hindenburg-Schleicher conference, Jan. 28, 1933, in Thilo Vogelsang, *Reichswehr*, *Staat und NSDAP* (Stuttgart, 1962), 490–91.
page 228
"After this breach of trust . . ." Hammerstein Memorandum in John Wheeler-Bennett, *Nemesis*, 280.
page 228
"If the new government . . ." Dorpalen 440.
pages 228–29
"Gentlemen, it is five minutes past . . . And now, gentlemen, forward with God!" Dorpalen 441–42.
page 230
"How on earth did he conjure . . ." Hoffmann 69.
page 230
Hitler-Papen: Papen 264.
pages 230–31
Frank account: Frank 129–30.
page 231
Heine quote, 1834. From Louis Untermeyer, *Heinrich Heine*, *Paradox and Poet* (New York, 1937), I, 230.

Chapter Eleven. AN UNGUARDED HOUR

page 232
Frau Goebbels story: Frau Goebbels section in Ziegler.
page 232
Papen quote: Ewald von Kleist-Schmenzin, "*Die Letzte Möglichkeit*," *Politische Studien*, *X*, 1939, 92.
page 233
New York Times, Jan. 31, 1933.

page 233
Schacht quote: NA, U.S. Dept. of State file, Berlin Embassy Report, Feb. 2, 1933.
pages 233–34
Party at Hammerstein's: Institut für Zeitgeschichte, ZS 105–5, Horstom Mellenthin; O'Neill 125–26.
page 235
"to avoid at all costs..." Heiden, *A History of National Socialism*, 216.
page 236
Hanfstaengl account: Interview, 1970.
pages 236-37
Hitler at Reichstag fire: Delmer, *Trail*, 187-88; Papen 268-69; Tobias 84.
page 237
"a ruthless settling of accounts...documents of the German people." Holborn, *Republic*, 183.
page 239
"I may say to the Communists..." Bewley 100–1.
page 239
Göring speech: Bullock 223–24.
page 239
Göring quote: Bullock 219.
page 240
Schacht quote: Interview with Schacht, 1963; Manchester 407.
page 241
"Authority is only a springboard..." Frank 156.
page 241
"like a timid newcomer..." François-Poncet 62.
page 242
"We consider it a blessing..." Dorpalen 466.
pages 242–43
Hitler speech: Baynes 426.
page 243
"We want the bill...your death knell has sounded." Bullock 229.
page 244
Isherwood account: Isherwood 180–81.
page 245
Hitler quote: E. De Felice, *Storia degli ebrei italiani sotto il fascismo* (Turin, 1961), 113.
page 245
"Little knots of passers-by..." Isherwood 183.

page 245
Hindenburg-Hitler correspondence: Walther Hubatsch, *Hindenburg und der Staat*, op. cit., 375–78.
page 246
"It is precisely for these young Germans . . ." Baynes 729.
page 247
"To gain political power . . ." Speech, July 13, 1933 in Baynes 848–85, 867–68.
page 248
"German socialism is directed by Germans . . ." Heinz 232.
pages 248–49
Hitler to Spengler: *Spengler Letters* 290.
pages 248–49
Richard Strauss received by Hitler: Koehler 67–68.
page 249
Hitler quote: F. Wagner 89.
pages 250–51
Hanfstaengls' trip to Obersalzberg: Egon Hanfstaengl, *Memoirs*, 216–29.
page 252
"We must make a break . . ." Papen 297–98.
page 253
Lord Allen quote: Martin Gilbert, *Plough My Own Furrow* (London, 1965), 340–41.
page 253
Hitler speech at Siemens plant: Berlin, Nov. 10, 1933.
page 253
"Tomorrow show your national . . ." Dorpalen, 474.
page 254
"the representative of the German state idea . . ." Bracher 231.
page 254
"We wish thus to conform to the spirit . . ." *Jahresbericht der Deutschen Mathematiker-Vereinigung* (Leipzig, 1934), XLIII, 81–82.
page 255
"The British were eager to get . . ." François-Poncet 122–23.
page 255
Hitler letter to Mussolini, Nov. 2, 1933; GFP, II, 63–64.
pages 255–56
Hanfstaengl to Mussolini: Hanfstaengl, *Out of the Strong*.
page 256
Mussolini quote: Bojano 30–31.

page 256
"They were not over three yards from me..." Knickerbocker 5–6.
page 257
"Mussolini stepped forth superbly..." Sisley Huddleston, *In My Time* (London, 1938), 309.
page 257
Wiedemann account: Wiedemann 32 (tr.).
page 257
Bojano account: Bojano 31.

Chapter Twelve.
THE SECOND REVOLUTION—"ALL REVOLUTIONS DEVOUR THEIR OWN CHILDREN"

page 259
"The Reichswehr is the sole bearer...," Schweitzer 244.
pages 260–61
Conference, Feb. 28, 1934: Unpublished memoirs of Field Marshal von Weichs in O'Neill 39–41; Höhne, *Order*, 96. "What that ridiculous corporal..." Helmut Krausnick, "Der 30 Juni 1934," in *Das Parlament 30 Juni*, 1954, 320.
page 262
Papen speech: Papen 305–7.
page 263
"He led me to his study..." The Lutze diary, in *Frankfurter Rundschau*, May 14, 1957.
page 264
"square accounts." Höhne, *Order*, 109.
page 264
Hitler phone call to Röhm: Holborn, *Republic*, 235.
page 264
"The Reichswehr is against us!" Höhne, *Order*, 112; Case against Josef Dietrich, Munich Provisional Court I, July 4, 1956, 58, 80.
page 264
"It was at last clear to me..." Baynes 321.
page 265
"This is the blackest day..." Case against Dietrich, op. cit., 77.
page 265
"Lock him up!" Gallo 207.

page 265
"You are under arrest . . ." Lutze diary, op. cit.
pages 265–66
Kempka account: Interviews with Kempka, 1971.
page 266
"somewhat tense but not visibly excited." CIC-PH interview of Wilhelm Brückner.
page 266
Lutze account: Lutze diary, op. cit.
page 266
Brückner account: CIC-PH interview, op. cit.; Kempka interview, 1971.
page 267
"I gave the order . . ." Baynes 321–22.
page 267
Epp account: Judgment on Josef Dietrich, Munich, May 14, 1957, 60.
page 268
"In a voice frequently . . ." Letter from Gruppenführer Karl Schreyer to Munich Police HQ, 4; Höhne, *Order*, 116.
page 268
Papen account: Papen 315.
page 269
Dietrich account: Interview with Dietrich, 1963.
page 269
"Select an officer and six men . . ." Höhne, *Order*, 117.
page 269
Frank account: Frank 149–51.
page 270
Execution of the six men: Judgment on Dietrich, op. cit., 15–16; Case against Dietrich, op. cit., 69–70, 72.
page 270
"Göring arrived in one of his . . ." Gisevius 156.
page 270
"He was foolish enough . . ." Wheeler-Bennett, *Nemesis*, 323.
page 271
Reference Karl Ernst: He was rumored to be involved in the mysterious murder of Hanussen, the astrologer, whose body was found in a forest near Stahnsdorf several weeks after his prediction of the Reichstag fire. There was some speculation that Hitler, reportedly incensed at the murder, took vengeance on Ernst. Hegner 21.

Curiously, another well-known astrologer was a victim

of the Röhm purge: Dr. Karl-Günther Heimsoth, a close friend of Gregor Strasser, whose correspondence with Röhm about homosexuality and astrology was given wide publicity in the 1932 attempt to discredit the SA and the party. Dr. Heimsoth's death could also have been related to the recent ban on all forms of professional fortunetelling in the Berlin area. The predictions of Hanussen and his successors were becoming an embarrassment to the Third Reich. In the horoscope published by Frank Glahn in February 1933, for instance, it was predicted that the Führer would not be able to form a viable government.

Hitler's horoscope, however, continued to fascinate many Germans and a number were circulated surreptitiously. Soon after the Röhm purge, Hans Blüher, a founder of the *Wandervögel* movement, met an astrologer friend, Count Finckenstein, in a Berlin restaurant to discuss a horoscope of the Führer. "My friend Ulrich looked cautiously around to see if anyone was listening to us," wrote Blüher in his diary. "Then he leaned towards me and whispered in my ear through a cupped hand: 'He's a homocidal maniac!' Ever since then I knew that Germany had sold herself into the hands of a murderer." Howe, *Urania's*, 109.

page 271
"For months I have been telling . . ." Dorpalen 479.

page 271
Death of Röhm: Statement by Lippert, *Stuttgarten Zeitung*, May 7, 1957; VB, July 1, 1934; *Süddeutsche Zeitung*, Mar. 30–31, May 11, May 14, 1947; *Frankfurter Rundschau*, May 8, 1957; Höhne, *Order*, 126–27.

page 272
Delmer statement: *Trail*, 235.

page 272
Hindenburg telegram: Wheeler-Bennett, *Nemesis*, 325–26.

page 273
Papen account: Papen 318.

page 273
Frank-Hitler: Frank 152–54.

pages 274–75
Hitler speech: Baynes 290–328.

page 275
"emergency defense measures of the state." Orlow II, 115.

page 275
"The inevitable has happened . . ." Ivone Kirkpatrick 297.

pages 276–77
Hitler at Hindenburg's: MY 262.
page 277
"We were in his study..." Raeder testimony at Nuremberg, 1946.
page 277
Oath: Wheeler-Bennett, *Nemesis*, 339.

Chapter Thirteen. TRIUMPH OF THE WILL

page 278
Thompson account: *Harper's Bazaar*, Dec. 1934.
page 279
Speer account: Speer 58–59.
page 279
Leni Riefenstahl account: Interviews, 1971.
page 280
"The German form of life..." Shirer, *Berlin Diary*, 19.
page 280
Frank account: Frank 154–55.
page 280
"The floodlit stadium gave the impression..." Speer, *Playboy*, 78.
page 281
Dodd comment: William Dodd 164.
page 282
"During these violent scoldings..." OSS interview of Friedelind Wagner: HSB 939.
page 282
Hitler to Wiedemann: Wiedemann 35 (tr.).
page 282
Hitler to Schröder: Zoller 101.
page 283
"withdrawal from the League of Nations..." GFP, III, 1043–44.
page 283
Eden account: *Facing*, 133, 134, 135.
page 286
Oka's account: Robert Ingrim, *Hitlers glücklichster Tag* (Stuttgart, 1962).
page 286
"If the British government..." Schmidt 32–33.

page 288
"He was of the opinion . . ." Wiedemann 35 (tr.).
page 288
"For me marriage would have been . . ." HSC 247–48.
page 289
Speer on Hitler's fear of cancer: Speer 104.
pages 290–91
Hitler to Reichstag: Baynes 732.
page 292
"formed a single community . . ." Orlow II, 138.
page 293
Hoesch to Eden: *Facing*, 338–39.
page 293
Eden to Baldwin: Ibid. 343.

Chapter Fourteen. "WITH THE ASSURANCE OF A SLEEPWALKER"

page 298
Hitler to Schmidt: Schmidt 41.
page 298
"Good Lord, am I relieved how smoothly . . ." Frank 204ff.
page 298
"The Germans, after all, are only . . ." Shirer, *Rise*, 293.
page 298
"His view is that, if a firm front . . ." Feiling 279.
page 299
Hitler speech: Prange 110.
page 300
Kirkpatrick comment: Ivone Kirkpatrick, *The Inner Circle* (London, 1959), 97–98.
page 300
Hitler to Frau Wagner: F. Wagner 127.
page 301
"Wedged between the powerful Soviet bloc . . ." *Ribbentrop Memoirs*, 59–60.
page 302
Owens quote: Mandell 227.
page 303
"It is better to consider and solve . . ." Gerhard Meinck, *Hitler und die Deutache Aufrüstung* (Wiesbaden, 1959), 234.
page 304
"Mussolini is the first statesman of the world . . ." Wiskemann 90.

page 304
"According to the English there are..." *Ciano's Diplomatic Papers* (London, 1948), 60.
page 305
"this Berlin-Rome line is not a diaphragm..." Ivone Kirkpatrick 347.
page 305
"We are already in a state of war..." IMT, IX, 40.
page 305
"The battle we are now approaching..." Shirer, *Rise*, 300.
page 305
"If I can marry her as King..." Windsor 332.
page 306
"carry the heavy burden of responsibility..." Windsor 441.
page 306
Hitler to Ribbentrop: HH 33.
page 307
"Both Grawitz and Bergmann..." Interview with Dr. Giesing, 1971.
page 307
Hitler speech: Baynes 1334–47.
page 307
Footnote: New York *Times* Book Review, Apr. 22, 1973.
page 308
"The goal of our education..." *Hans Schemm spricht: Seine Reden und sein Werk* (Gauverlag Bayerische Ostmark, 1935), 175–78.
page 308
Phipps report: CAB 27/599.
page 309
Hitler Youth: Siemsen 145, 154; interview with Lauterbacher, 1971; Lauterbacher testimony at Nuremberg, May 27, 1936, 534.
page 309
Wilson quote: Santoro 416.
page 310
"The bourgeois must no longer feel..." Ibid. 58.
page 311
G. S. Cox article in *New York Times Magazine*, Oct. 28, 1934.
page 311
Kennan comment: *Memoirs*, 118.

page 312
Göring quote: Speech, Oct. 28, 1936, reprinted in *Der Vierjahresplan*, Jan. 1937, 33–35.
page 313
Hitler quote: Santoro 423.
page 313
Schacht comment: *Account*, 98–99.

Chapter Fifteen. THE RETURN OF THE NATIVE

pages 315–16
Papen account: Papen 406–8.
page 316
"to forestall a coup..." Guido Schmidt interrogation, IMT, XVI, 152.
pages 316–19
Schuschnigg-Hitler first interview: Schuschnigg, *Austrian*, 12–19; interview with Schuschnigg, 1971.
page 319
Second interview: Ibid. 24–26; Keitel 57; IMT, X, 505.
pages 319–20
Third interview: Schuschnigg, *Austrian, 25–27.*
page 320
"The Jews were attacking..." Schuschnigg, *Brutal*, 225.
page 320
Hitler speech: Gedye 232.
page 321
Schuschnigg speech: Gedye 238–39; interview with Schuschnigg, 1971.
page 321
"Fundamentally, a close understanding..." Ibid. 85.
page 322
Henderson-Hitler meeting: N. Henderson 115–16.
pages 322–23
Schuschnigg-Keppler meeting: Schuschnigg, *Brutal*, 250.
page 323
Keppler report: Ibid. 249.
page 324
"We have prepared nothing..." Shirer, *Rise*, 335.
page 324
Hitler letter to Mussolini: GFP, D., I, #352.

page 325
Schuschnigg letter to Seyss-Inquart: Schuschnigg, *Brutal*, 264.
pages 326–27
Glaise-Horstenau account: IMT, XIV, 131–32.
page 326ff
Telephone conversations between Berlin and other cities throughout the chapter: Schuschnigg, *Austrian*, Appendix 290ff.
page 328
"professed to be ignorant . . ." Cadogan 60.
page 328
Halifax to Schuschnigg: BFP, 3rd, I, 13.
pages 328–29
Schuschnigg account: *Austrian*, 48–52; interview with Schuschnigg, 1971.
page 329
Schuschnigg speech: Shirer, *Berlin Diary*, 99; Guido Schmidt Trial Protocols, Nuremberg, 290.
page 330
"Now, get moving!" Grolmann affidavit, quoted in Eichstaedt, *Von Dollfuss zu Hitler* (Wiesbaden, 1955), 411.
page 330
Hitler proclamation: Santoro 102.
page 331
Guderian comment: Guderian 32.
pages 331–32
Freud story: Ernest Jones 294.
page 332
Gedye account: Gedye 299.
page 332
Telegram to Halifax: BFP, I, 44.

Chapter Sixteen.
"ON THE RAZOR'S EDGE"

page 334
Linge account: Linge #22.
page 335
Ciano account: Ciano diary, May 7, 1938; interview with Dollmann, 1971.
page 335
"was extremely successful in melting . . ." Dollmann 110.

page 336
Ciano account: Ciano diary, May 5, 1938.
page 336
Chamberlain letter, Mar. 20, 1938; Private Collection to be available at Birmingham University Library.
page 337
"even if France does not do so . . ." Louis Fischer 311.
page 337
"It depends upon you, Excellency . . ." Wheeler-Bennett, *Munich*, 57.
pages 337–38
Henderson-Ribbentrop: GFP, D, 11, 317.
page 338
Weizsäcker comment: Weizsäcker 135–36.
pages 338–39
May 28 conference: *Nazi Conspiracy and Aggression*, V, 3037-PS, 743–44; Wiedemann Testimony, Nuremberg, Oct. 24, 1945, 3; Braddick 22.
pages 339–40
Wiedemann account: Wiedemann 94 (tr.).
page 340
Hesse account: HH 40–51; letter, Hesse, 1974.
page 340
Beck memorandum: O'Neill 157–58; Wolfgang Förster, *Ein General Kämpft gegen den Krieg* (Munich, 1949), 98–102.
page 341
Maisky to Halifax: McSherry I, 63.
pages 341–42
Henderson letter: BFP, II, 257.
page 342
"You know I am like a wanderer . . ." Frank 320.
page 342
Göring speech: Nogueres 107.
page 342
Shirer account: *Berlin Diary*, 125.
page 343
Mussolini quote: Nogueres 116.
page 343
Chamberlain to Daladier: BFP, II, 314.
page 344
"I fell from Heaven!" L. B. Namier, *Diplomatique prelude* (London, 1948), 35.

page 344
Chamberlain on BBC: Nogueres 124.
pages 345–46
Hitler-Chamberlain meeting: Schmidt 92–93; Feiling 366–67.
page 345
Roosevelt quote: Ickes diary, Sept. 18, 1938.
page 346
Chamberlain-Daladier: BFP, II, 387–96.
page 347–48
Newton report: BFP, II, 416–17.
page 348
Hodža to Lacroix: Nogueres 148.
page 348
Newton report: BFP, II, 425.
page 348
Czech communiqué: Nogueres 155.
pages 348–49
Chamberlain to journalists: MacLeod 242.
page 349
First Chamberlain-Hitler meeting: Schmidt 96–97; GFP, II, 876; BFP, II, 472.
page 351
Schmidt account: Schmidt 99–100.
page 351
Second Chamberlain-Hitler meeting: Schmidt 100–3; BFP, II, 502; MacLeod 246; GFP, II, 907–8.
page 353
Chamberlain to cabinet: CAB 23/95, 42 (38); BFP, II, 510; Parkinson 41–42.
page 353
Sunday cabinet meeting: Parkinson 43; CAB 23/95, 43 (38); Barnett 540.
page 354
Daladier quote: Parkinson 47.
page 354
Chamberlain to cabinet: Parkinson 48.
page 354
Hitler-Wilson meeting: Schmidt 103; GFP, II, 555–57.
page 354
Hitler speech: Prange 114–15; Parkinson 52.
page 355
Bullitt phone call: Bullitt 296.

page 355
Wilson-Hitler meeting: BFP, II, 565; Schmidt 104–5; Bullock 410; GFP, II, 965.
page 356
House of Commons scene: MacLeod 249–50.
page 356
Bullitt letter: Bullitt 297.
page 356
Beneš message: BFP, II, 604.
page 356
"I have no need to mobilize . . ." I. Kirkpatrick, *Mussolini*, 383.
pages 356–57
Chamberlain to journalists: Nogueres 250–51.
page 357
"Our time is too valuable . . ." Schmidt 110.
page 358
Göring comment: G. M. Gilbert, *Nuremberg*, 88.
page 358
Shirer comment: Shirer, *Rise*, 418.
page 358
François-Poncet account: *Fateful*, 273.
page 358
Chamberlain letter: Feiling 377.
page 359
London *Times* comment: Oct. 1, 1938.
page 359
Chamberlain at 10 Downing St.: Feiling 381.
page 359
Syrovy announcement: Gatzke 214.

Chapter Seventeen.
CRYSTAL NIGHT

page 363
Schacht conference, Aug. 20, 1935: ND, NG-4067.
page 364
Streicher quote: speech before German Labor Front mass meeting, Oct. 4, 1935; ND, M-35.
page 364
Fromm quote: Fromm 235–36.

page 365
Grynszpan quote: Arthur Morse, *While Six Million Died* (New York, 1967), 222.
page 365
Heydrich teletyped orders: ND, PS-3051.
page 365
"must have been exceeded considerably." Levin 80.
pages 365–66
Göring testimony: IMT, IX, 277.
page 366
Hitler to Frau Troost: Interview with Gerdy Troost, 1971.
page 366
Hesse account: HH 59–61.
page 367
Göring quote: Levin 87.
page 367
Roosevelt news conference: Morse, op. cit., 231.
pages 368–69
Schacht account: *Account*, 134–37.
page 369
Hitler-Wiedemann: Wiedemann 146–47 (tr.).
page 370
Hitler to Chvalkovsky: *French Yellow Book*, 210; Krausnick 44.
pages 370–71
Foreign Ministry circular: GFP, IV, 932–33.
page 371
Hitler speech: Baynes 740–41.
pages 371–72
"During this month he plans . . ." Ciano 3.
page 373
"When I get worked up . . ." Schmidt 236.
page 373
Tiso-Hitler: BFP, IV, 439; GFP, D, IV, 243–45.
page 374
Chamberlain quote: BFP, IV, 250.
page 374
Hacha-Hitler: Schmidt 122; GFP, IV, 263–69; HSC 211; *French Yellow Book*, 96.
page 376
Hitler to secretaries: Zoller 91–92.

Chapter Eighteen.
THE FOX AND THE BEAR

page 377
Phipps note: BFP, IV, 596.
page 379
"You want to negotiate . . ." *Polish White Book*, No. 64.
page 379
Chamberlain statement: Bullock 444.
page 380
Hitler speech: Prange 303–4.
page 380
Canaris-Hitler: Gisevius 363.
page 382
"like a cannon ball." A. Rossi, *Deux ans d'alliance germano-soviétique* (Paris, 1949), 27.
page 383
Hitler-Hilger: Kleist 21–22; Gustav Hilger and Alfred Meyer, *The Incompatible Allies* (New York, 1953), 293–97; McSherry I, 149–50.
page 383
Hitler conference: GFP, D, VI, 574–80; Shirer, *End*, 233.
page 385
Message to Schulenburg: NSR 5.
page 385
Halifax to Maisky: CAB 23/100; Cabinet 33 (39).
page 386
Hitler-Kubizek meeting: Kubizek 287–89.
page 388
Hitler to Speer: Speer, *Inside*, 161.
page 388
Hitler-Burckhardt meeting: Burckhardt 378–88.
page 389
Hesse account: HH 71–74; interview with Hesse, 1971.
pages 389–90
Ribbentrop-Ciano meeting: Wiskemann 191–92.
page 390
Ciano-Hitler meetings: Dollmann 168; Schmidt 132–33; Wiskemann 194–98; Ciano 119–20.
page 391
Ribbentrop to Schulenburg: NSR 63.
page 392
Trade agreement: NSR 83.

page 392
"I have them!" Speer, *Playboy*, 88.
page 393
"one of the extraordinary figures . . ." HSC 38.
page 393
"If Stalin did commit a bank robbery . . ." Hitler to Baur: Baur section in Ziegler; interview with Baur, 1970.
page 393
"In actual fact, he identifies himself . . ." HSC 190–91.
page 394
This is not a verbatim account of the August 22 conference but based on notes taken by several officers present: GFP, D, VII, 200–6, 557–59; Shirer, *End*, 252–55.
page 395
Göring leads applause: IMT, IX, 492.
page 396
"Odd Moscow customs." J. von Ribbentrop, *Memoirs*, 111.
pages 396–97
Ribbentrop-Stalin meeting: Ibid. 111–13; J. von Ribbentrop, *De Londres à Moscou* (Paris, 1954), 147; NSR 72; Schmidt 137; interview with Richard Schulze, 1971; GFP, VII, 228.

Chapter Nineteen.
"A CALAMITY WITHOUT PARALLEL IN HISTORY"

page 400
"ingrown and Jewish . . ." Delmer, *Trail*, 386.
page 400
"The signing of the pact . . ." Hoffmann 113.
page 401
Schmidt account: Schmidt 142.
page 401
"to make a move toward England . . ." GFP, VII, 279.
page 401
Henderson-Hitler meeting: Ibid. 280–81; Schmidt 143.
page 402
Schmidt account: Schmidt 145–46.
page 402
Hitler-Attolico: GFP, VII, 286.
page 402–3
Hitler to Keitel: IMT, X, 514.
page 403
Schmundt to Warlimont: Warlimont 3.

page 403
Dahlerus phone call to Göring: Dahlerus 53.
page 404
"Why, at once, before hostilities begin." Wiskemann 206.
page 404
Hitler to Mussolini: GFP, VII, 314.
page 404
Hitler to Mussolini: Ibid. 232.
page 405
Dahlerus-Hitler: Dahlerus 60–62.
page 407
Dahlerus-Chamberlain: Dahlerus 72–73.
pages 408–9
Henderson-Hitler: GFP, VII, 332; N. Henderson 276; BFP, VII, 351, 381–82, 388.
page 409
Engel comments: Engel 61.
page 409
Henderson-Hitler: N. Henderson 280; Schmidt 149; BFP, VII, 393.
page 410
Dahlerus-Göring: Dahlerus 90–94.
page 410
Dahlerus-Chamberlain: Dahlerus 98–99.
page 411
Schmidt comment: Schmidt 150.
pages 411–12
Henderson-Ribbentrop: Schmidt 151–53; J. von Ribbentrop, *Memoirs*, 124.
page 413
Hitler to Mussolini: GFP, VII, 483.
page 413
"We only pity you people . . ." GFP, VII, 521.
page 414
Chamberlain speech: Feiling 415.
pages 414–15
Henderson-Schmidt meeting: Schmidt 157.
page 415
Schmidt at Chancellery: Schmidt 158.
page 415
Dahlerus-Göring: Dahlerus 129–30.
page 416
Henderson-Ribbentrop meeting: N. Henderson 300.

page 416
Chamberlain broadcast: Feiling 415–16; Colvin, *Chamberlain Cabinet*, 253–54.
page 417
Ribbentrop to Schulenburg: GFP, VII, 541.
page 417
Hitler to Mussolini: Ibid. 538–39.
page 417
"Now, all my work crumbles . . ." Zoller 175.
page 417
Hitler to Linge: Linge #15.

Chapter Twenty. VICTORY IN THE WEST

page 421
Hitler motto: Zoller 156–57.
page 422
Hesse-Hewel: Hesse, *Das Spiel*, Chap. 5; interview with Hesse, 1971.
page 423
Ribbentrop to Schmidt: Schmidt 162.
page 424
Heydrich to SS commanders, Sept. 21, 1939: ND, EC-307, PS-3362.
page 425
Hewel to Hesse: Hesse, *Das Spiel*, Chap. 5.
pages 425–26
Hitler memorandum: *Nazi Conspiracy and Aggression*, VII, 800–14.
page 426
"My attempts to make peace . . ." IMT, IX, 50; interview with Milch, 1971.
page 427
Müller account: Interview with Müller, 1963.
page 428
Brauchitsch-Hitler meeting: Halder Diary, Nov. 4–5, 1939; Brauchitsch testimony, IMT, XX, 575; Wheeler-Bennett, *Nemesis*, 471.
page 428
Krafft warning: E. Howe, *Urania's*, 169.

page 429
Elser account: Record of interrogation, *Der Stern*, May 10, 1966.
page 430
Hitler at Bürgerbräukeller: Interviews with Kempka and Wünsche, 1971.
page 430
"Now I am completely content!" Zoller 204. There is conflicting evidence on when Hitler learned of the bombing. Höhne wrote it was at the Munich railroad station (*Order*, 286). Herta Schneider and Kempka agreed it was near Augsburg (Interviews, 1971).
page 430
"What idiot conducted this interrogation?" *Schellenberg Memoirs* (London, 1961), 110.
page 431
Official version: Wheeler-Bennett, *Nemesis*, 481.
page 431
"for the first time he desired German defeat." Ciano 183.
page 432
Shirer comment: *Berlin*, 234.
page 432
Goebbels' propaganda methods: Interview with Naumann, 1971.
page 432
Goebbels' instructions: Boelcke 8.
page 433
"I doubt very much . . ." CAB 65/5; War Cabinet 30 (40).
page 434
War Directive: HWD 23–24.
page 434
"most daring and most important . . ." Rich I, 142.
page 434
Soviet mission to Berlin: Interview with Schlotterer, 1971; GFP, VIII, 722.
page 434
Hitler on Stalin: Zoller 178.
page 435
Hitler-Mussolini meeting: Schmidt 173; Ciano 223–24; Dollmann 183.
page 436
"You Germans have done the incredible again!" ND, 3596-PS; Shirer, *Rise*, 700.

page 436
Hitler-Brauchitsch: Assmann; Warlimont 77–78.
page 437
"beside himself with joy." Warlimont 79; interview with Warlimont, 1971.
page 437
Hitler on Milch: Irving, *Breach*, 88.
pages 437–38
Hitler's plan: Interviews with Wünsche, Below, Puttkamer, Manstein, 1970–71; Dietrich, *Hitler*, 81; Keitel 102–3.
page 438
"The swine has gone . . ." Allen Dulles, *Germany's Underground* (New York, 1947), 58–61; interview with Dulles, 1963.
page 438
"I was filled with rage." HSC 93.
page 439
"When the news came that the enemy . . ." Ibid. 94.
pages 439, 430
"I have always said . . ." London *Times*, Nov. 7, 1938.
page 441
Goebbels conference: Boelcke 42.
page 441
Göring incident: Engel 80; Irving, *Rise*, 89–90.
page 442
"Only fish bait will reach . . ." Engel 81.
page 444
"I have decided to stay . . ." *Belgian Rapport*, Annexes, 69–75.
page 444
"I have quite often in the past . . ." Engel 82.
page 445
Shirer account: *Berlin*, 422.
pages 445–46
French surrender: Schmidt 181–83.
page 447
"Now your work begins . . ." Interview with Giesler, 1971; correspondence, 1975.

Chapter Twenty-one. "EV'N VICTORS BY VICTORY ARE UNDONE"

page 448
Hitler to Hoffmann: Hoffmann 122.
page 449
Halder diary: July 13, 1940.
page 449
Delmer account: *Black Boomerang*, 10–11.
page 450
Conference, July 21: Ansel, *Hitler Confronts*, 163–65. Halder diary, July 22, 1940.
page 451
Jodl-Warlimont: Warlimont 111–12; interview, 1971; Ansel, op. cit., 181.
page 451
Conference, July 31: GFP, X, 370–74; Ansel, op. cit., 184–89; Shirer, *Rise*, 764–66.
page 452
Directives: HWD 37–38; *Führer Conferences on Naval Affairs*, 82–83.
page 453
"Neither type of fighter . . ." Irving, *Rise*, 101.
page 454
Göring broadcast: Ibid. 250.
page 454
Churchill speech: Churchill, *Their Finest Hour* (Bantam, New York, 1962), 282.
page 455
Hitler-Mussolini meeting: Ansel, *Hitler and Middle Sea*, 33; GFP, XI, 250–51.
pages 456–58
Hitler-Franco meeting: HSC 532; Schmidt 193–97; Hills, 345, 342; GFP, XI, 371–79; interviews with Puttkamer, Schulze (1971) and Serrano Suñer (1963); Linge #19; Keitel 126.
page 459
Franco to Pétain: Francisco Franco, *Discursos y mensajes del Jefe del Estado, 1951–54* (Madrid, 1955), 41.
pages 459–60
Hitler-Pétain meeting: Hamilton 231–32; Griffiths 271.
page 461
Engel account: Engel 88.

pages 461–62
Mussolini meeting: Keitel 126–27; Linge #19; Ciano 300; Ciano Minute, Oct. 28, 1940; Wiskemann 283; GFP, XI, 411–22.

Chapter Twenty-two. "THE WORLD WILL HOLD ITS BREATH"

pages 463–64
Ribbentrop-Molotov meeting: Schmidt 210–13; GFP, XI, 537–38.
pages 464–65
Hitler-Molotov meeting: Ibid. 542–61; Schmidt 213–19.
pages 465–66
Molotov-Ribbentrop meeting: GFP, XI, 562–70; Louis Fischer 431–32.
pages 465–66
Hitler speech: Flannery 107–9; Hitler, *My New Order* (New York, 1941), 901–24.
page 466
"When Barbarossa commences . . ." ND, 872-PS; Shirer, *Rise*, 822.
page 466
"struck a blow at the belief . . ." TAH 97–98.
page 467
Lochner account: *What About Germany?*, 122.
pages 467–68
Hitler and Yugoslavia: GFP, D, XII, 364, 369–75; Weizsäcker 25; Keitel 138–39; Jodl testimony at Nuremberg, June 5, 1946, 422.
page 468
"I was haunted . . ." TAH 97.
page 469
Hitler lecture: Keitel 134–36. Halder affidavit at Nuremberg, Nov. 22, 1945; Warlimont 160–61; Halder diary, Mar. 30, 1941.
page 471
Stalin notation: David Dallin, *Die Sowjetspionage* (Cologne, 1956); Carell, *Hitler Moves*, 59.
page 471
"wanted to try one more . . ." J. von Ribbentrop, *Memoirs*, 152.

page 471
"I do not intend a war . . ." GFP, XII, 66–69.
page 472
Jodl to Warlimont: Warlimont 140.
page 472
"had succeeded in infecting . . ." Guderian, 125.
page 473
Hitler to Hanfstaengl: *Out of the Strong*, 34.
page 473
"I was confronted by a very hard . . ." Hess 14.
pages 473–74
Background information on Hess: Interview with Hildegard Fath, 1971.
page 474
Events of May 10: Hess 19–21, 31–37; correspondence with Frau Hess, 1975.
page 475
Engel account: Engel 103–4.
page 475
"Oh, my God, my God!" Speer interrogation, June–July 1945, Field Intelligence Agency; Bodenschatz interrogation, May 30, 1945.
page 475
Hess letter: Hess 27; Dietrich, *Hitler*, 62–63.
page 475
"I hope he falls into the sea!" Schmidt 233.
page 476
"well, Hess or no Hess . . ." Douglas-Hamilton 163.
page 476
Frank account: Frank 411.
page 476
Ciano comment: Ciano 451.
page 476–77
Hitler did not think Hess mad: Interview with Schwaebe and Florian, 1971.
page 477
"True, I achieved nothing . . ." Hess 138.
page 478
Hitler-Oshima meeting: Interview with Oshima, 1966.
page 479
"I cannot demand that my generals . . ." Jodl testimony at Nuremberg, June 3, 1946, 308.

page 479
"These commissars are the originators . . ." Krausnick 519–20.
page 480
Tass communiqué: Werth, *Russia*, 125–26.
page 480
"No use beating an alarm." A. M. Nekrich, *June 22, 1941* (Moscow, 1965), 144–45.
page 480
Hitler-Frank meeting: Frank 408, 414.
page 481
Molotov to Schulenburg: GFP, XII, 1072.
pages 481–82
Hitler to troops: Carell, *Hitler Moves*, 4–5.
page 482
Molotov-Schulenburg meeting: Winston Churchill, *The Grand Alliance* (Boston, 1950), 366–67.
page 482
Ribbentrop-Dekanozov meeting: Schmidt 234.
page 482
Hitler's message: Ansel, *Hitler and Middle Sea*, 441.

Chapter Twenty-three. "A DOOR INTO A DARK, UNSEEN ROOM"

page 483
"We have only to kick . . ." Bullock 587.
page 483–84
"At the beginning of each campaign . . ." Zoller 160.
page 484
"to all intents and purposes . . ." Warlimont 180.
page 484
"Contrary to the opinions . . ." Leo Alexander, *Journal of Criminal Law and Criminology*, Sept.–Oct. 1948, 315.
page 485
"Strange is the calmness . . ." ND, RSHA IV-A-1, Operational Report, Sept. 12, 1941, No. 3154.
page 485
Conference, July 16: GFP, D, XIII, 149–56, 606–8. Interviews with Koeppen, Bräutigam and Leibbrandt, 1971.
page 486
Hitler-Ribbentrop meeting: U.S. State Dept. interrogation of Steengracht, Sept. 4, 1945.

page 488
Hitler-Mussolini meetings: Dollmann 191–92; Alfieri 159.
page 488
"In several weeks we will . . ." Zoller 160.
page 488
Table conversations: Interviews with Koeppen and Heim, 1971, 1974–75.
page 489
Sept. 17 conversation: HSC 58–60.
page 490
"They are brutes . . ." HSC 66.
page 490
"In a few days a youth . . . preservation of the species." Ibid. 69–70.
page 491
"Before I became Chancellor . . ." Fabian von Schlabrendorff, *Offiziere gegen Hitler* (Zurich, 1946), 47–48; Halder diary, Aug. 4, 1941.
pages 491–92
Hitler speech: VB, Oct. 5, 1941; Stein 78–82
page 492
Goebbels conference: Boelcke 186.
pages 493–94
Stalin speeches: Werth, *Russia*, 246, 248–49
page 495
Guderian account: Guderian 191–92.
page 495
Rundstedt-Hitler telegrams: U.S. interrogation of Rundstedt, 1945; Shirer, *Rise*, 861.
page 496
"I myself, for instance, am not . . ." Testimony of General August Winter at Nuremberg, June 8, 1946, 604.
page 496
"victory could no longer be achieved . . ." Percy Schramm 26–27.
page 497
"The United States and England will always . . ." Hillgruber, *Staatsmänner*, 300ff.
page 498
Hassell comment: Hassell 208.
page 499
Ribbentrop-Oshima meeting: Interview with Oshima, 1966; in-

tercepted message, Oshima to Tokyo, Nov. 29, 1941, ND, D-656.
page 499
Message to Oshima, Nov. 30, 1941: ND, 3598-PS.
page 500
Dietrich account: Dietrich, *Hitler*, 70–71.
page 500
Keitel account: Keitel 162.
page 500
Hitler to Hewel: Irving, *Hitler*, 354.
page 500
Directive: HWD 107.
page 500
Hitler to Bormann: TAH 87–88.
page 500
Hitler-Ribbentrop meeting: TMWC 297–98; Shirer, *Rise*, 894.
pages 501-2
Hitler to Reichstag: Prange 97, 367–77.
pages 501–2
"Stand fast, not one step back!" Keitel 166.
page 502
Brauchitsch-Keitel: Keitel 164.
page 502
Hitler-Halder: Halder 49.

Chapter Twenty-four. "AND HELL FOLLOWED WITH HIM"

page 505
"to make all necessary . . ." Göring to Heydrich, July 31, 1941, ND, PS 710.
page 506
Höss account: IMT, XI, 398.
pages 506–7
"but the first thing, above all . . ." HSC 91.
page 507
"From the rostrum . . ." Ibid. 108–9, 111.
page 507
"I am now as before a Catholic . . ." Engel 31.
pages 507–8
Frank account: ND, PS-2233; IMT, XXIX, 498ff.
pages 508–9
Wannsee conference: Eichmann minutes, ND, NG 2586; Hil-

berg 264–65; ND, PS-709; Krausnick 82–87; Röhl 163; interviews with Leibbrandt and Hesse.

page 509

After conference: *Life*, Nov. 28, 1960, pp. 24, 101.

page 509

"One must act radically . . ." HSC 238.

pages 509–10

Hitler speech: Prange 83.

page 510

Guderian-Hitler: Guderian 205–6.

page 511

"My prophecy shall be fulfilled . . ." *Keesings Archiv der Gegenwart*, 1940, 5409.

page 511

Fritzsche account: IMT, XVII, 172–73.

pages 511–12

Goebbels comment: *Goebbels Diaries*, 138.

page 512

"He plays cat and mouse . . ." *Goebbels Diaries*, 88.

page 513

Heydrich assassination: Jan Wiener, *The Assassination of Heydrich* (New York, 1969), 82–90; Höhne, *Order*, 494–95.

page 514

Merin quote: *Commentary*, Dec. 1958, 481–83.

page 514

Eichmann-Wisliceny: Wisliceny affidavit, Nov. 10, 1946; Levin 300.

page 517

Hitler-Paulus: Goerlitz, *Paulus*, 159–60.

pages 517–18

Hitler-Halder: Halder diary, Sept. 24, 1942; Keitel 184; correspondence with Halder, 1971; Shirer, *Rise*, 917–18.

page 518

Hitler-Zeitzler: Interview with Heusinger, 1971.

page 518

Zeitzler to officers: Warlimont 260.

pages 518

Sportpalast speech: *Keesings Archiv*, op. cit., 5657.

page 519

Jodl comment: "Answers to Questions Put to General Jodl," OCHM, MS #A-914.

page 520

"the God of war had now turned . . ." Percy Schramm 27.

page 520
Gehlen report: Gehlen 59.
page 521
"Führer himself completely unsure . . ." Percy Schramm 113.
page 521
Paulus to Schmidt: Goerlitz, *Paulus*, 210.
pages 521–22
Hitler to Paulus: Carell, *Hitler Moves*, 635.
page 522
Manstein to Paulus: Goerlitz, op. cit., 234; interview with Schmidt, 1971.
page 523
Paulus to Manstein: Goerlitz, op. cit., 236.
page 523
Conference, Dec. 12: Warlimont 292.
page 524
On breakout: Interview with Schmidt, 1971; correspondence, 1975.
page 524
Manstein-Paulus: Interview with Manstein, 1971; Goerlitz, op. cit., 277.
page 524
"this fellow Göring, this fat . . ." HH 152.
pages 524–25
Hitler-Zitzewitz: Carell, op. cit., 669; Goerlitz, op. cit., 264.
page 525
Paulus letter: Goerlitz, op. cit., 250.
page 526
Zeitzler to Paulus: Carell, op. cit., 670.
page 526
Schmidt account: Interviews with Schmidt, 1971.
page 526
Conference Feb. 1, 1943: Warlimont 300–6; Felix Gilbert 17–22.
page 527
De Gaulle quote: William Craig, *Enemy at the Gates* (New York, 1973), XV.

Chapter Twenty-five.
THE FAMILY CIRCLE

page 529
"You don't have to get excited . . ." Unpublished memoirs of Getraud (Humps) Junge; interview, 1971.

page 529

"After Stalingrad Hitler would not..." A. Zoller, *Hitler Privat* (Düsseldorf, 1949), 44–45.

pages 530

Goebbels speech: *Josef Goebbels Reden*, II, 1939–45 (Düsseldorf, 1971), 177–83.

page 530

Bormann letter: Bormann 6–7.

page 530

Lochner account: *Always the Unexpected*, 294–95.

page 531

Schlabrendorff account: Interview with Schlabrendorff, 1963.

page 531

Gerstdorff account: Interview with Gerstdorff, 1971; Gerstdorff correspondence, 1975; Peter Hoffmann, *Canadian Journal of History*, 1967.

page 532

Gertraud Humps (Junge) account: Junge, *Memoirs*.

page 535

"Either give up smoking or me." Interview with Herta Schneider, 1971.

pages 536–37

"If it be true today..." *Goebbels Diaries*, 354–59.

page 537

Hitler diet: Interview with Zabel, 1971.

page 538

On Citadel: Interviews with Manstein and Puttkamer, 1971; Guderian 246–47; Seaton 356; Gehlen 64–65.

page 538

Hitler-Mussolini: *Hitler e Mussolini*, 165–90; Alfieri 237–48.

pages 540–41

Hitler-Goebbels: *Goebbels Diaries*, 435–37.

page 541

Hitler speech: Prange 384.

pages 541–42

Skorzeny-Mussolini: Skorzeny, *Special Missions*, 70–90; interviews with Skorzeny, 1956, 1963, 1971; correspondence, 1975.

page 543

Hitler-Mussolini: F. Anfuso, *Da Palazzo Venezie al Lago di Garda* (Cappelli, 1957), 326–27; Zoller 180; J. von Ribbentrop, *Memoirs*, 170–71.

Chapter Twenty-six. "AND WITH THE BEASTS OF THE EARTH"

pages 545–46
Lammers account: IMT, XI, 52–53.
page 546
Frank comment: Interview with G. M. Gilbert, 1972; Gilbert, *Nuremberg*.
page 546
"was necessary in the interests of Europe." Piotrowski 281–82.
page 546
"People are now clinging." Krausnick 371.
page 547
Hitler to Himmler: Ibid. 123.
page 547
Hitler to Bormann: TAH 57.
pages 547–48
Warsaw ghetto: Hilberg 320–26; Ringelblum 310, 326; Stroop Report, ND 1061-PS.
page 548
Pius XII quote: Alexis Curvers, *Pie XII, Le Pape outragé* (Paris, 1964), 139.
pages 549–50
Morgen story: Interview, 1971.
page 551
Comments on Himmler: Höhne, *Order*, 30; interviews, Gudrun Himmler (1974), Wehser (1971).
pages 551–52
On Himmler: Toland, *Last*, 132–33; interviews with Hausser, 1963, Sündermann (1970), Richard Schulze, Milch, Wehser, Grothmann (1971).
page 554
"The SS commander must be hard . . ." *Die Zeit*, June 25, 1965.
page 555
Himmler speech, Oct. 4, 1943: ND, 1919-PS.
page 555
Himmler speech, Jan. 26, 1934: Interview with Gerstdorff, 1971; Kunrat von Hammerstein, *Spaehtrupp* (Stuttgart, 1963), 192–93; Smith and Peterson 201.
page 555
Himmler speech to Navy at Weimar, Dec. 16, 1943: Ibid. 201.

page 555
Himmler speech to generals at Sonthofen, May 24, 1944: Ibid. 202.
pages 556–58
Morgen story: Interview, 1971; Morgen testimony at Nuremberg, Aug. 7–8, 1946, 488–515.

Chapter Twenty-seven. THE ARMY BOMB PLOT

pages 561–62
Jodl speech: Shirer, *End*, 279–86.
pages 562–63
On air raids: Junge, *Memoirs*.
page 563
It had to happen: Interview with Günsche, 1971.
page 563
Speer account: Speer, *Inside*, 346–47.
page 564
"It will decide the issue . . . an end by political means." Interview of Warlimont by Major Kenneth Hechler, July 19, 1945, 5.
page 564
Rommel account: Carell, *Invasion*, 14–16.
page 566
"Now we can give them . . ." Linge #34; interview with Günsche, 1971.
page 566
Hitler conference: Interview with Warlimont, 1971; Warlimont 427.
page 567
Hitler to Göring: Irving, *Rise*, 285.
page 567
Hitler near Soissons: Hans Speidel, *Invasion* (Chicago, 1950), 93; Shirer, *Rise*, 1039–41; Speer, *Inside*, 356; OCMH, Speidel monograph.
page 570
"any such coup d'état . . ." Interview with Manstein, 1971.
page 570
"I believe it is my duty . . ." Desmond Young, *Rommel—The Desert Fox* (New York, 1950), 223–24.
page 570
"You are young . . ." Speidel, *Invasion*, op. cit., 71.

page 572

Steiner account: Interview with Steiner, 1963; Höhne, *Order*, 513.

page 573

Hitler to Schröder: Zoller 207–8.

page 574

Freyend account: *Walküre*, a TV special produced by Bavaria Atelier, Munich, and based on interviews with survivors; Zeller 302–3.

page 575

Heusinger account: Interview, 1971.

page 575

Puttkamer account: Interview, 1973. Günsche account: Interview, 1971.

page 576

Fellgiebel account: Zeller 345–48; *Walküre*, op. cit.

pages 576–77

Stauffenberg escape: Ibid.; Zeller 304, 344.

page 577

Hitler-Hasselbach: Interview with Hasselbach, 1971.

page 577

Hitler-secretaries: Junge, *Memoirs*.

page 578

Fellgiebel account: Zeller 346–48; Peter Hoffmann article on July 20 plot.

page 579

Keitel-Fromm: Zeller 306; Fabian von Schlabrendorff, *They Almost Killed Hitler* (New York, 1947).

page 579

Stauffenberg at the Bendlerstrasse: Zeller 307–9; *Walküre*, op. cit.

page 581

Remer account: Interview, 1971.

page 581

Hagen story: *Walküre*, op. cit.; Zeller 355; Bramsted 338–39.

page 582

Remer story: Interviews with Remer, 1971; Zeller 339–41, 355–56; Bramsted 339–40; *Walküre*, op. cit.; Speer, *Playboy*, 193; Oven diary, July 20, 1944.

page 584

Bormann message: Bormann 61–62.

page 584

Skorzeny account: Interview, 1971.

pages 585–86
Fromm-Beck: Zeller 315–18; Höpner testimony, TMWC, XXXIII, 299–530.
page 586
Teleprint message: Zeller 319.
page 586
Fromm-Remer: Interview with Remer, 1971.
page 587
Himmler at Goebbels: Zeller 339; interviews with Remer, 1971.
page 587
Fellgiebel to aide: Zeller 349.
page 587
Hitler quotes: Junge, *Memoirs*; interview with Christian, 1971.
page 588
Hitler speech: Zeller 342–43.
page 588
Goebbels quotes: Oven diary, July 21, 1944.
pages 588–89
Hitler-Eva Braun correspondence: Gun, *Eva Braun*, 179–80.
page 589
Hitler quotes: Junge, *Memoirs*; Zoller 193; *Walküre*, op. cit.
page 589
Guderian order of the day: Shirer, *Rise*, 1080–81.
page 590
Hitler-Giesing: Giesing, *Diary*; interview with Giesing, 1971.
pages 590–91
"The Stauffenberg family will be exterminated . . ." *Vierteljahreshefte für Zeitgeschichte*, Vol. 4, 1953, 363–94.
page 591
Trial and executions: Zeller 371–75; IMT, XXXIII, 2999, for testimony of Peter Vossen, shorthand secretary at trial; Shirer, *Rise*, 1070.
page 591
On film of executions: Speer, *Playboy*, 103; interview with Below, 1971; correspondence with Hasselbach, 1975.
page 592
Hitler to Keitel: Felix Gilbert 105–6; Warlimont 450–55.
page 593
Junge account: *Memoirs*.
pages 593–94
Giesing account: *Diary*.

Chapter Twenty-eight. THE BATTLE OF THE BULGE

page 595
Directive: HWD 197.
pages 595–96
Hitler special conference: OCMH, A-862, "The Preparations for the German Offensive in the Ardennes" by Percy Schramm; interview with Schramm, 1957.
pages 596–97
Giesing account: *Diary*; cardiograms in "Hitler as Seen by His Doctors," NA, USFET, OI/CIR/4.
page 597
Junge comment: *Memoirs*.
pages 598–99
Giesing-Hitler: Giesing, *Diary*; interview, 1971.
page 599
Dr. von Hasselbach does not believe that Giesing gave Hitler the double cocaine dose (correspondence, 1975).
pages 599–600
Giesing account: *Diary*; interview, 1971.
page 601
Rommel story: Speidel, op. cit., 152; Desmond Young, op. cit., 251–52; Milton Schulman, *Defeat in the West* (New York, 1948), 138–39; Zeller 378–79; Shirer, *Rise*, 1077–79.
page 602
Skorzeny account: Interviews with Skorzeny, 1957, 1963, 1971.
page 603
Model quote: Interview with Percy Schramm, 1957. Hitler-Rundstedt: Schramm, "Preparations," op. cit.
page 603
Hitler-Junge: Junge, *Memoirs*.
pages 604–5
Dec. 11 conference: Interviews with Manteuffel, Blumentritt and Percy Schramm, 1957; OCMH, MS #B-151, Manteuffel; Percy Schramm, op. cit.
page 606
Bradley-Eisenhower: Dwight Eisenhower, *Crusade in Europe* (Garden City, 1948), 350; interview with Bradley, 1957.
page 608
Manteuffel-Jodl: Interview with Manteuffel, 1957.

pages 608–9
Jodl-Hitler: OCMH, A858, "The Course of Events of the German Offensive in the Ardennes" by Percy Schramm.
page 609
Hitler-Göring: Frau Göring account in Ziegler.
page 610
Special meeting: Felix Gilbert 158–74.
page 610
Military conference: Percy Schramm, op. cit.; interview with Blumentritt, 1957.
page 611
Churchill-Eisenhower: Churchill, *Triumph and Tragedy* (Bantam, New York, 1962), 240–41.
page 612
Hitler-Guderian: Guderian 315; interview with Praun, 1971.
pages 612–13
Hitler-Junge: Junge, *Memoirs*.

Chapter Twenty-nine. "THIS TIME WE MUST NOT SURRENDER FIVE MINUTES BEFORE MIDNIGHT"

page 617
Hitler speech: Ausubel 46.
pages 617–18
Hitler lecture: Guderian 337; interviews in 1963 with two SS officers who were present but wish to remain anonymous.
page 618
Bormann letter: Bormann 168–69.
page 618
Hitler to Bormann: TAH 33–34, 38–41.
page 618
Hitler-Giesler: Interview with Giesler, 1971.
page 619
Hitler to Schröder: Zoller 230–31.
page 619
Hitler to Gauleiters: Interviews with Florian, Jordan and Scheel, 1971.
page 620
Kempka-Hitler: Interview with Kempka, 1971.
page 621
Speer account: Speer, *Inside*, 436–37, 440.

page 621
"If I ever lay hands . . ." Boldt 84.
pages 261–22
March 28 conference: Guderian 356–57; interviews with Puttkamer (1971), Freytag von Loringhoven, and Generals Thomale and Busse (1963).
page 623
Operation Sunrise: Interviews with Generals Wolff, Airey and Lemnitzer, Allen Dulles, Gero von Gaevernitz, 1963–64.
page 625
Stalin and Roosevelt messages: *Correspondence Between the Chairman of the Council of Ministers of the U.S.S.R. and the Presidents of the U.S.A. and the Prime Ministers of Great Britain during the Great Patriotic War of 1941–45*, II, 206–10.
page 625
Hitler-Carlyle story: Schwerin von Krosigk's diary (Shirer, *End*, 193). Carlyle is misquoted; the Czarina died on Jan. 5, 1762.
page 625
Hanussen's horoscope of Jan. 1, 1933, it will be recalled, predicted that Hitler would rise to power in thirty days and enjoy tremendous successes until the "union of the three" was broken. At this point his work would disappear during the spring of 1945 "in smoke and flames." Although Hitler often ridiculed astrology to his family circle, he had shown a genuine interest not only in Hanussen's horoscope but in that of Frau Ebertin in 1923.
page 625
Goebbels quotes: Semmler, op. cit., 192ff.
page 625
Ribbentrop quote: HH 218–19.
pages 625–26
Hitler proclamation: Max Domarus, *Hitler: Reden und Proklamationen* (Würzberg, 1962–63), 2223–24.
page 626
"Now, there's a beautiful woman!" Oven diary, Apr. 18, 1945.

Chapter Thirty.
FIVE MINUTES PAST MIDNIGHT

page 627
Hitler-Keitel: Keitel 197.
page 628
"I must force a decision . . ." Junge, *Memoirs*.

page 628
Hitler to secretaries: Zoller 247–48.
page 628
Footnote: *New York Times*, Apr. 21, 1945.
pages 628–29
Himmler-Masur: Norbert Masur, *En Jood talar med Himmler* (Stockholm, 1946); *The Memoirs of Doctor Felix Kersten* (Garden City, 1947), 284-86; Schellenberg 385–86.
page 631
Hitler to Steiner: Interview with Steiner, 1963; Cornelius Ryan, *The Last Battle* (New York, 1966), 426.
page 631
Bormann story: CIC-PH Document 03649, 12 Oct. 1945, Carlisle Barracks.
pages 631–32
Hitler collapse: Trevor-Roper 117–19; interview with Freytag von Loringhoven, 1963; Junge, *Memoirs*.
pages 632–33
Koller story: Koller diary, *Die Letze Monate* (Mannheim, 1949); Trevor-Roper 128–31.
page 633–34
Hitler's dismissal of Göring: Trevor-Roper 138–39; Toland, *Last*, 431–32.
page 634
Eva to Traudl: Junge, *Memoirs*.
page 634
Eva letter to Herta: Gun, *Eva Braun*, 209–10; interview with Herta Schneider, 1971.
page 634
Eva letter to sister: CIC-PH, Fegelein File, enclosure 18, Carlisle Barracks.
pages 634–35
Apr. 24 conference: Interview with Freytag von Loringhoven, 1963; Boldt 166–67.
page 635
Goebbels proclamation: *Drahtloser Dienst* (Nord), Apr. 24, 1945, BBC monitoring.
page 636
Hitler quotes: *Der Spiegel*, Jan. 1966.
pages 636–37
Reitsch-Greim story: Reitsch 229; U.S. interrogation of Reitsch, Oct. 8, 1945, "The Last Days in Hitler's Air Raid Shelter," Ref. AIU/IS/1.

page 637
Wenck account: Interview with Wenck, 1963.
page 637
Hitler quotes: *Der Spiegel*, op. cit.
page 638
Evening conference: Weidling Diary.
page 639
Reitsch account: Reitsch interrogation, op. cit.
pages 639–40
Hitler-Junge: Junge, *Memoirs*. Text of Hitler's two wills: ND 3569-PS; English translation, Stein 83–87.
page 642
Junge-Goebbels: Junge, *Memoirs*.
page 643
Frau Hitler-Junge: Junge, *Memoirs*.
page 643
"I will not fall into the hands . . ." Ibid.
page 644
Weidling-Hitler: Weidling diary.
page 645
Junge account: Junge, *Memoirs*.
page 645
Hitler-Günsche: Interview with Günsche, 1963.
pages 645–46
Günsche-Kempka: Interviews with Günsche and Kempka, 1963.
page 646
Baur-Hitler: Baur chapter in Ziegler; interview with Baur, 1970.
pages 646–48
Death of Hitler and Eva: Junge, *Memoirs*; interviews with Kempka and Günsche, 1963, 1971.
pages 648–49
Poem: Schirach 192.

Epilogue

page 650
"safe and well in Argentina." CIC-PH, Fegelein File, interrogation, Carlisle Barracks.
pages 650–51
Bezymenski quotes: Bezymenski 66.
page 651
Dr. Soggnaes account: Correspondence, 1973.

page 652
"Children, don't be afraid . . ." Bezymenski 63.
page 652
Kempka account: Interview, 1971.
pages 652–53
Naumann account: Interview, 1971.
page 653
Dr. Soggnaes account: Correspondence, 1975.
page 653
Dönitz to Himmler: Interview with Dönitz, 1963.
page 653
Schwerin von Krosigk to Himmler: Interview with Schwerin von Krosigk, 1963.
pages 653–54
Grothmann account: Interview with Grothmann, 1971.
page 654
Göring quote: Gilbert, *Psychology*, 109–10.
page 655
Ribbentrop quote: Gilbert, *Nuremberg*, 260.
page 655
Keitel quotes: Andrus 195–96; Gilbert, *Nuremberg*, 300.
pages 655–56
Günsche-Schulze: Interviews with Richard and Monika Schulze-Kossens, 1973.

Index

EUROPE
UNDER HITLER
0 Miles 300
N
Trondheim
NORWAY
Bergen
Oslo
Stavanger
NORTH SEA
NORTH IRELAND
IRELAND
GREAT
BRITAIN
DENMARK
Coventry
London
Amsterdam
Hamburg
RAVENSBRÜCK
ORANIENBURG
Bremen
BELSEN
Berlin
Hanover
HOLLAND
Dunkirk
ATLANTIC
OCEAN
Essen
GERMANY
Brussels
Cologne
ENGLISH CHANNEL
Cherbourg
Dieppe
BELGIUM
Rocky Nest
Leipzig
BUCHENWALD
Coblenz
Brest
NORMANDY
Compiègne
Wolf's Gorge
Paris
Troyes
Nuremberg
DACHAU
Montoire
Munich
Berchtesgaden
Innsbruck
BAY OF
BISCAY
FRANCE
SWITZERLAND
Ascona
Vichy
BRENNER PASS
Geneva
Trieste
Milan
Venice
ITALY
Hendaye
Toulouse
Genoa
Marseille
Toulon
St. Tropez
Florence
PORTUGAL
Madrid
Barcelona
Pescara
Lisbon
CORSICA
Rome
SPAIN
Anzio
Cassino
Naples
Valencia
SARDINIA
Malaga
MEDITERRANEAN SEA
Gibraltar
Tangier
Bizerte
SPANISH MOROCCO
Algiers
Bougie
Rabat
Oran
Bône
Tunis
PANTELLERIA
Casablanca
TUNISIA
MOROCCO
ALGERIA
Tebessa
Kasserine
MALTA

Hitler's Third Reich
German Conquests & Satellites
Italy & Vassals
Vichy France & Colonies
Hitler's Headquarters
CONCENTRATION CAMPS
KILLING CENTERS
SWEDEN
FINLAND
Helsinki
Stockholm
Tallinn
ESTONIA
Leningrad
Volkhov
Tikhvin
Vologda
Novgorod
Pskov
LATVIA
Riga
Velikiye Luki
Kalinin
Rzhev
Yaroslavl
VOLGA R.
Gorki
Kazan
Moscow
BALTIC SEA
LITHUANIA
Kaunas
Polotsk
Smolensk
Vyazma
Kaluga
Ryazan
Penza
Tula
U. S. S. R.
Saratov
Gdynia
Wolfs Lair
E. PRUSSIA
Mogilev
Bryansk
Orel
Voronezh
Danzig
POLAND
TREBLINKA
Poznan
KULMHOF
Warsaw
Brest-Litovsk
SOBIBOR
LUBLIN (MAIDANEK)
BELZEC
Gomel
Kursk
DON R.
Belgorod
Stalingrad
Kharkov
Kamensk
Kiev
Zhitomir
DNIEPER R.
Cherkassy
Dnepropetrovsk
Rostov
GENERALGOUVERNEMENT
Lvov
Cracow
AUSCHWITZ
Werewolf
Vinnitsa
Zhdanov
CZECHOSLOVAKIA
SLOVAKIA
Bratislava
Budapest
Cernauti
Krivoy Rog
Nikolayevsk
Odessa
Kerch
Krasnodar
Maikop
HUNGARY
ROMANIA
CRIMEA
Novorossisk
Sevastopol
Yalta
Ploesti
Belgrade
Bucharest
Constanza
BLACK SEA
Batum
YUGOSLAVIA
Sofia
BULGARIA
Istanbul
Salonika
Ankara
TURKEY
GREECE
Athens
Smyrna
SYRIA
RHODES
CRETE
CYPRUS
palacios

ABOUT THE AUTHOR

John Toland was born in La Crosse, Wisconsin, and spent his formative years in Westport, Connecticut. Educated at Exeter and Williams College, Toland worked his way through both prep school and college by playing bridge and running the college book store. He also spent four long summers traveling on freight trains all over the country, enjoying minor skirmishes with the law. During World War II he served as an assistant in the Army Entertainment Section, Special Services.

John Toland first wrote about Adolph Hitler in his bestselling THE LAST HUNDRED DAYS. Among his other books are BATTLE: THE STORY OF THE BULGE, SHIPS IN THE SKY, BUT NOT IN SHAME, the Pulitzer prize–winning THE RISING SUN, and INFAMY: PEARL HARBOR AND ITS AFTERMATH. Mr. Toland lives with his wife in Danbury, Connecticut.